Investigations
in the Workplace

Investigations
in the Workplace

Eugene F. Ferraro, CPP, CFE, PCI

Norman M. Spain, J.D., CPP, Legal Contributor

Auerbach Publications
Taylor & Francis Group
Boca Raton   London   New York   Singapore

Published in 2006 by
Auerbach Publications
Taylor & Francis Group
6000 Broken Sound Parkway NW, Suite 300
Boca Raton, FL 33487-2742

Library of Congress Cataloging-in-Publication Data

Ferraro, Eugene F.
     Investigations in the workplace / by Eugene F. Ferraro ; Norman M. Spain, legal contributor.
          p. cm.
     Includes bibliographical references and index.
     ISBN 0-8493-1648-0 (alk. paper)
     1. Employee crimes. 2. Investigations—Handbooks, manuals, etc. 3. Employee
     theft—Investigation—Handbooks, manuals, etc. 4. Personnel management—Handbooks, manuals,
     etc. I. Spain, Norman M. II. Title.

HF5549.5.E43F37 2005
658.3′8—dc22   2004065975

Taylor & Francis Group
is the Academic Division of T&F Informa plc.

Visit the Taylor & Francis Web site at
http://www.taylorandfrancis.com

and the Auerbach Publications Web site at
http://www.auerbach-publications.com

Dedication

With everlasting love and affection to my wife and best friend, Shelley, whose patience, encouragement, and faith made this work possible.

Contents

Preface

Successful workplace investigations are complex undertakings. They are time consuming and fraught with enormous potential for legal liability. When done properly, they combine an intricate mixture of skill, experience, and luck. Workplace investigations can also be expensive. Today's competitive world requires organizations of all sizes, both public and private, to manage their resources carefully. An improperly conducted workplace investigation can be expensive and ruin the careers of everyone who touches it. Few workplace activities invoke so much risk and, at the same time, so much opportunity.

For 24 years I have been a corporate investigator. For over two decades I have dedicated myself to the investigation of workplace crime and misconduct. This book is an attempt to share my knowledge and experience with others in my profession. My goal has been to provide both the novice and experienced investigator with the most insightful information possible. In the pages that follow, I have attempted to challenge conventional thinking and inspire a new approach to workplace investigations. I have resisted ordinary convention and sought new solutions to age-old problems. My hope is that, whether the reader is a professional licensed investigator or someone tasked by his employer to conduct an internal investigation, this work will shine new light on the reader's own process and investigation. I also hope this work serves to provide executives, human resource professionals, and employment lawyers new insights into the inner workings of what can become a truly professional workplace investigation.

The reader should know that I am more than a writer; I am a practitioner. The knowledge I offer in this book goes far beyond what is available in the current literature. I have drawn upon my years of practical experience to craft a work that dispels the myths and troublesome theories promulgated by the uninitiated. My intent has been to provide the reader with the story behind the methodology, rationale, and gritty practices that have made my workplace investigations soar. But most importantly, my intent has been to share. I want to give back to my profession and the many in it who came before me.

This book is designed for easy reading and use. I have provided an exhaustive table of contents to permit my readers to quickly find the information they seek. I have also provided innumerable references and an expansive appendix section. These and other features are intended to make this work more valuable to you. It is intended that the reader not read this book from cover to cover. Instead, you may go directly to the section that applies to your specific need or interest. Little should be lost in doing so. To help capture my salient points and simplify the learning process, I have also sprinkled the text with brief *Tips* and *Traps*.

Tip: Read my Tips and Traps to get the most out of this book. If you read nothing else, these little gems will help make your workplace investigations sparkle.

Disclaimer

Throughout this work I have attempted to avoid gender stereotyping or the preference of one gender over another. Any appearance of having done so was the product of my writing style and was not intentional. Hopefully my use of both genders does not create a distraction.

The case studies that have been used in this work are based on real investigations conducted by me or my organization. However, in order to protect the reputations of the guilty and the privacy of the innocent I have substantially altered some facts. Any similarity to real situations or real people is purely coincidental.

Acknowledgments

No work of any importance or value is possible without the help of others. This labor of love has been no exception. Two such people are my longtime friends and colleagues, Professor Norman M. Spain, J.D., CPP, and Dr. William C. Butler, Ph.D. Norman Spain, professor of assets protection and security at the College of Justice and Safety at Eastern Kentucky University, wrote Chapter 5 titled "Legal Challenges and Litigation Avoidance." Dr. Butler, a true friend and trusted co-worker, unselfishly contributed something to every chapter, but most significant was his contribution to Chapter 6, "Applied Strategies." Without the help of these generous professionals much of which you are about to read would not have been written with such grace and craft. I also thank my staff at Business Controls, Inc. Many of them picked up the slack while I toiled away on my manuscript and neglected them and our business. They include Steve Foster, COO; Kimberly Pfaff, Amy Slettedahl, and Meighan Laurie, all of our Behavioral Sciences Division; as well as my professional staff and the many investigators on our team.

I also thank my publisher, Rich O'Hanley at Auerbach Publications and Taylor & Francis Group. His professionalism, patience, and good humor are unmatched. Without his persistence and perseverance this book would truly not have been possible.

Most importantly I want to thank my loving wife, Shelley. She has sacrificed her time, shared her ideas, and patiently allowed me to quietly work in the peace and tranquility of our lovely home. Whether it was tending to our family affairs or doing the yard work while I sat and wrote, she did her job *and* mine. I love her completely and profoundly.

EFF
Pine, Colorado

Introduction

Large or small, organizations of all sizes routinely conduct internal workplace investigations. Though the objectives, and certainly the scope, of these undertakings vary widely, their principal purpose is that of objective *fact-finding*. Thus, the fact-finder must be fair, impartial, thorough, and certainly purposeful. Then to fulfill the varied objectives of the assigned investigation, the fact-finder must have a process. That process is called the *Process of Investigation*®.[1] Remarkably, however, most fact-finders, regardless of their level of experience, have little or no process. Their approaches are varied as are their results. Lacking an effective process, fact-finders often spend more time and resources than necessary, produce inconsistent results, and create unnecessary liabilities for those they serve. No investigation, regardless of its objectives or scope, can be successful if not properly engineered and driven by process.

Workplace investigations must have meaningful and well-defined objectives, be properly and lawfully executed, be fair and impartial, and the results accurately documented and communicated. In order for them to be effective, they must unfold incrementally and progressively in distinct phases. Each progressive phase is engineered to build on the phase that preceded it. Collectively, these phases are called the *Five Phases of Investigation*. They include

- Preparation and planning
- Information gathering and fact-finding
- Verification and analysis
- Determination and disbursement of disciplinary or corrective action
- Prevention and education

Due to lack of resources and experience, most fact-finders transfix on the second phase, that of information gathering. Unwittingly, they conclude their investigation after amassing an impressive collection of related facts, evidence, and conclusions. Though obviously important, what is overlooked denies those to whom they report a complete result and a thorough understanding of the very matter that precipitated the effort. By imposing process to otherwise disorganized, but seemingly important activities, the fact-finder creates the structure necessary to be uniquely effective. That process allows the fact-finder to transcend the unsophisticated and often tarnished image of corporate gumshoe and elevates him to the professional standing of corporate investigator, better yet, professional investigator.

Like most effective processes, the fact-finder's effort should also produce measurable results. First and most immediate is the return on investment, or ROI. The properly engineered investigation will often produce tangible, measurable results, such as the recovery of stolen property or money, the termination of dishonest employees or vendors, and, of course, successful prosecution and civil recovery, hopefully without litigation.

The process, however, goes beyond this and can even be engineered to allow the employer to recover the actual cost of the investigation from the transgressor. Unique also is the process's suitability to generate statistical results the fact-finder can use over time to measure effectiveness and ROI. Without process and structure, the fact-finder has no means to measure results and show value to the customer. The fact-finder must think in terms of process in order to be consistently successful. Long gone are the days when anyone could conduct a workplace investigation. Sloppy techniques, careless fact-gathering, and bending the law are no longer permissible in our litigious workplace. Neither the public nor our courts will tolerate the practices that just several years ago were considered "industry standards." Today you cannot get away with unethical and improper investigations, and if you try you will land yourself and your employer on the wrong end of a lawsuit.

When properly conducted, workplace investigations are complex affairs. They typically involve the convergence of many disciplines and an assortment of uncommon skills. More often than not, the investigator must have a comprehensive understanding of criminal, civil, and employment law. They also require a considerable investment of time, money, and patience by the employer. Then, finally, to ensure success, the process must be highly structured and flawlessly executed. Even the most sophisticated organization can find the task consistently challenging.

Therein lies the opportunity. Every organization, public or private, eventually finds itself in need of an internal investigation, be it the suspicious disappearance of tangible or intangible assets, the questionable ethical practices of an employee, or the troubling allegation of sexual harassment. Sooner or later, every organization is confronted with the need to gather evidence, interview suspects, and uncover the truth. With the ability to muster the necessary resources, deploy skilled fact-finders, and adhere to a disciplined process, any organization can conduct a successful workplace investigation. For the organization this outcome is manifold. For in addition to the above factors, workplace investigations are fraught with liability. Workplace investigations of even the simplest variety are not for the faint hearted. By definition they involve the investigation of people who have a relationship with the organization. Most often those people are employees. They are insiders. They are people whom the organization employs or with whom it does business. As such, they have special rights and expectations, and very often they carry a sense of entitlement. These considerations significantly add to the complexity of the fact-finding process and the manner in which the subject may respond to the investigation's findings and management's corrective actions. Regardless, the path is filled with legal obstacles and challenges. For the unknowledgeable and unprepared employer it is a virtual legal minefield. On the other hand, the totality of these complexities gives the properly prepared and equipped employer a decisive competitive advantage. The employer who is able to efficiently bring an end to a workplace substance abuse problem, catch thieving employees in the act, or obtain restitution from a dishonest vendor, without litigation or a public relations debacle, has a significant competitive advantage over the employer who cannot.

Several months ago the human resource director of a substantial clothing distribution operation called and indicated he needed my immediate assistance. Having provided him assistance in the past, I was eager to help. He told me that one of the firm's female executive assistants had received at least a dozen greeting cards from what appeared to be a disturbed anonymous admirer. All but two of the cards had been received via U.S. Postal Service. The two that had not, had been left at her desk. All of the cards were similarly themed and appeared to be part of a single set. Most disturbing, however, was that the handwritten message in each of the successive cards was increasingly disorganized and more bizarre, and the most recent message was outright threatening. My client asked that I help him identify the writer and determine the next course of action. We quickly discussed the investigation's objectives, a timeline, and several other administrative details, and then I got to work.

Given the facts I've just shared and several others I quickly uncovered, I determined the writer was most likely a current male employee. What's more, given that some of the cards were hand-delivered to the woman's desk, the writer also had access to the executive office area. With the use of simple forensics and some basic timeline analysis, I was able to reduce the suspect pool to a mere three people. Then after more interviewing and a little more digging, I identified the likely perpetrator—the corporate

IT (information technology) manager. I arranged to interview him and in less than 30 minutes he confessed. He also revealed that he had sabotaged a number of electronic management systems that if left uncorrected, would eventually cause significant financial and inventory distortions. The revelation was shocking, and my client quickly took corrective action. My client also now wanted the manager put behind bars. I agreed to look into the possibility of prosecution, and in the meantime the manager was placed on administrative leave, pending the determination of his fate.

Exercising its prerogative to search offices, desks, and workstations, while strictly following policy, my client authorized the systematic search of the manager's computer. The effort revealed that in addition to having spent a great deal of his time downloading pornography, the employee had also sent a huge number of inappropriate e-mail messages to several current and former female employees—a matter that had never been revealed by any of the recipients.

My client concluded he had enough evidence and terminated the manager. The former employee immediately hired an attorney and through her, he threatened to sue. It became quickly apparent that the attorney had not been provided the entire story. However, after several telephone conversations between the attorney and my client's employment law attorney, the whole matter dissolved and the former employee was never heard from again.

As promised, I did contact the local police and discussed the case. Although the matter involved the possible violation of both federal and state laws, law enforcement was not interested. Not only had some of the offenses occurred in several different jurisdictions (the cards were postmarked in one jurisdiction and received in another), none of the offenses involved a violent act and no one had suffered a monetary loss. In other words, the case involved too much work and not enough return on investment. Regardless, from the perspective of the employer, the case was a smashing success. Let's quantify the result:

- The anonymous "admirer" was identified and stopped, thus terminating a disturbing and potentially dangerous progression. The recipient and those who knew about the cards enjoyed great relief and satisfaction.
- Operational and financial management mechanisms that had been sabotaged were identified and could now be repaired.
- The perpetrator was swiftly separated from the organization without incident, litigation, or any public discourse or adverse publicity.
- The perpetrator received no unemployment insurance benefits and was never heard from again.

Additionally, the entire matter was handled quickly and economically. The lack of prosecution was not a failure. Had the district attorney taken the case, my client would have had to spend more time and money. Because the standard of proof for criminal prosecution (beyond a reasonable doubt) is so much higher than that of a workplace action (good faith investigation and reasonable conclusion), more time and money is always necessary to achieve it. In many instances the return on investment of employee prosecution just isn't there.

Without adequate process the success of the above investigation would not have been possible, nor would most workplace investigations. This book describes that process. Soon you will learn about this powerful mechanism and how it will allow you to engineer the most successful workplace investigations possible.

Let's get to work.

Note

1. The *Process of Investigation*® is the registered trademark of the author. Its use for any purpose is strictly prohibited without the prior written permission of the author.

About the Author

Eugene Ferraro has been a corporate investigator for over 23 years. Specializing in the investigation of employee dishonesty, substance abuse, and criminal activity in the workplace, he has conducted thousands of investigations for employers throughout the United States. He is also a published author and speaks frequently on the topics of workplace investigations and crime in the workplace. Mr. Ferraro has been designated a Certified Protection Professional (CPP) by ASIS International (formerly the American Society of Industrial Security) and has served as the chairman of its Workplace Substance Abuse Council. He is currently the program advisor for its Asset Protection Course II. He is also a member of the Association of Certified Fraud Examiners and is a Certified Fraud Examiner (CFE) and faculty member.

Mr. Ferraro is a former military pilot, intelligence officer, and graduate of the Naval Justice School. He is a frequent book critic for Security Management; and he completed a book entitled *Undercover Investigations in the Workplace* (publisher Butterworth-Heinemann).

Mr. Ferraro's affiliations include ASIS International, 1987; Association of Certified Fraud Examiners, 1988; Professional Private Investigators Association of Colorado, 1994; National Council of Investigative and Security Services, 1996; National Association of Professional Process Servers, 1996; and California Association of Licensed Investigators, 2001.

Chapter 1

The Process of Investigation

A. The Investigative Process

The process of investigation is fluid and dynamic. The approach must be reasonable and the investigator flexible. However, in order to be successful, every investigation must have a meaningful purpose and be executed ethically and lawfully.[1]

1. The Elements of a Successful Investigation

A successful workplace investigation in fact provides many dividends for the employer. In addition to uncovering facts and essential information needed to solve problems, a successful investigation helps restore order. It provides the employer the opportunity to analyze process and system failures and reengineer them to prevent future problems. However, in order to be successful every investigation requires the following elements:

- Management commitment
- Meaningful objectives
- A well-conceived strategy

- Properly pooled resources and expertise
- Lawful execution

Let's now examine each of these critical elements in detail.

a. Management Commitment

Because workplace investigations can be extremely complex and often involve potential litigation, a commitment by management is an essential component if success is to be achieved. From the very beginning, management must be prepared to commit the requisite time, patience, and resources in order to achieve its objectives. It is misleading and dishonest for the individual responsible for driving the investigative process, a person from this point forward we shall refer to as the project manager, to allow the employer (typically his employer or client) to believe anything less. To obtain quick results with little effort or with few resources is often impossible and even reckless. In accepting the assignment, the project manager must be prepared to accept responsibility and communicate honestly with the employer. Only with the proper information and a thorough understanding of the issues and options can the employer make decisions that are sound and appropriate. Anything less will diminish the return on investment and invite potential litigation.

Time

No two investigations are alike. Each has its own interesting characteristics and personality. Every investigation has a unique fact pattern and some extenuating circumstances that differentiate it from any other. The investigation's objectives, available resources, and a whole host of other things will impact the shape the investigation will take and the time necessary to achieve the desired results. Employers find this annoying. In the world of business, time is money—and money is what business is all about. From the employer's viewpoint, an investigation that consumes time consumes money as well. It is therefore in the project manager's best interest to manage time as he would any other resource.

Time Management

Time is a precious commodity. Each of us is allocated just so much; therefore, how we use it, by and large, is up to us. Because investigations are dynamic, the use of time and the allocation of it to any particular task is a critical aspect of project management. As we will see in later chapters, the project manager is responsible for, among other things, the establishment of the project's objectives. In doing so, he will define deadlines and milestones. It is he who will ensure that the investigative team remains on course and the project is accomplished in a timely fashion.

Over the years, I have used a variety of tools to assist me in managing my time and projects. Simplest of them is a journal. Whether kept in a small spiral-bound notebook or some electronic fashion, a simple journal allows the user to record his activities in chronological order. By comparing one's accomplishments to one's goals, the user obtains a very simplistic overview of where the project has been and where it needs to go.

Establishing and recording milestones can easily enhance the usefulness of the journal. For example, in writing this book I first decided its objectives. The objectives, once properly organized, became chapters. Each chapter was then organized into logical subcomponents. Simple manila folders were created for each chapter and significant sections thereof. The process is called outlining. Then, anticipating a book of approximately 120,000 words and knowing I could easily pen 1,000 words on a good day, I knew the first draft of the manuscript would require approximately 120 days to complete. Using the Properties feature of my word processor, I was able to easily determine my daily Word Count. Dumping the data into a spreadsheet application in which I had built a table and incorporated several formulas, I was able to precisely track my progress against the assorted milestones I had established for the timely completion of the manuscript. I have used the same process in the management of investigative projects.

Other tools of almost equal simplicity, but of far greater capability, are personal computer applications specifically designed for project management. The most popular of them is Microsoft® Project 2002 (Microsoft Corporation, Redmond, Washington). This inexpensive application is the world's leading project management program. It allows users to manage schedules and resources, communicate project status, and report project information painlessly. Using what Microsoft® calls dynamic scheduling, users instantly see the impact of a schedule or resource change on the overall project schedule milestones. The application also allows the easy conversion of existing task lists from Microsoft Excel and Outlook into Microsoft Project Plans. This flexibility allows the project manager to quickly and easily delegate tasks and monitor the progress of each team member. In subsequent chapters we examine some of the other tools now commercially available to assist with project management. But in the meantime, let me say a brief word about common sense.

No investigator can achieve success without some semblance of common sense. At times, however, I have seen so little of it among investigators that one might consider the term an oxymoron. Here's an amusing example

I received the other day via e-mail through a list-serve of West Coast private investigators of which I am a member:

Fellow Members:

I inadvertently deleted the form I had been using for recording new client information.

The form (like the one many of you probably use) contained such things as: Client name; Case#; Date; Nature of matter; Telephone number and so on. Before I undertake building another, I thought I would confer with you first. I am hoping someone would have one on hand and would be willing to share a copy with me at least as a template.

Your assistance is appreciated,

Sender's Name

See any problem with this request? Aside from the audacity to make such a request of his fellow colleagues (read competitors), this poor soul lacks common sense. If in fact he did truly delete his template, why didn't he just go back into his system and pull up a previously completed form from a prior case, save the document under a new name, delete the old client information, and save the *document as a template*! Or, if he hadn't kept electronic copies, why not go into an existing case file and *build a new template from a previously completed form from the file*! To top it off, the word "Intelligence" was one of three words comprising his organization's name.

Yes, common sense is necessary to achieve investigative success. Investigators that lack it ought to be reading something else. For those of you interested in forms, I will discuss them and their use in detail in Chapters 2 and 4.

Patience

A successful investigation also requires patience, a virtue few practitioners seem to have. The simple truth of the matter is that a proper investigation takes time. They frequently unfold in fascinating and often unexpected ways. Although the experienced project manager can influence the pace in which her investigation unfolds, there are aspects of it that may be uncontrollable. Undercover investigations are a perfect example. Undercover investigations are extraordinarily complex. They involve the careful selection and placement of an investigator. The investigator must then assimilate into the workforce. This phase of the investigation is called the relationship-building phase. Once assimilated, the investigator moves into the proactive phase. Once there, with the guiding assistance of her project manager, she begins to collect the information necessary to obtain the investigation's objectives. This takes time. The effort cannot be forced or willed. Despite the anxiousness of the other parties involved (the employer-client or law enforcement), the investigation must unfold at its own pace.

In the case of undercover investigations, experience has shown that the relationship-building phase is a four- to six-week endeavor. The proactive phase of the investigation may require an additional six to sixteen weeks. A whole host of variables will impact the length of the investigation, but in extreme situations the case may need to be run six months or more. The lack of patience will make an otherwise routine undercover investigation a daunting undertaking indeed.

Additionally, there may be events that impact the pace of the investigation that are beyond the control of anyone. Things such as illnesses, weather, holidays, schedules, and the unavailability of the players are all details that sometimes no one can control. In the case of undercover for example, the winter holiday season often creates challenges. In the aerospace industry, it is not uncommon for employers to shut their doors for the last two weeks of the year. It is precisely that time of year the undercover investigator can make her best headway. Holiday parties, dinners, and other seasonal events provide excellent opportunities to build relationships and gain confidences. The holiday spirit also increases complacency, making the gathering of otherwise useful information much easier. But in the aerospace industry, as in several others, as soon as the holiday spirit sets in, the organization shuts down and the workforce is not reconvened until shortly after New Year's. All the while, the meter continues to run for the employer-client. In order to endure such delays, the employer-client, as well as the investigators, must have patience.

Another example of the need for patience is in those matters involving the management of workplace aggression and potential violence. Often, the employer, upon discovery of the misconduct, wants to immediately discipline or terminate the transgressor. This, of course, is a common outcome in these types of matters. However, more often than not, the employer has not conducted a thorough investigation and has not met the standard of proof necessary to discipline or discharge anyone. For organizations such as mine, which specializes in managing these matters for employers, the rush to judgment and termination of the guilty by our clients is a challenge for us. In haste there is often waste, and in these types of cases, haste can also be very dangerous. Often there is no need to discipline or terminate. What is needed is a proper and thorough investigation. Facts need to be gathered, statements need to be taken, allegations need to be checked, and most importantly, barring an immediate danger to human life, the alleged aggressor has rights that must be respected and protected. It has been my experience that lack of respect has been a historical contributor to producing the very behaviors that are then in question.

Resources

The creation of wealth is the essence of business and the free enterprise system. Money is the lubricant that makes the system work. In addition to time and patience, a successful investigation requires the dedication of resources—real money. Regardless of the simplicity or complexity of an investigation, some investment of money is necessary. Like in the free enterprise system, money is an essential lubricant that in many ways makes the investigation possible.

My clients sometimes debate this. With all sincerity, they will sometimes contend that they could conduct the investigation under consideration cheaper and faster than I could. In rare instances this may be so. However, most often they have neither the skill nor the experience to conduct the investigation properly, much less materially achieve its specific objectives. The availability of manpower, equipment, and other resources does not ensure success. The mere fact that the organization already employs a security director, human resource manager, or house counsel does not mean that they or the organization is capable, qualified, or even has the time to conduct a proper investigation. Even if capable and qualified, it may make more economic sense to outsource the effort. Consider your own organization for a moment; does it have the human resources, talent, and time necessary to undertake a complex internal investigation? Probably not.

Allow me to put a finer point on it. Regardless of who does the investigation and whose resources and equipment might be used, somebody has to pay for it. Simply because the organization employs one or more of the professionals mentioned above, it does not mean they are free. The question the organization must ask is: is it more economic to undertake the project itself or to outsource it? In order to answer that question, a cost-analysis should be done.

Cost-analysis in this context is more than just running the numbers. Integral to the process is estimating to the finest degree possible, the return on investment (ROI). ROI should be one of the objectives of every investigation. The higher the ROI, the smaller the economic risk. What's more, the properly engineered investigation will have established milestones by which those driving the project will be able to periodically measure results, thus enabling them to reassess their plan and modify their objectives dynamically. As such, experienced investigators know cost-analysis is a necessary component of the preplanning phase of the project. Thus, the more complex the contemplated project, the more critical cost-analysis becomes. Here is a typical example.

Hypothetically suppose "our" organization suffered what appeared to be a fairly significant loss involving a "kick-back" scheme orchestrated by one of our purchasing agents. Preliminary information suggests that as a result of the scheme, over a period of a couple of years our organization overpaid several vendors more than $300,000. Our "security department" is brought to bear and its preinvestigation fact-finding effort reveals the overpayment is closer to $750,000.[2] Based on an organizational pretax net of 5 percent, analysis suggests that in order to have instead netted the $750,000, the organization would have had to increase sales by approximately $15 million. Depending on the organization and industry, this may or may not even be possible. Our analysis also suggests that the organization's inability to use that money elsewhere increased operating costs in the form of larger interest payments. Taking other facts into consideration and rounding the numbers, the loss actually exceeds $1.2 million.

Given that such matters lend themselves to recoveries of not only the losses, but in most instances the cost of the investigation, wouldn't it make sense to look outside for professional assistance?[3] Considering the burden on the organization's internal resources, manpower, and the distraction of a complex investigation of this sort, the smart move is to engage a qualified external resource. The outcome is likely to be better, and the organization can instead dedicate itself to what it does best—running its business.

The next question of course is what will be the cost? The answer is not an easy one. In the case of undercover, which is typically billed by the week, the organization (the client) and the service provider (the investigative vendor) together can determine the estimated length of the project and do the math. Other types of investigations require a little more analysis in order to determine the investment necessary to ensure success. Let's look at this process in a little more detail.

It is estimated that there are approximately 18,000 active private investigation firms in the United States.[4] Although it is nearly impossible to know for sure, it is widely accepted that the private investigation industry in the United States employs something on the order of 40,000 individuals.[5] Of those, only a small fraction are engaged in what have come to be called corporate investigations. Corporate investigations are those that specifically involve workplace issues. These include all types of crimes against the organization and, of course, policy violations by its employees.

Of those who claim to offer corporate investigative services, only a handful actually specialize in it. As such, the sample from which I am about to draw the following conclusions is relatively small, and thus there is some inherent inaccuracy in what I am about to offer. That said it is fairly safe to say the hourly fees charged by those offering corporate investigative services tend to be on the higher end of the scale for private investigation professionals. And although fees and pricing practices vary across the country, with some high cost-of-living areas such as San Francisco or New York skewing the data, most qualified corporate investigators who offer the service as their specialty charge something on the order of $250 per hour. Some organizations actually exceed $400 per hour for their top investigators. Associates and field investigator fees begin at about $150 per hour. On the whole, it is my experience that it is difficult, if not impossible, to engage a qualified corporate investigator of any sophistication for less than $200 per hour. For those readers interested in pursuing this line of work, that should be very good news. For purchasers of these services, it is equally good news.

Because corporate investigations in practice involve an understanding and appreciation of criminal law, civil law, and employment or labor law, few professionals actually have the skills necessary to deliver quality services. Those who do know its value charge accordingly for it. Conversely, some general practitioners (criminal defense, insurance investigators, and the like) may charge as little as $75 per hour, and some as little as $35 per hour. These professionals find it difficult to even imagine charging $200 per hour for their services, much less someone actually paying it. This gives the consumer of corporate investigative services a decided advantage. Simply by knowing the fee structure of the service offerer, one can generally tell his level of sophistication and experience. This is not to say that by paying more the client automatically gets more. However, the adage that one gets what one pays for certainly applies when choosing a corporate investigator.

The sophisticated vendor offers more. Professionals capable of delivering the type of services we are discussing also understand ROI. They have a fine appreciation for business and understand that a mutually beneficial engagement is only possible when the service provider is able to provide a reasonable ROI. Because most crimes against the business are property crimes, recovery is often possible. The professional corporate investigator knows this and will typically engineer his investigation to facilitate a recovery, to include, if possible, even his fees and expenses. Most private investigators have no appreciation for this aspect of the process. Many of them, particularly those with law enforcement background, will attempt to drive the process toward prosecution of the perpetrators. Such an effort or even the suggestion of prosecution, as an investigative objective, should be a red flag to the client. Unless it can be demonstrated to contribute to the desired ROI, prosecution should not be an objective and should not be pursued. In most instances, the pursuit of prosecution will consume unnecessary resources and contribute little to the outcome of the investigation.

Tip: Organizations intending to undertake an internal investigation of any size or complexity are generally better served seeking the services of an external resource to conduct the investigation. From the standpoint of time, money, and the best use of existing internal resources, it is more economical to outsource most corporate investigations.

---

b. Meaningful Objectives

No investigation of any complexity can be successful without meaningful objectives. The investigation's objectives define the fact-finders purpose, benchmark his progress, and provide the framework by which the project manager coordinates the effort to build his case. I am astounded by how many of my colleagues fail to appreciate this critical fundamental and begin their investigations without articulating or even contemplating their objectives. Those that do often still miss the point. The investigative objectives must be carefully articulated at the beginning of the process, where they establish the investigation's starting point and where it is intended to finish.

I embrace this concept to such a degree that it is my practice and that of my firm to begin every investigation by negotiating the effort's objectives with the client. By negotiating I mean that together we decide what it is we are pursuing, what information we are seeking, and the desired outcome. Together we talk through that which we are attempting to do, how we intend to do it, and who is responsible for what. The objectives make it clear that the investigation's purpose is proper and lawful. When properly articulated, they demonstrate that both the employer-client and the fact-finder have pure intentions, and that the length they will go to achieve success is reasonable.

I go so far as to describe the objectives in the investigative proposal I provide my clients. In doing so, I establish that I understand the needs and desires of the client. It also establishes benchmarks by which we can later measure our results. In fact, other than my case intake notes, the first document to be placed in my case file is a page on which I have detailed the investigation's objectives.

By articulating and recording the project's objectives early and placing evidence of them in my case file, I am also laying a defensive foundation against any claim of discrimination or some other form of investigative misconduct at the conclusion of the investigation. In the event of subsequent litigation and discovery, I want the plaintiff to be surprised. I want the plaintiff who has claimed discrimination, targeting, and abuse to sustain an early setback when handed documents that demonstrate from the start of my investigation that my intentions (and that of my client) were pure, honest, and reasonable. Practical experience has also shown that early setbacks for plaintiffs of this type tend to demoralize them. It tends to take some of the wind out of their sails. At the very least it demonstrates to them, and most importantly the court, that the defendant is no amateur and an easy victory is not likely. The objectives of almost all workplace investigations articulate the desire to

- Seek out and identify the true nature and scope of the problem.
- Identify who is involved and why.
- Gather any and all information in such a fashion as to allow the proper distribution of appropriate disciplinary or corrective action.
- Engineer the process in such a fashion that is least disruptive to the organization and its operations.
- Achieve the best possible return on investment.[6]

This is no small order indeed. However, taking the time to negotiate the objectives of the project in advance saves time and money. Moreover, as you have probably already recognized, the objectives stated above are nearly universal. Reflect for a moment on the last several workplace investigations you conducted or oversaw. Would these objectives have suited each of them? I suspect so. Imagine also the response of the decision maker(s) to whom you report if you had recited these objectives when your last assignment was handed to you. From a practical standpoint who could argue with them? Also note that these objectives, as I have penned them, speak in business terms. They demonstrate my appreciation of operations, corporate culture, fairness, and return on investment. They tell my client I understand his business and that I too am a businessperson. I don't think the objectives of any workplace investigation could be articulated any better.

c. Well-Conceived Strategy

The next key to success is the development and deployment of a sound investigative strategy. There are many different types of issues that call for a workplace investigation; therefore, I will forgo describing strategies for each of them here. However, the topic deserves some brief examination at least.

Effective investigative strategies involve more than mixing and matching investigative methods. The successful project manager needs process. That process must be sufficiently structured so it provides efficiency and the opportunity to measure results. However, the process must be sufficiently flexible so that it allows the changes of objectives and strategy. The project manager and her investigators must have the ability to change their objectives and modify their strategy as new information develops. My clients sometimes make this mistake. On numerous occasions I have had employer-clients tell me that they are interested in only catching the thieves or firing the drug dealers. Although I cannot argue with these objectives, upon discovery of other offensive workplace behaviors, these same clients do not want to address them. Knowing other egregious and actionable behavior is taking place, they will turn a blind eye to it because the investigation of those offenses "was not among our original objectives." How sad and how wasteful. Investigators make the same mistake. Because one offense or another was not included in their original charter, they ignore it. Their process is so structured; once the train has left the station, there is no changing its destination.

d. Properly Pooled Resources and Expertise

Nothing can derail a well-planned investigation more effectively than an organization's failure to support it with the proper resources. The failure to dedicate adequate resources results in a lengthier investigation that will assuredly fail to achieve the desired objectives. Here is an example.

Several months ago, the owner of a regional drug distribution operation called my office seeking my help. The owner claimed that several employees had come forward and alleged that co-workers were stealing. After discussing the particulars, it appeared to me that the allegations were credible and that an investigation would likely expose the perpetrators. I suggested the informants be interviewed so that all of the information possible could be extracted from them. As is often the case, the owner—now client—resisted. He said the employees had been promised immunity; furthermore, they were said to be unlikely to talk if confronted by an outsider. I told him in that case the only solution would be an undercover investigation. He resisted again. He said he did not have the time or the money for an undercover investigation. Although he believed his losses were approaching $40,000 a month, he wanted a faster, less-expensive solution. After more discussion and some debate, I acquiesced and agreed to surveillance. To my surprise the resultant surveillance produced results, and several employees were identified engaging in very questionable activity. I suggested they be interviewed. Given what we knew at the time, I proposed that investigatory interviews would likely yield admissions, and based on those admissions, the client could take the necessary disciplinary or corrective action. Again anxious to achieve a fast and more convenient result, my client insisted on involving the authorities. Incorrectly he believed that the police would pick up where we left off and solve his problem. He further professed that "police action" would produce an unqualified deterrent and discourage similar behavior by others in the future. The police agreed, but they insisted on verifying our result and doing additional surveillance themselves. After several weeks of inactivity on the part of the suspect employees, the police became tired of their surveillance and decided to confront them. They did, and even after using intimidation and the veiled threat of prosecution, not a single employee offered an admission. Thoroughly frustrated, my client shut the project down and paid our bill. Months later, as I typically do, I followed up and called him. He said his losses had diminished to a trickle but reluctantly admitted he had no peace of mind. He knew as I did, those responsible for the many months of theft were still in his employ. It was only a matter of time until they gathered the courage and once again resumed their old criminal behavior.

This scenario is common. Businesses and the people who run them, like most of us, are impatient. Workplace investigations are complex and as I said earlier in this chapter, successful investigations require the investment of time, patience, and resources. If your organization or client isn't prepared to make the requisite investment in each, your investigation will probably fail.

Tip: Obtain a commitment to obtain the resources you need up front. Decision makers very rarely change their minds. Even early success does not ensure you will be allocated more resources later.

---

e. *Lawful Execution*

Corporate investigators and those who conduct workplace investigations for their employers have enormous responsibility. The outcomes of their effort often impact the organizations they serve and the employees that work for them. The Process of Investigation® has no rule book (save this one), it is not governed by any oversight body, and it is not necessarily bound by criminal law or civil code. It and the people who conduct workplace investigations are governed largely by ethics. Usually not until someone complains or sues does anyone ever really scrutinize the typical workplace investigation or the people who performed it. Consider for a moment your own investigations. How many of those were ever really scrutinized and picked apart? Who critiqued you or your team? Certainly there must be exceptions, but by and large very few workplace investigations are looked at carefully. Unless someone challenges the outcome, is dissatisfied with the punishment, or realizes the effort was so glaringly defective, no one cares and no one looks. The case is closed and never looked at again. Not so for criminal investigations. Every aspect is examined.

2. The Six Methods of Investigation

Fundamentally, there are six basic methods of investigation available to those who conduct workplace investigations:

- Physical surveillance
- Electronic surveillance
- Research and internal audit
- Forensic analysis
- Undercover
- Interviews and interrogation

That's it. There are no others. Every workplace investigation uses one or more of these methods. The challenge then for the professional investigator is to select the method(s) most suitable for his particular circumstances and deploy it properly and efficiently. In many instances, the investigator will find that he must combine the methods in some fashion or mix and match them. It is only with knowledge and experience that the investigator can know which methods to use and when. It is this unique ability to combine these methods properly and efficiently that separates exceptional investigators from good investigators. Although I will describe each of these in finer detail in Chapter 3, let's look at each of them briefly here.

a. Physical Surveillance

In the context of workplace investigations, physical surveillance is nothing more than watching people, places, and things. Physical surveillance only requires two things: something to watch and someone to watch it. As such, physical surveillance is relatively inexpensive and easy to use. Those who have conducted surveillance know that as simple as it is, it requires skill and patience. Not everyone is capable of surveillance or doing it properly. In some instances, it requires sitting patiently in closed quarters, such as an automobile or van. In other instances, it requires following the subject as he drives about. This form of physical surveillance is called moving surveillance and requires even greater skill.

Physical surveillance, however, has its limitations. Because it is not interactive, that is, the observer has no interaction or communication with whom he is observing, the evidence physical surveillance produces is typically only corroborative. That is, it only supports or corroborates other evidence. Here's an example.

If I were to observe an individual remove from the rear door of his workplace a large, sealed corrugated box and secretly put it into the trunk of his vehicle under the cover of darkness, what did I actually see? Did I observe a theft? Absent any other evidence, what I observed was likely nothing more than an individual removing from the rear door of his workplace a large, sealed corrugated box and secretly putting it into the trunk of his vehicle. You see, absent any other information I don't know what the box contained, whether he had permission to remove it, or if the content of the box was even his. For this reason, physical surveillance can rarely be used for anything other than gathering corroborative evidence.

b. Electronic Surveillance

Electronic surveillance is similar to physical surveillance in that it too is nothing more than watching people, places, and things. However, unlike physical surveillance, electronic surveillance employs the use of electronic technology in order to improve the results. It too is relatively inexpensive and easy to use. Electronic surveillance can also be used in places and circumstances simple physical surveillance cannot. Because electronic surveillance uses technology such as video, covert cameras, and personal computer monitoring software, it can be used when and where physical surveillance is not possible. For example, if the subject of interest was deep inside a facility, say inside the employee break room, all the physical surveillance possible in the parking lot would never record the questionable activity in the break room.

However, therein lies the rub. Because electronic surveillance is possible in so many circumstances, users of it must be careful not to deploy it where its use might constitute an invasion of privacy. The courts have widely held that even in the workplace, employees enjoy a limited right to privacy, the limitations of which vary from jurisdiction to jurisdiction. Regardless, a worker's right to a reasonable expectation of privacy is universal, and to violate it may be both criminally and civilly actionable.

Electronic surveillance is also not interactive. Like physical surveillance it has no interaction or communication with whom it is observing or monitoring. As such, the evidence it produces is typically only corroborative as well.

c. Research and Internal Audit

The third method of investigation is the combination of research and audit. For the purposes of this work, we shall define research as that investigative activity involving the collection of information from public sources. Such sources include the Department of Motor Vehicles, the county clerk's office where criminal and civil records are stored, and the county recorder's office where all manner of records involving real estate transactions are recorded and kept.

Public records often afford the workplace investigator a huge source of information and, depending on the type of matter under investigation, possibly the very clues that may make his case. Take, for example, vendor fraud investigations. These frauds typically involve a dishonest purchasing agent who, without the consent or knowledge of his employer, establishes a business with which his organization then does business. In order to legitimize the business as a viable vendor, he must authenticate it by creating it legally. In most situations it must be properly organized as a corporation or a limited liability company (LLC). This permits the business to open business-banking accounts and perform other functions customary of a legitimate business. In order to do this, the principal must file certain documents with the secretary of the state in which the business operates. In doing so, public records are created, which are available to anyone for the asking. When suspecting vendor fraud, these are precisely the documents the investigator should seek.

On the other hand, the internal audit method is reserved for the examination of nonpublic records, such as those in the possession of the employer-victim. Such records include attendance, productivity, and financial records, and even prior investigations. Today, the amount of information organizations generate is staggering. Modern enterprises are far beyond merely watching the numbers; keeping records on customer wants, needs, buying patterns, and consumption; vendor capacity, capability, delivery time, and reliability; productivity, up-time, down-time, capacity, and even the amount of waste produced is common. No detail, event, outcome, or result is too small to document. In fact, modern management tools such as ISO and Six-Sigma require everything to be measured. Assuredly, no organization of any size is short on data.

The use of such data is manifold in many workplace investigations. Several years ago, I conducted an investigation for an aerospace manufacturer that suspected employee theft. The manufacturer produced a complex component used in jet engine fuel flow regulators. For some time, "per unit" production costs were escalating, yet supply prices and labor costs were stable. The waste stream seemed unchanged and "unit failure" rates were at an all-time low. Buried deep in the mass of information the client kept on its manufacturing process, we discovered that the production of each unit consumed three times the number of screws the unit actually required. Upon inspection of inventories we found no excesses nor did we discover any undocumented waste or failures. Purchasing records supported the findings; therefore, we began to dig even deeper. After taking a close look at each screw vendor, we discovered that two of them operated out of the same single-family residence. Further investigation revealed the home was that of one of my client's purchasing agents. In short order he was interviewed and readily admitted he had committed the crime. He further revealed that it was greed that had motivated him. He explained that after his screws were received and placed into inventory, he would steal them, repackage them, and resell them to his employer. We estimated that some screws had been repurchased as many as 20 times! Had the client not kept the detailed records it had, the case may have never been solved.

d. Forensic Analysis

Forensic analysis is the fourth method of investigation. It includes all manners of investigation that employ science or scientific method. In this category are bodily fluid analysis, chemical and substance analysis, fingerprint examination and comparison, computer forensics, various deception detection methods, and forensic document examination. For the purposes of our study, forensic analysis is the catch-all category where science and the investigator meet.

Some of the forensic tools available to investigators are rather interesting. One of the least familiar and more fascinating of them is Benford's law, a powerful fraud detection tool that predicts the frequency of numbers (digits) in some naturally occurring, unmanipulated groups of numbers. Engineers and mathematicians have long known of a simple but powerful mathematical model that quickly predicts the distribution of numbers for pointing suspicion at frauds, embezzlers, tax evaders, sloppy accountants and even computer bugs.[7] Frank Benford, rediscoverer of this phenomenon, was a physicist for General Electric who in 1938 recognized that certain "non-randomly behaved numbers in non-normally distributed data sets" behave in a very predicable fashion. Benford analyzed over 20,000

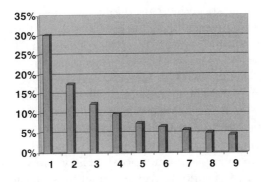

Exhibit 1.1 Benford's Probability Distribution of the First Digit in Non-Normally Distributed Data Sets

data sets of various categories and found that all of the seemingly disparate numbers followed the same first-digit probability pattern. Benford's probability distribution (in percentage) of the first digit of any database that meets the criteria described above is shown in Exhibit 1.1.

Thus, if we examined a data set composed of invoice amounts, Benford's law (which is scale invariant) predicts that 30.10 percent of the invoice amounts begin with the digit 1. Those amounts, for example, might be $1.29 or $17,031.81. Regardless, approximately 30 percent will begin with the digit 1; roughly 18 percent will begin with the digit 2, and so on. The data set that does not conform is thus suspect. My personal investigative use of this powerful forensic tool has consistently provided insight into corrupt data. In a case I will discuss in a later chapter, we'll see how it helped smoke out three dishonest vendors out of a group of over 200.

e. Undercover

Corporate undercover investigation is one of the most powerful methods of investigation. By definition it is nothing more than the surreptitious placement of a properly trained and skilled investigator, posing as an employee, into an unsuspecting workforce for the purpose of gathering information.[8] Undercover is one of only two forms of investigation that are interactive. That is, it permits the investigator to interact and communicate with those he is investigating. However, undercover is immensely complex and fraught with challenges. When conducted improperly, it can create unfathomable liabilities for both the employer-client and the investigator.

Undercover investigations are also time consuming and expensive. The typical investigation might take three to six months and cost as much as $100,000. Because of the cost and liability associated with undercover, I tell my clients that it should be used only as the option of last resort. After all other alternatives and solutions have been thoroughly contemplated, only then should undercover be considered. That said, I have personally supervised or managed over 1,000 undercover investigations in my career. I have successfully placed undercover investigators in nearly every working environment imaginable. Over the years, my undercover investigators have harvested trees, planted lettuce, built airplanes, sorted recyclables, emptied bedpans, refined oil, directed traffic, made bath tissue, tended bar, driven trucks, sorted mail, and slaughtered livestock. The only environment undercover usually not possible is one in which the employer is not hiring. Even then, undercover is sometimes possible.

But undercover is not for the faint-hearted. It requires a motivated and disciplined investigator and close supervision. It generally cannot be done in-house. Those who wish to use this method of investigation should always use a vendor—and good vendors are hard to find. Jump to Chapter 3 Section E if you are eager to learn more about undercover and how this fantastic investigative tool can and should be used. For the rest of you, let's move on to interviews and interrogations, indisputably the most powerful tools in the workplace investigator's tool chest.

f. Interviews and Interrogation

The sixth and final method of investigation is the systematic collection of information via interviews and interrogation. Unfortunately, these terms mean different things to different people. The term *interview* seems less harsh than *interrogation* to most people. It describes a process that is less formal, less structured. But *Merriam-Webster* defines these terms similarly, distinguishing interrogation as a process in which one "questions formally and systematically." But in actuality, the word *interrogation* is rarely used to describe a formal and systematic interview. Instead, when one uses the word *interrogation,* it seems to mean so much more. The thought of interrogation congers up images of an offensive and coercive interview during which the subject is harshly questioned under a bright light by law enforcement. It is stigmatized, carrying with it the inference or suggestion of coercion, intimidation, and trickery. Some even consider an interrogation to be unlawful. As such, I rarely use the word to describe my interviews. I don't like the inferences that are associated with it and don't care to offer qualifiers or explain myself every time I use the word. Hence, for the purposes of our study of the subject I will restrict my use of it.

Interviews conducted during workplace investigations fall into two categories. The less formal of the two is called an administrative interview. These include interviews of witnesses, bystanders, and others not or likely not culpable of the offense or matter under investigation. Investigative interviews, on the other hand, are reserved for those who we have very convincing reason to believe committed the offense or had direct involvement in it. Both forms of interviews are highly structured, but neither is confrontational or accusatory. Largely what distinguishes the two is the intended outcome. During administrative interviews we are simply looking for information. We are attempting to learn, gain insight, and collect information. During investigative interviews, first and foremost, we are seeking an admission. An admission is not a confession. A confession is a statement that includes an admission to all of the elements of the crime. In workplace investigations, confessions are not necessary. In order to discipline an offending employee in most instances, the employer need only prove the employee in question committed the offense. The employer does not need to prove or demonstrate things such as means, motive, or intent. Those elements of the offense are inconsequential and have no bearing on the employer's determination of guilt or culpability or the right to impose discipline. Armed with a properly obtained admission, an employer needs nothing more to take disciplinary or corrective action against the offender. The same is not the case for criminal prosecution.

Trap: Employers tend to overinvestigate. Many of them believe they must prove their case beyond a reasonable doubt. This extraordinarily high standard of proof is reserved only for criminal prosecution. In pursuing it, the employer expends more time and resources than necessary.

Like undercover, interviews are also interactive. They afford the investigator the opportunity to exchange information with the subject. Specifically, interviews afford the investigator the opportunity to determine the who, what, where, when, how, and why from the very person who was there. It provides the investigator the unique opportunity to peek into the mind of the offender. This benefit, combined with the opportunity to obtain an admission, makes interviews the most powerful from of investigation for those conducting workplace investigations.

3. The Five Phases of Investigation

Most workplace investigations unfold incrementally. That incremental, yet dynamic process is called the Process of Investigation.[9] The process includes five distinct phases:

- Preparation and planning
- Information gathering and fact-finding
- Verification and analysis;
- Determination and disbursement of disciplinary or corrective action;
- Prevention and education.

As we will learn, every proper workplace investigation requires the investigator to structure his investigation so that it systematically contemplates each phase. To do otherwise is insufficient, unprofessional, and possibly even negligent. The investigator who imposes process and structure on his investigation obtains better results and does so with more efficiency. What's more, it differentiates him as a professional. It affords him and his employer or client the benefit of ease in assessing and analyzing the result. As in the scientific community, process also permits peer review. In the community of employer–employee relations, others may review the investigator's efforts and are able to easily and accurately reconstruct that which the investigator found and how he found it. The ability to reconstruct the process and demonstrate its integrity and propriety lends it credibility. That credibility is the foundation on which all facts rest. An investigative process, like the investigator, without credibility is fatally defective. That defect potentially imposes a bar to the admission and ultimate use of otherwise admissible and actionable evidence. It is the implementation and ultimate integrity of this process that is the hallmark of the professional investigator.

a. Preparation and Planning

The first phase of process has already been discussed in some detail. It involves all of the "front end" activities and preparations that normally take place before fact-finding begins. It includes such activities as obtaining management's commitment, negotiating objectives, establishing a timeline, deciding a standard of proof, and pooling the necessary resources and expertise to do the job properly.

I take the preparation and planning of my investigations very seriously. I have learned from experience that the time and energy invested upfront pays big dividends later. For example, by negotiating and detailing objectives early, I am more easily able to lobby for the resources I need to do the job. Establishing a timeline and communicating it with the client before the project begins allows both the client and the investigator to better plan and budget their time. It also provides a clearer way to communicate expectations and often reduces later confusion. The adage "plan your work, then work your plan" works perfectly here. Without proper preparation and planning, successful workplace investigations are not possible. And sadly, even seasoned investigators overlook this important step. Have you ever intentionally traveled to a far-off destination without a strategy, itinerary, or map? It is not possible. You would never reach your destination. Why then would you undertake something as complex as an investigation without doing the same preparation and planning? Only a novice would gloss over this important step. Don't be foolish, plan your work, and then work your plan.

b. Information Gathering and Fact-Finding

I have already described in considerable detail the six methods of investigation. This phase of the investigation necessitates the investigator to combine these methods and deploy them in a precise sequence and measure. Tactically, the investigator mixes and matches the methods she determines appropriate at the appropriate time. This mix is largely predetermined during the planning phase. The investigative team, project manager, and client should together determine the investigative tools to be used and when they should be used. If you have ever conducted a workplace investigation, you probably did this and gave it very little thought. By front-loading the process with sufficient planning and mapping the investigative tools to be used, the objectives are usually easier to achieve and the investment necessary to achieve them is diminished.

The information-gathering phase of the process, however, is not an end, but a means. The purpose of this important phase is to gather the information necessary to move to the next phase—verification and analysis. This point is missed all too often by many in the industry. Many of my colleagues fail to appreciate that the successful gathering of information does not mark the end of the investigation. The successful gathering of information provides the foundation from which to move forward. Here is a good example.

Fact Pattern

Hypothetically, suppose our client (external or internal to our organization) suspected an employee violating her organization's policy regarding the use of the Internet during working hours. Specifically, the organization had credible evidence that the employee in question frequently viewed pornography at her workstation during scheduled work hours. Suppose also that during the preparation and planning phase, it was decided that should the suspicions be true, the employee would be terminated. You are asked to conduct the investigation and obtain the proof, should it exist.

Strategy

Given the objective to obtain the proof, the fact-finder must also know the standard of proof. The sophisticated fact-finder knows the standard of proof will drive his process and significantly determine the resources necessary to obtain the stated objective. Because only an employment action is sought, the standard of proof should be good faith investigation and reasonable conclusion.

The fact-finder then begins the information-gathering phase of the investigation. Using elementary computer forensics, he quickly finds temp files, trash bin items, saved images, and bookmarked Web pages related to or containing pornography, as defined by the organization's policy, on the subject's workstation. Is the investigation sufficient and has the fact-finder achieved the standard of proof selected? The answer will surprise you—it is yes to both questions. However, the investigator should not end his process here. He should move his effort to the next phase of investigation and interview the subject. The reason he should do this is twofold: (1) there is the possibility someone else used the subject's computer and left the evidence in question; (2) if the subject is guilty as suspected, an admission should be obtained.

In properly interviewing the subject, our investigator fulfills any due process rights the subject might enjoy, and if she provides an admission, it will be used as proof of guilt. The decision makers can then effectively discount or discard the evidence developed during the forensic analysis and hang their decision on the subject's admission alone. In doing so the subject is denied the opportunity to attack any aspect of the forensic portion of the process (assuming it was done properly and lawfully) or claim a material defect in the evidence. If she disagrees with the discipline, her only option is to overcome her own admission. In acting upon the admission only, the client has met the good faith investigation and reasonable conclusion standard and has significantly reduced that chance of an evidentiary challenge.

Tip: The information gathering and fact-finding phase of the investigation is not an end but a means. It affords the investigator the information he needs to interview the subject and successfully obtain an admission.

---

c. Verification and Analysis

As discussed above, the next phase involves the systematic interview of those identified during our information gathering and fact-finding. These interviews are called investigative interviews and are reserved for those who we have a very convincing reason to believe committed the offense(s) in question or had direct involvement in it. Many professional investigators and employers overlook this opportunity. They frequently forgo investigative interviews and opt for termination or even arrest. Although termination and arrest might remove the offender from the workplace, it is not a complete solution. Properly conducted investigative interviews often yield information not otherwise attainable by any other means.

A cooperative interviewee can provide information and intelligence spanning the term of his employment. Even a lengthy undercover would produce only direct evidence developed during the course of the investigation. A cooperative interviewee is likely to provide information regarding others as well. It is not unusual for a culpable offender to "give up" or "roll-over" on co-conspirators during an interview. This information is corroborative only. However, the accumulation of enough corroboration could justify the interview of an individual not identified during the information-gathering phase of the investigation. In substance abuse investigations, this is very common. The resultant expansion of information and intelligence and ultimate identification of many more additional offenders significantly enhances the ROI. I have had investigations in which my team began interviewing with information involving two employees and when finished had interviewed over 30. In one particularly memorable case a female employee identified 110 employees to whom she alleged sold cocaine at work. Sobbing as she discussed her transgressions, she said she was sure she had sold to additional employees, but could not remember their names!

As mentioned in the previous section, investigative interviews also yield admissions. From an employment law standpoint, properly obtained admissions constitute the best evidence an employer can obtain. Unlike criminal law, where admissions and even confessions often have only corroborative value, an employer needs only to proffer an admission to make his case. No other proof is necessary. An admission even trumps other evidence with which it conflicts. From an employer's perspective, there is no better evidence than an admission. Some of the best attorneys I know have failed to leverage this powerful opportunity. Don't make the same mistake. Whenever possible, follow your information gathering with investigative interviews.

In Chapter 3 I will go into detail how even an inexperienced investigator can become a successful interviewer. I will explain how to memorialize an admission and preserve it for evidentiary purposes.

Tip: Successful investigative interviews are largely predicated on the amount of information the interviewer
possesses before the interview. Bypassing the information gathering and fact-finding phase and going directly
to investigative interviews rarely produces results and
creates unnecessary liability for both the interviewer
and the client.

d. Determination and Disbursement of Disciplinary or Corrective Action

Following the second and third phases of the investigation, the project
manager should assemble the results and present them to the decision
makers. This typically involves reducing the findings into a concise report
and formally presenting it. To analyze, interpret, and detail one's work is
easier than it sounds if the project manager has the proper information
management processes in place. I will discuss these and other important
subprocesses later. What is important now is to appreciate what has been
achieved up to this point and its value to the client. Effectively the process
should have yielded

- Significant factual information regarding the matter under
  investigation
- Information identifying at least some of those involved and some
  idea of their purpose
- Corroborative information from investigative interviews regarding
  those involved from co-conspirators or witnesses
- Admissions from the wrongdoers regarding their transgressions

The investigative team has leveraged the initial information gathered
during the fact-finding phase into two additional sources of information:
that which was provided by the subject(s) and that which others said
about him. Armed with this wealth of information, the employer-client
can then easily and safely determine the equitable disbursement of discipline and corrective action. Let's look more closely.

In the instances in which admissions exist, decision making is simple.
Lacking admissions, the employer-client has corroborative statements from
those who made admissions as well as other evidence developed during

the fact-finding phase. Lacking any admissions, the employer-client still has the results from the fact-finding phase. Even in the face of a denial by any particular subject, armed with sufficient incriminating information, the employer-client is afforded the luxury to safely make a tough call if it applies a good faith investigation and reasonable conclusion standard. In other words, the process has engineered defensible fall-back options even in the worst case scenario—no admissions from anyone. This may all appear a bit esoteric, but I assure you these intricate machinations will not be missed on a trier of fact with any sophistication. At the very least, if challenged, the employer-client and the investigators will be able to demonstrate they employed a well-conceived process, one with structure, purpose, and fairness. It is one that optimizes professionalism and separates it and its principles from the typical bungling incompetents to which most judges and juries are accustomed. Plaintiffs and the attorneys who represent them love employers (and investigators) who lack process, fly by the seat of their pants, and make mistakes at every turn.

Regardless of the quality and sophistication of the process, the decisions regarding discipline and corrective action must be fair and equitable. Good evidence and an admission don't make a minor offense a capital crime. Conversely, punishing all offenders equally is not necessarily equitable. The punishment must first fit the crime, then like crimes must be punished equally. The failure to do so invites discrimination and disparate treatment claims. The successful prosecution of either can be embarrassing and costly.

Tip: The fact-finder should never play the role of decision maker or visa versa. In fairness to the subject and the process, separate the duties of the fact-finder and decision maker.

---

e. Prevention and Education

Tying the process together is the last phase, prevention and education. During this phase, the employer-client and investigative team join together to critique the effort, benchmark, identify best practices, and analyze their performance. Additionally, this employer-client–investigative team assesses the damage and attempts to sort out what went wrong in the first place. What was it that allowed the problem to occur and how can it be prevented in the future? This evaluation can be priceless. Clearly, if the organization continues the same practices, it is likely to get the same result again in the future. Such behavior is worse than pointless; it may also be negligent. Under the legal theory of foreseeability, negligence is compounded when a party should have reasonably foreseen an event that could have been prevented had that person taken corrective or preventative action. Organizations make the mistake often and in so doing may incur unnecessary additional liability.

Finally, the team should reduce its findings to some sort of recommendation. The recommendation often includes altering or modifying policies, changing or implanting new practices, and training for those who need it. Of all of the phases of investigation, this is the least utilized. Because investigations like those discussed are so complex and time consuming, it seems when they are completed everyone involved desperately wants to move on. I don't blame them. However, passing up the opportunity to learn from past mistakes and record best practices seems to be a heavy price to pay for simply wanting to close a file and move on to the next project.

B. The Differences between the Public and Private Sectors

My grandfather was a homicide detective in New York City for 30 years. He retired in 1952. During his career, he investigated unimaginable crimes and dealt with many horrible human beings. The experience left him bitter and cynical. But like many retired law enforcement officers of his time, he entered the private sector after he left the "job." He quickly found a job at a large racetrack as a security officer and ended up working there for many years. After he left the track and fully retired, he spent his time tending his tomatoes and making his famous Italian gravy. Every Sunday the entire family would gather at his home for a delicious dinner of spaghetti and meatballs. As a small child, I remember many times his reminiscing and telling wild stories of police chases and shoot-outs with gangsters. But of all his work, he loved most working at the track. I have since learned that he and retirees like him were the forefathers of modern industrial security. He and his generation pioneered the private security frontier and were among the first of those we call today security professionals. Interestingly, just two years after his first retirement, the American Society of Industrial Security was founded. Today the society has been renamed ASIS International and boasts almost 40,000 members worldwide. And like ASIS, the private security industry has come a very long way.

1. *An Historical Perspective*

The most significant change in private security is that it has become a true profession. No longer is it just a second career option or reserved for those coming out of law enforcement. It has become a profession in every regard. Secondary schools and universities now offer degrees in security management and even loss prevention. The profession has moved to accrediting and certifying select members who qualify. Designations such as Board Certified in Security Management and Certified Fraud Examiner are almost necessities for those in executive security management. Each segment of the profession offers its own designations and publishes its own periodical or journal. The men and women who make up the profession write, publish, and subject their work to peer review. These professionals meet, exchange ideas, and offer the results of their research to anyone willing to study them. It has been a marvelous and miraculous transition, and its impact on business and society has been significant.

Today nearly every organization, public and private, of any measurable size boasts at least one security management position. Larger organizations have security or loss prevention departments, and cutting-edge global enterprises have designated chief security officers (CSOs) to protect their assets and employees. These CSOs report directly to the chairman and enjoy all of the privileges and responsibilities of an organization's CEO, CFO, and COO. Never in the history of private security has the security professional experienced such recognition and importance.

This evolution, however, has come with a price. No longer can the successful law enforcement professional haplessly migrate from the public to the private sector after retirement as my grandfather did. Like the public sector, the private sector now demands more of its professionals and the men and women who manage them. Even advanced degrees and robust résumés are not enough. In order to transition from the public to private sector successfully, the individual needs an acute appreciation for business. Not just budgets, finance, and personnel management but a deep understanding of business and its purpose. That purpose, of course, is to make money and create wealth. Money is not a dirty word, and the creation of wealth is a worthy endeavor. The ability to create and accumulate wealth is the cornerstone of a free-market system. Although money is the oil that lubricates the system, it is the accumulation of wealth that provides our capital markets and makes possible the free enterprise as we know it. The mechanisms and apparatus that support it are not the same in the public sector.

2. Mission

Foremost of the many differences separating the public and private sectors is their missions. Public sector law enforcement's principal mission is the enforcement of public law. Over the past two decades, this mission has been expanded to include administration of public safety, crime prevention, substance abuse awareness, community service, and even revenue generation. However, job number one is to enforce public law. The principal vehicle used in pursuit of this mission is street enforcement and criminal investigations. Yes, law enforcement, both on the local and federal levels, does other important things. They make other significant contributions in other ways. But when one peels back the skin of the onion, one will find at the core—street enforcement and criminal investigations. With all due respect to the brave men and women in blue—what cops do best is put law-breakers in jail. Compare that activity and that which supports it to the purpose of business as I have described it in the preceding paragraph. Though not diametrically opposed, the principal missions of these important endeavors are vastly different. See for yourself. Look at your organization's mission statement or that of one of your clients. Does it contain the words *law enforcement, criminal justice,* or *prosecution*? Is it your organization's mission to prosecute its employees to the fullest extent of the law? Is it your client's mission to produce capital appreciation or to enforce public law?

As we drill into the private sector organization and come upon the security professional, we find that his mission is also vastly different from that of law enforcement. So different are the two, I oppose the use of the term "counterpart in law enforcement" when describing the function of the security professional. The law enforcement officer does not have a counterpart in the private sector. Even security officers are not responsible for the enforcement of public law. Their job, and important it is, is to observe and report. The corporate security professional is not the "company cop." Unfortunately for them and their organizations, many private sector security professionals see themselves as just that. These often very bright and capable people see their position in the private sector as an extension of their former roles in law enforcement. They intentionally retain the demeanor, that somewhat inflated self-confidence and that harsh cop-speak vernacular, they cultivated while on the job. Others in their organization call this collective behavior the "cop mentality." Because of it, they don't see the company cop as a peer. They perceive that individual as a corporate outsider and necessary nuisance. Tragically, many corporate security professionals relish this image. You know the type. You've met them and so have the executives in your organization—you know, those executives who evaluate your performance and measure your contribution to the organization. If they perceive you as the company cop, that is precisely how they will treat you and pay you. It's tragic and it's unnecessary.

Tip: Jettison the image of company cop. Talk like and act like the people in whose hands your career rests.

By confusing missions, however, the corporate security professional does more than damage his career, he damages his organization. While fixated on enforcing public law and putting workplace transgressors in jail, the security professional overlooks his organization's mission and purpose. He tends to forget that prosecuting dishonest employees contributes nothing to the organization's balance sheet and shareholder equity. In fact, in some cases the affect can be quite the opposite. Here's an excellent example.

My client, the corporate director of security for a nationwide auto parts distributor, was a retired FBI agent. A nice enough fellow, he was soft spoken, professional, and principled. He also hated crime and those who committed it. His purpose in life was to put law-breakers in jail. On numerous occasions I proposed we pursue restitution in lieu of prosecution. He would hear nothing of it. Then one day during an undercover investigation my firm was conducting for him he called and said he had just shut the case down. He said he was at the target facility and that the police were en route, and upon their arrival the guilty would be arrested. His plan was defective and I told him so. First, on what grounds might a misdemeanor offender be arrested; or for that matter, on what grounds might one be arrested for overstaying his break? Second, absent proper interviews, how might admissions be obtained? In other words, on what grounds would discipline be based? He retorted that those prosecuted would be disciplined and that arrest alone was cause for termination. The line went dead.

Sure enough, I later learned, the police showed up, lights flashing, and screaming sirens. Chaos ensued. Panicked employees leapt from windows, hurled themselves over fences and ran in every direction. The fact that many were illegal aliens didn't help the situation either. The police soon got the upper hand and took away those they had caught. Hours later an angry chief released the arrestees and apologized to each as they left his custody. The chief knew very well that his officers had made a terrible mistake. The arrests were unlawful, for probable cause did not exist. There was no proper justification for the arrest and search of these people. But the security director lost more than face. Shortly after the spectacle, the former arrestees sued their employer. The case was later settled and never went to jury. The settlement remains confidential but I do know that the former FBI agent and his second-in-command now work elsewhere.

Trap: Despite popular belief, employee prosecution is neither cost-effective nor a deterrent. In most instances, better results can be achieved by pursuing the organization's mission.

---

3. Advantages of the Public Sector

The second most significant difference separating the public and private sectors is the enormous power and authority the public sector has. Law enforcement and its companion, the criminal justice system, have at their disposal mechanisms and tools unheard of in the private sector. Let's briefly examine a few.

a. Powers of Arrest

Designated individuals in law enforcement and the criminal justice system have the incredible power of arrest. Unlike citizens, corporate security professionals, among them the police, district attorneys, and judges, can under a host of circumstances arrest people, subject them to a custodial interrogation, and even incarcerate them. By fulfilling a few simple requirements and with rather minimal justification, the public sector has the power to detain, forcibly question, and interrogate. In venues such as a properly convened court, the failure to answer a question or cooperate is a crime. The crime is called contempt of court and is punishable with incarceration. There is no equivalent in the private sector. Citizens can, under very special circumstances, make an arrest, but in doing so incur significant liability. To forcibly question or hold another against his will constitutes false imprisonment and is civilly actionable.

b. Search and Seizure

The public sector also has at its disposal the power to search people and seize property. The law permits one's person, property, and papers to be searched or seized by the government. Although the citizenry enjoys constitutional protections under the Fourth Amendment of the U.S. Constitution and elsewhere against abuse of this power, it is a critical tool in the conduct of criminal investigations and the enforcement of public law. The closest thing to it in the private sector is the ability of an employer to search its own property. Workplace searches of desks, lockers, and other work areas are permissible only where an employee does not have a reasonable expectation of privacy. The employer can substantially reduce the expectation of privacy by advising employees that such areas are subject to inspection, with or without notice; restricting private use of these areas by issuing its own locks and retaining duplicate keys; and crafting policies that limit worker's expectation of privacy and permit searches under any circumstances.

Regardless, the powers available to the employer pale compared with those of the government. The ability to search and seize property in the spirit of a criminal investigation or inquiry creates a huge differentiator between the public and private sectors.

c. Grand Jury and Special Inquiries

The ability to convene a grand jury and forcibly extract testimony, even with representation of the suspect absent, is unmatched in the private sector.[10] During such proceedings, a citizen's failure to cooperate may be ruled contempt, and failure to tell the truth may be deemed perjury. Although employees have an affirmative duty to cooperate in an organizationally sanctioned investigation, an employee may in fact refuse to cooperate (and face possible discipline) and has no obligation (other than an ethical one) to tell the truth.

Tip: An employee's refusal to cooperate in her employer's investigation is actionable. Under some circumstances, the termination of uncooperative suspects can be justified merely on their refusal to participate and answer an investigator's questions.

---

d. Prosecution and Punishment

Employers believe they can prosecute law-breaking employees, but they cannot. Unfortunately it is a widely held notion even in the private security

industry. Only the government can prosecute someone. Even more interesting is the fact that employers cannot even ask the government to
prosecute someone. In every jurisdiction of which I am aware, the
improper influence of the prosecution is in and of itself a crime. Furthermore, an employer's threat of prosecution may constitute criminal extortion.[11] Again, contrary to popular belief, the employer can only file a
complaint. It is the duty of the government to determine if a law has
been broken and, if so, what charges should be brought based on the
evidence available. In property crimes such as theft, if the employer were
the victim, it could swear-out a complaint and ask that the matter be
investigated. The authorities would then work the case and hopefully find
the suspect(s) and charge him. On the other hand, in matters involving
workplace substance abuse, even selling illegal drugs at work, the
employer is not the victim. The government is technically the victim and
no complaint is necessary. It is the sole discretion of the government
whether to pursue the matter. The employer cannot decide who or what
offenses can be prosecuted.

Successful prosecutions also result in punishment. The punishment is
designed to fit the crime and ranges from something as passive as a
suspended sentence up to and including execution. The private workplace
has nothing equivalent. And, employees are not punished, they are disciplined. The notion of workplace punishment does not exist in a free
society. However, many liberal triers of fact consider employee termination
the civil equivalent of capital punishment. As such, termination is frequently
considered extreme discipline and only used in extreme circumstances.

Workplace discipline also does not produce a public record. Criminal
prosecution, except that of minors, produces a criminal record capable
of following the offender his entire life. Not so in the workplace. Employee
discipline is a private matter and rarely should co-workers even be told
what discipline was meted out. In the interest of employee privacy and
confidentiality, workplace discipline stays in the workplace and any record
of it remains under strict employer control. Even perspective employers
find it difficult to learn the terms and conditions of an applicant's separation from a prior employer.

The public sector is not bound by such a construct. In addition to
some of the most powerful investigative tools available only to it, the
public sector is largely unconcerned about individual privacy and confidentiality. Of course its investigations are draped in confidentiality, but
the process and results are ultimately disclosed and made available to
public scrutiny. In fact, it is this public disclosure that keeps the system
sound and its participants honest. The public aspect of a criminal trial is
so critical to the fair and proper workings of the process that it is
constitutionally protected. The private sector is not bound by such rules

and procedures. Only if challenged must the employer make limited disclosures. Even then, special privileges abound, ensuring certain communications and evidence remain confidential.

e. Resources

The question whether the public sector or private sector has greater resources is debatable. Both sectors have operational and fiscal limitations. Both have manpower and technological limitations. But even today, Microsoft, which has a reported $50 billion cash reserve, could not outspend the U.S. federal government, which has a deficit of over $1 trillion. Nor could Microsoft field more people than the government. The total combined capability of all federal, state, and local law enforcement authorities in the Untied States is unmatched in the world.

On the microlevel I would also argue that the government, at the federal, state, or local level, can probably throw more resources at any particular case than almost any defendant. These same government resources probably can out-gun most corporations as well. There are examples, of course, to the contrary. The federal government has waged battle against the likes of Microsoft and IBM® (IBM Corporation, White Plains, New York) in federal court and substantially lost in several cases. In several of these instances the defendant threw more resources at the case than the federal government did and effectively overwhelmed the system. One case in point was the IBM antitrust case, which finally ended in the 1970s. During discovery, IBM provided over 100 million documents. Analysts at the time speculated that it would take the presiding authority 3,000 years just to read all of the evidence.

Tip: On the whole, the public sector has greater resources than most organizations or individuals. The availability of these resources and its manpower provide the public sector a significant investigative advantage.

---

4. Advantages of the Private Sector

In spite of the awesome powers of the government and the system that supports it, the private sector has some of its own unique set of privileges and advantages. I have touched upon a few already, but there are more, and some are remarkably powerful.

a. Due Process

The U.S. Constitution ensures and protects a host of important personal rights. By design, the Constitution protects the citizenry against government oppressions and intrusions. Contrary to the assertions of many advocates and commentators, it does not substantially protect us from one another. More precisely, it restricts the behavior and actions of government, not its citizens. One of the Constitution's more progressive protections is that of due process. Among other things, due process includes the right to know the offense(s) and crime(s) of which one is accused, the right to view and examine the government's evidence, the right to face one's accusers and examine them as well as any and all witnesses, the right to competent representation, and protection against self-incrimination. These rights are bolstered by volumes of criminal procedures and case law. Among that body of law is Miranda.[12]

Miranda

The *Miranda* decision, decided in 1966 by the U.S. Supreme Court, requires that those taken into criminal custody, and where probable cause exists that suggests the suspect committed a crime, be informed of their due process rights before being questioned.[13] Remarkably, employees, when questioned by their employer or the employer's agent (a hired consultant or private investigator) with regard to possible misconduct, have no such rights, even if the suspected misconduct is criminal in nature. Allow me to say it again: Regardless of the nature of the suspected offense, employees under investigation by their employer have no due process rights. The employer (or agents) has no duty to even tell the employee under suspicion the offense of which he is suspected or what evidence the employer might have against him. Furthermore, the suspected employee does not even have the right to representation. She may be entitled to an employee witness, but the law is yet to be clear on this point.[14] But the right to a lawyer or someone else from outside the organization does not exist. The theory goes that such encumbrances would impinge on the employer's prerogative to run its business as it sees fit and impede the necessary collection of information required to solve internal problems.

Employers must be careful, however. Although they have no legal duty to provide the subjects of internal investigations any due process, some triers of fact and jury members think otherwise. The appearance of treating the subject unfairly and the failure to comply with the reasonable requests of the subject may expose the employer to considerable liability. Even absent the rights of due process, it is expected that all people be treated fairly and provided all reasonable accommodations while under suspicion or when accused of misconduct.

Furthermore, the more the employer involves the government in its investigation, the greater these expectations. It is for these reasons that as a matter of practice, I avoid attaching agent status to my investigators whenever possible. The more control and influence law enforcement has over a workplace investigation and its investigators, the more agent-like the investigators become. Subsequent to the discipline, should an employee successfully argue the investigators were agents of law enforcement or that the use of them by law enforcement subjugated rights they might otherwise have enjoyed, portions if not all of the evidence gathered by the investigators could come under attack. A plaintiff (or in the case of criminal trial, defendant) might attempt a motion to exclude the "improperly obtained evidence." If the motion were successful, the entire investigation could be in jeopardy. More easily in an arbitration, where the rules of evidence are more lax, an arbitrator could exclude the grievant's admission or that of others simply on the belief that ample due process was not provided.

Tip: Avoid the appearance of being an extension of law enforcement and keep your portion of the investigation separate from that of the government. If prosecution is likely, remand your evidence only after you have received a court order to do so.

---

b. Entrapment

Employers shy away from undercover investigations for many reasons, but among the most common and unnecessary is the fear of entrapment. Employers and even the lawyers who represent them principally fear entrapment because they don't understand it. Contrary to popular belief, entrapment is not a crime. It is not an offense or something bad employers do to innocent employees. It is not something for which one might be punished or even admonished. Entrapment is nothing more than a criminal defense. The theory behind the defense suggests that an otherwise law-abiding citizen would not have committed the crime in question if the government or its agent had not improperly induced him. In order to prevail, the defendant must show the inducement was sufficiently improper and, absent the government's influence, he had no predisposition to the commit the crime.

Because entrapment is a criminal defense, only the government can entrap someone. An employer cannot entrap an employee, a private undercover investigator in the workplace cannot entrap a co-worker, and a private investigator cannot entrap another citizen. Only the government can entrap. What's more, the defense of entrapment can be used only after a defendant admits to the commission of the crime. That's right; one cannot claim entrapment and also claim innocence. A defendant cannot have it both ways. Let's look at an example of entrapment.

Suppose an undercover police officer posing as a life insurance agent suggests to an otherwise law-abiding prospect that she purchase unnecessary life insurance on a spouse and then kill her partner and redeem the policy. To cinch the deal, the undercover agent offers a policy priced well below market and offers to help plan the murder. Acting upon the opportunity, the would-be policy holder is immediately arrested and charged with conspiracy to commit murder or its equivalent. Our hypothetical defendant could easily raise the defense of entrapment and would likely prevail. Her marriage would be another matter, however.

Interestingly, a law enforcement agent's offer to sell an illegal drug to a citizen under most circumstances does not constitute entrapment and the defense is often unavailable to the defendant. Courts will usually insist that the prosecution show some predisposition to the crime, but the offer to sell an illegal substance alone does not constitute entrapment. Reverse stings, as these operations are typically called, have increasingly become the weapon of choice in the war against drugs. Simultaneously, civil liberty advocates have increased their opposition to them. Please note, however, reverse stings are not appropriate in most workplace settings and should not be typically used by the private sector.

Because entrapment is so misunderstood and stigmatized, workplace investigators should contemplate counters to the claim during the planning phase of their investigations. Of all of the types of investigation subject to the claim, undercover is the most likely. Because undercover is so interactive and the subjects of the investigation are in direct contact with the investigator, claims of entrapment following an undercover investigation are common. Countering the claim is easy but any counters used must be deployed during the investigation, not after. There are two counters that are particularly effective.

Establish That the Misconduct Was Preexistent

The undercover investigator can establish the misconduct was preexistent in numerous ways. The easiest way to accomplish this is for the undercover investigator to simply ask the subject how long he had engaged in the misconduct in question. Here's a simple example.

Suppose our investigator is investigating allegations of employee substance abuse. During a casual conversation during break, the investigator openly expresses interest in purchasing marijuana for the weekend. During the conversation one of the employee participants off-handedly offers to sell some to the investigator. The employee tells the investigator that she has several bags of marijuana in her possession and wishes to sell one or all for $25 each. To counter the potential claim of entrapment, the investigator should simply ask the seller if she had ever before sold marijuana at work. An affirmative response would demonstrate that the activity had taken place before the investigator had come on the scene. As such, the seller could not later claim she had been induced by the investigator to do something she had already done.

Establish the Motive of the Offender

You may recall earlier I mentioned that motive is an irrelevant element for an employer who is deciding discipline. Despite its usefulness for other purposes, an employer needs to neither know the motive nor consider it when deciding discipline. However, the disciplined employee may attempt to introduce motive when using the defense of entrapment. Because the defense necessitates the offender to show that his behavior was adversely influenced by someone else, the argument is bolstered if motive is shown to have been influenced as well. For example, suppose the offender who claims entrapment argues as part of his defense that he was both broke and lonely, and the offer by the investigator included the reward of money and friendship. These claims tend to support the defense and give it the credibility it needs—that is, were it not for the need of money and friendship and the influence of the investigator, the offender would not have committed the crime. Defeating this argument is easy.

The solution is to deploy the second counter with the first during the fact-finding portion of the investigation. All the investigator needs to do is establish the motive of the potential offender before the offense is committed. For example, in the hypothetical example above, had the investigator established that (1) the offender had committed the offense several times prior to the investigator entering the case and (2) the motive was profit as evidenced by a new vehicle the offender bragged he had just purchased with proceeds, the defense would handily be defeated. What's more, introducing this sort of evidence further incriminates the accused. Our hypothetical offender has not only had to admit he had committed the offense in order to use the defense of entrapment, but now he is stuck with the burden of explaining the purchase of his new pickup truck he has bragged so much about. He also has the additional burden of recovering his credibility. Remember, he claimed he was broke and needed a friend. The $35,000 red pickup he purchased before he had met the investigator will destroy his credibility and likely his case.

Tip: Entrapment is not a crime, it is a criminal defense. Only the government or an agent of the government can be properly accused of entrapment.

C. Significant Trends in the Private Sector

1. More Sophisticated Crimes and Perpetrators

I began conducting workplace investigations for employers before the advent of fax machines, cell phones, desktop computers, and the Internet. I recall vividly the office of my first corporate employer. It was a large West Coast investigation firm and I was a cub investigator haphazardly thrust into an undercover assignment in a large paper distribution facility. The office was set up newsroom style with rows of metal desks and no partitions. Atop each desk was an in basket, an out basket, and an IBM electric typewriter. The place was inefficient and noisy. But that was the way business was done back then. Several years later, after I had been promoted into management, I can remember arguing with the senior partner about the proposed purchase of the office's first fax machine. I embraced the technology, but he couldn't reconcile the need for the instantaneous transmission of documents when the organization had successfully used messengers and U.S. mail for nearly 50 years. "Besides," he said, "what could possibly be so important that a client needs it right now?" Can you imagine?

Today's workplaces, of course, are much different. But it requires no leap in logic to appreciate the fact that as the workplace becomes a more sophisticated environment, workplace offenses and offenders will also become more sophisticated. As employers heap on advanced processes, systems, and technology, the opportunity to exploit them is advanced as well. It is for this reason that today's security professional must also be more advanced. Those who reject the modern workplace and all of its modernity are doomed. The workplace investigator must also embrace the new and ever-changing workplace, for it is impossible to investigate today's modern workplace crimes without a fine understanding or at least an appreciation for the environment in which the alleged offenses occurred.

2. *Greater Use of Technology*

Technology by definition promises convenience and economy. When technology is properly crafted, the convenience and economy it provides combine and are offered up as solutions. Technological solutions improve efficiency and profitability. Intentionally, they also reduce headcount. Engineers are constantly looking for ways for machines to replace human beings. Unfortunately, however, from an asset protection and loss prevention perspective, two things happen: (1) the technology provides new opportunity for exploitation, and (2) the quantity of supervision decreases. There is a subtle dichotomy here: as the exposure increases, protections decrease. Look around your own organization. Don't employees have more access to just about everything, and isn't your organization operating with less supervision?

Furthermore, organizations have been tricked into thinking more can be done with less supervision. Consider for a moment a few of the "revolutionary," often "enterprise-wide" "leadership initiatives" the big name "thought leaders" have sold to America's "bleeding-edge" organizations designed to "empower" employees and create "world class organizations" "Built to Last."[15] It is sickening. I mean for heaven's sake, "Let's Get Real."[16] It seems that for more than two decades corporate America has been running around looking for "The New New Thing"[17] and has yet to find it. Maybe the chief executive should ask "The Millionaire Next Door,"[18] for she's certainly not going to find it while meandering down "The Road Less Traveled."[19] With all due respect, what some of these "change merchants" are peddling would not fly in most organizations even if strapped to a Titan missile if attempted. Although much of this new-era corporate "psycho-babble" and brainwashing nobly embraces employee relations and empowers individual contributors (see, I cannot help using some these terms either), the sad fact of the matter is most people do not care.

Forgive my cynicism, but my experience is that most employees do not want to be empowered, most employees do not want more responsibility, and most employees are neither prepared nor willing to make tough organizational decisions. By and large, today's employees couldn't care less about most of the stuff today's thought leaders think they are interested in. Largely what employees want is a safe, fulfilling job and a work environment in which they are appreciated and treated with respect. Think about it — if the average line employee or staffer wanted more responsibility or to take more risk, he would have started his own company. What has been created in many cases are work environments in which management has involved its employees in the business of running a business to a greater degree than the typical employee wants. Then, in order to capitalize on the dividend of reduced headcount the thought leaders and change merchants promised, they slashed the amount of supervision in their organizations—think quality circles and self-directed work groups. Rarely have these initiatives worked as anticipated. Instead they have served as expensive experiments. They often did nothing more than distract management and consume valuable resources. By reducing the quantity of supervision without necessarily improving quality, many of these well-meaning organizations created nothing more than fertile grounds for employee theft, dishonesty, and misconduct.

Let's not forget the technology component. As management reengineered itself, it often simultaneously embraced advances in technology. By design, technological advancements promise improved efficiency and quality. So is the case in most industries and workplaces. But as previously mentioned, new technology also means new vulnerabilities. As fast as the technology is deployed, villains will figure out how to exploit it to some criminal advantage. In some cases they will even go further and just steal the technology and the product it produces, as in the illegal practice of downloading music CDs off the Internet.

Tip: When deploying new technology, always attempt to identify exploitable vulnerabilities and address them before they are found by the criminally minded employee. Remind management that bleeding edge is often just that.

---

3. More Litigious Workforce

America is the most litigious industrialized nation in the world.[20] For all its greatness and potential, our society is also one wrapped in rules and regulations. Be it the placement of safety labels on household stepladders (has anyone ever really read them?) or the amount of vacation pay a terminated employee must be paid, we have decided that nearly everything we do, say, or think needs to be regulated. In the post–World War II era of regulation promulgation, we have passed more laws and regulations than were implemented during the previous 175 years. This tangled morass of increasingly contradictory rules, laws, and regulations is rapidly reaching critical mass. Even lawmakers are beginning to recognize the trouble they have created.[21] However, little has been done to solve the problem. Here's an example of one perplexing conflict.

The Americans with Disabilities Act (ADA; 42 U.S.C. 12101, 1990) stipulates employers must reasonably accommodate those with recognized or perceived disabilities. It also imposes an obligation to reassign work and make other accommodations to assist persons with disabilities or those recovering from injuries. This makes sense because early return-to-work policies reduce costs. However, if an employee is injured and an employer in an effort to reduce Workers' Compensation costs attempts to accommodate the employee and return him to an alternative or a light-duty position, the employer may very well violate the Family and Medical Leave Act (FMLA). The Department of Labor has taken the position that if an employee is entitled to leave because of a "serious health condition," which may include a Workers' Compensation injury, the employee is entitled to the same or equivalent position upon return. So, therefore, while the ADA and the employer's Workers' Compensation law may encourage rapid return to light-duty assignment, the FMLA allows the employee to refuse to do so.

Other opportunities for misstep abound elsewhere. Since its creation in 1970, the Occupational Health and Safety Administration (OSHA) has been hard at work creating a safer workplace for everyone. In doing so, the OSHA has published over 4,000 regulations, dictating everything from the height of a railing to the thickness of carpet. The maze of rules and often arcane regulations (how far a plank can stick out from the edge of a temporary scaffold) busy more than 2,000 inspectors and tens of thousands of attorneys who prosecute and defend the litigation that it has precipitated. Attempting to toe the line, industry has spent several hundred billion dollars on compliance alone.[22]

Arguably many of the laws and regulations such as Title VII of the Civil Rights Act and those mentioned above have made a safer and fairer workplace for Americans, but the net effect on the employer is more litigation exposure. People know it too. In Los Angeles County alone, over 3,000 civil law suits are filed each day! Only a mere fraction of these are employment related, of course, but the fact remains that Americans like to sue. Most disturbing is that the trend shows no sign of reversing.

4. *Expanded Rights and Protections of Employees*

Some, like Philip Howard in his compelling 1994 best-seller, *The Death of Common Sense*, have argued that to a certain degree, the expansion of rights is a zero sum game. That is, as the rights of one group expand, the rights of another contract. Zero sum theory applies well to aspects of economics, but as we look at the ever expansion of worker rights it seems to apply perfectly. Legislation such as Title VII, ADA, FMLA, and more recently HIPAA[23] has certainly provided much good. Few can argue against improving workplace safety or improving the treatment of employees. However, the cost has been the erosion of employer prerogatives and has caused an exponential increase in compliance costs. It is estimated that HIPAA compliance alone will cost employers between $40 and $66 billion.[24] The trend has eroded employer doctrines such as "at-will employment" to the point of meaninglessness. Few employers can terminate at will, much less hire whom they wish without contemplating the litigation potential of perceived inequality or unfairness. We have created a mess.

Sadly, even the employees don't win. Increased employer costs translate into fewer resources for research and development, fewer process and technology improvements, less profit, fewer investments, and ultimately, the creation of fewer jobs. It is a sad and pathetic cycle. Even the government loses. With less money in circulation and fewer people working, fewer taxes are collected. The net effect is a less competitive and weaker economy. No one wins when business is overregulated.

In the next chapter we will examine the fundamentals of fact-finding and how to engineer a proper workplace investigation.

Notes

1. E. F. Ferraro, *Undercover Investigations in the Workplace*, 1st ed. (Woburn, Mass.: Butterworth-Heinemann, 2000), 27.
2. Note I did not refer to this amount as the loss. The total loss is actually much greater. In order to calculate it, one must determine the cost of money, transaction and accounting fees, lost interest on the money, as well as the larger economic impact of not having the $750,000 drop to the bottom line. Remember, all economic losses (unless insured) are bottom line deductions.
3. Crimes of this type most often involve legitimate vendors; usually it is only one of its employees that is dishonest. As such, substantial recoveries are usually possible. As we will examine in the next chapter, recovery of the cost of the investigation is also very likely.
4. William C. Cunningham, *The Hallcrest Report II* (Hallcrest Systems, Inc., 1990).
5. *The Hallcrest Report II* estimates that the average private investigation firm employs something less than 1.5 individuals. The California Department of Consumer Affairs, which regulates the private investigation industry in California, estimates that the average investigation firm in that state employs 1.4 individuals. Under the department's supervision are approximately 18,000 licensed private investigators and/or agencies.

6. Principally derived from Ferraro, *Undercover Investigations in the Workplace*, p. 56, with permission.

7. M. W. Browne, *New York Times*, 1998; David Fisher, *Rules of Thumb for Scientists and Engineers* (Reed Elsevier, London, 1991); Robert Matthews, *New Scientist* (1999), http://www.newscientist.com/news.ns.

8. Ferraro, *Undercover Investigations in the Workplace*, p. 27.

9. The phrase the Process of Investigation® is the registered service mark of the author.

10. The statutes and rules that regulate the conduct of grand juries (or their equivalent) vary from state to state. My purpose here is only to demonstrate the power this tool affords the government and the lack of anything equivalent in the private sector.

11. For example, California Penal Code §§153 and 519 make it a crime to threaten criminal action to bargain or obtain the settlement of a civil matter.

12. *Miranda v. Arizona*, 384 U.S. 436 (1966).

13. I acknowledge that the current state of law with regard to when and precisely under what circumstances *Miranda* is required is in flux. As such, this brief treatment is offered for illustrative purposes only and should not be construed as a strict interpretation of the law.

14. A case in point would be *NLRB v. Epilepsy Foundation*. Epilepsy Foundation of Northeast Ohio, 331 N.L.R.B. No. 134 [2000]; on June 9, 2004 the National Labor Relations Board reversed this decision in IBM et al., 341 N.L.R.B. No. 148 [2004] and eliminated the right of an employee to have a witness present while being questioned by his employer.

15. James C. Collins, *Built to Last* (New York: Harper Business, 2002).

16. Mahan Khalsa, *Let's Get Real* (Salt Lake City, Utah: Franklin Quest Co., 1999).

17. Michael Lewis, *The New New Thing* (New York: Penguin USA, 2001).

18. Thomas J. Stanley, *The Millionaire Next Door* (New York: Simon & Schuster, 1999).

19. M. Scott Peak, *The Road Less Traveled* (Carmichael, Calif.: Touchstone Books, 1998).

20. FreedomWorks.org; http://www.freedomworks.org/processor/printer.php?issue_id=1535, March 2005.

21. U.S. House of Representatives Committee on Economic and Educational Opportunities, *Hearing: Conflicts and Inconsistencies in Workplace Regulations* (Washington, D.C.: GPO, 1995).

22. Philip K. Howard, *The Death of Common Sense* (New York: Random House, 1994), 12.

23. Americans with Disabilities Act of 1990, 42 U.S.C. 12181; The Family and Medical Leave Act of 1993, Public Law 103-3; Health Insurance Portability and Accountability Act of 1996, Public Law 104-191.

24. Advanced Medical Consulting, Inc., http://www.medical-billing-company.com/medical-billing/hipaa-costs-government.html, March 2005; Enterprise Systems Group, Inc., http://www.hipaaplus.com/abouthippa.htm, March 2005.

Chapter 2

The Fundamentals of Fact-Finding

A. The History of the Modern Fact-Finder

Unfortunately the public image of today's private investigator is not substantially better than it was 70 years ago. Portrayed by Hollywood as sleazy but awkwardly principled, former hard-drinking social misfits, private investigators as a lot have gotten a bad reputation. Be it for the silver screen or a primetime television series, the scriptwriters who pen these timeless masterpieces (that was a pun) tend to think that their private investigator, in order to be credible, must have been a military or law enforcement reject, once married to the perfect spouse (a lawyer usually) but screwed up the marriage like most things he touches, who is now on the brink of bankruptcy.

Modern literature hasn't done much for them either. Since masters such as Sir Arthur Conan Doyle created the unflappable and yet not infallible Sherlock Holmes, few authors have done much for the reputation of the private eye. The reason for this is not all that complex to comprehend.

1. The Lincoln Years and the Origin of the Secret Service

Prior to the assassination of Abraham Lincoln, private security was responsible for the protection of the president and other high-level dignitaries. The original Pinkerton's organization and others like it dominated the field, providing security not only for the heads of state, but the railroads as well. Contrary to popular myth, however, Lincoln's personal bodyguard was not a civilian. General George Crook, himself a victim of kidnapping and numerous attempts on his life during the war, was at Lincoln's side until about 6:30 P.M. the night of the assassination.[1] Following a long day and second trip to the War Department, Lincoln relieved Crook and told him there were men who wanted to take his life and that if it were to be done, it would be impossible to prevent.[2] At approximately 10:12 P.M. that evening Lincoln, while in the company of his wife, Mary, enjoying a show at the Ford Theater, was shot from behind by actor John Wilkes Booth. That shot was the beginning of the choreographed decapitation of the Union government in Washington. Later that evening, Booth's co-conspirators murdered Secretary of State William Seward and his son in their home and attempted to take the life of Vice President Andrew Johnson.

The legislature was not idle while the nation mourned. Just two months after the assassination of Lincoln, Congress approved the creation of the Secret Service Division. Although its principal mission was to suppress the growing problem of counterfeit currency, some in Congress had other ideas. Just two years after Division Chief William P. Wood was sworn in by Secretary of the Treasury Hugh McCulloch, responsibilities of the Secret Service were broadened to include "detecting persons perpetrating frauds against the government." This appropriation resulted in investigations into the Ku Klux Klan, nonconforming distillers, smugglers, mail robbers, land swindlers, and a number of other nefarious law breakers. However, it was not until the assassination of President William McKinley in 1901 that Congress informally requested the Secret Service to provide presidential protection.[3]

However, before the nineteenth century had drawn to an end Pinkerton's and Burns had already established themselves as America's premier private investigators. Pinkerton's, established in 1850, still claims to be this country's oldest PI firm. Burns, on the other hand, principally specialized in contract security services (although calling itself a detective agency), providing what in many parts of the western territories was the only form of law enforcement. The men and women who made up these organizations were professional and proud, and their powers were broad. Permitted to carry guns, wear badges, and enforce public law, these pioneers were among America's first lawmen. Today these companies are combined, employ approximately 125,000 in the United States alone, and still provide a broad selection of consulting and investigative services.[4]

2. The Texas Rangers

The role of the private sector changed substantially after the Civil War and the settlement of the West. The infant territories and states created their own governments and established their own law enforcement agencies. Among the most legendary were the Texas Rangers. In December 1836, the Congress of the Texas Republic (1836–1845) passed a law enabling President Sam Houston to raise a battalion of 280 mounted riflemen to protect the frontier. A month later a company of 56 brave volunteers left for the frontier. On January 29, 1842, President Houston signed into law the authorization for a company of mounted men to "act as Rangers" on what was then known as the southern frontier.[5] By the end of 1845, and just in time for Texas to join the Union, Texas Rangers had been dispersed throughout the territory. Already the Rangers' reputation was legendary. Rangers often acted as an army of one and brought justice and peace to the wild frontier. Their reputation for courage and honesty was exceeded only by that of their solitude. Often traveling alone for more than 100 miles on horseback, they chased down bandits, horse thieves, and bands of cattle rustlers and brought them to justice. However, the order and tranquility they brought to Texas did not last long.

Texas seceded from the Union and joined the Confederacy by action of a convention ratified on February 23, 1861. Texas immediately became a member of the Confederacy and remained so until the South surrendered in 1865. Interestingly, Texas and its Rangers were not readmitted into the Union until March 30, 1870. For most of the five decades that followed, the Texas Rangers were the only form of law enforcement for the centralized government of Texas.

3. The Creation of the FBI

The Federal Bureau of Investigation (FBI) claims it originated from a force of "Special Agents" created in 1908 by Attorney General Charles Bonaparte during the Theodore Roosevelt administration. Roosevelt and Bonaparte considered themselves "Progressives." They, like other thought leaders of their time, shared the conviction that efficiency and expertise, not political connections or influence, should determine who could best serve in government.[6] Both men believed that their Progressive philosophy should be applied to law enforcement as well. Yet their small group of Special Agents had neither a name nor a declared leader other than the attorney general.

The timing was perfect. The leanings of most Americans at the time were toward a responsive, centralized federal government coupled with an idealistic, reformist spirit. The Progressive generation (1900–1918) believed that government intervention was necessary to produce justice in an industrial society. Central to the Progressive movement was the conviction that in government and industry, professionalism coupled with the requisite expertise and governance would produce a just and fair society. Roosevelt personified the movement. His federal investigative force consisted of well-disciplined professionals, designed to fight corruption and crime, and memorialized his conviction.

On July 26, 1908, Bonaparte ordered ten former Secret Service employees and a number of Department of Justice investigators to report to Chief Examiner Stanley W. Finch and be sworn as Special Agents. This event is celebrated by the FBI as its official beginning.[7] Attorney General George Wickersham, Bonaparte's successor, named the newly created force of 34 men, the Bureau of Investigation on March 16, 1909. Simultaneously, the title of chief examiner was changed to chief of the Bureau of Investigation.

The absence of a federal criminal justice system handicapped the new Special Agents. The federal criminal statutes and the prosecutorial infrastructure of today did not exist. In many instances the Bureau of Investigation lacked jurisdiction when dealing with interstate criminal activity, and this became its greatest handicap. However, in June 1910 things changed. The passage of the Mann Act made it a crime to transport women over state lines for immoral purposes, a crime so reprehensible at the time the press dubbed it White Slavery. However, this often selectively enforced law allowed the Bureau of Investigation the opportunity to investigate and pursue criminals who evaded state laws but had not committed any other federal offense. In several short years the Bureau of Investigation grew to over 300 agents. It sprouted field offices across the nation and placed Special Agents in charge in each of them. Before America's entry into the Great World War in 1917, the nascent Bureau of Investigation had already placed into our lexicon investigative terminology still used today in both the public and private sectors. The Bureau of Investigation coined the terms *special investigations* (sometimes called SPs), *agent* (and a host of permutations that include *agent status, special agent,* and *special agent in-charge), field offices, working in the field, subject* (a more respectable substitute for suspect), and *subject of the investigation,* each of which remains in the investigator's lexicon today.

Well qualified to direct the Bureau of Investigation and friends with Warren Harding's Attorney General Harry M. Daugherty, William J. Burns was appointed as director of the Bureau of Investigation on August 22, 1921. Burns, a popular and highly visible Progressive who had previously successfully run his own detective agency for decades (William J. Burns International Detective Agency), appointed 26-year-old J. Edgar Hoover as his assistant director. Hoover, a graduate of George Washington University Law School, was aggressive and ambitious. He had worked for the Department of Justice since 1917 and had headed *enemy alien operations* (a place he likely developed his contempt for communism) during the war. Hoover was a savvy political animal and made many enemies under Attorney General A. Mitchell Palmer, investigating suspected anarchists and communists.

Burns resigned in 1924 at the request of Attorney General Harlan Fiske Stone because of his alleged role in the Teapot Dome Scandal. The highly visible and ruinous scandal involved the secret leasing of naval oil reserve lands to private companies. Burns retired to Florida and published detective and mystery stories based on his long and colorful career. He died in Sarasota, Florida, in April 1932.

When Burns stepped aside, Stone appointed the young Hoover to head the Bureau of Investigation. By inclination and training, the nattily dressed Hoover embodied the Progressive spirit. His appointment ensured the Bureau of Investigation would become the organization it is today. And like Hoover, in proper character, without the consent of the attorney general, Congress, or anyone else, he also renamed his organization the Federal Bureau of Investigation. Today his FBI has approximately 11,400 Special Agents and over 16,400 other employees who perform professional, administrative, technical, clerical, craft, trade, or maintenance functions. It is unarguably the most sophisticated and powerful law enforcement agency on the planet. But while Hoover was busy building his legacy, others were busy also.

4. The Birth of Corporate Investigations

On February 14, 1927, a department store collections manager and a close friend, the store's credit manager, incorporated what would be America's first modern detective agency. J. Edward Krout and Sam A. Schneider were fired when their employer, Roos Brothers, a fashionable metropolitan department store, learned they had been moonlighting as private investigators. Ambitious and visionary, the two San Franciscans saw an opportunity and decided to fill it. Realizing the public's perception of private detectives drew images of alcoholic misfits, hanging out at the free lunch counters of local saloons, Krout and Schneider envisioned a white-collar organization serving the needs of corporate clients. Schneider later characterized his early colleagues as "keeping their office in the sweat band of their bowler hats."

Krout and Schneider's timing could not have been much worse. Just two years they started their tiny company, the stock market crashed. Initially, the young entrepreneurs concentrated on debtor collection, utilizing their contacts in the credit field. However, as the depression wore on, the collection business became increasingly more difficult.

During much of the 1930s, the Golden Gate and the Oakland Bay bridges were under construction. Both of the construction companies that built them were Krout and Schneider clients. A worker injured while employed by one would often then go to work for the other. In 1932 Schneider, a photography buff with a makeshift darkroom in his home, secured a commercial motion picture rig. From an old black rag-top Ford, he filmed a malingering iron worker and the resultant motion picture evidence became the first to be admitted into U.S. Courts. It made front-page news in Oakland.

The only cameras available at the time used large rolls of film. Schneider described opening the camera in a dark room after an assignment and placing a paper clip on the roll to mark the end of that sequence before using the rest of the same roll on another assignment. Before Schneider's experiment, insurance companies relied on photographers with press cameras to document malingerers. The film was so slow that flashbulbs were needed to get a proper exposure. Needless to say, there was no element of surprise.

The process was revolutionized when Bell & Howell produced 16 mm magazine-loading cameras with double and triple turrets so that changing from wide angle to telephoto took only seconds. The operator had to estimate the light for exposure and also approximate the distance to the subject when setting the lens. Quite a different skill level than that required to operate today's high-resolution video equipment that can get usable evidence at nearly any distance in any light. The technology gave Krout and Schneider the leading edge and for decades it dominated the industry. In the 1950s it instituted one of the first employee-stock-ownership programs, ensuring built-in continuity of ownership and excellence of service. The firm was the first in the industry to offer paid vacations and medical benefits. Yet today, after more than seven decades, Krout and Schneider is still a leading advocate of the professional investigation industry and represents investigators and their causes across the nation and on Capitol Hill.

Elsewhere in the country others saw the opportunity as well. Most notable of them were the firms West Coast Detectives, opening its doors in Los Angeles in 1922, and Pendleton Detectives, operating in Jackson, Mississippi, in 1920. Both firms are still in existence today and play roles in the world of corporate investigations. The larger of the two, Pendleton Detectives, like so many corporate investigation firms, was founded by a former law enforcement officer. Founder Forrest C. Pendleton had been one of Wickersham's first agents and opened the bureau's New Orleans office, becoming its first Special Agent in Charge. Renamed the Pendleton Organization, the firm today provides both investigative and physical security services and remains a significant player in the deep South.

It wasn't until the 1980s, however, that the profession gained the name recognition and significance it enjoys today. Although every American city and many small towns had their share of private investigators, it was not until corporate America discovered illegal drugs had crept into the workplace that the need for corporate investigators was realized. Although illegal drugs were not new, their use and distribution in the workplace certainly was. The Research Triangle Institute's 1984 study, based on data collected in 1980, found the economic cost of the American drug problem was $46.9 billion, or the equivalent of $472 for every working adult in the country.[8] By the mid-1980s, nearly 300,000 Americans were behind bars for drug offenses, one in five were first-time offenders.[9] More than half of all federal inmates were behind bars for violations of federal drug laws. Yet law enforcement officials at both the federal and local levels continued to claim they were intercepting "only 10 percent" of all illegal drug shipments into the country. By 1988, the tragedy was manifold. An estimated 27,971,000 people in the United States aged 12 and up had used an illicit drug at least once in the previous year, and 14,479,000 were estimated to have used an illicit drug at least once in the previous month.[10] The call for help did not fall on deaf ears.

From Los Angeles to New York, investigation firms began to offer their services. The principal tool was undercover. Drawing from the public sector, firms of all sizes hired men and women with narcotics experience to attack the problem in the workplace. Organizations, such as Krout and Schneider in Los Angeles, then having nine offices on the West Coast; Professional Law Enforcement in Dayton, Ohio; Pendleton Organization in Jackson, Mississippi; and others in New York, began to place undercover drug investigators into some of the largest and most successful corporations in America. By 1990 collectively these pioneers and other like them had started to cut into the heart of the workplace drug problem. Combining covert surveillance and sophisticated interviewing techniques with the emerging science of undercover, they conducted thousands of successful drug investigations. Their visibility and effectiveness put corporate investigations on the map.

Although the 1990s did not bring an end to the war on drugs or the need for workplace drug investigations, the go-go 1990s created yet more opportunities for corporate investigators. With full appreciation for the effectiveness of using private sector investigators, America's public and private institutions began to demand more. By 1990 most of the firms that had chosen to specialize in workplace drug investigations found themselves doing other types of workplace investigations as well. The demand for specialized investigators mushroomed as employers and the attorneys who represented them began to confront an ever-increasing number of workplace harassment and discrimination claims. Institutionalizing the claim of sexual harassment and the passing the Americans with Disabilities Act (ADA; 42 U.S.C. 12101, 1990) precipitated an expansion of employee rights that has not relented to this day. These expanded rights, though proper and due, have created a legal minefield for employers the likes of which had not been seen in the industrial age. The alleged violation of those rights and oftentimes unwitting missteps by employers have precipitated an avalanche of lawsuits that today have clogged our civil courts. The misfortunes of employers, however, created unfathomable opportunities for skilled corporate investigators. Like convenience stores, boutiques specializing in these unique types of investigations sprang up all over the country.

Corporate fraud, waste, and abuse created additional opportunities. For nearly a full century, investigation of corporate misconduct and financial shenanigans had been left to the public sector. Early adaptors such as Krout and Schneider saw the need and quickly fielded attorneys and other professionals as project managers and specialized corporate investigators. The ability to provide high-end investigative solutions to an ever-growing client base provided the opportunity to build powerful firms never before seen in the private sector. Advances in communications, computer technology, and forensic science created a new industry, one built on professionalism, know-how, and technology. The phenomenon gave birth to service organizations specializing in everything from due diligence to money laundering to gray market goods. Along with the growth of the industry came professional societies and trade associations to support it. Specialized training gave way to certification programs and accredited college curriculums. In a mere decade, the thousands of men and women who today call themselves corporate investigators have institutionalized the trade and professionalized beyond the wildest dreams of history makers, Alan Pinkerton and William Burns.

B. The Role of the Fact-Finder

1. The Fact-Finder Defined

No discussion regarding the role of the fact-finder would be complete without first defining the term. The fact-finder is the central figure in the fact-finding process. Of the assorted members of the investigative team (see Chapter 4), the fact-finder in many regards defines the outcome of the investigation. In less complex investigations, the fact-finder may single handedly fulfill the role of investigator, counselor, and decision maker. Although this is not advised even in the simplest investigations, circumstances sometimes dictate that the *investigative team* be composed of a single individual. Optimally, the fact-finder is one of numerous individuals who, working together toward common objectives, makes up the team that ultimately drives the investigation from start to successful conclusion.

a. Skill

The first characteristic the fact-finder should have is skill that is matched to the type and nature of the project to be undertaken. The fact-finder should have the requisite skill necessary to achieve the desired objectives. For example, a fact-finder possessing only the training and skills associated with the investigation of sexual harassment would likely be unsuited to undertake a complex substance abuse matter. Conversely, someone with the training and skills associated with only workplace substance abuse investigations would be equally unsuited to investigate complex frauds or financial crimes against the business. There is, of course, crossover of skills and many qualified fact-finders may have the skills necessary to investigate all types of workplace investigations. Regardless, the outcome of the project will be largely driven by the skill of the fact-finder and his ability to bring to bear that skill and all prior training in an orderly and effective fashion. Just as one would not ask an ophthalmologist to perform heart surgery, it is essential to match the skill of the fact-finder to the type of investigation undertaken.

Trap: Insisting on or allowing a fact-finder without the proper skills to conduct an important investigation is a recipe for disaster. Resist the temptation to use just any fact-finder. For best results, match the skill of the fact-finder to the type of project undertaken.

---

b. Experience

Some argue that experience trumps skill. However, I believe experience is an integral component of skill. It is experience that allows the properly trained and skilled fact-finder to overcome unusual and oftentimes unexpected circumstances that invariably arise during an investigation. It is true that good judgment comes from experience and experience comes from bad judgment. But the experience must be of the proper type. Like skill, experience in sexual harassment investigations may not translate well in complex substance abuse investigations. Employers typically make this mistake.

Oftentimes, organizations hire individuals with law enforcement experience to run their security or loss prevention functions. Though on its face this seems to make perfect sense, confusing the *experience* of one responsible for the enforcement of public law with that which is required of corporate asset protection and loss prevention is a serious mistake. Contrary to popular belief, the sad fact of the matter is that there is very little experience crossover between the public and private sectors. Yet this mistake is made everyday. A whole host of organizations, large and small, intentionally seek out and hire those with prior law enforcement experience for corporate security positions. It is my opinion that the skill and experience of most law enforcement professionals does not match that needed by the private sector. Similarly, human resource professionals are often asked to perform investigative tasks of which they have no experience either. Here's a good example.

The matter began with an anonymous tip from a concerned employee. The employee, using his employer's anonymous incident reporting mechanism, in this case, a toll-free hotline, reported that a small group of co-workers had been co-opted by a foreman and were regularly assisting him to divert material from a large jobsite to a relative's home. The concerned individual (CI) also reported that the thieves frequently drank on the job and that on more than one occasion the foreman had nearly wrecked a company vehicle while driving when impaired. The report was quickly passed up the chain of command and soon was on the desk of the CEO. He immediately called my office and requested advice. As the reader might image, I suggested some fact-finding was in order. Work orders, time cards, and inventories needed to be examined. The first order of business when allegations of this sort are received is to somehow substantiate them. I outline for the CEO an appropriate plan and he instructed me to coordinate the effort through his director of human resources, a woman with whom I had worked previously. In a short time, together we were able to corroborate some of the allegations and uncover additional irregularities. We quickly packaged the results and recommended that my team interview the suspected transgressors. The CEO, however, balked. Concluding that his human resources director better knew the personalities involved, his organization's process directed her to conduct the interviews. Experienced as she was with routine internal investigations, she had never confronted or interviewed anyone suspected of such serious offenses. Reluctantly, she proceeded and resultantly failed miserably. Not a single individual made an admission. Instead, each accused her and the organization of conducting a witch hunt. Inexperienced in conducting difficult investigatory interviews, she visibly demonstrated her uneasiness and lack of experience. She was unable to overcome the most meager denials and quickly found herself defending the investigation and all of the evidence it had produced.

Tip: When available, use experienced fact-finders. Match both the skill and the experience of the fact-finder to the specifics of the investigation. Experience in law enforcement and human resources does not make one an experienced fact-finder.

c. *Impartiality*

Impartiality is the innate ability to separate one's self and self-interests from the investigation and its outcome. It is not a common trait, nor is it human nature. Because the human spirit is possessive by nature, we tend to take ownership (and pride) in the things we do. The greater the investment of time and resources, the greater that ownership becomes. Investigations are no different. The professional fact-finder must divest herself from any interest in the outcome of the investigation. This is not to say one may not be interested in the outcome or take pride in her work. No, the fact-finder must instead be impartial and not allow her loyalty and self-interests to interfere with the fact-finding process or the investigation's ultimate outcome. This unique characteristic is the trademark of a true professional.

There are two effective ways the fact-finder can demonstrate her impartiality. The first is to not decide the investigation's objectives. By removing herself from deciding objectives, it is reasonable to conclude that the fact-finder has little interest in the outcome. By not deciding the objectives of the investigation, the fact-finder has no vested interest in the effort's outcome. She has no agenda to prosecute. The second way the fact-finder can demonstrate her impartiality is by excluding herself from any decision-making process at the conclusion of the investigation. By not being party to the decisions regarding discipline or corrective action, the fact-finder has no say in the outcome. The fact-finder has isolated herself to the solitary role of fact-finder. She is neither judge, jury, nor prosecutor. And without interest in the investigation's objectives or its outcome, it is nearly impossible to be accused of any bias or prejudice. To claim that she has any partiality is illogical and offends the evidence to the contrary.

d. Ethical

It would be fair to argue that impartiality is an ethical characteristic. However, my use of *ethical* in the context of describing the necessary characteristics of the professional fact-finder is far more expansive. The *American Heritage Dictionary* defines ethical:

> eth·i·cal (ĕth′ĭ-kəl) *adj.*
>
> Of or dealing with ethics.
>
> Being in accordance with the accepted principles that govern the conduct of a group, esp. a profession.[11]

As this definition suggests, ethics is a collection of "accepted principles that govern" a particular group or profession. In this case the operative term is *profession*. In order to be professional the fact-finder must adhere to an assortment of guiding principles any reasonable person or trier of fact would embrace as proper. Actions such as truthfulness, honesty, and impartiality collectively constitute ethical behavior. To be ethical requires the fact-finder to behave in such a fashion as to protect the rights of those under investigation, obey the law, and protect the integrity of the process. For example, if the fact-finder uncovers exculpatory evidence, exonerating his subject, he brings it forth and reveals it. If the fact-finder hasn't found the evidence to accuse his subject, he does not conduct an accusatory interview of that subject. If the fact-finder knows the employer is likely to discharge an offender who makes an admission, the fact-finder does not tell the subject an admission will cleanse his soul and that his job will be protected if only he makes a "confession."

> Tip: Conduct your investigations the way you would wish someone else would conduct them if you were the accused. Treat all of your subjects with respect and dignity. Remember: a reputation of being ethical takes years to develop and moments to destroy.

e. Fair

Fairness is in the eye of the beholder. In workplace investigations that person may be your boss, the director of human resources, the CEO, or a judge. In order to be effective, the fact-finder must be fair. But fairness takes many forms. To be honest and ethical may in fact be fair. But to be fair to the individuals one investigates is paramount and a trait of a true professional.

Fairness may comprise being truthful to the one we are interviewing. When he asks what evidence we may have against him, it means telling him the truth. It is not embellishing the quantity or quality of that evidence. It is not telling him the evidence is irrefutable when we know it is not. It is not telling him he may not leave when in fact he has the right to do so. It is not telling him that everyone knows he is guilty when it is only you who thinks so. Being fair is being honest. It is being professional in our actions and with our words. Being fair results in the ability to look at ourselves in the mirror and not be ashamed of ourselves, our actions, or our organization.

f. Deliberate

Last, the fact-finder must be deliberate. His actions must be purposeful. He must not prosecute some personal agenda or grievance. The fact-finder must act with reason and reason his actions. The fact-finder that is deliberate is decisive. He works his plan and plans his work. His process has purpose and meaning. Each action has a method and end. All actions have meaning and are engineered to fulfill an end.

The professional fact-finder does not waste time or resources. If his plan is flawed, he confronts the defects. He rectifies his shortcomings and is always conscious of his objectives. Everything he does is a means toward a fair, honest, and ethical conclusion.

2. Gather Facts and Evidence

That the fact-finder engages in the collection of information is intuitively obvious. What may not be so obvious is the way he goes about it. From the first chapter we learned that one of the essential elements of a successful investigation is the crafting of meaningful objectives. The objectives of the investigation will drive what facts and evidence are to be gathered. For example, if one of the objectives of the investigation is to determine who was responsible for the disappearance of $1,000 from the office safe, we might start by creating a list of the facts and evidence necessary to meet that objective, effectively, creating an *investigative task list*. In no particular order, here is a partial list:

- Determine who had access to the office that contained the safe.
- Determine who had access to the safe.

- Determine who discovered the loss and when.
- Determine who put the $1,000 into the safe.
- Determine who last saw the $1,000.
- Confirm that the $1,000 was actually put into the safe.
- Determine the source of the $1,000 and why it was stored in the safe.
- Determine cash handling and security procedures.
- Determine cash audit procedures and responsibility.
- Determine if the procedures were followed (if not who violated them and why).
- Determine who knew the $1,000 was in the safe.
- Determine if those who knew the $1,000 had shared that information with anyone else.
- Determine if other similar losses had ever occurred and if so, obtain the details.

This is not an exhaustive list. But as you can see, the simple exercise of listing the facts and various pieces of information surrounding *just* the circumstances of this hypothetical loss has significantly focused our effort. Additionally, if we were able to obtain the desired information, we would substantially reduce the size of the suspect pool, if not identify the primary suspect. Other pieces of the puzzle also fall into place as well. For example we may discover process failures, or the lack of adequate controls—information that might be critical to formulating a prevention strategy for the future.

In situations in which the subject matter or circumstances are far more complex, the process can be modified by creating subtasks for some of the action items on our task list. Experienced investigators will find that over a period of time workplace investigations of similar types take on similar themes. By tracking these recurring themes, the workplace investigator, over time, will create for himself a portfolio of forms, checklists, action items, and processes for each of the assorted investigation types he has conducted. In Chapter 6, "Applied Strategies," I will demonstrate this in some detail. I will also provide some of the tools I have developed, saving you time and resources.

3. Document and Catalogue

The fact-finder must next document and catalogue that which she has gathered. In some orderly and easy-to-use fashion, she must organize, tag, label, and store her evidence. Concurrently, she must document her efforts and those of her team members (should she be directing the effort of others) and begin preparation of a final report. In the case of simple matters this effort is rather straightforward and almost intuitive. However, complex matters require a great deal more organization. I for one have handled matters involving tens of thousands of documents and scores of evidentiary tidbits. Absent a structured process and high degree of organization, the production of a 1,500 page report would not be possible.

a. Creating and Using an Investigative Journal

Using a journal has been briefly mentioned earlier. The investigative journal might be a three-ring binder in which all notes and collateral documents can be placed. The items are placed in the binder in the order in which they are created or developed. Preliminarily "sticky notes" can be used as temporary tabs. Later, as the investigation begins to take shape, tabbed separators can be inserted to help segregate and organize the information. A separate evidence folder or something similar should be used to store all original documents. Only copies should go into the binder. Eventually, additional binders can be created if necessary. Document storage boxes can then be labeled and used to store the binders, evidence folders, and anything else of importance. Evidence labels, rubber stamps, Bates Stamp (a sequential numbering device), and bar code labels can all be used to mark, identify, and further organize the materials.

b. Unleashing the Power of the Computer

The personal computer is available as well. Using standard office applications such as word processors and spreadsheets, the fact-finder can electronically organize his information and thoughts. The fact-finder can create files, folders, and databases to create and organize task lists, records, documents, and reports. Products such as CaseMap and TimeMap can further help the fact-finder organize himself and his investigation. Both of these powerful software applications are available from CaseSoft (www.casesoft.com) a division of DecisionQuest, one of the nation's largest and most respected providers of litigation support. Though designed for the legal profession, CaseMap can be equally useful to the fact-finder for managing large investigations. The software allows the user to organize and explore facts, the cast of characters, the issues, and all of the legal aspects of the case. It provides the fact-finder with the ability to electronically perfect link-analysis and pull together a cogent expression of his findings. TimeMap is an enhancement that allows the user to create chronology visuals. Because TimeMap plugs into CaseMap, the combination of the two makes a powerful investigative tool capable of handling the most complicated cases.

Another useful tool is a product called The Case File. The Case File is an information collection and organization tool composed of investigative forms, checklists, and report templates. The product includes an actual sample case file and a CD or zip-disk with all of the forms, checklists, and templates in MS Word® (Microsoft Corporation, Redmond, Washington) and in Rich Text Format (.rtf). The documents are professionally formatted and neatly organized. Because they are electronic, they can be easily manipulated and customized. The user license allows unlimited use and duplication of the documents. Both novice and experienced investigators will find The Case File an invaluable tool. It is available from InfoQuest Investigators at www.thecasefile.com. Exhibit 2.1 summarizes the contents of my version of The Case File.

It is easy to see that The Case File program contains many useful items. The real value, however, is that it provides case file and project management standardization. The standardization facilitates easier file review and easy case file sharing or reassignment, and when used in its electronic form, it permits computer entry of data and notes.

This excellent project management tool does have one shortcoming. The electronic forms have been created as text documents and do not use form fields. As such, as the user enters data, the format of the document changes and alters its appearance. A skilled user can overcome this by highlighting the desired blank space and replacing it with a form field. This can be tedious, but done incrementally as the fact-finder uses the documents, over a period of time he will have created an inventory of very powerful tools.

Before moving on to describe the contents of the typical case file, let's briefly discuss some aspects of computer file management. Anyone who has conducted investigations and used a computer has encountered the difficulty of managing the information. Establishing some structure to the process easily rectifies this nuisance. Because current computer technology typically organizes information using directories and files, a "file" system is relatively easy to create. Conceptually, the computer's data storage capability is similar to that of file cabinet. A storage device, be it a hard drive, CD, or flash mechanism, is effectively the file cabinet. The device can sometimes be partitioned into smaller units so that system applications can be segregated from data. Using the example of a typical hard drive it might be organized as shown in Exhibit 2.2.

Note that the user has segregated his application files. He has placed them in what has been identified as the Program Files folder. Other folders have been created for other purposes. One of them is the Workplace Investigations folder. In it, he has sorted his investigations by region and location. In this example the user is responsible for five locations in one region, shown in Exhibit 2.3 as region 4. However, because he is on a

Exhibit 2.1   Sample Case File

Section / Forms	Notes and Instructions
"Case/Subject"	
Contract of retainer	This is included because this same file is used as a complete package by private investigators. You may modify this to be a contract you use for outside investigators or just remove it from your folder.
Specialized incident report	See the "Bonus Forms" section. Use the appropriate one for criminal, civil, or tort investigations.
Subject data file table of contents	Shows category and line number of the main "Subject Data File" and allows you to show which areas of information are provided, needed, and completed.
Subject data file	A 35-page fill-in-the-blank dossier on the subject of your investigation.
Addendum sheet	The "Subject Data File" is line numbered. Use the addendum for overflow information or for annotation.
Table of contents	Shows layout and organization of the Investigative File.

"Theory"

This section is grouped in the first section with your subject and case. As you start the case with what you already know, you use the "Theory" section to list what you need to know.

The to-do list	General area to list necessary activity. Check its completion, and delegate.
Case activity game plan I	A comprehensive checklist of sources to be used in gathering info.
Case activity game plan II	A "to do" list organized by activity rather than source.
Quick-scan contact log	A list of people you will talk with on a regular basis or use to match people, phone numbers, e-mail, etc., with each other.
Other contacts— Client	People associated with your client that the investigator may or should contact.
Other contacts— Subject	People associated with the subject who are friendly to the investigation. OR, people such as the subject's attorney.
Time line	Use to develop time relationships of factors leading up to an incident, or comparisons of witness testimonies, etc.

"Data"

Data section cover sheet	A fill-in-the-blank "table of contents" to list information reports and documentation that have been gathered and stored in the folder itself. Underneath the cover sheet place items such as photocopies from court records, surveillance reports, witness interviews.

Exhibit 2.1   Sample Case File (Continued)

Section / Forms	Notes and Instructions

"Activity"

This section will give you your investigative report and investigation invoice in rough draft format

Daily activity chart	This is your billing diary. Use it to show all hours and expenses as well as to show when each activity occurred or was performed. Make only single-line entries here.
Journal entry starter page	Use as a model for lengthier notes when an entry on the Daily Activity Chart needs explanation greater than its single-line entry. For example take notes re: "Phone call with client." Simple notebook paper is placed behind this model and used to continue with notes.

"Communications and Correspondence"

Client data sheet	Discretionary use based on the investigator's relationship to your client. If it is an outside investigator, YOU may well be the "client" listed on this form. If this is an in-house investigation and the person assigned to the investigation is privileged to contact the client directly, then use this form. Otherwise, disregard and remove.
Correspondence log	Similar to the one in the "Case Workbook" but focused on correspondence generated by and from the investigation directly.
Contacts address register	General purpose contact list for miscellaneous entities involved in case.

"Clerical"

Evidence envelope	Use for photos, receipts, business cards, file backup diskettes, etc.
Evidence tracking sheet	For tracking documents or evidence not stored in the folder.
Outside vendors	Track contact with vendors.
Clerical activity checklist	Contact roster for any outside assistance, e.g., forensic lab.

Source: Courtesy The Case File, Paul Purcell © 1999.

networked system shared by multiple users, their regions are visible, though not necessarily electronically accessible to him. We also see that the location folder identified as San Diego contains four subfolders, one for each year the system has been in use.

The year 2003 contains six subfolders. Each of these represents a separate investigation. For simplicity and easy identification each of these

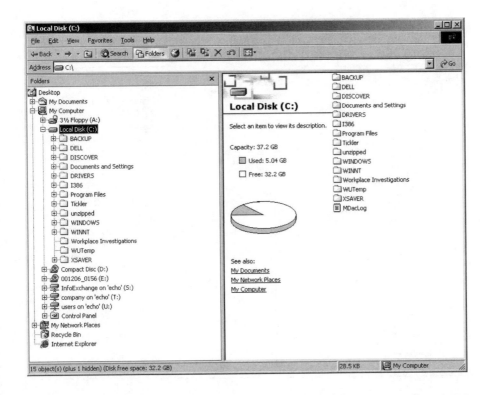

Exhibit 2.2   Organization of Electronic Files

projects has been named and a two-letter identifier has been appended to indicate the type of investigation conducted. He has used the following system to identify the investigation type:

- FD—Fraud
- SA—Substance Abuse
- SH—Sexual Harassment
- UC—Undercover

I have found further sorting unnecessary. To create subfolders for each type of investigation for the respective cases is not productive. Unless one manages a huge number of cases, further sorting wastes time and actually makes locating a particular project more cumbersome.

Within each project folder he has organized his information even further. (See Exhibit 2.4.) Here we see that the user has created six subfolders in which he can sort and file documents and other items. The way he has organized his information allows for quick filing of his work product and enables him to easily locate any item.

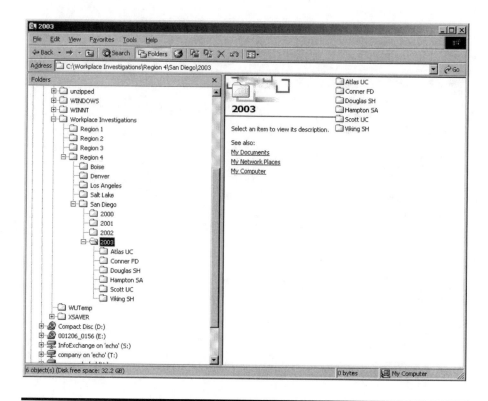

Exhibit 2.3   Organization of Electronic Project Files

Because large or complex projects tend to generate a large number of documents, how you name electronic files also deserves some consideration. The system used may vary depending upon the type of documents being named. For example, the Correspondence folder might contain letters, memoranda, and faxes. Hypothetically, the documents in a multifile folder might be named as follows:

- Fredrickson, Robert 01.doc
- Fredrickson, Robert 02.doc
- Fredrickson, Robert 03.doc
- Fredrickson, Robert fax 01.doc
- Fredrickson, Robert memo 01.doc
- Fredrickson, Robert memo 02.doc
- Gross, David 01.doc
- Gross, David fax 01.doc
- Gross, David memo 01.doc
- Gross, David memo 02.doc

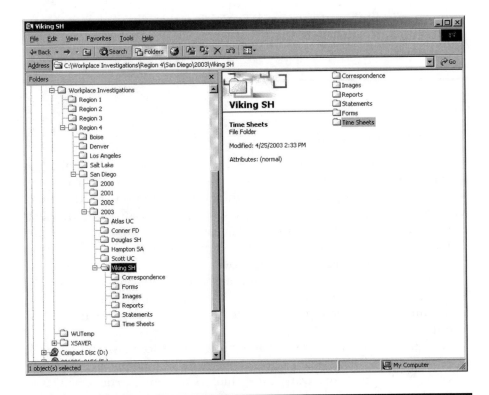

Exhibit 2.4   Organization of Working Files

This method uses the recipients name (last name first) as the primary identifier, followed by the type of document (no document description is the default for letter), followed by a number representing the sequential order in which the documents were created. Instead of trying to create a document name that is descriptive of the document's contents, for example: Letter to Robert Fredrickson regarding the motion for summary judgment dated August 22, 2003, from Eugene Ferraro.doc, this method is easy to use and offers a universal methodology that can be deployed consistently across the entire enterprise. This method can also be used for naming files contained in the other folders. It has been my method for years and I have yet to find a better one.

Tip: Impose organization and structure on your electronic file folder and file system before you begin your investigation. Structure your document management process such that it allows your work product to be easily filed and retrieved. Exercising discipline during the early phases of the project can save time and frustration later.

c. Creating a Case File

The organization of the physical case file on the other hand is largely a matter of preference. *Organization,* however, is the operative term. Without sufficient organization, even the best fact-finder is handicapped. Without the ability to organize one's self and work product, the fact-finder puts the success of the project in jeopardy. Lost documents, misplaced pieces of evidence, and disorganized files are the hallmarks of an amateur. Professionals don't misplace documents, keep messy case files, or lose stuff. They are organized and their work product looks like it. They are usually able to put their hands on any item in their possession, at any time. An integral component to this level of organization is the case file.

Over the years I have used a variety of case file formats. The simplest, of course, is the plain manila folder. I prefer something a little more versatile. Today, my organization uses multipart tabbed folders, similar to those used in the health care profession. They are made of heavy stock, have an expandable spine, and have sturdy document fasteners inside. They are made in a host of colors and are available at most stationary or office supply stores. For ease of recognition, one could color-code project types. For example, all fraud cases would be kept in blue folders, sexual harassment cases in green folders, and so on. Using colored folders also makes finding case files easier when searching for misplaced files in a busy office.

The contents of the case file should be organized. The file is not just a repository for documents, notes, and miscellaneous papers; it is a tool. Like all tools, if properly used, the case file will make one's work easier. As previously mentioned, there are case file organizing systems that are commercially available. Such systems are sometimes helpful, but are not absolutely necessary. If constructing one's own case file system from scratch, the following should be considered in advance:

- Number of potential cases in a given year
- Typical type or types of cases normally handled
- Size and complexity of the typical case
- File distribution and management

- File retention.
- Compatibility with existing file management systems.

Although all of these aspects of the system need to be given fore-thought, case file retention deserves special attention. How long one should retain case files is debatable. Federal law regulates record retention in a variety of areas. For example, aspects of the Occupational Safety and Health Act (OSHA) require some records to be kept the length of the employee's tenure plus *30 years*, and records pertaining to the Employee Polygraph Protection Act such as why a test was administered and its corresponding results must be retained only three years. Statutory record keeping under Title VII of the Civil Rights Act of 1964 is less straightfor-ward. The Equal Employment Opportunities Commission (EEOC), which is responsible for enforcement of Title VII, does not require that any record be created, but once created, rules require the record be retained for one year from the date personnel action was taken. In the event a formal charge or lawsuit is filed, all relevant records must be kept until "final disposition." The confusing and often conflicting array of state and federal requirements makes record retention policies complicated and burdensome. Compliance and enforcement of such policies is even more burdensome. As such, many employers keep everything forever. I for one think something a little more reasonable is in order.

I recently conducted a nonscientific survey of licensed investigators who specialize in workplace investigations that revealed that most intend to retain their files indefinitely. On average, those that stated they peri-odically purge their files said they do so about every seven years. On the other hand few employers stated they intended to retain case files indef-initely. Those who stated they periodically purge their files said they do so about every five to seven years. Only a few of the investigators and employers said they have systematic record destruction procedures. Fewer still could explain what those procedures were.

My suggestion is to retain case files not less than five years. Absent a clearly defined system, in most instances after five years case files tend to be misplaced, lost, or accidentally disposed in the normal course of business. When someone leaves or changes position, very rarely are they asked to surrender investigative case files and materials pertaining to past investigations. Usually the stuff just gets thrown out. Establishing a policy requiring indefinite retention creates an unnecessary administrative burden and potential liability for the organization. With such policies in place, the organization that cannot produce a file when needed can be accused of a cover-up or worse. Conversely, the systematic destruction of files can also raise questions. However, a reasonable policy that is consistently applied is tough to attack and can usually be defended.

Tip: Case file retention practices deserve thorough consideration before implementation. Retention of case files for five years from the date of closure is considered the minimum. However, retention policies that exceed seven years are difficult to manage and often do not work.

The next issue is that of what to place in a case file. At a minimum the file should have four sections. Exhibit 2.5 identifies these sections and briefly describes the contents of each.

Obviously, the type of investigation will drive the sections to be included and their contents. The reader will note that these sections differ from those described in Exhibit 2.1. Need, preference, and the objectives of the investigation will dictate the construction and contents of one's files. What should not be overlooked is structure and consistency. Devising a workable format and using it consistently will facilitate organization and structure to the investigative process. Improved efficiency and better investigative results will be the byproduct.

4. Report Findings to Higher Authority

The fourth role of the fact-finder is to report his findings to a higher authority. The fact-finder should not be a decision maker in the process of deciding discipline. In order for the investigative process to be credible, the fact-finder and decision maker should not be one in the same. The fact-finder's role should be strictly that of fact-finding. His process should be driven by the objectives of the investigation with the intention of providing his result to a party outside of the project team. As a practical matter, the fact-finder should report to someone not actively involved in the investigation.

This of course is easier said than done. In small organizations it is nearly impossible. Even in large organizations there may not be the bandwidth to support the hierarchy of separate powers and responsibilities. Similarly, very complex or sensitive investigations involving organizational members at the corporate or "C level" may preclude distinctive roles of the participants. In these instances other safeguards to ensure fairness and impartiality are necessary. One of them is the use of outside counsel.

Lawyers are expensive and the decision to hire one should be made very carefully. Few organizations engage them without having a very special

Exhibit 2.5   Case File Contents

Activity and administration section	Daily activity log detailing all activities, time and expenses; case fact sheet; list of objectives; engagement letter (if applicable); initial notes and case intake information.
Clerical or record keeping section	Time sheets; subcontractor engagement agreements and invoices; expenses records; and any other productivity management tools.
Notes and work product section	All notes and investigator generated work product, except final reports and communications with those outside the investigative team.
Reports and communication section	All reports, investigative summaries, and communications that are prepared for review by a higher authority or nonmembers of the investigative team.

need or desire. However, in the case of workplace investigations, outside counsel can bring so much to the process that their use should be considered every time an investigation of any substance is contemplated. The properly selected attorney will have the legal knowledge and experience insiders don't. Competent outside counsel will have resources and time to oversee a complex investigation and more than likely will have handled similar situations and challenges in the past. Outside counsel should be able to provide the counsel and advice needed to make the best decisions when they need to be made. Outside counsel will also be viewed as more impartial. Although by definition outside counsel is an advocate, that person is still an outsider and will not be carrying the baggage an individual internal to the organization might. Nor will outside counsel have had the past experiences and interactions with the subject, witnesses, or others involved in the investigation. Usually outside counsel will lack the *history* that might cloud judgment and impartiality. Furthermore, outside counsel can be the voice of reason. When temperatures rise and emotions begin to surface, the properly selected attorney can be the voice of reason and the corporate therapist who quiets the waters. He or she can also assuage egos, expose hidden agendas, and mediate differences.

Inside counsel can often do these things as well. But in many instances, inside counsel lacks some of the specific expertise necessary to do the job properly. Additionally, most staff attorneys are not litigators. They haven't the training or the experience (or the time) to prosecute or defend an action. In other instances, house counsel is already a witness. His participation began at the onset, before the matter came under investigation. He coached human resources, wrote letters to opposing parties, or interviewed participants and witnesses. He is conflicted, still able to advise and participate, but because of his vested interest in the organization, he is subject to the charge of impartiality and self-interest.

Outside counsel offers something else—the ability to protect the investigative work product and result from discovery. If litigation is under way or anticipated and the investigation is performed under the direction and supervision of counsel, the work product is protected from discovery and the requirement to be produced. Under the doctrine of the *work product privilege*, all the fact-finder does and produces is privileged. Furthermore, all of the communication between the employer and the attorney is privileged as well. Like the attorney–work product privilege, the doctrine of attorney-client privilege protects attorney-client communications from discovery. And for good reason—in order to preserve the integrity of our legal system, it is held that the attorney's effectiveness is significantly impacted by his ability to communicate confidentially with his client. Under the privilege even the client's admission of guilt is protected. In the case of workplace investigations, all aspects of the matter can be protected. Damaging statements, memos, and other communication created during the investigation can be withheld as evidence once the privilege is invoked. Unfortunately, this powerful protective tool is often overlooked and underutilized.

Like many good things, the privilege has its limitations. It is only a tool. It is not a shield. One cannot hide behind it in order to deceive or cover up criminal activity. One cannot use evidence he holds privileged in the prosecution or defense of his case and not disclose it to the other side. In workplace investigations it can create an unexpected dilemma. If, for example, an employer who possesses information provided by a confidential informant wishes to use it to discipline an employee, he cannot claim that the information is privileged. In order to use the information the employer has to disclose it if challenged. The operative term here is *if challenged*. Absent a challenge, the employer is likely to be able to consider and use any evidence he wishes, regardless of its source. The easiest work-around to the confidential informant dilemma is not to use the informant's information directly. Instead, use the information provided by the informant to further the investigation from another direction. That is, the informant's information is only used as intelligence. With it, the project manager can engineer another investigative solution, then produce the results of that effort as the primary evidence for the purpose of deciding discipline.

The reader should not confuse outside counsel's role with that of a decision maker. Outside counsel, like the fact-finder, plays a functional role that does not include making decisions regarding discipline. If at all possible, the decision maker should have no role other than deciding discipline. Segregating the role of the participants reduces the likelihood of claims of impartiality and unfairness. Because the standard of proof of good faith, reasonable conclusion is so low, appearances of impartiality or unfairness can jeopardize the credibility of the entire process.

5. Provide Recommendations When Asked

The temptation to provide recommendations should be resisted. Instinctively, most fact-finders conclude their process by providing recommendations to those to whom they report. Many very experienced investigations do this as a natural course of business. However, by offering recommendations, the fact-finder has the ability to influence the decision maker. In doing so, the fact-finder places his credibility in jeopardy.

At first blush this assertion is counterintuitive. A reasonable person could easily contend that by his very position, the fact-finder is influential. The fact-finder enjoys great autonomy and is able to take his investigation wherever he wishes and include or exclude whatever evidence he sees fit. Furthermore, it can be argued that of all the interested parties, the fact-finder is the most qualified to make recommendations, for it is he (and his team) who is closest to the facts. All of these propositions are true. However, a proper investigation should have engineered safeguards into the process to ensure that the fact-finder's efforts are focused and reasonable. Here are a few of those safeguards:

- The fact-finder and project team are driven by established process, not personal agendas (review the first chapter for more details).
- The Process of Investigation clearly defines the fact-finder's role and the limits of his authority.
- From the onset, the investigative effort is driven by clearly articulated and well-defined objectives.
- The fact-finder and the entire investigative effort are overseen by a designated higher authority (usually outside counsel). As such, the fact-finder is responsible to him, not necessarily the decision maker.
- The decision maker is bound to a standard of proof established before the investigation began.

These safeguards diminish the fact-finder's ability to pursue his own agenda, spin facts, and influence the decision maker. This construct may appear contrived, however, absent some sort of structure and defined process, including the delegation of responsibilities, the acting parties are defenseless. Only with a well-conceived and defined process can the participants assert impartiality and fairness. Good looks and a bright smile won't do it. Experienced employers will agree—in the end, it is the process that will be challenged at trial, not the malfeasant employee who brought the suit.

Another problem arises when a fact-finder makes recommendations. As the title suggests, the fact-finder is one who seeks out and uncovers facts. Her work product should be factual and grounded in objective determinations. Conversely, recommendations are subjective. By combining objective findings with subjective recommendations, the fact-finder's work product can no longer be claimed purely factual. In effect, it is tainted—not intentionally, but nevertheless it is tainted. Of course, the fact-finder could clearly segregate her findings of fact from her recommendations, but when pressed while under oath, she would have to admit her work product was not entirely factual. Albeit, with hesitation she would have to admit that she had been somewhat subjective and not all that she had provided the decision makers were facts. This damaging testimony could be cleaned up during cross-examination. However, regardless of the qualifiers added, it still does not sound good. The point I am making is simple, there is no need or advantage in providing recommendations. When the fact-finder makes recommendations it tends to diminish her credibility by impugning her impartiality.

Possibly the biggest problem recommendations create are instances when the recommendations are not acted upon or rejected. If the recommendations are not protected by an attorney–work product privilege, they are subject to discovery. Later, long after the investigation has been concluded, recommendations can come back to haunt an organization. Here is a good example.

Suppose the postinvestigation recommendations made by a fact-finder included improvements to exterior lighting. Say the fact-finder concluded that better lighting in the employee parking lot would reduce the chance of future vandalism to both the company property and employee vehicles. However, because of cost or other priorities the improvements are never made. Then, sometime later, tragedy strikes. A female employee is brutally attacked in that same parking lot while leaving the facility late at night. She then sues alleging the organization did not do enough to protect her. Her causes of action might include inadequate security, negligent security, and employer negligence. During the discovery phase of the litigation the long-forgotten recommendations of our otherwise well-meaning fact-finder are uncovered. Among his recommendations of course is the recommendation to improve the lighting in the very parking lot in which the attack took place. The report and its recommendations would support her allegations and further demonstrate that the attack was even foreseeable. Foreseeability would point directly to her employer's negligence, for the theory propounds that the employer knew of the risk and ignored it. In doing so, the employer was negligent and thus liable.

When proven, negligence and foreseeability impart huge exposure to the employer. The exposure is expanded further when the plaintiffs' demands include compensatory and *punitive* damages. As the name suggests, punitive damages are awarded to punish the defendant. It is not uncommon that punitive damages are awarded in large multiples of the compensitories. Making the matter even more painful, some states such as California prohibit insurance from paying compensatory damages. In such states, these damages are paid directly by the defendant.

Tip: The fact-finder should resist the temptation of making recommendations. The tradition of providing the decision-maker with recommendations is unnecessary and tends to diminish the credibility of the fact-finder and increase the employer's liability.

C. The Objectives of the Investigation

As stated in the first chapter, no investigation of any complexity can be successful without meaningful objectives. The investigation's objectives define the fact-finder's purpose, benchmark his progress, and provide the framework by which the project manager coordinates and builds his case. The objectives become the foundation on which the investigation rests.

The lack of objectives, or those that are poorly crafted, contributes to disorganization and lack of focus. Investigations without clearly defined objectives tend to lack focus. They wobble and seem to go nowhere in particular. They waste time and resources. Conducting an investigation without purposeful objectives is like taking a road trip without a map. It is hard to image setting off to one's intended destination without a plan as to how to get there. Worse yet would be to start the journey not even knowing the destination. Investigations are like journeys. They have a starting place and a destination. The Process of Investigation is the means to reach that destination.

1. Determining the Objectives

Experience has shown that carefully crafting the objectives at the onset of the investigation provides substantial dividends later. In addition to setting the project's course, carefully articulated objectives contribute substantially to one's ability to defend the process should it be later challenged. As mentioned in the previous section, angry plaintiffs not only take issue with their punishment, but the process that led to it as well. In these contests, the employer and his investigators are intentionally put on the defensive. They are forced to justify every action and decision associated with their process. Seemingly insignificant remarks, conversations, and decisions can be contorted until they appear as conspiracies driven by racism and hatred. At the very least, the defendants are made to look foolish. The plaintiffs will seek opportunities to point out the defendant's poor judgment, lack of sophistication, and biased thought processes. In the end, the employer's best intentions are made to look prejudicial and unfair. Regardless of how egregious the behavior that led to the discipline, the plaintiff who can show that his employer's investigative process was defective will have a substantial advantage. He will retain the offensive for as long as the employer has to defend its process. Like many high-profile criminal cases of late, it eventually becomes difficult to determine who is actually the suspected offender. Experienced advocates know that when they can put the process on trial, their clients usually win.

All of these complexities are unnecessary in the case of workplace investigations. Not only is the standard of proof lower, but the facts and contentions are usually less complicated. Moreover, the probability of a successful assault on the process is inversely proportional to the complexity of the investigation. That is one reason why capital cases are so difficult to successfully prosecute, and workplace discipline cases should be so easy to win. Like most things, the more complex they are, the more vulnerable they become. It is for this reason I am so adamant about front-loading the investigative process with an ample dose of planning and preparation. More often than not the fact-finder does not fully know the breadth of the problem he is about to investigate. Without adequate planning upfront and properly laying a foundation before starting, the fact-finder and his customer could be in for some real surprises. Here is a frightening example.

Several years ago an attorney representing a large restaurant chain contacted me and requested assistance in the investigation of a sexual harassment claim. The attorney indicated that a female employee had alleged that her manager had repeatedly made lewd and inappropriate comments in her presence and had attempted to fondle her while he was intoxicated. Realizing that sexual harassment claims tend to be contagious and one claim often precipitates others, we recommended initiating the groundwork for a containment strategy. Containment strategies vary in design and purpose, but in potentially large and complex situations involving sexual harassment claims, they are used to prevent an avalanche of false and frivolous claims by dishonest employees eager to cash-in on the opportunity of big settlements. Here are the fundamental components of such a strategy:

1. Quantify the complainant's claims and tie down his or her story.
2. Quickly interview and obtain statements from all witnesses and tie down their stories.
3. Identify and interview other potential complainants early.
4. Communicate and affirm the organization's sexual harassment policy to the workforce.
5. Provide the opportunity for any employee to make a formal complaint or anonymously report an issue of concern.

This strategy prevents opportunists from jumping on the bandwagon in the event the matter goes to settlement or trial. By minimizing the potential for false claims the organization expends fewer resources during its investigation and ultimately pays smaller damages.

Unfortunately in this particular case the employer would hear nothing of it. Fearful, that our proposed strategy would precipitate ill will and potentially create a public relations problem, the employer chose to quietly interview the complainant and her alleged harasser. Word quickly got out and rumors flew that the employer had offered a huge settlement. In no time, the employer was hit with complaints from over 120 additional employees. Across the enterprise, dishonest employees, eager to obtain some quick cash, brought charges against the employer. It was a can of worms. When it was all said and done, only a few of the complaints were proven to have any veracity. Yet it cost the employer hundreds of thousands of dollars and countless hours both of which could have been better used building the business.

Tip: Containment strategies are used to prevent opportunists from jumping on the bandwagon in the event the matter under investigation goes to settlement or trial. By minimizing the potential for false claims, the organization expends fewer resources during its investigation and ultimately pays smaller damages.

The importance of sound objectives cannot be overemphasized. Although the objectives vary from case to case, the objectives of almost all workplace investigations articulate the desire to

- Seek out and identify the true nature and scope of the problem.
- Identify who is involved and why.
- Gather any and all information in such a fashion as to allow the proper distribution of appropriate disciplinary or corrective action.
- Engineer the process in such a fashion that is least disruptive to the organization and its operations.
- Achieve the best possible return on investment.[12]

As mentioned in the previous chapter, this is no small order. But, taking the time to carefully determine the objectives of the project in advance saves time and money. Moreover, as you can easily recognize, these objectives are nearly universal. From a practical standpoint it is nearly impossible to disagree with them. And that is an important point. If later the investigative process is challenged or comes under scrutiny, the investigation's objectives will most certainly be questioned. The objectives and motives of the investigative team and those who determine discipline will all be scrutinized. A plaintiff will look for vulnerabilities and weaknesses in the process and the manner decisions were made. The plaintiff will search for evidence of ulterior motives and unlawful conduct. But image how disappointed he'll be when he finds that one of the first actions of the process was establishing fair and very reasonable objectives. Experience has also shown that early setbacks for plaintiffs of this type tend to demoralize them. It tends to demonstrate to them, and most importantly the court, that the defendant is no amateur and an easy victory is not likely.

I am so convinced of the importance of establishing and memorializing the objectives of the investigation at the beginning of the project, a list of my investigative objectives is one of the first documents placed into my case files.

a. Seek Out and Identify the True Nature and Scope of the Problem

In many situations, the nature and scope of the problem are not fully known before the investigation begins. What may appear to be the simple theft of petty cash may in fact be part of a massive fraud. A simple accounting error may in fact be one component of a massive embezzlement scheme that has spanned decades. The fact-finder rarely knows the full scope and nature of the problem about to be investigated until it has been investigated. As such, this seemingly simple and logical first objective is one of the most important.

b. Identify Who Is Involved and Why

In order to solve a workplace problem created by people, one needs to know who created it. Note that this objective does not include the identity of a suspected offender. The objective *determine if John Jones was involved* is improper. It is accusatory and suggests a bias or some predetermined conclusion. It is also difficult to defend if challenged. The object in part, is to identify the responsible party, not determine the involvement of one particular person. When the stated objective singles out an individual or group it becomes suspect. It creates an appearance of targeting and lays the foundation for future discrimination and bias claims.

This objective also seeks to determine *why* the offender was involved. Although determining the *why* does not necessarily need to be known in order to determine guilt, it is often essential if one expects to prevent the problem from recurring. Knowing the motivation and causation helps the organization engineer long-term solutions with safeguards against recidivism. Knowing the *why* behind the behavior makes achieving the last object on our list possible.

c. Gather Any and All Information in Such a Fashion as to Allow the Proper Distribution of Appropriate Disciplinary or Corrective Action

This objective speaks to how the information is collected and packaged. It also speaks in part to the way the decision makers make their decisions. First, the investigation must be conducted ethically and lawfully. In order to use the results, the information collection process must not only be effective and efficient, it must be done well within the boundaries of ethical and lawful behavior. Additionally, the results must be packaged such that it allows the decision makers the opportunity to make fair and consistent decisions regarding discipline or corrective action. The equitable disbursement of discipline is essential in order to defend against claims of disparate treatment or discrimination. Not only must the investigation appear fair, the distribution of discipline must also appear fair.

d. Engineer the Process in Such a Fashion That Is Least Disruptive to the Organization and Its Operations

It is pointless (and potentially damaging to one's career) to offer a cure that is worst than the disease. Fact-finders and their project managers who get carried away with themselves and their investigations jeopardize their investigations and the customer's well-being. Placing the employer in a position that requires him to shut down, displace people, or significantly disrupt operations is not good business. It's stupid. The investigation must be engineered so that it is least disruptive to the organization and its operations. It is the duty of those driving the investigative process to manage their process so it does not interfere with that of others. The project manager should always have his customer's best interests in mind when making decisions and taking action. Furthermore, thinking and planning in these terms demonstrate to the customer a particularly high level of sophistication. They demonstrate that the project manager understands business and the needs of his customer. They also demonstrate a degree of professionalism that is not expected of most investigators.

e. Achieve the Best Possible Return on Investment

Employers are more likely to conduct investigations that provide a return on investment. Yes, some investigations such as those precipitated when sexual harassment is alleged are mandated by law; others, of course, are just the smart thing to do as in the case of the mysterious disappearance of property. But if the investigation can be engineered to provide a substantive return beyond the obvious, it is more likely to be embraced by the organization and given the funding it deserves. The return should be measurable and defined as an objective. Determining it will be the focus of the next section, but before we move on let's examine briefly how and when objectives should be altered.

2. Modifying the Objectives

In order to be successful the process of investigation must be fluid and dynamic. Because facts can alter outcomes, the objectives of the investigation must be flexible. Situations change and the fact-finder must be able to adapt. As information and facts are developed, the true nature of the problem becomes increasing clear. It is logical, therefore, that if the nature of the problem under investigation is not what it was thought to be, then the objectives of the investigation must change with it. To do otherwise makes no sense. Steering a rigid course, no matter how well planned in advance, will not get one to his desired destination if his destination has changed. In other words, the investigative process cannot be so rigid and single-purposed that it cannot be altered when necessary.

Changing the investigation's objectives is easy. To do so, one only needs to restate them. The key, however, is to memorialize the fact that they have changed. For all the reasons stated earlier in this chapter, once the objectives have changed, the changes must be documented. All that is necessary is a note or memo to the file. Supporting arguments and some discussion relative to the reason for the change is recommended. Referencing file notes or other documents is sufficient. These simple actions speak volumes about the thought process and the mindset of the fact-finder. They demonstrate a professionalism that appreciates the finer nuances of fact-finding and intelligent and purposeful investigation. It says of the fact-finder, "I know want I'm doing and recognize my responsibility."

Trap: When changing the objectives of an ongoing investigation, document the new objectives and what necessitated the change. Failure to do so could later create the appearance of bias, unlawful discrimination, and prejudice. Remember, when taken to task it is the process that goes on trail, not the offender.

D. Potential and Intended Outcomes

The outcome of the investigation is inextricably related to the objectives. In fact, it is the potential and intended outcomes that largely determine the objectives. There are, of course, a number of outcomes, but in the final analysis there are but three that are truly viable: prosecution, termination, and restitution. Each of these will determine to some degree how the investigation is engineered and, to a much more significant degree, the process of investigation itself. For example, an investigation designed to prosecute offenders will consume more time and resources, for prosecution requires a higher standard of proof. Alternatively, if the intent is simply to terminate those who have violated their organizations' polices, the process will require less time and resources and will likely achieve its objectives more easily. The outcome of the investigation in this sense really speaks to the expectations of the organization for which the investigation is being performed.

1. Prosecution

Of all of the expectations an organization might have, prosecution is the one that first comes to mind when the misconduct is criminal. It is widely held that criminal conduct should not go unpunished. The greater the pain, the more the organization yearns for justice. The pursuit of it can consume an organization and its focus. However, criminal prosecution is often justified, and many organizations consider it a civil duty. Many organizations also believe prosecution is an effective deterrent. Others simple pursue it because they don't know what else to do.

However, employee prosecution is expensive and risky. Although our criminal justice system is arguably the best in the world, it is imperfect. It is slow and cumbersome. Moreover, in many ways it is designed to provide more rights to the accused than to the victim. Our system assumes innocence until proven guilty and provides that the accused receive fair and adequate due process. The right of due process is constitutionally ensured and buttressed by volumes of criminal procedure and decisions such as *Miranda*.[13]

When an employer blends prosecution with an employment action such as termination, it unwittingly extends rights to the offender that he would not otherwise enjoy. The right of due process is one of them. Due process, among other things, is the right of the accused to know the charge(s) brought against him, to examine the evidence, to cross-examine witnesses, to provide a defense, and to be represented by competent counsel. Surprisingly, employees enjoy many rights in the employment context, but the right to due process is not among them. That is, in taking an employment action, an employer has no affirmative duty to disclose its evidence, produce witnesses, allow the accused the opportunity to explain his behavior, or even permit representation. Barring a contractual obligation or past precedent to the contrary, the employer can discipline and fire at will. This remarkable fact is lost on many employers. They mistakenly assume that an employee accused of workplace misconduct must be shown the evidence against him or her and be told the identity of any witnesses. Employers frequently cringe when, during the course of an internal investigation, the subject requests representation. Unnecessarily, attorneys representing the interests of the employee are permitted to enter the process. They gain access to information that would otherwise be unavailable and are permitted to scrutinize the finest details of the employer's process. It is unnecessary and employers should not permit it.

The pursuit of criminal prosecution by the employer is likely to have similar effects. By co-mingling its attempts to prosecute with an employment action the employer exposes its process to discovery, the production of witnesses, and increases its potential for civil litigation. Experienced criminal defense attorneys may use the criminal prosecution process to "put the nose of the camel under the tent" and gain access and insight into the employer's investigative process in ways that would otherwise not be possible. The "free discovery" available to them during the prosecution permits the assessment of the employer's case from a civil perspective. Defects in the employer's process, such as evidentiary mishandling, breaks in the chain of custody, and conflicting statements by witnesses that are immaterial to the prosecution, can become the seeds of a civil action.

Criminal prosecution is also expensive. The standard of proof to obtain a criminal conviction (beyond a reasonable doubt) requires more time and resources to achieve than that which is necessary to discipline an employee (good-faith investigation, reasonable conclusion). The criminal investigation must be nearly perfect to achieve a conviction. Conversely, an employer's investigation must only be fair and reasonable in order to justify discipline. This fact is frequently overlooked. In the heat of the moment, while emotions are high and the pain is the greatest, employers instinctively involve law enforcement for the purpose of prosecution. Involving law enforcement is often the correct thing to do. However, if the matter does not require it and it does not provide a distinct return on investment, the employer should consider alternatives.

Prosecution's higher standard of proof necessitates a more rigorous investigation. All of the elements of the crime must be proven beyond a reasonable doubt. Proving details such as motive, intent, and state of mind may be necessary. Demonstrating these elements requires more time and resources. More witnesses must be interviewed, more evidence must be gathered and catalogued, and the employer must be prepared to spend more time in court. The belief that law enforcement will handle all of these things properly and conduct a complete and proper investigation for the employer is not realistic. Law enforcement has neither the time nor inclination to root out all of management's ills and shortcomings. Its mission is to enforce public law and bring offenders to justice. It has no duty to share with the employer all that its investigation has uncovered, nor does it need to determine root causes or process failures that created the criminal opportunity or those that made the loss possible. Often law enforcement will not reveal to the employer the identity of informants or others involved in the crime. Law enforcement is also able to cut deals with some offenders in order to make cases against others. This may leave in the workplace other undesirable criminals who were not worth the trouble. In other situations, the offenders may be offered immunity in order to obtain convictions against nonemployers. In these cases, no information is shared with the employer, no property is recovered, and no problems are solved. Time and resources are wasted and all that is achieved is that a few criminals in the community are put behind bars and the employer is left holding the bag. Moreover, a defective prosecution can create huge liabilities for the employer.

An employer that links its corrective action to prosecution unnecessarily raises the standard of proof. If the defendant is found not guilty of the very offense for which his employer had fired him, he may have a civil claim against the employer. The argument goes like this: how could the employee possibly be fired for the very offense for which the government found him not guilty? Of course the standard of proof used to determine the two is quite different. However, if the employer fired the employee because he was arrested or charged with a crime allegedly committed while at work, he has self-imposed the higher standard of proof on the employment action. In other situations, those arrested on suspicion of a workplace crime are not charged. This outcome is equally devastating to the employer and will frequently precipitate claims of false arrest against the employer. Even though the employer did not make the arrest, merely acting as a facilitator, doing as little as permitting the arrests to take place in the workplace, it can be asserted that the police were agents of the employer. As such, the employer is then vicariously responsible for their behavior. The causes of action brought against the employer might include defamation, intentional infliction of emotional distress, conspiracy, false arrest, and false imprisonment. In these cases, the more intertwined the relationship between the employer and law enforcement, the greater the potential liability for the employer.

Contrary to popular belief, employee prosecution is not an effective deterrent. This may be the most contentious point made in this book and I suspect many readers will disagree. However, I firmly hold that prosecution is not an effective deterrent and largely a waste of time. Although there are many exceptions, most workplace offenders who find themselves in the criminal justice system are first-time offenders. After spending hundreds of hours and countless dollars of taxpayer and employer money, most of these offenders will receive little more than a slap on the wrist. With the nation's jails and prisons already overflowing, these small-time and often first-time offenders will rarely be put behind bars. Probation and community service are usually the best that can be expected. In rare cases, restitution orders are handed down and even then, the offender is ordered to prepay only a fraction of what he or she has stolen. Because the offenses are usually nonviolent, probation is typically unsupervised and rarely enforced. The entire outcome is often a complete disappointment for the employer.

Even in the case of career criminals, prosecution is not an effective deterrent. As anyone in law enforcement will attest, the career criminal sees incarceration as little more than the cost of doing business. Life behind bars for months or even years is simply something they know comes with the job. They accept it and expect it. The occasional run-in with the law or an employer is seen as a minor inconvenience and nuisance. In some circles, doing time for one's crime is even perceived as a right of passage. These pathetic souls sometimes even decorate their bodies with jailhouse tattoos so as to display them someday in public as a badge of honor. Among the more notable are teardrops tattooed to the corner of the eye. Each tear represents a five-year stretch. Think about that next time you meet or see someone with three teardrops tattooed on his or her check!

Moreover, few co-workers learn from the mistakes of others. The presumption that other employees will fear going to jail or falling under the harsh hand of the law is absurd. Remember the criminal element we are discussing is arrogance. They believe those who are caught and punished are stupid. They do not see their employer or the government as wise and powerful. They perceive us a meek and pathetic. Those that are caught are viewed as incompetent. What's more, by removing the weak from society it creates more room for them. Fewer employees stealing from their employers only means less competition and more opportunity. When an employer removes from its workplace a drug dealer and leaves behind the abusers, no deterrent is created. More often than not the abusers will celebrate. Unwittingly the employer has created a business opportunity for one of the abusers. He or she can now step up and fill the void and takeover the former dealer's enterprise. Furthermore, some of the abusers will have likely owed the dealer money. Now that he is gone, their debts are "forgiven" and he will likely never be repaid. Such an outcome is a win-win situation for everyone except the dealer and the employer. Making matters worse, the new dealer is likely to be more aggressive and potentially more violent than the experienced dealer he replaced. Attempting to establish a reputation and name for himself, he will be tempted to use intimidation and violence to assert his authority over his new client base. And like many new businesspeople entering the market for the first time, he will likely undercut the competition on price in order to establish himself and grab market share. Like the misguided entrepreneur, in doing so all he will likely do is destabilize the market and put more product in it than there is demand to consume. The impact on the employer can be devastating.

Many years ago a client of mine who was a frequent user of undercover asked that we sprinkle several operatives into a location at which we had just completed a very successful investigation. The location had had a long history of employee substance abuse and consistently underperformed. After the necessary logistical preparations, we inserted two fresh undercover investigators into the workforce. On his first day at the facility, a co-worker, who introduced himself as a source of premium marijuana, approached one of the new operatives. He told our investigator that the employer was a regular user of undercover and that if he was going to be involved with drugs at work he ought to be careful. He told our investigator he could be trusted because after no less than three prior investigations he had never been caught. In his words he was *cool*. The young entrepreneur eventually went on to sell our investigator a small amount of marijuana and was eventually terminated for it. However, before losing his job, he had bragged to our operative that the prior investigations performed by the employer had identified and removed only the most careless dealers and users. He said that the removal of these dealers, while leaving behind many of their customers, had created a vacuum. He was very proud of himself to have seen the opportunity and have filled it so quickly. Sadly, by deciding to remove only the dealers and the most serious users, my client had unwittingly only made the workplace substance abuse even worse.

Tip: Employee prosecution is expensive and time consuming. It is not an effective deterrent and rarely provides an acceptable return on investment. The decision to prosecute should be made for business reasons only.

---

2. Termination

Termination, the second potential outcome, is decidedly the most common. The most serious of workplace transgressions uncovered by employers almost invariably result in termination of employment. The decision to terminate is often an easy one. With sufficient evidence it is usually also a safe one. But because termination is considered the employment equivalent of capital punishment, the decision to terminate must be made carefully. The unequal and inconsistent application of its policies and the failure to follow established precedents can give rise to claims of disparate treatment and discrimination. Regardless of the amount of evidence an employer may have, the decision to terminate should not be made hastily or impulsively. Under most circumstances, there is no need to rush to judgment.

In most circumstances the decision to terminate should be made methodically. The fourth phase of investigation, determination and disbursement of disciplinary or corrective action, as described in the first chapter, contemplates this potential outcome and identifies it as a component of the investigative process. Behind the decision, however, should be a process of incremental steps leading to it and the resultant action. Here are the typical steps:

- *Step 1:* Ensure the fact-finding effort is complete and that the decision maker(s) has (have) been provided all of the information available.
- *Step 2:* After review of organizational policies regarding the offenses in question, decide the appropriate discipline for each type of offense.

- *Step 3:* Separate offenders (if more than one) into groupings of similar offenses.
- *Step 4:* Sort offenders in each group by the quality of evidence against them.
- *Step 5:* Systematically match the choice of discipline to the corresponding group of offenders in each grouping of offenses. First apply the harshest discipline to those of whom the best evidence exists. Incrementally repeat the process until discipline has been decided for each individual.
- *Step 6:* Review the result to ensure the fair and equal treatment of each offender. Double check the quality of evidence in each case, ensuring the standard of proof used has been met. Compare decisions to past precedent. Consider any extenuating or special circumstances for each offender. Document process and determinations.
- *Step 7:* Dispense the discipline.

Steps 1 and 2 are self-explanatory; however, the others require some amplification. In Step 3 the offenders (if more than one) are separated into groupings of similar offenses. Organizational policy, precedent, and the findings of the organization determine the offense categories. Hypothetically in a fraud case the offenses might be:

- Misappropriation by deceit and deception
- The intentional misapplication of customer credits
- Use of petty cash for personal purposes
- Unauthorized cancellation of active invoices

Notice that only the first offense is actually a potential violation of the law (misappropriate by deceit and deception is actually the definition of fraud). The others are policy or work-rule violations. Regardless, in this hypothetical example all four offenses were uncovered and each of them was deemed actionable.

An investigation of sexual harassment might hypothetically uncover:

- Inappropriate and unwanted touching of a co-worker
- Repeated use of inappropriate and profane language in the workplace
- Failure to enforce the organization's sexual harassment policy

Here none of the offenses is criminal, but all three are policy or work-rule violations, at least for hypothetical purposes. The last is most interesting. Here, the mere failure to enforce a policy is a policy violation and thus deemed actionable.

Step 4 is a little more complicated. Here the employer must categorize the assorted types of proof he may have and weight them. For example, in workplace investigations the highest and most valuable form of proof is a properly obtained admission. Under most circumstances it alone is enough evidence to justify discipline. The next general category of proof is the other evidence generated during the investigation. It may include video, fingerprints, documents, or recovered property. The statements of witnesses would also fall into this category. Most often evidence in this category is direct evidence, although circumstantial evidence may very well fall into this category if sufficiently strong. The third category would likely be all other circumstantial evidence and the statements of other offenders and conspirators. Intuitively one might think that the statements of other offenders and conspirators would have great weight and would be considered very valuable, and that is true *in criminal cases*. In employment cases, however, witnesses cannot be forced to testify nor can deals be cut in order to obtain their testimony. As such, the reliance on such witnesses for testimonial purposes is iffy at best. Even if they are willing to testify, they likely have a self-interested motive to recant or lie. Inherently, these witnesses can rarely be relied upon, and thus, their value is usually limited.

The "Discipline Distribution Chart" shown as Exhibit 2.6 is an example of how the evidence can be sorted and applied to a collection of possible offenses. Admissions are given the highest consideration and circumstantial evidence, in this case the *statements of others* is given the least. Note that in this example, admissions were obtained from both offenders but for different offenses. In deciding the equitable distribution of discipline, the chart facilitates the comparison of offenders and offenses, while illuminating the quality of evidence in each case. Moreover, it provides for a permanent record of how the discipline decisions were determined. The equitable distribution of discipline in complex cases involving a large number of offenders would be nearly impossible without this valuable tool.

Tip: Admissions alone are enough evidence to justify discipline. When properly obtained, admissions trump all other forms of proof.

---

3. Restitution

Of all of the investigative outcomes possible, restitution is the one least considered by employers. Remarkably, restitution is relatively simple and

Exhibit 2.6 Discipline Distribution Chart

	Misappropriation by Deceit and Deception	Intentional Misapplication of Customer Credits	Misuse of Petty Cash	Unauthorized Cancellation of Active Invoices
Jones, William				
Admission	Yes	Yes	No	Yes
Direct evidence	Altered documents	Altered documents	None	Altered documents
Circumstantial evidence	Statements of others	Statements of others	Statements of others	None
Stevens, James				
Admission	No	No	Yes	No
Direct evidence	None	None	Altered documents	Altered documents
Circumstantial evidence	None	None	Statements of others	None
Employee Name				
Admission				
Direct evidence				
Circumstantial evidence				

yet powerfully effective.[14] When properly used, the employer cannot only often recover his losses, but the cost of the investigation as well. Restitution allows for exponential returns on the investigative investment made by the employer. When properly crafted, there is no better outcome at the conclusion of a workplace investigation.

Restitution has many forms. The simplest of them is the repayment or return of that which was taken. This usually requires very little effort and is easily arranged. In its most complex form, restitution can involve contractual agreements, civil judgments, and court orders. In extreme cases, offenders may be forced to pay not only compensatory or actual damages but punitive damages as well. Illustrative of this are actions brought under the Racketeer Influenced Criminal Organization Act (RICO), which statutorily permits the trebling of damages. Originally enacted as a weapon to be used against organized crime, this powerful statue has been increasingly used by plaintiffs to hammer defendants in civil actions. Under most circumstances in which the employer can quantify damages and attribute intentional losses directly to the action (or inaction) of an employee, restitution is possible. Remarkably, all that is necessary is an agreeable offender and a mechanism to bind the offered to his agreement.

In addition to recovering an actual loss or damages, the employer can often recover the cost of the investigation. Even in cases in which the loss is insured, recovery for the cost of the investigation is often compensible. That is, the employer's investigative costs are included in the settlement or attributed to the deductible. In either situation, the employer is made whole for both its loss and the investigation of it. Fidelity claims, as they are called, are usually easy to make and recover. Often the employer need not even show the precise amount of the loss, but only a rough number. Although the deductibles are traditional large, usually not less than $25,000, losses attributable to ordinary inventory shrinkage are not covered and settlement is usually fast and painless. Policies usually require full employer cooperation to include the production of witnesses and documents and full subrogation rights. Subrogation rights allow the carrier to assume the role of the victim and pursue the offenders for the purpose of recovery. Fidelity policies also often require the employer to make a crime report, file charges, and report the alleged loss to them within 30 days of its discovery. These stipulations allow the carrier the best chance of bringing an action against the parties responsible and the greatest opportunity of a successful recovery from them.

Even when losses are not compensible or are less than the deductible, recoveries are still possible. As stated earlier, all that is necessary is an agreeable offender and a mechanism to bind him to his agreement. Attorneys should be used to draft these agreements. Because they constitute a contract, they must contain certain elements in order to be enforceable. Alternatively, a poorly crafted admission in which the offender offers to repay his employer, but which contains no terms may also constitute a contract. However, if improperly structured the contract may be unenforceable while barring further civil or criminal action. Many states also honor verbal contracts. Colorado, my home state, for example, permits oral contracts and allows the enforcement of them. Engaging the offender in ordinary discussion and accepting his plea for forgiveness and repayment of that which he has admitted stealing could constitute a verbal contract. The contract could be enforceable and preclude any chance of a prosecution or an insurance company's ability to recover the loss.

Another potential exposure for the employer is the claim of extortion. Law prohibits the threat of criminal prosecution in order to obtain a civil settlement in most states. As such, the demand for restitution in lieu of criminal prosecution in many parts of the country is both criminally and civilly actionable.[15] Therefore, in negotiating a settlement the employer must be careful not to even imply that restitution may influence its decision to prosecute or even report the matter to the police.[16] However, inexperienced employers and unsophisticated investigators do this frequently. Many an investigator, usually the principal of his firm, has boasted to me how he or she obtained an admission and promise to pay restitution under the threat of prosecution. Not only is this bad form and unethical, it is most likely illegal. Use of this unsophisticated tactic is cheap and unprofessional. No one should do it.

Trap: Using the threat of criminal prosecution in order to obtain an admission or the promise to pay restitution is extortion. In most states it is a crime and both criminally and civilly actionable. It is inappropriate to use threats to obtain the cooperation of any subject during the course of a workplace investigation.

E. Evidence Collection and Preservation

Of equal importance to case file management is evidence management, a topic on which entire books have been written. Because evidence is available in so many forms, it is not practical to examine the topic in its entirety here, nor do I intend to so. However, the subject should be discussed briefly.

1. The Definition of Evidence

Evidence is any type of proof that when presented is materially capable of proving or disproving a contention or fact.[17] In order to be used or admissible, the evidence must be material to the matter in question. Thus, materiality speaks to the relevance of the evidence. Direct evidence is that means of proof that tends to show the existence of a fact without the intervention of proof or any other fact, and is distinguished from circumstantial evidence, which is often called *indirect* evidence. Circumstantial evidence is inferential by establishing a condition or premise from which the existence of the principal fact may be concluded by reasoning. By nature, all presumptive evidence is circumstantial. However, all circumstantial evidence is not presumptive, as it leads to necessary conclusions instead of probable ones.[18]

2. Hearsay Evidence

Hearsay evidence does not proceed from the personal knowledge of the witness, but from the mere repetition of what the witness has heard others say. When the source that had allegedly been heard is not available to testify, hearsay evidence is typically not admissible. One exception is when the defendant's conduct is in issue or is relevant; statements made in his presence by which his conduct can be inferred are admissible when the defendant makes no denial.[19] By their very nature, most statements and declarations (statements taken under oath) are hearsay when the author is unavailable as a witness. Such documents are *double-hearsay* if they include reference to statements made by the accused. However, statements and declarations made by the accused (assuming they were properly attained) constitute the highest quality of evidence available in workplace investigations.

Trap: Many employers and the investigators who work for them pursue the standard of proof beyond a reasonable doubt and self-impose rules of evidence that are exceedingly strict. Thus, excluded is evidence that otherwise would be admissible in the typical workplace investigation. Lowering the standard of proof eases the rules of evidence and permits the use of evidence otherwise not admissible.

3. Admissibility and Materiality

In many regards the admissibility, and often the materiality, of evidence is tied directly to the standard of proof. For example, in unemployment insurance benefit eligibility hearings (sometimes called UI hearings) nearly all forms of evidence are admissible. Administrative law judges hearing these cases will usually allow the introduction of any and all evidence, and in my experience, even evidence of questionable origin (read "fabricated"). Procedure requires such evidence to be *weighted* (not weighed) and accorded the consideration it deserves. All this makes for rather loose proceedings. But that is the intent. Because representation is optional in these venues, the rules are relaxed in order to ensure fairness to those who do not have representation. Most arbitration hearings are similar. It is usually the arbitrator who establishes the "rules of evidence" and determines what is admissible and what is not. As such, the outcomes of arbitrations are highly unpredictable. The following is a fine example.

Some time ago, one of my undercover drug investigations resulted in the termination of over 30 employees. All but one of the employees were members of a collective bargaining agreement and were entitled to grieve their discipline. The grievances ultimately resulted in arbitration. The arbitrator, well known for the liberal application of his authority, allowed the admission of all forms of evidence and claims. Although all of the grievants had provided written admissions during the investigation detailing their transgressions, he allowed them to recant or alter them substantially during the hearing. He allowed the argument that the admissions obtained without a union representative present were coerced. He ignored the fact that many of the admissions were corroborative to one another and that several of the grievants admitted that even if a union representative had been present, their statements to our investigators would not have been substantially different. He also allowed the union to raise the issue of discrimination. Although fully two-thirds of the workforce were minorities, less than a third of the grievants were. To cap it off, he allowed several of the grievants to introduce statements written by them asserting their own innocence! The final travesty of justice was served when the arbitrator rendered his decision and ordered of all of the grievants to return to work.

The rules of civil and criminal procedure do not allow for such injustices. Both in civil and criminal court, the rules of evidence are codified and for the most part adhered to. Uniquely, workplace investigations are subject to the rules of evidence imposed by the employer. Short of legal challenge, the employee enjoys the prerogative of deciding both the standard of proof and the rules of evidence in deciding workplace issues. The challenge is to balance the need for fairness and maintaining workplace order. The employer's decisions regarding discipline must be lawful, fair, impartial, and consistent.

4. Spoliation of Evidence

Spoliation is the destruction of evidence and it constitutes an obstruction of justice. Spoliation is also the destruction, or significant and meaningful alteration, of a document or instrument.[20] The rules of evidence impose an obligation to retain and produce evidence deemed admissible and relevant in criminal and civil matters. The intentional and sometimes even the accidental destruction of evidence may be unlawful and civilly actionable—and for good reason. The destruction of evidence very often provides one party an advantage at the expense of another. Recent cases involving the employees, and in some instances the agents (outside accountants and auditors) of public companies, intentionally destroying documents and critical records demonstrate the consequences. Litigation and criminal indictments of both the organization and the responsible parties are not uncommon. Worst yet may be the damage to the organization's reputation and the loss of public confidence in the markets. The destruction these acts can cause can be incalculable. Even the destruction of evidence during a simple workplace investigation can have grave consequences.

During the investigative process, should items such as e-mails, notes, and apparently extraneous documents be discarded, claims of spoliation may later arise. In emotionally charged cases such as those involving the claim of discrimination or sexual harassment, accusations about the destruction of evidence are common. Furthermore, they are difficult to disprove. The mere fact the alleged document (which may have never existed) cannot be produced inferentially suggests that it was destroyed. In most cases, only testimony can be used to prove the document didn't exist (think of personal notes and how one would prove they or portions of them didn't exist). If credibility of the witness(es) used to prove the document didn't exist is in question, the charge of spoliation has a good chance of gaining traction. If so, the credibility of the witness(es) will suffer further damage.

Tip: In the course of investigation, do not destroy anything that may later be considered evidence. The destruction of evidence is considered an obstruction of justice and may be a crime or civilly actionable. At the very least, it looks bad.

---

5. Evidence Retention

For many of the reasons stated earlier, evidence retention and preservation have become popular topics. The mishandling and misplacing of evidence can be catastrophic. The investigative process must contemplate this issue from the onset. Reconstruction of evidence is time consuming and expensive. It is best to handle it properly from the onset. The favored tool in workplace investigations used to catalogue and preserve evidence is the evidence file.

An evidence file may be nothing more than a manila folder in which evidentiary documents are placed for safekeeping. Accordion folders, corrugated boxes, file cabinets, or safes may also be used to store evidence.

Exhibit 2.7   Evidence Tracking Sheet

#	Date Received	Description	Quantity	Received From	Received By	Disposition
1	9-12-03	Hard drive # 74223415099-SH03	1	Jones, L.	Ferraro, E.	Retained
2	9-15-03	CD (marked as # EVID 2314-01)	1	Parker, B.	Ferraro, E.	Retained
3	9-16-03	CD (marked as # EVID 2314-02)	2	Parker, B.	Smith, T.	Retained
4						
5						
6						
7						
8						
9						
10						
11						
12						
13						
14						

On the extreme end of the spectrum is the evidence locker or compound. Regardless of its form or construction, the purpose is the safe storage of evidence.

In addition to containing evidence, the evidence folder should contain a document used to identify and track the evidence within it. Variations of this form are largely a matter of preference. Exhibit 2.7 represents a partially completed evidence tracking sheet.

In 2001 the Securities and Exchange Commission fined six U.S. securities firms a total of $10 million for failing to produce e-mails (yes, e-mails) in the course of an investigation. Although companies can destroy any document they wish if in compliance with the law, many find they don't even know what documents they had or which ones they have destroyed. According to a survey by the American Bar Association, 83 percent of member respondents said their corporate clients had no comprehensive data-retention plan. Seventy-five percent said their clients did not even know e-mail and other e-documents could be used in litigation. DuPont, an early adaptor, says its systematic document management program has saved it an average of $300,000 per litigation case—easily funding its program.[21]

Trap: Even the routine and scheduled destruction of documents pursuant to an established document management program is not foolproof. Administrators should routinely conduct inspections to ensure compliance.

---

6. *Chain of Custody*

The transfer of evidence from one party to another should be carefully documented. Each person who handles or takes control of evidence must be recorded, creating what is called the *chain of custody*. The chain of custody, sometimes called the *chain of evidence,* is a document that at a minimum identifies each custodian, when he received the evidence, and to whom he transferred it. The chain of custody must not be broken. That is, there cannot be gaps during which the evidence was unaccounted for or out of the control of a custodian of record. A chain of custody that is broken exposes it to challenge and jeopardizes the admissibility of the evidence. Exhibit 2.8 is a sample evidence custody form.

Exhibit 2.8   Evidence Custody Form

EVIDENCE CUSTODY FORM
COLLECTION INFORMATION

DATE: _____

TIME: _____

LOCATION: _____

SUBJECT'S NAME: _____

DESCRIPTION OF EVIDENCE: _____

_____

_____

NAMES OF PERSONS HANDLING EVIDENCE

1. _____   Time/Date: _____

2. _____   Time/Date: _____

3. _____   Time/Date: _____

4. _____   Time/Date: _____

5. _____   Time/Date: _____

6. _____   Time/Date: _____

7. _____   Time/Date: _____

The sloppy handling of evidence exposes both the fact-finder and the evidence to credibility challenges. Claims of evidence tampering, alteration, or contamination are possible when evidence is mishandled. Fact-finders should not handle or use originals during their investigation. Whenever possible, copies, photographs, or models should be used in lieu of the actual evidence. Never place an original piece of evidence in the hands of the subject. Knowing the value of the evidence and its implications, the subject may be tempted to destroy it.

Tip: Establish a chain of custody for each piece of evidence. Do not take originals into the field. Use copies, photos, and models instead of the actual evidence.

In the next chapter we are going to examine how the fundamentals of fact-finding are actually put to use. Some of what you are about to learn will surprise you.

Notes

1. J. Winik, *April 1865* (New York: HarperCollins, 2001), 155, 220.
2. Ibid., p. 220.
3. U.S. Secret Service Web site, http://www.ustreas.gov/usss/history.shtml, 2002.
4. Pinkerton's Burns Web site, http://www.pinkertons.com/company-info/default.asp, 2002.
5. Texas Department of Public Safety Web site, http://www.txdps.state.tx.us/director_staff/texas_rangers/, 2002.
6. Author's note: It was the application of this philosophy to every aspect of government Roosevelt touched that made the first modern president.
7. The Federal Bureau of Investigations Web site history page, http://www.fbi.gov/libref/historic/history/origins.htm.
8. H. J. Harwood, D. M. Napolitano, P. L. Kristiansen, and J. J. Collins, *Economic Costs to Society of Alcohol and Drug Abuse and Mental Illness: 1980*, Research Triangle Institute, Research Triangle Park, NC, June 1984.
9. E. Nedelmann and J. S. Wenner, "Toward a Sane National Drug Policy," *Rolling Stone Magazine* (1994): 24–25.

10. *National Household Survey on Drug Abuse* (Washington, D.C.: National Institute on Drug Abuse, 1988).
11. *The American Heritage Dictionary of the English Language*, 3rd ed. (Boston: Houghton Mifflin, 1994).
12. Principally derived from E. F. Ferraro, *Undercover Investigations in the Workplace*, 1st ed. (Woburn, Mass.: Butterworth-Heinemann, 2000), 56, with permission.
13. *Miranda v. Arizona,* 384 U.S. 436 (1966).
14. Ferraro, *Undercover Investigations in the Workplace*, p. 45.
15. California Penal Code §§153 and 519 make it a crime to threaten criminal action in order to obtain the settlement of a civil matter.
16. Ferraro, *Undercover Investigations in the Workplace*, p. 46.
17. J. John Fay, *Encyclopedia of Security Management* (Woburn, MA: Butterworth-Heinemann, 1993), 291.
18. Martin Roth, *The Writer's Complete Crime Reference Book* (Cincinnati, Ohio: Writer's Digest Books, 1990), 271.
19. Ibid., p. 277.
20. H. C. Black, *Black's Law Dictionary,* 6th ed. (St. Paul: West Publishing, 1997), 1257.
21. Ashby Jones, *AmLaw Tech,* http://www.law.com/index.shtml, 2002.

Chapter 3

The Methods of Investigation

Fact-finders conducting workplace investigations have six fundamental investigative methodologies at their disposal:

- Physical surveillance
- Electronic surveillance
- Research and audit
- Forensic analysis
- Undercover
- Interviews and interrogations

It is the responsibility of the investigative team to select the appropriate methodologies and use them properly to achieve the investigation's objectives. Although each method of investigation may be used alone, the best investigative results are usually achieved by combining them in some logical fashion. The fact pattern of a particular situation combined with the skills and experiences of the investigative team should determine which methods should be used and in which order. In some situations these decisions will be intuitively obvious. In some situations the task will be more difficult. The investigative team may need to ponder the applicability of each method and its practicality relative to the achievement of the project's objectives. For example, if the matter under investigation is the vandalism of employee restrooms, electronic surveillance (specifically covert cameras) might at first blush seem to be an appropriate method of identifying the perpetrator(s). However, upon closer examination it becomes obvious that the use of cameras in restrooms has privacy implications and may be very inappropriate. Additionally, the investigative team should realize that even appropriate methods may not be practical or even work if used. For example, while undercover may appear appropriate to solve the vandalism problem described above, it may not be practical because of the location of the restroom and its accessibility to nonemployees.

Before making final decisions regarding the use of one or more methods of investigation, the investigative team should consider the following regarding each method contemplated:

- Appropriateness
- Practicality
- Expedience
- Potential results
- Cost
- Legal implications

In some instances there is no perfect method or combination of methods. On occasion, my team and I have had to make tough decisions when determining which methods to use. In these situations we sometimes were unable to select the best method(s) and were left with the only method available.

A. Physical Surveillance

1. Physical Surveillance Defined

Surveillance is simply the careful watching of people, places, or things. It need not be covert but often is. It is probably also the oldest form of investigation and was very likely the most widely used method until the advent of the Internet. It is also fundamentally simple. All that is needed to conduct surveillance is something to watch and someone to watch it. Physical surveillance also differs from other forms of surveillance including *electronic* surveillance in that it involves the use of a human observer. And because is it inherently simple it is also relatively inexpensive. This and other aspects of physical surveillance often make it the method of choice for the inexperienced fact-finder when contemplating a workplace investigation.

It is also not uncommon for organizational decision makers and those that counsel them to embrace the idea. Not knowing what else to do, surveillance often sounds like a good idea. And why not—it is simple, expedient, and inexpensive. Moreover, "maybe we'll learn something." Surveillance in these situations also *feels good*. It gives the decision makers and the investigative team a sense that they are doing something. The illusion, however, is just that. *Feel good* investigations rarely produce worthwhile results or achieve the stated objectives. They amount to little more than an exercise that keeps the participants occupied. Even when these undertakings produce some seemingly worthwhile evidence, additional investigation or reinvestigation is often necessary. Here is a good example.

The manufacturer of machined auto parts knew his organizational culture was dysfunctional, but did not fully grasp the extent of it until the organization began to renegotiate a simple labor agreement. The vice president of labor relations got his first clue during an afternoon visit with some of the plant production employees. While visiting the plant, every individual complained that management was overbearing and condescending. Collectively they complained that they were overworked and unappreciated. They also reported that the plant manager was often off-site or absent all together.

Recognizing the need for additional information, the vice president hastily hired a local private investigator and placed the plant manager under surveillance. The surveillance quickly revealed that he spent the better part of nearly every day away from the plant visiting and entertaining customers and doing other odds and ends. Nothing particularly strange about that; however, something was unusual. Without failure, upon his return to the plant he meandered through the employee parking lot doing the most incredible thing—he picked up empty alcohol containers. The vice president then did what he should have done first; he sat down and had a chat with the plant manager.

Without hesitation, the plant manager admitted he spent the better part of each day off-site. He explained that business development and customer relations were an important part of his job. He also explained that for some time he suspected an employee substance abuse problem. The suspected problem was impacting productivity, quality, and employee morale. He told the vice president that everyday he found empty alcohol containers in the employee parking lot. He said his employees had complained to him *that management was overbearing and condescending—collectively they complained that they were overworked and unappreciated.* He also said that without more efficiency and a larger customer base, the viability of his plant was in serious question. The seasoned vice president of labor relations stood and glanced out the window, mindlessly gazing into the employee parking lot. As he was thinking of what to say next, he saw two young employees toss what appeared to be empty beer cans from the window of a parked pickup truck.

Tip: Physical surveillance is deceivingly simple. Do not default to it when other methods of investigation are readily available and obviously more practical.

2. Stationary and Moving Surveillance

Physical surveillance can be conducted while stationary or while moving. In either case, the fact-finder's task is the same. He is watching either someone or something. His obvious purpose is to collect useful information, which furthers the investigative process. The choice that his surveillance will be stationary or moving is usually not his. Rather, it is the behavior of the subject and other factors that dictate the type of physical surveillance he will use. Those factors include

- The subject's ability to move from one location to another
- The likelihood the subject will leave one location for another
- The likelihood that the object being watched will leave one location and be moved to another

Other considerations include the number of subjects to be watched, the likelihood of additional subjects showing up, the likelihood of one or more of the subjects leaving at the same time, and finally, that what is being watched is inherently mobile and that movement is a function of its purpose (i.e., a delivery truck). In most instances the determination is obvious. In those in which it is not, the fact-finder weighs his options and makes the best choice possible. It is therefore no surprise that more often than not, physical surveillance involves the use of automobiles.

Automobiles (including trucks and vans) are almost the perfect tool. They are readily available, are rarely appear out of place, provide ample cover, are easy and inexpensive to operate (think airplanes), and are convenient. Most physical surveillance, whether it is stationary or moving, is done from an automobile.

a. Stationary Surveillance

Of the two forms of physical surveillance, stationary surveillance is the most common. Not only is it suitable in most circumstances, but it is easy as well. Often the most difficult task for the fact-finder is staying awake.

For convenience, most surveillance is done from a vehicle. Vehicles, be they cars, vans, or trucks, provide both a means of transportation to the intended surveillance site and cover. The vehicle is thus a critical piece of equipment. Selecting a suitable vehicle and maintaining it are often central to the success of the effort. However, the selection or choice of vehicle has historically been overemphasized. Law enforcement, often with a larger budget for such things, tends to be a bit more extravagant. For them, the use of sophisticated vans or sport-utility vehicles is common. Sporting sophisticated cameras, recording equipment, periscopes, and a host of creature comforts, these hi-tech vehicles are expensive and more than is ever needed for the typical workplace investigation. More often than not, the fact-finder needs only a vehicle that provides reliable transportation and adequate cover, and sometimes that is not even necessary.

An investigator with whom I worked years ago did all of his surveillance from an impeccably maintained Volkswagen Cabriolet. He used the sporty convertible with top down for nearly every assignment given him. Over lunch one day I asked him how was it that he consistently shot some of the best video in our office. He replied, "Who'd suspect me?" It was true. Norm was a handsome, well-tanned man, driving a Volkswagen convertible—who would have thought he would have the time or interest in watching anyone except maybe a beautiful woman? Norm understood that it wasn't the vehicle that allowed a successful surveillance; it was the investigator behind the wheel. Correspondingly, over the years my teammates have used every type of vehicle imaginable.

On some occasions we have had to use preplaced vehicles from which to conduct our surveillance. In these instances, it was not practical to move our vehicle in and out of the target area. Instead, after careful planning, we preplaced our vehicle exactly where we wanted it and left it. On some occasions, with the cooperation of our client, we ran electrical power to the vehicle (sometimes a trailer) in order to provide electricity for our equipment and to power the necessary creature comforts required under the conditions. These stationary surveillance posts make sense when there is absolutely no need for mobility. Using a vehicle, truck, or trailer already in place is best. However, if this option is not possible, the preplacement of one is a very suitable alternative. Because people (and bad guys) do not tend to notice things that are ordinary or expected, preplaced stationary vehicles make for excellent cover for surveillance. They do pose one problem the reader probably has already recognized: how does one get to and from the concealment of the surveillance position without being noticed?

The most common method is called the *drop*. Using another inconspicuous vehicle, the surveillance investigator(s) is driven to the surveillance position and *dropped*. If possible, drops are made under the cover of darkness. For obvious reasons, a night drop and pick-up has many advantages. However, in some instances the drop must occur in daylight. Regardless, the fact pattern and common sense determine the time and methodology. On rare occasions I have even created distractions to divert the attention of would-be observers seeing my team enter or leave its surveillance position. In some instances all that is needed is a staged tire change. On one occasion, I actually hired an ambulance and paramedics and staged an emergency to distract would-be observers. In yet other instances, all that was needed was an attractive female delivery person or an annoying salesman.

Another variant of the drop is to place the surveillance vehicle with the investigator already concealed in it. With proper planning and equipment, the surveillance vehicle can be driven to the target location where a breakdown is staged. The driver and perhaps even a passenger get out and attempt to repair the vehicle. After an apparently fruitless attempt to repair it, they give up and try pushing it. Moving the vehicle into the precise place desired, sometimes while in full view of the intended subjects, the driver and his exasperated companion abandon the vehicle. Inside and *covered* is the surveillance team. Alternatively, the surveillance investigator can simply meander up to his preplaced surveillance vehicle and climb in. In some situations this works very well, in others it is out of the question.

Stationary surveillance is not without its hazards. In addition to being uncomfortable and boring, it can also be dangerous. In some places such as Los Angeles routine surveillance can rarely be done from a van. In many of Los Angeles's neighborhoods vans of any kind draw attention and are considered suspicious. In rougher neighborhoods (that's an interesting oxymoron) a parked van will invariably draw gunfire. In the late 1980s a surveillance investigator with whom I worked was the victim of *two* drive-by shootings in a single day while on surveillance. Although violence of this sort is not common, the attention and inherent suspicion drawn by vans when used for surveillance is not. Vans, especially those that look like a tradesman's van, can also be the target of burglars. On numerous occasions my surveillance vans have been broken into while manned. We have always been able to scare away the would-be thieves, but at a cost. Invariably the incident drew unnecessary attention to our team. Be they curious onlookers drawn from the neighborhood or the police, the surveillance is usually burned. At the very least, it is necessary to assume a new position or switch out vehicles. Most experienced fact-finders who have done any significant amount of surveillance agree that the impulse to use vans and an employer's insistence that his fact-finders must have surveillance vans at their disposal is wrong-minded. Vans tend to be more difficult to maneuver and park. Because they are often larger than other vehicles, they tend to stand out. Even when disguised with a sideboard sign and a racked ladder or two, vans still draw attention. When selecting a vehicle to be used for stationary surveillance, consider all aspects of the situation. Just because Hollywood thinks vans make great surveillance vehicles doesn't mean they are.

Tip: The use of vans for stationary surveillance is not always necessary. Often, vans draw too much attention and appear suspicious. Do not conform to conventional thinking and insist your fact-finders must use vans to conduct their surveillance.

Not all stationary surveillance must be done from a vehicle. In fact, in some circumstances the fact-finder need not even be covered. Successful surveillance has been done from a park bench, a beach blanket, a café table, a playground, and even a jail cell. My investigators have done surveillance while snow skiing, surfing, skateboarding, golfing, and writing parking tickets. The limitations are only bound by the imagination of the investigative team and the fact-finder, and occasionally the fact-finder can be rather creative. Years ago I had such an investigator, and he nearly landed us in court.

Tomas was energetic and always eager to please his supervisors. He was also very creative and as such, frequently successful in obtaining the evidence requested of him. However, like many of the best surveillance professionals I have known over the years he had a peculiar quirk—he occasionally made very bad decisions. On this particularly memorable occasion, Tomas was tasked with obtaining video evidence of an alleged malinger performing manual labor while on full disability. Allegedly, the claimant was working part time as an auto mechanic while receiving undeserved benefits. Upon his arrival at the claimant's alleged place of work, a small independent repair shop, Tomas concluded that the only suitable location from which to obtain the evidence he was seeking was from inside a nearby church. Finding the church locked and normal entry impossible, Tomas engaged his tiny brain and decided the best course of action was to break in to the church. Using a coat hanger, in broad daylight, our genius broke in and took up a perfect surveillance position in the steeple. To no one's surprise other than his, Tomas was swiftly arrested and whisked away to the county jail for processing. Fortunately, we were able to arrange his quick release, and with a small donation to the church, we were able to have the charges dropped. Unfortunately, the effort—in spite of its cost and inconvenience—produced no useful evidence. Today Tomas runs his own successful investigative agency in Los Angeles, and the media frequently seeks his "expertise."

In addition to conducting surveillance from churches we have set up in hotel rooms, restaurants, train stations, convenience stores (inside the self-serve coolers actually), airports, and abandoned buildings. The places from which stationary surveillance can be conducted are limited only by the creativity of the fact-finder. However, no discussion regarding surveillance is complete without mentioning *privacy* and the reasonable expectation of it (this will be examined more thoroughly in Chapter 5, "Legal Challenges and Litigation Avoidance").

Privacy

The *right of privacy*, as it is often called, and privacy rights in general were first contemplated in the Fourth Amendment of the U.S. Constitution as a protection against unreasonable searches and seizures. Decades later, the implications of the Fourth Amendment are still being interpreted by the courts at both the federal and state levels.[1] The constitutions of at least ten states address the right to privacy or recognize a right to freedom from intrusion into one's private affairs. Among them, the California constitution states in Article I, Section I, "All people ... have inalienable rights. Among these are enjoying and defending life and liberty ... and pursuing and obtaining safety, happiness, and privacy."

Whether statutorily provided or created by the courts, the right to privacy imposes restrictions on the fact-finder and his efforts. Categorically, physical surveillance is permissible in all places except those where the subject might enjoy a reasonable expectation of privacy, or where prohibited by law or a mutually recognized agreement. Relative to the workplace, such places include restrooms, locker rooms, and any space in which the employee exclusively controls access. Offices, vehicles, desks, lockers, tool boxes, and the like are places in which the employee could have a reasonable expectation to privacy barring unfettered access by the employer. The employer can and should reduce the expectation of privacy by deploying a search policy and notifying employees that all work areas and spaces are subject to search. The employer should also prohibit the use of personal locks to secure offices, desks, lockers, and tool boxes.

A reasonable expectation does not usually exist in such work spaces as lobbies, break rooms, smoking areas, or other common areas. Surveillance in these areas is generally permissible. Surveillance outdoors in parking lots, shipping and receiving areas, and other similar areas is also generally permissible. Problems arise, however, outside the workplace. Watching employees in public places and areas outside the workplace where employees (and others) do not have a reasonable expectation of privacy creates few problems. Conversely, peering through open doors and windows of a private residence does. Fact-finders should also resist the temptation to peek through fences and other barriers surrounding private property. Even when invited, entry onto or into private property via a pretext may give rise to a privacy claim. Moreover, one who intentionally intrudes, physically or otherwise, upon the solitude or seclusion of another or into his private affairs or concerns is subject to liability for invasion of privacy, if the intrusion would be highly offensive to a reasonable person.[2] For this reason and others employment attorneys often play a useful role during the preparation and planning phase of the investigation. Counsel should be consulted prior to the initiation of any surveillance when the issue of privacy is evident or in question.

Trap: Even when no apparent expectation of privacy may exist, labor contracts and case law may require an employer to bargain prior to the surveillance of employees. Fact-finders are well advised to consult other members of the investigative team before initiating any form of workplace surveillance.

---

b. Moving Surveillance

Moving surveillance is a powerful variation of stationary surveillance. Unlike stationary surveillance, moving surveillance involves actively following the action (or subject) from place to place, crime scene to crime scene. Motorized vehicles typically provide the means of transportation; however, bicycles or even walking may be used. In addition to the obvious complexities of following someone or something undetected, moving surveillance can create challenges not typical of other forms of investigation. Among them is the issue of *jurisdiction*.

Jurisdiction

Jurisdiction is the authority by which a court acts, and the territory over which its authority extends.[3] By its very nature, moving surveillance permits the action to move from one jurisdiction to another. As the action unfolds in different jurisdictions, the investigation increases in complexity. Rules, policies, practices, and laws may vary from one jurisdiction to the next. For the fact-finders, licensure, insurance, and reporting requirement issues may arise as well. Moving surveillance is difficult in the first place, but as the players change, their mode of transportation changes and their activities change, and the complexities of case management exponentially increase. Throw in the added complexity of multiple jurisdictions, and project management can become a daunting task. Jurisdictional considerations further complicate the matter when prosecution is an objective. If the crime(s) was committed in multiple jurisdictions, the demands of competing law enforcement agencies, district attorneys, and governmental agencies must all be managed. Search warrants, arrest warrants, and evidence procurement (and sharing) become increasingly challenging for the investigative team. And as the complexity of the investigation increases, so too does its demand for resources. In very complex situations, the demand for resources can outstrip the employer's ability to provide them. This harsh reality further demonstrates why the preparation and planning phase of the project is so important. Unfortunately, some of the best practitioners in the industry have little appreciation for this not-so-subtle aspect of the process.

Multiple Tails and Teams

Moving surveillance is often best accomplished when more than one surveillance investigator is used. Using multiple teams to tail the subject reduces the chance of being detected and the possibility of losing him. Positioning the investigators so they can easily respond to the movement of the subject is of course necessary. Each team member must also anticipate the movement of the subject and his intentions. Using more than one surveillance investigator also allows for a *looser tail* and unexpected actions by the subject. When properly orchestrated, using a team produces better and more predictable results that often offset the higher cost they produce. Multiple tails also increase the complexity of the effort. Paramount to their success is effective communications.

Communications

Like most technologies, communications have made huge strides in the past decade. Years ago when I first entered the trade, two-way radios were the only electronic means of communication available to the surveillance investigator. I recall the first radio installed in my vehicle was so large "the box" had to be put in the trunk. Another box was crudely installed under the dash and a handheld microphone enabled me to talk to one other team member at a time. Contacting others required switching frequencies and hoping they were "up," or on that frequency. Radios were not provided to junior investigators and they were forced to communicate with hand signals. As crude as the methods were, we conducted many successful surveillance operations and usually got the evidence we were seeking.

Today investigators have a host of communication choices, all of which are inexpensive and dependable. Among the most popular devices is the cell phone. Cell phones are inexpensive and easy to use. What's more, just about everybody has one. They provide an efficient and secure means of communication and today they work almost anywhere. A popular variant of the common cell phone is the Nextel system. Like cell phones these devices can be used to make cellular calls, but they also provide the means to be used as two-way radios with other subscribers on the system. Call and radio conferencing is also possible, making Nextel a popular communication choice where it is available. The tool's effectiveness is further improved with the use of headsets and their easy-to-use hands-free features.

However, good communication tools are only part of the equation. Smooth operations and success also require a communication plan and discipline. Having to fumble around for a phone list, not knowing a contact's number, or unnecessary chatter is disruptive and unprofessional. A good communication plan and the disciplined use of one's tools can make the difference between success and failure.

Tip: Do not take communications for granted. Like every other aspect of the investigative process, a communication plan deserves careful consideration, and its use should be integrated into the investigative plan.

Tracking Devices

Global Positioning Satellite (GPS) technology is a remarkable technology. Using satellites in geosynchronous orbit about 35,000 miles above the surface of the earth, GPS allows someone to reliably identify his location within several meters anywhere on the planet. For less than $100 you can purchase a small handheld device that will enable you to identify a person's location, land navigate, or find your way when lost. The technology is even more exciting when used in workplace investigations. Here is how it is typically used.

Contrary to that which is portrayed in some movies, only the most expensive GPS technology allows one to track a target in real time. In order to do so, a GPS device and transmitter must first be attached to the target vehicle. The receiver is then placed in the tracking vehicle. The receiver is connected to a computer or display monitor. Using preinstalled software the system will display the position of both vehicles overlaid on a map of the area. As theoretically simple as it sounds, these systems are technologically complex and expensive. Moreover, they tend to be less than reliable where they might be most useful, such as in high-density urban areas. Because they typically rely on low energy transmitters to conserve battery power and use line-of-sight communications, they are vulnerable to electronic interference and loss of reception. I have only seen the technology work as it is portrayed in movies in the movies.

Other systems are even more complicated and expensive. Similar to those used on some commercial vehicles, the GPS uploads data to a satellite. These systems as used in commerce allow the precise tracking of the vehicle and two-way communication between the operator and his base. Speed, fuel state, and maintenance data are also uploaded and made available to the base station. These systems require a constant and reliable source of power and unless specially configured cannot operate on batteries. They also require large antennas to be placed atop the vehicle. In sum, this technology does not easily lend itself to the typical workplace investigation.

The more common and far less expensive technology also requires a GPS device to be placed on the target vehicle. However, instead of a transmitter, a recording device is attached to it. The whereabouts of the vehicle cannot be determined contemporaneously with its movement. Instead, the recorder is periodically recovered (or replaced), and its data is downloaded for analysis. Again, using software provided by the manufacturer, the route, speed, destination, and other aspects of the vehicle prior to travel are made available. These systems work well and have many applications. However, there are significant drawbacks. Here are a few of them:

■ The device must be placed on the target vehicle without detection.
■ The device must be placed so that the GPS can receive the necessary satellite data. This usually requires it to be placed atop the vehicle or someplace near its exterior.
■ The device has a limited operating time.
■ The batteries can power it only for several days.
■ The use of the technology has serious privacy implications.

The first four considerations should be self-explanatory, so I will address only the last. Although current case law addressing vehicle-tracking devices used for investigative purposes is limited, that which is currently available suggests that placing a tracking device on a privately owned vehicle without the owner's knowledge is probably actionable. The civil causes of action theoretically could include trespass, invasion of privacy, and even intentional infliction of emotional distress. What is clear is that electronically tracking a private citizen as he goes about his private affairs, whether in his vehicle or not, likely constitutes an invasion of privacy at some level. Interestingly, however, is that the conduct of physical surveillance does not. Barring another limitation, whether the observer was visible to the subject or not does not alter its permissibility. Apparently the fact that the observer is physically present is the differentiator.

Conversely, placing tracking devices on a company vehicle driven by an employee does not pose the same problem. Because the employer owns (or controls) the vehicle, the employee driver doesn't have the same expectation of privacy as when the vehicle is his own. This significantly expands the usefulness of this tool. Nevertheless, the privacy implications always need to be considered prior to the initiation of any surveillance, particularly those associated with a workplace investigation.

3. Evidence Collection and Preservation

The purpose of surveillance is to gather evidence. Because it employs the use of observers, the evidence it renders is visual in nature. Without a mechanical means to preserve that which is observed, the surveillance investigator must rely upon his memory and notes in order to reproduce what he has seen. Although this practice is effective, it is not perfect. The recollection of the observer is subject to challenge, and ample studies have demonstrated that eye witnesses are inherently unreliable.[4] Even the trained observer who has taken copious notes can sometime make mistakes and have difficulty recalling the finer details of what he has observed. Thus, the case is made for augmenting his effort by some mechanical means. The favored method, of course, is using cameras.

Of all of the types of cameras currently available, those that employ digital technology are preferred. Because these cameras are readily available and relatively inexpensive, they are widely used by today's professional fact-finders. Cameras in the +1.5 mega-pixel range are preferred because of their high resolution. Common features on the higher-end equipment include auto-focus, auto-exposure, conventional zoom, digital zoom, and some form of low light capability. However, the most significant feature is the ability to download images and video to a personal computer. Once downloaded, the evidence can be duplicated, edited, filed, printed, and instantaneously transmitted to others via the Internet. The capability of this technology is mind-boggling. Moreover, its versatility and applicability make it the perfect workplace investigation tool. But a good camera alone does not ensure the proper collection of evidence. The following is offered to provide a better understanding of this technology, but it is not a comprehensive treatise on the subject of photography or the collection of photographic evidence and digital imagery.

a. Camera Technology

Photographs are the result of mechanical, optical, and chemical manipulations (emulsion chemistry and development variations) of light. Once the resultant chemical reaction is "fixed," an indelible image is produced. Alternatively, digital imagery enables the capture of light electronically. The pixilated image it produces is nearly a perfect reproduction of the subject or scene at the moment it was captured. By their very nature, both technologies can be prone to distortion and intentional manipulation. Accordingly, a photograph is never a perfect rendition of the object(s) it portrays. It is merely a two-dimensional representation of three-dimensional forms that always contains distortions in size, color, shape, and other attributes. Unlike the human eye, a photograph does not see with depth perception. The job of the evidence photographer is thus to minimize the various types of distortion and show as much detail as possible. In order to produce acceptable images for evidentiary purposes, the following types of equipment are suggested.

Conventional Cameras

Select a camera that is easy to operate and, if possible, one with which you are familiar. Use a totally automatic camera if nothing else is available. In emergency situations, use a single-use (disposable) camera if necessary, but remember the optics of these cameras are usually poor and objects shot less than four feet away will likely be out of focus. Consider using a tripod and keep fingers and straps away from the lens and camera face.

Of course, the camera of choice will have variable settings and allow the user to control f-stop and shutter speed. Some very good, yet inexpensive cameras have programmed settings for close-up (still life/evidence), portrait (middle-distance/slow moving or still), sports (fast action), and scenery. These work well and are capable of capturing very high-quality images, even when used by an amateur. Experienced fact-finders recognize film is cheap (even cheaper when purchased in quantity) and use an entire roll of film for each subject of interest.

Initially, photograph the evidence or item in question the way it is found. Do not move it or change its orientation. Then, reposition the object if necessary to reveal additional detail. For relatively small objects photographed indoors, use a medium reflectance blue or gray background, such as a sheet, and fluorescent (not tungsten) lighting. If photographing documents, first photograph a piece of paper on which you have printed your name, your organization's name, your location, the date and time, the case number (if assigned) and a description of the item. If your photographs are ever lost, or you forget when, where, or why the images were taken, this one picture could prove to be invaluable.

When shooting outdoors, properly light your subject and the area around it. Get as much light on the subject as possible. Photograph everything at the scene and around it regardless of whether you think it is relevant at the time. The devil is in the details, and many experienced crime scene investigators will attest that things first thought to be unimportant later often prove to be invaluable. Also, do not attempt to photograph everything in one frame. Photograph each piece of evidence separately, then their position relative to the others. Create a collage. Start in the center and work outward.

Do not forget to use the flash. Take some photographs using the flash even if it is daylight and the subject is outdoors. The flash will help to evenly distribute light and fill in dark areas. If the camera permits manual settings, bracket the exposures with respect to light exposure. Make it a practice to shoot a few photographs with larger and smaller aperture settings (f-stops) and faster and slower shutter speeds. Do this after a few photographs have been taken with the automatic setting. With this combination of settings, the proper exposure will most likely be achieved and your chances will be improved of obtaining the perfect picture.

If possible select a camera with a 50 mm focal length lens. These lenses are common and most quality single reflex lens (SLR) cameras are sold with one. Wide-angle (25–35 mm or shorter) or telephoto (75 mm or longer) lenses can be useful, but should be used only as ancillary perspectives after the standard 1-1 50 mm lens photographs have been taken.

If the camera has manual focus, focus on a point directly in front of the object being photographed. If shooting an entire scene or panoramic view, do not focus on infinity but rather on an object in the foreground about 20–30 feet in front of you. This will likely put everything into focus including the background.

Another good practice is to take your photographs in groups from three distance categories: close-up, intermediate, and distant (to capture the overall scene). These categories vary with respect to what is being photographed, but generally close up means within about one half to two feet, intermediate means about two to ten feet, and distant means beyond about ten feet to capture the entire setting that has relevance. In doing so shoot your initial photographs "head-on." Once the basic orthogonal view (perpendicular to the object) photos have been taken, take photographs from other perspectives. And do not forget to shoot your subject from above if possible. An overhead perspective is particularly useful when taking pictures of a crime scene. However, objects and scenes often do not lend themselves to photographing from above.

Footprints, tire-tread impressions, and other low-relief evidence may have to be photographed at very low angles (almost parallel to the ground) to see the detail. Avoid shooting into the light source or into that which is back-lit, as this tends to fool the camera's light meter into thinking there is too much light. Photographs taken under these circumstances will be nearly useless. For objects that must be stood on end or stabilized while photographing, use modeling clay for support. Keep some in your equipment bag.

Another important consideration when photographing evidence is *scale*. Improper perspective tends to make objects look smaller or larger than they actually are. To overcome this anomaly place one or more items of know size near the object being photographed. Plastic, colored rulers (English or metric) that have bold dark numbers work very well. The color of the ruler can also serve as a color guide for the identification of a type of evidence, where it was found, or by whom. A ruler not only provides scale, but also reveals the actual size of the object being photographed, thus accomplishing two tasks. If a ruler is not available, place a pen or other common object such as a coin in the scene.

Remember to keep notes. Record the details of the entire effort in a notebook. Record your camera settings too. Document every imaginable detail including weather condition, temperature, and visibility. If in doubt, write it down.

Here are a few more pointers when using conventional camera equipment:

- Use fresh color film and batteries.
- Store unused film and batteries in the refrigerator to keep them fresh and extend their serviceability beyond their expiration dates.
- Do not leave film or batteries in the closed confines of a vehicle. Heat and even indirect sunlight will damage film and reduce the battery life.
- Take 50 percent more film than you intend to use and bring spare batteries.
- Film speed (a rating of ability to capture light) should be ASA 200 or 400. When shooting stationary object use a slower speed (slower speed film is less grainy and allows for higher resolution).
- A faster film, ASA 800, should be used in low-light environments or when shooting dark objects. Conversely, a slower speed film (ASA 100) can be used for bright objects and bright outdoors environments.

Tip: Have your film developed as soon as practicable. Do not discard any original photographs or negatives. Retain them in your case file. The intentional destruction of photographic evidence can give rise to the claim of spoliation and could bring the credibility of the fact-finder into question.

Digital Imaging

Digital imaging has come remarkably far in a few short years. Good quality equipment is inexpensive and easy to use. A high-end outfit can be purchased for less than the cost of a good SLR. In just a few hours, someone with little or no photographic experience can produce nearly perfect digital images. The better cameras allow viewing of recorded images right on the camera. These same cameras have enormous utility, and depending upon the recording media used, some can capture more than 600 images without reloading.

In addition to shooting remarkable images in all kinds of environments and circumstances, digital cameras permit the downloading of images to computers. There, images can be viewed, edited, and stored. Captured images can even be transmitted to others via the Internet. The newest technology incorporates digit cameras into cell phones. This arrangement allows the wireless transmission of images to anyplace at anytime instantaneously! Captured digital images can also be inserted into reports, incorporated in a slide presentation, or viewed on almost any television. Several manufacturers have also incorporated features that permit the recording of short video clips and sound.

Of the many considerations to be evaluated when selecting a digital camera, one of the most important is the type of media it uses. Digital cameras with removable media are preferred. Like the film used in conventional cameras, removable media allows the reloading of the camera once the media has reached its capacity. My preferred media is the CD. CDs have a higher capacity than memory sticks and do not require a peripheral in order to upload the images contained on them when viewing on a personal computer. A "disk" containing images can be shared with anyone with a computer and CD drive. CDs also can be stored flat, making them easy to place and keep in a case file.

The guidelines provided in the prior section on the use of conventional cameras and evidence collection similarly apply to digital cameras and do not need to be covered again. However, some discussion regarding the editing of digital images is necessary. Because digital images are so easily edited and modified, they are subject to evidentiary challenge. In order to be admissible, the images must first be "fair and reasonably accurate representations" of that which they depict. Second, it is imperative the images are handled properly. Like the handling of all evidence, a chain of custody should be established from the moment the images are captured. The original medium on which the images were recorded should be preserved in its original state (another consideration in favor of selecting cameras with removable media). Several duplicates of the original should then be made, and these too should be preserved as evidence. An additional copy should be retained and only the images from it are to be edited, modified, or enhanced. During this process, detailed records should be kept as to what was done to each image and how the images were used in the investigation. The fact-finder should maintain sufficient records to allow the precise re-creation of the images used as evidence. Then, in the event of discovery, copies of the original medium can be produced as well as a record detailing how the images were modified and by whom.

The assertion that digital images or video recordings are inadmissible as evidence is nonsense. The admissibility of digital imaging has been well tested in the courts.[5] Still, the technology is frequently questioned and those opposing it invariably raise *Kelly-Frye* challenges.[6] The *Kelly-Frye* decision mandates the exclusion of evidence derived from test results or conclusions generated by a "new scientific machine, mechanism or instrument, which is unproven or experimental" from evidence. *Kelly-Frye* applies only to novel devices and processes and does not apply to expert medical testimony or an expert's reliance on medical literature, statistical data, or epidemiologic studies. In two noteworthy cases, the courts determined that digital imagery is neither new nor unproven.

In the *State of Washington v. Eric Hayden*, a 1995 homicide case, in spite of a rigorous *Kelly-Frye* challenge and the claim that digital images had been manipulated, the court authorized the use of digital imaging and the defendant was ultimately found guilty. In 1998, an appellate court upheld the conviction.

In the *State of California v. Phillip Lee Jackson*, a 1995 case, the San Diego Police Department used digital image processing on a fingerprint during a double homicide investigation. The defense challenged the evidence and requested a *Kelly-Frye* hearing. The court ruled it was unnecessary, asserting that digital image processing is a readily accepted practice in forensics and that "new information was not added to the image."

Like all evidence, in order for digital imagery to be entered into evidence, it must be entered via a witness. The credibility of the evidence is tied to the credibility of the witness. If the witness is credible and the chain of custody is intact, the evidence, if relevant, should be admitted. In the case of workplace investigations, admissibility is even easier. Because the standard of proof (good faith investigation/reasonable conclusion) is so low, so are the rules of evidence. If the fact-finder or witness can credibly certify that the digital image(s) offered is a "fair and reasonably accurate representation" of the item or scene in question as it existed at the time the image(s) was captured, the image(s) should be given all of the evidentiary consideration it deserves. The claim that the image(s) *could have been* altered is bogus, and absent some reasonable proof, entirely incredulous. Without credible substantiation, such claims should not even be entertained. Moreover, the concern that unfounded claims may potentially tarnish the value of one's evidence should not preclude the fact-finder from taking advantage of this technology. Merely suggesting that evidence *could have been* altered is a smokescreen and no reasonable trier of fact will fall for it.

Just what amount of alteration or modification of a digital image is actually acceptable? The legal answer is as complex as the technology that produces the image, so allow me to simplify it. Outright alteration of the image that materially changes that which it represents is clearly improper. For example, adding a mustache to the face of an individual who is unmustached is patently improper. Likewise, removing something or someone from the image would be equally inappropriate. Generally speaking, enhancements or modifications that actually *enhance* the quality of the image or improve its usefulness are acceptable. Such enhancements might include enlarging the image or brightening it. Care should be exercised not to materially alter the image or that which it portrays. Furthermore, to make any modification without sufficient purpose could diminish the value of the evidence and bring into question the credibility of the fact-finder responsible for it.

Tip: Before enhancing a digital image that has evidentiary value, first consult with another member of the investigative team. The person that is most likely able to provide the most reliable input is the team's attorney. Only alterations that enhance the quality of the image or improve its clarity are permissible.

Video

Video imaging technology has been commercially available for nearly four decades. Unlike its predecessor, which captured images on light-sensitive film via a chemical reaction, video captures moving images electronically. Although recording formats vary, the images are typically recorded on a form of magnetic tape or disk. The video file, once created, can be either viewed with the camera or exported to a monitor or a compatible television, or to a computer. Software enables the user to cut, edit, or enhance the video. Still images can be captured and exported into reports or presentations. The technology is remarkable and its applicability to workplace investigations is limited only by the imagination of the investigator.

The quality of today's video equipment is so advanced and so inexpensive there is no excuse not to employ it when appropriate. Quality outfits can be had for less than $400 and are available at any big electronics store. Although recording formats vary widely, all cameras come with the software and cabling necessary to output to a standard VHS recorder. Once recorded in VHS format, the video can be viewed on any VHS player or VHS-capable television. The functionality, ease of use, and low cost make video technology the perfect investigative tool. Regardless of how or why it is created, video evidence should be treated like all other evidence. Once created it should not be materially altered or destroyed. Because of its ease of use, the tendency is to shoot more video than is necessary, creating the temptation later to erase that which is deemed unusable or duplicative. This should *not* be done. All evidence, good or bad, should be preserved until the matter in question has been properly adjudicated or settled.

Among professional investigators, it is often debated whether recorded video should be date and time stamped. The technology of most video cameras allows the date and time to be recorded over the image while recording. Innocuously, the data are displayed in a corner of the image. Although this function is very useful, it also has its drawbacks.

Several years ago I deployed a team of two investigators to watch the rear doors of a client's manufacturing facility. The client had received information from an anonymous source that several employees were regularly removing company property through the rear emergency exists during their breaks. My investigators took up positions in a tree line on some high ground immediately behind the building. As alleged, at about 8 P.M., two employees slipped out one of the rear doors carrying what appeared to be some of their employer's product. As expected, they placed the property into the truck of the parked car and quickly reentered the building. The entire event was captured on video by one of the investigators. Later, at the end of the shift, one of the individuals returned to the vehicle and drove off. The next day the video was taken into the office for viewing. The video was sharp and perfectly captured the faces of our two apparent thieves. However, my investigator had not properly set the camera's date/time feature and as a result our "evidence" showed the event had occurred five years prior at two o'clock in the morning. Fortunately, our client allowed us to interview the two and both provided written and tape-recorded statements containing detailed admissions. They were both terminated based on their admissions, and our video was fortunately never produced or used.

Today, unless specifically agreed upon with my client, it is my practice not to date/time stamp video created during an investigation. Even with the best procedures and taking all the necessary precautions, date/time stamp errors do occur. The result is often embarrassing or worse. Moreover, video evidence is only as good as the credibility of the investigator who recorded it. If the video must eventually be entered into evidence, it will be done through the testimony of the investigator who shot it. That investigator can then attest to the date and time the video was recorded as well as to what it represents. This practice is far better than having an investigator occasionally introduce his video and explain why the date and time shown on it are incorrect. Such testimony tends to diminish the credibility of the evidence and the investigator.

Another interesting aspect of video evidence is how often a trier of fact expects an employer to use it. Unfortunately since the 1980s, the public as well as many triers of fact expect video evidence to be produced if video would make the issue at hand easier to prove or disprove. Sadly, many people have come to believe video makes the case, and conversely, if the event was not recorded on video, it is likely more difficult to prove. This dogma was memorialized for most Americans during the Rodney King case in Los Angeles. This high-profile yet unfortunate case demonstrated the riveting, raw power of amateur video. Night after night, millions watched in horror as a black motorist was horribly beaten by white law enforcement officers. With less than 60 seconds of video, the nation was conditioned to believe that video evidence makes a case. For employers this has created a troubling dilemma. It has been my experience that administrative law judges and, more troubling, arbitrators have come to expect employers to make their case with video. Frequently, these otherwise intelligent people conclude that if the complainant or grievant was not caught on video, the employer's case is somehow weak. The logic I have heard goes something like this—*considering the seriousness of the alleged transgression, would it not have served the employer (and the process) better to memorialize the misconduct on video, especially if the behavior, as alleged, occurred more than once? How difficult would it have been to capture the event on tape?* Is that so? Consider the following complexities confronting the employer who decides to use video. The employer would have to

- Precisely know when and where the event was to occur.
- Arrange to have an invisible observer there when it occurred or have a covert system covertly installed to record it.
- Consider and manage lighting and other environmental issues.
- Address a host of privacy issues.

If the workforce was protected by a collective bargaining agreement, the conduct of covert surveillance may have to be bargained and union notified of it, and the effort would have to be funded.

Furthermore, in the event incriminating evidence was gathered, it would have to be considered only corroborative. The employer has no way of knowing exactly what the video captured. Although it may record an employee sniffing a white powder up his nose, it doesn't identify the white powder. In most cases, physical surveillance, regardless of its form, produces only corroborative evidence. As such, it must be augmented by some other form of investigation and evidence gathering. Usually, that evidence is primary and any video would support it.

Remember also under most circumstances an audio recording cannot be made to accompany the video. The employer might be lucky and actually capture suspicious activity on video, but not know what was being said by those involved at the time. Imagine the suspected offending employee, while later viewing the employer's video, assisting by offering, "Yeah that's me, and right there is when I said to my co-conspirator, 'Screw the company, I'm gonna steal this place blind,' then I put the stuff in the trunk of my car and drove off." In all likelihood upon viewing any incriminating video the testimony offered by the accused employee will be limited only by his imagination and that of those who represent him. I have had several cases during which we obtained video of an employee snuffing a white powder into his nose using a short straw and compact mirror who later testified under oath he was putting either flour or talcum powder up his nose. A very cynical arbitrator in one of these cases later wrote in an unpublished decision "the grievant's claim that he consumed flour through his nose is difficult to believe. However, the employer offered nothing contrary to this assertion except a poor quality [video] of the alleged event and the 'expert' testimony of its paid investigator who testified the grievant had admitted to him that the white powder was indeed cocaine." Ultimately, the arbitrator in his infinite wisdom concluded that the employer had insufficient proof the grievant had violated its substance abuse policy and ordered him to return to work.

Tip: Video evidence can be very compelling but is not always practical to obtain. The investigative team should consider if and how video should be used. Regardless, even the best video evidence is often only corroborative and is best used to augment other direct evidence.

b. Surveillance Vehicles

No discussion regarding workplace surveillance is complete without addressing the use of surveillance vehicles. By and large the use of specialized vehicles that have been configured specifically for surveillance use is overrated. The notion that proper surveillance requires a customized vehicle is false on several levels. Many professional investigators invest tens of thousands of dollars into vans or utility vehicles to later find they enable them to produce evidence that is only incrementally better than that possible without the vehicle; and in spite of the costs incurred, the vehicle produces little if any return on investment. However, professional investigators and law enforcement agencies are often lured into a seductive fascination with high-tech gadgetry and invest in expensive vehicles and equipment when the simplest of solutions may have worked better.

Moreover, as anyone who has worked the field will admit, bad guys are suspicious. Vans with tinted windows, antennas, and unusual devices on their roofs attract attention. Most criminals are also paranoid. They have watched enough television to conclude that those who might oppose them will use all of the technology available to watch them and their activities. Consider your own belief system for just a moment. Where did you get the notion that surveillance requires a van or other specialized equipment? How many customized surveillance vehicles have you actually been in? I would venture that your answer was *never*, and the last time you saw one used was on television or in a movie. True, isn't it? The bad guys are no different. They expect us to watch them, and they expect us to be in vans with tinted windows, antennas, and unusual devices on the roof.

Tip: Save the money and don't rent or buy a surveillance van. The bad guys expect us to use them. Use a nondescript vehicle that provides adequate cover and is easy to drive and maneuver. While your subject is looking for vans, you can be watching him from the back seat of your Saturn wagon.

B. Electronic Surveillance

1. Electronic Surveillance Defined

Electronic surveillance is similar to that of physical surveillance except that it replaces the human fact-finder with electronic technology. Generally, it is relatively easy and inexpensive. Be it the placement of covert cameras in a work area or the installation of surveillance software on the subject's computer, the mechanics of electronic surveillance are relatively simple. Unlike the investigative method of *forensic analysis*, which largely involves taking the investigation to the laboratory (or conversely taking the laboratory or its technology to the investigation), electronic surveillance involves inserting the technology *into* the investigation. In that sense, the technology isn't so much used to analyze evidence; it is instead used to *create* it. Here is an actual example.

My client was the human resources manager for a multinational law firm with whom I had worked for many years. During my initial consultation she revealed that several female employees working at the firm's Chicago office had complained they had found on numerous occasions a translucent sticky substance in the athletic walking shoes they frequently left under their desks. Several of the women speculated that the substance might be semen. The investigative solution was simple: identify the unknown substance and install covert video equipment in a spot likely to be hit next. Upon acceptance of our proposal, we put our plan into action. First, we secured several specimens and field tested the unknown substance. Characteristically, the substance illuminated under the light of a handheld ultraviolet lamp, suggesting that it was semen. We, of course, established the necessary chain of evidence and retained the specimens as evidence. Next, we installed several covert video cameras in areas we thought to be likely targets. Several days after the installation we recorded our first suspicious event. The video revealed a young male employee rummaging under a female coworker's desk, selecting one of her athletic shoes, dropping his trousers, and with some amount of fuss, ejaculating into the shoe. After redressing, our subject returned the shoe under the desk. Our client easily identified the subject and we interviewed him. By only suggesting we had video of the act, he quickly made a full admission and was subsequently allowed to quietly resign.

The case is noteworthy from two perspectives. First, although the owners of the shoes thought they knew what the sticky substance was, and several had suspicion as to who had put it there, the employer did not act precipitously but, instead, conducted a proper investigation. Second, even with rather conclusive video evidence, the employer took its investigation to the next level. Deciding that the video in this instance, though very compelling (read "incriminating"), was only corroborative, the employer allowed the subject the opportunity to explain his actions. In doing so, the employer fulfilled any "due process" obligations it might have, and at the same time obtained a detailed admission of the offense. Properly, the employer used the subject's admission in deciding his fate. This simple but very carefully orchestrated investigation saved my client time and resources. What's more, the discipline it invoked was reasonable, fair, and defensible.

Electronic surveillance, however, includes more than just the use of covert cameras. It also includes the use of

- Electronic access control technology
- Computer and activity monitoring
- Alarms with electronic warning and monitoring technology
- Covert voice communication interception and monitoring
- Any electronic capturing or monitoring technology that can be reasonably used as a fact-finding tool

Because of recent advances in technology, these tools are inexpensive and relatively easy to use. The greatest challenges facing the fact-finder are selecting the technology that fits the need and then deploying it properly. Additionally, the fact-finder must address a host of privacy issues and ensure that the intended investigative plan does not run afoul of the law or organizational policy. Before we examine these complexities, let's look a little closer at the technologies themselves.

a. *Electronic Access Control Technology*

Commercially available electronic access control systems and the technology that supports them are uniquely suited to aid the fact-finder. Because these systems are designed for access control management, they enable the recording of who comes and goes in the spaces they monitor. Additionally, they record the time and date the entrance or exit occurred. When it is available, the fact-finder can use this information to identify those who accessed a particular area at any particular time. Assuming the individuals in question used their own access devices (key, card, or fob), the fact-finder can readily separate individuals of interest from his universe of suspects. In some instances the technology will allow the fact-finder to pinpoint a single individual, advancing the investigation instantly. However, with the opportunity comes several limitations:

- Not all workplaces have electronic access control systems.
- Where systems exist, not all work areas may have adequate coverage.
- Contrary to established policies, employees often share their access control devices.
- Employees frequently tailgate one another when entering or exiting controlled spaces, corrupting the accuracy of any electronic record created.
- System limitations can significantly reduce the accuracy and usefulness of any records.
- Records may be stored for only a limited period.

b. Computer Use and Monitoring

The monitoring of workplace computer use has been the topic of countless editorials and articles in recent years. And, while monitoring the use of computers in the workplace is lawful and appropriate under most circumstances, many employees find the intrusion offensive and counterproductive. In 1999, International Data Corporation estimated that businesses worldwide spent over $62 million on Internet monitoring and filtering software and predicted the number to rise to over $550 million by the year 2005. In 2001, the Privacy Foundation reported that employee monitoring, as measured by the sales of surveillance software, increased at least twice as fast as the number of U.S. employees with Internet access. It estimated the sale of employee monitoring software to be about $5.25 per monitored employee per year.[7]

For the purpose of managing workplace productivity and monitoring employee behavior, employers of all sizes frequently monitor their employees' use of the computers they provide them. At the user level this is extraordinary simple. Microsoft offers a versatile tool called Windows Explorer® with all of its Windows® and Windows NT® operating systems. Using the Histories feature users are able to see what files had been opened, which applications had been used, and where the user of that machine had gone on the Internet as far back as two weeks. The Histories feature is also available if MS Internet Explorer® is loaded on the machine in question, and searching it is possible unless the file has been *emptied* by the user. The Histories feature is a particularly useful tool when the fact-finder needs to quickly examine how a particular system was recently used. Unless the system was password-protected and the password was not compromised, the fact-finder cannot be sure who used the machine, only how it was used.

Beyond simple system tools, a host of commercially available tools are also available. Of them, the most common are software applications, which are loaded locally and reside hidden on the user's fixed drive. Generically called *spyware*, these inexpensive and easy-to-use applications allow an administrator to covertly monitor and record the activities of anyone using a system on which they are installed. The features and sophistication of these tools vary. Some record only the applications and files accessed by the user. Other more sophisticated applications record every keystroke and periodically capture screen shots, effectively allowing the administrator to retrace every action of the user and see much of what she saw while using the system. One popular application sold as a tool for parents desiring to monitor their children's use of a home computer allows the administrator to see all incoming and outgoing e-mail to and from the machine on which it is installed. Additionally, the application covertly forwards copies of the e-mail traffic to any recipient designated by the administrator, including himself. According to the Privacy Foundation, the most popular software packages are Websense® for tracking Internet use and MIMEsweeper™ for monitoring e-mail.[8]

It should be noted that while these tools have many useful investigative applications, many computer users know they exist and some take offensive measures to defeat them. Free Internet downloads are available that enable users to identify the presence of these monitoring applications on their system and disable them. Moreover, while the applicability of this technology is intriguing, the privacy implications are considerable. Because of the reasonable expectation of privacy enjoyed by most employees, fact-finders must use such tools cautiously. The existence of such an expectation would significantly reduce the ability to use this tool and any evidence it may capture.

Trap: Organizational policy and state law may significantly limit the fact-finder's ability to monitor employee computer use. Consult with other members of the investigative team before accessing anyone's computer other than your own.

---

c. Alarms Using Electronic Warning and Monitoring Technology

Many professional workplace investigators I know have never used this technology. Although widely used by law enforcement, the application of this technology in the workplace is surprisingly rare. Effectively, this technology allows the remote and often wireless arming of doors, windows, safes, cash drawers, file cabinets, or virtually anything so that when the item is opened, moved, or somehow disturbed, a monitor is covertly notified. Upon notification, the monitor, usually an investigator or fact-finder, responds accordingly. Law enforcement agencies across the country successfully use this technology every day in the prosecution against the war on drugs. Because illegal drugs are often transported from place to place by mail or package service, alarms can be inserted in intercepted shipments. The alarm transmits a wireless signal when the package is opened. The police can then respond at the precise moment the contraband is physically in the hands of the recipient, thus making a case for receipt and possession.

Similarly, the technology can be used in workplace investigations. Given the proper fact pattern and circumstances, objects of any type or size can be covertly armed and monitored. When used properly, the fact-finder can identify the precise moment an event occurs and respond accordingly. I have even used this technology successfully outdoors. In one particular case we used motion detectors and trained them on large pieces of industrial equipment kept in an outdoor storage facility. The motion detectors were programmed to send a wireless text message to a team of investigators waiting nearby if one of the invisible beams was broken. We coordinated the effort with the authorities who agreed to standby. Several days after the equipment was installed, my team received their first alarm. They quickly descended on the facility and arrived with the police right behind them. The perpetrators were literally caught in the act of preparing a piece of equipment for removal.

d. Covert Voice Communication Interception and Monitoring

The information technology revolution has irreversibly changed the way we communicate and do business. Never before have employers had so many ways to monitor their employees' behavior. Not only can employers monitor their employee's communications, they can now know their exact whereabouts. The technology available offers a host of amazing investigative options for the fact-finder. Although the opportunities are plentiful, so are the risks. For the inexperienced and untrained fact-finder, voice communication interception and monitoring provides for a legal minefield that only a masochist would attempt to enter. The Omnibus Crime Control and Safe Streets Act of 1968 (Title III) prohibits private individuals, organizations, and employers from intentionally intercepting or recording wire or oral communications. Amended as the Electronic Communications Privacy Act of 1986, 18 U.S.C. §§2510-2520, states: "[A]ny person who willfully uses, endeavors to use, or procures another person to use any electronic, mechanical, or other device to intercept an oral communication when ... such use or endeavors to use ... take place on the premises of any business or other commercial establishment the operations of which affect the interstate or foreign commerce ... shall be punished." There are several exemptions:

- Where there is consent of one party to the communication
- Where an employer uses a telephone extension to monitor an employee in the ordinary course of business, which can include
  - Providing training on interaction with the public
  - Determining whether an employee is discussing business matters with a competitor
  - Determining whether an employee is making personal telephone calls
  - Monitoring calls for mechanical or service purposes[9]

The amended act of 1986 also prohibits the interception of wire communications, including e-mail. Section 2515 reads: "Whenever any wire or oral communication has been intercepted, no part of the contents or such communications and no evidence derived therefrom may be received in evidence in any trial, hearing, or other proceeding in or before any court, grand jury, department, officer, agency, regulatory body, legislative committee, thereof if the disclosure of that information would be in violation of this chapter." Clearly, law makers intended to extend employee privacy rights to include the protection of electronic mail and messaging. Only in the arena of workplace drug testing has the clash of employer interests and individual rights been more vivid.

The United Nations Committee on Crime and Criminal Justice recently tagged employees as the greatest security threat to employers.[10] Many employers agree. A survey released by the American Management Association in April 2001 revealed that 78 percent of U.S. firms monitor employee communications in some fashion. The survey also found that two thirds of the new survey respondents cited legal liability as the most important reason for their monitoring.[11] My personal experience is that most employers monitor because they suspect employee misconduct or are simply curious. Statutorily, these reasons are insufficient. Citing the exemptions above, an employer's options are extremely narrow. However, creative employers have not surrendered.

One very practical workaround is the implementation of a monitoring policy. By establishing a policy that notifies employees of the employer's intent to monitor, and insisting employees consent to it as a condition of employment, exemption (1) above is satisfied. Employers with such a policy should be able to monitor as they choose.

Trap: Although a properly constructed monitoring policy may satisfy federal law, it may not satisfy state law. Many states require all parties to a communication provide consent before it can be monitored. Employers desiring to intercept and monitor employee workplace communications should first consult a competent employment law attorney. The intricate web of federal, state, and local statutes provides big opportunities for legal missteps.

What Can Be Monitored?

What can be monitored is limited only by one's imagination. Most frequently intercepted and monitored are voice and e-mail communications. In the case of voice communications, the principal tool is the telephone. Although some employer's may occasionally listen in, others record all telephone activity. The legal problems persist. Even with the consent of the employee, the employer may not have the consent of the other party. You may recall the problem Linda Tripp had recording her friend Monica Lewinski. Although Washington, D.C., adheres to the federal standard of requiring one-party consent, Maryland requires the consent of *all-parties*. Thus, Maryland claimed that Tripp violated state law by not obtaining Lewinski's permission to record their telephone conversations. Other states, such as Florida, have asserted the same provenance over calls coming into their states. (Go to http://www.pimall.com/nais/n.record-law.html to determine if recording in your state is permissible.)

Tip: Regardless of the situation, know the law before you record the telephone conversation of anyone.

Intercepting and monitoring e-mail may also be regulated by state law. As such, rummaging through e-mail could be risky. Still employers do it all the time. The effort is time consuming and often futile when one does not know what to look for. A better method is to ask the subject or a cooperative witness to provide it. Many fact-finders overlook this simple but effective method of information gathering. In many instances, recruiting the assistance of a cooperative party is the most practical approach. If your investigation leads you to believe e-mail messages may be helpful, ask someone to provide the information you are seeking. Alternatively, if you find yourself in a situation where an interception or monitoring policy does not exist, ask the subject for permission to conduct a search. Unless the individual has something to hide, he will generally grant permission.

Monitoring Computer Use

Employers know workplace computers can improve productivity and efficiency. As common as they are today, it is difficult to imagine an office without them. However, the misuse of workplace computers has been a growing problem, and employers of all types are increasingly concerned. Be it shopping online, catching up on news and sports, or viewing pornography, employees with computers are using them for many things deemed improper while at work. The problem is epidemic. One employment lawyer recently told me that an investigation by one his clients found pornography on over 70 percent of the employer's desktop computers. In Chapter 6, "Applied Strategies," I discuss in some detail the tools available to monitor computer use. These tools are very powerful and very inexpensive. They are abundant are readily available via the Internet. Use your favorite search engine and search for *spyware*. For less than $50 one can purchase any number of easy-to-use applications that can be remotely installed on a target machine without the user's knowledge. Fact-finders ought to be aware that these tools should only be used when the employee computer user has no expectation of privacy. This can easily be achieved by flashing a warning notice upon boot up. Additionally, the employer should publish a policy stating that it reserves the right to monitor computer use at anytime, for any reason. The policy should clearly state that employees do not have any expectation of privacy while using company computers and that the employer may inspect them and the system's contents at anytime. Some employers go even further, prohibiting the use of company computers for any personal purpose.

Tip: Consult competent counsel before searching an employee's computer or monitoring workplace computer use.

The fact-finder should also consider hiring an expert. Because computer technology changes so rapidly, it is nearly impossible for the average fact-finder or even the professional corporate investigator to keep up with the breathtaking pace of our ever-changing technologies. The endless array of computers, PDAs, cell phones, digital cameras, digit records, scanners, and, of course, the Internet are marvelous inventions.

C. Research and Audit

1. The Fundamentals of Research and Audit

Incorrectly many fact-finders use the terms *research* and *audit* interchangeably. In doing so, they mislead themselves and those they serve. For the purpose of workplace investigations the method we shall call *research* defines work involving the collection and examination of public records. Records such as those found at the county clerk's office or local department of motor vehicle epitomize the sort of documents and records accessed while conducting research. On the other hand, *audit* applies to those records and documents internal to the organization—specifically the examination of documents and information that would not normally be available to someone outside the organization. These might include attendance records, productivity reports, accident reports, and personnel files.

The employment of research and audit as an investigative method is analogous to an archaeological dig. The fact-finder must first decide what he is looking for and then where to begin his digging. Then, it is a matter of poring over documents and selecting those that are material to the matter in question or appear to have some evidentiary value. Such fact-finding may yield a wealth of information about a particular individual, group, or event. Among other things, research and audit might be used to determine

- The time and place an event occurred
- The ownership of a property or business
- The identity of witnesses

- The attendance or work history of an individual
- The principals and attorney of record for a business
- The driving history of an individual
- The assets or net worth of an individual or entity
- The legal relationship between parties
- The criminal history of the subject or a witness

Carefully and with purpose, the fact-finder can use the sources available to seek out and identify information relative to the matter under investigation. In doing so, she gains a better understanding of the events and their relationship to the parties involved. Quite ironically, many very experienced fact-finders do not use research and audit as an integral component in their investigations. However, absent a process and the proper use and integration of the methods of investigation, one's effort is little more than a complicated journey with neither a destination nor a map to get there. Only by perseverance and a large dose of luck do investigations by happenstance ever produce meaningful results. This is shameful and unnecessary. The value of an objective, fair, and competent investigation is that it permits the accurate determination of facts not otherwise known.

In most situations, this is far more easily said than done. Federal, state, and local laws control to some degree what the fact-finder can and cannot do when conducting his investigations. Penalties for violating these laws can be stiff; as a result, many fact-finders play it safe and do very little research or auditing. Even experienced attorneys make this mistake. In one such case, an attorney friend of mine asked for our assistance in dealing with the employee of a client who had threatened his supervisor. It was alleged that the employee had threatened to beat the supervisor with a baseball bat. Following a brief discussion regarding objectives, timeline, and such, I requested my friend's permission to do a background check on the subject and the alleged target. On both counts he resisted, claiming there would be little to learn from public records, especially in the case of the supervisor. Speaking for his client, all he wanted from us was to address the threatener. After some debate, he acquiesced. A quick search of Arizona criminal court records revealed our slugger had two prior convictions for assault with a baseball bat, one of which was against a police officer. So not only did our threatener prefer to use bats to settle disputes, he had little respect for authority. The supervisor's record was clean, giving additional credibility to his allegation. As expected, "Babe Ruth" admitted his transgression when we confronted him and was subsequently allowed to find employment elsewhere.

This case illustrates the value of research and audit and the importance it often plays in seemingly routine investigations. Before going further, let's briefly examine a few more significant statutory prohibitions and restrictions affecting this important method of investigation.

2. Specific Statutory Prohibitions and Restrictions

a. Antidiscrimination Laws

Employers are prohibited in most situations from making any oral or written employment inquiry that directly or indirectly identifies characteristics protected by federal law (either Title VII, §42 U.S.C., Americans with Disabilities Act or Fair Employment and Housing Act). Both direct questions about protected status and the use of indirect inquiries that disproportionately impact members of a protected group are prohibited. The protected groups are

- Race
- Color
- National origin
- Ancestry
- Sex
- Pregnancy, child birth, or related condition
- Marital status
- Religious creed
- Physical handicap (includes drugs or alcohol abuse)
- Cancer or related condition
- Age over 40

Although the federal statutes (and comparable state statutes where they exist) provide protections to these *protected classes* in all employment contexts, many associate them with only hiring decisions. However, the outcome of workplace investigations frequently results in discipline or corrective action. If management's postinvestigation decisions appear to have an adverse impact on a member of one these protected classes, a charge of discrimination is likely. As such, the unnecessary accumulation of facts relative to an individual's membership in a protected class, such as noting the subject is pregnant, has no relevance to the issue in question, and the fact-finder is setting himself up to be challenged. If brought to task, he may be forced to explain why he collected information about the subject that was not relevant or material to the matter in question. These situations are particularly troublesome. On the one hand, the fact-finder is forced to defend his motive and process. On the other hand, he has to prove his intentions were not discriminatory. Such situations can put the investigation's credibility at stake and change the employer's role from moving party to defendant.

b. The Federal Fair Credit Reporting Act

It is undisputed that the Federal Fair Credit Reporting Act (FCRA) as amended in 1997 has far-reaching implications for employers who decide to conduct workplace investigations. However, the impact on such investigations was not realized until the Federal Trade Commission opined on the subject in response to what is now known as the "Vail Letter" (April 1999). In that opinion, the FTC concluded that all workplace investigations, regardless of their purpose or objective, when conducted by a third party (identified as Consumer Reporting Agencies or CRAs in the FCRA) for an employer, are subject to compliance with the FCRA. However, the FCRA has since been amended and as of March 31, 2004, third-party investigations of workplace misconduct are exempt from the act.

c. Arrest and Criminal Records

It is unlawful for most public employers to *ask* a job applicant to provide information concerning an arrest or detention that did not result in a conviction. Employers can ask about an arrest with respect to whether the individual is out on bail or if there is a case pending final disposition. There are exceptions applicable to health care facilities regarding arrests for sex offenses and the possession of narcotics.[12] In most jurisdictions, an employer can obtain criminal history records for employment purposes without restriction. Even the Fair Credit Reporting Act does not impose any restrictions unless the employer engages a third party to gather the information for it. Moreover, I am unaware of any statute that prohibits an employer using criminal record information pursuant to ongoing workplace investigation. The question then is one of relevance. What relevance might there be for existence of a criminal record to an internal workplace investigation? The answer is as varied as the criminal code itself. In other words, *it depends*. It depends, of course, on the nature of the matter, extenuating or special circumstances, whether the employer is public or private, and a whole host of other variables.

Because of the lack of materiality, the employer cannot necessarily discipline an employee upon learning he has a criminal record. Unless the employer can credibly argue that the conviction impairs the qualifications of the individual, discipline would likely be improper. However, if the employer can prove the employee had made a material misrepresentation regarding the existence of a record, knowledge of the record is actionable. For example, say the employee had checked the "No" box on his employment application in response to the question: Have you been convicted of a crime within the last seven years? Subsequently, for whatever reason, the employer discovers the employee in fact had a felony conviction for burglary at the time he completed the application. The falsity of the representation made on the application would likely justify his discharge.

Most employers protect themselves against such eventualities by (a) disclosing to applicants that errors, falsehoods, and misrepresentations of any sort on an employment application are grounds for disqualification or termination; and (b) conducting a thorough search of criminal records before making an offer of employment. There is no codified statute of limitations regarding the actionability for misrepresentations found on an employment application. However, employment law attorneys with whom I have had the pleasure to work generally agree that a discovery made more than three years after the date of employment is about as far as an employer should go.

The question remains, what circumstances make knowledge of a criminal conviction record valuable to those conducting a workplace investigation? For reasons other than those stated above, typically a record has only anecdotal value. It provides only a backdrop or historical perspective. Depending on the nature of the crime and any evidence of recidivism, it may demonstrate a propensity or preference for a certain type of crime or behavior. That being the case, one cannot conclude that a history of past criminal activity ensures future criminal activity. The existence of a record, however, does impact the credibility of the subject. A history of criminal mischief, hooliganism, and run-ins with the law tarnishes the credibility of an individual. Although in and of itself the existence of such records may not be enough to find guilt, they immensely assist the employer that uses a good faith investigation/reasonable conclusion standard for its workplace investigations. So powerful is such information, that it can be the tipping point between a determination of guilt and inconclusiveness. Note I did not use the word innocence. Inconclusiveness means open to doubt, where innocence proffers nonguilt even virtuousness. An employer has no duty to determine one's innocence. The determination of inconclusiveness or simply *not involved* is as far as an employer must go. Thus, an employee's claim of vindication by his employer's determination of anything other than guilty is false. Unlike the formal determinations made in a court of law, an employer's determination that "we think he probably did it, and she likely had nothing to do with it" is perfectly acceptable. Given that the employer met the standard of a good faith investigation and reasonable conclusion, such determinations are not only defensible, they are in fact proper.

d. Medical Records and Drug Testing Results

A host of federal and state laws regulate how and when an employer can require an applicant or employee to provide a urine specimen for drug testing purposes or to submit to a physical examination.[13] The law equally determines how this information can be used in a workplace investigation. Most employee medical information and drug test results are protected from disclosure by privacy provisions in the statutes that regulate them. The fact-finder is advised, before seeking these types of records, to first seek the advice of competent counsel.

3. Sources of Information

The following is offered not as an all inclusive list of sources of information the fact-finder may use, but instead as a high-level overview of some of the more typical places and venues information of value can be found. Newcomers to the profession should visit their local reference librarian for assistance. Of course, the Web-enabled should go directly to the Internet. Search engines such as Google® and Yahoo® make for perfect starting places.

Tip: Google.com is the world's number-one search engine. Google is fast and effective. Each day it receives tens of millions of search requests from users around the globe. Here are few search tricks used by power-users:

- To find a person's phone number, type in "name" + "city" + state abbreviation.
- To obtain a business address, type in the business's phone number.
- To obtain a business phone number, type in Company name + "contact us".
- To get the lowest price on a product, type in Model + "price comparison".

Google ignores most common words and characters such as "where" and "how," as well as certain single digits and single letters, because they slow down a search without improving the results. Google will indicate if a common word has been excluded by displaying details on the results page below the search box.

If a common word is essential to getting the results desired, users can include it by putting a "+" sign in front of it. (Always include a space before the "+" sign.)

Another search method is a called a phrase search. To conduct a phrase search put quotation marks around two or more words. Google also supports the logical "OR" operator. To retrieve pages that include either word A or word B, place an uppercase OR between the words or terms.

---

a. Criminal Courts

Criminal records, including arrest, conviction, and punishment information, are maintained on the federal, state, county, and local levels. Most of these records (at least for now) are public and available to anyone upon request. These records are normally managed by the court clerk's office in the respective jurisdiction. There are approximately 3,500 counties in the United States and each of them maintains some form of criminal records management system as do all of the municipalities that adjudicate criminal matters on the local level. Contrary to popular belief (and myth), there is not a centralized public repository where these records are compiled for the convenience of the public. Several states compile records statewide. Most do not. In order to be ensured that a subject does not have a record, all jurisdictions must be individually searched! The effort is time consuming and frequently impractical.

Over the past two decades an entire industry has been created that compiles these records and makes them available to the public on a per use or subscription basis. The records are regularly updated and available to the paying customer via the Internet. This solution allows researchers to search a large number of venues quickly and inexpensively. The drawbacks include

- The questionable accuracy of the records
- Possible incompleteness of the records[14]
- The irregular frequency with which these records are updated[15]

It should also be noted that criminal records are indexed by name and date of birth. There is pending legislation on Capitol Hill that would require record custodians to remove dates of birth on all criminal records.

The legislation proposes that by removing the dates of birth, the privacy interests of the *convicted* would be better protected. Because criminal record indexes do not reflect Social Security numbers, removing the dates of birth would make it impossible to positively identify individuals or their records. When this unintended consequence was brought to the attention of the California senator who proposed the legislation, her response was a very smug "So ..."

b. Civil Courts

Civil disputes that result in litigation produce public files that are segregated by plaintiff and defendant. Here researchers will find all civil actions to which their subjects have been a party as well as any judgments, notices of default, restraining orders, or unlawful detainer actions against them. Of these records, those regarding divorce often contain the most information. If one's investigation includes searching for assets, this is the perfect place to look. Because all of these records (unless otherwise protected) are public, they may be used as a source for investigative research.

c. Department of Motor Vehicles

The records maintained by a state's Department of Motor Vehicles are protected by the Driver's Privacy Protection Act and are not generally available to the public. However, with the proper release, such as that which may be part of a general release on an employment application, an employer may access these records. This is an excellent place to obtain information regarding an individual, his driving record, and ownership of vehicles. All states maintain them on a statewide basis. Thus, a single search covers an entire state.

d. Secretary of State

The office of the Secretary of State performs a number of administrative functions. Among these is the recording and supervision of all organizational entities that reside in its state. Included are corporations, professional corporations, limited liability companies, nonprofits, and partnerships. Most states do not require a sole practitioner doing business in his own name to register. Filings include the names of all officers, street addresses, and agents for process of service. This is a particularly good place to search if the fact-finder suspects the subject is a corporate officer or has an interest in an enterprise. Also found at the Secretary of State's office are the licensing authorities for the various professions. Nurses, doctors, building contractors, and even mattress rebuilders must be licensed in most states. If the matter in question involves those who must be licensed, it is often worth the effort to check if the subject is licensed or ever has been.

e. Bankruptcy Records

All bankruptcies are handled at the federal level in Federal Court. These records are public and often reveal valuable information about one's ability to handle his financial affairs, ownership and interest in businesses, location and value of assets, and other information about an individual or organization. Federal law prohibits employers in most instances from taking an adverse action against an employee or applicant based on the filing of bankruptcy or a history of bankruptcy.

f. Credit Reports

Section 604 of the Fair Credit Reporting Act (also known as Public Law 91-508) details the permissible uses and circumstances under which one can access consumer credit reports. It specifically states that a consumer reporting agency (as defined earlier in this chapter) may furnish a consumer report under the following circumstances and no other:

■ In response to the order of a court having jurisdiction to issue such an order.
■ In accordance with the written instructions of the consumer to whom it relates.
■ To a person who the CRA has reason to believe intends to use the information in connection with a transaction involving the consumer on whom the information is to be furnished and involving the extension of credit to, or review of, collection of an account of the consumer.
■ To a person who the CRA has reason to believe intends to use the information for employment purposes.
■ To a person who the CRA has reason to believe intends to use the information in connection with the underwriting of insurance involving the consumer.
■ To a person who the CRA has reason to believe intends to use the information in connection with the consumer's eligibility for a license or other benefit granted by a government instrumentality required by law to consider an applicant's financial responsibility or status.

■ To a person who the CRA has reason to believe otherwise has a legitimate business need for the information in connection with a business transaction involving the consumer.

Workplace investigations may fulfill several of these circumstances and lawfully entitle the employer to a consumer credit report. However, in reality the large consumer reporting agencies (credit bureaus) that manage these records will not release them to an employer without a good reason and a properly crafted release. Exhibit 3.1 is an example of a proper release. As mentioned elsewhere in this chapter, the time to obtain the release is during the application process, not the night before you launch your investigation.

The value of a consumer credit report to the fact-finder is debatable. The payment and collection history of a consumer is unlikely to have any materiality in the typical workplace investigation. However, a history that shows a consumer's (our subject) inability to pay his debts could possibly create the motive of theft or diversion. Though a poor credit history and theft may have a cause and effect, unless proven otherwise, they are mutually exclusive.

g. Other Places to Search

The fact-finder has other places to search as well. A quick look in the front of the phone book reveals all of the government agencies and regulatory authorities available to a particular area. Additionally, using only a telephone, the diligent fact-finder can

■ Verify a current address or residence.
■ Obtain Social Security number verification.
■ Verify one's education and claim of advanced degrees.
■ Verify previous employment.
■ Determine ownership of a business or enterprise.
■ Determine real estate ownership.
■ Determine watercraft and aircraft ownership.

Recent American Psychological Association research revealed that as many as 67 percent of all job candidates provide some untruthful information on their job applications. In one study, applicants were asked if they had ever supervised others using a fictitious piece of equipment. Of the 221 applicants questioned, 76 (34.4 percent) stated they had. Other independent studies reveal that as many as 50 percent of all applicants inflate their educational and managerial experience. With such statistics,

Exhibit 3.1   Release and Notification of Intent to Obtain a Consumer Credit Report or Investigative Consumer Report for Employment Purposes

I understand that, in conjunction with my application for employment with Business Controls, Inc., the company may request a consumer credit report and/or an investigative consumer report from a consumer reporting agency, and that any such report(s) will be used solely for employment-related purposes. I understand that if a report is requested, the source of the report will be Business Controls, Inc., located at [state full address of the business].

I understand that the nature of this investigation will be to determine if I possess the minimum qualification and background necessary for the position for which I have applied. I further understand that the scope of this investigation may include but is not limited to a Consumer Credit Report and/or an Investigative Consumer Report, which may include inquiries into an applicant's consumer credit, character, general reputation, personal characteristics, and mode of living. I understand that if Business Controls, Inc., hires me, the company may request a consumer credit report and/or investigative consumer report about me for employment related purposes during the course of my employment. The scope of that investigation will be the same as the scope of a pre-employment investigation, and the nature of such an investigation will be my continuing suitability for employment, or whether I possess the minimum qualifications necessary for promotion or transfer to another position. Any effort by Business Controls, Inc., to that investigation will be done in accordance with Section 606 of the FAIR CREDIT REPORTING ACT, Public Law 91-508. Business Controls, Inc., is licensed and insured where required. For more information about my rights and the investigative process described above, I may contact Business Controls, Inc., at [state phone number] M–F, 8:00 a.m. to 5:00 p.m. MST.

I have read and understand the "Summary of Rights under the Fair Credit Reporting Act", prepared pursuant to 15 U.S.C. section 1681(g)(c). If I am applying for employment in the state of California or if I am a resident of California at the time of applying for employment, I have read and understand the summary of the provisions of California Civil Code section 1786.22. I have read and fully understand the above notice/release. I hereby authorize the release of all information pursuant to Section 606 Fair Credit Reporting Act, Public Law 91-508.

_____

Applicant's Name (please print)

_____   _____

Applicant's Signature   Date

I would like to receive a free copy of any Consumer Report on me that is requested.

_____ Yes   _____ No

it is obvious that the employer must do everything possible when screening applicants. The same is true for the fact-finder who is undertaking a workplace investigation. Failing to conduct a thorough background of one's subjects, witnesses, and even confidential individuals used as informants is often careless. It also may be unprofessional. Moreover, this type of fundamental fact-finding adds very little to the overall cost of a project.

h. Records Internal to the Organization

For most of this section I have focused our analysis on the examination of records, which are principally found external to the organization. For many, the method of *research* congers up images of the hard-drinking, gruff gumshoe who seems to put his nose everyplace it does not belong. Today, however, professional researchers command big salaries and are well-respected members of the corporate investigation community. So visible is their contribution, often overlooked are the organizational fact-finders tasked to dig into the files and archives of their employees. For our purposes, this form of research is called *auditing*. It is the examination of records and information found internal to the organization. As already mentioned earlier in this section, these records might include attendance records, productivity reports, accident reports, and personnel files.

More generally they constitute information, records, reports, and data points, which are generally not available to those outside the organization. As such, the procurement, handling, and distribution of this information deserve special consideration. Protecting the information from accidental disclosure is merely one consideration. Another consideration, one that I think is most critical, is that of unwanted disclosure through discovery. By wrapping counsel into the process early, the work product produced by the investigative team can easily be protected. By asserting and maintaining either the attorney-client or attorney–work product privilege, some if not all of the team's findings would be protected. Even trade secrets that were not otherwise properly protected that find their way into investigative files may have to be disclosed. This dilemma and its consequences unfortunately are often overlooked.

Tip: Safeguard work product from unwanted disclosure by protecting it using either the attorney-client or attorney–work product privilege. Memorialize the decision in writing and mark all documents accordingly.

Trap: The unintentional or careless mishandling of privileged documents could undermine the privilege. Establish an organizational policy addressing the issue and ensure it is consistently enforced.

Another challenge is deciding which records or documents to procure. Organizations produce mountains of data. Financial reports, safety statistics, customer profiles, and on and on; in fact, it is rare a single person knows of all of the information his organization accumulates and retains—much less why. Recognizing this, the fact-finder is well advised to rely on others to help him to decide what sort of information might be useful to him. I have frequently asked a client to introduce me to all department heads, just so I could ask what sort of data they collect and what type of reports they generate.

D. Forensic Analysis

Forensic analysis is the fourth method of investigation. It includes all of the assorted forms of information gathering and analysis that employ science or scientific method. In this category are bodily fluid analysis, chemical and substance analysis, fingerprint examination and comparison, accident and incident reconstruction, computer forensics, various deception detection methods (including polygraph), and forensic document examination. For our purposes, forensic analysis is the catch-all category where science and the investigator meet. Let's examine a few of them.

1. Chemical Analysis

a. Drug Testing

Recent figures show that nearly half of all Fortune 500 companies do some kind of drug testing. Today, those who are not testing are simply hiring the rejects of others. Testing, however, is not without risk, nor is it foolproof. Although drug testing is a valuable tool in the employment screening process, it can serve a number of investigative purposes as well. When misused, this powerful tool can bring claims of invasion of privacy, slander, wrongful termination, and employment discrimination. Before launching a sweeping substance abuse program that includes drug testing, consult an experienced employment law attorney.

Employment drug screening involves the use of chemical tests to detect the presence of the metabolical byproducts of selected drugs in the human system. The testing determines if certain metabolites are present in a given human specimen. The specimen is usually a liquid, such as blood or, most typically, urine. However, the specimen may be hair, saliva, perspiration, tears, or even a fingernail clipping. For employment purposes the object is not to determine if the subject is "under the influence" at the time the specimen was collected, but to merely determine if a particular metabolite is present in the specimen. To this end, urine is the most common type of specimen used. Because urine collection in nonintrusive and the specimen requires little special handling, urine testing has become the gold standard (no pun intended) in the world of workplace drug testing and illegal drug detection. Once collected, the specimen is typically tested several ways. Today, most laboratories conduct initial screening via thin layer chromatography (TLC). The test is relatively inexpensive and easy to perform. If a substance of interest is detected, a confirmatory test is performed. Typically used for confirmation and quantitative purposes is gas chromatography mass spectrometry (GCMS). Though more expensive than TLC, the accuracy and efficiency of GCMS is unmatched. Most laboratories confirm all initially positive tests with GCMS.

The accuracy of today's drug testing technology has received a great deal of attention and is occasionally still questioned by those who oppose workplace drug testing. However, the claims of inaccuracy and fear of "false-positives" is largely unfounded. Claims have also been made that the tests are inherently unreliable because they are subject to interference from foods, beverages, therapeutic drugs, and normal human metabolism. The majority of these claims are without merit and experience has shown an employer using prudent collection and handling protocols can easily overcome many of the routine challenges associated with drug testing.

For readers not familiar with drug testing and the current state of the technology, the following is a partial list of the issues one should consider before instituting a drug testing program or using drug testing for investigative purposes:

- Does the organization have a policy regarding how and when drug testing should be used?
- How will the subject of false-positives and false-negatives be addressed?
- Are processes and protocols in place to ensure testing and evidence integrity?
- What level of concentration will be used to determine a positive test result?
- Who will receive the results and how will they be used?

■ Will confirmatory testing be performed and by whom?
■ How will challenges be handled?

In situations when workplace drug policy violations are suspected, simple drug testing is often not a proper investigative solution. Drug testing policies, state and sometimes local law, and collective bargaining agreements frequently affect an employer's prerogative to use drug testing for investigative purposes. Additionally, fact-finders are reminded that with the exception of alcohol, drug testing by its very nature is not capable of determining if a subject is impaired at the time he or she provides a specimen. Naive employers and their fact-finders can succumb to the temptation of using drug testing as an easy way to detect illegal drug use on the job. However, current technology is unable to tell when a substance was consumed; it can only determine that the substance *was* consumed. Metabolite concentrations provide no reliable indication as to when the substance was consumed. As such, the mere presence of a metabolite in a specimen is not proof the corresponding substance that produced the metabolite was consumed at work or during working hours.

Ill-conceived drug testing strategies pose another interesting paradox. What if the suspected abuser is tested and the result is negative? Regardless of evidence to the contrary, the employer faced with such a dilemma may have to resign himself to the fact that it proved the suspected offender's innocence, effectively immunizing the employee against the possibility of discipline.

Tip: Workplace drug testing is complicated and fraught with legal liabilities. If an investigation sufficiently proves on-the-job substance abuse, do not attempt to further affirm your findings with drug testing. Remember also that conventional drug testing is incapable of proving whether a suspected employee has sold or purchased an illegal drug. Drug testing can only determine if a particular metabolite is present in the specimen tested.

---

b. Other Forms and Uses of Chemical Analysis

My experience may be different from other workplace investigators; however, my use of other forms of chemical analysis has been limited. Over the years I have had the occasion or need to have a suspected specimen tested in order to identify the substance. The reasons for analysis have been as varied as the substances themselves. I have had the occasion to test for suspected semen, feces, urine, blood, gasoline, poisons, pesticides, and a host of other toxic substances.

2. Accident and Incident Reconstruction

Accident and incident reconstruction when done properly is a science. Volumes have been written on the subject and every industry has a small legion of experts who specialize in nothing but accident and incident reconstruction. As with all other sciences, the professionals who have dedicated themselves to accident and incident reconstruction have their own vernacular, methods, technologies, professional societies, journals, and means of learning their craft.

Of the most famous and well-funded professionals specializing in this field are those who work for the National Transportation Safety Board (NTSB). The experts from the NTSB investigate all types of public trans-portation accidents. Of them, some of the most talented are those who specialize in aircraft accident reconstruction. Whether the aircraft in ques-tion crashed over land or sea, the reconstruction experts from the NTSB gather the pieces and put the aircraft and its contents back together. See Exhibit 3.2 from the NTSB Web site.

If your investigation calls for accident or incident reconstruction, hire an expert. Unless the matter under investigation is routine and the outcome of your investigation is of little consequence, under most circumstances, experts should be retained.

3. Computer Forensics

Computer forensics is a relatively new field. It was not until the advent of the personal computer (PC) that computer forensics leaped into the world of modern investigations. Computers and the more common PC are both the target of criminals and the tool of criminals. Today, few financial crimes are committed without the use of a computer. Conversely, computers can be the objects of evidence or the tool of the investigator.[16] If used for no other reason than storing information or preparing reports, computers are used in almost all workplace investigations. Familiarity with them and their capabilities is essential to the fact-finder. Because so many aspects of business involve the use of computers, the fact-finder who is technologically challenged and unwilling to adapt to our ever-changing technological world will quickly become obsolete.

Exhibit 3.2   Mission of the NTSB

The National Transportation Safety Board
The National Transportation Safety Board was established in 1967 to conduct independent investigations of all civil aviation accidents in the United States and major accidents in the other modes of transportation. It is not part of the Department of Transportation, nor organizationally affiliated with any of DOT's modal agencies, including the Federal Aviation Administration. The Safety Board has no regulatory or enforcement powers.

To ensure that Safety Board investigations focus only on improving transportation safety, the Board's analysis of factual information and its determination of probable cause cannot be entered as evidence in a court of law.

The NTSB "Go Team"
At the core of NTSB investigations is the "Go Team." The purpose of the Safety Board Go Team is simple and effective: Begin the investigation of a major accident at the accident scene, as quickly as possible, assembling the broad spectrum of technical expertise that is needed to solve complex transportation safety problems.

The team can number from three or four to more than a dozen specialists from the Board's headquarters staff in Washington, D.C., who are assigned on a rotational basis to respond as quickly as possible to the scene of the accident. Go Teams travel by commercial airliner or government aircraft depending on circumstances and availability. Such teams have been winging to catastrophic airline crash sites for more than 30 years. They also routinely handle investigations of certain rail, highway, marine and pipeline accidents.

During their time on the "duty" rotation, members must be reachable 24 hours a day by telephone at the office or at home, or by pager. Most Go Team members do not have a suitcase pre-packed because there's no way of knowing whether the accident scene will be in Florida or Alaska; but they do have tools of their trade handy—carefully selected wrenches, screwdrivers and devices peculiar to their specialty. All carry flashlights, tape recorders, cameras, and lots of extra tape and film.

Source: http://www.ntsb.gov/abt_ntsb/invest.htm, July 2004.

For the purpose of this text, I will limit my examination of computer forensics to the use of the computer to uncover and analyze potential or relevant evidence. In this context the computer can be used to acquire, preserve, analyze, catalogue, and present evidence. Computers are the end-product of more than 150 years of industrial evolution. These complex machines are engineering miracles that store and process information in the form of numbers. Those numbers are expressed as binary numbers, either a one or zero where one is the state of a closed switch and zero the state of an open switch. In this manner, digital computers are essentially a collection of switches that when energized are capable of opening and closing in a tiny fraction of a second. The information they store and process is nothing more than a numerical expression (thus the term *digitized*). Ingenious methods have been devised to digitize all types of information. For instance, the English alphabet has been digitized into a standard code known as ASCII.

Computers allow the replication of information with exact precision. Unlike other technologies using analogue media such as photography, reproduction of digital information can be done on-demand without degradation. Digital copies are, thus, exact duplicates of the original. Not surprisingly, this causes some evidentiary challenges. For example, how does one differentiate a copy from an original, or how does one know when an original has been altered?

Computer data, by their very nature, lend themselves to manipulation and corruption. Because electronic data files are not fixed and essentially exist in a dynamic state, the bits and bytes that compose them can be rearranged or erased almost at will. To appreciate this unique aspect of digit information, imagine if the oil paintings of the great masters were *dynamic paintings*. By merely touching a Renoir or Monet with a dry paintbrush, one could alter its appearance. Each human who touched the painting—changed it! Barring special precautions, that is precisely what happens when one merely opens and views a computer file. From an evidentiary perspective, the dynamic nature of digital information significantly elevates the complexity of collecting and managing it.

a. *Computers as Targets of Crime*

Given human nature, the attack of a computer with criminal intentions probably occurred the same day the computer was invented. This possibility has not gone unnoticed. As briefly mentioned in the Introduction of this book, one of the traditional functions of corporate security is to identify organizational vulnerabilities before they are criminally exploited. In this regard, the security profession has sometimes disappointed. However, I believe in the case of computer security, the profession has risen to the occasion. In spite of the fear mongering and negative press, the truth of the matter is that our digital world is largely safe. That is not to say digital crime does not exist. Of course it does. But our computers and the networks to which they connect are not leaking sieves. If that were the case, our lives would be in complete chaos. Industry and government as we now know it could not exist without adequate computer security. In spite of some privacy advocates and their fear-mongering, our most intimate personal information is not easily available for the world to see. Identity thieves are not waiting for us in every corner of cyberspace. Our

Exhibit 3.3   Top 10 Viruses of 2003

Name	Number of Interceptions	Description
SoBig.F	32,000,000	"Re: Your wicked screensaver"
Swen.A	4,000,000	Masquerades as a Microsoft security update
Klez.H	4,000,000	Comes disguised as free inoculation tool
Yaha.E	2,000,000	Free screensaver
Dumaru.A	1,100,000	Bogus Microsoft security patch
Mimail.A	1,000,000	Bogus PayPal e-mail and URL to capture credit card info
Yaha.M	900,000	Delivers DOS attack against remote machines
SoBig.A	800,000	Harvests e-mail addresses
BugBear.B	800,000	Captures victim's key strokes and disrupts network printers
SirCam.A	500,000	Deletes files and consumes disk space

Source: CFO Magazine, 2004.

libraries are not under constant electronic surveillance, and corporations are not recording our every keystroke. Big Brother has yet to breathe his first breath *and no, the sky is not falling*. However, computer attacks are real and some systems are vulnerable. The more disruptive of these are computer viruses and worms.

Spam and malicious code in the form of viruses and worms are the modern evils of our electronic world (see Exhibit 3.3). According to security specialist MessageLabs, in May 2004 spam accounted for 50 percent of all business e-mail traffic in the United States for the first time. In November 2003, in response to the SoBig and Blaster viruses, which exploited vulnerabilities in its software, Microsoft offered a $250,000 reward to anyone who could lead it to those who created the viruses. Experts believe that criminals will next combine spam with viruses. Hackers have already given the scheme a name, dubbing the mass distribution of spoofed e-mail messages with return links that appear to come from reputable businesses, *phishing*. Some customers of eBay, PayPal, and other online vendors have already been victims. As one IT security manager put it, "It will only get worse. The Internet will remain wild and dangerous well into the twenty-first century."

The digital security organization SANS reported, "A few software vulnerabilities account for the majority of successful attacks because attackers are opportunistic—taking the easiest and most convenient route."[17] According to the report, criminals exploit flaws with common attack tools knowing that some organizations have not adequately protected themselves. Frequently these attacks are indiscriminant and the casualties are more often victims of chance than victims of choice. In this sense, computers are both the targets of crime and the tools of crime.

b. Computers as Tools of Crime

Dishonest bookkeepers and hackers use computers in a similar fashion. They both use the computer as a tool to commit a crime. As mentioned above, most financial crimes today involve the use of a computer. In most situations, a computer (or a subsystem) stores the targeted information and the criminal uses another computer to access it. The target information ranges from intellectual property to personal information. The perpetrator then uses the stolen information to commit another crime. The crimes include

- Theft of trade secrets and other intellectual property
- Banking and financial manipulations
- Embezzlement
- Identity theft
- Sabotage
- Fraud

The investigation of these assorted crimes can be complex and expensive. The fact-finder must have the requisite skills and hardware to perform his investigation. He must also properly catalogue the evidence he uncovers and establish a proper chain of evidence. While working he must also take the necessary precautions to not alter the medium in which the evidence resides. Anything that causes the subject medium to change could completely invalidate its evidentiary value. Moreover, the intentional alteration or destruction of evidence (spoliation) may be unlawful and subject the fact-finder, his team, and even counsel to criminal sanctions.

c. Computers as Investigative Tools

Computers can also be used to collect and store evidence and to conduct research and compile information. Computers can similarly be used to process information and evidence as well as present it and can also be used as an investigative management tool as described elsewhere in this book (see Chapter 4, "Project Management and Case Development"). As such, computers have become essential tools used to conduct modern workplace investigations. Few investigative functions can be performed without touching a computer.

In addition to using the computer for simple computations and writing reports, the computer can be used for evidence preservation. Forensic imaging tools allow the fact-finder to create perfect mirror images of electronic media. The mirrored copies can then be analyzed and the originals preserved as evidence. Forensic imaging tools abound. In the Windows environment these include Guidance Software's EnCase® and Access Data's forensic tool kit FTK®. There are also hardware devices, such as the ImageMASSter by ICS and the forensic SF-5000 by Logicube-Forensic.com, designed specifically for the task of forensic imaging. These tools prevent Windows from automatically overwriting each file's time and date stamp as the file is being accessed. This is critical because a file's time and date stamp is often important evidence. Knowing exactly when a particular file was last accessed can be a critical piece of information when establishing a timeline or reconstructing a chain of events.

Forensic tools such as EnCase and FTK also allow recovery of deleted files and data. Using a "keyword" search, these tools can recover blocks of unallocated data containing the remnants of files, which have since lost their structure due to deletion. This is particularly useful in recovering formerly viewed Web pages, and sometimes even the information typed on them by the user of the computer.

Tip: Before examining data stored on a computer, ensure proper consent has been first obtained. In most instances unless an employer has provided proper notice, employees may have a reasonable expectation of privacy relative to the information on a computer provided to them by their employer. If unsure if such a right exists, seek the advice of competent legal counsel.

Trap: There is a significant difference between intercepting and accessing electronic information. The interception of electronic information in transit may be subject to federal and state wiretap statutes. Generally, accessing stored data is not.

Also commercially available are spyware applications, which track the activities of a computer user while using machines on which the tool is loaded. Spyware is typically loaded to the file allocation tables (FAT) of the computer's hard drive. This scheme makes the application invisible to anyone attempting to look for it. The more sophisticated of these applications not only create a history of the user's activities, some can even be programmed to take periodic screen-shots and transmit them to another party. Alternatively, electronic keystroke loggers typically just record the keystrokes of the user. Although both of these technologies may be useful to the fact-finder, privacy issues abound. Before loading these tools onto an employee's computer, seek the advice of an attorney first.

Here a few places some of these tools can be found:

- www.guidancesoftware.com
- www.accessdata.com
- www.datarecoverysoftware.com
- www.ics-iq.com
- www.forensic-computers.com
- www.logicubeforensic.com

4. Forensic Document Examination

To the layperson, a document is simply a piece of paper, but to the fact-finder it is something much more. Because commerce is driven by the exchange of information, most business activities involve the creation and use of documents. Consider your organization for just a moment. Identify a single legitimate process that does not involve paperwork or documentation of some form. It is nearly impossible to think of one. Paper abounds in our "paperless" world. Commerce of all sorts depends on it. This reality makes document examination a component of almost every workplace investigation. By their very nature, documents are created to convey information. Although documents can be created to convey accurate information, some documents can be created for other purposes. Wrongdoers can alter, destroy, substitute, and fabricate documents. Depending on one's intent, almost anything is possible. From the fact-finders perspective, documents often hold the key to uncovering and proving workplace misconduct.

Several years ago I was asked to assist in a complex fraud investigation. The client-employer who had requested the assistance explained it had uncovered evidence of vendor and payroll fraud, which had apparently gone on for years. The dollar amount of the loss was significant and the problem appeared to involve several upper-level employees. Following some preparation and planning and a little preinvestigation, it was evident that a separation of duties issue existed in the organization's finance department. One person managed accounts receivable, accounts payable, and payroll. This individual had added three ghost employees to the payroll and over the years paid them thousands of dollars. Greedy and not satisfied with taking home the pay of four people, the fraudster had created several fictitious vendors whom she also paid frequently. The house of cards collapsed when our contract document examiner concluded that a single hand had endorsed all of the payroll checks in question as well as the checks paid to the phony vendors. Although there were numerous ways to unravel the two frauds, a document examiner with handwriting analysis expertise was able to quickly reduce our suspect pool to a single individual.

The premise that no two people write exactly alike is generally accepted within the forensic community and has been accepted by the courts and criminal justice system for more than a century.[18] Because the act of writing is a reflex action executed by habit, a practiced writer is able to think and write simultaneously. One thinks more of the words than the letters that are used to create them. Over time, the skill of writing becomes so innate it can control other parts of our body. Try this simple experiment: while sitting at a desk and your feet flat on the floor, begin to slowly move your right foot (if right-handed, left foot if left-handed) in a counter-clockwise fashion so that it rotates in a small circle with a diameter equal to the length of your foot. Now, with a pen in your right hand (left hand if left-handed), begin to draw circles in a clockwise fashion. Few people can perform this exercise properly.

As our writing skills develop, we develop individualized character-istics and styles. Some of these characteristics are barely detectable. However, most of us can read a single handwritten word of just three or four letters and instantly determine if it is our own handwriting. In fact, most people can recognize the handwriting of several people, usually family members and several co-workers. It is the combination of an individual's unique writing characteristics and style that allows experts to match handwriting samples. In order to make a match, the expert will need to examine both the document in question and *exem-plars*. The exemplars are writing samples of known individuals. In the case of workplace investigations they might be *undictated*, such as those obtained from an employment application, memos, letters, reports, ship-ping or receiving documents, work orders, and most any other papers common to the workplace; or *dictated*, that is, produced at the request of the fact-finder. In most instances, given a sufficient sample and a sufficient quantity of quality exemplars, a qualified handwriting expert can either make a match or eliminate suspicion. However, handwriting analysis is not a perfect science. The fact-finder should do as much as practicable to corroborate the findings of a handwriting expert with other forms of evidence.

Document examiners do other things besides compare handwriting samples. Forensic specialists with expertise in inks, paper, typewriter ribbons, ink jet and laser printer technology, and document duplication technologies are available and can be used when appropriate. Documents can also be examined for mechanical impressions, such as check writer imprints, embossed seals, rubber stamps, accidental indentations, charring, and soiling. Documents can be examined for the presence of latent fingerprints. Document examinations should be done before fingerprint processing because chemicals used in the process may preclude some document examinations. And while on that subject, the fact-finder should be reminded that all documents should be handled properly. Documentary evidence, like all evidence, should be preserved in the same condition it was found. It should not be folded, torn, marked, soiled, stamped, written on, or handled unnecessarily. When possible, documents should be placed in plastic envelopes and sealed. This will preserve fingerprints and any microscopic evidence on the item that may exist. The exterior of the envelope can then be marked accordingly and the chain of evidence established. Should the document require distribution or inclusion in a report, make a photocopy of it and use only the copy. The original should remain "bagged and tagged" and kept in a secure place until it is needed.

For more information about how forensic document examiners can be used, contact the American Society of Questioned Document Examiners at www.asqde.org or the American Board of Forensic Document Examiners at www.abfde.org. For additional resources enter *forensic document examiners* into your favorite Internet search engine.

Another form of document analysis is graphology. Graphology uses someone's handwriting to assess his personality. Many consider graphology to be based more on fantasy than science. Graphologists believe that handwriting reveals the inner workings of the mind. They also believe that writers, even with concentrated effort, cannot hide or disguise their inner self. Although the courts have not banned the use graphology for preemployment screening purposes, its use in court is not widely accepted. As such, fact-finders should use it cautiously.

5. Deception Detection

Man's pursuit of the truth and the detection of deception has been an endless endeavor. Recorded history reveals that the ancients employed ingenious methods to separate truth-tellers from liars. Some methods, such as the dunking of suspected witches, were simply cruel and illogical. Others carefully leveraged the human psyche and exploited the subconscious inability to maintain innocence when guilty. Of all the forensic deception detection tools available today, the most well known is the polygraph. Similar to the methods employed by our ancestors, the polygraph allows a peek into the subject's mind as well as his body. According to Dictionary.com:

> [The polygraph is an] instrument designed to record bodily changes resulting from the telling of a lie. Cesare Lombroso, in 1895, was the first to utilize such an instrument, but it was not until 1914 and 1915 that Vittorio Benussi, Harold Burtt, and, above all, William Marston produced devices establishing correlation of blood pressure and respiratory changes with lying. In 1921 an instrument capable of continuously recording blood pressure, respiration, and pulse rate was devised by John Larson. This was followed by the polygraph (1926) of Leonarde Keeler, a refinement of earlier devices, and by the psychogalvanometer (1936) of Walter Summers, a machine that measures electrical changes on the skin.

Since its invention, the polygraph and its use have been controversial. The polygraph is most widely used today by law enforcement. More than half of the large police departments in the United States use the polygraph for preemployment screening.[19] For decades the law enforcement community has successfully used polygraph testing as an investigative tool. Law enforcement has traditionally used the polygraph to

- Verify the statements of witnesses and victims.
- Establish the credibility of witnesses.
- Evaluate truthfulness.

In the private sector, the polygraph is most effectively used to help exonerate an innocent person suspected as the result of circumstantial evidence. In fact, this is the only way I use polygraph testing today. For example, instead of testing the most obvious suspect, I typically would test everyone else in the possible pool of suspects. This strategy will likely accomplish several things: (1) exonerate the innocent, (2) help achieve the standard of proof necessary to take disciplinary action absent an admission, and (3) remove the possibility that the suspect will refuse a polygraph test and subsequently claim the discipline he received was not because of his guilt but instead because he had refused to take the test. To appreciate the latter, the reader should know that disciplining an employee for refusing to submit to a polygraph exam is unlawful.[20]

> Trap: Requesting an employee, on whom one already has sufficient evidence to justify discipline, to submit to a polygraph exam is very risky. Should the individual refuse and then be disciplined, he may claim his treatment was unlawful. It would appear that he was disciplined for refusing the exam, not his misconduct. The employer would then need to explain why it wanted the test, when it already had sufficient evidence to justify and sustain the discipline. Under these circumstances, the discipline would likely appear retaliatory and thus unlawful.

a. The Employee Polygraph Protection Act

The Employee Polygraph Protection Act of 1988, 29 U.S.C. §§ 2001-2009 virtually prohibits all private sector preemployment polygraph testing. The act (sometimes referred to as the EPPA) bars most private-sector employers from requiring, requesting, or suggesting that an employee or job applicant submit to a polygraph or lie detector test, and from using or accepting the results of such tests.[21] The EPPA further prohibits employers from disciplining, discharging, or discriminating against any employee or applicant: (a) who refuses to take a lie detector test, (b) based on the results of such a test, or (c) for taking any actions to preserve employee rights under the EPPA.

The EPPA contains several limited exceptions to the general ban on polygraph testing, one of which permits the testing of prospective employees of security guard firms. A second exemption is for employers that manufacture, distribute, or dispense controlled substances. The third exemption is the most important to private employers. It permits the testing of current employees who are reasonably suspected of involvement in a workplace incident that resulted in economic loss or injury to the employer's business.[22] Thus, in situations involving a *specific issue* of economic loss or injury wherein an employer has reasonable suspicion of a particular employee, the employer may test. In order to do so, however, the employer must:

1. Be engaged in an ongoing investigation involving economic loss or injury to its business.

2. Be able to show that the employee to be tested had access to the property in question.
3. Show it has a reasonable suspicion the employee to be tested was involved in the incident.

The EPPA goes further; in part, it requires the employee be given written notice of the date, time, and location of the test and what is to be asked at least 48 hours before the examination. The examiner must not deviate from the questions originally proposed and may not offer conclusions or opinions that are not relevant to the purpose and stated objectives of the test. Furthermore, neither the polygraph test results nor an employee's refusal to submit to an exam can provide the sole basis for discharge, discipline, a refusal to promote, or any other form of adverse employment action.

Given the complexities of the EPPA and the negligible utility of the polygraph, I have used it fewer than six times in my 23-year career. Although, some of my colleagues swear by it and use it frequently, I think it is more trouble than it is worth. However, there is one way it can be used very effectively and with very few complications.

Suppose the matter under investigation is the unexplained disappearance of several hundred dollars from the company safe. Also suppose our preliminary investigation has revealed that five employees had access to the safe during the time in question. However, for various compelling reasons, four of the five can be eliminated as suspects and two of them have credible reasons to suspect the fifth. The fifth employee for additional reasons is also our primary suspect. Instead of proposing our suspect submit to a polygraph exam, ask the other four to do so. We explain that they are not suspects but that we want to affirm the suspicions they have regarding the actual subject and exonerate them if possible. As would be expected, all four provide nondeceptive answers with two confirming their original suspicions. We then interview our subject. Using the findings of our investigation and the results of the polygraph tests, the subject may have little choice but to admit (assuming of course he is in fact guilty) to the theft. The psychological burden of guilt and knowing the other four "passed" exams will likely be too much for him, and he will be unable to maintain his claim of innocence. However, even if he does, our hypothetical employer can still easily justify the discipline of him. The employer has met a good faith investigation and reasonable conclusion standard, by clearing four of the five individuals who had access to the safe. Confident that no one else had access, it is now obvious the one who was not polygraphed is the guilty party. Under the circumstances, as unfair as he may think his employer's process was—*failing to polygraph someone* is not a recognized cause of action. Thus the angry employee who desired to sue would be left to assert that his employer did not meet the standard of a good faith investigation and reasonable conclusion *and* the polygraph exams it had administered were unreliable. The employee, however, before getting an attorney, probably demanded that he too be allowed to take a polygraph to prove his innocence, creating the ultimate dilemma of why he once thought it was reliable and demanded to take one and then later asserts it to be unreliable when administered on other people.

Tip: The polygraph should never be offered to those we suspect of guilt; only to those we are sure of innocence. If we terminate a party that refuses to take a polygraph when our investigation points to his guilt, he may claim he was disciplined for unlawful reasons while an employer's decision *not* to administer a polygraph is not a recognized cause of action.

Over the past eight decades, over 250 studies have been conducted on the accuracy of the polygraph. The preponderance of these studies indicates that when a properly trained examiner uses established testing procedures, the accuracy of the determinations made by polygraph examiners is above 85 percent for specific issue circumstances.[23] The polygraph's accuracy and the determinations made by the examiner can be influenced by the emotional state of the examiner, the examinee's psychological and medical state, and the contemporaneous use of drugs or alcohol by the examinee. Because of the complexities surrounding the use of the polygraph, the investigative team should seek the advice of competent employment law counsel.

b. The Voice Stress Analyzer

The subject of voice stress analysis as a tool to detect deception has been the subject of study for years. The National Institute for Truth Verification claims to be the manufacturer and sole source of the Computer Voice Stress Analyzer (CVSA).[24] The CVSA is sold only to law enforcement agencies and according to the Institute more than 1,200 public agencies use the CVSA. However, the use of this technology has been limited in the private sector. The EPPA and the state laws that mirror it place significant restrictions on lie detector "or similar" tests.[25] Accordingly, employers and private sector fact-finders should use caution when considering the use of any deception detection technology.

It should be remembered that although seemingly powerful technologies might exist, there are no "silver bullets" for those undertaking a workplace investigation. Extreme care should be used when deciding if a new or unproven technology should be used. Do your homework and seek the advice of counsel before deciding your final course of action.

6. Forensic Psychology

Many consider forensic psychology the intersection where psychology and criminal investigation meet. Forensic psychology concerns the application of psychological theory, knowledge, skills, and competencies to the pursuit of civil and criminal justice. Similar to the other forensic methods mentioned above, it too is a tool. When properly used it allows a peek into the mind of the subject and permits the fact-finder a fundamental understanding of *why* the subject of his investigation behaved in the manner he did. It has applications in a wide array of environments both clinical and corporate. Within the corporate environment, a working knowledge of the subject's mindset is sometimes essential in order to manage and predict the future behaviors of those under investigation. In matters involving threats of violence in the workplace, it is frequently imperative to understand the motivation of the aggressor. Armed with a psychological appreciation for the way environmental stressors impact behavior, the fact-finder and his team can better engineer an intervention strategy. The professionals that provide this type of assistance are specialists. It is a mistake to presume that any attending physician, family psychologist, or EAP (employee assistance program) counselor can provide the forensic assistance necessary for most workplace investigations.

The clinician qualified to provide assistance must be properly trained and have the requisite experience to conduct psychological forensic assessments. The fact-finder has a duty to ensure the resources brought to bear are qualified to perform the task assigned. These qualifications might include credentials in the field of forensic psychology, formal education, and practical experience. Of these, practical experience may be the most important. The clinician without experience in complex workplace investigations will have difficulty balancing the opposing interests of the parties and rendering advice that is legally defensible. My organization, for example, employs two full time forensic psychologists. As members of our behavioral sciences team, they have the forensic qualifications stated above *and* specific training and experience regarding the process of investigation. Thus, they are able to engineer investigative solutions that meld their capabilities with a sound investigative strategy.

Tip: Although forensic psychology does not play a role in every workplace investigation, the fact-finder should be familiar with this tool and be able to use it when appropriate.

7. *Other Forms of Forensic Analysis*

The forms of forensic analysis and their application to workplace investigations are as assorted as the underlying science itself. It is the responsibility of the professional fact-finder to know something about these technologies and their suitability for a particular investigative purpose. One need not be a scientist or a forensic expert in order to select the best tool for the job. The fact-finder need only know the technology exists and its general capabilities and limitations. The forensic expert should then be tasked to conduct the analysis and render a finding. The fact-finder should drive the process. His job is to select the best tool; it is not necessary that he also be able to use that tool.

Tip: Because the realm of forensic analysis is broad and technical, fact-finders should sometimes hire and use experts. It is acceptable to use resources outside the investigative team and for them to be involved in the information-gathering process. In some instances, it is absolutely necessary.

E. Undercover

1. *Undercover Investigations Defined*

As discussed in the first chapter, corporate undercover investigations are nothing more than the surreptitious placement of a properly trained and skilled investigator, posing as an employee, into an unsuspecting workforce for the purpose of gathering information. However, undercover investigations are complicated and are not suitable in all environments.

The chief distinction between undercover and other forms of investigation is that the undercover investigator does not conceal her presence or attempt to pass unnoticed. What is concealed is the investigator's true identity and true function. Other than interviewing, undercover investigation is the only form of interactive investigation. This unique quality allows the skilled undercover investigator (properly identified as the operative) not only to gather information concerning a workplace problem, but to learn the purpose behind the actions of those involved.[26]

Because undercover investigations are filled with complexity and opportunity, they are fraught with liability. In significant ways, a successful undercover investigation will encompass many of the other methods of investigation. For these reasons and others, our examination of undercover investigation will be considerably deeper than some of the other methods of investigation. I strongly recommend the reader read this section, even if she has no intention of ever using undercover as an investigative tool.

2. When Should Undercover Be Used?

Although on its face undercover appears deceivingly simple, it is in fact the most complicated and demanding form of investigation available. It is fraught with legal complexities, and if improperly executed, it can create enormous liability for both the employer and the fact-finder. Undercover also requires the investment of time, patience, and resources. It requires a highly structured process and a flawlessly detailed plan. And because the undercover investigator (operative) does more than periodically collect information and mingle with informants, these complex investigations require some degree of social interactivity and usually participation in at least some of the activities of the subject group or individual. Association with the subject may be close and continuous, as in performance of a daily work assignment, or periodic and coincidental, such as when the investigator meets the subject at a scheduled recreational activity or when he occasionally takes the same public transportation. Resultantly, the competing demands of safety, immunity, entrapment, privacy, and the pursuit of information often collide creating a tangled web of considerations and legal complexities. For these reasons and others, undercover investigation is not for everyone or every organization.

However, undercover serves a very specific purpose and, as previously mentioned, enables the collection of information and ultimately resolution of problems not possible by any other means. The specific structure of the undercover operation and its objectives must be dictated by the nature of the information sought. Consequently, it is widely held that undercover operations are not a panacea, and they should be used only in the most aggravated circumstances. In short, undercover investigation should be the exception not the rule and should be contemplated when no other options are available. The following are situations that have historically lent themselves to the use of undercover:

- When there is consistent, reliable information suggesting employee misconduct or criminal activity but insufficient detail to permit appropriate corrective action or the identification of those involved
- When misconduct or losses are known to occur in a specific area, but there is no information as to how they occured or who is responsible
- When there is a strong suspicion or actual indicators of on-the-job alcohol or illegal drug abuse or drug dealing in the workplace
- When there is a strong suspicion or actual indicators of on-the-job impairment due to alcohol or illegal drug abuse, yet supervision is nonresponsive or incapable of intervening
- When it is necessary to compare actual practices with required or supposed practices and routine auditing is not possible
- When there is a high probability the use of undercover will produce the desired results and all other options have been ruled out

3. When Undercover Operations Are Not Appropriate

There are situations, regardless of the circumstances, in which an undercover investigation is inappropriate. Here are a few circumstances for which undercover is not suitable:

- The investigation of protected union activities
- The investigation of any activity permitted or protected by any governmental statute, rule, or regulation or otherwise protected by a union agreement or contract
- When some other form of investigation or fact-finding will likely produce the same results while consuming less time and resources

It should be noted that the use of undercover should not automatically be ruled out simply because a workforce is unionized. It is permissible for an employer to use undercover and even place undercover investigators into a union setting as long as the investigation does not impinge upon the lawful and protected activities of that union or its members. It should also be noted that some situations that might produce information useful to the employer would be among the most inappropriate for an undercover investigation. Trying to determine the relative strength of a union organizing campaign by identifying the workers sympathetic to the union is a perfect example. This type of information is not lawfully available to the employer, and any covert effort to obtain it could be determined to be an unfair labor practice. Such determinations may give rise to employer sanctions and will likely adversely impact long-term employee relations.

Tip: Undercover is a tool, not a weapon. It should not be used for improper or illegal purposes. Because of its complexity and cost, it should only be used when all other investigative options have been ruled out.

Clearly, undercover should not be used to gather or collect information of personal or confidential nature or to offensively intrude into the private lives of anyone where a reasonable expectation of privacy exists. Such efforts are actionable and may give rise to legal claims against the employer and its agents.

4. Selecting a Vendor

Although law enforcement can conduct workplace undercover investigations, most often law enforcement has neither the time nor resources to conduct an investigation properly or for any meaningful duration. Similarly, most employers are not equipped to conduct an undercover investigation. As such, most employers turn to private agencies that specialize in undercover. Users should consider the following when selecting an undercover vendor.

a. Licensing

All but several states license private investigators and their agencies. A failure to obtain the proper license can result in criminal charges against the investigative team and in some cases the investigative results rendered may even be excluded from evidence at trial.

b. Training

The agency selected should provide professional training and rigorously screen its investigators. Most of the better undercover agencies have some form of structured training for their investigators.

c. Experience

Ensure the agency as well as the employees they assign to your investigation have the experience necessary to do the job properly. If possible, interview them and demand answers to difficult questions regarding their knowledge and experience with investigations of the type under consideration.

d. Reputation

Reputations vary widely in the industry. Qualified agencies are well known in the business community and are active in their professional associations. Request references and check them thoroughly. Ask about the firm's litigation and claims experience. A reputation of sloppy work, high-profile lawsuits, and big settlements is undesirable and possibly indicates process deficiencies.

e. Willingness to Testify

All undercover investigators must be willing to testify and see their cases through to their fullest completion regardless of the circumstances. Sometimes that means testifying in court or before an arbitrator. An unwillingness to testify could be nothing more than fear and inexperience. Less-experienced agencies sometimes claim they don't want to compromise the identity of their undercover investigators. Others claim it is too dangerous. Both claims demonstrate a lack of experience and professional sophistication—do not hire them.

f. Reports

As the reader should now recognize, reports are an important part of every investigation. As such, detailed reports should follow all undercover efforts. The information provided in a report should be complete, concise, and correct. Ask for samples and examine them thoroughly before selecting a vendor.

g. Insurance

Most quality agencies carry general liability and errors and omissions insurance. In fact, most states that license investigators require insurance in some form. Bonding is not enough protection. In order to be safe and to protect your organization, require the agency under consideration to provide a Certificate of Insurance naming your organization as an additional insured. Also, ensure the coverage is *occurrence*, not *claims-made*.

h. Willingness to Involve the Police

As discussed extensively in the previous chapter, employee prosecution is not always necessary and is complicated and often expensive. As such, the decision to prosecute should be made for business reasons only. However, a good agency knows its limitations and when to involve law enforcement. Investigations involving illegal drugs, for example, cannot be done without the assistance of the police. Ask the agency to provide law enforcement references. Also, ask the agency about its success with criminal prosecution. The answers will provide some idea as to how many cases the agency has run and where problems arose. A low prosecution ratio should not patently disqualify a vendor. Instead, examine the organization in its totality before making your selection and making a contractual commitment.

i. Attorney Involvement

The best undercover agencies insist on the involvement of their client's attorneys. The attorney's role is an important one, and the attorney should play an active role during most of the investigation. Sophisticated undercover vendors know that an attorney will contribute to the smoothness of the investigation and coincidentally protect its interests as well as the interests of client.

5. Selection of the Undercover Operative

Following the selection of a vender, the next step is to select the investigator(s) who will actually be placed undercover. Undercover operatives come in all shapes, sizes, and colors. They also vary in experience and ability. Assist the agency in selecting an investigator who will blend into the target workforce, and arrange to provide that investigator a position that will allow him the greatest degree of mobility and interaction with the greatest number of employees. Some the best positions for the undercover include

- Material handling and expediting
- Shipping and receiving
- Mailrooms
- Customer service

- Uniformed security
- Some on-site contractor capacity

The investigator must "fit in" with the workforce he intends to join. The following items should be considered, both in relation to the cover position and to the workforce demographics: experience and skill, education, apparent socioeconomic dynamics, apparent lifestyle, age, gender, ethnicity, and skills.

Largely, today's professional corporate undercover investigators are well educated, properly trained, and highly motivated. Quality agencies thoroughly screen, train, and test their operatives on a regular basis. Most are college degreed and have prior law enforcement or military experience. Typically, in order to be hired, the investigator must not only have intelligence, but also demonstrate she can think quickly and has the street sense to comfortably mix with the intended workforce. Because the undercover investigator must often work entry-level positions, she must also have the personal fortitude and stamina to work unusual hours and physically demanding jobs. Often doing the work others refuse to do, or working excessive hours in extreme conditions, the professional undercover investigator must put aside her emotions and personal comfort and remain focused on the investigation's objectives.

The best agencies also routinely drug test their employees. Because the investigator may never know when she will be exposed to illegal drugs or substance abuse, she must constantly be screened to ensure her continuous credibility and discourage carelessness. Short of a life-threatening circumstance, the operative must never use or even sample illegal drugs when offered them. To do otherwise threatens her safety, health, and credibility, and potentially jeopardizes the entire investigation.

Unlike law enforcement, professional investigative agencies cannot use snitches, informants, and substance abusers with criminal records or drug problems. Although the standard of proof is higher for criminal prosecution, arbitrators, administrative law judges, and other triers of fact are intolerant of convicted criminals informing on others while trying to save themselves. Interestingly, the use of such individuals is one of the more interesting dichotomies of our criminal justice system.

The selected investigator must also have strong communication skills. Not only must he make daily written reports detailing his day's activities, but he must be able to effectively communicate verbally with his supervisor and occasionally with the client-employer and the police. The selected operative will also likely have to testify. His cases may eventually yield criminal prosecutions, terminations, and other employment actions. Compelling testimony is essential for successful prosecution and winning civil actions and is a skill that usually must be taught. In order for the investigation to be successful, the operative (and the team that supports him) must be able and willing to testify effectively and professionally.

Trap: When selecting an operative it is a mistake to place more emphasis on the age, color, and sex of the individual than his experience and skill. The experience and skill of the undercover investigator should be the determinant qualifications when selecting an undercover investigator.

---

6. Operative Placement

Once selected, the undercover investigator should not be placed in a position for which he does not have the requisite credentials, prior experience, or ability to perform the job. For example, the operative should not be placed in a position requiring some form of licensure if the investigator does not actually possess the required license. If the position is within an unskilled labor force, typically filled by persons with less than a high school education, the operative's style or mannerisms should not betray a college education, or his spending habits suggest greater resources than are typical for such job-holders. The operative should also have the skills and abilities required for the job he will be performing. If he lacks these, sometimes remedial training can be provided before he is inserted into the job.

Temporary positions, on the other hand, offer all of the upside with very little lasting downside. Increasingly throughout the American workplace, temporary workers have come to make up a larger portion of the workforce. No longer seen as scabs, incompetents, or the unskilled, temporary labor makes up an important and beneficial portion of America's labor pool. As such, the temporary workforce makes for easy entry as well as an excellent cover for the undercover investigator. Because organizations that use temporaries are accustom to some turnover and a constant stream of new faces, the undercover investigator posing as a temporary can quickly infiltrate the workforce and assimilate with little or no difficulty. In order to improve the chance of a successful placement, it is sometimes tempting to use a *political hire*. These are hires based on contrived relationships that claim to be politically or economically grounded. For example the cover story might be that the applicant-investigator is a board member's niece or worse yet he is the CEO's son or nephew. Another foolhardy ruse is one in which the applicant-investigator claims to be a friend of a friend of a friend. This invariably raises suspicion and gives rise to too many potential questions and problems.

Another unsophisticated placement technique is for someone of unquestioned authority in the organization to command that the applicant-investigator be hired. This may in fact get the investigator hired. However, once there, no one will likely talk to him or her. Most employees don't like people who got their job because they knew somebody important. People like to think they work for an employer that is fair. When somebody, particularly someone new to the organization, gets a job in a competitive environment because he knows somebody, it bothers most people. In most workplaces these sorts of political hires don't work for placing undercover investigators. They attract too much attention, create suspicion, and tend to cause the investigator to be alienated.

Consequently, for these and other reasons under no circumstances should a position be created for the investigator. To do so will likely bring unnecessary suspicion upon him and will likely lengthen the duration and the expense of the investigation. Regardless of the circumstances, the undercover investigator should be treated like any other employee and should not receive any preferential treatment or special considerations.

There are two specific entry schemes by which the investigator can be placed into his cover position. The first is known as a *cold hire*. In a cold hire, the investigator applies for a position and is processed as any other applicant. Without exerting any influence over the process or the people who manage it, the operative is hired and placed into the desired position. This type of entry is preferred but is often the least practical. Often it is not possible for the operative to obtain the desired position without the help of the client-employer. This type of entry is called a *controlled hire*. When a controlled hire is used, the system is covertly manipulated to the extent necessary such that the operative is hired and smoothly placed into the desired job and location.

Proper placement of the operative is crucial to the investigation because the job selected must permit the pursuit of the project's objectives. As an illustration, if diversion of finished goods at the shipping platform of a distribution center were suspected, the required cover job would be one that would give the investigator maximum opportunity to be on or near the shipping operation. A position of checker or loader would be perfect. Alternatively, working in the front office would likely be useless.

The position must also allow the operative sufficient mobility. In order to effectively network and obtain the desired information in the shortest amount of time, the operative must be placed into a position that allows him to interact with the largest number of employees and still perform the responsibilities of his cover position. As a general rule, the cover position should be one that affords the investigator mobility and flexibility. It should also involve the fewest controls and restraints possible. Above all, however, it should be a job in which the investigator will appear ordinary and usual. In this regard, although management may be tempted to create a job (particularly a salaried or exempt payroll position) for the operative, the sudden presence of a new face in a totally new job may appear suspect and will attract unnecessary attention.

7. Deciding the Number of Operatives to Use

As a very general rule, it is recommended that one undercover investigator be used per every 500 employees. For example, if the workforce is 1,500 people, it is recommended that three undercover investigators be placed into the workforce. It is unrealistic to expect a single individual to network a group larger then 500 people. In some environments such as hospitals, although they allow a great deal of mobility, the workforce is highly compartmentalized. The higher the degree of compartmentalization and the less mobile the cover position, the greater the number of investigators required. Using multiple investigators also tends to make the project move faster. Although the investment is greater, typically the speed in which the desired information is obtained more than makes up for the additional cost of the added investigator(s).

8. The Cover Story

The operative should also have a plausible cover story. The cover story is the explanation of how the investigator came to obtain his position. In some situations, the level of detail may be quite superficial, and in other cases, the history may be quite involved. Generally, the more intimate the personal association between the investigator and members of his work group, the greater depth of the cover story. The cover story must not only explain the investigator's qualifications for the particular job, but also offer a convincing account of how the job was obtained as well as something about the investigator's past. Each situation will require specific cover story details but will likely include at least some details of the operative's actual past. That is, the operative should have held a similar job previously, or at least be familiar with it.

The cover story must be complete enough to permit the investigator to take all actions contemplated by the investigative plan. For example, if it is necessary to ask an employee suspected of theft to go and meet the operative's alleged fiancée, then he must have a fiancée. Or, if the operative claims to own a custom sport utility vehicle, then he must have such an automobile or have access to one.

Tip: If using a vehicle is necessary, ensure it cannot be traced to the investigator.

Routine documents supporting the cover story should be carried if possible. However, no documentation indicating the investigator's actual identity should ever be carried while on the assignment.

Trap: Inexperienced agencies tend to overemphasize the importance of the operative's cover story. Cover stories should be uncomplicated and easy to remember.

---

9. Case Management

Assuming the investigator has been successfully placed into the target workforce, she will first engage in what is commonly called the *relationship-building phase*. During this phase of the investigation the operative will learn her job, become familiar with her surroundings, and make acquaintances. The investigator should resist the temptation to press for information or appear too inquisitive. Doing so will create suspicion and will hamper her ability to gather useful information later.

In order to be successful during this phase, the investigation must be worked hard and managed. A simple operational plan and an eager investigator are not enough. In addition to clearly defined objectives, the investigation requires not only the proper pooling of resources and expertise, but also flawless execution. The mechanism that fulfills these requirements and makes this complex process possible is succinctly called *case management*. Sophisticated workplace undercover investigations are managed at five distinct but interrelated levels. The management of each level is left to the following participants: the operative, the project manager, the client-employer, the attorney, and law enforcement. Each participant plays a distinctly different role, yet coordinating and communicating every effort with his teammates. In practice this case management team becomes the investigative team.

a. The Operative

Of all of the investigative team members, the operative enjoys the greatest amount of responsibility while maintaining the highest degree of visibility. Indeed, without an undercover investigator, no undercover investigation can take place. Although the others listed above play important roles, the undercover investigator singularly will likely make or break the case. Thus, the proper management of his assignment is paramount. It is his ability to think, plan, and execute, under often difficult and dangerous circumstances, that makes the investigation possible.

b. The Project Manager

The project/case manager also plays a significant role in the outcome of the investigation. The project manager should be responsible for the day-to-day administration of the case as well as the daily supervision and administration of his operatives. The project manager also has the responsibility of maintaining regular contact with the client-employer as well the others involved in the case. In this respect the project manager functions as the vehicle through which all case information flows and is disseminated.

In order to be effective, the project manager should have certain attributes. He should be good a communicator, have exceptional writing skills, and a sound background in investigations and case management. Prior law enforcement or military experience, though helpful, is not absolutely necessary nor should it be considered a prerequisite. Some of the best case managers with whom I have worked had no prior law enforcement experience. Regardless, the best project managers are those who have high ethical standards, understand the intricacies of civil and criminal law as it applies to the investigative process, and have terrific people skills.

The project manager must also be patient. He knows that projects that drag on for months can be boring and sometimes very frustrating. He also knows that the operative's cover position can be hard, dirty, and tiring. Under such circumstances the operative needs to be closely monitored and coached. The project manager must supervise and motivate the operative and keep the assignment on track. The project manager must also ensure that the client and law enforcement are both continuously updated and kept abreast of the operative's progress and direction of the project. For the case manager this daily coaching, motivating, and communicating can be tiring and sometimes boring.

By limiting the number of operatives a project manager supervises to six or less, the manager is allowed the time he needs to properly administrate each investigation, keep the appropriate parties informed, and still live somewhat of a normal personal life. Experienced users of undercover recognize this and typically ask how many cases the project manager assigned to their case is running. Conversely, if the project manager does not regularly run undercover, she probably lacks the experience to effectively manage a complex assignment. A lack of experience and inadequate training and support, combined with an already full schedule, make proper case management almost impossible. Ensure the case manager assigned to the case not only has the ability to do the job properly, but also has the time.

c. The Client-Employer

Contrary to practices of many practitioners, the client-employer role in the selection of the operative should be limited. Unless the employer contact (the person responsible for the routine interface with the project manager) regularly runs undercover or has extensive experience supervising operatives, his role in direct project management should be limited. Supervising an undercover investigation is difficult and time consuming. A single operative can consume the full attention of a manager for an entire day. So unless that manager has no other responsibilities, case management is best left to others. Second, getting too close to the project blurs one's view of it. In this regard the client contact best serves his client (usually his employer) by keeping the investigation at arm's length, monitoring it but not directly managing it. By getting too close to the investigation the client contact also becomes an active participant. Although this may seem appropriate, it is actually problematic because the greater the active participation in the investigation, the greater the ownership and responsibility. Therefore, unless the client contact is prepared to assume some of the collateral liability associated with case management, he is safer only monitoring it.

For efficiency, only one representative should be designated as the primary point of contact for the client. Through this individual all information passes into and out of the organization. By restricting the number of individuals in the loop and requiring all information flow through a single point of contact, confidentiality is protected and the risk of accidental compromise is significantly reduced. Because fewer people have access, the investigation is easier to manage and the result is often better. Management by committee does not work when it comes to undercover and should be avoided.

This designated point of contact should have the authority to make policy decisions and spend the organization's money. The individual should be of strong character and, of course, be trustworthy. A common test is to consider whether the individual selected would make a good witness. Even the best cases can unravel, and when they do, the point of contact will surely be required to testify.

The designated party should also be accessible. Often, particularly in small, closely held organizations, the owner(s) wants to be intimately involved. However, these individuals usually don't have the time or patience necessary to do the job. They have busy schedules and often travel, making continuous communications almost impossible. Usually the best person for the job is an executive from either the security or human resources department. These individuals usually have both the experience and professional acumen necessary to do the job right. They also have the time and are relatively accessible. In many instances they have filled a similar role in the past.

Trap: The greater the active participation in the investigation, the greater the ownership and responsibility. Therefore, unless the client-employer is prepared to assume some of the collateral liability associated with case management, she is safer only monitoring it.

---

d. The Attorney

Of all of the team members involved in case management, the attorney is the least utilized and least understood. Many vendors and their clients never even consider involving an attorney in their undercover investigations. This remarkable lapse in judgment is evidenced by the lawsuits these ill-fated investigations sometimes precipitate. The organization that relies on itself or its vendor for legal counsel during an undercover investigation imposes unnecessary risk on itself. However, just any attorney will not do. The counsel selected must be an employment law specialist. She must be experienced in the finer aspects of employment law, have defended employers in cases involving employment claims, and have an appreciation for the complexities of criminal prosecution and its impact on employer liability.

For the participating attorney to be effective it is best she join the team during the investigation's planning phase. By her participating early and taking responsibility for information management and dissemination, the work product of the investigators may be protected from later discovery should the production of documents ever be necessary. This form of sophisticated prelitigation preparation is unique to the private sector. Those in law enforcement are rarely challenged by discovery motions and demands. In fact, in most criminal cases the prosecution usually wants more evidence admitted than does the defendant. Thus, it may seem peculiar to protect information and evidence during a workplace investigation even when prosecution is anticipated. However, a workplace investigation may uncover information the employer may not wish to reveal. Moreover, the employer may have a duty to protect the identity and the contribution of some of the individuals involved in the investigation. Sometimes there are things a company simply does not what to make public. Remember, civil and criminal actions by their very nature allow discovery. If the business has not protected itself and its investigation, some or all of the investigative results could be made public.

In addition to the work product protections provided by the participating attorney, she may also be able to provide some useful advice. Unlike the other members of the project management team, the attorney is uniquely qualified to address employment, contract, and prosecutorial questions as they arise. It is not wise for the employer to rely upon its vendor or the police for legal advice. Not only are neither of them legally qualified to give it, but the simple fact of the matter is that they are not lawyers. All lawyering should be left to the lawyers. And although it is frequently claimed lawyers only slow down the process and unnecessarily restrict the cunning fact-finder, they also share some of the political liability when they help make decisions. The value of this infrequently considered benefit should not be underestimated. If by chance the project gives rise to a civil action, defending the project is far easier if everyone has simply followed the advice of counsel.

e. Law Enforcement

Law enforcement plays an important role in some, but not all, workplace undercover investigations. In cases involving illegal drugs, no drug purchases can take place without the approval and involvement of law enforcement. In other types of cases law enforcement may provide resources, manpower, and intelligence, and in some instances actively participate in the supervision of the operative.

However, law enforcement's role should be limited. As the line between a private workplace investigation and public law enforcement begins to blur, legal responsibilities and liability begin to shift. The more law enforcement becomes involved in the undercover investigation, the more the operative becomes an agent of the police. If agent status is in fact bestowed upon the investigator, the rights of those he investigates are expanded. Significant among those rights is that of due process. Furthermore, if agent status is achieved, the criminal defendant can bring forth the defense of entrapment if appropriate.[27]

10. Communications

The investigative team, however constructed, cannot function without effective communications. No investigative plan or strategy, regardless of its detail and forethought, can be implemented without deliberate and effective communications.

a. Written Reports

Aside from the telephone, written reports are the most fundamental form of communication used during undercover investigations. Even before the operative is placed, the generation of reports should begin. Although practices vary, most vendors providing undercover investigation services require their operative to make daily reports. These daily reports in their most basic form detail the *who, what, when, where, how,* and *why* of the investigator's daily observations and experiences. Generated by the operative at the end of his workday, the reports are then transmitted to the project manager for review and dissemination. The formats for these reports are as varied as the organizations that use them. However overwhelming, most follow some sort of chronological format starting with the operative's arrival at work and concluding with his return home. Whatever the format selected, it must be easy to read and use, and above all accurately describe the observations and experiences of the operative.

Organization of the report is extremely important as well. A poorly organized report may contain accurate facts, but if they are entangled with trivia or buried within paragraphs dealing with useless information, they may be overlooked or their importance undervalued. A simple timeline or chronological format is probably the most basic form of operative report. Used for decades, this format is still popular. Typically written in the first person, the operative chronicles his daily activities. Brief and to the point, this report format tends to preclude the operative from providing a great deal of detail. As such, those who prefer this type of report insist their investigators periodically augment them with some form of supplemental report.

The process, however, should not necessarily be bound to a rigid chronological rendering if another form seems more appropriate. The essential point is that the information contained in the report must be organized in such a way that the facts follow one another in logical sequence, and the material related to a particular incident or event can be easily located and understood. In writing his report, the investigator should assume that the reader knows absolutely nothing about the case other than what he will read in the report provided. Partially stated facts that assume a certain degree of familiarity on the part of the reader are vulnerable to misinterpretations and confusion. They can also be a source of embarrassment, particularly when there is a need to recall supporting details months after an incident has occurred and no report or reliable record exists. Additionally, ambiguous words or phrases may force the reader of the report to rely on his judgment to interpret the report. For example, descriptions such as "tall," "a large amount of drugs," "early morning," or "usually" are relative terms forcing the reader to guess what the writer means. The use of simple, direct language will enhance the accuracy and clarity of the report. The operative's reports should be clear, concise, and complete.

One of the most popular formats used is the structured narrative. This simple, yet sophisticated format still allows the information to be presented in chronological order, yet it permits more detail to be included. Exhibit 3.4 illustrates this modern report format. Notice the simplicity and readability. Respectful of the typical reader, military time is not used, giving the report a much more professional and business-like attribute. Also eliminated are words such as agent, suspect, and perpetrator. For security purposes, the identity of the operative is also protected. The use of a unique and confidential code in place of his name allows the report's author to be identified and authenticated.

Also notice that the narrative report is written in the third person. This format permits the report to be edited by a second party (the project manager) while retaining its accuracy and readability. It also precludes any future debate as to who authored it or who subsequently edited it. The project manager can attest to its accuracy and explain any differences between his report and the operative's originals. The version he authored would not look like a polished operative report pawned off as an original.

Note also that each entry is a stand-alone paragraph preceded by an alphanumeric code. These codes allow the project manager to later merge the operative's daily reports and then sort them by topic. Electronically, the case manager can quickly prepare a report for the investigative team with the contents sorted chronologically and by topic. This report is called an *investigative summary report*. These reports are provided to the appropriate members of the investigative team in place of daily reports and their third-person format.

Investigative summary reports can be periodically prepared depending upon the needs and desire of the team. Typical, however, are summary reports prepared every ten days the operative has worked. This allows the accumulation of enough information to make the report readable

Exhibit 3.4 Sample Operative Report

Case Name:	Hawks
Case Number:	000-000-000
Date:	Thursday, October 12, 2003
On Clock:	6: 00 a.m.-3:00 p.m. (8.0)
Off Clock:	10:00 a.m.-11:00 a.m. (1.0)
Off Clock:	3:00 p.m.-4:00 p.m. (1.0)
Off Clock:	0.5 (report writing)
Expenses:	Social Activities $7.00 for beer, $1.00 tip

B-16 Questionable Activities: On Thursday, October 12, 2003, at approximately 7:45 a.m., while in the production area, the operative observed Ben Stevens (machine operator/temporary) leave his assigned machine accompanied with Sonny Herman (production supervisor). Stevens and Herman enter the supplies closet and closed the door behind them. Both employees remained in the closet for approximately three minutes. Stevens then returned to his machine. Herman departed from the department.

E-23 Messages from Management: On Thursday, October 12, 2003, at approximately 10:00 a.m., while in the production area, Chris Watts (floor supervisor) informed the production department that Friday, October 13, 2003, was going to be a 12-hour mandatory shift due to excessive customer orders. Watts warned all the production employees not to be absent or tardy. Approximately 15 production employees complained about the overtime to Watts. Watts stated to everyone that it was normal to work long hours the first quarter of the year. The meeting ended and production resumed work without further discussion.

B-2 False Time Records: On Thursday, October 12, 2003, at approximately 1:10 p.m., while in the production area, John (last name unknown/janitor/temporary) was observed clocking in three time cards. The operative asked John to whom the time cards belonged. John explained they belonged to other janitors (names unknown) who were late. John appeared to be nervous and uncomfortable when answering the question. No further questions were asked due to John's behavior. John departed from the area and discontinued the conversation.

Note to topic: John is a Caucasian male, approximately 22 years of age, 6'1", 200 pounds, brown short hair, brown eyes, and wearing a blue janitorial jumpsuit uniform and white tennis shoes.

A-4 Sale of Marijuana: On Thursday, October 12, 2003, at approximately 1:15 p.m., while in the receiving department, Ronny Sanders (receiving clerk) handed what Sanders identified to be an ounce of "bud" (marijuana) to Mike Lance (forklift operator) in exchange for $25.00 (two $10 bills and one $5 bill). Lance placed the marijuana in his right side pants pocket. Lance thanked Sanders and exited the department through dock door 11. Sanders stated that Lance buys marijuana from him once a week at work. Sanders was then paged over the intercom by Tony Lucas (receiving manager) to receive an order at dock door 14. Sanders responded to the page and discontinued the conversation. No further details were disclosed by Sanders concerning the marijuana transaction.

Exhibit 3.4   Sample Operative Report (Continued)

B-17 Sabotage: On Thursday, October 12, 2003, at approximately 3:30 p.m., while at J. J.'s Bar & Grill (Tampa, Florida), Kenny Sanchez (truck driver) stated that he and two other driver's (names unknown) frequently puncture their work truck tires to avoid driving to certain delivery locations (locations unknown). Sanchez further stated that he has punctured the tires on his assigned truck on three occasions in a 12-month period. Sanchez changed the topic of conversation because Randy Clark (shipping lead) sat at the table with the operative and Sanchez. The conversation was changed to current affairs and sports. No further information was obtained.

Submitted by: A4567B

and provide context. To prepare the report more frequently does not allow enough content and makes analysis of what has actually taken place more difficult.

Another report that is typically produced during an undercover investigation is what is generically called the *special report*. Special reports document a special event or something other than that done in the normal course of the investigation by the operative. A good example is an instance in which surveillance is used to supplement the undercover or document someone's activity relative to the investigation but not necessarily directly involving the operative. These supplemental reports can also document significant events, which may be distinguishable from the daily activities of the operative. For example, a district attorney may require a stand-alone special report for each drug purchase the operative makes. As a matter of evidentiary clarity she may not want everything the operative reported on a particular day introduced into evidence. She may therefore insist that in addition to the operatives daily reports prepared for his agency, he prepare a special report detailing solely the drug purchase in question and the events leading up to it.

b. Electronic Communications

In today's digital age, electronic communications in many ways have replaced traditional methods of communication. E-mail to a large degree has replaced the use of mail and other physical means of moving information. Because e-mail is fast and inexpensive, it is the preferred method of communications for much of the business world. E-mail is perfectly suited for workplace investigations. Operative reports uploaded to his employer's network at the end of his day can be downloaded, edited, and within minutes of receipt, sent to an awaiting recipient anywhere.

Additionally, electronic reports can be augmented with digital images, PDFs, and even video if available. Operatives can even capture images while on the job using their cell phones (those equipped with that capability) and instantly send them to their project manager.

The question of e-mail security and confidentiality should not go unmentioned, however. Since its inception, the security of e-mail has been a valid concern. Users know that no system is absolutely secure and free from unwanted interception. And although many e-mail users fear interception of their confidential message traffic, the real vulnerabilities are within their own networks. Hackers have correctly claimed the only network that is truly secure is one that is powered down and disconnected from the outside world. For these and other obvious reasons, e-mail and the other forms of electronic communications (including facsimiles) should be used only when appropriate security protocols are in place. One simple security precaution is encryption. Encryption software is simple to use and inexpensive.

Tip: The investigative team that uses e-mail as a communication tool should take the necessary precautions to prevent its interception and compromise. E-mail may also become evidence and subject to legal discovery. As such, the intentional destruction of it may be unlawful.

---

c. Telephone Communications

Telephone communications, whether conventional or wireless, are a necessary component of nearly all workplace investigations. In addition to providing a daily written report, the operative should talk to the project manager every day. This link allows the investigator to expound upon his written report and efficiently team-consult with the project manager. By telephonically communicating every day, the operative and the project are kept on track and closely monitored by management. Then, using the telephone or e-mail, the case manager can communicate with the other members of the investigative team. Daily communication is necessary for the case to run smoothly and be properly managed. Without frequent and consistent communications, successful undercover is not possible.

11. Case File Management

Case file management and format are largely a matter of preference. However, the system chosen should be simple and efficient. Because undercover investigations tend to generate a lot of paper, large three-ring binders work well as document holders. The file may be divided into five sections. One for each of the following:

- ■ Section 1: Operative Daily Reports
- ■ Section 2: Investigative Summary Reports
- ■ Section 3: Special Reports
- ■ Section 4: Correspondence
- ■ Section 5: Invoicing and Expenses

The binder holding the documents should be marked confidential. However, no reference to the operative or the investigation should be on the outside cover. Even a code name or case number on the outside of the file could arouse suspicion and invite someone to look inside. As with all workplace investigations, reports, files, and other investigative materials should not be left lying about or accessible to unauthorized persons.

At the completion of the investigation all case files and evidence should be retained. Original notes, reports, and investigative summaries should not be destroyed. Electronic folders and files should be downloaded, burned to CDs or other media, and safely stored. Digital images, spread sheets, and databases can also be downloaded to CDs and stored for safekeeping. Although duplicate information and files can be deleted in order to save disk space, original documents and files should be retained.

12. Drug Investigations

There is no workplace problem more complex or dangerous than on-the-job substance abuse. The problem of workplace substance abuse is a debilitating and infectious disease. Left unaddressed, it can consume an organization. Because of the risk it poses to the organization and its people, workplace substance abuse investigations should be conducted by experts. Those unfamiliar with substance abuse and complex workplace investigative methods should not conduct these investigations alone. One of the many challenges these types of investigations pose is separating those employees who are simply abusing while on the job from those who are selling while on the job.

In order to separate the users from the dealers, the operative must eventually buy drugs from those willing to sell them. Because dealers need customers, they are usually not hard to find. In most workplaces, the substance abusers know exactly where to go for their drugs. Because drugs are so easy to purchase from workplace dealers, the operative must exercise care. It serves no purpose to cause a naive user to become a dealer. Because the operative enters the workplace with specific objectives, training, and money, drug purchases are not particularly difficult to make. As such, guidelines should be established to manage and direct the operative during this important stage of the investigation.

a. Guidelines for Workplace Drug Purchases

The guidelines established for workplace drug purchases are not a matter of public policy or law. Effectively they are self-imposed by the investigative team. With the investigation's objectives clearly in mind, the team should decide the rules of engagement. The agency providing the operative will certainly have policies and guidelines for its investigators, but surprisingly, law enforcement will likely have none. With the exception of those law enforcement agencies that routinely assist in private sector drug investigations, most agencies haven't considered what should or should not be done. And because each case is unique, there are few hard and fast rules. Here are some points as guidance.

Qualify the Dealer

In order to overcome an allegation of entrapment (actually not a crime, but a criminal defense), the operative should qualify each person from whom he intends to purchase drugs. Qualifying is simple. First, the operative should establish that the behavior or activity in question was pre-existing; that is, it was taking place before the operative came on scene. By establishing that the suspected employee-dealer had dealt prior to the operative's approach, the dealer's later claim that he was induced to engage in an activity in which he had previously not been involved can be negated. Next, the investigator should establish why the dealer wants to sell to him. The perfect motive would be financial gain. Regardless, by establishing proper motive the dealer is denied any reasonable attempt to claim that he was improperly induced to engage in an activity that he knew was wrong and had never before been involved.

Manage All Drug Purchases

All workplace drug purchases should be done under the control and supervision of law enforcement. Although this is not always possible, every attempt should be made to ensure law enforcement is aware and approves every drug purchase in advance. Without the appropriate approval and immunity it provides, the operative exposes himself to criminal prosecution for his simple possession, transport, or purchase of any controlled substance. To avoid this potentially embarrassing legal predicament, all workplace drug purchases should be coordinated with the appropriate authorities in advance.

Avoid Off-Premises Purchases if Possible

Under most circumstances an employer cannot control what an employee does on her own time. This fundamental right to privacy precludes an employer's intrusion into the private lives of its employees. Thus, under most circumstances the employer should not permit its investigation to veer into the private lives of its employees, even if the activity in question is substance abuse or illegal drug dealing. The focus of the workplace investigation should be workplace issues and misconduct, not the enforcement of public law.

Investigators Should Not Be Permitted to Use Illegal Drugs

Short of a life-threatening situation, the undercover investigator should not use illegal drugs during the assignment. To do so would affect his health, impair his credibility, and threaten the success of the entire project. To help preserve the operative's credibility, routine drug testing of the operative should be performed. Using a combination of periodic hair and urine testing can demonstrate that the investigator is not a substance abuser and has not used an illegal drug.

b. The Importance of Drug Purchases

Drug purchases give drug investigations credibility. Without the benefit of a drug purchase it can be hard to demonstrate the scope and severity of the problem. However, never should the lack of a drug purchase be considered fatal to the overall success of a workplace drug investigation. Many factors and situations may arise precluding drug purchases. For example, a qualified dealer might insist that all drug purchases take place off company premises at locations he alone would take the investigator. This scenario is simply too dangerous and the dealer who insists on these terms may never be purchased from. In other situations, the dealers might insist that the operative use his drug before finalizing the purchase. Under these circumstances the investigator again may be forced to forgo an otherwise acceptable purchase. Regardless, the properly engineered investigation contemplates these situations during the planning phase and identifies alternatives.

c. Supporting Investigation

As mentioned above and elsewhere in this book, the properly engineered investigation contemplates the totality of the problem to be investigated and the circumstances surrounding it. Not all drug investigations permit drug purchases. In some workplaces, hardcore drug dealers sell only to established subordinate dealers, thus making purchases from them impossible. In other instances, dealers refuse to be seen possessing either their wares or money. Sometimes they employ elaborate schemes where they hide the drugs someplace where they have some control (such as an unlocked vehicle) or inside the workplace. Then, after receiving payment, they direct the customer to the location of their merchandise. For these reasons and others, the investigation must allow for more than just undercover. More often than not, some form of support investigation is needed to assist the investigator and his team.

Of all of the additional aids available, surveillance is the simplest and most useful. Using either physical or electronic surveillance the operative's efforts can be augmented. Drug use, purchases, and other drug-related activity can sometimes be captured on video or film. If properly orchestrated, drug purchases can take place openly in an employee parking lot or other common area. Well-placed surveillance teams can then document and video-record the transaction. In states permitting voice recording, the operative can be wired in advance so that both audio and video evidence can be obtained. When this is possible, the case can be made on the investigator's testimony, the testimony of eye-witnesses (the surveillance team), and the recordings. If later the suspected dealer is interviewed and admits his misconduct, the totality of the evidence is virtually overwhelming and so compelling that even the most creative defense counsel will be unable to save the employee's job, much less keep him out of jail.

The investigative team should not overlook other methods of investigation either. Workplace drug investigations lend themselves to an assortment of other investigative methods. The creative investigative team should use every tool available if practicable. From the forensic use of chemical testing and ion scan technology to the use of trained narcotics dogs, the process of investigation should consider the use of every information-gathering tool available.

d. Employee Prosecution

The use, the sale, the possession, and the manufacture of most of the drugs of abuse are strictly regulated in every state in this country and in most of the world. It is logical that those who are caught violating the law be punished. If the chief objective of the investigation is the elimination of workplace substance abuse, before leaping at the opportunity of employee prosecution, the investigative team should first determine how it will help achieve its principal objective. In most jurisdictions, only dealers can or will be prosecuted. The criminal justice system in most parts of this country hasn't the capacity to prosecute every user. In workplace drug investigations, the users are almost never prosecuted.

Employee prosecution is also complicated and expensive. Although it is counterintuitive, prosecuting employees is more expensive than any of the other alternatives available to the employer. Successful prosecution requires time, resources, and a great deal of patience. Documents, evidence, and witnesses will have to be produced. Court appearances, depositions, and testimony are often required. Then, after lengthy delays and extensive plea bargaining, our imperfect system often renders nothing more than a mere slap on the wrist.

Tip: If the investigation's objectives include prosecution be sure it's necessary. Most importantly, make sure the value of employee prosecution is carefully calculated when determining the investigation's overall return on investment. Surprisingly, employee prosecution rarely provides any measurable return.

For more information on the subject of employee prosecution please refer to Chapter 2, "The Fundamentals of Fact-Finding."

13. Theft Investigations

Undercover theft investigations begin like any other undercover investigation. However, special care should be exercised during the planning phase. Because not all investigators are created equal, particular care should be given to selection of the investigator. Although important in any investigation, the selection of the right operative in theft cases is critical. Theft investigations are difficult and demanding. In most instances they require an investigator who is both talented and experienced.

Like the drug investigations detailed above, strategy and tactics play an important role in almost every successful theft investigation. Once the operative is properly placed and is sufficiently acclimated to his new environment, his fact-finding effort can become more focused. Because most employee theft is a very private matter, unlike substance abuse, which is very social by nature, the investigator must creatively place himself in a position to be noticed. The investigator must become visible and accessible to those who are stealing. Because the identity of the perpetrators is not always known at the beginning of the investigation, this can be particularly difficult and time consuming. Instead, the operative should try to attract the dishonest employees to him. Carefully creating the appearance of having criminal tendencies may be enough. Often by indicating that he (the investigator) is a substance abuser, he can attract others with criminal involvement. That being the case, the undercover investigator looking to solve a theft problem should first look for a substance abuse problem. Once fully aligned with the substance-abusing element of the workforce, the investigator can then seek out those involved in the theft with near impunity. It will not seem peculiar for the investigator who has been accepted by his marijuana-smoking co-workers to talk about theft. Thus, by seemingly placing himself in the middle of the client-employer's substance abuse problem, the operative can gain direct access to those involved in theft or the diversion of company assets.

a. The Use of Associates and Other Third Parties

The third party for this purpose is just another investigator who poses as a shady associate of the operative with criminal connections. Depending on the need, this associate could be the purchaser of stolen property; in other cases he could be the purveyor of stolen property. And like so many criminals, he can be made to appear to have involvement in whatever criminal activity makes money. Easily, this additional investigator can maneuver onto the scene and assist the undercover when needed. In theft investigations it is perfectly acceptable for the operative to steal. But because her credibility is at stake, all of her theft activity should be done with an explicit purpose and be preapproved. Stealing for the sake of stealing or simply proving it can be done is inappropriate and risky. But if it is necessary to help the operative's credibility, controlled stealing is permissible and creates no technical or legal problems for either the investigator or the assignment.

b. Other Techniques and Approaches

Everybody likes to get something for nothing and criminals are no different. Offering small appliances at seemingly ridiculous prices is one such rouse to enhance the operative's criminal credibility. Event tickets are another popular give-away or item to sell to co-workers. Although it should go without saying, introducing guns or contraband is dangerous and may be unlawful. Safety is job number one. Don't allow the investigator to do anything that will diminish the safety of the workplace or do anything else that is unlawful or otherwise inappropriate.

c. Buy-Busts and Sting Operations

The buy-bust is a case closing technique in which the subject is arrested at the moment he is either buying or selling the property in question. Usually the other party to the transaction is a member of law enforcement or a designated agent. Upon some prearranged signal, the subject is confronted and arrested on the spot. In theft cases, like most drug cases, the technique works best toward the end of the investigation. Usually by design, the true identity of the undercover operative and law enforcement's agents is exposed. Arresting the offender(s) at this stage of the investigation precludes the loss or destruction of valuable evidence or chasing down dangerous and possibly armed offenders later.

Sting operations, on the other hand, are similar, but the use of the term generally connotes a longer, more complicated investigative effort. Sting operations usually involve more elaborate setups than buy-busts. Sometimes these involve the actual setup and operation of a business as a front or place where stolen goods are sold or traded. Because of their complexity, good sting operations are usually expensive and time consuming.

d. Corroborating Evidence

In most theft cases corroborating evidence beyond that provided by the undercover investigator is often useful. The most common and economic form of corroborating evidence is videotape. If the crimes under investigation can be videotaped or recorded, doing so should be seriously considered. In most theft investigations this is surprisingly easy. If the property in question is being stolen and resold by the thieves, the investigation can be engineered to buy some of it. Because a key element of the crime is physical removal of the property, arrange for the thief to deliver his stolen wares outdoors. Specifically, instruct him to meet outside the facility, warehouse, or physical structure where the property originated. The organization's controlled parking lots are fine, in fact preferred. The parking lot is usually controlled enough to make it safe. Plan ahead, arrange to park surveillance teams next to or nearby the investigator's vehicle. The investigator should arrange to meet the subject in the parking lot near or at his (the operative's) vehicle. By carefully choreographing the action, the investigator and the subject can be placed in perfect position to be videotaped. The stolen property, the money exchange, and entire event can be documented.

Only one thing can improve this already solid case and that is tape-recording the dialogue of the operative and the suspect employee at the time of the transaction. Federal law permits the tape-recording of any conversation as long as one party to the conversation is aware it is being recording. However, state laws regarding tape-recording vary. Most states are more restrictive and require all parties to be aware the conversation is being tape-recorded. Be aware of the fact that because the party without knowledge has committed a suspected crime, it does not obviate any rights he might otherwise enjoy.

e. Multiple Transactions

As in drug investigations, multiple transactions make a stronger case. As a matter of practice always try to conduct more than one transaction with each player. Multiple transactions help eliminate the claim that the activity was spontaneous and or some sort of anomaly. Multiple transactions help prove the perpetrator is a true offender and not just someone who made a one-time mistake. Multiple transactions also help destroy the claim of entrapment and make the case look better. Putting aside the claim of entrapment, multiple transactions give all parties concerned (except the subject, of course) the confidence needed to justify prosecuting the case. Be it an employer hoping to terminate the offender or the criminal justice system attempting to make a convincing prosecutable case, multiple transactions enhance the case against the offender. Similar to drug investigations, multiple offenses speak volumes to the mindset and intention of the perpetrator.

f. Recoveries

Recoveries can be a big part of theft investigations. Because undercover investigations permit a high degree of interactivity with the offenders, they permit the gathering of information not generally otherwise obtainable. Of obvious value is the determination of who is stealing and what it is they are taking. But of equal value is *why* they are stealing and how the stolen property is being disposed. If other parties are receiving the property, it is possible some form of civil recovery can be effected. A properly conducted investigation should reveal the identity of any third parties (receivers, for example) and to what degree they are involved. Once identified, the investigation can be engineered to allow recovery from them as well as the principal perpetrators. Not only can property or consideration for the property be recovered, but so can some of the costs of the investigation.

A recovery of costs will significantly increase the return on investment of any workplace investigation, not just undercover.

14. Case Closure

Every workplace undercover investigation eventually evolves to where the production of useful information reaches the point of diminishing return. In some instances, the investigative effort has met every objective and the undercover investigator identified every perpetrator. More common, however, is something short of this perfect outcome. Typically, the investigation simply reaches the point where it has yielded enough information to permit the removal of the operative and the investigation to move to the next phase. Generally, the properly engineered investigation has anticipated this eventuality and has designated and allocated the sources necessary to properly move the effort forward. The next phase of the investigation is called *verification and analysis* and it usually involves interviewing the offenders identified during the information-gathering phase. For more information about this important phase of investigation, see that section in Chapter 1.

a. Employee Interviews

Employee interviews are a key component of any successful workplace investigation. In fact, in many regards, the undercover portion of the investigation could be considered only a vehicle by which the investigative team reaches the point where employee interviews are possible. In other words, the information developed by the operative serves as a foundation, which enables the proper selection of candidates for interview. However, unlike most general investigations where the interview process over time closes in on the perpetrators, these interviews begin with those most involved and work toward those less involved. Interviews are the most critical component of the entire undercover investigation. Failure to conduct employee interviews following a successful undercover investigation is the equivalent of professional negligence. Those who are familiar with this powerful tool will attest that more than 75 percent of the total information gleaned during the investigative process is derived from employee interviews. Investigative teams that don't effectively use this powerful tool are not properly serving their customers and deny them the result they paid for and deserve. In the next section I will detail how these interviews should be conducted and how the investigative team can derive the most value from them.

b. Operative Removal and Extraction

The timing and method of the removal of the undercover investigator is one of the most frequently debated subjects among those who use undercover. However, the answer is simple—the operative should be undercover as long as possible. In instances where interviews follow the undercover effort, the operative should stay in place until such time he is named by enough interviewees as a co-offender and it would seem illogical that he too would not be called up and interviewed. To remove the operative sooner will only bring suspicion upon him. If he is removed before the interviews begin, it may appear that he was an informant.

As a general rule, if the undercover investigator is not compromised or otherwise exposed, he can be very valuable if left in place. Often after the disciplinary and corrective action is taken by the employer, offenders who have not been exposed will become complacent. Some offenders will even brag that they slipped through management's investigative net.

Another option is to place a new undercover investigator into the staff replacing the group just terminated. Although for some time, most new hires will be suspect; the skilled investigator placed this way can often get information otherwise not possible by other means. Whatever the circumstances, the investigative team should not rush to pull the undercover investigator. Fact-finders are reminded that the purpose of undercover is the development of information. As long as the operative is gathering information, he should be kept in place.

c. The Disbursement of Disciplinary and Corrective Action

Following the interview process the investigative team should compile all of the information gleaned during the investigation and prepare a report. The report will assist the decision makers in determining the appropriate discipline and corrective action. The report should separate the investigative findings into three elements:

■ That which was developed by the investigator(s)
■ That which was provided by the employee during an interview
■ That which was provided by others during their interviews

If an interviewee made an admission against interest, it would serve as the best evidence against him. For employment purposes, a properly obtained admission is the only evidence needed to decide discipline. Unlike the criminal justice system, the admission is all that is needed in employment cases.

From an employee relations standpoint it is often best to allow those who have been selected for termination to be allowed to resign instead. Though the option does not offer any legal protections, allowing the offenders to resign permits them to leave with some element of dignity. Experience shows that employees who are fired, even for just cause, often leave angry. And angry people can be dangerous people. Anger that is not managed can precipitate more misconduct and even violence. It is also true that those who are allowed to resign typically don't pursue unemployment benefits or file grievances. Once the discipline and corrective action has been taken, all files, records, tapes, and evidence should be provided to the custodian of record for storage and safe-keeping.

F. Interviews and Interrogation

There are few skills more important to the fact-finder than the ability to obtain information through effective interviewing. Although volumes have been written on the subject, in this section we will examine interviewing as an investigative tool in workplace investigations. As mentioned in the Chapter 1, the terms *interview* and *interrogation* mean different things to different people. Often these terms are used interchangeably, confusing both the user and the public. However, according to some professionals there are significant distinctions.[28] Readers familiar with the Reid Technique® know this popular method defines an *interview* as nonaccusatory. The technique uses the interview to gather information. Alternatively, the technique proposes that the *interrogation* is accusatory and its purpose is to gain the truth.[29] I respectfully disagree with this distinction and the use of the terminology in this fashion. Although I have the utmost respect for the proponents and users of the Reid methodology, I think the technique provides the fact-finder limited value in the context of most workplace investigations. Instead of arguing the point or criticizing my professional colleagues, I suggest the reader research the Reid Technique and decide which method is best. I also suggest the reader examine other popular methodologies. In fact, there are many. However, the methodology I offer herein has been tried and tested by me. My process is the product of 23 years and thousands of workplace interviews. It represents that which my associates and I have learned and perfected while working in dozens of industries, investigating all types of misconduct, and dealing with innumerable personalities and cultures. Moreover, my methods have successfully withstood grueling legal challenge time and again. Please read with an open mind and use the method that works best for you. There is no one method that fits every fact-finder's needs.

1. Administrative Interviews

There are two types of interviews that may be conducted in the course of a workplace investigation. The first and most basic is the *administrative* interview. Administrative interviews, like Reid's interview, are designed for the purpose of gathering information. Administrative interviews are generally reserved for those who are not materially involved in the matter under investigation but are tangentially associated with it. This might include witnesses, informants, friends, associates, and other people possessing relevant information. In the workplace, these people may be someone responsible for a process or critical functions, such as accounts receivable clerk, payroll manager, or production supervisor. Anyone other than the suspected offender(s) can be asked to participate in an administrative interview.

a. The Purpose

The purpose of administrative interviews is to gather information otherwise not available. Administrative interviewers provide insight into a process, situation, or event. Generally, administrative interviews are casual, yet professional. As with all workplace interviews, the subject should be treated with respect and dignity. The tone should be polite and conversational. Because the subject is asked to cooperate and volunteer information, the interviewer should not fire questions at the interviewee. Instead the interviewer should ask open-ended questions and allow the subject to provide explanatory responses in a conversational manner. The interviewee should do more *explaining* than just offering answers. The interviewer should be seeking insight as well as facts.

b. Determining Who Should Be Interviewed

Determining who should be interviewed is sometimes more complex than it might first appear. Employers often suggest everyone be interviewed. Interviewing *everyone* is not a strategy. It consumes time and valuable resources, and it is wasteful. The investigative team should consider the project's objectives, time constraints, and budget before agreeing to interview everyone. A better approach is to first determine what information is needed and then interview those who possess it.

For example, recently during a complex fraud investigation I was conducting, my client asked that all of his employees be interviewed. Although it is true my firm is in the business of conducting workplace interviews, to interview everyone was not in my client's best interest, and I told him so. Instead, we selected those who we believed had the best information concerning the matter under investigation and were likely the most credible. Then, very tactically we decided the order in which they should be interviewed. In the final analysis this approach proved to be very productive and cost effective.

Tip: Before conducting administrative interviews determine who likely has the information sought, and among them, who is most likely to provide it. Remember, even innocent people will not always be cooperative or tell the truth.

---

c. Selecting the Interviewer

Good interviewers are conversationalists. They like to talk and most importantly they like to listen. Not all fact-finders should be considered interviewers. Good interviewers are professional and disciplined. They embrace structure and process. In selecting an interviewer, his skills, training, and experience should be mapped to the intended interviewee or project. Generally, men should be selected to interview men, and women should be selected to interview women. This is not absolutely necessary. However, experience shows that matching the gender of the interviewer and interviewee often eliminates the need for a witness and is often less stressful for the interviewee.

The interviewer should also have some knowledge and experience regarding the matter under investigation. Such qualities reduce the steepness of the learning curve and tend to accelerate the investigative process. Moreover, the properly qualified interviewer is less likely to be misled by an interviewee or to misunderstand what he is being told.

The interviewer should also have empathy. The ability to appreciate and understand the feelings of others is virtuous. Every interviewer should be kind, gentle, and understanding. There is no need to be tough or unsympathetic.

d. The Location of the Interview

The location of the interview should be convenient to all parties. The location should be comfortable and private. However, unless absolutely necessary, the interview should not take place in the interviewees office or immediate work area. Generally, such locations provide too many potential distractions to the interviewee and offer inadequate privacy. A borrowed office, conference room, or some other place that is mutually agreeable to the parties is often the best.

If at all possible the subject should not be interviewed in his home. Circumstances often make this choice convenient. However, the interviewer should resist the temptation and choose another location. One's home is very private and is usually not suitable for the purpose of conducting a workplace investigation. Moreover, in the home of the interviewee, the interviewer is strictly a guest and has no control over the environment. Pets, television, family members, and visitors can be distracting and disruptive. Additionally, the home interview poses privacy and safety issues. Before agreeing to interview someone at home, carefully consider other alternatives.

e. Documentation

Because the principal purpose of an administrative interview is to collect information, the interviewer should take notes. Like all interview notes, that which the interviewer documents should be accurate and concise. Notes should include the date of the interview, its start and finish time, and the name of the interviewer. As a matter of practice some interviewers document their questions as well as the subject's answers. I have not found that to be necessary. In most instances, by accurately documenting the subject's answers, the questions that preceded them are obvious. The questions can be structured and, in some instances, prepared in advance. Sexual harassment investigations generally lend themselves to structured questions prepared in advance. Accident investigations, on the other hand, may not. The fact-finder's preinvestigation will help determine the line of questioning and the order in which the questions should be asked. Helpful to the interviewer will be an outline containing some case facts and some information about the person being interviewed. The outline does not need to be formal and might contain the following:

- Name of the interviewee
- Date and time of interview
- Location of interview
- Type or description of incident in question
- Location of incident
- Known witnesses
- Relation of those witnesses to the subject
- Interviewee's job title
- Interviewee's known location at the time of the incident

Like all investigative notes, the notes of the interviewer should be written using a black ink pen on white lined paper (photocopies better than blue ink on yellow paper). They should be neat and legible. The interviewer's notes should not contain any subjective comments or observations. The notes should be an objective reflection of what the subject said. At the completion of the interview the notes should be kept in a safe place. No notes (unless copies of originals) should be destroyed. Although many in public sector law enforcement destroy their notes after they have rendered their report, doing so in the private sector is bad form and should not be done. Destroying notes tends to raise questions later and makes it appear that whoever destroyed them might be hiding something.

> Tip: All interview notes should be retained. Do not destroy notes, documents, evidence, or case files until the matter has been completely adjudicated and all possible opportunities of appeal have expired.

When appropriate the interviewee should be asked to provide a statement. The statement may be prepared by either the interviewer or the interviewee. It may be handwritten or prepared using a computer. Regardless, the document should be authenticated by the interviewer and interviewee and dated. Authentication may be achieved with a signature or more formally with a notarized signature. The nature of the matter under investigation and importance of the statement should determine the appropriate protocol. If the subject is unwilling to provide a statement, one should be prepared for him and then the subject should be asked to sign it. If he refuses, ask that he read it and determine if it accurately reflects that which he said. If he agrees that it is accurate and yet still refuses to sign it, the interviewer should annotate such and sign it.

> Tip: If an interviewee refuses to provide a statement or sign one prepared for him, he should be asked why. Often his concerns can easily be addressed and an otherwise hesitant interviewee will become agreeable.

Important elements in an administrative statement include:

- Subject's name;
- His position or job title;
- Location of the interview;
- Acknowledgment that the statement was voluntary;
- The relevant facts, including the who, what, when, where, and how of the incident or matter in question;
- Why the interviewee cooperated and was truthful;
- An affirmation of the accuracy of the facts provided;
- The signature of the interviewee;
- The signature of a witness (usually the interviewer).

The affirmation of the accuracy of the facts provided might read as follows: "I have written, read, and understand the above __ number of lines and declare that they are true and correct. If later called upon to verify the information set forth in this statement, I will do so confidently."

f. Confidentiality

Confidentiality is important to most workplace investigations. At the beginning of an administrative interview the interviewer should tell the interviewee that the matter to be discussed is confidential and that it and the interview should be treated as such. Most interviewees will understand the need for confidentiality and will be agreeable to these terms. If they are not, they should be asked why. In matters such as the investigation of a sexual harassment allegation, confidentiality is almost always necessary. If so, it is acceptable for the interviewer to insist on it. If the interviewee is still hesitant, the interviewer should consider terminating the interview until a later time.

Trap: Although an employer can consider the refusal to cooperate or keep a matter confidential to be insubordination, it is not advisable to discipline for it. Best advice: discontinue the interview and develop another investigative strategy.

---

2. Investigatory Interviews

Investigatory interviews are complex undertakings. They are psychologically demanding and require a high level of mental concentration. They require a great deal of planning and preparation and typically culminate the fact-finding and information-gathering phase of most workplace investigations. Investigatory interviews are highly structured interviews conducted for the purpose of learning the truth and obtaining an *admission*. Similar to administrative interviews, investigatory interviews are nonaccusatory. Typically, the subject is either known to have committed the offense in question, or the interviewer has very good reason to believe that he has. An admission differs from a confession in that a confession typically includes all of the elements of the offense. The elements might include such things as motive, intent, state of mind, and capacity. An admission is a simple statement of guilt. For disciplinary purposes, an employer need only make a reasonable determination of guilt. The employer need not prove all of the elements of the crime in order to impose corrective action. Therefore, a properly obtained admission from the offender meets the employer's burden of proof. For this reason, it should be no surprise that employers place great value on an admission. Only uninformed or misguided employers attempt to prove all of the elements of a crime and obtain confessions.

a. Why Most Offenders Tell the Truth

For most people, telling the truth is instinctual. On the other hand, lying seems to be learned. One learns to lie through conditioning. For example, a child frequently disciplined for misbehaving might equate punishment with telling the truth. In the same fashion, the same child might eventually learn that lying tends to prevent punishment. If this conditioning continues we could expect the child to eventually conclude that lying is an acceptable behavior, and when used properly, it can prevent undesirable outcomes in some circumstances. This is not the type of person one would hope to marry.

Fortunately, most of us have learned that "honesty is the best policy." Intellectually we know that sometimes telling the truth "hurts." On other occasions, telling the truth may result in severe punishment and very undesirable consequences. But experience shows that all things being equal, most people in our society tell the truth. That is a good thing. Much of the normalcy in our lives depends on us and others consistently telling the truth. Be it in personal relationships or in interactions with our employer and co-workers, our criminal justice system, our tax system, or everyday commerce, exchanging the truth with those with whom we interact enables our society to function properly. Truth-telling builds trust and improves the quality of our lives. It also improves the efficiency of society. Imagine a society where no one could be trusted. One in which every communication, message, label, advertisement, every spoken or written word could not be trusted and had to be vetted. What an awful, wasteful place that would be to live.

It is not a secret that the outcome of the investigatory interview is likely to result in discipline. This potential outcome is not lost on the interviewee. Even the most honest and well-meaning offender may be tempted to lie in order to avoid punishment. To be successful, the interviewer must be able to provide the interviewee a credible reason to believe that cooperating and telling the truth will benefit him. That is, the interviewee must be motivated to tell the truth. That motivation or incentive must be sufficient to overcome the potential benefits of lying. On both the conscious and subconscious levels, the interviewee conducts a risk-benefit analysis. If the benefits of telling the truth outweigh the benefits of lying, the subject will tell the truth. Classic responses indicating just the opposite include these:

- "The way I was raised ..."
- "My Daddy told me to never ..."
- "You know, I've got a family to feed."
- "Why would I lie?"
- "You haven't shown me anything. Where is the proof?"
- "If I did it, prove it."

These responses provide incredible insight into the mind of the interviewee. Here is what is likely not said when these responses are offered:

- *"The way I was raised ...* I am guilty and learned that lying works! People who tell the truth always get punished."
- *"My Daddy told me to never ...* I am guilty but my Daddy taught me to never tell the truth, truthful people are stupid."
- *"You know, I've got a family to feed ...* I am guilty. But if I tell the truth and lose my job, feeding my family will be more difficult."
- *"Why would I lie?* Let me count the reasons: save my job, avoid punishment, protect my reputation, stay out of jail, keep my kids, keep the money I've stolen, save my marriage, and get over on a chump like you!"
- *"You haven't shown me anything. Where is the proof?* I am guilty and I am stalling. Even if you show your proof to me, I'll claim it proves nothing. Moreover, if you show me your evidence now, I will be able to fabricate a better alibi and lie my way out of this mess."
- *"If I did it, prove it.* I am guilty and I know you know it. But I suspect your proof against me is weak and you need me to confess.

I've learned that by challenging my accuser, I almost always go unpunished."

Tip: People lie because they believe that lying provides more benefits than telling the truth. The interviewer needs to appeal to the interviewee on the conscious and subconscious levels and convince him that telling the truth is more beneficial than lying.

---

b. The Location of the Interview

Assuming we have decided whom to interview and who should interview them (if not go back to the section "Administrative Interviews" above), the next step is to determine where the interviews should take place. As with administrative interviews, investigatory interviews should not be conducted in the subject's office or work area. A neutral location on or off organizational premises is best. Although I have conducted interviews in hotel lobbies, noisy restaurants, landfills, and automobiles, the best places are quiet, private, and comfortable to both the interviewer and interviewee. Conference rooms, meeting rooms, and private offices are best.

Once the location is decided, it should be properly prepared. If possible, the furniture in the room should be arranged so that the interviewee will sit closest to the door. The interviewer should sit so that there is no obstacle between him and his subject. If the room contains a desk, the interviewer might sit behind and configure the remaining furniture so that the subject will sit to the side of the desk instead of in front of it. If a witness is to be present, she should be placed so as to be out of view of the subject yet not sitting behind him or block the room's exit.

Knickknacks, heavy objects, unnecessary documents and paperwork, sharp objects, and other distractions should be removed from the desk or table if present. Any visible clocks, valuables, or other distractions should also be removed from the room. Blinds should be drawn and windows covered in order to provide adequate privacy. The extent to which windows are covered should be considered carefully. The interviewer should balance the quest to provide adequate privacy with the possible appearance of trying to isolate the interviewee. A poorly chosen location can give rise to the annoying allegation of being "interrogated tirelessly in a windowless room."

c. The Introduction

I recommend that workplace investigatory interviews begin with a proper introduction. In most instances the interviewee will not be told of his interview in advance; therefore, it will be necessary that some form of structured introduction be made. The introduction should be made by someone other than the interviewer. A supervisor, manager, or someone of authority over the interviewee is appropriate. Because the most serious offenders are typically interviewed first, the element of surprise still exists. It should be maintained if possible. The first interviewees are usually the easiest to obtain admissions from and very often the most cooperative. However, a proper introduction is still necessary. Because the interviewer is not always known by the interviewee, the following introduction may be appropriate: "[Name of interviewee] this is [name of interviewer]. He and his team have conducted an investigation for us and he wishes to share some of the results of that investigation with you. We expect and appreciate your cooperation."

This introduction properly introduces the interviewer by name and subtly instructs the interviewee to cooperate. Notice that the party making the introduction does not tell the interviewee that the interviewer has questions for him. Instead the interviewee is told that information will be shared with him. Telling someone he will be questioned puts him on guard. It encourages that person to anticipate what will be asked and to prepare a response.

d. Theme Development and Discussion

Investigatory interviews should be very structured. Every interviewer should develop a structure and methodology that can be consistently and efficiently used. The discussion phase of the interview should be designed to move the interviewee to the point where she eventually volunteers the truth and makes an admission.

The theme should offer the interviewee some rationale as to why an investigation was conducted and what led the fact-finder(s) to believe the interviewee was culpable of an offense. The theme must be credible and not misrepresent the truth. It might begin with something like this: "As you know, this organization has had a long-standing policy addressing sexual harassment and improper behavior in the workplace. Sometime ago, it came to the attention of management here at this facility that that policy had possibly been violated. First, human resources received anonymous reports that something was going on. Then, several employees came forward and made complaints. One of those employees went so far as to submit a complaint in writing. As such, management decided to undertake a formal investigation. Today I am going to share with you some of the things we learned during that investigation."

Notice that the interviewer has made no accusations. He has succinctly summarized what the suspected violation under investigation is and some of the evidence already accumulated. It sounds sincere and confident. Also notice how this same script could be used for other purposes. By substituting *substance abuse* for *sexual harassment* the entire theme is altered: "As you know, this organization has had a long-standing policy addressing substance abuse and improper behavior in the workplace. Sometime ago, it came to the attention of management here at this facility that that policy had been possibly violated. First, human resources received anonymous reports that something was going on. Then, several employees came forward and made complaints. One of those employees went so far as to submit a complaint in writing. As such, management decided to undertake a formal investigation. Today I am going to share with you some of the things we learned during that investigation."

Next the interviewer should disclose his role in the investigative process. He might say something like this: "My role in that investigation has been that of an information gatherer. I am not a decision maker. My purpose was to collect information and seek out the truth. The information I have gathered has been packaged in the form of a report and given to those who will make decisions regarding discipline or corrective action. I am only an information gatherer."

By clearly stating that the interviewer is only an information gatherer and not a decision maker, the interviewer is making it clear that he has no control over the outcome of the investigation and any discipline the interviewee may face. There is no implication that the interviewer has any control over the future employment of the subject. The interviewee's later claim that the interviewer told him he could save his job would not be credible. Thus, the claim that the interviewee was improperly induced to make an admission cannot be made.

Next, the interviewer should provide some idea as to how the investigation *could have been* conducted. In doing so the interviewer should avoid the temptation to exaggerate the quality or quantity of his evidence. The interviewer should generally describe the methods of investigation available to him and explain that using one or more of them, he learned that the subject had some involvement in the issue under investigation. Note that if the interviewer cannot say this truthfully, it should not be said. If that is the case, maybe the subject should not be interviewed.

Remember, investigatory interviews are reserved for those who are either known to have committed an offense or whom the interviewer has very good reason to believe that he has. The interviewer at this moment is proposing the interviewee is guilty. Without disclosing any of his evidence, the interviewer is telling the subject he knows he is guilty. Cleverly, he asks the interviewee to justify his misconduct: "Using one or more of the methods I just described, we learned you had some role in the problem here at work and on more than one occasion violated our policy against [name the misconduct]. What is not known at this time is why you behaved the way you did and if you fully recognize why the policy is so important."

With confidence and conviction the interviewer is affirming the results of his investigation. He is not asking if the subject is guilty, he is asking *why* he is guilty. Unlike other popular methods of interrogation, the interviewee is not asked a string of leading questions or subjected to an obviously contrived conclusion offered up following a transparent interview. I have found that most people are not so easily convinced that an interviewer has evidence of their guilt simply because an investigator says he does. Most people, even those who have no intention of lying, want to be convinced that evidence exists. Only by explaining how an investigation might be conducted and offering some detail regarding the methods of investigation can we hope to convince a reluctant interviewee to come clean and make an admission.

Next, the interviewer needs to impose some conditions to allow the interview to go forward. Appropriately, those conditions involve honesty. The conditions might be framed like this: "In order for us to discuss this matter and for you to have the opportunity to explain what took place, you need to agree to do two things. Both have to do with honesty. The first is to agree to be honest with me, and the second is to agree to be honest with management (the decision makers)."

And here it is, the first question asked during the investigatory interview: "Can you promise to be honest with me?" Notice that until this point the interview has been a monologue. The interviewer has asked no questions or prompted the interviewee to respond to his statements. The first question asked is if the subject can be honest—when delivered properly it is almost impossible for the interviewee to answer no. Moreover, to reply no, in and of itself is telling and reveals more about the individual than if he dispassionately answered yes. By affirming a commitment to be honest with the interviewer and his employer, the interviewee has given the interviewer something to return to if the subject subsequently denies guilt. Should that occur, reminding the subject of his commitment to be honest causes him to make a conscious choice between honesty and the potential commission of two offenses, the one in question *and lying*. It is permissible for the interviewer to tell the interviewee that lying is the more serious offense if it in fact is. The interviewer can also remind the interviewee that the interview cannot continue unless the interviewee is truthful. The dialogue might go like this: "If you cannot be truthful about what took place, this interview cannot take place. The decision makers will then have to decide your fate without your input … you may not have the chance to explain why you behaved the way you did."

If the interviewee is agreeable and agrees to be truthful, the interviewer can then begin to explore the matter in question. Suggesting the subject start at the "beginning," the interviewer can methodically move from the events leading up to the incident to the actual incident. By stressing the need to understand the motives behind the subject's every action, the interviewer can adhere to his conviction of the subject's guilt without being accusatory. Although understanding motive and intent is not necessary for the employer to achieve its standard of proof, asking questions about the subject's thought processes and intentions allows him the opportunity to save face by rationalizing his behavior. The interviewer can even help in this regard. The interviewer might suggest: "I have no reason to believe you did this to hurt [name of person or company]. Sometimes people do things they later regret. I think the reason this happened was because you did not think it through. You had good reason to be angry and just made a bad a decision. Is that not correct?"

During this entire exchange the interviewer and his witness should be taking notes. The date, start time, and the time of any breaks should be documented. All notes should be neat and legible. They should be retained and become part of the case file.

Once the subject has made his admission and provided all of the pertinent details surrounding the misconduct, he should be questioned regarding the misconduct of others. If he is knowledgeable of others and their transgressions he should be thoroughly questioned about them. The interviewer should systematically document the who, what, when, where, how, and why regarding each individual the subject provides knowledge about. This information can then be added to that developed during the second phase of the investigation. In doing so, the investigative team can make real-time decisions regarding the interview of others and continue to build its information base.

e. Obtaining a Written Statement

Just as with administrative interviews, statements play an important role in investigatory interviews. If the interviewer has been gentle and empathetic, most interviewees will not resist when asked to provide a written statement. Those who object should be asked why. In some instances the interviewee is afraid of how the statement will be used or if others, including co-workers, will see it. In other instances the subject may simply be unable to write. It is acceptable for the interviewer to write or prepare the statement for the subject if asked. Doing so does not diminish the value of the statement or its usefulness. Even statements written by the subject but unsigned are useful. Statements written or prepared by the interviewer and read by the subject, but unsigned, are still useful. Even a statement torn up by the subject is useful and should be retained. Here are the elements that the interviewer should encourage the subject to include in his written statement:

- A description of the precise nature of the misconduct
- Details of when, where, and the last time the event in question occurred
- The known or observed misconduct of others
- The motive for subject's actions
- The motive for the subject's cooperation and participation in the interview
- An acknowledgment that the subject understands that he violated company policy or the law
- An acknowledgment that the subject understands that because of his actions he may disciplined or discharged (or prosecuted if applicable)
- Documentation of why the subject has decided to be honest knowing the possibility of discipline (or prosecution)
- The subject's opportunity to add anything to the statement in his own words
- An affirmation as to the truthfulness of the statement and the reliability of its contents

In the event the subject is completely opposed to a written statement in any form, the interviewer should prepare an *addendum*. An addendum is a statement prepared by the interviewer (or any investigator, for that matter) detailing a particular occurrence or event. This underused tool is particularly suitable for investigatory interviews. It permits the contemporaneous capture of information not possible by other means. What's more, addenda can be used as admissible evidence. For example, suppose the interview begins very cordially, the subject readily makes an admission, and then suddenly has a change of heart. He becomes belligerent and even abusive. Before the interview has been completed the interviewee summarily leaves and walks off the job. The interviewers would document this is detail. The report would include all of the information the decision makers would need to appreciate what took place, what was said, and who said it.

Tip: If the subject refuses to provide a written statement offer to provide one for him. In any case, the interviewer can prepare an addendum and document what took place and the subject's admission if provided.

f. Tape-Recorded Statements

I frequently also create a tape-recorded statement. After I have obtained a written statement, I arrange for a decision maker to join the interview and with a tape recorder in plain view, I attempt to have the interviewee repeat his admission on tape. This enables me to capture the mood and tone of the interview and eliminate a future claim that the admission was made under duress or obtained improperly. Again, using a pre-prepared checklist I attempt to engage both the interviewee and the decision maker. Exhibit 3.5 lists some of the items on my checklist.

My questions are asked so as to allow the subject to answer without a simple yes or no response. I attempt to obtain as much dialogue between the subject and me as possible. I want to permit a listener to have a very good appreciation for the atmosphere within which my interview took place. Following the tape-recording, arrangements are made to have the decision maker place the interviewee on administrative leave. Instead of deciding discipline on the spot, the decision maker is permitted time to analyze what was said by the interviewee and the totality of the information gathered during the entire investigation. Additionally, other interviews may be necessary. Those interviews may produce additional information regarding the subject and may impact any disciplinary decisions. Delaying the decision to discipline also allows the employer the opportunity to examine all of the evidence and make fairer, less disparate decisions. Postponing the disbursement of disciplinary action until after the completion of the entire investigation also allows the employer time to prepare final checks, draft discharge notices, and make the appropriate internal disclosures.

Trap: Tape-recording an interview has its risks. Interviewers should not tape-record their interviews unless they have been properly trained and have the requisite experience to do it properly.

Exhibit 3.5   Pre-Prepared Checklist

☐ Have everyone else present identify him- or herself by name, position, and employer.

☐ Establish that subject understands English and is aware that he or she is being tape-recorded.

☐ Establish subject understands why he or she has been investigated and is being interviewed.

☐ Establish that subject was treated fairly.

☐ Establish that I am an information gatherer not a police officer.

☐ Establish that subject was not imprisoned and that he or she could leave at any time.

☐ Establish if the subject requested counsel.

☐ Establish that subject was not denied use of the telephone, food, drink, or the restroom.

☐ Establish why the subject did or did not want representation.

☐ Review the methods of investigation that could have been used and state that one or more of them were used to gather information about the subject.

☐ Establish that subject agreed to two conditions in order to participate in the interview.

☐ Establish that I am only an information gatherer, not a decision maker.

☐ Establish that no threats or promises where made.

☐ Establish possibility of termination or prosecution or other action as appropriate.

☐ Establish that subject understands that his or her cooperation does not guarantee favorable treatment or continued employment.

☐ Establish why subject has been honest.

☐ Have subject identify his or her signature on the statement and then read the statement.

☐ Review information provided by the subject regarding others.

☐ Allow the decision maker to ask any questions.

☐ Allow subject to ask any questions or add anything to his or her statement.

☐ If the interview goes beyond a reasonable length of time, state why.

☐ Ask the subject not to discuss the investigation or his interview with others that may be involved.

☐ Ask the subject if everything he or she has just said on tape is true and correct.

☐ Establish date and time and that the recorder was not turned off during recorded portion of the interview (or if it was, why).

☐ Offer the subject the last word.

3. Overcoming Objections and Denials

It is human nature to resist doing something that is uncomfortable. Even under the best of circumstances, admitting one's transgressions to a stranger or someone of authority is uncomfortable. Whether the stakes are large or small, it is not fun to admit one's mistakes. The greater the consequences, the greater the temptation to minimize one's guilt or deny guilt completely. Those who are guilty frequently try to distance themselves psychologically from the offense. They will frequently refer to the victim in the third person, awkwardly avoiding the use of his or her name or revealing their connection to him or her. For example, Patsy Ramsey, the mother of murdered child celebrity JonBenet, has repeatedly referred to her slain daughter as *that child* when speaking in public. Curiously, Mrs. Ramsey seemed unable to bring herself to say *my baby* or *my JonBenet*. More recently, Scott Peterson, the philandering cad accused of murdering his pregnant wife and unborn son, when talking to the media said of his wife, "A lot of people want her to come home." Peterson also seems to have had difficulty saying, *I want my wife to come home to me.* These pathetic souls are so consumed by apparent guilt, they are unable to personally identify with those who were once the most important people in their lives. In another murder case involving a child victim, the stepfather suspected of molesting and then killing the toddler told the police, "I would never hurt that child." Notice that the suspect substitutes the word *hurt* for *murder* and *that child* for the child's name. In a recent case of mine, an office manager, suspected of stealing an envelope stuffed with cash that had been pushed through a door slot after the close of business, repeatedly told my interviewer, "I did not see the money on the floor." A curious answer for anyone asked *did you take the money.* Again, analyze what the subject is saying. First, he was not asked if he saw the money; he asked if he *took* the money. Second, the money was never on the floor, the *envelope containing the money* was on the floor. Factually, the manager's response was truthful. However, he failed to answer the question. Similarly, Mrs. Ramsey truly never killed *that child*—no, but she may have killed *her daughter.* Exhibit 3.6 lists a few of the more common psycholinguistic differences frequently encountered when dealing with truthful and deceptive individuals.

Fortunately, given the opportunity, most people will be truthful and admit guilt. Lying is not a natural behavior and must be learned. Liars lie for a host of reasons. Some experienced liars know that sometimes lying works and doing so absolves them of the consequences of their misconduct. Others lie because of fear. They may fear punishment, losing their jobs, their homes, even losing a loved one. But admitting one's guilt often

Exhibit 3.6   Comparison of Truthful and Deceptive Behaviors

Truthful	*Deceptive*
Rich in details.	Vague, few details.
First person singular, past tense.	Inconsistent first person singular. Speaks in both present and past tense.
Uses possessive pronouns such as, "My daughter."	Lack of possessive pronouns. Instead says, "The child."
Proper characterization of the victim, "My daughter."	Improper characterization of the victim, "She."
Appropriate emotions at the right time.	Inappropriate emotions. No emotions at all.
Wants truth known. Actively seeks to find it.	Wants truth hidden. Claims to seek the truth, but actions indicate otherwise.
Tries to assist and focus the investigation.	Provides little useful information; attempts to broaden the investigation. Casts a wider net than is necessary.
Committed to innocence and alibi.	Not committed to innocence or alibi. Will offer multiple alibis. Passive when asked tough questions.
Expressive and speaks with conviction.	Detached and evasive.
Admits the opportunity to commit the crime.	Denies the opportunity. Overstates inability to commit the crime.
Argues actual innocence. Identifies facts that support innocence.	Argues legal innocence. Raises legal defensives, while ignoring the facts.

involves the loss of face. When other people know we have done bad things, we are embarrassed. We know people will think differently of us if they know the bad things we have done. As such, there are enormous pressures to hide the truth, minimize our malfeasance, and lie. It has been my experience that in workplace investigations, most people lie because they are afraid. In order to obtain an admission from these individuals one must determine what they fear.

In the context of investigatory interviews the best way learn what one is afraid of is to ask. The question might be proposed as follows: "[First name of interviewee], it is not uncommon in these circumstances that people are afraid of losing their jobs, going to jail, or being shunned by their friends. However, most often our worst fears never come true. Are you afraid you will be fired?"

By approaching the obstacle in this fashion I have articulated some of the common fears people face in these circumstances. Even if my suppositions are incorrect, I will likely draw the interviewee out and encourage him to tell me his fear. Once the fear is identified, in most instances it can be addressed. Although it is improper to minimize the seriousness of the offence or the possibility of punishment, the interviewer can put these matters into proper perspective. For example, the fear of losing one's job is not as frightening if the person knows other employment is readily available. Alternatively, the fear of going to jail may be exaggerated and not even a mere possibility. Only talking about them can the interviewer address the interviewees fears and possibly overcome them.

A denial can also be overcome by appealing to the subject's sense of integrity. A rational person knows that lying often makes matters worse, lying ultimately complicates things, and in the end the truth almost always prevails. Here is one approach to meet this challenge: "While I cannot tell you what will happen when this investigation is over, the worst mistake someone can make is lying when others know he is guilty. Your decision not to tell the truth will not minimize what you have done. It will not make it go away or remove your guilt. In addition to what you already have done, you will have to deal with the prospect of being known as a liar. Which behavior do you think management least likes, [state the offense] or lying?" This creates a fascinating psychological dilemma for the interviewee. It is similar to what I call the *liar's paradox*. The liar's paradox goes like this: "In order to avoid punishment for breaking one policy, you chose to break another. Giving that choice more thought, which policy do you believe to be more important, the one you broke or our policy against lying?"

Another question to ask someone who clings to his innocence in the face of considerable evidence against him is: "Then how is it we can know with certainty you are not lying today?" This question causes the subject to ponder the gravity of his or her guilt without calling the person a liar. In response to questions as to whether the interviewer is calling the interviewee a liar, the answer might be: "No. However, in light of the amount of evidence which points to your guilt, it is impossible to understand how you are innocent."

This line of questioning will frequently elicit a tacit admission. This type of admission comes in a variety of forms. Within the answer provided by the interviewee, he only will imply or infer guilt. Exhibit 3.7 lists some deceptive responses.

The last question I ask someone who cannot find the ability to tell the truth begins with a statement: "In spite of the evidence against you, by maintaining your innocence you give up three very important things. They include (1) the opportunity to offer any mitigating circumstances

Exhibit 3.7 Deceptive Responses

"O.K., then show me the evidence."	An innocent person knows there is no evidence and would not ask to see something that does not exist.
"If I am guilty, then why haven't they fired me?"	This question tests the interviewer's confidence in his evidence. It also suggests that the interviewer has convinced the interviewee of the quality of his investigation or the evidence it produced.
"Show me what you've got and then I will tell the truth."	This is a trap. The interviewee has no intention of telling the truth but wants to see the evidence against him. No quantity of evidence will cause this interviewee to provide an admission.
"Tell me the names of the people who talked about me and then I will cooperate."	This is also a trap. The interviewee wants to know the interviewer's source of information in order to size up the quality of evidence against him.
"I am not going to say anything because I don't trust the company."	This is likely a lie. What the interviewee is really saying is that he is certain that the only thing between him and the prospect of discipline is his admission.
"I'd like to cooperate but I need more time to think about it."	Innocent people do not need time to formulate a statement of innocence; only guilty people do.
"I did not do this. But if it makes any difference, I will repay the money."	An innocent person rarely will say this. An innocent person finds it unconscionable to pay for something he has not done.

which might help explain your action and in turn potentially reduce the punishment; (2) the opportunity to ask for a second chance; and most important, (3) the opportunity to say you are sorry. Most troubling to management is your failure to say you are sorry."

Then ask the question: "If you were a decision maker in this instance who would you forgive: the person who admitted he had made a mistake and said he was sorry, or the person who hides behind a lie?" An answer of "I don't know" is a tacit admission of guilt, and should be thought of as such. If the subject answers correctly and says, "The person who told the truth," the interviewer should ask "Then why haven't you told the truth?" For some employers that may be too close to offering leniency in exchange for an admission. Some employers may even think it is patently coercive. However, I think the question is legitimate. It contemplates human nature's distinction between right and wrong and our compulsion to say we are sorry when we have indeed made a mistake. To blunt the assertion that the question is coercive, the interviewer should make it clear that he is not offering leniency in exchange for an admission. Instead, the interviewer should tell the interviewee that all he is seeking is the truth.

Notes

1. E. F. Ferraro, *Undercover Investigations in the Workplace*, 1st ed. (Woburn, Mass.: Butterworth-Heinemann, 2000), 202.
2. *The National Employer* (San Francisco: Littler Mendelson, 2002), 706.
3. Martin Roth, *The Writer's Complete Crime Reference Book* (Cincinnati, Ohio: Writer's Digest Books, 1990), 283.
4. Reid Inbau and Jayne Buckley, *Criminal Interrogations and Confessions*, 4th ed. (Gaithersburg, MD: Aspen Publishers, 2001), 41.
5. Andre A. Moenssens, James E. Starrs, Fred E. Inba, and Carol E. Henderson, *Scientific Evidence in Civil and Criminal Cases*, 5th ed. (Westbury, NY: Foundation Press, 2003).
6. *People v. Bui*, 86 Cal. App. 4th 1187, 1196, 2001.
7. Andrew Schulman, *One-Third of U.S. Online Workforce under Internet/E-Mail Surveillance*, available from www.privacyfoundation.org (2002).
8. Ibid.
9. Ferraro, *Undercover Investigations in the Workplace*, p. 214.
10. Victor Woodward, *E-Mail, Privacy and the Workplace*, available from http://dominopower.com/issues199809/privacy001.html (2001).
11. "Employers Watching Computer Use for Legal Liability, AMS Survey Finds," *Daily Labor Report* (BNA) 153 (2001): A5.
12. California Labor Code §§ 432.7 and 432.8.
13. The Rehabilitation Act of 1973, 29 U.S.C. §§793, 794 and California's Fair Employment and Housing Act, California Government Code §12900-12996; additionally, see California's Confidentiality of Medical Records Act, California Civil Code 56.1, and Americans with Disabilities Act.
14. Sources suggest that even the FBI's National Crime Information Center (NCIC) database is incomplete. These sources claim that less than 65 percent of all jurisdictions contribute information to NCIC and at least half of those records are incomplete or inaccurate.
15. One nationwide source of which I am familiar has not updated some of its records for over two years.

16. Charles A. Sennewald and John K. Tsukayama, *The Process of Investigation*, 2nd ed. (Woburn, Mass.: Butterworth-Heinemann, 2001), 309.
17. For an example, see http://www.sans.org/topten.htm/ (July 2000).
18. *Bank of Weston v. Saling*, 33 Ore. 394, 54 Pac. 190 (1898).
19. John J. Fay, *Encyclopedia of Security Management* (Woburn, Mass.: Butterworth-Heinemann, 1993), 554.
20. Employee Polygraph Protection Act of 1988, 29 U.S.C.
21. *The National Employer*, p. 730.
22. Ibid.
23. Fay, *Encyclopedia of Security Management*, p. 554.
24. See http://cvsa1.com/index.php (August 2002).
25. Employee Polygraph Protection Act of 1988, 29 U.S.C. §§ 2001-2009.
26. For an in-depth study of undercover investigations in the workplace, the reader is encouraged to obtain a copy of Ferraro, *Undercover Investigations in the Workplace*.
27. Contrary to popular belief, entrapment is not a crime, but instead a criminal defense. Only the government or an agent of the government can entrap a citizen.
28. Inbau and Buckley, *Criminal Interrogations and Confessions*, p. 5.
29. Ibid., pp. 6 and 8.

Chapter 4

Project Management and Case Development

A. The Investigative Team

In order for a workplace investigation of any complexity to be undertaken, an investigative team must be constituted. The team members must possess the skills necessary to drive the project forward and achieve its objectives. They must have experience and some working knowledge of the matter to be investigated. They do not need to be technical experts. However, they must understand the process of investigation and how to engineer a proper investigation. If the members of the investigative team possess these characteristics, their effort will be productive and fair.

As described in the previous chapter, it is the responsibility of the investigative team to select the appropriate methodologies and properly use them to achieve the investigation's objectives. Because of the multitude of complexities and opposing interests of the many parties likely to be involved, the selection of the correct team members is critical to the success of the investigation. Although every investigation is different and the fact pattern that precipitated it varies, the structure of the investigative team does not. At a minimum, the team should include one fact-finder and one decision maker. Only in extreme circumstances should one person fill these two positions. In order to impart impartiality and impugn a sense of fairness, one person should not share these two important roles. Any reviewing party or trier of fact will likely have difficulty reconciling the apparent conflicts of interest if one person plays the role of detective, prosecutor, judge, jury, and executioner. It is the separation of these duties that makes our criminal justice system so effective. It is logical, therefore, that in workplace investigations when practicable more than one person should participate. Here we will examine some of the more traditional participants in modern workplace investigations.

1. The Fact-Finders

To one who has never conducted a workplace investigation, it might seem unnecessary to put structure to the investigative process and designate a team to drive it. However, even experienced practitioners make this common mistake. I have spoken with seasoned professionals who described their process as "A little of this and little of that." Remarkably, as experienced as they were, they had not put any process around the most important activity associated with their profession. Successful fact-finders need to have an appreciation for the process of investigation and know how to use it. A little of this and a little of that is not sufficient.

Fact-finders also need organizational skills. I have worked with very capable investigators who were horribly disorganized. Not only was their work disorganized, but their lives were disorganized. As I look back on my experiences with them, the disorganization of their investigations was a carry-over from the disorganization in their private lives. This is not acceptable. Complex workplace investigations are important affairs. Their outcome often impacts many people. The results these investigations produce will influence decision makers who will likely make career-altering decisions. In extreme instances, their decisions may even impact their subjects' lives. The fact-finder has a duty to produce the most professional, honest, fair, and economic result she can. Disorganization and the inability to effectively manage information significantly reduces the ability of the investigator to achieve a proper result.

Beyond skill, knowledge, and organization, the fact-finder must also be ethical and fair. The philosophy that the end justifies the means has no place in workplace investigations. Trampling the rights of those we investigate, improperly collecting or creating evidence, and disregarding the law are not permissible. As the fact-finder goes about her business she has the duty to protect the integrity of the process and the rights of those she investigates. Violating the rights of one individual effectively violates the rights of all people. Using techniques that trick, trap, and mislead those whom we investigate should not be tolerated. Fact-finders of all stripes have the ethical responsibility to protect the rights of everyone involved in their investigation. Just because the matter under investigation will not be prosecuted does not give a license to disobey the law or sidestep one's ethical responsibilities.

2. The Project Manager

As the name suggests, the project manager supervises the overall investigative effort. This individual is tasked with keeping the project focused and directed. The project manager is the glue that binds the other team members and keeps the investigative objectives in focus. In internal workplace investigations this person is usually someone with investigative experience who has organizational decision-making authority. Such individuals include high-ranking human resource professionals, security or loss prevention professionals, or someone from the organization's legal department. In small organizations it may be someone from operations or administration. For investigations using outside resources, outside counsel or a qualified vendor may serve as the project manager.

The project manager also has the responsibility for intrateam communications. He can disseminate information and keep the other team members informed. Using tools such as e-mail, the project manager can disseminate reports, provide updates, and query the team when decisions need to be made. All reports and communications should flow through the project manager. He should be the custodian of all documents, files, records, and evidence produced during the investigation. Other than personal notes or working documents retained by the other members of the team, the project manager should be the one person who has everything. In the event documents or information must be provided to an outside party (such as the police or a prosecutor), the task should be performed by the project manager. The project manager should also prepare and present the final report, if appropriate, to the decision makers. That report as well as the others that are typically produced during the investigation will be described later in this chapter.

Because of the responsibilities and the demands, selecting the right project manager is critical to the success of the investigation. Sloppy, carefree project managers add little to the project's outcome. The project manager should also have the time to do the job properly. Selecting someone who already has a full workload or travels extensively may not be the best choice because that person has little time to invest in the project or manage it properly. The inability to periodically meet with the team, supervise its investigators, and handle the day-to-day functions of proper project management will frustrate the effort and impact its overall outcome. Good project managers are hands-on professionals and active participants. Here are some of the routine functions of the project manager:

- Day-to-day fact-finder supervision
- Periodic report preparation and dissemination
- Timekeeping and record administration

- Law enforcement liaison;
- Expense and budget management;
- Team communication;
- Project coordination;
- Mission achievement.

The project manager achieves success through the proper management of the resources available to him. He ensures that the project's objectives are achieved on time and on budget.

3. Employment Law Counsel

Central to the project's litigation avoidance strategy is the team's attorney. Of all of the team members, the attorney is least utilized and least understood. I am constantly surprised by client-employers who seek my firm's assistance yet have not involved their attorneys. Because most workplace investigations have the potential of producing results that lead to the discipline or termination of workers, legal advice is necessary throughout the entire investigative process. In order to navigate through the legal minefield of state and federal employment laws, the investigative team needs the support and counsel of competent legal advisors. Employers that fail to put attorneys on their investigative teams expose themselves to unnecessary risks. It is inadvisable to delegate this important function to the project manager or a vendor. Doing so puts the organization's assets at risk and may even jeopardize the careers of all those involved.

Not just any attorney will do. The team's attorney should have experience in employment and labor law and understand the intricacies of complex workplace investigations. She may be in-house or from outside the organization, but most important is having experience regarding workplace investigations. I have worked with very competent employment law attorneys who lacked solid investigative experience. Although they certainly understood employment and labor law, they frustrated the investigative effort by assuming the role of project manager. They became overinvolved in the project and became more of a participant than an advisor.

This is counterproductive in two regards. First, the attorney turned project manager or worse yet, fact-finder, runs the risk of being a witness in her own case. It is legally impermissible for one to represent another and be a witness in the same matter. The apparent conflict such an arrangement creates diminishes the credibility of both "advisor" and the "witness." Should the investigation's result later be challenged and litigation ensue, opposing counsel might look for ways to conflict-out the employer's lawyers. By successfully causing the employer's lawyers to cross over and become witnesses in their case, more cost and effort is added. Moreover, the attorney-client privilege may be challenged and attorney–work product protections may come into question. The second adverse consequence of using an attorney that lacks investigative experience is a very practical one. Lawyers lacking the proper experience tend to overanalyze and theorize. They tend to experiment and sometimes make very poor recommendations. I have had attorneys make ridiculous suggestions such as, "why not just let the police arrest them at work," as if the ability to arrest can be turned on or off with a magical switch. I have also had inexperienced attorneys suggest that employee interviews were not necessary because "most people do not confess anyway." Although the fees experienced attorneys charge may be greater than those of less experienced attorneys, in the long run the overall investment will be less if the right attorney is selected.

Employers should also be wary of attorneys and accounting firms that offer investigative services. Several of the nation's largest law firms now offer investigative services. Some even have SIUs (special investigative units), a concept borrowed from the insurance industry. Though marketed as value-added client services, I think for some of these firms they are nothing but revenue centers. They are cunning ways to train young attorneys and generate billable hours. Few of these "investigators" have any real investigative experience and fewer have effective interview skills. Moreover, is a guilty offender likely to be willing to talk to an attorney? When confronted by an attorney, most people become scared and less cooperative. They will demand to speak to an attorney or union representative. The results will likely be less than desirable.

Tip: Do not hire law firms that offer investigative services. Let the lawyers practice law and the professionals do the rest.

The big accounting firms have also gotten into the act. It is fascinating; all the big firms seem to have suddenly discovered a new market—workplace investigations. Like several of the big law firms, most of the large accounting firms have even created SIUs. Some firms now offer their clients everything except janitorial services. There is just no end to the marketing creativity of some professionals. More remarkable is the fundamental lack of ethics and respect for the law some of these people have.

The head of the SUI of one of the larger accounting firms recently told me about one of his biggest successes. While at a national gathering of the investigative industry's top professionals, my esteemed colleague proudly relayed that he had extorted a business executive. He said his accounting firm had been hired to investigate the background of a high-profile American executive (an idea as ridiculous as hiring a background screening company to provide accounting services) and help settle a piece of litigation of which the executive was the plaintiff. Using "police contacts" in Canada and the United States, he claimed he learned the subject was the father of an illegitimate child. He boasted that he ultimately confronted the executive in Florida (a state that requires investigators be licensed, which my storyteller was not) and threatened to tell the man's family about the illegitimate child if he did not drop the lawsuit. He claimed the "guy dropped the suit like a hot potato." Laughingly, he said that his boss was so impressed with the speedy result that he "value-priced" the project at more than $36,000, while the fees, if calculated on an hourly basis, were closer to $5,000. My colleague summed it all up for me and said that if had he known "it was this easy in the private sector, I would have left law enforcement years ago."

The story outraged me and I have not talked to the man since that time. Many professionals that dabble in the corporate investigative industry think it is easy. They have no qualms about breaking the law, working without a license, extorting people, or cheating their clients. It is offensive and troubling. Bad facts make bad law. The reckless disregard of the rules by a few can result in consequences that affect everyone in the industry.

Tip: Do not hire law-breakers. If hiring an external resource to provide investigative services, ensure the resource is qualified and adheres to the ethical standards you would expect of any professional service provider.

---

4. The Decision Makers

No workplace investigation is possible without ultimately involving decision makers. Decision makers are the people who decide the fate of the wrong-doers. When practicable they should play no other role in the investigation. By segregating their duties from the others on the investigative team, the result and corresponding discipline (if any) will appear fairer and more impartial. The decision makers should have the fortitude and character to make sound decisions. They should be individuals who have a vested interest in the investigation's outcome or direct relationship to the parties whose fate they may be deciding. Additionally, they should be knowledgeable of their organization's policies and practices. Most importantly, they should be people who are capable of being credible and informed witnesses. Should the investigation later be challenged, it will be the decision makers who will have to justify the resultant discipline. They will have to articulate how the decision-making process unfolded and the rationale for the punishment.

It is easy for the role of the decision makers to expand in the course of an investigation. It is not uncommon that they are tempted to become involved in the fact-finding and process of investigation. Although some decision makers will be qualified to perform these functions, it is best that they leave those efforts to others on the team. For example, if a decision maker were allowed to select the employees who should be interviewed, it could later be argued that he had an ulterior motive in his selection. This is a common claim in arbitration. The union representing the grievants might suggest the decision makers wanted certain employees interviewed because they hoped they might admit to something for which they could justify discipline when attempts to do so by other means was not possible. The motive proffered by the union might be the desire to discriminate or harass. The case then becomes more complicated for the arbitrator. The mere appearance of an ulterior motive on the part of the decision makers looks bad and requires an explanation when no justification was necessary in the first place. The whole affair creates unnecessary complications and fuels what would otherwise have been a nonissue.

Common sense also suggests that the decision makers know the rules. I had a case many years ago that resulted in the discharge of a tenured employee for consuming alcohol at work. During the arbitration, which followed the termination, the HR manager who had made the termination decision, upon cross examination was asked if the employer had a policy that prohibited drinking on the job. To the astonishment of even the union attorney who asked the question, the manager said he did not know! The arbitrator ultimately reinstated the employee, correctly finding that if the HR manager did not know if the company had a policy regarding drinking, it was logical the grievant did not either.

5. Supporting Members

The addition of supporting members to the investigative team will in part be decided by the fact pattern of the matter under investigation. If forensic evidence collection is necessary, forensic experts should be recruited and added to the team. If specialized investigators are needed, they should be added as well. Additionally, clinicians, technicians, and other experts may be needed. The investigative team should consider the need for external assistance as early in the process as possible. Because outside expertise is not always available at the drop of a hat, some planning is necessary early on so as not to later delay the process for the lack of necessary support.

The most common form of external support is law enforcement. Should prosecution be an objective, law enforcement will undoubtedly play some role. That role, however, should be carefully considered and managed. Allowing law enforcement to play too much of a role and intentionally or unintentionally making the fact-finder an agent of law enforcement may entitle the subject(s) the rights he or she would not have otherwise enjoyed. For example, the Bill of Rights provides a host of rights to those suspected of criminal misconduct. These rights, collectively called *Due Process* rights, protect citizens against governmental abuses. For example, citizens accused of a crime are entitled to a speedy trial and may not be subjected to unreasonable search of their person, property, or papers. However, the Constitution and the Bill of Rights protect us against abuses committed by the federal government, not those committed by another citizen. As an extension of the government, law enforcement may not do certain things in the course of an investigation. Some of these actions, such as the search of an employee's desk without a search warrant, are not unlawful per se if done by a private employer. If the private fact-finder works in concert, in accordance, or in cooperation with law enforcement, agency may be triggered. If so, even though the fact-finder may not be a member of law enforcement or working on behalf of the government, the subject may have some due process rights.[1] In addition to these rights, the subject may also later claim entrapment. Entrapment is a criminal defense, which claims that government officers or agents induced an otherwise honest citizen to commit a crime not previously contemplated. Entrapment does not result from an act of inducement by a private citizen.[2] Thus, one citizen cannot entrap another.

Another consequence of investigator agency is the potential need to Mirandize those arrested, detained, or questioned.[3] If the fact-finder is indeed an agent of law enforcement, it may be necessary to provide a Miranda warning to those he interviews. The following is the Miranda warning:

- You have the right to remain silent.
- Anything you say may be used against you.
- You have the right to contact an attorney.
- If you cannot afford an attorney, one will be provided for you.
- Do you understand these rights as I have given them to you?[4]

The mere utterance of such a warning to an employee in the course of a workplace investigation by a fact-finder could have a chilling effect.

Concerned about the criminal implications, an otherwise cooperative individual might have second thoughts. Additionally, the failure to provide the warning could nullify anything the subject might say. Agency imposes a host of additional consideration on the fact-finder and his process, and most are easily evaded simply by avoiding a close relationship with the police.

That said, police involvement is necessary in some workplace investigations. As described in detail in previous chapters, some investigations do have criminal implications and require the assistance of law enforcement. Substance abuse investigations are a good example. It is unlawful to buy, possess, or sell a controlled substance without proper licensing or government approval. The typical fact-finder does not enjoy immunity simply because he is investigating a suspected crime. Retired law enforcement personnel are not immune either. One's prior government service does not provide immunity when conducting an investigation in the private sector. However, many private sector investigators who have prior law enforcement experience conveniently overlook this technicality. On more than one occasion I have lost business to such an individual. Incorrectly they told the prospect that they could do things that were patently unlawful for either of us to do. Unwittingly the prospect accepted their claim and hired them.

Trap: Private sector investigators with law enforcement backgrounds must still obey the law. Such individuals enjoy no special privileges or immunity. Only properly authorized law enforcement officials can immunize someone or their investigative activities. Under no circumstance is immunity implied or transferable.

When cooperating with law enforcement, the investigative team should have a clear understanding of law enforcements expectations and plans. An untimely arrest or take-down could significantly compromise one's investigation. If for no other reason than safety, all parties involved should clearly understand the plan and course of action. At no time should one party or another be left in the cold and not know what the other(s) is doing. Investigative teams that fail to adequately plan, plan to fail.

Project managers should also be leery of law enforcement agents who put their objectives before that of the employers. Private sector investigators and decision makers are reminded that law enforcement's charter is different from that of most employers. Law enforcement's principal mission is to enforce the law and bring law-breakers to justice. I have never read anything like this in the mission statement of a private employer. If your objectives are not in line with those of the agency for which you are working, discuss the differences. Ensure the project plan allows both parties to reasonably pursue their objectives. In most instances differences can be negotiated. Law enforcement professionals are usually eager to serve the public particularly when those asking for help take the time to appreciate their needs and are willing to work cooperatively.

B. Investigative Proposals

It is remarkable how many professionals undertake a workplace investigation without preparing a written plan. I would speculate few licensed corporate investigators regularly prepare them. I would be surprised if any HR professionals prepare a written investigative plan. It is hard for me to imagine how one might expect to get to an intended destination without some sort of roadmap. The most practical roadmap for those intending to undertake a workplace investigation is the investigative proposal. An investigative proposal is a written document that describes the nature of the matter to be investigated and the intended investigative plan. This important document provides the investigative team the direction it needs. It states the project's objectives and how the investigative team intends to attain those objectives. Other than routine, one-dimensional investigations, such as employment background checks, every workplace investigation should not begin without a written plan in place. Literally, these plans propose the intended actions of the investigative team. They provide the investigative process the structure it needs to remain on track and achieve its full potential. Investigative proposals also provide those that manage the organization's purse strings the information they need in order to make informed decisions regarding the investment necessary to pursue the objectives and the potential return on that investment.

Equally important, the investigative proposal serves as a fundamental component of the employer's overall litigation management and prevention strategy. It is a document that can later be produced to demonstrate that the project's objectives were pure and well intended. What better way to show the employer's good intentions than to produce a document that was prepared before the investigation that states its objectives and intended strategy? No other tool better serves this purpose than the investigative proposal. Remarkably, very few professionals ever use one.

Although an investigative proposal can be and sometimes is nothing more than a list of objectives and a brief sketch of how one intends to achieve them, the investigative team is better served by rendering something more. The basic investigative proposal should contain the following elements:

- A description of the matter to be investigated
- The project's objectives
- Recommended course of action
- Logistical considerations
- The expected investment or budget
- Estimated return on investment

I have crafted proposals that were less than two pages in length. Most, however, are on the order of six to fifteen pages. Remember though, my projects tend to be out of the ordinary. Employers do not typically hire me or my organization to investigate routine matters, nor should they. Regardless, the length of the investigative proposal will be driven by the complexity of the matter to be investigated and the detail necessary to articulate the proposed solution. Here is a sample investigative proposal:

Scope

For some time, executive management at the XYZ Corporation has had concerns regarding employee theft and dishonesty. Information recently obtained from anonymous sources and several vendors suggests a serious problem may exist and that a large number of employees may be involved. Additionally, several employees have confidentially identified a number of co-workers they suspect are stealing frozen food products during the second and third shifts.

It is the intention of the XYZ Corporation to maintain a workplace free of employee dishonesty and workplace crime. As a result, executive management desires to undertake an investigation of the allegations and determine the true nature and scope of the problem, should one exist.

Objectives

1. Investigate the allegation of employee theft and dishonesty and determine the true nature and scope of the problem.

2. Gather any and all information concerning the problem so as to allow management the opportunity to enforce XYZ's policies and take appropriate corrective or disciplinary action.

3. Conduct the investigation so that the process is least disruptive to the organization and its operations.

4. Engineer the entire process such that it provides the organization the highest return on its investment.

Recommendations

1. *Preparation and Planning*: Conduct a preinvestigation and preliminarily corroborate the allegations of employee misconduct to the extent reasonably possible. Identify possible witnesses, cooperative employees, and additional sources of information to help facilitate a cost-effective, yet confidential fact-finding process.

2. *Information Gathering and Problem Identification*: Confirm initial inventory variances and access control records for the months of October and November 2004.

Interview the three vendors who initially came forward and obtain written statements from those willing to provide them.

Interview both employee informants and obtain written statements if possible.

Conduct covert physical surveillance over two consecutive weekends between the hours of 5:00 P.M. and 6:00 A.M. Document vehicle traffic in motor yard with video, and record license plate numbers on all noncompany vehicles entering and leaving yard during surveillance.

Run license plates and identify vehicle owners.

Conduct complete inventory of Freezers 1 and 2 on December 1, 2004.

Contact local law enforcement and request assistance as appropriate.

3. *Verification and Analysis*: Arrange for the corporate security manager and her team to interview those employees believed to be most involved. Obtain written statements from each interviewee if possible. Place all interviewees on administrative leave until completion of investigation and decisions regarding discipline (if appropriate) are made. Coordinate effort with corporate legal.

4. *Disbursement of Disciplinary and Corrective Action*: Compile results and prepare final report. Provide one copy of report to corporate HR and one copy to corporate legal. Allow corporate HR to decide discipline, and provide input only if requested.

5. *Prevention and Education*: Given what little is known at this time, preventative and educational strategies cannot be formulated now. Upon completion of the third phase of the process as described above input will be provided to corporate security and HR.

Logistics

Confirm composition of investigative team. Ensure corporate legal approves investigative proposal and is available first week of December.

Review current labor contract and recently revised work rules.

Review prior investigation and all 2004 incident reports.

Contact vendor and arrange for covert physical surveillance. Ensure master services agreement is still in force.

Notify corporate security department and request local law enforcement be contacted.

Ensure general manager reviews the investigative proposal and approves budget.

Investment

1. *Preparation and Planning*: No cost.

2. *Information Gathering and Problem Identification*: Estimate $ for research and employee interviews.

Estimate $ for vendor interviews.

Estimate $ for covert surveillance.

Estimate $ to conduct December inventory.

Estimate total investment: $

3. *Verification and Analysis*: No cost. Employee interviews to be conducted by local security personnel.

4. *Disbursement of Discipline and Corrective Action*: No cost. However, replacement workers may need to be hired. Based on facts as now known, three new hires will likely be necessary. Estimated cost: $

5. *Prevention and Education*: Investment unknown at this time.

Return on Investment

Given the amount of the estimated inventory losses as calculated over the past six months, it is estimated that if the investigation achieves its objectives and the losses are stopped, the XYZ Corporation will recover its investment in 45 days. Additionally, a recovery is possible. Vendor #1 has already indicated interest in cooperating and has preliminarily agreed to repay $XXX and contribute $XXX toward the proposed investigation.

Anticipated Questions and Answers

Q. How long will the investigation take?

A. As currently scoped, the project should be completed in less than 21 business days.

Q. Does the organization have any past practices relative to disciplining employees for theft and dishonesty?

A. Yes. Last year two employees were terminated for stealing frozen products, specifically work rule #5. Both employees grieved and their cases went to arbitration. The arbitrator upheld both terminations.

Q. Are there any employee privacy issues that should be considered before proceeding?

A. No. All surveillance will be conducted outside the facility and will be restricted to the motor yard. Currently there is no plan to search employee lockers or work areas.

Note that this investigative proposal is very clear and succinct. The author has clearly laid out his plan and detailed his intentions. He frankly stated potential issues and clearly addressed them. Also notice the confidence this plan exudes. The author has clearly and thoroughly thought through his process and carefully walked the reader (most likely a corporate decision maker) through it from start to finish. He has thoughtfully laid out his intentions and addressed any questions the decision maker might have. Like a fact-finder's report, it is clear, concise, complete, and very professional.

C. Mission Management

One of the key responsibilities of the project manager is mission management. Although the investigation does not have a mission per se, collectively its objectives constitute its mission. By definition, the project manager is the glue that binds the investigative team and drives the investigative process. She is responsible for team communications, report dissemination, and mission accomplishment. She is the person who ultimately gets the job done.

The project manager also is responsible for managing the other team members. Though each member should be a professional in his or her own right, the project manager should ensure that team members' skills are put to proper use and their time used efficiently. Keeping the project moving ahead and the members functioning as a team is demanding. The project manager must have the skills to lead and delegate.

One of the more challenging aspects of the job is managing anxious decision makers. Successful businesspeople are used to having things done when they want them done. Typically, they want things done sooner rather than later. Because workplace investigations by their very nature involve important business issues and possibly the discipline of employees, some cases tend to be emotionally charged. Some cases are at times sensitive merely because of the nature of the matter. For example, allegations of sexual harassment require employers to undertake their investigations in a "timely fashion." Allegations of potential violence or threats against an individual also necessitate some urgency. Decision makers tend to want all investigations to be conducted quickly and usually place a premium on accomplishing the mission swiftly. This is not always a bad thing, but by and large, a quality investigation cannot be rushed. Conducting a proper investigation is similar to baking a cake, merely increasing the oven's temperature does not decrease the baking time. Instead, it ruins the cake. Some investigations are easily ruined by trying to increase the speed of the process. Shortcuts, sloppy work, and haste all make for very poor quality investigations.

Several months ago a client engaged my firm and requested assistance in identifying the writer of several very inappropriate greeting cards sent to the administrative assistant of the firm's president. From the written contents of the cards it was clear the author was either a current or former employee. As is typically the case in these matters, each subsequent missive was incrementally inappropriate and as expected executive management wanted the perpetrator caught and caught quickly. We were able to quickly whittle the suspect pool down to several individuals and hastily started background investigations on them. We also obtained handwriting exemplars from our client and sent them off with the cards to our handwriting expert. In the meantime, another nasty card was received and management was livid. They wanted somebody's head. Against my better judgment they succeeded in talking me into interviewing the three suspected authors. Without the results from our handwriting expert, we interviewed the three and all three denied any knowledge of either the writings or who might be responsible. However, we did not tell the interviewees that the writings in question were in the form of cards. We told our subjects that the president's assistant had received a series of threatening communications that had been handwritten. Two of the subjects assumed the communications were letters and adamantly denied writing the letters. The third interviewee, the VP of finance, told my interviewer he did not write "those cards." Bingo!—but still no admission. Anxious to put the matter to rest, the decision makers went ahead and fired the VP. He, of course, threatened to sue and left with considerable commotion, elevating the decision makers' anxiety even further. Two days later our expert called and reported that she believed beyond any doubt that the VP was in fact the author. Hallelujah! Because evidence gathered after-the-fact is admissible in employment cases, we at least now had something on which to hang our hat in the event he sued. Painfully we also believed that if we had had our expert's opinion before our interview of the VP, we would have likely turned him and obtained an admission.

The VP never sued nor was he ever heard from again. This case demonstrates: (1) regrettably, even experienced professionals like me can sometimes be influenced to make poor decisions, and (2) hastily executed investigations tend to yield poorer results than those that are properly baked.

Tip: Haste makes waste. Investigations that are removed from the oven when only half-baked, usually taste like it.

D. Report-Writing

Report-writing is considered by many shear drudgery. I tend to like it. The more one writes, the more they seem to like it. Regardless of one's preference, report-writing is a necessary function of all fact-finders. In Chapter 3 I describe in detail the preparation of undercover reports. General investigative reports, however, are quite different. Here I will provide the fundamentals of basic report-writing and review what I consider to be the best practices.

Good reports evolve from good notes. Note-taking is a learned discipline. Accurate and complete notes allow the report-writer the ability to write clear, concise, and complete reports. As you will read in Chapter 3, notes frequently become part of the investigative case file and should be retained. One's notes should be written in black ink and be legible. The use of shorthand or symbols is acceptable as long as the note-taker can later accurately decipher his work. Destroying notes after a report has been rendered is not advisable and may lead to questions later regarding the investigator's motives. The same is not so for report drafts. Attorneys will occasionally recommend all drafts be retained. In all the years I have been in practice, I have not once been asked to produce a draft. On the other hand, the request for notes is rather common and should be anticipated.

1. Bulletized Summary Reports

For many years I prepared my reports in narrative form. With practice and considerable diligence one can produce easy-to-read, well-written

Exhibit 4.1   Sample Bulletized Report

Interview of Mr. Erik Spicer
Saturday, August 21, 2004
Mr. Spicer stated:

- He is the Vice President of Finance and has been an employee of Marathon Press ("Marathon") since August of 1983.
- He currently works at the Houston, Texas, office located at [full address].
- Before joining Marathon he worked for Random House as an auditor for approximately fifteen years at its New York headquarters.
- He reports to Mr. Charles L. Davidson, President and C.E.O., and has done so for the past eleven years.
- On Monday, August 16, 2004, he arrived at work at approximately 7:30 a.m. and opened the office for he was the first to arrive (see Exhibit C, Access Control Log dated August 16, 2004).
- Upon entering the business's executive office area in order to go to his office, he noticed Mr. Davidson's office door was open and his desk lamp was on.
- Looking into Mr. Davidson's office expecting to see him, he saw, instead, Ms. Rene Williams at his credenza with what appeared to be a contract file in her hand.

narrative reports. However, narrative reports are tedious and time consuming to write. Narrative reports also tend to lend themselves to inclusion of subject remarks and the occasional conclusion. Alternatively, today most of my reports are in the form of bulletized summations. I have found this format easy to write and easier for my reader to read and use. Exhibit 4.1 contains a sample.

Notice if you will how easy this reads. It is fluid and easily tells the story. Additionally, the reader can quickly and efficiently find and extract what he wants. Also notice that this format eliminates the common redundancies of the typical narrative report such as the subject's name, place, and date. Overwhelmingly my clients have grown fond of this format as well. Moreover, it can be used for nearly any type of investigative report and any type of situation. I strongly recommend you try it if you are currently not using it.

The bulletized summary reports also easily lend themselves to the insertion and use of references, exhibits, and footnotes. Because I like to use footnotes in my reports, the bulletized summary report allows me to quickly insert a few words that otherwise might not fit or flow smoothly in the body of the report. Exhibit 4.2 contains a sample.

Neatly, the footnote allows me to quickly provide additional information and context to what may appear to be an otherwise ordinary piece of information. Footnotes used in this fashion make the report interesting

Exhibit 4.2 Bulletized Report Entry with Footnote

■ Looking into Mr. Davidson's office expecting to see him, he saw instead, Ms. Rene Williams at his credenza with what appeared to be a contract file in her hand.[1]

[1] This is particularly interesting because Ms. Williams has key to neither the executive office area or Mr. Davidson's office. Additionally, record research shows that Ms. Davidson was supposed to be on vacation the entire week of August 16, 2004.

and more readable. Attorneys have used footnotes for years, isn't it about time professional investigators and fact-finders do also?

Bulletized summary reports can be quickly and easily redacted. Redacted reports are sometimes required when providing information to the authorities or others who are not members of the investigative team. In order to protect confidentialities and in some cases privacy, redacted reports are sometimes necessary. Deleting individual bullets or groups of bullets is easy and fast. The same cannot be said when redacting narrative reports.

2. Other Report Formats

Not every type of investigative effort lends itself to the bulleted narrative format. For some activities a simple activity log or journal is very suitable. The physical surveillance report in Exhibit 4.3 is a good example.

This report format is also simple and easy to read. Chronologically, the investigator has recorded what he has observed. Notice also his writing style is crisp and clean. It even has a little snap to it. Through this report and any accompanying videotape or digital images, the reader is provided a clear understanding of exactly what the investigator observed. See Appendix C for a complete version of this surveillance report. You will also find in the appendix section several other interesting report formats you will probably find useful. The determination of which report format to use is largely driven by the type of activity reported upon and the writers personal preference.

Tip: Select a report format that best serves your purpose. Use a format that you find easy to prepare and your customer finds easy to use.

Exhibit 4.3   Sample Surveillance Report

INVESTIGATIVE DETAIL

At approximately 9:45 a.m., two surveillance investigators departed for the subject's residence located at 123 Any Street, Glendale, California.

At approximately 10:31 a.m., investigators #1 and #2 arrived at 123 Any Street, Jane Doe's residence. Investigator #1 established a position one block east of the residence located on Smith Avenue. Investigator #2 was positioned on Jones Street, two blocks west of the residence. From these two positions, we were able to view the garage, the south side of the property, and the front door of the residence.

At approximately 10:49 a.m., Jane Doe was observed exiting her garage in her white Cadillac (CA license plate 2N3249). Jane Doe drove west on Smith Avenue; moving surveillance was initiated by both investigators and cautiously maintained.

At approximately 11:05 a.m., Jane Doe arrived at the General Store located at 43 Doe Street, Glendale, California. Jane Doe exited her vehicle and entered the store.

At approximately 11:29 a.m., Jane Doe was video taped by investigator #2 as she exited the General Store. Jane Doe then entered her vehicle. [11:29:10 a.m.]

Here are a few additional suggestions regarding reports:

■ Ensure every report is clear, concise, and complete. The report should be a stand-alone document that can be read and understood by anyone.

■ Prepare your report so it tells a story. It should have a beginning, a middle (or body), and an ending. Make sure your story is complete and precisely expresses that which is being reported upon.

■ Ensure your report objectively represents your investigative result. Subjective commentary and recommendations, even when appropriate, do not belong in an investigative report.

■ Do not use military time. Other than those with military or law enforcement experience, most people are unfamiliar with military time. It is professionally arrogant to use it when your customer cannot translate it.

■ Do not use law enforcement terminology. Do not use terms such as agent, suspect, perp, busted, or any other form of cop-speak. It is unprofessional and makes for lousy reading.

■ Do not use abbreviations or acronyms unless properly explained.

■ Do not address the subject solely by his or her last name. Address the subject properly in the body of your report and use Mr. and Ms.

- Use footnotes to provide supplemental information or context.
- Use footers on all of your reports. It looks professional and helps identify pages that have been separated from the original document.
- Clearly mark the classification (i.e., COMPANY CONFIDENTIAL; ATTORNEY WORK PRODUCT) on each page of your report.
- Consider writing your reports in the third person, past tense. The use of first person should be reserved for statements, addendums, and affidavits.
- Spell check and proofread all reports before submission.

3. Executive Summaries

Another component of an investigative report is the executive summary. All of the interim and final reports my firm produces include an executive summary. The executive summary is a concise synopsis or snapshot of the entire contents of the report. It might include the identity of the person who requested the investigation and why he or she requested it, who performed the work, and some indication of the overall result. I insist my firm's executive summaries not exceed one page. Exhibit 4.4 shows an example. If you are interested, go to Appendix D and see a complete version of this report.

By holding the report-writer to one page he is forced to be concise, complete, and correct. I know from experience clients and decision makers often haven't the time or inclination to read a comprehensive report. A report produced as the result of a complex fraud or substance abuse investigation can sometimes exceed 1,500 pages. We have produced reports exceeding 3,000 pages. Busy people don't have the time to read a report this size. What's more, large reports are difficult to use. It is hard to find the information one wants in a huge report. Most decision makers want to get to the bottom line. The best way to do it is by way of an executive summary. Respect your reader; include an executive summary in your next investigative report.

4. Recommendations

When providing a service it is customary to offer one's customer recommendations at the completion of a project. In the security industry, providing a recommendation is often the central objective of the assignment. However, relative to workplace investigations, recommendations should be provided only when requested. To do otherwise may increase the customer's exposure by recommending corrective action, which can

Exhibit 4.4   Sample Executive Summary

EXECUTIVE SUMMARY

On December 15, 2003, Mr. John Smith of XYZ Company ("XYZ"), Denver, Colorado, contacted *Business Controls, Inc.,* and requested investigative and consultative assistance in a matter involving alleged employee and vendor misconduct at the newly opened box plant in Anytown, California. According to Mr. Smith, several employees at the Anytown facility alleged the plant manager and his plant superintendent had knowingly authorized contractor overcharging and were engaged in other inappropriate activities, much to the determent of the organization. Mr. Smith also stated that independent financial analysis of the box plant's start-up costs and other indicators (see Exhibit A) suggested something was terribly wrong.

The resultant investigation involved on-site information gathering, employee and contractor interviews, and the detailed analysis of hundreds of records, invoices, purchase orders, and requisitions. During the process, plant manager, Mr. Paul Jones admitted he had accepted personal services from a painting contractor for which he did not pay and authorized the overpayment of several hundred thousand dollars in invoices. His superintendent, Mr. Robert Miller admitted to have accepted $2,200.00 in cash from one contractor (Mr. William Redkin of Handy Services), who himself admitted paying it. Additionally, two other contractors admitted they had overcharged for their services to varying degrees or failed to maintain adequate records to justify their invoices.

The total economic impact and scope of the fiscal misconduct uncovered at the Anytown facility has been impossible to determine. The lack of proper record keeping, internal process failures, and managerial negligence at the location has frustrated any effort to accurately quantify the damage. However, demonstrably the loss exceeds $500,000.00.

---

or may never be taken. For example, suppose your investigation reveals that the subject's crime was largely possible because of inadequate lighting. You then recommend that lighting be improved, but your customer fails to improve it for some reason. Then someone is later assaulted in that same area. The victim, learning of your recommendation, might claim that the attack was preventable because your customer knew the lighting was poor yet did not correct it.

The other aspect of recommendations is that they are subjective. An investigative report should be objective. Co-mingling subjective recommendations within an otherwise objective investigative report makes it difficult to differentiate opinions from facts. Doing so will confuse the reader and possibly diminish the value of the report. Instead, prepare a separate document containing your recommendations. I call this document an after-action report. Exhibit 4.5 contains a sample of an after-action

Exhibit 4.5   Sample After-Action Report

PERSONNEL SCREENING

It is often said that the employees make or break an organization. Consequently, a company's success depends on the quality of its people. No other element more greatly impacts our productivity, competitiveness, and profitability than our people. Effective preemployment screening is the only proven technique to ensure quality people are consistently brought into the organization. In this case, a few of the employees involved in substance abuse and other misconduct should not have been hired.

Recommendations:

■ Review current preemployment drug testing protocols. During the course of the undercover investigation several employees boasted that they were illegal drug users and had beaten the drug test. A qualified clinician should examine the collection site and the laboratory conducting the test. Audit periodically to ensure process meets needs and expectations.

■ Retain the services of a preemployment screening and background investigation firm. Several of the individuals examined during our investigation had criminal histories, including convictions involving violence and substance abuse. Have each candidate thoroughly screened before an offer of employment is made. The background investigation should include at minimum: a seven-year criminal conviction history (examine both felonies and misdemeanors), a driving record history, and a public filing history (notices of default, civil judgments, tax liens/bankruptcies). Check other states where the applicant lived over the past seven to ten years. According to most state highway enforcement agencies, driving histories are the single best place to search for, and identify, a history of substance abuse.

■ During the preemployment interview, ask penetrating questions that reveal the applicant's ability to solve problems, resolve conflicts, and communicate ideas.

■ Have the current employment application reviewed by counsel to ensure it meets current legal standards and asks nothing unlawful. Ensure the application contains an enforceable release of liability and that it provides the necessary protection for conducting background investigations and drug testing.

report. To see a complete version of this report go to Appendix D. Also see Chapter 2 for more information about making recommendations.

Tip: Following your investigation, provide recommendations only if asked. Do not include recommendations in your investigative report. Report your recommendations separately in a stand-alone document. That document is called an after-action report.

E. Electronic Communications

Electronic communications are a growing part of today's workplace. The use of e-mail is nearly universal and as important as the telephone to many organizations. E-mail is efficient, free, and perfectly suited as a communication tool in most workplace investigations. For all of its benefits, e-mail also has some disadvantages:

- It is not secure. Unless precautions are taken, it is subject to potential interception and being read by other people.
- Unwanted distribution is difficult to manage. A recipient may forward e-mail to unauthorized parties if precautions are not taken.
- It is discoverable. In the event of litigation, all electronic communications (and records thereof) exchanged during the investigation may be subject to possible discovery and production.
- Deleted e-mail can often be recovered.

Precautions can be taken to minimize some of these risks. For example, encryption technology can be employed to reduce the potential of unwanted reading of e-mail. Additionally, e-mail retention and management protocols can be established to ensure the timely elimination of unwanted e-mail. A client of mine recently learned the value of such a protocol. According to my client contact, his firm was forced to produce nearly 500,000 e-mails; one copy in both paper and electronic forms.

Electronically transmitting reports is another problem. It is common practice to simply attach a report to an e-mail message. This exposes the report to the same risks described above. Protecting the document with a password or by other means is helpful but by no means a perfect solution. A better solution is to store the report on a secure server with restricted access. A link to the report can be sent via e-mail and upon

Exhibit 4.6   Sample Confidentiality Warning

Every e-mail leaving our offices includes this warning.

> **CONFIDENTIALITY WARNING:** This e-mail is for the confidential use of the intended recipients only and may be protected by the attorney–work product privilege. Any unauthorized review, access, copying, dissemination, distribution, or use of the content of this message/information is strictly prohibited by Federal Law. Attempts to intercept this message or distribute it without authorization are in violation of 18 U.S.C. 2511(1) of the Electronic Communications Privacy Act (ECPA). Fines, imprisonment, and/or civil damages may be imposed for violations.

receipt, the recipient follows the link and uses a user name and password to access the document. My firm uses this technology and our clients are very satisfied with it. Additionally, with a little programming, processes can be established that record when the report was accessed and by whom. Our system additionally tells us if the client has copied or printed the report.

Every e-mail should contain a confidentiality notice. The purpose of the notice is to warn those who view the e-mail that it is indeed confidential and intended only for a particular recipient. Exhibit 4.6 shows the confidentiality warning my firm currently uses.

> Tip: Electronic communications are efficient and economical. However, users of this technology need to take the necessary precautions to protect the communication from interception and unauthorized use.

F.   When and How to Use Outside Resources

Using outside resources to assist with or conduct one's internal workplace investigation is an acceptable practice. Some investigations are too complex to be conducted by resources organic to the organization. Sometimes the use of an external resource is appropriate to ensure fairness and confidentiality. High-profile sexual harassment investigations would fall into this category. Another example would be employee substance abuse where the only investigative solution might be an undercover. Regardless of the issue, sometimes it makes more sense to have someone external to the organization perform the investigation than to expend the time and resources to do it internally. In addition to a cost-benefit analysis, the most important consideration should be whether the organization has the skill and experience necessary to do the job properly.

Employers are frequently tempted to undertake an investigation for which they are not qualified. Driving forces include ego, pride, inadequate budgets, and ignorance. I frequently witness instances where an employer undertakes an investigation and is able to only partially complete it. Without an investigative plan or any sort of process, it just investigates. This is wasteful and frequently counterproductive. Readers who are professional investigators will likely have had assignments that were as much about cleaning up someone else's mess as they were about fact-finding. My firm is frequently engaged after our client has interviewed everyone vaguely associated with the problem and is puzzled why nothing of value was learned. If you are an employer and contemplating undertaking a complex investigation, please consider the following:

- Do you or your organization have the necessary skills and experience to do the job properly?
- Do you have the equipment and technology to do the job properly?
- Do you have an investigative plan and have you committed it to writing?
- Is undertaking an investigation the best use of your time and resources right now?
- Have you properly considered a contingency plan if something goes wrong?
- Is there someone else more qualified or better suited to do the job?

If after answering these questions, you think your organization should still go it alone, then by all means go for it. If you are not a decision maker in your organization and investigations are typically assigned to you, ask your boss these questions. Insist the organization honestly conduct a little self-analysis. Just because the organization has not traditionally used outsiders to assist it with its internal investigations is not a reason to not use someone now.

Selecting the right external resource, however, is not an easy task. In addition to the traditional corporate investigation firms offering such services, today law firms, accounting firms, and HR organizations of all stripes offer investigative services. The task of selecting the right vendor can be challenging and time consuming. Here are a few of the things you should consider when selecting a vendor.

1. Licensing

Most states license those who sell investigative services. In California for example, even HR consultants must have a private investigator license to conduct workplace investigations. Failure to be properly licensed can result in criminal charges against the investigative team, and in some cases the investigative results rendered may even be excluded from evidence at trial.

2. Training

Ensure the vendor selected has the training and skills to do the job properly. The vendor selected should provide professional training and rigorously screen its investigators.

3. Experience

Ensure the vendor as well as the employees they assign to your investigation have the experience necessary to do the job properly. If possible, interview them and demand answers to difficult questions regarding their knowledge and experience with investigations of the type under consideration.

4. Reputation

Reputations vary widely in the industry. Qualified vendors should be well known in the business community and be active in their professional associations. Request references and check them thoroughly. Ask about the firm's litigation and claims experience. A reputation of sloppy work, high-profile lawsuits, and big settlements is undesirable and possibly indicates process deficiencies.

5. Willingness to Testify

A willingness to testify is mandatory. Sometimes that means testifying in court or before an arbitrator. An abject unwillingness to testify demonstrates a lack of experience and professional sophistication—do not hire them.

6. Reports

As you should now recognize, reports are an important part of every investigation. As such, detailed reports should follow all investigative efforts. The information provided in a report should be complete, concise, and correct. Ask for samples and examine them thoroughly before selecting a vendor.

7. Insurance

Not all vendors carry general liability and errors and omissions insurance. However, most states that license investigators require insurance in some form. Bonding is not enough protection. In order to be safe and protect your organization, require the vendor under consideration to provide a Certificate of Insurance naming your organization as an additional insured. Also, ensure the coverage is occurrence, not claims-made.

8. Willingness to Involve the Police

As discussed extensively in Chapter 2, employee prosecution is not always necessary and is complicated and often expensive. As such, the decision to prosecute should be made for business reasons only. However, an experienced vendor knows its limitations and when to involve law enforcement. Ask the vendor to provide law enforcement references. Also ask about its success with criminal prosecution.

9. Attorney Involvement

All professional organizations providing investigative services insist on the involvement of their client's attorneys. The attorney's role as described in some detail in this chapter is an important one and the attorney should play an active role during most of the investigation. Sophisticated vendors know that an attorney will contribute to the smooth running of the investigation and coincidentally protect the vendor's interests as well as the interests of the client.

G. Ethics

According to the *Protection of Assets Manual*, professional ethics are those rules of conduct by which members of a profession regulate their conduct among themselves and with all other persons with whom they deal in their professional capacities.[5] These rules exist in addition to the precepts of ethical and moral conduct that society at large observes and those required by our laws and courts. For any profession to be indeed professional, standards for behavior and conduct, which guide its members, must be recognized. The investigative profession is no exception.

Lawyers have long recognized the need for such guidance. Nearly 100 years ago the American Bar Association published its Canon of Ethics. Today, the Bar's Code of Professional Responsibility offers both ethical guidance and standards for members. The Code provides for strict sanctions, including disbarment in extreme cases, for rule-breakers. The security profession first established rules of professional conduct in 1957. The profession's premier society, the American Society for Industrial Security (recently renamed, ASIS International) promulgated these rules in order to provide guidance to its member and to professionalize the society.[6] These guidelines were revised in 1980, but in their original form they still offer, to some degree, guidance for the professional fact-finder. Here is a loose summary of them:

I. We will endeavor to perform our professional duties in accordance with the highest moral principles.

II. We will direct our concerted efforts toward the support, protection, and defense of liberty and justice for all.

III. We will thwart those that seek to change or destroy our democratic government.

IV. We will strive to strengthen our government through security and conserving resources.

V. We will protect property, employees and assets of our employers.

VI. We will observe strictly the precepts of truth, accuracy, and prudence.

VII. We will respect and protect confidential and privileged information.

VIII. We will promote programs designed to raise standards, improve efficiency and increase the effectiveness of security.

IX. We will work together to achieve our collective objectives.

X. We will strive to work with and assist one another.

More recently, Kitty Hailey, a licensed California investigator, wrote the first published code of ethics for private investigators. Her work, *Code of Professional Conduct: Standards and Ethics for the Investigative Profession,* has been widely acclaimed by the investigative industry, and several trade associations are considering adopting her code. According to her publisher's Web site:

> People come to a private investigator to seek help. Lawyers will use an investigator on cases, a businessman may hire an investigator to investigate fraudulent transactions with his company, or an investigator may be hired by a convicted felon to prove his innocence. The job of the investigator is to provide the necessary assistance in a manner that is both accountable and complete. Nothing, however, stops the unethical practitioner who takes advantage of those for whom he or she works. *Code of Professional Conduct* has been prepared to advance the reputation of the profession and insure that sufficient effort is afforded each client. A majority of the professional investigator associations already invoke a code of ethics. Although similar in many respects, they also vary greatly. Kitty Hailey has compiled, compared, and contrasted the various doctrine of these codes. They have been categorized and restated with emphasis on clarity and simplicity of language.
>
> Many of these international, national, and state ethical codes are individually lacking in content. Together, they are an all-encompassing platform that establishes a level to which the investigator can aspire. The bar is high. But the profession demands the most diligent, honest and professional conduct be afforded those who pay for the services of the investigator.[7]

Hailey's code was written for the professional private investigator and much of it addresses investigator–client relationships. The fundamental theme is honesty, integrity, and truthfulness. Even if you are not a private investigator, I highly recommend you read her book. In the meantime, here is a sample code I think most fact-finders ought to consider:

- ■ Treat all people with respect and dignity.
- ■ Conduct all business with uncompromising honesty and integrity.

- Always remain loyal to your mission and customer.
- Embrace change, diversity, and teamwork.

I think you will agree that these four simple rules can provide most of us the moral compass necessary to negotiate any ethical dilemma. And to be sure, ethical dilemmas will arise. Do not believe that because a situation arises and you have to stop and think and make an ethical choice, you are weak or are ethically challenged. On the contrary, if you never have to think twice or question your choices, you are indeed ethically challenged. Good fact-finders are thinkers and good thinkers examine all the choices. Just because you considered or even thought of an alternative choice does not mean you have a problem with ethics. It is natural to consider the alternative. By the very nature of the fact-finder's work (investigation of the misconduct of others), it is easy to reflect on the alternative. The defect is making the wrong choice.

Years ago while in navy flight school one of my instructors told me, "Always fly like the CO [commanding officer] is in your backseat." I never forgot it. Conduct your investigations like your commanding officer is in your backseat.

Notes

1. L. A. Tyska and J. F. Lawrence, *Investigations: 150 Things You Should Know*, 1st ed. (Woburn, Mass.: Butterworth-Heinemann, 1999), 54.
2. Ibid.
3. Ibid., p. 127.
4. Ibid.
5. *Protection of Assets Manual* (Santa Monica, Calif.: POA Publishing, 2000), 25-1.
6. Ibid., p. 25-3.
7. See http://www.lawyersandjudges.com/productdetails.cfm?PC=1089 (August 22, 2004).

Chapter 5

Legal Challenges and Litigation Avoidance

NOTICE: The information presented in this chapter is not meant as legal advice. It is meant only for educational purposes. Readers in need of legal assistance should seek the advice of competent legal counsel.

From the onset, the fact-finder must be thinking of one destination: the Courtroom, prepared to defend the purpose, scope, and methods of investigation in the courtroom.

A. Jurisdiction over Workplace Investigations

Traditional private sector fact-finders conduct investigations for their employers or contract for a fee to conduct investigations for others. The types of investigations conducted and the legal constraints upon private sector fact-finders are often different from those of public sector investigators acting with police powers. Whereas public sector investigators are primarily concerned with violations of criminal codes, private sector investigators conduct a wider variety of workplace investigations, including internal, administrative, civil, and criminal investigations. These investigations fall under the jurisdictions of various federal and state courts and agencies, and there are a variety of evidentiary tests used in these different proceedings to determine the reasonableness of the investigative processes, the merits of the information gathered, and the justifications for adverse actions taken against employees based upon the investigative outcomes.

1. Jurisdiction

Jurisdiction refers to the authority of a state or federal court to hear a case. In order to preside over a case a court must have both *subject matter* and *in personam* jurisdictions. Subject matter jurisdiction refers to authority over the matter in dispute, and *in personam* jurisdiction refers to authority over the person. For example, assume a warehouse employee who worked for a Jacksonville, Florida, company injured his back at work and pursued a workers' compensation claim. Subsequently, his employer's investigator trespassed upon the employee's property, in Jacksonville, while attempting to video the employee digging a trench in his backyard. If the employee filed suit for $100,000 against the investigator and company for invasion of privacy, he would do so in the Florida courts because they have subject matter jurisdiction over a wrongful trespass committed within the state, and *in personam* jurisdiction over the employee, investigator, and employer. Of course, the courts of other states have neither jurisdiction over the trespass or parties in this case.

The state and federal courts have exclusive jurisdiction over many areas of law and concurrent jurisdiction over areas of mutual interest. Of interest here, the federal courts have jurisdiction over cases involving the federal government, constitution, and laws; and concurrent jurisdiction over civil cases involving state law issues between parties from different jurisdictions (such as states) that involve damages greater than $75,000. Under the doctrine of *pendant jurisdiction,* the federal courts, in the interest of judicial efficiency, may decide cases that involve both state law issues and substantial federal issues when the parties and facts are the same. When deciding state law issues, the federal courts follow the laws of the states. The state courts exercise exclusive jurisdiction over legal disputes involving state law issues regardless of the magnitude of damages when there is no diversity of jurisdiction. State courts also have exclusive jurisdiction over state law issues when there is diversity of jurisdiction and damages are less than $75,000, and concurrent jurisdiction with the federal courts when there is diversity of jurisdiction and damages are greater than $75,000. The vast majority of workplace lawsuits against private-sector fact-finders involve state law issues and are decided in state courts.

Returning to the case study, assume the employee's home was in Georgia rather than Florida and the employee was still seeking $100,000 in damages. Because the requested damages are greater than $75,000, and the plaintiff-employee is from Georgia and the defendant-company is from

Florida, there is now diversity of jurisdiction and the state and federal courts have concurrent jurisdiction. The employee could file the lawsuit in Georgia because it has *in personam* jurisdiction over the employee and store investigator in the state and subject matter jurisdiction over wrongful trespass committed within the state. Or, the employee may elect to file the case with the federal courts. The defendant, if sued in Georgia, may accept the jurisdiction of the Georgia courts or it may file a motion to have the case transferred to the federal courts. If the case is tried in the federal courts, it will apply the law of Georgia to decide the issues.

Jurisdiction also refers to the authority of an agency, board, commission, department, or other public administrative body to initiate, investigate, or review a complaint. Different federal and state administrative bodies have jurisdiction over the conduct of private sector investigators and private employers. For example, the National Labor Relations Board (NLRB) and Equal Employment Opportunity Commission (EEOC), respectively, have the authority to review charges against employers and their agents of unfair labor practices and discriminatory practices. State human rights commissions may also review discrimination complaints. State workers' compensation commissions and unemployment boards routinely analyze the adequacy of evidence derived from workplace investigations when deciding the merits of employee benefit claims. Federal and state labor departments too may investigate claims against employers and factfinders for violating labor codes. Decisions rendered by administrative bodies are subject to judicial review by appropriate federal and state courts.

2. Evidentiary Burdens and Standards

Every federal and state judicial and administrative tribunal has established burdens and standards of proof. Here, burden of proof refers to the duty of a party to present evidence, whereas standard of proof refers to the level of evidence that must be presented to prevail. The elements of proof are the specific facts that must be proven for each cause of action.

In criminal proceedings, for example, the police must show probable cause to obtain a search warrant or make an arrest, and prosecutors must establish guilt of an accused beyond a reasonable doubt. Probable cause means evidence sufficient for a reasonable person to believe a crime has been committed and the suspect committed it. Guilt beyond a reasonable doubt is the highest standard in the judicial system. It means there is certainty in the minds of jurors and judges. The elements that must be proven are those of the alleged crimes as set forth in the penal codes of the jurisdictions.

In order to prevail in a civil case, the plaintiff must establish fault by only a *preponderance of the evidence*. This means when the competing evidence of the parties is weighed it must tilt in favor of plaintiffs. If the evidence tilts the other way, the defendants prevail. The elements of proof are those of the alleged wrongful acts (e.g., invasion of privacy, malicious prosecution) as set forth in the judicial decisions and statutes of the jurisdictions. By understanding the elements of the actions that might be filed against them, discussed throughout this chapter, fact-finders can conduct themselves in an appropriate manner and minimize their liability exposures.

In a discrimination lawsuit there is a *shifting burden of proof*. First, the employee must establish *prima facie* discrimination, which means he is a member of a protected class and adverse employment action was taken against him. Second, the burden then shifts to the employer to show a *legitimate business reason* for the alleged adverse employment action. Thereafter, the burden shifts back to the employee to show by a preponderance of the evidence the reason set forth by the employer is a *pretext* to hide the alleged discriminatory action. For example, assume a company fired a female production employee for suspected theft of company tools. The employee filed a sex discrimination complaint. She alleged she was discharged [the adverse employment action] because of her status as a female [membership in a protected group]. In response, the company introduced testimonial evidence by coworkers who observed her taking the tools. In response, the employee claimed she borrowed the tools. Further, she introduced evidence that male employees routinely took tools home to work on personal projects and they were never disciplined. Was the firing justified or was it really a pretext by the company to cover up discrimination?

Although the evidentiary standards in workers' compensation and unemployment hearings vary by state, the initial burden is generally upon employers to prove employees are disqualified from receiving benefits. One level of proof in some states is *substantial evidence*. This means facts sufficient to support a reasonable conclusion, although others might reach a different conclusion. In workers' compensation hearings, for example, employers in these states are required to provide substantial evidence an injury *did not arise out of and in the course of employment,* the benefits were *procured by fraud,* or some other disqualifying conduct. Similarly, employers need to produce substantial evidence showing *willful misconduct* or *just cause* to disqualify unemployment applicants. Interestingly, parties that lose at the agency level and appeal to the courts often must satisfy higher standards of proof. For example, they may have to prove the agencies' decisions were *clearly erroneous* or *outside their statutory authority*. The reason is the courts give deference to the expertise, interpretation of facts, and decisions of the agencies.

In addition to knowing the burdens and standards of proof necessary when bringing actions, employers and their fact-finders need to know what level of evidence will enable them to successfully defend their conduct. For example, in malicious prosecution lawsuits, fact-finders may defend their actions by showing they acted upon probable cause. They and their employers may defend against discrimination complaints by showing they acted for legitimate business reasons. Parties may defend against defamation lawsuits by showing their comments were privileged and the communication had a legitimate business purpose. Because there are so many different claims that may be raised, many discussed in this chapter, the key issue is that fact-finders understand these claims and understand the burdens and standards the courts and regulatory agencies will impose to evaluate their evidence and their conduct.

3. Multiple Agency and Court Review

It is important to remember that the vast majority of workplace investigations are never contested and therefore are not reviewed by outside agencies and courts. Nonetheless, one cannot forget that any investigation may be subject to review if an aggrieved employee files an administrative complaint or lawsuit. Further, depending upon the facts, a single investigation and resulting disciplinary action may be reviewed by multiple agencies and courts.

Hypothetically, assume a white male, union employee, 47 years of age with 25 years of service, was terminated after a lengthy investigation for theft of company property. Further, the employee was not given notice of nor provided union representation during a confrontational investigative interview. The employer signed a criminal complaint and the ex-employee was found not guilty at his criminal trial. Based upon these facts, the employee could file a union grievance that he was terminated without cause, an unfair labor practice charge that he was not provided union representation, and an age discrimination complaint that the criminal charges were trumped up as a pretext to discharge him. He also might file a claim for workers' compensation benefits for emotional distress suffered when he was unjustly accused, and a separate claim for unemployment benefits on the grounds he did not engage in disqualifying misconduct. Finally, he might sue for false imprisonment, defamation, malicious prosecution, emotional distress, and assault had his interview been conducted improperly.

This is not to say the employee would win any or all of the charges, but the employer and fact-finder would have to respond to each agency and court per the respective charges. In response to the union grievance, the employer would have to convince an arbitrator that it had just cause to terminate. Regarding his right of representation complaint before the NLRB, the employer would need to show it did not violate his right to representation on the grounds the employee never requested representation. Addressing the EEOC issue, the employer would have to prove it had a legitimate business reason to terminate and did not engage in age discrimination. Before the state unemployment board, it would have to establish employee willful misconduct to prove ineligibility to collect unemployment benefits, as well as establish that the misconduct was sufficiently egregious so as to harm the interests of the employer. Regarding the workers' compensation claim, the employer would need to prove any emotional distress suffered was a self-inflicted result of the employee's misdeeds or beyond the scope of statutory protection. To defend against the false imprisonment and assault claims, the employer must prove that it did not detain the employee against his will, nor did its agents do or say anything that constituted assault. It may also need to substantiate that it acted in good faith and had probable cause to sign the complaint to defend against the malicious prosecution claim. Regarding the emotional distress allegation, the employer would need to show it did not act in an extreme and outrageous manner during the investigation, interview, and termination. The actual responses of the fact-finder before the different agencies and courts might range from providing investigative documents to testifying at official hearings and proceedings.

The harsh reality of the situation is that even a simple case may be very complex when all the underlying variables and liabilities are examined. Although few workplace investigations result in administrative complaints and lawsuits, the potential exists in every investigation. Thus, it is imperative that fact-finders understand their rights and duties, respect the rights of those they investigate, and understand the standards and burdens of proof used in the different proceedings.

In conclusion, both federal and state courts and administrative agencies have exclusive and concurrent jurisdictions over various aspects of workplace investigations. Investigators, in order to perform their duties effectively, should become familiar with the courts and agencies that have jurisdictions over their investigations and learn about the different burdens and standards of proof. To do otherwise is unprofessional and potentially expensive.

TIP: To maximize effectiveness and to minimize liability of an investigation, a fact-finder must understand the burdens and standards of proof of the agencies and courts for the jurisdiction.

B. Preparatory Legal Considerations

From a liability risk management perspective the "preparation and planning phase" of an investigation is a critical stage. It is the foundational stage; if not properly set, there is a greater probability the investigation may not achieve its objectives, but will waste time and resources. As a review, the following critical issues should be, at a minimum, addressed during this phase: (1) the legal duty to investigate, (2) investigator selection, (3) investigative objectives, (4) evidentiary burdens, and (5) documentation controls.

1. The Legal Duty to Investigate

One of the first issues an employer should address is to determine whether it has a legal duty to conduct the intended workplace investigation. In most circumstances, the decision to investigate employee misconduct in the workplace is left to the discretion of the employer. The underlying reason is that the victim of the misconduct in the majority of cases is indeed the employer. Whether the loss is of a type or magnitude that concerns the employer sufficiently enough to allocate resources to investigate is a business decision left to the discretion of the employer based upon its calculation of return on investment (ROI), as discussed elsewhere in this book.

There are circumstances, however, where an employer may have a legal duty to investigate employee misconduct. That is, in these cases the decision to investigate is no longer discretionary. A duty to investigate, for discussion purposes here, may arise from statutes and regulations, contracts with employees, and common law duty to properly screen and supervise employees.

First, for example, a few statutes and regulations impose a duty upon most employers to investigate under limited circumstances. Civil rights laws prohibit various forms of workplace discrimination. This general duty includes a secondary duty to conduct thorough and timely investigations of harassment complaints by employees.[1] Also, the general duty clause of the Occupational Health and Safety Act (and similar clauses under state plan programs) requires employers to maintain an environment "free from recognized hazards that are causing or are likely to cause death or serious physical harm to his employees."[2] If an employee demonstrates a propensity toward violence and the employer fails to investigate, the employer might be cited for violation of the general duty clause if the employee later injures another. In a situation where the organization is the alleged perpetrator, for example, defrauding the government or investors, and is facing criminal prosecution in federal court, under the Federal Sentencing Guidelines the court may reduce the severity of its penalty if the employer investigated the alleged misconduct in a timely manner.[3]

Further, employers in certain regulated industries have a duty to investigate specific types of incidents. For example, healthcare providers must investigate cases of patient abuse; pharmaceutical companies must investigate missing controlled substances; financial institutions must report certain financial transactions, losses, and irregularities; and officers and boards of public trade corporations now have a greater duty to ensure the accuracy of their financial statements.

Second, employers have an implicit duty to conduct reasonable inquiry when investigating suspicious behavior of union and other not-at-will employees. Union and personal contracts of employment usually contain clauses that stipulate discipline, and termination must be based upon *cause, just cause, good cause,* or other similar standards. These contracts place the burden upon employers to produce sufficient evidence to sustain the appropriate disciplinary actions. Implicit in this condition is the requirement of a reasonable investigation. Failure to do so may leave an employer in a position where it loses a grievance hearing or breach of contract lawsuit because it cannot meet its contractual evidentiary burden.

Third, many courts recognize common law claims of negligent hiring and negligent supervision. Negligent hiring occurs when an employer hires an untrustworthy employee into a position of trust and the employee subsequently injuries another. A position of trust is one where others are highly dependent upon the employee to perform his duties in a reasonable and safe manner. Negligent supervision occurs when an employer has or should have knowledge that an employee is unfit for duty or for performing his duties in an unsafe manner. For example, allowing an intoxicated employee to operate a company vehicle or failing to properly intervene when an employee threatens another may expose employers to liability based upon their failure to investigate further and take appropriate remedial measures.

In *Salinas*, the Supreme Court of Texas affirmed a taxi company could be held liable for the negligent hiring of a taxi driver who was screened by the police.[4] The police check failed to reveal the employee had committed multiple felonies. The driver sexually assaulted a female customer. Because of the high trust customers place in taxi drivers, the company was held to an ultrahigh duty of care in hiring and was not permitted to shift its responsibility and liability to the police. In *Saine*, the Supreme Court of Arkansas held a cable company could not be sued for negligent hiring but could be sued for negligent supervision and retention.[5] The company hired a cable installer who brutally sexually assaulted and attempted to murder a customer in her home. The company did check with two past employers, verified he had an honorable military discharge, and administered a drug test prior to hiring. But, the company did not follow up on an earlier female customer's complaint that the employee made sexual advances and her allegation that he left windows unlocked and later attempted to break into her home.

In *Yunker*, the defendant company rehired a man who had spent five years in prison for the murder of another employee (the circumstances of this case were never set forth).[6] He was twice transferred to new facilities after he had some encounters with co-workers. At the last facility, he was terminated for threatening a female subordinate. He murdered her a few days later in her front yard. The Appeals Court of Minnesota affirmed the dismissal of the negligent hiring claim on the grounds it would undermine the public policy of rehabilitation to find an employer was negligent for hiring a felon. But, it reinstated the family's negligent retention claim.

In conclusion, the decision to investigate must be made based upon a determination of whether the employer owes a legal duty to investigate or, in the absence of a legal duty, on a determination of ROI as discussed elsewhere in the text.

2. Investigator Selection

The selection of the right investigator(s) is critical. The investigator and his team should have a combination of experience, education, and continuing professional development sufficient for the level of sophistication of the investigation. An experienced individual, with a successful record of prior investigations of similar nature and complexity, is more likely to appreciate the time and resources necessary to complete the project properly; be more familiar with the appropriate agencies and courts that may review the investigative process; and possess more insight as to the legal duties owed, standards of proof required, and overall liability risks. This is not to say that employers cannot call upon less experienced investigators, for it may be very appropriate to use less seasoned investigators so long as they are properly supervised. Selection of an investigator or investigative team, either employee or outside contractor, is an important decision that employers should make with care.

a. Liability for Employee Investigator Misconduct

What is the liability of an employer for the misconduct of its investigator? Under the *doctrine of respondeat superior,* a principal is vicarious liable for the actions of its agent that are committed within the scope of employment or engagement. An employer-employee relationship is a principal-agent relationship as the employer has control over the methods of work and performance outcomes. An employee-investigator conducting a workplace investigation on behalf of the company is an agent of the company, and the employer may be held liable for any misconduct.

b. Liability for Contract Investigator Misconduct

A contract investigator is in most cases an independent contractor of the client principal. An independent contractor does work for a principal, and the principal controls the performance outcome. However, unlike with an agent, a principal does not exercise the same degree of control over the methods of performance. An independent contractor performs the work according to its methods or the methods of its trade or profession. Under the *independent contractor rule,* a principal is not liable for the conduct of the independent contractor on the premise the principal does not exercise substantial control over the contractor's methods.

For example, in *Paradora*, the plaintiff, a worker on disability benefits, sued an insurance company for the alleged verbal abuse of investigators working for the private investigative firms it retained to conduct routine activities checks.[7] The Appeals Court of Massachusetts affirmed the insurance company was not liable for conduct of the independent investigators because the insurance company:

> provided no instruction or protocol to … the investigators as to the manner it wanted work on its behalf conducted … did not supervise the … investigations or ask for amplification of reports that were filed by … the investigators … and the investigators billed the agencies that hired them, not CNA (the Defendant), and were paid by those agencies … the conclusion compelled by the evidence is that CNA contracted out work to them when needed and left to them the manner and means.

However, a principal may be held liable for the acts of an independent contractor if the principal retains control over the contractor in the contract for service or actively exercises control over the activities of an independent contractor. A principal might also be held liable if it knows the contractor is engaged in misconduct and ratifies this conduct by not taking appropriate action to stop further similar conduct. In *Greenbaum*, when interviewing an employee suspected of theft, a private investigator placed his chair in front of the door in the manager's office, twice told the employee he could not leave, and even once shoved him back into the chair.[8] The Court of Appeals of Georgia, in affirming a judgment for false imprisonment against the company, noted the defendant could be held liable for the conduct of the investigator on the grounds the "defendants actually exercised a power of direction and control over the interrogator at the time of plaintiff's detention." Specifically, the court commented on the fact noted that the store manager and investigator had planned the interrogation together, and it was the manager who had determined when it was over.

c. Contractual Shifting of Liability Risk

As a means of managing liability risks, principals and independent contractors may include certain provisions in the contracts for service. For example, a contract may require the independent contractor to carry a specified amount of general liability, errors and omission, or other insurance coverage. Further, the principal may require proof of insurance and notification of cancellation. Either party may require the other to indemnify the other for any third-party claims and lawsuits arising out of performance of the contract. If there is a dispute over proper performance of the contract, the parties may stipulate the maximum damage exposure to each other. From the perspectives of the employer and contract investigator, the more clearly the roles, objectives, and risks are defined at the beginning of the relationship the more probable the investigative process will be conducted in a reasonable and professional manner.

3. Investigative Objectives

The investigative objectives set the focus and tenor of an inquiry. The objective of an investigation is not to get the money or the suspect, to show who runs the business, or to make an example of the suspect. In *Kelley*, for example, the Massachusetts Court of Appeals, in affirming a $36,000 judgment for abuse of process against a company, was not impressed with the company investigator, who testified "his job was to make sure he got the ninety-six dollars and nine cents."[9] This and similar statements are the antithesis of a professional investigation and set the stage for unnecessary liability.

The objectives of an investigation must be lawful in purpose, scope, and methods. An employer should have a clear, legitimate business purpose for launching a workplace investigation. The scope of the inquiry, too, should be limited to the legitimate purpose of the investigation. The methods of investigation must also be lawful. For example, while an employer may have a right to conduct criminal background checks on job applicants, a decision to investigate the criminal backgrounds of only minority applicants is a discriminatory and unlawful purpose. Similarly, during an undercover investigation into suspected employee on-the-job illegal drug use, it may be within the scope of the investigation to observe and report on suspect union employee involvement, but it would clearly be outside the scope of the investigation to also report on their lawful union activities. Finally, the philosophy "the ends justify the means" is not acceptable. The methods of inquiry must be reasonable. Employers may have the right to conduct investigative interviews with their employees, but regardless of how serious the offense it would be clearly unlawful to physically or coercively detain the employees against their will in order to interview them.

Tip: A professional workplace investigation is a tool. It is a lawful inquiry, reasonable in scope and methods, conducted by a qualified individual or team to systematically identify, collect, and document material evidence about a legitimate workplace concern. Like most tools, a workplace investigation is something that should never be misused.

---

4. Identifying Standards of Proof

Inherent in the issue of determining the investigative objectives is identifying the applicable burdens and standards of proof to be placed upon the process. For example, if an organization's investigation is noncriminal in nature, it makes little business sense to devote extra resources necessary to achieve the criminal burden of proof beyond a reasonable doubt. As noted earlier, a decision to terminate a union employee may, depending upon the language of the bargaining agreement, be satisfied by showing cause, just cause, or good cause. If an employee files a claim for unemployment benefits, the company may prove ineligibility by merely establishing the employee's willful misconduct. The key point is that at the beginning of an investigation, the employer should be cognizant of the standards and burdens of proof that it may need to prove: to bring an action against the employee and to defend its conduct should the employee later make a claim against it. One overlooked and sometimes costly risk in this process is an employer will assume a higher standard of proof than necessary to achieve the legitimate objectives of the business.

For example, assume a manufacturer receives an anonymous tip on its hotline that a few employees at a small facility are taking inventory from the plant after hours. It is a violation of company policy to be on site during non-operating hours without authorization. It is also a violation to remove property without authorization. The manufacturer conducts a routine inventory audit and discovers an unexplained 10 percent inventory variance at one of its small plants. The company president tells the corporate security manager to investigate. When asked, he states he does not want to prosecute the employees. The security manager contracts with an experienced licensed private investigator in that state to conduct video surveillance of the plant after hours. Three days later, the investigator provides video evidence of three persons entering the plant after hours and removing several cartons. All three are readily identifiable as employees. Their duties do not entail being on site after hours nor the removal of property. Herein lies the issue, should the company spend further funds to gather more video evidence, to track the property removed, to catch the employees in the act, and to prove employee theft beyond a reasonable doubt? Or, should the company cease the video surveillance, interview the employees to verify their unauthorized presence and removal of boxes, and terminate them for violation of company policy? An intelligent response to this situation can only be made if the fact-finder understands the legitimate intent of the president and applicable burdens and standards of proof necessary to protect the interests of the company should the employees file wrongful discharge and other civil actions, or seek unemployment benefits.

5. Documentation Control

Almost every investigation will produce some records even if it is as simple as a note on a calendar about a call from a concerned employee or verbal disciplinary meeting with an employee. Records produced during workplace investigations and resulting disciplinary actions are often discoverable during administrative and judicial proceedings. This includes notes on calendars, field notes, e-mail messages, investigative reports, conference notes, disciplinary actions, and other documents produced as the result of the investigation, disciplinary action, and postinvestigative analysis. Proper documentation control procedures for creating, labeling, copying, tracking, distributing, and retaining investigative documents should be established. Without such ground rules there are risks. Documentation may be produced that is immaterial or even harmful to an investigation; investigative documents may be inadvertently intermixed with other records and create problems locating and editing them when requested in litigation; vital evidence may not be properly documented; sensitive information may be too broadly distributed; and critical documents may be lost. Ideally, documentation controls should be established before any specific investigation and reviewed in the preparation and planning phase. In the alternative, ground rules should be established in this phase before the information and fact-finding phase begins.

6. Confidentiality

It is a recommended practice in the planning stage of an inquiry to remind all of the participants, especially those who do not normally participate in investigations, that the information uncovered and discussed is to remain confidential, shared with only those who need to know in performance of their duties. The accidental exposure of an employer's investigation or investigative results is almost always undesirable. If employees become aware of critical information or investigation before its completion and some form of formal communication by management, it may adversely impact morale and productivity. Customers or suppliers may also feel resentful of having been a part of the investigated activity and may choose to discontinue their relationship or patronage. Public exposure of a compromised investigation may spark resentment, an onslaught of painful adverse publicity, and law suits. The failure to timely remind all parties, at the outset and throughout the inquiry, of their duty to retain confidentiality can only harm the investigative process and enhance the liability risks.

C. Information Gathering and Fact-Finding Considerations

The confluence of federal and state laws, regulations, and judicial decisions makes the information gathering and fact-finding phase the most dynamic and complex, and the highest risk phase of the investigation. Fact-finders must be sensitive and responsive to a complex mixture of constitutional, administrative, civil, and criminal laws that proscribe behavior, standards, and burdens of proof. Uninformed fact-finders may unduly restrict their methods of investigation, expend unnecessary time and resources to achieve an unnecessary standard of proof, or engage in high-risk conduct that increases their employers', their clients', and their own personal liability exposure. The next several sections address fact-finding liability concerns in more detail.

D. Constitutional Considerations

The Fourth Amendment of the U.S. Constitution guarantees "The right of the people to be secure in their persons, houses, papers, and effects, against unreasonable searches and seizures." The Fifth Amendment guarantees the right against self-incrimination, and the Sixth Amendment provides the right of legal counsel in criminal proceedings. Under the *exclusionary doctrine*, evidence obtained in violation of these constitutional rights may be ruled inadmissible in criminal proceedings. Employers and employees are often confused about the constitutional protections afforded employees during workplaces searches and investigations. Employees often believe they enjoy constitutional protections against workplace searches and are entitled to be advised, based upon the landmark U.S. Supreme Court decision in *Miranda*, of their constitutional rights to remain silent and to have legal counsel present when interrogated.[10] Collectively these rights among others constitute the right of *due process*. Employers, on the other hand, are frequently uncertain whether they are bound by the prohibitions of the Constitution and precisely whether due process rights should be afforded a suspect employee.

The federal and state courts (which are obligated to abide by the decisions of the federal courts in this area of law) have been petitioned by numerous criminal defendants to apply federal constitutional rights to private sector investigatory matters. The courts have consistently held that there must be *state action* (government involvement or entanglement) to invoke the protections of the Constitution. As a rule, private parties are not viewed as state agents nor is their conduct viewed as state action. The courts, under most circumstances, view corporate and private investigators as private parties engaged in private actions.

1. Self-Incrimination

In *Antonelli*, a contract security officer searched the car of a dock worker and found stolen imported merchandise worth thousands of dollars.[11] The employee made several self-incriminating statements at the scene. He was convicted at trial and appealed the use of the self-incriminating statements to the security officer. The appeals court stated:

> there was no governmental knowledge or instigation of, influence on, or participation in any of the actions surrounding the taking of appellant into custody, which produced the statements unsuccessfully sought to be suppressed prior to trial ... the Fifth Amendment privilege against self-incrimination does not require the giving of constitutional warnings by private citizens or security personnel employed thereby who take a suspect into custody.

The U.S. Court of Appeals affirmed the admission of the incriminating statements and the conviction.

Similarly, in *Green*, an employee made several incriminating statements when "interrogated" by a company investigator without being advised of his constitutional rights. He objected to the use of the statements at his criminal trial.[12] The Court of Common Pleas of Pennsylvania noted:

> The overwhelming authority from other jurisdictions supports the position that "Miranda" warnings need not be given by a private security officer prior to questioning a suspect taken into custody. This Commonwealth has never squarely decided the issue. "We believe ... the guarantees of the Fifth Amendment are intended as limitations upon governmental activities and not on private individuals," thus the "Miranda" warnings need not be given by persons other than governmental officials or their agents.

2. Search and Seizure

In *Simpson*, a union employee refused to open his lunchbox for a routine search by plant security at the end of the workshift.[13] He was resultantly suspended. He requested unemployment benefits for the time of his suspension. The referee granted him benefits on the grounds he had "good cause" to refuse the search based upon his belief the search violated his federal and state constitutional rights against unreasonable searches. On review, the full board reversed the decision and the employee appealed. The Commonwealth Court of Pennsylvania rejected the circuitous logic of the employee who argued the board's denial of benefits was "state action" because it deprived him of his constitutional right against unreasonable search. The court stated:

> It is firmly settled that the Fourth Amendment of the United States Constitution applies only to the actions of governmental authorities, and is inapplicable to the conduct of private parties. ... The same is true of the search and seizure provision in the Pennsylvania Constitution. ... It follows, then, that the right the claimant seeks to establish against his employer, a private entity, is not a right that arises from the constitutional provisions.

The court affirmed the employer's search did not violate either the federal or state constitution.

When acting as private parties in private matters private sector investigators are not engaged in state action and thus are not governed by the constitutional prohibitions against unreasonable searches, self-incrimination, and right to counsel. But, there are exceptions to this general rule.

3. Joint Action and Public Function Exceptions

The courts have stated a private party may be held to constitutional standards when acting jointly with a public party to perform a public function. Hypothetically, assume a fact-finder had uncorroborated information that an employee was dealing drugs out of his company locker. Now consider two alternative scenarios. First, assume the fact-finder, per company policy, directed the employee to open the locker and found what were later to be proven to be controlled substances. The fact-finder then conducted an investigative interview, never advised the employee of his constitutional rights, and the employee provided a full admission. The fact-finder called the police to the facility and turned over the drugs and the details of the signed admission. In the second alternative, assume the fact-finder called the police and together they opened and searched the employee's locker and found the suspected drugs. The fact-finder and detective jointly interviewed the employee, never advised the employee of his constitutional rights, and he admitted the drugs were his. In this alternative, will the drugs and confession be admissible at the employee's criminal trial? How would a court make this determination? One way is to look at the level of government knowledge and involvement before and during the time, and to look at the motives of the private party.

In the first alternative, the government was unaware of and played no role in the search or subsequent interview. Further, the company fact-finder acted to protect the interests of the employer. His turning the evidence over to the police did not make him a state actor or agent. Therefore, there is no government action and the evidence and admission should be admissible. In the second scenario, the government played a very direct and active role in both the search and interview that followed. Also, although the investigator was acting to protect the interests of the employer, it appears that he was concurrently acting in a public capacity. Because the fact-finder was an active participant and effectively acting as an agent of the government, there is a significant probability that many courts would apply constitutional prohibitions when evaluating the admissibility of evidence under the second scenario.

Note, there is a difference between the police directing or participating in workplace searches and interviews versus being apprised of lawful private sector investigations or standing by as witnesses.[14] Private sector investigators also need to recognize that there is an enhanced probability, but not certainty, that their conduct may be subject to constitutional prohibitions if they are off-duty police working security or have special police commissions.[15]

Tip: Fact-finders, as private parties engaged in private action, are not normally subject to federal constitutional prohibitions. But, these prohibitions might apply if they have special police commissions or are off-duty police officers working security.

As discussed later, the proper remedy for unreasonable searches by private parties is a civil suit for invasion of privacy. Similarly, if an employee is unable to leave an interview conducted by a fact-finder, the appropriate remedy is a civil suit for false imprisonment.

4.   State Constitutional Issues

A state constitution may set forth similar prohibitions to the federal constitution regarding unreasonable search and seizures, and the right against self-incrimination.[16] The states almost universally follow the lead of the federal courts in requiring state action to invoke these protections.[17] However, a state Supreme Court may interpret a state constitution as granting greater rights than provided under the federal constitution. For example, in evaluating whether to suppress the admissions and evidence obtained from a shoplifting suspect after he had requested to talk with a lawyer and refused to waive his constitutional rights, in *Muegge,* the Supreme Court of Appeals of West Virginia found the state shoplifting detention law vested private merchants with state powers.[18] It stated: "[W]e find that the security guard was not acting in a purely private fashion, but under the mantle of state authority and that, therefore, the protections of ... the West Virginia Constitution apply to her dealings with the appellant."

Three states have held private security personnel acting under merchant detention statutes were vested with state power. But, two of the three have since reversed their stance. There is debate whether the remaining state, West Virginia, has or has not.[19] Nonetheless, workplace searches and employee interviews are not normally conducted under specific state statutory authority and are not viewed as state action.

It should also be noted that a few state constitutions provide a specific right of privacy. As shown in the following examples, this right may be worded independently of or incorporated in the state prohibition on unreasonable search and seizure. Here are two examples.

California Constitution, Article I, §1

All people are by nature free and independent, and have certain inalienable rights, among which are those of enjoying and defending life and liberty; acquiring, possessing, protecting property; and pursuing and obtaining safety, happiness, and privacy.

Hawaii Constitution, Article I, §5

The right of the people to be secure in their persons, houses, papers and effects against unreasonable searches, seizures and invasion of privacy shall not be violated.

An important issue in the few states that recognize a state constitutional right of privacy is whether it protects against both unreasonable government and private party intrusions. In *Hill* a collegiate diver challenged the National Collegiate Athletic Association drug-testing program on the grounds it violated her state constitutional right of privacy.[20] The Supreme Court of California affirmed that the provision applied to intrusions by private parties because the constitution has been amended, in part, to protect against businesses collecting and misusing personal data. It adopted a shifting burden test to determine if the invasion was unreasonable. First, the plaintiff must show a legally protected privacy interest, a reasonable objective expectation of privacy under community norms, and a serious breach of that privacy. The burden then shifts to the defendant to establish it had a legitimate competing interest or justification for the intrusion. The burden then shifts back to the plaintiff to show a less intrusive means available to achieve the competing interest. Applying this test, the court ruled the NCAA had a legitimate interest in requiring college athletes to submit to drug testing and the program was not unreasonably intrusive because it contained many procedural safeguards. The exact effect of this decision on workplace investigations in unknown, in part, because the objective expectations of privacy in the workplace might be somewhat reduced. Nonetheless, of relevance here, fact-finders need to be aware of and sensitive to investigate procedures that may violate an applicable state constitutional right of privacy.

E. Federal Law and Employee Rights

The U.S. Congress has enacted several labor laws in order to reduce labor strife and promote national economic welfare. Of special interest here, the National Labor Relations Act (NLRA) guarantees employees the right to engage in "concerted activities" that foster labor organization and collective bargaining.[21] The NLRA defines and prohibits "unfair labor practices" by employers and unions, and vests the National Labor Relations Board (NLRB) with authority to receive complaints, investigate, hear, and decide alleged violations under the statute.[22] The Labor Management Relations Act (LMRA) places exclusive jurisdiction over labor disputes in the federal courts.[23] State courts are preempted from deciding disputes that fall under the jurisdiction of the NLRB. Rulings of the NLRB may be appealed to the federal appellate courts.

1. Unfair Labor Practices

The NLRB has identified two broad workplace investigative practices it considers unfair labor practices, under section 8(a), that are in violation of employee rights, as set forth in section 7 of the NLRA. Specifically, section 7 guarantees employees the "right to self-organization, to form, join, or assist labor organizations, to bargain collectively through representatives of their own choosing, and to engage in other concerted activities for the purpose of collective bargaining or other mutual aid or protection." These practices deal with the employees' right of union representation during disciplinary hearings and employer investigations into protected concerted activities.

2. Union and Coemployee Representation

The landmark case affecting workplace interviews is *Weingarten*.[24] It is based upon an unusual set of factual coincidences. Here is what happened. Based upon a report that a food counter employee was stealing cash, a company investigator, without advising store management, watched the food service operation for two days. He observed no thefts. The investigator introduced himself to the store manager and told him of his investigation. Coincidentally, the manager stated another employee just reported the suspect had just paid only $1.00, the price of a small box of chicken, for a $2.98 large box of chicken. The investigator interviewed the suspect employee. Her requests for a union steward to be present were denied. The investigator confirmed her explanation that the company was out of small boxes and that she had used a large box for her order. He apologized for any inconvenience and prepared to leave. The employee then started to cry and spontaneously said the only thing she had ever taken were her free lunches. She had been with the company for approximately eleven years and had worked nine of those years at a store that provided free lunches. The last two years she had worked at a new store that by company policy did not provide free lunches. The investigator began to question her further and calculated she owed about $160 for lunches she had taken. Her requests for a union steward to be present were denied in this session too. The investigator ended his investigation after he checked with the corporate office and could not verify the no free lunch policy had ever been communicated to the employees at the current store. The investigator and store manager told her the matter was closed; no disciplinary action was taken against her, and she was asked not to discuss the matter with anyone. A short while later she revealed the entire matter to a union representative. The union, concerned about the chain of events, filed an unfair labor practice complaint on the grounds the employer had refused her requests for a steward to be present during the interviews. The NLRB held that union employees upon their request are entitled to union representation during interviews that they reasonably believe might lead to discipline. The denial of this representation was an unfair labor practice. On appeal the U.S. Court of Appeals disagreed and reversed the decision.

The case was appealed. On appeal, the U.S. Supreme Court affirmed the NLRB decision that union employees are entitled upon request to union representation during investigative interviews that they reasonably believe might lead to discipline. The Court found, however, a fact-finder is not bound to advise the union member of this right. If the employee requests and insists upon representation, the investigator may advise the employee that the interview may be discontinued. The employee may waive this right and participate in the meeting without representation, or forgo the interview and the opportunity to present his side of the matter. The Court said that in such circumstances, the employer is free to continue its investigation, with or without the interview, and to take appropriate disciplinary action based upon the information it is otherwise able to derive. The Court also said if an interview is conducted with a representative present, the interviewer is not obligated to bargain with that representative, and that the role of the representative is to assist the employee but not to answer the questions.

However, the role of the representative in not one of a "passive observer." In *Pacific Telephone and Telegraph*, the NLRB ruled it was an unfair labor practice for the company to not advise two employees, who were to be disciplined for the unauthorized installation of a telephone in one's home, and their union steward the purpose of the meeting after they requested to know before it was conducted.[25] Further, the court held it was an unfair labor practice to deny the employees and steward (and two other employees and steward in a companion case) a preconference meeting once a steward requested it. The request did not have to come directly from the employee. But, in *Southwest Bell* the U.S. Court of Appeals held the right of representation was not violated when a union steward was asked not to interfere with the questioning but was permitted to consult with an employee before the investigatory meeting and was free to make comments, suggestions, and clarifications after the interview.[26]

By permitting union representation in investigatory interviews while restricting the role of the union representative, the NLRB and courts are attempting to balance the right of employees to engage in concerted activities for mutual protection with the right of the employers to investigate and to take reasonable measurers to protect their properties and businesses.

Before concluding this section, it should be noted the right of non-union employees to coemployee representation can quickly change. In 2000 the NLRB ruled non-union employees were entitled to coworker representation; the U.S. Court of Appeals upheld this decision in 2001; but in 2004 the NLRB reversed its position and returned to the long standing view the right of representation did not extend to non-union employees. Since this is not the first time the NLRB has briefly flirted with granting non-union employees a right of coemployee representation, fact-finders should note the NLRB often reflects the labor policy of the president and this issue might arise again when changes in administration occur.[27]

Tip: While non-union employees are generally not entitled to coemployee representation, employers should contemplate such request during the planning and preparation phase. Refusing representation can be risky. It can raise other issues about motive, methods, and trust. If it is granted, there are other issues. Is it a coemployee of choice? What if the coemployee is also a suspect? What is the role of the coemployee? These are decisions best answered before raised in an interview.

---

3. Investigations into Protected Concerted Activities

The NLRB and the courts fully recognize the right of employers to take reasonable measures to protect their businesses and to investigate suspicions of misconduct by all employees, but such investigations may not include overly broad or intrusive surveillances, interviews, undercover operations, and other investigative inquiries that infringe upon or "chill" the employees' rights to organize, collectively bargain, and engage in other protected concerted activities.

In *Parsippany*, the U.S. Court of Appeals concurred a hotel had a "legitimate business interest" in protecting its guests, however, it affirmed that it was an unfair labor practice for an employer during a labor organization drive to beef up its security staff and then have those officers conduct surveillance in the workplace on the employees that advocated the union.[28] In *Unbelievable,* the U.S. Court of Appeals affirmed it was an unfair labor practice when the chief of security eavesdropped on a conversation between an employee and union representative talking in a break room that was an authorized area for visits.[29] Further, it was an unfair practice when the employer expelled the representative based upon what was overheard.

When employees engage in protected organizational and protest activities, the documenting of these activities by video recording of participants may be viewed as an unfair labor practice to coerce or intimidate employees from exercising their rights. When those activities include threats, vandalism, violence, or other unlawful activities, employers are justified in enhancing surveillance activities. But, enhanced surveillance activities should not focus on or be overly inclusive of lawful activities of union members.

In *Horsehead Resource Development Company*, the company, based upon volatile contract negotiations and in anticipation of a lockout or strike, installed a camera at its front gate and in two vehicles that were used for interior patrols.[30] The evening after the last negotiation session, the hotel where the company negotiators were staying received a bomb threat. Later that evening the plant mysteriously lost its power and lights on two occasions, and the old office trailer was set on fire. On the first day of the lockout the company discovered several acts of sabotage and a drawing of a rifle scope aimed at a man labeled "Yankee Scab." The front gate camera was left on the first day and thereafter it "was turned on whenever company personnel ... crossed the picket line to enter or leave the plant." After someone attempted to run a manager off the road, the cameras in the vehicles were used during the escorting of the shuttle vans between the plant and hotel. These cameras were also used to observe union members who were peaceful and off company property as "they parked their cars, gathered to talk in the shade, or moved to and from the picket shack and the portable restroom."

The cameras also documented acts of:

Misconduct on the part of four employees that was sufficiently serious to justify their discharge. [The misconduct involved placing "jackrocks" (six-pronged objects constructed from bent nails) and roofing nails in the road to puncture tires, using a slingshot to shoot ball bearings at a truck and through the windshield of a car, and spitting in the face of a security guard as he drove through the picket line.]

The union filed unfair labor charges against the company for its use of the cameras. The U.S. Court of Appeals held:

It was clearly not an unfair labor practice to photograph the four miscreants. Likewise, the videotaping of company vehicles crossing the picket line and the use of camera cars to patrol the plant perimeter and escort replacement employees did not interfere with employees' protected concerted activity. These were justified precautions against potential violence.

For the most part, however, the picketing seems to have been peaceful. To the extent that the Board's finding of an unfair labor practice was based on surveillance that went beyond videotaping the access to front gate, the plant perimeter and the company cars, we conclude that it was supported by substantial evidence. The surveillance of union members who were in no way engaged with company personnel or property, but were merely talking among themselves or moving to and from the picket shack and the portable restroom, was unjustified. We are satisfied that it was within the Board's province to find that [the company] went too far in its surveillance.

In *California Acrylic Industries* the U.S. Court of Appeals held it was an unfair labor practice for an employer to videotape a lunch hour meeting between employees and union representatives talking on a public sidewalk.[31] Allegedly, the company felt "something might happen" and videotaped to protect against possible union vandalism and trespass. The court affirmed this was insufficient justification in light of the chilling effect of videotaping upon employees in the exercise of their protected rights.

In *National Steel and Shipbuilding Co.*, the company placed a camera on a tripod on top of a building to monitor a gate and large parking lot where the unions, which were working without a contract, conducted rallies every morning with about 100 persons present.[32] The company monitored these rallies for approximately four months. Even though there were three to four security officers stationed at a guard station next to the gate and there were two permanent cameras, the company tried to justify the decision to install the extra camera based upon a history of strikes every four years for the past twelve years and acts of violence during those strikes.

The U.S. Court of Appeals affirmed the NLRB ruling that the use of this extra camera was an unfair labor practice because the incidents of violence cited were too remote in time and occurred during strikes, and the union was actually working without a contract and was not out on strike. The court and NLRB rejected the company's argument there was no tendency to coerce by its use of the camera on the grounds at least 100 employees showed up every morning and the company had never taken any reprisal action against any employees. The court stated this did not prove the other 2,900 employees didn't feel coercion and the lack of disciplinary action did not prove there was no fear of reprisal.

In conclusion, video surveillance should be restricted to documenting destructive and unlawful employee activities in progress. Also, when there is a reasonable objective basis for anticipating disruptive behavior a company may engage in limited videotaping of protected activities, for example, video recording a truck entering a plant when employees in the immediate past have blocked the entrance or video recording managers entering a plant when they have been threatened or attacked in the recent past.

4. Federal Preemption and State Tort Actions

As noted, the LRMA preempts state courts from deciding issues that fall under the jurisdiction of the NLRB. One issue of relevance here is whether a union employee may sue an investigator and employer in state court for tortuous conduct under state law, for example, invasion of privacy, false imprisonment, or emotional distress. The deciding factor in this type of case is whether the union contract does or does not need to be interpreted to determine whether the alleged tortuous conduct was committed. If the union contract does not need to be interpreted, then the aggrieved employee will be permitted to proceed with the state tort claim(s). If the union contract needs to be interpreted, the claims must be preempted and decided under federal labor law. The answer to whether a contract does or does not need to be interpreted depends upon the alleged tort(s) and the contract language.

In *Hanley*, a cashier failed to properly enter seven of eight transactions in a blind security test where money was left on her register.[33] After signing an admission that she often saved the money for the end of her shift and used it to balance the register but never for personal gain, she was terminated. She filed suit. She claimed she was "interrogated" in a backroom, verbally detained even though she wanted to leave, threatened with arrest, and promised no other action would be taken if she confessed.

The Supreme Court of Montana held the LMRA §301 did not preempt her state tort claims because it was not necessary to interpret the union-management contract to decide the issues of false imprisonment, intimidation, emotional distress, slander, and employer negligence. It reinstated the suit against the company.

In *Blanchard*, the company, based upon information provided by employees and police, hired an outside firm to conduct an undercover investigation.[34] Months later, two other investigators were retained to interview employees implicated in the investigation. The employees were interviewed in an office where all the windows were covered with paper. Allegedly, each was falsely told there was substantial evidence of their individual drug use, advised they would be terminated if they left the interviews, promised they would not be discharged if they confessed, and told they had the right to union representation. Twelve employees, who made self-incriminating statements, were discharged. Four of the employees, whose discharges were affirmed in binding arbitration, filed suit. In part, the suit contained state tort claims of intentional infliction of emotional distress, false imprisonment, invasion of privacy, and fraud (false promise that no other action would be taken against them). The company argued the tort claims were preempted by the LMRA. The U.S. District Court held the privacy claim was preempted because the labor contract contained language pertinent to the use of controlled substances. The false imprisonment claim was also preempted because the alleged threat of termination for failing to answer questions pertaining to violations of work safety rules required an examination of the company authority under the labor contract to direct the activities of the employees and to investigate and take appropriate disciplinary actions for violation. The court also ruled the allegations of fraud and emotional distress, if fraud was first proven, might be decided without reference to the labor contract, and it permitted plaintiffs to continue with these two claims.

In *Cramer*, the employer, a large trucking company concerned about driver drug use and dealings, installed cameras in the restrooms used by its drivers, both female and male.[35] Employees in two separate lawsuits, one a class action and other with 282 plaintiffs, filed invasion of privacy and emotional distress claims in state court. The company removed the cases to federal court on the grounds they were preempted under the LMRA because the company was allowed under the collective bargaining contract to use cameras in employee theft and dishonest cases. The U.S. Court of Appeals held it was not necessary to interpret the labor contract to decide these cases. The conduct of the company was in violation of the state criminal code. Further, the collective bargaining agreement could not make illegal conduct under state law legal. Absent any federal question, the appeals court remanded the consolidates cases back to state court for further adjudication on the merits of the claims.

5. Union Contract Restrictions

Fact-finders in unionized environments should review the union contract before undertaking an investigation. Specifically, the contract will set forth the burden upon the employer to justify progressive discipline and terminations. Common requirements set forth in these contracts include such terms as *cause, just cause, good cause,* and other similar language. Although the exact meaning of these terms may vary, all of them place a burden upon the employer to produce evidence to support the discipline. A termination may be subject to arbitration if the union appeals.

Other restrictions may be placed upon workplace investigation in a unionized environment. For example, an employer and union may contractually agree that company investigators will advise union members of the right to union representation prior to disciplinary interviews. Further, both parties may agree that no investigative disciplinary interviews will be conducted without a representative and even a stenographer being present. A union and employer may agree that a union member cannot be questioned about the conduct of another union member. Further, a union and company may agree whether drug testing or use of drug dogs will or will not be permitted. The important point is that workplace fact-finders must be aware of and abide by any pertinent conditions negotiated into the collective bargaining agreements.

6. Arbitration

Binding arbitration is a process where two or more parties (usually management and union, but such clauses are with more frequency being inserted in management and professional contracts) contractually agree to use an independent party to review and decide disputes between the parties. Arbitration decisions are generally final and may be appealed to the courts only on very limited grounds. Usually, arbitrators are not bound by earlier decisions of other arbitrators on the same issues, and thus arbitration decisions are sometimes quite unpredictable.

Employers and unions use this process to settle grievances under the management-union contract. Most disciplinary arbitrations focus not upon the methods of investigation but upon whether the company met the necessary standard of proof. Nonetheless, these decisions may affect how workplace investigations are conducted. An arbitrator, for example, may influence an investigative method by finding a company did not have sufficient evidence, based upon a single documented incident of property removal, to prove the employee stole rather than borrowed the equipment. As a result, company investigators may alter their investigations to include multiple observations of property removal in order to meet the standard of proof established by the arbitrator. Where applicable, company investigators should take time to review past arbitration decisions for guidance on acceptable practices and burdens of proof.

7. Civil Rights Law

A number of federal laws prohibit various forms of workplace discrimination and harassment. The major act is the Civil Rights Act of 1964 (often referred to as Title VII).[36] It prohibits employers from engaging in unlawful employment practices relating to hiring, firing, promoting, and altering the terms and conditions of employment because of race, color, religion, sex, or national origin. It also vested enforcement authority in the Equal Employment Opportunity Commission (EEOC) but did not preempt state law. Other important federal laws include:

- The Civil Rights Act of 1866
- Age Discrimination Employment Act
- Equal Employment Opportunity Act
- Rehabilitation Act
- Pregnancy Discrimination Act
- Americans with Disabilities Act
- Civil Rights Act of 1991

Collectively these laws prohibit other forms of discrimination and harassment, strengthen the enforcement authority of the EEOC, and authorize compensatory and punitive damages and attorney's fees in certain instances. In addition to the federal laws, all 50 states and many local authorities have similar antidiscrimination laws, and some of these laws may include other categories of protected persons.

At the fact-finding stage of an investigation, the major impact of civil rights laws that prohibit employment discrimination and harassment is twofold upon workplace investigations. First, employers have an affirmative duty to investigate employee allegations of discrimination and harassment. Second, fact-finders must be careful not to engage in or use discriminatory methods of investigation.

a. Duty to Investigate

EEOC guidelines provide that employers should "investigate promptly and thoroughly" all credible allegations of sexual harassment.[37] This statement balances and puts equal value on two competing criteria that employers should consider for all discrimination and harassment investigations. It does not permit an employer to sacrifice timeliness for thoroughness, nor to sacrifice thoroughness for timeliness. Instead, the burden is upon an employer to initiate the investigation in a timely manner and to keep it moving forward to a timely conclusion. But, the conclusion must be based upon a reasonably thorough investigation into the facts. This normally includes interviewing the complainant, witnesses, and alleged harasser, and reviewing other relevant documents and available evidence. It may also include identifying other complainants or witnesses who have not stepped forward. More complex allegations and number of persons involved, variations in work schedules, and other factors will, in part, determine the length of an investigation.

For example, in *Fuller,* the U.S. Court of Appeals found an employer's investigation of a sexual harassment complaint was seriously deficient in several respects.[38] The employer failed to timely interview the harasser, giving him time to prepare his defense, and the investigator often accepted the harasser's side of the issue without taking reasonable steps to confirm, including failing to check telephone records available to him. The employer disregarded evidence in support of the complainant, and failed to interview a key witness in favor of the complainant.

Similarly, in *Valdez*, the court was critical of the "remarkably shoddy" internal company investigation.[39] The company received an anonymous EEOC complaint of sexual harassment by "top management" at one of its stores. The personnel manager who received the complaint assigned it to the zone manager who himself had a questionable history involving alleged sexual harassment. He, in turn, assigned the investigation to the manager of the store where the harassment had allegedly occurred. In the analogy of plaintiff's counsel, it was as if the fox was guarding the hen house. The store manager never contacted the law firm representing the complainant and named on the EEOC complaint for more details; when he interviewed employees, he asked only about the conduct of his assistant manager; and he never allowed the assistant manager to respond to the allegations in writing. The assistant manager was terminated within two days of the start of the investigation. The assistant manager, who was a Salvadorian, filed a national origin discrimination complaint. Although the case facts were very complex, the U.S. District Court sharply criticized the shoddiness of the employer's investigation. It disapproved of the decision to assign the investigation to the zone manager who had a questionable history and, as it came out in trial, who had also stated on two occasions a desire to fire the plaintiff because there were too many "wetbacks" working for the company. It also doubted the selection of the store manager, who was a prime suspect himself, to conduct the investigation. It wondered about the manager's thoroughness and objectivity for focusing only on the assistant manager and failing to gather more facts.

And, it criticized the company for terminating the assistant manager when he didn't even work at the store at the same time the complaintant worked there. The court found the company had discriminated against the manager when it terminated him.

As a final comment, an important consideration for employers is that a prompt and thorough investigation of a harassment complaint accompanied by appropriate and timely remedial action provides the employer an affirmative defense in subsequent litigation. But note, the issue of whether temporary remedial measures need to be taken before or during the investigation is a separate issue. Depending upon the severity of the allegations, sensitivities of the parties, and level of immediate supervision, an employer may need to take temporary measurers before an investigation is completed.

b. Discriminatory Practices

Discriminatory investigative practices include those that are discriminatory on their face and those that are neutral on their face while discriminatory in impact. For example, it would be discriminatory practice on its face for a company to check for criminal histories of only minority job applicants. Similarly, all factors being the same, it would be a discriminatory practice for a company to interview only white males and not minority employees who had access to stolen company property. But, this does not mean everyone has to be interviewed if there is legitimate evidence for interviewing some and not others. Similarly, if as part of an internal investigation an employer searched only the purses of women employees and not the briefcases of male employees, this may be a discriminatory investigative practice unless there was a legitimate reason for such a search pattern. The simple fact of the matter is that investigative methods should not on their face be discriminatory.

Other investigative practices may be neutral (nondiscriminatory) on their face but may have a discriminatory impact. A workplace investigation procedure that is neutral on its face might include something so simple as interviewing only hourly employees and not management staff who had access to missing property or areas where suspected illegal drugs were found. The distinction between hourly employees and salaried managers is not discriminatory on its face. But, hypothetically, what if all the managers were white males and all the hourly employees were female minorities? Further, assume the investigation was inconclusive and the company elected to terminate all the hourly employees. If a complaint was filed and the employer (and his fact-finder) could not articulate a legitimate reason for interviewing only minority hourly employees, the underlying investigation and subsequent adverse employment action might be vulnerable to claims of discrimination. Investigators need to remain sensitive to the potential for engaging in direct and indirect discriminatory investigative practices.

Tip: Fact-finders need to be sensitive to the totality of the investigative environment as not to be influenced by or to engage in practices that are discriminatory on their face or impact, including bias remarks, selection of suspects, and investigative reporting.

---

8. Select Federal Statutes

The following statutes have been discussed elsewhere in this text. The purpose here is to provide a brief foundation in each and to highlight their relevancy to fact-finders.

a. Employee Polygraph Protection Act

The Employee Polygraph Protection Act (EPPA) prohibits private sector employers from administering polygraph examinations, creates limited exemptions where it may be used, and sets forth very specific rights of employees who refuse or agree to take the test.[40] Specifically, it is illegal under the act for a private employer to "require, request, suggest, or cause any employee ... to take or submit to any lie detector test," or to "discharge, discipline, discriminate against in any manner ... or threaten to take any such action," against any employee who, "refuses, declines, or fails to take or submit to any lie detector test." Thereafter, it creates a few specialized exceptions for businesses dealing with national security, pharmaceuticals, and protection of key public facilities. It also permits private employers to use the polygraph for "ongoing investigations involving economic loss to the employer," where the employee had access to the missing assets and the employer has other "reasonable suspicion" that the employee was involved. The act also places certain conditions upon employers and details rights of the employee, including the right to refuse and withdraw permission, notification of the specific grounds for reasonable suspicion, and other rights.

For example, in *Wiltshire*, the defendant bank conducted an extensive investigation into the unauthorized wire transfer of $1.5 million.[41] It recovered the funds only because another bank intercepted the transfer when it became suspicious. But, the defendant bank had to pay a few thousand dollars in administrative fees for the transaction. Based upon information provided by the FBI, access to funds, use of an outdated time stamp, and knowledge of fund transfer protocol, the bank narrowed its investigation to a manager, the plaintiff. During employee interviews, the manager was the only suspect who stated it was necessary to put a date stamp on a debit transfer. The bank asked the manager to take a polygraph. Per the statute, he was allowed 48 hours to decline and he did so on the second day. Approximately two weeks later, based upon existing information, the bank terminated his employment for lack of confidence in his ability to protect bank assets. He claimed his termination was based upon his refusal to take the polygraph, and he filed suit for violation of the EPPA. The bank countered that he was fired based upon the information it had and not his refusal to take the polygraph. The court, per the statute, found it was an ongoing investigation, he had access, and there was economic loss (the loss of use of funds for a few days and the fee). Further, the court concluded the bank had reasonable suspicion to request the manager take the polygraph test. But, the court found the notice provided the manager was deficient because it didn't adequately describe with "particularity" the bank's basis for it suspicion. The notice for reasonable suspicion stated "You were present on Dec. 7, 1990 when the wire transfer was sent. You had access to all necessary documents and stamps to create item and place it in basket for transmission." The bank argued that there was sufficient particularity and notice principally based upon the multiple interviews that it had had with the plaintiff.

The Supreme Court of New York County, New York, disagreed and held the verbal notice was insufficient because Congress was specific that the reasonable suspicion notice must be set forth in writing. Because the bank failed to comply fully with the notice requirement, the court found the bank violated the EPPA when it requested the plaintiff to take the polygraph. Addressing the issue of his termination, the court added: "Citibank's suspension and termination of plaintiff were barred by EPPA §3 (29 U.S.C. § 2002[3]) unless Citibank can prove at trial that plaintiff's failure to take the polygraph test played no part in the decision either to suspend or fire him." The court denied the bank's motion for summary judgment.

In another interesting case, *Lyle*, the U.S. District Court held the defendant hospital did not qualify for the ongoing investigation exemption for economic loss.[42] The hospital vice president who was investigating the theft of funds from a doctor's locker asked the plaintiff, a technician in the surgical area where the theft occurred, to take a polygraph. He refused and subsequently was terminated. He sued for violation of the EPPA. The hospital filed for summary judgment on the grounds it qualified for the ongoing investigation exemption. The court held it did not because the doctor, not the hospital, had suffered economic loss. In addition to the federal statute, employers and fact-finders need to recognize that many states have laws that restrict the use of polygraphs as well.[43]

Tip: The use of the polygraph and other similar devices is highly regulated by federal and sometimes state laws. Fact-finders should never discuss, suggest or request the use of such devices, even if never intending to do so, with interviewees without full understanding of these laws.

---

b. Fair Credit Reporting Act

The Fair Credit Reporting Act was enacted by Congress to place reasonable procedural controls on Consumer Reporting Agencies (CRA) that balance the needs of commerce for fast and reliable consumer information regarding a consumer's credit worthiness and character versus the rights of individual consumers to accuracy and confidentiality.[44] A CRA refers to a person or business that engages in the "Practice of assembling or evaluating consumer credit information or other information on consumers for the purpose of furnishing consumer reports to third parties." It is important to note a public agency, such as a police department or court, that keeps public records is not a CRA.

There are two types of consumer reports: a *consumer report* and *investigative consumer report*. A consumer report pertains to a person's "credit worthiness, character, general reputation, personal characteristics, or mode of living ... which is used or expected to be used in establishing the consumer's eligibility for [among other things], *employment purposes.*" An investigative consumer report expands this information to include "personal interviews with neighbors, friends or associates ... or who may have knowledge concerning any such items of information." The term "employment purposes" means "a report used for the purpose of evaluating a consumer for employment, promotion, reassignment or retention as an employee."

In order to obtain and use information from a CRA for employment purposes, an employer must give notice to the consumer, obtain the consumer's written permission, and verify this information to the reporting agency. If it is an investigative consumer report, the employer must also identify it as such, provide an explanation why the information is sought, and give notice that the consumer may submit a request for a complete disclosure about the nature of the investigation and its methods. If an employer takes adverse action based upon a consumer report, the employer has further duties prior to the action including providing the consumer with a copy of the report and a document that again outlines his or her rights. After the adverse action there are further notification requirements placed upon an employer. Of interest here, the FCRA, as amended in 2003, excludes certain communications between a CRA and employer regarding investigations into employee misconduct, breaches of written policy, and compliance with and regulations, and rules of self-regulated organizations. If adverse action is taken upon the communication there is a duty to provide a summary of the "nature and substance" of the report. It is essential that employers and CRAs abide by the FCRA.

c. Federal Sentencing Guidelines

In order to reduce the disparity of sentences defendants received for similar offenses by the federal courts, the Federal Sentencing Commission was established to provide uniform guidelines.[45] Of interest here, the Federal Sentencing Guidelines provide guidance on how the *culpability* score of a convicted *organization* (e.g., business) is to be calculated. The higher the culpability score, the greater the severity of the financial penalty assessed against the organization. The score is increased if "high-level personnel … participated in, condoned or were willfully ignorant of the offense." Further, it may be increased if the organization has a prior history of similar offenses, it violated a court order, or it obstructed the government investigation. An organization may lower its culpability score if it has an "Effective Program to Prevent and Detect Violations of Law." The score may also be lowered if the organization self-disclosed the offense, cooperated in the government investigation, and accepted responsibility.

Employers should enact corporate codes of ethics, provide all employees appropriate training, and provide internal reporting mechanisms for employees to report concerns, including suspicions of criminal conduct by high-level personnel. Further, employers should conduct reasonable follow-up investigations when presented with credible accusations. The failure to implement these counter-measures and the failure to investigate high-level misconduct can expose an organization to severer penalties in the federal courts.

F. State Tort Law Issues

The majority of workplace investigative-related lawsuits are civil tort actions under state law. However, fact-finders should be aware that although very similar in nature, there are variations in the laws of the 50 states, the District of Columbia, Puerto Rico, and other territories. When crossing jurisdictional lines investigators should be sensitive to these variations.

1. Assault and Battery

The majority of workplace investigations do not involve the use of force by the fact-finder. Nonetheless, if private sector investigators unnecessarily threaten to or use unnecessary or unreasonable force, they may be sued for assault and/or battery.

An assault occurs when one party creates a reasonable apprehension in the mind of another of a forthcoming, imminent offensive touching. An assault does not require that there be any contact. An assault may be physical, verbal, or a combination of both. A verbal threat combined with apparent capability to hit, slap, shove, or smash, or a similar threat can certainly be sufficient behavior by a fact-finder to constitute an assault. Making a fist, glaring, lunging, swinging, grabbing at, and other similar body motions may also constitute an assault. Of course, verbal threats coupled with aggressive body motion make for an even stronger impression of an assault.

Battery is the intentional touching by one party of another that is offensive in nature. The touching may be either directly or indirectly upon the other. For example, it would be battery if a frustrated fact-finder directly slapped an uncooperative employee. Likewise, even though the investigator never touched the employee, it would be battery if the investigator kicked the chair out from underneath an uncooperative employee, causing him to fall to the floor.

For example, in *Warren*, a company security representative and private investigator "interrogated" an employee for failing to properly enter a $1.00 transaction during an anonymous honesty and efficiency check.[46] The two men questioned the plaintiff about the incident and continued to press the issue of whether she had taken other money. They threatened her with arrest if she did not sign a confession with an estimate of the amount she took. They told her the arrest would be an embarrassment for her family, on several occasions refused to let her leave, and on one occasion the private investigator grabbed her on the arm to prevent her from leaving. She wrote a confession as dictated by the private detective but never entered the amount. Later, she claimed she did so under duress in order to be allowed to leave the interrogation. The Court of Appeals of Texas held the "findings of the trial court clearly establish … assault and battery as against the defendant," private investigator.

2. False Imprisonment and False Arrest

When conducting workplace interviews fact-finders need to be sensitive to the issues of false imprisonment and false arrest. False imprisonment occurs when one denies another the voluntary freedom of movement. The denial may be by verbal or physical means.

For example, in the aforementioned *Warren* case, both of the investigators involved denied the plaintiff's requests to leave, and the private investigator grabbed her arm to prevent her from leaving.[47] Not only did the private investigators commit assault and battery, the evidence clearly showed both falsely imprisoned the employee against her wishes.

False arrest is arrest without legal justification. Whenever there is a false arrest, there is false imprisonment. Workplace investigators rarely make citizen's arrests of employees. But, nonetheless, they need to avoid creating an impression that the subject is under arrest by claiming to have police authority, stating the subject is under arrest, or unnecessarily restraining the individual.

3. Defamation

Defamation is the single most frequently cited complaint in civil lawsuits against employers. A defamatory statement is a false statement of fact published by one party, either by spoken or written means or conduct, to a third disinterested party that impugns the community, business, or professional reputation of another. A false allegation that a party committed a crime is such a grievous act that it is considered *defamation per se*. That is, the remark is presumed to be so injurious to one's reputation that damages need not be proven.

There are two types of defamatory statements: *slander* and *libel*. Slander refers to defamation by the spoken word or conduct. For example, an employee might claim he was slandered when he was handcuffed or verbally accused of dishonesty in front of co-workers. Further, a suspect employee might claim defamation when a fact-finder made inquiries of co-workers about him that inferred he was involved in the alleged incident. Libel refers to written statements or pictures that are defamatory. An employee, for example, might claim he was libeled in the fact-finder's report to his employer's managers.

Defendants may raise several affirmative defenses to suits for defamation. First, *truth* is a defense as defamation entails the publication of a false statement. Assume an employee was arrested in the workplace and sued for defamation; a showing that the arrest was lawful would defeat the allegation of defamation. Second, *nonpublication* is also a defense; in other words, the alleged defamatory statement was never communicated to a third disinterested party. For example, if an investigator accused an employee of selling drugs during an investigatory interview with just the two of them present, in a suit for defamation the investigator could defend on the grounds there was no publication to a third party. In some states intraorganization communications (communications within a business) are considered nonpublished on the premise a business is a single legal entity.

The third defense, the one most commonly used in workplace investigations, is *privileged communication*. Privileged communications are either absolute or conditional/qualified. As a matter of public policy, to protect the interest of the public at large over the interest of the individual, *absolute privileged communications* are protected even if false and made maliciously. Statements made in legislative and judicial proceedings usually enjoy an absolute privilege. Assume a fact-finder accused an employee of stealing funds or assets at a criminal trial, the employee was found "not guilty," and the employee sued for defamation. Because the accusation was made in a criminal trial, it would be an absolute privileged comment. But note, there may be other sanctions taken if a witness lies under oath (perjury), lies in an official report (false statement), or maliciously initiates criminal prosecution (malicious prosecution).

Conditional or qualified privileged communications are protected if made in good faith to an interested party. An interested party, in the context of workplace investigations, is someone who needs to know in performance of his duties. For example, if a fact-finder told an employee's superior that an employee was using illegal drugs while on the job, in most jurisdictions this statement would be considered a conditional privileged communication so long as the fact-finder was acting in good faith. But, the statement would no longer be privileged if the investigator told his family and friends (clearly disinterested parties) or acted maliciously (intentionally lied about the truth of the allegation).[48]

An employer, in *Nipper*, received an employee hotline tip that a store manager was flashing a gun, working under the influence of drugs, allowing her boyfriend to stay in the store for hours at a time, and permitting birthday parties in the store.[49] A company investigator interviewed store employees based upon this tip and a documented $30,000 loss of inventory. The interviews were conducted in a back room with an open door; employees were told the information was confidential and told the scope and nature of the inquiry. After confirming in the employee interviews the information set forth in the hotline tip, the investigator interviewed the manager. After the manager admitted to allowing her boyfriend to visit, bringing a gun to work, and taking medication that made her sleepy, the company terminated her. She sued. In part, she claimed she was defamed when the investigator interviewed the other employees. The Supreme Court of Alabama noted communications between employees acting within the proper scope of their duties "do not constitute a publication." Here, the investigator was acting within the scope of his employment; he spoke only with employees "only to the extent reasonably necessary to investigate the hotline complaints and the inventory loss." Therefore, there was no publication and no defamation. It affirmed judgment for the company.

In *Gaumont*, the Court of Appeals of Ohio held a contract investigator enjoyed a qualified privilege to discuss an employee suspected of theft of company tools with a deputy sheriff from another county.[50] The sheriff was an interested party because he had previously investigated a burglary of tools at the employee's home and the contract investigator wanted to know if the deputy had noticed any company tools during his search of the residence. Of note, the states are split on whether statements made to law enforcement personnel are absolute privileged communications or are conditional privileged communications.[51]

Defamation lawsuits are sometimes based more on office rumor than the words or conduct of the investigators. As a rule, companies are not responsible for office gossip and rumors. For example, in *Ashcroft,* a private duty nurse was arrested in a hospital gift shop for shoplifting.[52] She claimed that she lost referral business because of alleged defamatory statements by the security officers. However, she cited "no specific statement published by defendants to her prospective employers." Rather, she admitted to basing her allegations on speculation and "rumors by way of the grapevine." The Ohio Court of Appeals affirmed summary judgment for the hospital.

In *Paolucci*, the Court of Appeals of Ohio held a nurse discharged for violation of work rules was not defamed when two security officers escorted her off hospital property in plain view of others.[53]

Crump is an unusual case that illustrates the need for investigators to be careful not only with whom they speak but in what they say.[54] Crump worked as head receiver for dry goods at the defendant's warehouse. His job was to verify proper delivery of ordered goods and to reject unordered and defective goods. Rejected goods were to be returned to the delivery driver or placed in the company salvage pile where they might be repackaged or given to the warehouse employees. Company policy held that if property was removed, the employee taking it had to obtain a property pass signed by a supervisor. The plaintiff had been with the company 18 years when he was terminated for breach of company policy. Specifically, he rejected two cases of breakfast food; the driver refused to take the goods back and told the plaintiff to take them for his grandchildren. The plaintiff offered to share the items with co-employees and kept them by his desk to take home. He admitted he violated company policy by not placing the merchandise in the salvage area and properly obtaining a property pass, instead he had issued himself one. He sued for defamation on the grounds he was called a "thief" in a meeting attended by the company director of warehousing, director of loss prevention, and a loss prevention specialist. Further, in two written reports prepared after the incident he was referred to as a "problem employee." The trial court awarded the plaintiff both compensatory and punitive damages for defamation. The company appealed.

The Supreme Court of Vermont affirmed that the company enjoyed "a conditional privilege for intra-corporate communications to protect its legitimate business interests." But, the court noted this privilege might be lost if the company acted with reckless disregard for the truth or acted with ill will in violation of the discharged employee's rights. Here, the court affirmed there was reasonable evidence to support the verdict. The court noted the rejected merchandise did not belong to the company, since it did not have to pay for it, therefore, the company's characterization of the plaintiff's conduct as theft might reasonably be interpreted by a jury as showing a "reckless disregard both for the truth and for plaintiff's rights." Further, the court noted the company acted outside its privilege when it made an oral report to the security manager for the trucking company and spoke with the driver and another employee of the trucking company.

> Tip: Exercise care when communicating the results of an investigation to others. Prior to dissemination, be certain it is made in good faith, without malice or careless disregard for the facts, and there is a justifiable business purpose for the recipient to know.

---

4. Invasion of Privacy

The right of privacy emanates from three sources of law: constitutional, statutory, and common law. Having previously discussed federal and state constitutional privacy rights in workplace investigations, this section addresses statutory and common law rights of privacy enjoyed by those in the workplace.

a. State Statutes

State statutes, in some form or another, afford the right of privacy in all 50 states. There are essentially two types of statutes: statutes that protect a general or specific right of privacy and statutes that restrict different methods of intrusion or investigation.

For example, under the laws of Massachusetts person "shall have a right against unreasonable, substantial or serious interference with his privacy."[55] Similarly, Rhode Island by statute guarantees four specific rights of privacy (three of interest here) that are often guaranteed under the common law of other states.[56] These rights include the right to be secure from unreasonable intrusion upon one's physical solitude or seclusion, unreasonable publicity given to one's private life, and publicity that reasonably places another in a false light before the public.

In *Williams*, a payroll clerk was terminated after an investigation into the cashing of forged payroll checks.[57] The investigation included both private and federal investigators. During the course of the investigation, she was asked to account for her activities on the day when some checks were cashed. She had had an abortion and some complication thereafter, and this fact came to light in response to this inquiry. She sued under the general privacy statute of Massachusetts. First, she claimed her privacy was invaded by the accusations of theft against her. The court rejected this claim on the grounds the defendants had conducted a good faith inquiry that warranted further investigation. Second, she claimed publication of a private fact. The Superior Court of Massachusetts noted this statute covered the publication of highly personal or intimate information to an employer, but this disclosure had to be weighed against the employer's legitimate business interests. Here, the court held there was no publication of private fact because it was reasonable for the employer to question her regarding her activities on the day the checks were cashed and the employer had no idea this inquiry would elicit personal information of this nature. The court granted summary judgment to the defendants with regard to all privacy claims.

In California, in addition to a state constitutional right of privacy as discussed earlier, there are numerous statutes that protect specific information. For example, the Labor Code of California provides employers "shall make reasonable efforts to safeguard the privacy of the employee as to the fact that he or she has enrolled in an alcohol or drug rehabilitation program"[58] or "has a problem with illiteracy."[59]

California, as many states, also prohibits or restricts certain methods of investigation. For example, the Civil Code of California specifically prohibits the physical trespass upon the land of another with the intent to capture visual, sound, or other impressions of the plaintiff engaged in personal or familial activities where the trespass is "offensive to a reasonable person." The same law also restricts the use of a "visual or auditory enhancing device" without any trespass to capture visual or audio impressions of a person engaged in similar activities where the plaintiff had a reasonable expectation of privacy and the attempt is "offensive to a reasonable person."[60]

Similarly, under the Penal Code of California it is a crime to intentional amplify or record confidential communications of others without the consent of all parties,[61] and it is unlawful to install a "two-way mirror permitting observation of any restroom, toilet, bathroom."[62] In *Cramer,* for example, the United States Court of Appeals ruled that federal labor law, LMRA §301, did not preempt the more than 280 plaintiffs from pursuing their privacy claims under California law against the company for violating state law by installing two-way mirrors and video–audio recorders in men's and women's restrooms to detect drug usage.[63]

The intent here is not to attempt to cover the multitude of statutes that guarantee general or specific rights of privacy, nor is it to discuss all the different statutes that restrict various methods of gathering information. The purpose is to alert fact-finders (and those who employ them) that they need to understand the privacy-related statutes of the jurisdiction in which they operate.

b. Common Law Right of Privacy

Employees also enjoy various degrees of common law right of privacy under the judicial decisions of the respective state courts. There are three different tort actions for invasion of privacy of interest to workplace fact-finders: invasion of privacy—false light; invasion of privacy—publication of a private fact; and invasion of privacy—intrusion upon seclusion. The first two actions deal with how investigative information is managed, whereas the third tort action deals with the method of gathering information.

False Light

False light invasion of privacy is similar to defamation. But, there are differences. Defamation involves injury to one's reputation, whereas a false statement involves emotional distress suffered by the party. Defamation may occur with publication to just one other party, whereas a false statement involves publicity.[64] A false statement is one made with reckless disregard for the truth that attributes highly objectionable characteristics, beliefs, or conduct to an individual and places him before the public in a false position.[65] Publicity means the statement was made before the public or shared with a sufficient number of persons that it is likely to become public knowledge.

In *Aranyosi*, several employees were terminated when the company elected to contract out their duties.[66] During an exit meeting a few of the employees made modestly veiled threatening remarks. That evening two intruders, dressed in camouflage, confronted a plant security officer, placed a gun at the officer's head, made threats against the plant manager, and stated there was a bomb in the plant. The police were contacted. The police learned from the plant manager and other employees about the threats of a few terminated and even remaining staff, such as: "What goes around, comes around"; "You will reap what you sow"; "Y'all [sic] better watch your backs"; and "I will make sure the same thing happens to you … and your family." One employee was even quoted as saying that "he received a vision about the warehouse blowing up." The local newspaper, based upon information provided by the police, reported the incident and bomb threat (no bomb was found) and published, "Company officials said they had been threatened earlier that day by several of the 14 employees who officials laid off." The plaintiff-employees filed suit, in part, alleging false light invasion of privacy, as the information made it appear that they had participated in the threats and attack. The court held there was no false light publication on the grounds the company did not act unreasonably in relating the comments of the employees and events of the day to the police who were summoned to investigate the aggravated battery and bomb threat. It granted summary judgment on this issue for the company.

The outcome was different in *Lee* where a long-term employee was accused of being involved in theft.[67] Two company investigators and police detectives went to search his home. Ultimately, three other police detectives, an officer, and 12 to 15 employees were involved. More than 400 items valued at over $50,000 were taken from the home, placed in the yard, inventoried by the police, and put in a truck rented by the company. The company kept the items in secured storage, but somehow 37 items not listed on the police inventory were co-mingled with the items seized. Several persons saw the search in progress and the local papers covered the story. Ultimately, the county prosecutor refused to prosecute the case. Lee filed civil suit. In court, the items that Lee identified as his were returned and the 37 co-mingled items were returned to the company. The court awarded Lee over $1.6 million in damages, in part, for false light invasion of privacy. The Supreme Court of Arkansas affirmed.

Most cases, of course, do not involve the public media. But, it is not necessary for the media to be involved for a plaintiff to file a false light claim. In *Bine,* an employer installed a camera in its parking lot after reported acts of vandalism and stationed an officer with a handheld camera in the lot.[68] The officer observed a suspicious person around a vehicle that had been previously vandalized. He checked the car and noticed it had been recently scratched. The officer identified the plaintiff as the suspicious person (the record was not clear whether any of the incident was recorded on videotape). The plaintiff denied any involvement but was terminated. In order to deal with rumors about the termination, the plant management told a number of employees that the plaintiff was in fact terminated for vandalism. The plaintiff filed suit, in part, for false light invasion of privacy. The trial court granted summary judgment to the employer. The Supreme Court of West Virginia held there was a dispute of material fact as to the truth of the allegation. It noted, "The spreading of such information, if false, could constitute a valid false light claim." The court remanded the case to the trial court.

In *Smith*, discussed earlier, a purchasing agent was suspended pending her decision to resign or take a demotion for her abuse of vacation leave.[69] At that time she was escorted off company property by the investigator. Smith claimed false light invasion of privacy on the grounds it "left her co-workers free to speculate that Smith had been disciplined for something more egregious than vacation day violation, such as fraud or graft." The court rejected this circuitous argument that she was placed in a false light because the company did not publicize the true reason for her demotion or escort off its property.

Publication of a Private Fact

There are facts (truths) about people that are private and the law recognizes a tort action for invasion of privacy when such facts are given publicity and such disclosure is highly offensive to a reasonable person.

In *Johnson*, the employer, based upon reports of employee drug use and large inventory losses, hired a contract investigative firm to provide undercover operatives in its warehouse.[70] The agents, based upon what they saw and heard, reported on the personal lives of some of the employees, including information about children, domestic violence, pending divorces, sexual partners, personal health, future employment plans, and even characterizations of some employees as alcoholics. The employees filed suit, in part, for publicity of a private fact. The trial court entered summary judgment for the defendants. The Appellate Court of Illinois stated the information could be viewed as private because the agents obtained it through deception, communication to the employer could be considered publicity, and its disclosure might be highly offensive to a reasonable person. The appellate court reversed and remanded the issue to the trial court.

Note, the commenting about a private fact in front of others does not always mean the speaker has given publicity to the matter. In *Dietz*, a jewelry clerk was "interrogated" about an unauthorized discount provided a customer who was upset about the length of time it took to be served.[71] During her interview, the company investigator stated that Dietz had personal credit problems. Present in the room were a female manager who was serving as a witness and a security officer who was monitoring the CCTV system and was not a party to the session. The court denied the reference to her credit difficulties with the two employees present amounted to publicity of a private fact. The Court of Appeals of Indiana affirmed summary judgment in favor of the defendants on this issue.

In *Shattuck*, the plaintiff, who worked at a resort, was raped while on break and the attack was captured on video.[72] The company immediately reported the incident to the police. In order to determine if the rapist was an employee the company showed the video to select managers. It also showed the tape to another rape victim (who was not attacked at the resort) and the police officer investigating that case. The plaintiff claimed this showing was an unreasonable publication of a private fact. The Supreme Court of Utah ruled the company's showing of "the video to a discrete number of persons for the legitimate purposes of a criminal investigation" did not qualify as a public disclosure.

Intrusion upon Seclusion

Intrusion upon seclusion refers to an intentional intrusion by another upon the physical solitude or private affairs of another that is unreasonable and highly offensive to a reasonable person.[73] Employees enjoy a degree of privacy in the workplace but the level of privacy afforded them must be balanced with the legitimate interest of the employer in running its business. There is a long list of intrusion of seclusion cases on a variety of issues that impact workplace investigations. The following cases cover traditional off-premise and on-site cases, and more recent cyber privacy issues.

In *Johnson v. Corporate Special Services, Inc.*, a contract investigator staked out the plaintiff's house to observe if the plaintiff was engaging in any physical activity that would disqualify him from receiving benefits under workers compensation.[74] As the court noted, at no time did the investigator try to observe or peek into the home. One evening, during the surveillance, the investigator was questioned by the police. He was asked to explain his presence, which he did. The plaintiff noticed this encounter and continued to watch the investigator who relocated to another close-by spot. The plaintiff, subsequently, pulled his car in front of the investigator's vehicle and confronted the investigator, who pulled his weapon and withdrew. The plaintiff sued for assault and battery, and invasion of privacy. The trial judge granted summary judgment on the invasion of privacy claim in favor of the defendant and the jury found in his favor on the assault and battery claim. The plaintiff appealed the invasion of privacy claim. In affirming judgment for the investigative firm, the Supreme Court of Alabama used a two-part test: it looked at the "means" of intrusion and "purpose" of the intrusion. It stated parties to personal claims should expect some investigation into their claims and loss of privacy related to the claim. It found the purpose of the investigation was lawful and the outside surveillance did not intrude into the privacy of his home.

However, not all outside investigations are reasonable or lawful. In *Souder*, the Court of Appeals of Louisiana held the plaintiff, who had filed a workers' compensation claim, did state a privacy cause of action against investigators for the constant surveillance of his home, use of binoculars, trespass to property, and peeping into windows.[75] The last conduct was in violation of the state "Peeping Tom" statute and the court noted that any investigation outside the lawful bounds of state law is unreasonable.

The Georgia Court of Appeals, in *Stevens*, found similar conduct by detectives, conducting surveillance of a plaintiff in an automobile accident case, actionable.[76] The investigators peeped through hedges adjoining her property, trespassed upon her property, peeped into windows, eavesdropped upon conversations and cut a hole in the hedges, and closely followed her about in public areas. They were so aggressive and blatant in their tactics that her neighbors became suspicious of and shunned her. Even after being advised by legal counsel for plaintiff of the emotional duress caused, the intensity and tactics of the investigators did not change.

But, in *Saldana*, the Court of Appeals in Michigan ruled it was not an intrusion upon the privacy of an employee, who was suspected of malingering on disability, when investigators watch his home, walked by the house to look in open windows, observed the home with a telephoto camera, talked with the garbage pickup crew, and pretended to be a process server to look inside the home.[77] One justice on the three-judge panel dissented on the issue of the camera use, as he felt it created a triable issue of fact. Interestingly, the investigator sent a letter to the employee's physician but, fortunately for the investigator, the doctor never replied.

In another off-premise case, *Sowards*, the Court of Appeals of Ohio affirmed it was an intrusion of privacy when an employer searched a hotel room it had reserved for an employee–driver who used the same room on a regular basis.[78] The court noted the employee had a reasonable expectation of privacy because he was the only person in the room, he had a key to it, and it was not used for company business. The court also rejected the good faith investigation defense of the company because an invasion of privacy need not be made maliciously or intentionally to be actionable.

Investigators also need to be sensitive to their activities in the workplace. The seminal office search case is not a private sector case. In fact, the case is based upon the Fourth Amendment of the U.S. Constitution (which we know does not apply to private sector searches unless there is state action). But, it was decided by the U.S. Supreme Court and the underlying logic of the case has been used as a frame of reference by many courts.

In *O'Connor*, a state hospital searched the desk, filing drawers, and office of a physician who had used the office for over 17 years.[79] There was debate whether it was investigative (into professional improprieties including sexual harassment) or noninvestigative (inventorying state property). The U.S. Supreme Court noted the protections of the Fourth Amendment apply to noncriminal searches. But it ruled the requiring of public employers to obtain a warrant and to establish probable cause to conduct workplace searches was too cumbersome. Instead, in order to balance the government employee's "not insubstantial" expectation of privacy with the "substantial government interests in the efficient and proper operation of the workplace," the court adopted a two-part reasonableness standard:

> Under this reasonableness standard, both the inception and the scope of the intrusion must be reasonable; Determining the reasonableness of any search involves a twofold inquiry: first, one must consider "whether the ... action was justified at its inception," ... second, one must determine whether the search as actually conducted "was reasonably related in scope to the circumstances which justified the interference in the first place."

Although this decision dealt with the application of the Fourth Amendment to government employer searches, the logic of the U.S. Supreme Court provides strong guidance toward determining the reasonableness of private sector searches as well.

In *Simpson*, discussed earlier, an employee refused to participate in a lunchbox inspection because he strongly felt it violated his human and constitutional rights of privacy.[80] After having rejected the constitutional arguments, the Commonwealth Court of Pennsylvania looked at his property right of privacy in his lunchbox versus the reasonableness of the employer's request. Concluding the request to inspect was reasonable, based upon past practice even without a written policy, the court stated Simpson had a duty to cooperate and his failure to do so could not "be predicated upon asserted common law personal and property rights ... the employee has waived those rights as a basis for noncompliance; he waived them when he voluntarily assumed the legal relationship with his employer."

In *Clement*, the defendant company, without admission of fault, settled a claim that it had invaded the privacy of plaintiffs when it, based upon rumors of employee drug use, placed a concealed camera in a men's locker room.[81] In *Trotti*, managers open an employee's locker and searched her purse while looking for a missing watch, which they had no reason to believe she had taken, and a missing price-marking gun.[82] Because the employee was allowed to put her lock on the locker and the company did not advise employees the lockers were subject to search, despite the manager's claim it did, the court felt there was sufficient evidence the employee had a reasonable "expectation that the locker and its contents would be free from intrusion and interference." The Court of Appeals of Texas further affirmed there was sufficient evidence the employer acted with malice when the manager originally denied the search and misrepresented that employees were advised of the search policy. (Note, the court reversed the trial court judgment in favor of the plaintiff on grounds the jury instructions were deficient and it remanded the case for a new trial.)

In *Johnson v K Mart*, also discussed earlier, the undercover agents reported on the personal lives of the employees, and the court held they had stated a cause of action for publication of a private fact.[83] The court also found the employees had a cause of action for intrusion upon seclusion. It felt there was sufficient evidence that a jury might find the methods and scope of the investigation to be an offensive intrusion. Specifically, the court expressed concern about personal information being gathered on and off company property, about it being gathered by deception, its lack of relevancy to the legitimate interests of the business, and the company never stopped this practice. It reinstated the employees' privacy claim.

McLaren is one of the first e-mail cases to deal with employee privacy as it relates to an internal company investigation.[84] The company suspended the employee pending a sexual harassment and inventory investigation. He requested access to his e-mail to gather evidence to disprove the allegations against him. He also asked that the company not tamper with his workstation and e-mail files. Subsequently, he filed suit for invasion of privacy. He claimed the software allowed him to password protect his e-mail files (separate from the network password protection) and that this protection gave him an expectation of privacy, symbolically speaking, similar to the expectation *Troitti* enjoyed in a company locker once she put her personal lock on it. He argued that the decryption of his password and distribution of it (presumably to other company employees) by the employer represented a serious intrusion and interference with his privacy. The Court of Appeals of Texas rejected the locker analogy, noting that the locker was specifically for the employee to store personal items, whereas the computer was provided by the employer for his work and "the e-mail messages contained on the company computer were not McLaren's personal property, but were merely an inherent part of the office environment." The court added that even if he had a reasonable expectation of privacy it would be outweighed by the company's compelling interest in investigating and resolving the accusations of sexual harassment and inventory issues given that he had indicated some of the e-mail messages were relevant to the investigation. The Court of Appeals of Texas affirmed the trial court's dismissal of the case for failing to state a cause of action.

Tip: There are three different tort actions for invasion of privacy; fact-finders must understand how each might affect an investigation.

---

5. Emotional Distress or Outrage

Many cases against investigators contain claims of emotional distress or outrage. In general, in order to prevail on a claim of this nature the plaintiff must prove the defendant acted in an outrageous and highly offensive manner that was highly probable of inflicting severe emotional distress upon another. In some states, plaintiffs may have to show physical manifestations of the duress.

In *Agis*, a restaurant manager called a staff meeting, told everyone that there was stealing going on, and stated he was going to fire everyone present starting with the letter "A" until the thief stepped forward.[85] In a misguided move, using discipline in lieu of fact-finding and verification, he summarily fired Agis who immediately became hysterical. She suffered anguish and lost wages. She filed suit for intentional infliction of emotional distress but the court granted summary judgment to the defendant because the state did not recognize a cause of action for emotional distress without physical injury. The Supreme Court of Massachusetts reversed. It held the plaintiffs, the waitress and her husband, did state, even without physical injury, a cause of action for intentional or reckless infliction of emotional distress and it reinstated their claims.

In *Bodewig* a customer accused the plaintiff, a young sales clerk, of taking four $5.00 bills she left on the checkout counter while she went to get a sale item. The manager intervened. He pulled out the clerk's apron pockets, checked the area around the register and found nothing. He offered to check her register and the customer demanded he do so.

The register balanced perfectly. The customer continued to cause a commotion and would not leave. Finally, the manager told a female assistant manager to take the clerk to the restroom and search her. The assistant manager offered to allow the customer watch the search. The clerk stripped to her underwear with the two watching her. The customer, when asked, said the clerk did not have to remove her underwear since she could see through it. That evening the customer found the money in her purse, called the mother of the clerk [whom she knew], and called the store. Plaintiff sued for outrage. The trial court granted summary judgment for the store and customer. The Court of Appeals of Oregon found there was sufficient evidence a jury might find the manager, "after concluding that plaintiff did not take the customer's money, put her through the degrading and humiliating experience of submitting to a strip search ... that the manager's conduct exceeded the bounds of social toleration and was in reckless disregard of its predictable effects on plaintiff." It also held there was sufficient evidence a jury might conclude the customer intended to humiliate plaintiff. It remanded the case for trial.[86]

In *Olivas* an employee's missing paycheck was cashed at a local liquor store. Coworkers accused the employee's brother who also worked for the company. An employee made copies of some employee pictures, showed them to the liquor owner, and accused the brother of theft and forgery. The owner signed a criminal complaint against the brother. Other employees accused the brother in their conversations, with the victim and brother's landlady. The brother was fired. The criminal charges were dismissed. The brother filed suit. The Superior Court of Connecticut denied the company's motion to strike plaintiff's claim for emotional distress. The court held that the discharge taken with the accusation of theft and forgery could amount to "extreme and outrageous conduct."[87]

In *Tenold* the plaintiff worked for defendant's railroad company that was part of its forestry operation. Plaintiff obtained approval from the site security supervisor to remove some railroad ties. The site security supervisor told him to check the price with the company. Plaintiff assumed this meant he could pay for the items later. The next day, the same supervisor gave him permission to use company equipment to remove the ties. A week later, a contract security officer, who lived on-site, told the site security supervisor the plaintiff had delivered some railroad ties to a ranch. The site security supervisor reported it to his superior and a company security supervisor. The company security supervisor directed a deputy sheriff (the company paid the county for the deputy to be assigned fulltime to patrol the company's property) to investigate. The deputy sheriff told the ranch owner that plaintiff had taken 600 ties. The site security supervisor interviewed two employees who stated they had helped deliver the ties and reported that plaintiff told them that he intended to pay for the ties. The site security supervisor did not pass the later remark on to his company superiors or the deputy.

A union representative, the site security supervisor, and his manager met with plaintiff who admitted taking the ties but stated he had permission from the site security supervisor. The manager reported to his superiors the plaintiff admitted taking the ties and "he really offered no excuses or reasons for taking the ties without paying for them." The company terminated plaintiff's employment. The deputy sheriff cited plaintiff for criminal theft. His report did not indicate plaintiff's claim he had permission to take the ties and intended to pay for them. Plaintiff was indicted but the district attorney dismissed the charges after he learned some of the confiscated ties did not belong to the company and had been paid for by plaintiff. Plaintiff filed civil suit against the company. Evidence was presented that the site security supervisor bore ill will toward plaintiff. An employee testified that two years earlier the site security supervisor had stated, "there's more than one way to get rid of [plaintiff]." The company security supervisor testified another manager involved in the investigation had stated, "I don't care what the court system does or anything else, that I--I will have the man's job." He also noted the site security supervisor had stated plaintiff was a drug addict and he had caught plaintiff with marijuana two years earlier. The site security supervisor's foster son even testified he overheard his father state plaintiff was a drunk, a drug user, and had a methamphetamine lab in his home. The jury awarded damages of approximately $2.4 million against the company for defamation, malicious prosecution (discussed later), and intentional infliction of emotional distress, and $150,000 in damages against the site security supervisor for defamation and intentional infliction of emotional distress. The Court of Appeals of Oregon affirmed there was sufficient evidence for a jury to conclude defendants engaged in an extraordinary and intolerable campaign to defame, terminate, and prosecute plaintiff.[88]

In conclusion, investigators must be careful to not engage in outrageous conduct that is highly likely to inflict severe emotional distress upon suspect employees. Unreasonable investigative methods and interrogations include such activities as gathering immaterial personal information on employees, threatening employees with arrest, shouting at and physically threatening employees during interrogations, and similar conduct.

Clearly, fact-finders must be careful not to engage in intentional outrageous conduct that is highly likely to inflict severe emotional distress upon an employee. Unreasonable investigative methods and interrogations are unacceptable. This includes such activities as gathering immaterial personal information on employees, threatening employees with arrest, shouting at employees during an interrogation, and similar conduct. Also, an employee might file suit against an investigator and employer for negligent infliction of emotional distress where the employer failed to reasonably train and supervise the employee in performance of the investigation. Here, too, the conduct of the defendant must be extreme and highly probable of inducing severe emotional distress.

G. Negligent Investigation

1. A New Tort Action

Most lawsuits against fact-finders and their private employers involve specific claims of injury, such as, defamation, invasion of privacy, wrongful discharge, malicious prosecution, and emotional distress. In recent years, plaintiffs have added a new tort action for negligent investigation. The courts have not universally endorsed this concept because it often conflicts with the employment at-will doctrine and other available legal remedies. For example, assume an at-will employee is suspected of criminal conduct. The company conducts a shoddy investigation, terminates the employee, and unsuccessfully prosecutes. Further, the company tells co-workers he was fired for theft. Should he be able to sue for negligent investigation when the company could have terminated him under the employment at-will doctrine without ever investigating the matter? Also, because he can sue for defamation and for malicious prosecution, many courts question the need to recognize a new tort action for negligent investigation.

In *Sears*, the plaintiff worked as an independent insurance agent.[89] He had been with the company several years when a policyholder wrote to the company and stated the agent, an insurance adjuster, and a local contractor were engaged in a fraudulent kickback scheme. The company looked at his files, determined a few might be suspicious, and hired a private investigator. The investigator never obtained any direct evidence against the plaintiff but still advised the company he should be considered a suspect because of two suspicious claims. The company fired the plaintiff, and it reported him to several federal and state law enforcement and regulatory agencies. The adjuster and contractor were indicted, and the contractor was convicted. The authorities never pressed charges against the plaintiff, and the insurance licensing board refused the company's efforts to have his license suspended.

Sears, who claimed the investigation destroyed his local reputation, sued and won damages for negligent investigation and emotional distress. The appellate court affirmed damages for emotional distress, and it affirmed a cause of action for negligent investigation but overturned the judgment for insufficient evidence. The Supreme Court of Texas stated the conduct of the defendant in conducting the investigation and reporting its suspicions to the authorities did not amount to outrageous behavior.

There was "certainly no evidence that (defendant) knew the reports to be false or manipulated the findings so that Sears would be subject to criminal or other liability." The court, in a case of first impression, also declined "to recognize a negligent-investigation cause of action in this circumstance, because to do so would substantially alter the parties' at-will relationship."

The Appeals Court of Massachusetts affirmed the denial of a negligent investigation claim in *O'Connell*.[90] The plaintiff, a former bank teller who had left to take a higher paying position with a new company, was charged sometime afterward with theft of $4,800. The theft involved a single transaction posted, in her last few days, to two different accounts. The transaction occurred at the window of a teller trainee working adjacent to plaintiff. The investigation of the theft was difficult because the plaintiff's daily journals for the day of the theft were missing (misfiled by the bank with the trainee's records) and the time clocks on the bank videotapes were out-of-synch with the transaction logs. As a result, the investigator did not further analyze the video. When interviewed by the bank she stated she did not work the teller line where the checks were cashed but the video showed she did. The bank concluded she was the only person on that line who had enough knowledge to make the transactions. After she was charged, her attorney prevailed upon the bank to retain a handwriting expert. He concluded the writing on the documents was not the plaintiff's. A municipal judge found her not guilty. The plaintiff sued. During the civil trial the videotape, which the bank denied having, resurfaced, and the plaintiff and bank together carefully synched the film with the teller's transactions. It showed a hand, not the plaintiff's, reaching in to enter the fraudulent transaction. Regarding the plaintiff's negligent transaction claim the court held the duty of investigation ran to the party requesting the investigation and not the party under investigation. Although the party under investigation might be injured, the appeals court stated "the law makes remedies available—actions for defamation, malicious prosecution, and tortuous infliction of emotional distress." (Several months later the bank filed charges for other thefts against the male supervisor of the teller trainee.)

In *Devis*, a bank, in the belief that plaintiff was attempting to cash a stolen check on the account of a customer who had posted a warning about stolen checks, called the police.[91] The customer had written separate checks to a Davis and a Devis, and Davis stole some blank checks. When Devis attempted to cash a lawful check, he was arrested. Based upon the bank's failure to properly check his identification, he sued for negligent investigation and defamation. The California Court of Appeal affirmed summary judgment for defendant bank. Under state law, reports to the police are part of a judicial proceeding and privileged communications when made in good faith. The appeal court, in a case of first impression, stated, "The privilege must extend to actions based on negligent investigation, for if it did not, the privilege for reports to the police would be eviscerated."

In conclusion, the courts have been reluctant to recognize a new and distinct common law cause of action for negligent investigation on the grounds that it conflicts with the employment at-will doctrine, and that there are other established legal remedies available to plaintiffs.

2. Implicit and Explicit Duties to Investigate

Although the courts have been reluctant to recognize a new common law action for negligent investigation, there are circumstances where employers have overarching duties that contain explicit or implicit duties to investigate. A duty to investigate, for discussion purposes here, may arise under statute, regulation, employment and labor contracts, and tort law governing the duty to hire and supervise employees. Further, as noted, a failure to investigate may enhance liability exposure for other tort actions.

First, for example, civil rights statutes and regulations prohibit various forms of workplace discrimination. This broad duty includes the obligation to investigate complaints of harassment. As noted in *Fuller* and *Valdez,* the courts were critical of defendant employers for their deficient investigations. In *Fuller,* because of a lack of investigative thoroughness and timeliness, the employer was unable to show it took appropriate remedial measures.[92] In *Valdez,* the shoddy investigation resulted in the wrong employee being terminated.[93] When coupled with other facts, the court found the company had engaged in national origin discrimination. Also, for example, the general duty clause of the Occupational Health and Safety Act (and similar clauses under state plan programs) requires employers to maintain an environment "free from recognized hazards that are causing or are likely to cause death or serious physical harm to his employees." If an employee demonstrated a propensity toward violence, which the company did not investigate, and later the employee injured or killed another employee, the employer might be cited for violation of the general duty clause. The failure to investigate or to do a reasonable investigation may be an explicit or implicit issue in administrative and judicial proceedings when an employer owes a broader statutory duty to employees.

Second, regarding the duty to properly hire and supervise employees, in *Salinas,* the employer was found liable for the negligent hiring (i.e., failing to do a reasonable background investigation) of a taxi driver who had a felony record and later assaulted a customer.[94] In *Saine,* the Supreme Court of Arkansas held a cable company could be sued for negligent supervision and retention based upon its alleged failure to investigate a female's complaint about a cable installer who subsequently assaulted and attempted to murder another female customer.[95]

Third, regarding the issue of a contract duty to investigate, employers need to remember that not all employees are at-will. There are countless arbitration decisions under collective bargaining agreements against employers who have failed to properly investigate and satisfy their burden of establishing cause, good cause, or similar standard when seeking to discipline and terminate employees for their misconduct. Fourth, the case of *Mendez* illustrates the enhanced risk of employers being held liable for other torts based upon a failure to reasonably investigate workplace incidents.[96] Here, the Appeals Court of Massachusetts affirmed a defamation judgment against defendant employer based upon its failure to "verify its truth, in circumstances where verification was practical."

In conclusion, the courts have been reluctant to recognize a separate cause of action for negligent investigation when plaintiffs are at-will employees and where other remedies are readily available. But employers and investigators must remain sensitive to the fact there may be an explicit or implicit duty to investigate under certain statutes and regulations, contracts of employment, and common law torts for negligent hiring and supervision.

Tip: Failure to conduct reasonable investigations might lead to lawsuits for negligent hiring and supervision, and increase the risk of defamation, emotional distress, and other tort claims.

H. Claims Arising from Employee Verification Interviews

The verification and analysis phase is still an inquiry phase but it is different in the sense that it is based upon previously gathered information and its primary focus is upon the suspected wrong-doers. Before conducting investigative verification interviews with employee suspects, fact-finders need to understand the following issues:

- Constitutional warnings
- Labor law right of representation
- False imprisonment

- Assault and battery
- Defamation
- Emotional distress
- Admissibility of confessions

Further, fact-finders should be open-minded and recognize that the beginning of the verification process does not necessarily mean the fact-finding phase is completely concluded, for any verification process has multiple possible outcomes. It may not provide any additional material and relevant information; it may produce evidence that confirms known information; it may provide information that contradicts known information; it may provide information that may or may not need further investigation or corroboration; and it may provide a combination of the aforementioned outcomes. Investigators must be sensitive to the possibility that further fact-finding may be necessary after conducting verification and analysis investigative interviews. Since the first six issues listed have been previously discussed, generally only the key points will be summarized here.

1. *Constitutional Warnings*

Generally, as noted earlier, private sector investigators acting as private parties in private matters are not required to advise employee suspects of the constitutional Miranda rights to remain silent and to legal counsel. As the Court of Common Pleas of Pennsylvania stated in *Green*, "the overwhelming authority from other jurisdictions supports the position that 'Miranda' warnings need not be given by a private security officer prior to questioning a suspect taken into custody and the guarantees of the Fifth Amendment are intended as limitations upon governmental activities and not on private individuals, then the 'Miranda' warnings need not be given by persons other than governmental officials or their agents."[97]

Although it happens infrequently, if fact-finders operate as agents of or jointly with law enforcement, the courts may find their conduct to be state action and impose constitutional protections. In *Tarnef*, the Supreme Court of Alaska held that a signed confession obtained by a private arson investigator working for an insurance company was governed by the Fifth Amendment right against self-incrimination.[98] Prior to interviewing the suspect, who was in prison for another crime, the arson investigator meet with the authorities and promised to provide them a copy of any statement obtained. The authorities aided the private investigator in gaining access to the correctional facility. The suspect signed a five-page confession. Immediately afterward the investigator reported back to the authorities. The arson investigator, who was a former police officer, claimed he advised the suspect of his constitutional rights but the waiver was defective because it did not contain this notice. In the words of the court, "we hold under the facts of this case that [the insurance arson investigator] was required to give a Miranda warning and secure the defendant's waiver of rights before undertaking interrogation of appellant." Note, unlike most workplace investigations, here the suspect was clearly in custody.

In *Elliott*, a hospital security officer, who was a retired city police officer, was dispatched to a car in the hospital parking lot that was reported to have a gun in it.[99] He was told the city police had also been dispatched. The security officer was the first to arrive on the scene. He observed the gun in the locked car. At the same time the vehicle owner, who was also a security officer, arrived. The security officer asked the owner if it was his car and gun. The owner replied in the affirmative, opened the car, and gave the gun to the security officer. At that time a police officer arrived and the hospital security officer turned the gun over to him. The police officer asked the owner if it was his gun and whether he had a permit. The owner replied it was his gun and he did not have a permit. The police officer arrested him. The Supreme Court, Queens County, New York, held the hospital security officer's conduct was governed by the constitution because he acted in "coordinated private-public law enforcement ... investigation of a crime incident. The parking lot investigation and response here, by the hospital security officer, did accommodate police objectives." However, the court found the owner voluntarily turned the gun over to the security officer. It also ruled his statements were admissible in court because the owner was not in custody at the time he was questioned and the security officer's questions were routine field investigative inquiries. Therefore, the hospital security officer was not required to advise the owner of his Miranda rights.

2. Assault and Battery

An assault occurs when a party, who has apparent capability, creates a reasonable apprehension in the mind of another of an imminent and offensive forthcoming touching. For example, if an investigator made verbal or physical gestures to intimidate or threaten an employee during an investigative interview, this conduct may be sufficient to support a claim of assault. A battery is an intentional touching that is highly offensive in nature to a reasonable person. There is no requirement there be physical injury. The injury is the offensive touching. If an investigator bumped, pushed, jabbed, grabbed, or threw an object at an employee, a court might find such conduct sufficient to support a battery claim. Most workplace assault and battery claims involve the shoving or pushing of employees into meetings or the grabbing and holding on to prevent employees from leaving investigative interviews. It should be noted too, some courts use the terms assault and battery interchangeably.

In *General Motors Corp.*, the security staff at a plant entrance stopped an employee, who was suspected of stealing small radio components, in order to question him.[100] The employee testified an officer reached out and grabbed his arm and he pulled it away; a second officer grabbed his arm and he twisted away again; and he was finally detained "by a number of guards 'and, you know, like nudging me through the door or shoving me,' I guess what you call nudging or shoving blocked his path." The security supervisor testified that he asked the employee to enter the security office; the employee responded with profanity and protests that the company was calling him a thief; that neither he nor any of the officers touched the plaintiff; and that it was against company policy to do so. The trial court found the plaintiff's testimony to be more persuasive and found the officers assaulted the plaintiff. The Court of Special Appeals of Maryland affirmed both compensatory and punitive damages.

In *Blailock*, the Supreme Court of Mississippi ruled an employee could sue her employer and supervisor for assault and battery based upon the allegation the employee was grabbed on the arm and pushed toward an office by her supervisor who wanted to conduct a disciplinary interview.[101] Similarly, in the previously discussed case of *Warren*, the Court of Civil Appeals of Texas affirmed an assault and battery claim against a defendant investigator when he reached out and grabbed the plaintiff's arm to prevent the plaintiff from leaving the interrogation.[102]

a. Sympathetic Touching

The potential liability for assault and battery raises the issue of whether an investigator should reach out in sympathy and touch a suspect during an interview, such as patting a suspect's hand, knee, or shoulder. Indeed, touching may be a powerful means of communicating empathy and willingness to listen. But, it may also be perceived differently. The key issue may not be what the investigator intended but how the employee perceived the touch. When an investigator touches an employee, even with a sincere intent of expressing sympathy, in a manner that goes outside of normal business physical contact, such as a handshake, the employee may interpret or at least allege that it was an unreasonable and offensive touching amounting to battery. Investigators should carefully weigh the risks.

3. False Imprisonment

False imprisonment, as defined earlier, occurs when one person denies another by verbal or physical means his voluntary freedom of movement. For example, in the previously discussed case of *Warren*, the investigator falsely imprisoned the plaintiff when he denied her requests to leave and grabbed her arm to prevent her leaving. In *Caldor*, a juvenile employee was detained in an interrogation room with two investigators.[103] One stood behind him blocking his access to the door. When he attempted to leave, he was told to "sit down or we'll help you sit down." When he attempted to use the phone in the room, he was told "to put the damn phone down." The interrogation lasted from approximately 6:45 until sometime past 11:00 P.M. The Court of Appeals of Maryland affirmed judgment for false imprisonment.

In *Hampton*, one investigator bumped the employee while another investigator stood in front of the door to prevent him from leaving.[104] The Court of Appeals of Georgia noted that a false imprisonment did not have to be by physical restraint but could also be by "words, acts, gestures, or the like, which induce a reasonable apprehension force will be used if plaintiff does not submit." The appeals court reinstated the claim of false imprisonment and derivative claims for punitive damages and attorney fees.

In *Smith*, a purchasing employee went skiing while claiming to be on a vendor call that had been canceled.[105] She was interviewed for approximately three hours by two company investigators for vacation abuse under company policy. She was given a notice that she was not suppose to discuss the investigation with anyone other than authorized parties. Smith denied the abuse and noted that upon her return to the office she had sent a note to payroll to record the day as a vacation day. About two weeks later, she had lunch with a co-worker who was also a subject of the investigation and the vendor they were to visit, and they discussed the investigation. The next day she was reinterviewed and she walked out of the meeting. About a month later the company gave her the choice or resigning or accepting a demotion for violation of the vacation policy, failing to cooperate in the investigation, and discussing the case with nonauthorized persons. She accepted the demotion and filed suit against the company. In part, she claimed the two investigators falsely imprisoned her because one of the investigators "yelled at her and repeatedly called her a liar ... slammed the note on the table at one-point." The United States District Court thought the alleged conduct of the investigator was "disagreeable" but noted Pennsylvania law required there be "verbal threats" if there was no violence in the confinement. Because the room was unlocked, she was never threatened or physically restrained, never asked to leave, and had walked out of the second interview, the court granted summary judgment for the company.

a. Economic and Moral Compulsion

An interesting issue is whether an employee may be falsely imprisoned if he stays out of concern about losing his job (economic necessity) or feels a need (moral compulsion) to stay and clear his name. Although one's reputation is important and the loss of a job may inflict serious economic harm, the general rule is that these factors alone are insufficient to support claims of false imprisonment.

For example, in *Wright*, a loss prevention agent interviewed an employee suspected of underringing items.[106] The employee never attempted to leave and he was never threatened. He felt compelled to stay to clear his name and he was concerned that if he left he might be arrested. The U.S. District Court rejected these facts as being sufficient to support a claim of false imprisonment and granted summary judgment for the defendant.

In *Johnson v. United Parcel Services, Inc.*, an employee was interviewed for approximately three to four hours concerning theft and drug dealings.[107] He was not physical detained, verbally threatened, or confined in a locked room. Nor did the investigators act in anyway to block an escape. He stayed based upon "a statement leading plaintiff to fear that he might lose his job should he leave." He filed suit, in part, for false imprisonment. In granting summary judgment for the defendant corporation, the U.S. District Court stated, "The restraint that resulted simply from plaintiff's fear of losing his job is insufficient as a matter of law to make out a claim of false imprisonment."

b. Precautionary Protocols

Fact-finders can easily decrease the risk of successful suits for false imprisonment by taking certain precautionary measures. They should be able to show the employee was given notice he was free to leave at anytime; the employee was seated closest to and had unobstructed access to the door (provided safety of the investigator is not an issue), which was unlocked; there were not an excessive number of company representatives present; and the investigative interview was conducted in a reasonable manner and voice without threats, yelling, profanity, and similar conduct. It is important that an investigator properly document an interrogation, not only the content of the interview, but also the process, such as room, location of parties, start and end times, persons present, breaks and amenities, and other material information.

Tip: When conducting an employee verification interview, the fact-finder should allow the employee unobstructed access to the door, speak in a moderate voice, and avoid physical gestures that infer the employee is not free to leave.

---

4. Defamation

Defamation, as described earlier, refers to a false statement of fact published by one party to a third disinterested party that impugns the business, professional, or community reputation of another. Libel refers to written defamation, and slander refers to defamation by the spoken word or conduct. Defenses to defamation lawsuits include truth, nonpublication, absolute privileged communication, and qualified/conditional privileged communication.

a. Precautionary Protocols

In order to minimize their risk exposure, fact-finders need to exercise prudent common sense prior to, during, and after investigative verification interviews. In the preinterview stage, requests to meet with suspect employees should be neutral or nonaccusatory in nature to minimize the risk of premature publication of the accusations to disinterested parties. Hallway, lunchroom, and other public area conversations regarding the investigations and with suspects should remain neutral in nature. In the interview phase, whenever reasonably possible, investigative interviews should be conducted in private offices or work areas where other disinterested employees cannot overhear the discussions. The number of company agents present during an investigative interview should be restricted to persons who serve a necessary function, such as the investigator and witness, to minimize the risk of excessive publication.

In the postinterview phase, notes, written reports, and oral briefings should similarly be shared with only interested parties. This often includes the employee's superiors and select staff, such as human resources and security, if necessary to perform their duties. Investigators should be careful to avoid personal conclusions (which is different from accurately reporting and properly crediting statements of persons interviewed) and to use terms in all reports that accurately describe the suspects' conduct and that can be proven. This will reduce the risk of a court finding an investigator acted with malice and lost either the intracorporate or qualified privilege defenses to communicate derogatory information with interested parties.

b. Escorting of Employees

Investigators should conduct themselves in a normal, reasonable manner when escorting employees to and from investigative interviews, off company property, and when inspecting employee possessions. The following cases highlight a few of the risks.

In *Uebelacker*, a manager and two large subordinates confronted an employee in his office cubicle.[108] The manager told the employee that he was fired and to clean out his belongings. When the employee attempted to go to the personnel office, the manager blocked his path, grabbed him by the arm and spun him around, and later pushed down the phone disconnect button to prevent him from calling the personnel office. The manager even refused the employee permission to use the restroom. Subsequently, he relented but had the employee escorted. The encounter lasted approximately an hour and was witnessed by co-workers. The Court of Appeals of Ohio affirmed judgment for false imprisonment, emotional distress, and defamation.

Similarly, in *Caldor*, the Court of Appeals of Maryland affirmed a store security manager, who lacked probable cause to arrest, defamed a juvenile employee whom he had handcuffed and paraded through the store before patrons and other employees.[109] If an employee is to be handcuffed, a practice that has liability risks, the investigators should have probable cause to arrest or lawful need to restrain (e.g., the employee was violent).

It should be noted, however, the courts have generally held the reasonable escorting of employees off premises and searching of their possessions are not defamatory acts. In *Paolucci*, the Court of Appeals of Ohio held a nurse discharged for violation of work rules was not defamed when two security officers escorted her off hospital property in plain view of others.[110] In *Rolsen*, a store loss prevention manager and detective escorted an employee who was eating lunch in the mall through the mall and through the store where she worked.[111] Many employees in the mall and store knew the loss prevention staff even though they were nonuniformed. She was interviewed for suspected theft of a watch she wore to lunch, suspended, and escorted off the property by the human resource manager and store detective. Later that evening she was fired. She was kept under surveillance when she returned that night to pick up her possessions. She sued, in part, claiming defamation based upon this conduct. The Ohio Court of Appeals held the security and management staff did not act in an outrageous manner to support a claim she was defamed. The rationale behind this and other similar decisions is the courts' view that the reasonable escorting of employees off-site and the inspecting of employees' packages as common security practices do not infer the employees were engaged in criminal conduct.

5. *Duty to Investigate an Alibi*

A critical issue often overlooked by fact-finders is the lawful duty to investigate an alibi or other information favorable to the subject. The alleged failure to verify an alibi is in actuality an allegation the fact-finder was negligent in conducting the investigation. As discussed earlier, the majority of courts are reluctant to create a new tort action for negligent investigation. Such a tort action conflicts with the widely accepted doctrine of employment at-will. In addition, many other tort actions are available to plaintiffs who allege wrongful investigator conduct, including defamation, malicious prosecution, emotional distress, and wrongful discharge.

Nonetheless, fact-finders should be sensitive to the need to conduct additional fact-finding when suspects offer reasonable alibis or verifiable information. The failure to do so may not expose an investigator and employer to new liability but may add validity and strength to other claims for defamation, emotional distress, wrongful discharge, and malicious prosecution. A failure to conduct further reasonable inquiry may also lend credence to a plaintiff's claim for punitive damages based upon the reckless or malicious conduct of the investigator.

For example, the court, in *Mendez*, held an employee accused of theft was defamed by the company, an alcohol beverage distributor, when the plant manager, at the direction of the company president, fired the employee for theft and advised the employee's supervisor and union steward.[112] Prior to firing the employee, the president, on his way to breakfast, drove by the plant before it opened and saw the employee, a janitor, loading a box into the trunk of his car. The box was a type used by the company. After breakfast the president told the plant manager he had observed the employee stealing and to "take care of the matter."

Hereafter the facts are in dispute. The employee claimed he was called by the plant manager to the president's office and told he was being fired for theft. He further stated that he attempted to explain he took an empty box from the trash to hold the tools in his car, and he offered to open his car to be inspected. The executives declined. In contrast, the plant manager stated he fired the employee shortly after leaving the president's office, and it was sometime afterward the employee offered to have his car searched. Regardless of the sequence of events, without any further investigation the employee was discharged per company policy. The plant manager told the reason why to the supervisor and union steward. The employee sued the president and company for defamation. The jury found the president had not defamed the employee but the company did. The company appealed on the grounds the verdicts were irreconcilable.

The Appeals Court of Massachusetts affirmed judgment for the plaintiff employee. It held both the president and plant manager were privy to discuss the sensitive allegation, but it went on to state:

> We think that the evidence warranted a finding that broader
> dissemination of the charge against [the employee] without an

effort to verify its truth, in circumstances where verification was practical, amounted to a "reckless disregard" of [the employee's] rights and of the consequences that [might] result to him.

The conditional privilege to disseminate a serious charge may be lost, not only by knowledge of its falsity, but also by reckless disregard whether it is true or not. Reckless disregard does not necessarily imply that the charge has a flimsy base. Here, clearly, it did not. Recklessness can also be shown by a failure to verify in circumstances where verification is practical and the matter is sufficiently weighty to call for safeguards against error.

Further, as discussed earlier, when an employment relationship is not at-will the duty to verify an alibi or other evidence favorable to a suspect might be implicit in a contractual relationship such as a collective bargaining agreement. Likewise, there might be an implicit duty to verify alibis and other information in select statutes and regulations, such as antidiscrimination laws. The duty to investigate an alibi may include the obligation to properly document it too. In *Tenold*, the Oregon Court of Appeals awarded about $2.5 million against defendant company for malicious prosecution, defamation, and emotional distress because, in part, the security staff did not properly report plaintiff's alibi to upper management or authorities.[113]

6. Allegations of Discrimination

The potential for employees to claim discrimination raises other management-investigative issues. For example, assume a suspect employee claims he is the victim of discrimination because his conduct is no different from the conduct of other employees. Notice the suspect did not claim innocence but merely that others have engaged in similar conduct without being confronted or disciplined. How should an employer handle this allegation? Should the employer ignore or investigate the allegation? Should it continue to move forward with the investigation and corrective action, and treat the allegation as grounds for separate investigation? Or, should the employer delay corrective action and conduct further investigation of the allegation?

There is no simple answer. The decision must be made on a case-by-case basis by weighing the totality of information available. Regardless, when counter-claims of discrimination or similar claims are made, employers must recognize that the dynamics of an investigation may have changed and it may well be the company that will have to show it acted reasonably (e.g., it had a *legitimate business reason* for taking corrective action). A legitimate business reason may include the duty to investigate an alibi or other relevant information before taking the investigation further.

Nonetheless, employers and investigators should be cautious not to feel compelled to investigate every conceivable piece of evidence regardless of how remote. For example, in *Stockley*, the court refused to find a manager was defamed in an internal investigation when the company allegedly failed to interview a witness favorable to him.[114] The court noted the company had interviewed approximately 20 other persons. Relevant factors in deciding when a reasonable investigation has been conducted include the status of the employee (at-will versus employment contract), the possibility of an implicit statutory or regulatory duty, the applicable burdens and standards of proof, the thoroughness of the current investigation, the strength of the existing evidence, the ease and convenience of follow-up investigation, and similar factors.

7. Admissible Confessions

The admissibility and evidentiary value of any signed confession/admission may be challenged in a courtroom of law. In order to be admissible a signed confession must be made knowingly and voluntarily without undue duress, coercion, threat, or promise. A court may exclude a confession or admission that was obtained by duress, deceit, or false promise. Even if admitted as evidence, a jury may give little credence to the confession if it feels the plaintiff signed it as a result of abusive interrogation tactics, such as the interrogator yelling, threatening, intimidating, demanding a confession, or even dictating the wording of a confession. Because a confession may be extremely damaging to an employee's case, investigators should assume all plaintiffs will challenge the admission or credibility of their confessions.

A coerced confession may actually backfire on the investigator. In *DeAngelis*, the plaintiff, a 17-year-old cashier, sued her employer for false imprisonment.[115] Based upon the accusation of another employee who claimed the two split a false refund, the loss prevention district manager interviewed the employee for four hours in the evening. During the interview the plaintiff "was lectured about theft, shouted at, frightened, charged with theft and forced to admit to a crime she did not commit." The New Jersey Superior Court, Appellate Division, expressed its view of the investigator's conduct and the value of the confession when it stated, "The coerced false confession, the evil that concerned the Miranda court, evidences the outrageous nature of defendants' conduct." The appeals court affirmed punitive judgment for false imprisonment.

There are many factors that influence the admissibility and credibility of confessions, including age (e.g., youth and old age), experience, language skills, mental health, intelligence, conduct, and even requests of an employee. The number of management and investigative staff present, demeanor of the investigator, seating arrangements, location and room conditions, time of day, length of interrogation, breaks, and communications with outside parties may also be factors. An admissible and credible confession is the product of a reasonable investigative environment and process. The process may not be duress free, nor should it include undue coercion, trickery, or false promises.

Tip: Investigations can take quick turns. An alleged failure to investigate an alibi, a discrimination claim, or an allegation of a coerced confession can undermine the credibility of a fact-finder and the investigative findings. Be professional, be prepared, be objective, learn the facts, document the facts, report the facts, and let the facts speak to the allegations.

I. Claims Arising from Employee Disciplinary Actions

Liability risks associated with the discipline or corrective action phase of the investigative process include the continuing risks of defamation (and the newly established risk of self-published defamation), emotional distress, wrongful discharge, and malicious prosecution. In addition, fact-finders must be prepared to meet the evidentiary burdens of arbitration, unemployment, and workers' compensation hearings.

1. Defamation

Employees may claim they were defamed based upon false and excessive publication internally within a company and for false and derogatory reports made externally to outside parties, such as the police, unemployment boards, workers' compensation commissions, and media. As noted earlier, internal company discussions and reports regarding employee misconduct are usually protected by the intracorporate publication rule or a conditional privilege. Remarks and documents provided to government agencies are usually viewed as absolute or conditional privileged communications. Intracorporate and conditional privileges may be lost if a communication is not made in good faith (e.g., communications made with malice or reckless disregard for the truth of the matter) or if communicated to a disinterested party. Not to be overlooked, alleged defamatory comments must first be published.

In *Chappelle*, the defendant company initiated an investigation of an employee based upon an unusual pattern of no sales and voids.[116] He was interviewed for slightly over one hour by a regional loss prevention investigator with the store's loss prevention manager as a witness. He was advised the meeting was voluntary and that he was free to leave at anytime. The door was left unlocked. The suspect verbally confessed, signed a promissory note, and wrote the following confession:

> Over the last 5 or 6 months I have rang 5 transactions where I have rang the transaction for my self in order to generate a receipt so I could leave the store with unpaid merch[andise]. The approximate loss to Robinsons May by doing this is 500 dollars. I knew what I did was wrong[,] so I am willing to pay back the company for the loss. I am terribly sorry for what I have done and feel terrible[,] that is why I feel it is right to pay this back to the company.

After he affirmed his confession with the human resource manager, his employment was terminated. He filed suit, in part, for defamation. The plaintiff alleged he was defamed when an investigative report was forwarded to the Store Protection Association. The trial court held the evidence of defamation was insufficient to send to a jury and granted *nonsuit* in favor of defendant store. The plaintiff appealed. The Appeals Court of California noted, "Here it was uncontroverted that appellant stole merchandise. The only dispute was the amount taken." It stated: "The trial court ruled that appellant failed to meet his burden of proof for defamation. We agree. Appellant claimed that an internal case report was forwarded to the Store Protection Association, but there was no evidence that defendants actually transmitted the report. Defamation requires a publication." The trial court further ruled that the claim for defamation "is barred by the defenses of truth and qualified privilege. It did not err. Truth is an absolute defense to defamation." The Appeals Court of California affirmed judgment for defendant merchant.

Crump, as noted earlier, illustrates the need for employers to be careful about using unsubstantiated conclusions in internal discussions and reports.[117] Crump was the warehouse receiver who was terminated for taking defective goods home in violation of company policy. He successfully sued for defamation based upon the allegation he was called a "thief" in an internal meeting involving the warehouse director and two loss prevention personnel. Further, in two post-incident reports he was labeled a "problem employee" despite the fact he had been with the company for 18 years and had no other personnel actions taken against him. The Supreme Court of Vermont affirmed judgment against the company. It found the company lost the intra-corporate publication privilege based upon evidence showing a "reckless disregard for the truth or ... ill will in violation of the plaintiff's rights."

In *Present*, the plaintiff, a brochure production manager, was terminated after a thorough internal investigation initiated by his new director based upon complaints of the manager's subordinates.[118] Separate employees explained how the plaintiff divided large vendor invoices into smaller invoices to bypass audit controls, took a leather jacket and developed personal film at company expense, and directed a subordinate to have a vendor buy the plaintiff a $900 watch and bill it to the company. The vendor confirmed it had done so for fear of losing business. After the director made his report, in-house legal counsel reinterviewed and took affidavits from the parties. The plaintiff was confronted. He offered no reasonable explanation and was suspended. After two other vendors confirmed they falsely billed the company to cover for items they bought the plaintiff, the company terminated the plaintiff's employment. Corporate security and internal auditors then conducted independent investigations. Security presented its findings to the police. The plaintiff was charged with seven misdemeanors. He was acquitted on one count and the jury could not reach a verdict on the other six charges. The district attorney dismissed the charges rather than retry the case. The plaintiff filed suit for defamation and malicious prosecution (to be discussed later).

In part, he claimed the employees and vendors lied and defamed him, and the company defamed him when it reported the allegations to the police. The trial court denied defendants' motion for summary judgment. The Supreme Court, Appellate Division, New York stated:

> As defendants asserted in their summary judgment motion, all of the challenged statements are undoubtedly covered by a qualified privilege. This being the case, it was incumbent upon plaintiff to raise an issue of fact as to whether defendants acted with constitutional or common-law malice, which he failed to do.
>
> A good faith communication upon any subject matter in which the speaker has an interest, or in reference to which he has a duty, is qualifiedly privileged if made to a person having a corresponding interest or duty. The common interest privilege

covers statements by employees to management about another employee's job-related misconduct. The same is true of statements by an outside vendor or independent contractor. This qualified privilege also extends to reports to the police or the district attorney's office about another's suspected crimes. If the person passing on the information has a good faith belief in its truth, he is shielded from liability for defamation, even if a more prudent person would not have reported it or the information turns out to be false.

Essentially, to overcome the privilege, the plaintiff needs to challenge the good faith of the defendants by showing that they acted with malice. A speaker exhibits constitutional malice when he makes a defamatory statement while knowing that it is false or recklessly disregarding whether it is false. The plaintiff must set forth evidence to support the conclusion that the defendants entertained serious doubts as to the truth of the statement.

The court went on to compliment the thoroughness of the investigation, the direct knowledge of the employees and vendors, the cross-checking and consistency of evidence from the different sources, and the extensive documentation. Based upon the good faith shown by defendants, the Supreme Court, Appellate Division, New York, granted summary judgment to defendants.

In *Kelly*, the plaintiff was accused of assisting the spouse of another employee to steal merchandise and was terminated.[119] After the company dropped the criminal charges and she was awarded unemployment benefits over the objection of the company, the plaintiff sued her employer, manager, and co-workers for defamation. She argued the outcomes in the criminal and administrative proceedings were proof the defendants lost any qualified privilege they had to share the allegations against her. The Court of Appeal of Louisiana affirmed summary judgment for the defendants except for the alleged statements by one co-worker. It held the manager did not lose his qualified privilege because he communicated in good faith with persons who participated in the investigation, were in the plaintiff's chain of command, the company's lawyer, and its unemployment representative. Absent any evidence other than the plaintiff's speculative allegation the employees conspired to "frame her to divert suspicions [of theft] from themselves," the court also affirmed the employees who reported the alleged misconduct of plaintiff did not abuse their privilege when they spoke with management, police, and unemployment representative. But the court did find the alleged comments, if proven, of one employee to her mother and roommate would fall outside the conditional privilege.

In *Layne*, the Appellate Court of Illinois affirmed an employer's statement to the police that an employee had threatened, harassed, and assaulted a co-worker was an absolute privileged communication.[120] In *Beauchamp*, a company terminated all five store managers for "failure to protect company assets" after it conducted a three-month investigation and could not isolate the cause of a $150,000 inventory shortage.[121] One manager filed for unemployment benefits. The company contested on the grounds he was "not a prudent manager" and his "failure to protect company assets." Because the company did not establish the manager was at fault for the losses, he was awarded benefits. He claimed he was defamed in the unemployment hearing and filed suit. The appeals court affirmed the accusations by the company were not defamatory per se (note, the company did not accuse him of theft) and the employee failed to show the statements were false or the company acted with malice. It noted the company acted under a "qualified business privilege" and:

> the statements made by [the company] to persons at the Department of Employment Security were certainly relevant to the determination of unemployment compensation and made to persons with a legitimate interest therein. The testimony at trial concerning the defendant's extensive investigation as to the lost inventory provides the required element of good faith.

In conclusion, most communications to police, unemployment boards, workers' compensation, and similarly interested outside parties are privileged communications. In some jurisdictions statements in judicial and administrative agency proceedings are absolutely privileged communications, whereas in other jurisdictions these statements are conditional privileged communications. So long as employers act on a good faith belief of the truth of the matter and not with careless disregard for the facts or reasonably discoverable facts, employers should be protected when sharing information with interested external agencies. Second, employers generally have a conditional internal privilege to share adverse employee information with union stewards, supervisors, managers, and select staff such as security and human resources if this information is needed by them to perform their duties. In the alternative, employers may defend on the grounds of truth or nonpublication for intracorporate communications. Nonetheless, investigators should be careful to avoid prematurely labeling suspects as having engaged in criminal conduct. Instead, investigators should report the allegations as reported and the facts as documented, and refrain from reaching unsubstantiated conclusions in their oral and written investigative reports.

a. Self-Published Defamation

There is a little-known tort action for *self-published* defamation. These cases normally involve employees who have been terminated for misconduct and who repeat the reasons for their discharges to potential employers. In order to prevail, a plaintiff must show a defamatory statement, compelling facts that made it reasonably foreseeable plaintiff would republish the derogatory statement, and actual self-publication to a third party.

The majority of states that have reviewed this doctrine have rejected it primarily because it conflicts with the at-will employment doctrine. That is, discharged at-will employees could tell potential employers the stated reasons they were fired and then sue their former employers. There are other concerns, too: employees might purposely repeat such allegations; statutes of limitations might be extended with each republication; and employers might feel compelled to fire employees without comment rather than use constructive discipline to improve employee performance.

For example, in *Sullivan*, the plaintiff was a part-time neonatal nurse at defendant's hospital and at another hospital that was setting up a neonatal unit.[122] The plaintiff told a co-worker that she had taken some new angiocaths, used to start infant IVs, from the defendant's hospital to the other hospital. The co-worker reported her. She denied the allegations. The hospital terminated her. She applied for positions with two other hospitals and revealed the reason for her discharge. She was not hired. She filed suit for self-published defamation. The trial court granted summary judgment to defendant hospital on the ground the plaintiff failed to prove publication. The appeals court reversed. It held the state would recognize the tort of self-publication defamation in the employment context. The hospital appealed.

The Supreme Court of Tennessee rejected the self-publication doctrine because it would chill employer-employee communications, negatively impact grievance procedures, cast an unfair doubt of silence over persons who were discriminatorily discharged, create a cause of action of negligent investigation in conflict with at-will employment, and unreasonably stretch the state statute of limitation. The court also concluded the lower standard of proof used in the self-publication doctrine conflicted with the higher standards in the state statute governing the right of employers to share employee information. Under the self-defamation doctrine an employer might be held liable for its negligence in failing to undercover the truth, whereas the state statute shielded employers from liability except in circumstances where an employer shares information that is "Knowingly false; Deliberately misleading; Disclosed for malicious purpose; Disclosed in a reckless disregard for its falsity …; or Violative of … employment discrimination laws."

A few states have recognized self-publication defamation.[123] Many, perhaps all, of these have retained the qualified/conditional privilege of employers to communicate in good faith with their employees. In *Theisen*, for example, the plaintiff was a security director who was terminated for leaving a sexual harassment phone message on the voice mail of a nurse.[124] He claimed self-publication defamation in that he felt compelled to tell his family, friends, and potential employers the alleged reason for his discharge to get their support for his personnel appeal and to obtain future employment. In the words of the state supreme court, the trial court granted summary judgment to the defendant hospital on the grounds "an employer is entitled to qualified immunity for statements made to an employee to protect the employer's interest, and that the privilege extends to situations in which the employee feels compelled to repeat such statements." The Supreme Court of Iowa affirmed the hospital had not acted outside its privilege. It found the original communication

> was made in good faith, based on the identification of [plaintiff's] voice by four persons. [The hospital] had an undisputed interest in the subject of the statement, which was made as part of a sexual harassment investigation. And the statement was made during a closed-door meeting with [plaintiff's] supervisor and the director of employee services, a proper time and place to discuss such an accusation with limited parties. Thus [the hospital's] statement easily falls within the criteria necessary to establish a qualified privilege as a matter of law.

In *DeWald*, the employee plaintiff put some loose wood in two shopping carts, showed it to the assistant department manager, paid the reduced price he was told to pay by the assistant manager, and loaded it into his truck.[125] The store loss prevention manager saw him loading the wood, spoke with an assistant manager, and then told the plaintiff to pay more for the excess wood he had beyond three bundles, or unload it from his truck. Later, the employee left without unloading or paying for the alleged excess wood. He returned the next morning with the wood still in his truck. The loss prevention manager and two store assistant managers interviewed the employee. He was terminated. The loss prevention manager walked him out of the store through the front door even though an employee exit was closer, unloaded the wood from the truck, and refunded the employee's money. At this time, co-workers overheard the loss prevention manager state the plaintiff was fired for taking more wood beyond that which he paid. The assistant managers stated in his personnel file that the plaintiff was discharged for "theft of firewood and a fraudulent act." About a month later the loss prevention manager and assistant store manager in a employee meeting stated the plaintiff was "terminated for stealing firewood and had to be dealt with in the same fashion as [the company] dealt with other shoplifters." The latter comment meant he was escorted out the front door as other shoplifters to make an example of him and to intimidate fellow employees. In subsequent job interviews the plaintiff, in response to the question why he had left his former employer, stated he had been fired for theft and fraud.

He filed suit for defamation, including compelled self-publication defamation. The trial court granted summary judgment for defendant employer and employees. The plaintiff appealed. The appeals court reversed. It noted that when job applicants are asked why they left their former employment there is *compulsion* to reveal the reasons for failure to do so or lying could be grounds for denial of employment or termination. The court held the plaintiff offered evidence on each element of his defamation claim and the company did not "conclusively establish[ed] that the defamatory statements were either substantially true or that their publication was a privileged communication." The Court of Appeals of Texas remanded the case for further proceedings on the issue of self-publication defamation.

> Tip: When responding to employee complaints and claims for benefits, employers enjoy a good faith privilege to share investigative information with government agencies, including state unemployment and workers' compensation commissions, and federal agencies such as the NLRB and EEOC.

---

2. Wrongful Discharge

The vast majority of private sector workers are at-will employees. Under the *employment at-will doctrine,* which is recognized in all jurisdictions, an employee may accept and leave a position at anytime, and an employer may hire and discharge an employee at anytime for any reason, no reason, or even a bad reason. This doctrine is a major but sometimes surmountable barrier for employees who believe they were unjustly discharged. As discussed here, not all employers serve at-will, and there are several exceptions to the employment at-will relationship.

a. Union and Personal Employment Contracts

Not all employment relationships are at-will. Union members, for example, work under collective bargaining agreements, and an employer must show cause, just cause, good cause, or similar evidence to terminate. Failure to satisfy the requisite burden may result in an arbitrator directing the company to reinstate a terminated union employee with or without back pay and benefits. Similarly, some executives and professionals have personal contracts of employment that restrict the rights of employers to cause discharges. A terminated employee may file an arbitration grievance or a breach of contract lawsuit against the employer and force the employer to show cause or pay the full benefits of the contract.

b. Implied Contract of Employment

One exception to the at-will doctrine is an *implied contract of employment*. In union and personal contracts of employment, the terms and conditions of employment have been negotiated and agreed to by all concerned parties. In contrast, an implied contract is one that arises based upon facts that would lead a reasonable party to conclude a contract right exists. Many of these cases involve oral statements by managers and the disciplinary procedures and standards set forth in employee handbooks and personnel manuals. Sometimes at-will employees claim these unilaterally issued publications by employers are binding contracts of employment and they were fired outside the disciplinary provisions. Employers may defeat these claims by inserting appropriate notices in the documents (e.g., the manuals are not contracts of employment and the employment relationship remains at-will).

c. Whistleblower and Similar Statutes

Many states have whistleblower statutes that prohibit retaliatory discharges against employees who report illegal company acts (e.g., tax fraud and illegal dumping). The breadth and depth of protection varies by statute. Some protect only employees who actually report the criminal conduct to the authorities. Other statutes, as a means of shielding employees from preemptive terminations by their employers, also protect those employees who were about to report the criminal conduct. Some statutes protect employees when reporting violations of a specific law, whereas other statutes protect employees for reporting a wide variety of employer criminal conduct under the penal code. These statutes may not apply when employees report criminal acts that are unknown to company executives. When an employee qualifies for protection under a statute, the burden usually shifts to the employer to show the termination was for reasons separate from the employee's protected status.

d. Public Policy

Many states recognize an action for wrongful discharge in *violation of public policy* (i.e., the discharge is harmful to the larger interests of the public). In order to prevail, employees must often prove a *clear and compelling reason* the discharges violates the public interest. Usually this interest must be based upon the constitution or statutes of the state, although a few states recognize judicial public policy. This doctrine allows the courts to intervene when other remedies may not be available. For example, assume an employee filed a workers' compensation claim and was shortly thereafter falsely terminated for theft, the employee might argue the discharge violated public policy because it was a pretext to deny him benefits and to deter co-workers from filing for workers' compensation benefits.

e. Discriminatory Discharges

Terminated at-will employees might claim their discharges were illegally based upon race, nationality, color, sex, religion, age, disability, or other protected classification. Once an employee shows prima facie discrimination (member of a protected class and adverse employment action), the burden shifts to the employer to show a legitimate business reason for the discharge. The burden then shifts back to the employee to prove the proffered reason is a pretext. At-will employees who are members of protected groups may claim their discharges were discriminatory, shifting the burden to the employers to show legitimate business reasons (facts supported by the investigations) for the terminations, thereby shifting it back to the employees to show the investigative findings were pretexts.

f. Covenant of Good Faith and Fair Dealings

The *covenant of good faith and fair dealings* is a contract law doctrine. It implies all parties to a contract have a duty to act accordingly. A small minority of states have applied this doctrine to wrongful discharge cases to prevent employers from unfairly denying employees benefits they have or are near earning. For example, assume a sales representative made a large sale and was entitled to substantial upfront and continuing commissions and he was shortly thereafter fired for embezzlement. He might file a wrongful discharge suit claiming his discharge was a pretext by the company to avoid paying his commissions in violation of the covenant of good faith and fair dealings.

g. Case Discussion

In *Dewald*, an employee was terminated for alleged theft of firewood. He had paid the reduced price for the unbundled firewood (a common practice by the store) that he was told to pay by the assistant department manager.[126] Later that day the loss prevention manager, at the direction of the assistant store manager, told him to pay more or unload it. He left work and returned with the wood the next day. The company gave him his money back and fired him for theft. Although the Court of Appeals of Texas reversed the summary judgment in favor of the defendant store on the issue of defamation, it affirmed judgment on the issue of wrongful discharge. The employee argued he had an expressed agreement based upon a company policy of providing three warnings prior to termination. The court held employee practices and employee handbooks standing alone without expressed agreement do not alter an at-will employment relationship. Here, the company had disclaimers the handbook was intended to provide only guidelines, it was subject to change, and it did not create any contract rights.

In *French*, the plaintiff employee, an inventory stocking crew leader, was discharged after he signed a confession to knowingly eating a small amount of food and not paying for it.[127] He alleged his confession was coerced by a private investigator. The company fired him. He filed suit claiming the company "breached an express contract of employment, … an implied-at-law covenant of good faith and fair dealing," and tortuously discharge him in violation of public policy. The trial court granted summary judgment for the company. He appealed. The Iowa Supreme Court, first, noted an exception to the employment at-will doctrine arises "when a contract created by an employer's handbook or policy manual guarantees an employee that discharge will occur only for cause or under certain conditions." But, it rejected the employee's claim because the handbook contained language it was for "information only," the company "reserves the right to change or terminate any or all of [policies, procedures] at any time" and "Just as you retain the right to terminate your employment at any time, for any reason, [the company] retains a similar right." Second, the Iowa Supreme Court stated the plaintiff "urges us to adopt a cause of action for breach of an implied covenant of good faith and fair dealing, a theory that we expressly rejected. In rejecting this theory, we joined the majority of jurisdictions that have considered it." Third, the employee argued the coerced confession violated "Iowa's policy against suborning perjury and the prohibition against making a false charge of dishonesty" and the policy that "every person is presumed innocent until proven guilty." The court did not discuss the alleged coercion, instead it rejected his public policy argument on the grounds the case did not involve a criminal charge, perjury, or the presumed innocent doctrine. The Iowa Supreme Court affirmed judgment for the company.

In *Mead*, the defendant company terminated an employee over an unspecified incident at a convenience store and the employee filed suit.[128] She claimed, in part, breach of an implied contract of employment. The company responded that its employment application governed the case and she was an at-will employee. It filed a motion for summary judgment. The Superior Court of Connecticut denied the motion on the grounds there were material facts in dispute about the nature of the employment. Specifically, it stated the manager's alleged remarks "about security, longevity, and promotion opportunities which, factually, contradicts the at will employment relationship."

In *Theisen*, discussed previously, a director of hospital security was suspected of making an obscene phone call that was left in the voice mailbox of a nurse.[129] After four employees identified the voice as the director's, the hospital requested he submit an exemplar of his voice for voice pattern analysis. He refused based upon an attorney's advice it violated the state polygraph statute. The hospital terminated his employment. The director filed suit, in part, alleging his discharge was in violation of public policy because it violated the state polygraph act that prohibited employers from requesting or requiring an employee to submit to a polygraph examination. The court granted summary judgment to the defendant hospital. The director appealed. The Supreme Court of Iowa found the voice pattern analysis as requested was not to detect deception. Instead, the device was to be used as a means of identification, much as fingerprints and photographs. Because he was not going to be asked specific questions for determination of truth, his discharge did not violate the public policy of the state. The court affirmed judgment for the hospital.

In *Wholey*, a long-term at-will store security manager filed a lawsuit for wrongful discharge in violation of public policy.[130] After having given the security manager permission to install a camera in the office of the store manager who was suspected of theft, the security director told him to remove it before it was activated. Shortly thereafter, the store manager fired him. He filed suit and won damages of $166,000 for wrongful discharge. The Court of Special Appeals of Maryland reversed. It held there was no clear legislative or judicial mandate that an employee investigate or report a co-employee's criminal conduct, therefore, his discharge did not violate the public policy of the state.

Similarly, in *Morris*, a long-term at-will employee claimed he was wrongfully terminated in violation of public policy.[131] He argued the company failed to conduct a reasonable investigation and it falsely accused him of misappropriating funds. The Supreme Court of Connecticut affirmed he failed to state a recognized cause of action because a mere negligent false accusation did not violate a clear constitutional, statutory, or judicial public policy.

In *Koller*, a nurse on separate occasions reported two doctors for abusing patients.[132] She threatened to report the abuse to the state if the hospital did not address the issues. Over the next 18 months, she reported retaliatory abuse by the physicians. The hospital proposed to initiate a staff training program in response to her complaint. She quit. She filed suit for wrongful discharge under a constructive discharge argument (i.e., working conditions were so bad a reasonable person would feel compelled to quit). She argued her constructive discharge violated the "about to report" section of the state Whistleblowers' Protection Act. The Court of Appeals of Michigan affirmed judgment in favor of the hospital on the grounds the plaintiff could not show with clear and convincing evidence she was protected under the statute given the long lapse of time, 18 months, between her first statement that she would report the abuse until the time she resigned.

In *Vaillancourt*, an assistant store manager with a bi-polar disorder was granted a leave of absence.[133] Later, she returned to work on a reduced work schedule to accommodate her disability. Due to staffing shortages, she frequently worked over her scheduled hours. One day when working late, she was told by an associate that two customers had just shoplifted. She and a security officer followed the suspects outside the store and told a police officer who detained the suspects and recovered the items. She was terminated for violating the "Four Steps of Proof" policy of the company that required a manager to witness the theft. She filed suit for failure to accommodate and wrongful discriminatory discharge. The trial court granted summary judgment for the store.

The appeals court reversed. It found there was sufficient evidence to go to trial to determine if the store did offer reasonable accommodation in light of the fact that accommodation is an ongoing requirement (i.e., the question of whether her working longer than approved by her doctor was a triable issue). Reference the discriminatory discharge claim, the appeals court noted her manager reported she did not train the plaintiff on the policy until after the incident. There was testimony the regional manager had been condescending and hostile to her accommodation needs. Further, the regional manager did not inform the management staff that reviewed the incident that plaintiff had not been trained prior to the incident. In addition, there was evidence the company had not fired other assistant managers who violated the policy. The Court of Appeals of California remanded the case to the trial court.

In conclusion, although most employees are at-will and may be terminated at anytime for any, no, or poor reasons, fact-finders still must be cognizant of wrongful discharge claims. When employees establish that their services are not at-will or they qualify under an exception to the employment at-will doctrine, wrongful discharge claims shift the burden to the employers to offer sufficient evidence to sustain the terminations.

Tip: Under the employment at-will doctrine employees may be fired at anytime for any reason. But, there are exceptions to this rule that employers need to understand and to consider before discharging employees.

---

3. Malicious Prosecution

Before deciding to bring criminal charges against an employee, an employer should understand the civil tort action of malicious prosecution. It is a civil action designed to protect persons from being unjustly prosecuted. In order to prevail on a malicious prosecution claim the plaintiff employee must prove the defendant employer or investigator initiated or continued a criminal proceeding without probable cause and for a malicious purpose, and the criminal proceeding terminated in favor of the accused employee.

When analyzing these cases the courts focus on the issues of initiation and continuation, probable cause, malice of the accuser, and decisions in favor of the accused. In addition to a not guilty verdict, possible verdicts in favor of the accused cover a wide range of actions, including a dropping of charges by the employer, a decision to not prosecute by the district attorney, and a dismissing of the charges on merit by a judicial officer. The existence of probable cause is often based upon the good faith belief of the employer or investigator at the time or it may be based upon the beliefs of a reasonable person in the same situation at the time. If a grand jury indicts the employee on the same evidence and not evidence later acquired, this is a very strong but refutable presumption of probable cause. Malice is closely linked with but separate from the issue of probable cause. The absence of probable cause supports a conclusion of malice by an employer, but malice must be further proven by a showing of a reckless disregard for the facts to a specific ill will directed at the accused employee.

The time when a criminal proceeding is actually initiated also varies by jurisdiction. Generally, the reporting of information to the police is not an initiation of a criminal proceeding if the police have the opportunity to conduct an independent investigation. However, the known inclusion of false information or the withholding of material information from the police may convert the reporting party's action into an initiation. The signing of a criminal complaint by an employer and the insistence of having an employee arrested on the scene by a police officer are acts that increase the probability the courts will find the employers initiated the criminal proceeding. Finally, the continuation of a criminal proceeding refers to an employer's ongoing duty after initiating a criminal proceeding to timely disclose to the authorities any subsequently discovered material information that favors an accused and diminishes existing probable cause. Failure to do so may be viewed as evidence of malice toward the accused.

In *Wright*, a customer was stopped leaving a store with approximately $50.00 of merchandise for which she had paid only a $1.05.[134] The customer signed a statement the employee (plaintiff) who underrang the items had participated in prior misconduct. This later part of the statement was based upon information the customer's husband, who worked at the store, told her. The husband later denied making such a statement. The employee was interviewed for approximately one and a half hours. The police were called. A detective took a statement of the store loss prevention agent. Without any further involvement by the company or further investigation by the police, ten days later the police arrested the plaintiff for shoplifting. He was acquitted and sued, in part, for malicious prosecution. The company filed a motion for summary judgment. The U.S. District Court held the company did not initiate the arrest of the plaintiff. The company played no more active role than reporting the offense. The police elected to engage in no further investigation and to initiate charges. Further, it found the company had probable cause to report the incident to the police based upon the merchandise recovered versus the purchase price paid. The probable cause was strengthened by the allegation of the customer against the plaintiff. The court granted summary judgment on the issue of malicious prosecution in favor of the company.

In *Binns*, the company appealed an award of $750,000 compensatory and $2 million punitive damages for malicious prosecution and abuse of process.[135] The company pressed criminal charges against the employee for theft of lay-away payments. The evidence against the employee consisted of numerous cancellations of customers' final payments by the employee and the lack of overage in her cash drawer when she balanced the count. The company contacted the police. A detective reviewed the files, copied some transactions, and obtained an arrest warrant for the employee. A year later the prosecutor *nolle prossed* the case for lack of evidence. The plaintiff successfully sued for malicious prosecution and the company appealed. The Supreme Court of Arkansas focused its analysis on the testimony of the employee's expert. He testified the company's computer software in use at the time would not have shown an overage in the system when the last payment was canceled even if she did not remove the payment. He also thought the two managers who investigated the problem probably believed they had probable cause to believe she stole the funds, and they probably did not act with "ill will, spite, or a spirit of revenge." The Supreme Court of Arkansas found the managers had "honest and strong suspicions" that the employee was taking funds from the register. It reversed the judgment against the company and it held the company was entitled to a directed verdict because the plaintiff failed to prove either the absence of probable cause or the existence of malice.

In *Sisney*, a company vice president had a check issued to himself, told the cashier to record it as a cash advance, and because the president was absent, signed the president's name followed by his name—"Ballou by Sisney."[136] The company contacted the police and reported the vice president was embezzling company funds because he did not have the authority to sign the president's signature, nor had he ever done so in the past. The prosecutor refused to prosecute the case when he found out the vice president on four prior occasions had issued and signed similar checks, a fact the company withheld. The court held there was sufficient evidence to prove the company maliciously initiated criminal proceedings against the accused.

When money turned up missing out of a cash register, a store manager filed an initial police report, followed by two company investigators, which named the plaintiff as the prime suspect.[137] Subsequently, the company investigators learned another employee had access to the missing money, she had access to other missing funds, and creditors were calling her at work. The company investigators never shared this information with the police. The police arrested the first employee. She was found not guilty and sued the company for malicious prosecution. The trial court granted summary judgment for the defendants. The Maryland Court of Appeals reversed. It ruled there was sufficient evidence for the plaintiff to pursue a malicious prosecution claim against the company and remanded the case for trial.

When reporting suspect employee criminal activities to the authorities, employers should make full and timely disclosure of all known facts and subsequently discovered facts material to the cases. Further, they should not hastily sign criminal complaints, nor press the authorities (including officers on the scene) to make arrests in order to make examples of the employees. Employers should refrain from labeling employees as criminals; rather they should simply share known facts that the police may conduct independent investigations to determine if probable cause exists to arrest or obtain an arrest warrant. Before actually signing criminal complaints, fact-finders should reaffirm they have conducted good faith investigations and reasonably believe they have probable cause to support the complaints.

4. Emotional Distress/Outrage

Employees who are terminated or prosecuted by their employers may reasonably be expected to add claims for emotional distress/outrage. As previously discussed, these claims may be for the intentional or negligent infliction of emotional distress. In order to prevail on a claim of intentional infliction of emotional distress, a plaintiff must prove the defendant acted in an outrageous and highly offensive manner that was highly probable of inflicting severe emotional distress upon another. In a negligence case, plaintiffs may also have to prove physical impact, risk of imminent physical impact upon themselves, or physical manifestations of the distress. These claims in investigation cases are usually based upon abusive investigative interviewing practices and the reckless disregard for the truth of the information obtained during the investigation.

In *Agis,* as discussed earlier, a restaurant manager in response to employee theft terminated employees in alphabetical order in order to force the thief to confess. The Supreme Court of Massachusetts felt this action, even without physical injury, was sufficient to support a cause of action for intentional or reckless infliction of emotional distress. It reinstated the claims against defendant.

In *Olivas,* the Superior Court of Connecticut held an employee could sue his employer for emotional distress on the grounds the discharge taken with the accusation of theft and forgery could amount to "extreme and outrageous conduct."[138] Here, after a paycheck was stolen and cashed at a liquor store, an employee of the company made comments to the liquor storeowner that the employee plaintiff stole the check and committed forgery. Allegedly, other employees accused the plaintiff and told his landlord. Later, the criminal charges against the plaintiff were dismissed.

In *Tenold,* the Court of Appeals of Oregon affirmed $2.4 million against the company for defamation, malicious prosecution, and intentional infliction of emotional distress, and $150,000 in damages against the site security supervisor for defamation and intentional infliction of emotional distress.[139] This case involved the employee who was arrested for stealing company railroad ties. The criminal charges were dropped after the company could not show evidence of ownership and the employee was able to produce receipts for some of the ties. The employee claimed he had been given permission to take the ties and pay for them later. There was evidence a site security supervisor and another manager bore ill will toward the employee. The manager had stated he wanted his job, and the security supervisor accused him of being a drunk and drug user, and operating a methamphetamine lab. The company investigative reports did not accurately reflect the exculpatory statement of the accused employee. The appeals court held these facts were sufficient evidence for a jury to conclude the defendants had engaged in an extraordinary and intolerable campaign to defame, terminate, and prosecute the plaintiff.

Disciplinary actions based upon unreasonable investigative methods and interrogations expose businesses to the increased risk of lawsuits for infliction of emotional distress. Fair disciplinary actions that are based upon reasonable inquiry are far less likely at the disciplinary phase to expose employers to claims of emotional distress.

5. *Unemployment Claims*

Unemployment compensation is a state-administered program designed to provide temporary financial relief for workers who lose their jobs through no fault of their own. If an employer wishes to challenge an employee's claim for benefits, the burden is generally placed upon the employer to prove the employee's actions constituted misconduct, willful misconduct, or similar disqualifying conduct as defined by state statute.

For example, Florida defines misconduct as:

(a) Conduct demonstrating willful or wanton disregard of an employer's interests and found to be a deliberate violation or disregard of the standards of behavior which the employer has a right to expect of his or her employee; or

(b) Carelessness or negligence to a degree or recurrence that manifests culpability, wrongful intent, or evil design or shows an intentional and substantial disregard of the employer's interests or of the employee's duties and obligations to his or her employer.[140]

In Illinois misconduct is defined as "the deliberate and willful violation of a reasonable rule or policy by the employing unit."[141]

The degree of evidence required to be produced by an employer varies by state. A frequently referenced standard is *substantial* evidence.[142] Substantial evidence is sufficient to support a decision even though others might reach a different conclusion. Some courts will not overturn an unemployment board's decision unless it is clearly contrary to the overwhelming weight of the evidence[143] or against the manifest weight of the evidence.[144]

In *Cabreja*, the claimant was a hospital janitor.[145] A security officer observed her accepting an empty bag from a suspect ex-employee under surveillance, going into a locker room, and returning the bag filled with hospital cleaning supplies to the suspect. She was terminated and denied unemployment benefits. An appeals court affirmed there was substantial and credible evidence to support the unemployment board's decision the claimant employee engaged in misconduct and was disqualified from collecting benefits. In the words of the board, as affirmed by the Supreme Court, Appellate Division, New York, "We find significant the credible eye-witness testimony of the security guard who personally observed the transfer of the shopping bag which contained the stolen hospital property."

In *Hurlbut*, the Missouri Court of Appeals ruled a convenience store manager violated the reasonable rules of her employer when she and her subordinates failed to include a cash register tape with the daily count of the cash box.[146] The absence of the detail tape impeded the company from determining the actual date and time of a cash shortage. The appeals court affirmed there was sufficient evidence to support the denial of benefits.

Similarly, in *Frey*, the Commonwealth Court of Pennsylvania affirmed there was substantial evidence of willful misconduct by an employee who left a piece of paper with the combination on top of the office safe.[147] The fact she claimed that she left it for another employee and asked it be placed in her mailbox did not relieve her of her duty.

a. Off-Duty Misconduct

The general rule is that off-duty conduct of employees is not relevant to employers. But, when there is a nexus or connection with the duties of the employee, the off-duty conduct may be grounds for denial of unemployment benefits. These cases normally involve conduct that breaches a necessary trust or reflects negatively upon the reputation of the company.

In *Montellanico*, the claimant was the supervisor of hourly workers.[148] He scheduled workers and processed unemployment and other claims. He was also treasurer of the employees' credit union where he was arrested for making fraudulent loans. The credit union operated completely independent of the company. Upon hearing of his arrest, the company suspended and later terminated him before there was a conclusion of the criminal proceeding. Based upon his admission to the authorities that he had made fraudulent loans the unemployment board found this conduct related directly to his duties as hourly employee supervisor. Applying a two-prong test where the employer must show the employee's off-duty criminal conduct was inconsistent with acceptable behavior and it reflected upon his ability to perform his duties, the Commonwealth Court of Pennsylvania held that the claimant's conduct threatened if not totally destroyed the requisite trust between himself and the hourly employees. It affirmed the denial of benefits.

In *Conseco,* the employer, in response to thefts in the workplace, instituted a criminal records check of employees.[149] The claimant signed the authorization. She worked the midnight shift and had unrestricted access to five buildings. Her job entailed the printing of customer claim checks. Later, she was arrested for shoplifting. She pled not guilty. The company discovered the arrest when it conducted her background check. It terminated her employment. She filed for benefits. The company argued the employee breached a necessary trust. The hearing deputy denied her benefits. An administrative law judge reversed on the grounds there had not been a final adjudication and therefore no proven disqualifying conduct. The company appealed. It introduced evidence that the employee later pled guilty. Nonetheless, the board found the company's evidence was too attenuated to prove she was terminated for just cause related to work. The company appealed. The appeals court found there was substantial evidence to support the board's decision. It affirmed the company did not establish work-related just cause.

6. Workers' Compensation

The purpose of workers compensation is to provide financial benefits and medical care for victims of accidental injuries arising out of and during the course of employment. At the time of discipline employers should determine whether they will contest the awarding of benefits. If they do, the burden is generally upon an employer to establish the injury did not arise out of and in the course of employment, an employee is malingering and able to return to work, or employee fraud. One popular investigative method in workers' compensation cases is surveillance with video cameras. Employers and investigators must recognize that although video evidence is often invaluable there are restrictions upon its use and limits to inferences that might be drawn from the evidence.

For example, in *Combined Insurance Company of America,* the employer had photographic evidence of an employee jumping into a pool and bending over a lounge chair.[150] This video evidence was reviewed by the employer's medical expert. He testified the employee was able to return to work. This evidence, however, was stricken from the record when the employer failed to authenticate it by having the photographer testify as the parties had agreed.

In *Anthony,* a private investigator observed a widow beneficiary of a deceased worker had an overnight male visitor.[151] A second investigator placed surveillance on the home and videotaped the widow (she was 60 years of age and her husband had died approximately ten years prior) and the male early in the morning standing on the front porch hugging twice and kissing once. The employer requested the discontinuance of death benefits on the grounds she had entered into a meretricious relationship. The claimant testified that the male lived in her home while he was remodeling his home, a period that lasted for approximately 20 months, and that they did not have a sexual relationship. Further, medical testimony was introduced that the male was a diabetic and suffered from erectile dysfunction. The workers' compensation judge cut off benefits on the grounds the two lingering kisses were "not the type of kiss the majority of Pennsylvanians give to their platonic friends." Noting the parties did not admit to the relationship and there was no child conceived out of the relationship, the court held the video evidence was insufficient to establish substantial evidence of a carnal relationship. Even though it recognized employers were in a difficult situation, finding substantial evidence of such a sensitive nature without invading the privacy of the persons, it reversed the board's denial of benefits.

In seeking to use video evidence, investigators must be prepared to authenticate the evidence. They may enhance the strengths of their cases, although it may not always be practical or possible, by obtaining multiple videotapes of suspects engaged in disqualifying behavior before seeking to disqualify them.

In conclusion, the primary liability issues that arise from employee discipline are defamation including compelled self-published defamation, emotional distress, wrongful discharge, and malicious prosecution. Further, at this stage of the investigation the burden is upon the employers to produce evidence to prove disqualifying employee conduct to deny or terminate the awarding of workers' compensation and unemployment benefits.

Employers may minimize the liability risks and enhance their successes in administrative hearings by sharing adverse information in good faith on a need-to-know basis only; administering fair and impartial discipline; properly documenting all evidence and making full and timely disclosure to law enforcement authorities when filing criminal charges; and obtaining documentation of repeated or serious disqualifying behavior when challenging unemployment and workers' compensation benefits.

J. Prevention and Education

The final phase of the investigative process is Prevention and Education. When reaching out to inform and change employee behavior, an important question for employers is how much information regarding an investigation and disciplinary action should be shared with coworkers? The primary liability concerns are lawsuits for defamation, false light invasion of privacy, and emotional distress.

1. Defamation and False Light Invasion of Privacy

Both these actions have been discussed earlier. In review, defamation occurs when one party publishes a false statement of fact to a third disinterested party and the statement is injurious to the community, business, or professional reputation of the named party. False light invasion of privacy involves the emotional distress suffered by the party based upon the publicity of a false statement.[152] A false statement is one made with reckless disregard for the truth that attributes highly objectionable characteristics, beliefs, or conduct to an individual and places him before the public in a false position.[153] Publicity means the statement was made before the public or shared with a sufficient number of persons that it is likely to become public knowledge.

In *Bine*, previously discussed, the plant manager, in order to deal with rumors, told a number of employees the plaintiff was fired for vandalism. Plaintiff filed suit, in part, for false light invasion of privacy. The trial court granted summary judgment to the company. The Supreme Court of West Virginia held there was a dispute of material fact as to the truth of the allegation. It noted, "The spreading of such information, if false, could constitute a valid false light claim." The supreme court reversed and remanded the case to the trial court.[154] In *Garcia*, the human resource manager held two staff meetings and told coworkers of plaintiff that based upon a "thorough investigation" [an anonymous phone call] plaintiff was observed shooting up cocaine. Plaintiff sued for both defamation and false light invasion of privacy. The jury found in her favor on both counts. The trial judge vacated the judgment. U.S. Court of Appeals reversed. It affirmed there was sufficient evidence to support both claims.[155]

Where these cases involved oral statements made by management, *Stock* involved two written statements released by management to employees. As noted earlier, plaintiffs were new contract security officers who were accused of cheating in their basic training class. They were denied access by the electric company to the nuclear facility where they were to be assigned. The company investigation did not conclusively prove which employees had cheated. Yet, the company released two statements to its employees. The first memo by the plant manager stated the ten officers were denied access because they were involved in cheating while in training. It also stated the company would not tolerate such conduct and that this incident did not reflect upon the current security staff. The second statement appeared in the monthly nuclear department newsletter. It stated the company had rescinded the unescorted access of ten security guards because they broke the bond of trust by violating the testing code. It added that it was a difficult situation for all, the company felt sympathy for the officers and families, but the rescission of access privileges was the right thing to do. The officers sued the company for defamation. Since the communications made it appear as if all the officers were cheating, the jury found the officers were defamed and awarded each officer $46,500. The Court of Appeals of Wisconsin affirmed the judgment.[156]

The risk for companies that attempt to explain or justify specific disciplinary actions to coworkers is that the underlying investigations will not support the alleged defamatory and false light statements. A safer alternative is to not make any internal public statements. For example, in *Smith*, the U.S. District Court rejected plaintiff's claim that she was put in false light when she was escorted off company property and the company "left her coworkers free to speculate that Smith had been disciplined for something more egregious than vacation day violation, such as fraud or graft." Similarly, in *Szot*, an insurance agent, who was terminated for falsification of applications for insurance coverage, claimed, in part, defamation based upon the "rumor mill" among other agents regarding her termination. Since the plaintiff did not produce any evidence the company told the other agents of the reason for her discharge, the U.S. District Court granted summary judgment to the defendant company.[157]

It is more difficult to sue an employer for not saying anything than it is to sue for the confidential remarks published beyond a need-to-know basis. In the alternative, if an employer feels the information must be shared, before sharing it, the employer should carefully consider: why it is necessary to share this information; who will be told; what is the legitimate business reason for sharing this information with each employee; how will it enable each employee to better perform his duties; and will the investigative facts support the truth of any statements made? From a business perspective, the employer should also ask: will the benefit from this sharing exceed the liability risks to be incurred? In the final analysis, it is more difficult to sue for silence than for words spoken.

2. Emotional Distress

When companies openly discuss employee misconduct and name the parties involved or give facts sufficient that co-workers may identify the involved employees, there always exists the possibility the named employees will claim defamation, false light invasion of privacy, and infliction of emotional distress. The claims may be for negligent infliction or intentional infliction. Assuming the plaintiffs can offer proof of severe emotional distress with physical manifestations if required, the focus at trial will be upon the defendant's conduct and whether it was outrageous in nature. A determination of outrage might include review of the defendant's motives for releasing the information, the integrity and reliability of the information discussed, and the parties to whom it was released. Malicious or reckless motive, known falsity or reckless disregard for the truth of the information, and overly inclusive sharing of information are factors that may support findings of employer outrage. Good faith intent to educate employees to prevent future similar incidents, reliable and documented information, and focused training programs for concerned employees are factors that will mitigate the risks of adverse judgments for infliction of emotional distress.

In relaying case facts to co-workers, in order to prevent future problems, an organization may defend its action by showing the release of information was done in good faith and communicated to only those employees who needed to know in order to properly perform their duties. However, it is imperative that managers and investigators carefully consider the need to openly discuss case facts versus the risks of defamation, false light invasion of privacy, and emotional distress lawsuits. An employer's good intentioned release of information to quell employee rumors or to reinforce company values may expose the company to undue risk if the investigative foundation for the statements is incomplete or flawed. In the alternative, a company may ask an employee to voluntarily sign a release and waiver from liability for the company to share the case file with co-employees so they will not make similar mistakes.

K. Litigation Avoidance and Employee Dignity

Sound planning and superb execution are two key elements of a litigation avoidance strategy. As detailed at length in this chapter, poor planning, aggressive fact-finding, careless communication, and poor disciplinary and corrective judgment frequently produce substandard results and litigation.

There is another equal if not more important critical factor that cannot be overlooked: the attitude of the fact-finder. An objective fact-finder who understands the liability risks and conducts an inquiry in a manner that respects the dignity of all employees is more likely to be respected and less likely to be sued.

1. Awareness and Liability Avoidance

Employers and their fact-finders need to recognize the complexity of federal and state laws and regulations that are woven throughout every phase of modern workplace investigations. These laws impose affirmative duties upon employers to restrict the purposes of their investigations to lawful objectives, to confine the scope of inquiry to legitimate business interests, and to use only methods of investigation that are lawful in nature. When personal reputations, incomes, jobs, promotions, and personal freedom are at stake, the liability risks are real, and employers must properly identify and manage these overlapping risks.

2. Employee Dignity and Liability Avoidance

The Process of Investigation is an approach that is founded upon a balanced respect for employee and employer rights and dignity. It respects the right of the employer by providing a fair and equitable process to make reasonable inquiry into wrongful workplace behavior that is harmful to the interest of the employer and ultimately to the employees. The process respects the rights and dignity of all employees, not merely those who are the subjects of investigations, to a reasonable scope of inquiry, an objective inquiry, verification of facts, and fair discipline and corrective action when appropriate. The seeds of litigation will find it difficult to take root, grow, and spread in an investigative environment that is reasonable in scope, methods, and outcomes.

Tip: The most effective ways for fact-finders to mitigate litigation and liability are to intelligently plan and carefully execute the plan, and at all times to be objective, straightforward, fair and respectful of all employees, including suspects, throughout the Process of Investigation.

Acknowledgment

This chapter was graciously contributed by Norman M. Spain, J.D., CPP, Professor of Assets Protection and Security at the College of Justice and Safety at Eastern Kentucky University. Professor Spain, a former Fulbright Fellow, is a member of ASIS International and the Program Advisor for ASIS International's Asset Protection Course III. He speaks frequently on the subject of investigator liability and investigation related litigation.

Notes

Citations for quotations within quotes cited herein have been omitted.

1. *Fuller v. City of Oakland,* 47 F.3d 1522 (C.A.9 (Cal.) 1995) and *Valdez v. Church's Fried Chicken, Inc.* 683 F. Supp. 596 (W.D. Tex. 1988).
2. Occupational Health and Safety Act, 29 U.S.C. §654.
3. Federal Sentencing Guidelines (§8C2.5)(f) and (g).
4. *Salinas v. Forth Worth Cab and Baggage Company,* 725 S.W.2d 701 (Tex. 1987).
5. *Saine v. Comcast Cablevision of Arkansas, Inc.,* Supreme Court of Arkansas, No. 02-1388, Oct. 23, 2003.
6. *Yunker v. Honeywell, Inc.,* 496 N.W.2d 419 (Minn. App. 1993).
7. *Paradoa v. CNA Ins. Co.,* 672 N.E.2d 127 (Mass. App. Ct. 1996).
8. *Greenbaum v. Brooks,* 139 S.E.2d 432 (Ga. App. 1964).
9. *Kelley v. Stop & Shop Companies, Inc.,* 530 N.E.2d 190 (Mass. App. Ct. 1988).
10. *Miranda v. Arizona,* 384 U.S. 436, 86 S.Ct. 1602, 16 L.Ed.2d 694 (1966).
11. *United States v. Antonelli,* 434 F.2d 335 (C.A.N.Y. 1970).
12. *Commonwealth v. Green,* 1973 WL 15308 (Pa. Com. Pl. 1973).
13. *Simpson v. Commonwealth, Unemployment Compensation Bd. of Review,* 450 A.2d 305 (Pa. Cmwlth. 1982).
14. For a short and insightful discussion of some of these points, see *U.S. v. Leffall,* 82 F.3d 343 (10th Cir. 1996).
15. *U.S. v. Dansberry,* 500 F. Supp. 140 (N.D. Ill. 1980).
16. For example, see West Virginia Constitution, Article III, section five (right not to be compelled to be a witness against himself) and section six (right to be free from unreasonable searches and seizures).
17. *Simpson,* supra at 13.
18. *State v. Muegge,* 360 S.E.2d 216 (W. Va. 1987).
19. See California, *People v. Zelinski,* 594 P.2d 1000 (Cal. 1979); Montana, *State v. Helfrich,* 600 P.2d 816 (Mont. 1979); and West Virginia, *State v. Muegge,* 360 S.E.2d 216 (W. Va. 1987). However, two states have since reversed their positions: Proposition 8, passed by California voters in 1982; and Montana rulings, *State v. Long,* 700 P.2d 153 (Mont. 1985) and *State v. Christensen,* 797 P.2d 893 (Mont. 1990).
20. *Hill v. National Collegiate Athletic Association,* 7 Cal.4th 1 (1994).
21. National Labor Relations Act, §157. "Rights of employees as to organization, collective bargaining, etc. [Known as §7 rights]

Employees shall have the right to self-organization, to form, join, or assist labor organizations, to bargain collectively through representatives of their own choosing, and to engage in other concerted activities for the purpose of collective bargaining or other mutual aid or protection."

22. 29 U.S.C. §158. **Unfair labor practices** [Known as §8(a) and §8(b) unfair labor practices].

    (a) Unfair labor practices by employer. It shall be an **unfair labor practice** for an employer—

    (1) to interfere with, restrain, or coerce employees in the exercise of the rights guaranteed in section 7 [29 U.S.C. §157];

    …

    (4) to discharge or otherwise discriminate against an employee because he has filed charges or given testimony under this Act; …

    (b) Unfair labor practices by **labor** organization. It shall be an **unfair labor practice** for a **labor** organization or its agents—

    (1) to restrain or coerce (A) employees in the exercise of the rights guaranteed in section 7 [29 U.S.C. §157]: …

23. Labor Management Relations Act: §301, as codified in [29 U.S.C. §185]: §185. Suits by and against labor organizations—(a) Venue, amount, and citizenship

    Suits for violation of contracts between an employer and a labor organization representing employees … may be brought in any district court of the United States having jurisdiction of the parties, without respect to the amount in controversy or without regard to the citizenship of the parties.

24. *NLRB v. J. Weingarten, Inc.*, 420 U.S. 251 (1975).
25. *Pacific Telephone and Telegraph Co. v. N.L.R.B.*, 711 F.2d 134 (9th Cir. 1983).
26. *Southwest Bell Telephone Co. v. NLRB*, 667 F.2d 470 (5th Cir. 1982).
27. *Southwestern Bell Telephone Co. v. N.L.R.B.*, 667 F.2d 470 (5th Cir. 1982). See: Epilepsy Foundation of Northeast Ohio, 331 N.L.R.B. No. 92, at 1, 2000 WL 967066 (July 10, 2000) ("Board Decision"); Epilepsy Foundation Of Northeast Ohio v. NLRB, 168 L.R.R.M. (BNA) 2673, 144 Lab.Cas. P 11,129, United States Court of Appeals, District of Columbia Circuit, Decided Nov. 2, 2001; and IBM Corp., 341 NLRB No. 148 (06/09/2004).
28. *Parsippany Hotel Management Co. v. NLRB*, 99 F.3d 413 (D.C. Cir. 1996).
29. *NLRB v. Unbelievable, Inc.*, 71 F.3d 1434 (9th Cir. 1995).

30. *Horsehead Resource Development Co., Inc. v. N.L.R.B.,* 154 F.3d 1093 (6th Cir. 1998).
31. *California Acrylic Industries, Inc. v. NLRB,* 150 F.3d 1095 (9th Cir. 1998).
32. *National Steel and Shipbuilding Co. v. NLRB,* 156 F.3d 1268 (D.C. Cir. 1998).
33. *Hanley v. Safeway Stores, Inc.,* 838 P.2d 408 (Mont. 1992).
34. *Blanchard v. Simpson Plainwell Paper Company,* 925 F.Supp. 510 (W.D. Mich. 1995).
35. *Cramer v. Consolidated Freightways Inc.,* No. 98-55657, No. 98-56041, No. 98-56154, (U.S.C.A. 9th Cir. En Banc), 2001 U.S. App. Lexis 19157.
36. 42 U.S.C. 2000e et seq.
37. Policy Guidance on Current Issues in Sexual Harassment, *Equal Employment Compliance Manual* No. 120 (Oct. 25, 1988).
38. *Fuller,* supra at 1.
39. *Valdez,* supra at 1.
40. Employee Polygraph Protection Act, 29 U.S.C. §§2001-2009.
41. *Wiltshire v. Citibank,* 653 N.Y.S.2d 517 (N.Y. Sup. 1996).
42. *Lyle v. Mercy Hospital Anderson,* 876 F. Supp. 157 (S.D. Ohio 1995).
43. For example, see Alaska [Alaska Stat. §20. 10.037] and Delaware [19 Del Code. Ann. §704].
44. 15 U.S.C. §1681 et seq.
45. 2001 Federal Sentencing Guidelines (§8C2.5).
46. *Kroger Company v. Warren,* 420 S.W.2d 218 (Tex. Civ. App., 1967).
47. *Kroger,* supra at 46.
48. Restatement (Second) of Torts, §§600-605A.
49. *Nipper v. Variety Wholesalers, Inc.,* 638 So.2d 778 (Al. 1994).
50. *Gaumont v. Emery Air Freight Corp.,* 575 N.E.2d 221 (Ohio App. 1990).
51. For an extensive discussion on this topic, see *Caldor, Inc. v. Bowden,* 625 A.2d 959, 330 Md. 632 (Md. 1993).
52. *Ashcroft v. Mt. Sinai Medical Ctr.,* 588 N.E.2d 280, 68 Ohio App.3d 359 (Ohio App. 8 Dist., 1990).
53. *Paolucci v. Robinson Memorial Hospital,* 1995 WL 236743 (Ohio App.) [Unpublished].
54. *Crump v. P & C Food Markets, Inc.,* 576 A.2d 441 (Vt. 1990).
55. Mass. Gen. Laws Ann. ch. 214 §1B.
56. General Laws of Rhode Island Annotated, 9-1-28.1
57. *Williams v. Brigham & Women's Hosp., Inc.,* 14 Mass.L.Rptr. 438, 2002 WL 532979 (Mass. Super.).
58. California Stat. Ann., Labor Code §1026.
59. California Stat. Ann., Labor Code, §1042.

60. California Stat. Ann., Civil Code, §1708.8 (a) and (b).
61. California Stat. Ann., Penal Code §632.
62. California Stat. Ann., Penal Code §653n.
63. *Cramer,* supra at 35.
64. Restatement (Second) of Torts §652D. Comment (a).
65. Restatement (Second) of Torts §652E.
66. *Aranyosi v. Delchamps, Inc.,* 739 So.2d 911 (La.App. 1 Cir. 6/25/99).
67. *Wal-Mart Stores, Inc. v. Lee,* 74 S.W.3d 634 (Ark. 2002).
68. *Bine v. Owens,* 542 S.E.2d 842 (W.Va., 2000).
69. *Smith v. Bell Atlantic Network Services, Inc.,* 1995 WL 389697 (E.D.PA.).
70. *Johnson v. K Mart Corporation,* 723 N.E.2d 1192 (Ill. App. 2000).
71. *Dietz v. Finlay Fine Jewelry Corp.,* 754 N.E.2d 958 (Ind. App. 2001).
72. *Shattuck-Owen v. Snowbird Corp.,* 16 P.3d 555 (Utah 2000).
73. Invasion of Privacy—Intrusion Upon Seclusion (Restatement (Second) of Torts, 2d. §652B). One who intentionally intrudes, physically or otherwise, upon the solitude or seclusion of another or his private affairs or concerns, is subject to liability to the other for invasion of his privacy, if the intrusion would be highly offensive to a reasonable person.
74. *Johnson v. Corporate Special Services, Inc.,* 602 So.2d 385 (Ala. 1992).
75. *Souder v. Pendleton Detectives, Inc.,* 88 So.2d 716 (La. App. 1956).
76. *Pinkerton National Detective Agency v. Stevens,* 132 S.E.2d 119 (Ga. App. 1963).
77. *Saldana v. Kelsey-Hayes Company,* 443 N.W.2d 382 (Mich. App. 1989).
78. *Sowards v. Norbar, Inc.,* 605 N.E.2d 468 (Ohio App. 10 Dist. 1992).
79. *O'Connor v. Ortega,* 480 U.S. 709 (1987).
80. *Simpson,* supra at 13.
81. *Clement v. Sheraton-Boston Corporation,* Commonwealth of Massachusetts, Superior Court Department, Civil Action No. 93-0909-F, settlement entered 1/8/98.
82. *K-Mart Corp. v. Trotti,* 677 S.W.2d 632 (Tex. App. 1 Dist.,1984).
83. *Johnson,* supra at 77.
84. *McLaren v. Microsoft Corp.,* 1999 WL 339015 (Tex. App.-Dallas).
85. *Agis v. Howard Johnson Co.,* 371 Mass. 140, 144 (1976).
86. *Bodewig v. K-Mart, Inc.,* 635 P.2d 657 (Or. App. 1981).
87. *Olivas v. DeVivo Indus., Inc.,* 2001 WL 282891 (Conn. Super.).
88. *Tenold v. Weyerhaeuser Co.,* 873 P.2d 413 (Or. App. 1994).
89. *Texas Farm Bureau Mut. Ins. Companies v. Sears,* 45 Tex. Sup. Ct. J. 1245 (Tex., 2002).
90. *O'Connell v. Bank of Boston,* 640 N.E.2d 513 (Mass. App. Ct. 1994).

91. *Devis v. Bank of America* (1998), 65 Cal.App.4th 1002, 1008, 77 Cal.Rptr.2d 238.
92. *Fuller,* supra at 1.
93. *Valdez,* supra at 1.
94. *Salinas,* supra at 4.
95. *Saine,* supra at 5.
96. *Mendez v. M.S. Walker, Inc.,* 528 N.E.2d 891 (Mass. App. Ct. 1988).
97. *Green,* supra at 12.
98. *Tarnef v. State,* 512 P.2d 923 (Alaska 1973).
99. *People v. Elliott,* 501 N.Y.S.2d 265, (N.Y. Sup. Ct. Queens 1986).
100. *General Motors Corp. v. Piskor,* 340 A.2d 767, (Md. App. 1975).
101. *Blailock v. O'Bannon,* 795 So.2d 533 (Miss. 2001).
102. *Warren,* supra at 46.
103. *Caldor,* supra at 51.
104. *Hampton v. Norred & Associates, Inc.,* 454 S.E.2d 222 (Ga. App. 1995).
105. *Smith,* supra at 71.
106. *Wright v. Montgomery Ward & Co., Inc.,* 814 F. Supp. 986 (D. Kan. 1993).
107. *Johnson v. United Parcel Services, Inc.,* 722 F.Supp. 1282 (D.Md., 1989).
108. *Uebelacker v. Cincom Systems, Inc.,* 608 N.E.2d 858 (Ohio App. 1992).
109. *Caldor,* supra at 51.
110. *Paolucci,* supra at 53.
111. *Rolsen v. Lazarus,* 2000 Ohio App. LEXIS 4466.
112. *Mendez,* supra at 106.
113. *Tenold v. Weyerhaeuser Co.,* 873 P.2d 413 (Or. App.,1994).
114. *Stockley v. A.T. & T Information Systems, Inc.,* 687 F. Supp. 764 (E.D.N.Y. 1988).
115. *DeAngelis v. Jamesway Dept. Store,* 501 A.2d 561 (N.J. Super. A.D. 1985).
116. *Chappelle v. Robinsons-May, Inc., et al.,* California Court of Appeal, Second District, Division 6, 2d Civil No. B150130, Dec. 18, 2001 [Unpublished].
117. *Crump,* supra at 54.
118. *Present v. Avon Products, Inc.,* 253 A.D.2d 183, 687 N.Y.S.2d 330 (Sup. Ct. App. Div. 1st 1999).
119. *Kelly v. West Cash & Carry Building Materials Store,* 745 So.2d 743 (La. App. 4 Cir. 1999).
120. *Layne v. Builders Plumbing Supply Company, Inc.,* 569 N.E.2d 1104 (Ill. App. 1991).

121. *Beauchamp v. Eckerd's Drugs of Louisiana, Inc.,* 533 So.2d 390 (La. App. 4 Cir. 1988).

122. *Sullivan v. Baptist Memorial Hospital,* 995 S.W.2d 569 (Tenn., 1999).

123. Stephen P. Pepe and Scott H. Dunham, *Avoiding and Defending Wrongful Discharge Claims,* §2:09 Reference Checks—Defamation In Employment Setting. Callaghan & Company (1987–1991); Clark Boardman Callaghan, a Division of Thomson Information Services, Inc. (1991–1997); and West Group (1998–2000).

124. Theisen v. Covenant Medical Center, Inc., 636 N.W.2d 74 (Iowa 2001).

125. *Dewald v. Home Depot,* 2000 WL 1207124 (Tex.App.-Dallas) [Unpublished].

126. *Dewald,* supra at 135.

127. *French v. Foods, Inc.,* 495 N.W.2d 768 (Iowa, 1993).

128. *Mead v. Deloitte & Touche LLP,* 2000 WL 1337662 (Conn. Super.).

129. *Theisen,* supra at 134.

130. *Sears, Roebuck and Co. v. Wholey,* 779 A.2d 408 (Md. App., 2001).

131. *Morris v. Hartford Courant Company,* 200 Conn. 676 (Conn. 1986).

132. *Koller v. Pontiac Osteopathic Hospital, et al.,* Court of Appeals of Michigan, No. 229630. May 21, 2002.

133. *Vaillancourt v. The Gap, Inc.,* Court of Appeal, First District, Division 3, California. No. A096201. (Marin County Super. Ct. No. 174776). Oct. 15, 2002. [Unpublished].

134. *Wright,* supra at 117.

135. *Wal-Mart Stores, Inc. v. Binns,* 15 S.W.3d 320 (Ark. 2000).

136. *Sisney v. Sha-Tec Foods, Inc.,* Pottwatomie County District Court, Okla., No. C-89-291 (Sept. 16, 1989), reported in 33 ATLA L. Rep. 74 (March 1990).

137. *Brown v. Dart Drug Corporation,* 551 A.2d 132 (Md. App. 1989).

138. *Olivas v. DeVino Indus., Inc.,* 2001 WL 282891 (Conn. Super.).

139. *Tenold v. Weyerhaeuser Co.,* 873 P.2d 413 (Or. App., 1994).

140. Florida, 443.036(26)(a) and (2).

141. Illinois Unemployment Insurance Act, 602A.

142. For example, see *Cabreja v. Mount Sinai Medical Center,* 535 N.Y.S.2d 149 (N.Y.A.D. 3 Dept. 1988) and Frey v. Unemployment Compensation Review Board, 589 A.2d 300 (Pa. Commw. 1991).

143. *Hurlbut,* supra at 93.

144. *Ray v. Department of Employment Security Board of Review,* 614 N.E.2d 196 (Ill. App. 1 Dist. 1993).

145. *Cabreja v. Mount Sinai Medical Center,* 535 N.Y.S.2d 149 (N.Y.A.D. 3 Dept. 1988).

146. *Hurlbut v. Unemployment Review Board,* 589 A.2d 300 (Pa. Commw. 1991).

147. *Frey v. Unemployment Review Board,* 589 A.2d 300 (Pa. Commw. 1991).

148. *Montellanico v. Unemployment Compensation Board of Review,* 558 A.2d 936 (Pa. Commw. 1989).

149. *Conseco v. Review Board of Indiana Dept. of Employment and Training Services,* 626 N.E. 2d 559 (Ind. App. 1993).

150. *Combined Insurance Company of America v. Workers' Compensation Appeal Board,* 754 A.2d 59 (Pa. Commw. 2000).

151. *Anthony v. Workers' Compensation Appeal Board,* 823 A.2d 1046 (Pa. Commw. 2003).

152. Restatement (Second) of Torts §652D. Comment (a).

153. Restatement (Second) of Torts §652E.

154. *Bine,* supra at 68.

155. *Garcia v. Aerotherm Corp.,* 202 F.3d 281, 1999 WL 1244486 (10th Cir. (N.M.)) [Unpublished].

156. *Stock v. Wisconsin Electric Power Company,* No. 93-0522, Court of Appeals of Wisconsin, March 9, 1994.

157. *Szot v. Allstate Ins. Co.,* 161 F.Supp.2d 596 (D.Md., 2001).

Chapter 6

Applied Strategies

A. The Method of Multiple Working Hypotheses

All investigations should have structure, and in order to achieve the desired objectives, the search for meaningful facts must be systematic and organized. That structure is called the process of investigation. The process enhances the effectiveness of deciphering and reconstructing past events, and it allows others who follow in the footsteps of the fact-finder to independently validate his conclusion(s).

However, sometimes there is enough missing or insufficient evidence to preclude the declaration of absolute certainty of any conclusion. Some would argue that even admissions of wrongdoing are questionable given the possibility of coercion and duress. Nonetheless, by using the method of multiple working hypotheses, the fact-finder can significantly improve the likelihood that his conclusions, answers, and solutions are viable and consistent with the actual facts of the case. Paul Campos, Esq. (University of Colorado) correctly and succinctly assessed the role of science in society by noting that *normal science* continually undergoes tiny adjustments at the margin of an accepted theory until a paradigm shift suddenly occurs and the accepted theory is revised or discarded. Campos states, "Science is not and can never be about truth with a capital *T*. Science—that is, the development of useful theories based on logical inferences drawn from empirical observations—isn't designed to discover what is true in any fundamental metaphysical sense. It is designed to develop useful ways of thinking about practical problems and it is extraordinarily good at achieving this goal."

Whether the fact-finder is tasked with a criminal defense investigation or a complex fraud, like the scientist, his charter includes the collection of high-quality evidence, obtaining a complete understanding of the phenomena (discovering "truths"), understanding the cause-and-effect, and solving problems in a creative manner. This scientific approach stimulates our latent creativity and fosters ideas. It permits us to maximize our efforts and improve our results. It also imparts an element of professionalism, which often eludes many sectors of the craft.

A helpful starting point is to clearly articulate the fundamental problem. How we state and define that problem will significantly affect how we proceed. Using simple examples, we might ask why has the investigation been requested; why did a concerned individual come forward with information alleging the criminal activity of others; or does the requestor (or customer) have a legitimate need for the information desired and how does that information help him or her. Understanding the answers to these underlying questions will allow the fact-finder to position his investigation and freely develop multiple plausible hypotheses. This sort of free-association and reflective contemplation prevents the fact-finder from clinging to a single and seemingly reasonable, yet rigid, theory or hypothesis. This process also helps the investigator to winnow order out from the chaos.

According to Osterburg and Ward, "To the extent that criminal investigation is perceived as part and parcel of a more universal kind of inquiry, we will have succeeded."[1] All legitimate and well-conceived investigations, whether "good-faith" corporate, civil, or criminal, follow a systematic process that remarkably parallels the scientific method. All investigations, especially those that are complex, benefit from the scientific method; that is, they are impartial, objective, thorough, accurate, and viewed from all angles. This is not to say that good scientific methodology is not a synthesis of science, art, humanities, intuition, and organizational skills. Indeed, successful attorneys, prosecutors, investigators of all types, reporters, and detectives are unwitting scientists. These professional fact-finders have a sincere desire to uncover the totality of facts available and are eager to understand the inner workings of the phenomenon under investigation. Successful fact-finders must have a dedicated excitement and passion about the process of discovery. It should relentlessly motivate them to establish covert links among the assorted elements before them. They should also understand that exact answers to their problems may not always be obtainable. *Moreover, not all cases are solvable.* No doubt we all live in a world awash in uncertainty, but we need to have some basic concepts of how to confidently deal with it.[2] The mere fact that an outside investigator has been retained to evaluate or solve a corporate workplace issue could signify that either the solution may be unexpected or the consequences unforeseeable.

The thought processes, or investigative *mindset*, employed by the fact-finder is similar in that the investigative logic invoked links the truth of the conclusion to the truth of the supporting claims. It is this common logic of investigative methodology and analytical strategy that allows the investigation to conclude successfully. Euripides (484–406 B.C.) understood that the fountainhead of knowledge is doubt and challenge when he said, "Man's most valuable trait is a judicious sense of what not to believe." It is recognized that the role of some investigators is to collect information, that is, to obtain physical evidence, interview people, and access records. The role is not to draw conclusions or make subjective interpretations. However, the importance of critical thinking and creativity for these investigators is likewise vital because it pertains to the quality of evidence collected.[3]

The desire to find additional information and make our cases stronger while approaching but never fully attaining the complete story is a recurring theme in many investigations. This is evidenced in the words report writers sometimes use, words that give the writer the room to wiggle. Qualifiers such as *almost, apparently, about, supposedly, may, might, maybe, may have, relatively speaking, perhaps, substantially, mostly, usually, fairly, big, small, relatively significant (or insignificant), some, somewhat, sometimes, plausible, reasonably believe, presumably, could, more-or-less, expected, roughly, assume, estimated, approximately, possibly, unlikely,* and, of course, *allegedly* sometimes suggest the fact-finder's inability to understand and explain the relevance of every fact he has accumulated. My suspicion is that this vague vocabulary has found its way into the lexicon of the investigative world because of the inherent uncertainty of the craft and the practitioner's nagging desire to explain all that cannot be explained.

Likewise denoting doubt, phrases such as *the unlikely probability, chances are good,* and *the odds are against it* are statistically oriented and tend to quantify the amount of uncertainty. Risk qualifiers, moreover, imply an element of doubt while they subtly attach a probability to a potential outcome. Thus, the opportunity for misinterpretation is manifold. For example, the clinician that performs a dangerousness assessment of a paranoid schizophrenic, psychopathic criminal may conclude that there is a high probability of the subject hurting someone. However, without additional explanation and an understanding of basic probabilities, one would not know that the real risk potential to a randomly selected individual is actually infinitesimally small, even if the criminal were not incarcerated or monitored. The communications of the fact-finder (and most other professionals), therefore, need to be more precise. The casual use of qualifiers and certainty–uncertainty statements lend themselves to misunderstandings and abuse. If improperly used, they tend to trick the reader into a sense of understanding when in fact no such understanding exists.

Tip: Be careful when using qualifiers and certainty–uncertainty statements. Because they are so deeply fixed in our lexicon, fact-finders must be cautious and not abuse them or ever hide behind them.

---

1. Index of Suspicion

From the moment basic client-provided information is received, the fact-finder must begin to make links or connections from the information and data provided. Depending on the fact-pattern and the matter under investigation, this might be done by using one or more of the following:

- Invoking the principles of fundamental science (physics, chemistry, mathematics, biology) and related sciences (such as medicine, physiology, meteorology, geology, astronomy, psychology, sociology, and criminology)
- Separating objective empirical facts from subjective inferences
- Conducting experiments (deductive reasoning) for verifications and cause-and-effect relationships while searching for root causations
- Constructing creative working hypotheses as explanations (inductive reasoning) and therein exploring all possibilities and alternatives
- Generally interpreting the data and identifying trends and patterns
- Assigning subjective probabilities to the evidence quality and resultant multiple working hypotheses

Subjective probabilities, based on the strength of one's belief, are frequently assigned to investigative conclusions.[4] Subjective values rather than objective probabilities are preferred when the amount of direct evidence available during the investigation is limited. Objective probabilities, on the other hand, must be calculated using stoichiometric formulas, such as coin-toss outcomes where the number of times an event occurs (frequency) in the total set of possible outcomes can be predicted with relative certainty.

To be successful, the use of objective probabilities as an investigative method requires some basic attributes of the fact-finder. The most intangible of them is an *index of suspicion*. Instinctively, upon receipt of a new assignment, fact-finders of all experience levels tend to immediately and quite naturally form an opinion regarding motive, intent, and the profile of the perpetrator. Thus, based on initial and nearly always incomplete information, several opinions are quickly formed; collectively I call them our *index of suspicion*. For better or worse, these preliminary opinions are prejudiced because they are based almost entirely on experience and training. And logically, with more experience and training, the accuracy of our index improves. The clear advantage of a refined index is that it saves time and resources. For example, the seasoned homicide detective who instantly recognizes the tell-tale indicators of a serial killer the moment she steps into a crime scene is able to quickly direct her resources and maybe capture the killer before he strikes again. Or take the experienced fraud examiner who is able to examine merely a handful of receipts and recognize what will later be proven to be a clerk's lapping scheme. Intuitively and efficiently he organizes the fact-pattern offered him and with little conscious effort renders a key determination. That index of suspicion or "investigative nose" can be remarkably precise.

Not long ago a long-time client of mine called in search of some advice relative to an apparent serious theft problem. Noticeably frustrated, she explained that her firm had been the victim of a series of thefts of which the perpetrator(s) had taken nearly a dozen notebook computers and almost the same number of PDAs from the offices of attorneys in her firm. The incidents appeared random; however, most of them occurred after hours and only on a few of the many floors the firm occupied. For a host of reasons, she suspected the cleaning crew. Intuitively I disagreed. From the fact-pattern she offered me, I, too, suspected someone whom the firm trusted, but instead suspected that this was the handy-work of a security officer. Analysis of the officers' tour schedule and access control records allowed us to quickly isolate several suspects. Again, based on intuition and many years of experience, I had the officer I suspected interviewed by one of our most experienced interviewers. With little coaxing, the officer revealed he had "purchased" several computers and PDAs from a former colleague with whom he had worked. He said he suspected they were stolen but informed no one. The local authorities were immediately looped in and a search warrant was obtained for the officer's apartment. A search of his apartment discovered more than ten computers and all of the missing PDAs. He readily admitted to the thefts and criminal charges were filed.

Although the above example illustrates the effectiveness of proper investigative and interviewing techniques, it also illustrates the importance of having a good index of suspicion and allowing one's intuition to help guide the process.

Exhibit 6.1   Suspected Credit Card Transactions

Date of Transaction	Debit Card Account Number	Expiration Date	Type of Account	Name Used	Amount
10/19/2000	XXXXXXXXXXXX5307	Feb-05	Visa	R Boltin	$2576.00
11/8/2000	XXXXXXXXXXXX5307	Feb-05	Visa	R Boltin	1344.94
12/6/2000	XXXXXXXXXXXX5307	Feb-05	Visa	R Boltin	545.17
12/20/2000	XXXXXXXXXXXX5307	Feb-05	Visa	R Boltin	920.23
3/12/2001	XXXXXXXXXXXX5307	Feb-05	Visa	R Boltinetti	1,500.00
4/18/2001	XXXXXXXXXXXX5307	Feb-05	Visa	R Boltinetti	1,310.51
5/29/2001	XXXXXXXXXXXX5307	Feb-05	Visa	R Boltinetti	1,644.46
7/25/2001	XXXXXXXXXXXX5307	Feb-05	Visa	R Boltinetti	2,451.84
6/11/2002	XXXXXXXXXXXX5307	Feb-05	Visa	R Boltin	4,202.56
7/16/2002	XXXXXXXXXXXX5307	Feb-05	Visa	R Boltin	3,975.96
12/23/2002	XXXXXXXXXXXX5307	Feb-05	Visa	R Boltinetti	4,145.67
2/12/2001	XXXXXXXXXXXX6711	Mar-03	MasterCard	R Wolkin	941.10
5/7/2001	XXXXXXXXXXXX6711	Mar-03	MasterCard	R Wolkin	1,847.04
6/18/2001	XXXXXXXXXXXX6711	Mar-03	MasterCard	R Wolkin	3,424.00
9/7/2001	XXXXXXXXXXXX6711	Mar-03	MasterCard	R Wolkin	3,248.38
2/21/2002	XXXXXXXXXXXX6711	Mar-03	MasterCard	R Wolkin	5,566.66
10/30/2002	XXXXXXXXXXXX3578	Feb-03	Visa	R Voltin	4,910.10
1/15/2003	XXXXXXXXXXXX3578	Feb-03	Visa	R Voltin	4,104.00
2/28/2003	XXXXXXXXXXXX3578	Feb-03	Visa	R Voltin	6,785.10
4/16/2003	XXXXXXXXXXXX3578	Feb-03	Visa	R Voltin	6,022.05
5/9/2003	XXXXXXXXXXXX3578	Feb-03	Visa	R Voltin	9,837.38

The disadvantage of forming an opinion and drawing conclusions too quickly is that it may lead the fact-finder down the wrong path, wasting time and resources. But, intuition, based upon the investigator's knowledge, training, and experience, is a valuable attribute. Intuition is an internal feeling or hunch that things are either normal or not normal. It is the beginning of the hypothesis-forming stage of the investigation, hopefully leading to higher degrees of proof. The fact-finder ought to ask himself if there are significant perturbations or disturbances to the system; on balance, do the facts make sense and what sense do they make? Exhibit 6.1 provides another interesting example. This spreadsheet summarizes actual fraudulent transactions performed by a bookkeeper (sufficiently modified to protect the guilty). The perpetrator employed the simple, yet often difficult to uncover scheme of misapplying customer credits. In this instance she applied them to her personal debit cards while recording the credits to names of fictitious customers. What does your intuition tell you from the scant information provided? Intuitively, the experienced fraud examiner will likely suspect:

- That because of the comparatively large size of the first transaction on October 19, 2000, it is not likely to be the first. The experienced fact-finder would not be satisfied that this was the earliest fraudulent transaction and would instinctively dig deeper. Why? Because he would know from experience that perpetrators of crimes like this tend to steal small amounts first and progressively steal larger amounts over time. This was in fact the case in this investigation.
- That the fictitious customer names used by the perpetrator have a hidden significance. Realizing the vague similarity of the names, he would intuitively suspect they are similar to a name familiar to the perpetrator. In fact in this case the perpetrator's last name was Volker. What do you suppose the initial *R* represents?

This fascinating examination of limited information demonstrates that experience combined with a modest dose of intuition can often yield extraordinary results.

Successful fact-finders also know prejudices must be separated from intuition. Here are two tests that emphasize this point:

- In a fair coin-toss experiment with three equal independent tosses, what is the probability that heads would show three times?
- In a biased black-and-white-sided coin-toss, knowing that the black will come up 70 percent of the time when tossed, on which color would you bet in multiple tosses?

Although the answers to these questions may not be intuitively obvious, the fact-finder who has a large capacity for exceptional intuition is the one who has an innate understanding of logic and the ability of making order and sense from a wide array of information. The intuition is an expression of probability and reflects the investigator's current state of knowledge about the problem being worked. This sort of fact-finder sees things others do not; that is, he demonstrates that unique creativity we sometimes call *genius*. Intuition is an attribute that is usually derived from lifelong personal experiences and not necessarily from formal education. As such, incisive insight is a corresponding attribute that allows the prediction of events and the ability to visualize unexpected patterns, periodicity, or structure amid apparent chaos. Concurrently, if the initial information is not accurate or contains imperfect data, the final conclusion cannot be accurate. A small initial uncertainty may compound itself, or propagate, as the investigation unfolds. The scientist who suspects apparently false or bad data and dismisses them believing that they are actually systematic or random errors (uncertainties) in his measurements may actually be ignoring the discovery of an important principle. Systematic errors affect all measurements in the same way, such as a slow-running clock or a radar gun reading three mph high (fast); such errors may be difficult to detect unless comparisons are made to outside standards. Similarly, the fact-finder who fails to note and record that the employee-suspect in a retail theft case has a cousin who also works for the victim's business in its bookkeeping department may compromise the entire investigation or, at a minimum, waste valuable time and resources. The outcome of many an investigation can hinge on the smallest of details. The experienced fact-finder knows this and rarely overlooks anything or dismisses a coincidence. Consider this example.

On September 23, 1999, NASA's Mars *Climate Orbiter*, a $125 million spacecraft launched in December 1998, was descending into orbit around Mars. However, the Lockheed Martin Astronautics team had programmed English units of measurement into the satellite's software, using miles, feet, and pounds of gravitational force. NASA's team, however, used metric units, such as kilometers, meters, and newtons of force, in their software development. Ultimately, the egregious blunder caused the spacecraft to crash on the Martian surface because it was about 60 miles (96.6 km) closer to the planet than realized and orbit could not be achieved. A replacement spacecraft will cost about three times as much and take years to build and resend.

This incredible failure was due to a simple sophomoric mistake—the lack of error detection in information transfer. But the debacle does not end here. On December 3, 1999, the Mars *Polar Lander* spacecraft, worth about $165 million, crashed on the Martian surface due probably to premature deployment of its landing pods—a mistake now known to have been easily correctible with simple software updates. Other outrageous scenarios similar to the Mars mishaps, albeit not as sensational, are frustratingly too numerous.

Not surprisingly, there are many attributes other than possessing good intuition and a good index of suspicion that fact-finders need if they expect to conduct reasonably successful investigations. Just as an expert witness must show expertise via skill, knowledge, education, experience, and training, so too must the fact-finder. This expertise includes the ability to make accurate estimates and specify the limits of uncertainty. Ergo, my earlier test questions (which I have not forgotten). Making accurate estimates is difficult for most people. They tend to overestimate their ability at arriving at a correct value. That is to say, they have more confidence in their ability than their information or knowledge warrants.

If we were to ask 1,000 people to guess the number of beans in a clear-glass, five-gallon jar, the results would be disappointing because the players would provide only one value and most of them would be much too high or low. Our beans are the small white navy beans about 8 mm long by 5 mm wide by 3 mm thick, or about 2,478 beans in the 453-gram bags (I actually counted). Thus, the actual number of beans in the jar is 89,616 (I will spare you the math). A correct estimate would be a range of values, or the limits of uncertainty, corresponding to *beyond a reasonable doubt* and believed to encompass the actual number of beans. Because we need to be more accurate in our estimate, our guess might be 70,000 beans plus or minus 25,000. Even if the participants were instructed to provide a range of values to demonstrate their uncertainty, the range of values would likely be too narrow.

An interesting twist on this experiment would be to ask 500 players (group 1) if the number of beans is more than or less than 15,000 and then ask the remaining 500 players (group 2) if the number of beans is more or less than 165,000. Group 1 will likely estimate an average between the real value and 15,000. Group 2 will alternatively estimate the average between the real value and 165,000. The difference between averages is remarkably somewhere around 75,000 beans! This phenomenon is called the anchoring effect, and it demonstrates the strong influence of an uninformed outside or fictitious source when forming a determination. The investigative process is vulnerable to this phenomenon as well. It requires the fact-finder to precisely articulate the problem, collect and sort information, articulate credible hypotheses, objectively weigh the facts and scrutinize each hypothesis, and finally, present a result in terms of what is truly known and what is uncertain. In this process, careful observations and accurate measurements or trials that contribute to the basic information are made while irrelevant information is discarded. Predictions are made about these trials or experiments as to what should be expected if a particular scenario is truly reasonable and viable. Risks, odds, chances, or probabilities are ultimately calculated or estimated. In the intuitive mind this is sometimes accomplished in the subconscious. Intuitively and seemingly effortlessly, the *geniuses* among us are able to reduce the information to its most basic value and wondrously render a solution.

So, do you have the answers to my test questions? Here they are: In the coin-toss experiment the answer is that three heads in three tosses would occur with a $p = 0.125$ probability. Perform this experiment ten times and the coin-tosser has an excellent chance that he will toss three heads consecutively at least once. Intuition might suggest that the odds are more favorable, that of perhaps one-third ($p = 0.333$). Each independent flip of the coin has a probability of 0.5 of being a head and hence multiplication of 0.5 three times ($0.5 \times 0.5 \times 0.5$) gives the answer. If this same coin is tossed twice, what is the probability that it will come up heads twice? It is not an intuitive 50-50 chance but, rather, a 0.25 probability. The probability of tossing two heads in four flips is not the intuitive $p = 0.5$ but, rather, 0.375. In four tosses there are 16 possible combinations of heads and tails, and in only six of these are there two heads. Similarly, the probability of tossing four heads in four tosses is only 0.0625. What is the probability of tossing three heads and three tails in six tosses? Once again, the intuitive answer of a 50-50 chance is wrong. The answer is that in the 64 possible outcomes this combination occurs a mere ten times, or $p = 0.156$ (about 15.6 percent).

The answer for the black-and-white-sided coin-toss betting experiment is that by betting 100 percent of the time on black the bettor wins 70 percent of the time versus only 58 percent of the time if he bets on black 70 percent of the time.

Tip: These coin-toss examples demonstrate objective predictions by mathematical deduction. We can make similar predictions during our investigations and with a high degree of certainty assign probabilities to certain outcomes.

---

2. The Scientific Method

The scientific method is a process that helps explain natural events and other less natural phenomena. The scientific method allows the formulation of rules that govern the interaction of evidence, argument, and hypothesis.[5] More specifically, the scientific method is a system of advancing knowledge by judging probability.[6] It permits the formulation of a question, collecting data about it through observation and experiment, and testing a hypothetical answer.[7] Without trained observations, measurement, focused experimentation, and logical reasoning, modern science could not be distinguished from vague philosophical conjecture. Thus, the use of the scientific method in one's investigations allows the distinguishable and defensible separation of fact from pure speculation. Each hypothesis or alternative viewpoint provides a stimulus for probing but cannot be more extraordinary than the facts themselves. Moreover, the scientific method only *approximates* the truth of any observable phenomenon. Science deals with probabilities and not absolute certainty; that is, one hypothesis seems for the moment more correct than another.

Hypotheses are always tentative and a new test may quickly invalidate a well-worn theory. If the hypothesis withstands the test of time and becomes a theory or law, it is still subject to change and or rejection. Therefore, scientific explanation is never-ending because the explanation produces only an approximate and convenient working model or paradigm of the world as it is understood at any particular time. Jon Norby has stated, "All reliably constructed scientific explanations are best viewed by their creators as works in progress." He continues: "This basic intellectual stance remains necessary both for essential humility and for the very possibility of scientific advance. Forensic scientists must develop an intellect not too sure of what must remain uncertain, not too uncertain about what must remain sure."[8] Fact-finders, too, operate in a dynamic environment; they must not only invoke the traditional science or methodology, but remain open and sensitive to the nontraditional. For stimulating ideas about complexity and nontraditional scientific approaches see Stuart Kauffman's intriguing work, *Investigations*.[9]

The scientific approach to understanding and solving problems is often viewed as the only logical way of thinking and, arguably, as the basis of all real knowledge. The basic principles of how to think systematically and logically and yet remain creative are not esoteric. The most creative people are not necessarily the most intelligent people. Creative fact-finders have a desire to pick apart problems and ask questions to find more problems and maintain their skepticism. Their questioning is continuous and intense. Their method is dynamic, causing the underlying understanding and logic to evolve.

The scientific method in various forms has been developed and debated by hundreds of intellectuals and philosophers since the time of Plato and Aristotle. The scientific revolution, with its professional academies and societies, first blossomed 300 to 450 years ago and transformed scientific inquiry. Copernicus, Kepler, Galileo, Descartes, Bacon, Harvey, and Newton were some of the then modern European thinkers, astronomers, and mathematicians of their time. They broke with religious dogmas and were responsible for man's first revolution in thinking. Knowledge of physics, chemistry, biology, and anatomy, for example, led to giant leaps in experimental methods and technological innovations. A solid understanding of the scientific method and creative thinking process is as appropriate and essential for complex civil, criminal, and workplace investigations as it is in theoretical nuclear physics, statistical probability, or modern forensic psychology.

Anyone familiar with the famous fictional character Sherlock Holmes knows about scientific deduction. But is Sherlock's logic really deductive reasoning, or is it inductive reasoning or perhaps both types?[10] Let us briefly examine these two important terms and see how the total sum of all experience and knowledge is derived from a circular or iterative reasoning path between the two.

Deductive reasoning is the prediction of results, or at least a logical rationale, from known causes, that is, from a general principle or theory comes a specific understanding. Logically, one theory follows from another. If the premise is true and the argument is valid, then the conclusion is true. I can deduce that if I mix potassium nitrate, sulfur, and charcoal in certain known proportions and light the mixture with a match, it will burn fast or explode. I can predict this result because I have empirical knowledge and perhaps own a chemistry book containing basic information about the way these ingredients react when mixed and ignited. I can also deduce that I must die someday because this premise is based upon the premise that all men are mortal. Similarly, I can deduce that if I stick the pointy end of a metal screwdriver into a live 120-volt electrical outlet, then certain undesirable consequences will follow.

On the other hand, *inductive reasoning* is to logically infer from the specific to the general, that is, induction provides an interpretation of causes from the results. Even if the premise is true and the argument is reasonable, the conclusion might be false. When we use inductive reasoning, we infer a general rule from specific facts or experiences. For example, if I am investigating a suspicious explosion that occurred in a chemistry lab and upon inspection find the ingredients of gunpowder (a potential explosive) and a Bunsen burner (a potential ignition source) nearby, I might inductively reason that someone had attempted to make gunpowder and accidentally blew himself up in the process. However, this conclusion could be woefully incorrect. A more thorough investigation might reveal that intruders had forced their way into the lab, bringing with them an explosive device that *they* detonated in order to cover up another crime they had committed while at the scene.

If I stand on the rim of the Grand Canyon in Arizona and wonder how the canyon formed, I must use inductive reasoning because I cannot conduct an experiment at this very instant in time and place to "prove" that the Colorado River carved the canyon, but I do understand the concepts (principles) of erosion by running water, the regional uplift of the Colorado Plateau, and the consequential incisive down-cutting to reach sea level by the river. On the other hand, I may have conducted laboratory flume experiments with running water to calculate the rate of erosion in bedrock given a certain volume and velocity of water and suspended sediment. As I begin to understand the cause and effect in this example, that is, before I start to analyze the creation of the Grand Canyon, I might wonder if the Colorado River is in the canyon because the land is the lowest area topographically, or the area is the lowest because the river is there. If I find a new principle of nature, that is, one that most scientists accept, this principle can thus become the basis for further inferences and the reasoning becomes deductive again. This iterative or feedback-loop process is the basis for why man gains knowledge. All past events must be explained using inductive reasoning, and the absolute truth of the claim is never guaranteed by the truth of the conclusion.

This fundamental principle of cause and effect must be understood in nearly all investigations. The hypothesis proposed must logically connect an often-confusing host of variables before possibly making a prediction. Take, for example, the hypothesis *a rapidly falling barometer of 29 inches of mercury to less than 28 inches on the coast of Louisiana indicates heavy rain and an imminent hurricane*. The barometric trend does not cause the weather but reveals the effect of very low atmospheric pressure. Obviously, the impending hurricane is the cause of the low barometric reading because even if one were to manually reset a rapidly falling barometer to 29 inches of mercury, the rain and hurricane would likely still materialize. *Likewise, setting a barometer on a sunny day to 28 inches will not cause a hurricane.*

If the number of packs of cigarettes smoked per day is proportionally related to the number of cups of coffee consumed per day, then people who do not drink coffee will never smoke. This hypothesis and cause and effect are more complicated. I know people who do not drink coffee but who do smoke cigarettes, and thus the hypothesis is false. Although a research study may be conducted in order to determine if coffee drinking and cigarette smoking are somehow correlated, does it seem possible that the use of one causes the use of the other? Does the hypothesis apply to both males and females? Are age, general health, lifestyle, geographic location, caffeine content, or phase of the moon even necessary considerations? We could control one variable, say coffee, as the independent variable, and measure/observe how the other dependent variable, cigarette smoking, changes with varying coffee consumption, but there may be hidden confounders or undetected influences that lead to uncertain results. There may, of course, be no associations or cause and effect. There may also be variables working synergistically and unpredictably, thus, leading to scientific imprecision.

Trap: The fact-finder's intuition must be tempered, for not all things are as they first appear. A careless rush to judgment wastes time and resources. The successful fact-finder learns to harness his intuition and only use it to his best advantage.

---

3. The Purpose of Creating and Testing Hypotheses

Forcing the investigator's *unbiased* mind into a logical process that develops numerous rival, and sometimes contradictory, but plausible generalized working hypotheses is the key to successful investigations. As previously noted, it stimulates creativity, cultivates objectivity, promotes thoroughness, and leads to an understanding of causation. Multiple hypotheses construction is a powerful method that stimulates the systematic classification of facts and data, hence fostering incisive insight into the association of evidence.[11] Any premature ideas about guilty or responsible parties are not held to be partial by the investigator who is forced to think about all possibilities. We can all cite examples of situations where premature theories and false conclusions tend to degenerate into adopted and ruling theories due to the intellectual affection for the theory by its originator. Many times a simple hypothesis leads to a single cause, whereas the phenomenon really involves several causes and an equal or greater number of effects. Thus, each hypothesis should generate its own parallel or subinvestigation. Having several possible explanations gives us the insight to see the interaction of the causes being researched or investigated.

Frederic Jueneman stated:

> Everything must be subject to scrutiny, right down to the most fundamental postulates. To my mind, any of the disciplines—the sciences most of all are but a collection of observations. With an accretion of observations, a working hypothesis may present itself; but if one doesn't persist in questioning the conclusions drawn from the observations, and continually replenish the supply of alternatives, the *ad hoc* hypothesis will tend to evolve into a theory, and from thence into a principle, and finally—with tender loving care—develop into a fully grown dogma. And heavens forefend! We've got enough of those running around loose as it is.[12]

The mind of the fact-finder and his alter ego, the hypothesis-creator, must scrutinize everything, be open to all possibilities, and not rule out coincidences. Nothing should be without question. Albert Einstein once said, "If at first the idea is not absurd, then there is no hope for it." Although facts supporting coincidences can be easily found, one must accept that significant coincidences actually do occur in investigative work. Just because there might be *an improbability* for certain events to occur in a certain order does not automatically rule out the hypothesis. Several general examples of coincidences in the public record are both instructive and entertaining.

In the mid-1970s, an Ohio man won the state lottery and then moved to Florida where he subsequently won that state's lottery. One might intuitively think that if this incredibly low probability value were injected somehow into a criminal case, any jury would find that the lottery winner could not have accomplished this feat beyond a reasonable doubt. In reality, the man's chance of winning in Florida was not diminished or changed whatsoever by his prior win in Ohio. Likewise, a gambler who always bets on the same favorite number on the roulette wheel and believes that each time the number does not win the chances that it will win improve, does not understand independent events and probability. A gambler who keeps doubling her money on a favorite number will likely go broke long before the number wins.

What is the probability of getting any specific combination of five cards in a poker hand? In each hand the probability (p) is the same—about one chance in slightly less than 2,600,000, or $p = 0.000000385$. Each hand has an equal chance of being dealt, and thus, it is a remarkable combination, a highly unlikely event, and hence, a coincidence. Surprisingly, the probability of being dealt four aces plus any other card is much higher, or about one in 50,000 ($p = 0.00002$). Here is a surprising example from Paulos: If a thousand similarly addressed envelopes and a thousand similarly addressed letters were all randomly shuffled, then the probability that a blind person would put at least one letter into its correct envelope is $p = 0.63$ or 63 percent.[13] The lesson for investigators is that what may appear to be an impossible event can actually be predicted, and the chance that it will occur is much higher than ordinary intuition might suggest.

The possibility or probability that coincidences and random events can and do occur must be built into the multiple hypotheses constructed by the fact-finder. Paulos said it best when he succinctly opined, "The paradoxical conclusion is that it would be very unlikely for unlikely events not to occur."[14] Few people would have predicted the massive electrical blackout a few minutes past 5 P.M. on November 9, 1965, that affected about 30 million people in about an 80,000-square-mile area that included New Hampshire, Vermont, Massachusetts, Connecticut, Rhode Island, New York, Long Island, and parts of Pennsylvania.[15] A transmission line relay about the size of a coffee cup malfunctioned because it had not been adjusted properly at a Niagara Falls, New York, power station. Subsequently, power surges and overloads crippled the distribution network in the affected area, causing the collapse of entire power grid. Life came to a virtual standstill for up to 13 hours in one of the most heavily industrialized and populated areas of the world. The ensuing chaos forever changed the lives of those affected. Due to the creation of the North American Electric Reliability Council in 1968, similar failures were guaranteed never to happen again. However, because the power grids were overextended and the systems that supported them were not sufficiently upgraded and could not keep pace with demand, on August 14, 2003, a few minutes after 4 P.M. EDT, another blackout, the largest in U.S. history, occurred in a triangular area from New York City to Ottawa, Quebec, Canada, to Toledo, Ohio (about 95,000 square miles). Within nine seconds the safeguards and firewalls failed and the power outage cascaded through this area affecting about 50 million people.[16] Fortunately, there were no riots or hysteria but a lot of stunned and stranded *refugees.* Analysts concluded that the power network had become more complex than anyone had realized. They also indicated that the cause of the power failure may have been simply a tree falling on a high-tension line in Ohio and tripping off a generator. *The failure to trim a single tree likely caused 263 power plants to go down with an economic punch of over $6 billion.*

Another coincidence, or more correctly *randomness of events,* example was the November 7, 2000, U.S. presidential election. Here are the facts.

Only 50.7 percent of those eligible to vote voted. This was the third-lowest percentage since 1932. A total of approximately 105,376,300 votes were cast for all candidates. Hence, about 102,500,000 eligible U.S. citizens did not vote. In the final popular vote, Al Gore received 51,003,894 or 48.41 percent, George W. Bush received 50,495,211 or 47.89 percent, and Ralph Nadar received 2,834,410 or 2.69 percent. Where there are 3,097 counties in the United States, only one of these counties *finally* decided the outcome of the election. This county was in Florida, which had 25 electoral votes at stake. Prior to the Florida count, Gore had 255 electoral votes and Bush had 246. In the final count, about 5,956,430 votes were cast in Florida with Gore receiving 2,912,253, Bush receiving 2,912,790, Nadar receiving 97,488, Buchanan receiving 17,484, and Browne receiving 16,415. The final difference between Bush and Gore in Florida was 537 more popular votes for Bush; this gave 5 more electoral votes to Bush who won the election. Legal challenges cut Bush's lead to 327 votes. Four counties began recounts with deadlines set by the Florida secretary of state. Requests for extensions were denied. During the confusion, one county gave Gore a gain of 567 votes and another county gave Gore a gain of 188 votes. Absentee ballots, overseas military, and incompletely punched ballots were all disputed and added more confusion. Bush's lead was ultimately reduced to 154 votes by December 8, 2000. Gore then lost a Florida Supreme Court appeal to recount two additional counties. Overturning the Florida Supreme Court, recounts were rejected by the U.S. Supreme Court in a 5 to 4 decision based on the rationale that time had run out. On December 12, 2000, Florida finally declared Bush the winner of its 25 electoral votes. In this legal quagmire, dozens of county, state, and federal lawsuits were filed. Decisions were appealed, overturned, and sustained. Hundreds of motions were filed in the process. If only one voter in every 200,000 in Florida had changed his or her vote to Gore, or if one judge had changed his or her decision on any one of these motions, or if one court decision had gone the other way, the presidential outcome may have been different. Again, we see where a host of unexpected events, if sequenced properly, can create the appearance of a *coincidence* and can have monumental consequences and even affect the course of U.S. and world history.[17]

Sometimes coincidences may only seem like remarkable occurrences; for example, what is the probability that each human on the earth today has breathed at least one molecule of oxygen or nitrogen contained in the air that Julius Caesar exhaled in the year 44 B.C. just as he was assassinated and said, "Et tu Brutus"? Ordinary intuition might tempt one to make this a very small number. However, in actuality the calculated probability is greater than $p = 0.99$.

4. Creativity

All fact-finders must possess a modicum of creativity. This attribute, although touched on much earlier in this book, has been purposely emphasized because of its importance and correlation to one's ability to devise multiple working hypotheses. There are thousands of tests to ascertain one's general level of creativity; two are presented here.

The first is a simple self-test. In her article, Laura Berman cites psychologist E. Paul Torrance who devised the following test.[18] In ten minutes list all of the unusual uses imaginable for junked automobiles. The most common 14 answers to this creativity test are: make them into art objects, make one good auto from several, use as a pretend car on children's playground, make into chairs, repair for demolition derby, use as a safety warning for drivers, use for practice in teaching auto mechanics, use as a flower planter, fix up for racing, repair and sell, sell for scrap and spare parts, use tires as swings, smash with hammer for tension-reducer, and recap the tires and sell them. Any of these answers score zero and all others score one point each. A score of 1–5 shows very little originality; 6–14 points is the average score; and 16 points or more indicates highly original thinkers.

An even shorter creativity test is to ask someone to add all the numbers from 1 to 100 in five minutes. The average person will actually try to add each successive number but will run out of time. On the other hand, a creative person will realize that 1 plus 100 is the same (101) as 2 plus 99 as is 3 plus 98 and 4 plus 97, and so on. Thus, the fast solution is to simply multiply 101 times 50 to obtain the answer of 5,050.

You may have heard of the well-known and long-lived example of creativity that is used by physics professors to stimulate students into thinking about creative ways to use a simple barometer. The challenge is this: explain how to calculate the height of a tall building using a barometer. A creative student's answer might be to lower the barometer over the edge with a string while standing on the roof and then measure the length of the string (which equals the building's height). Other equally correct answers include:

1. Take the barometer to the roof, drop it over the edge, time its descent, then using the formula: distance = 1/2 AT^2, where A is the acceleration of gravity and T is time;
2. Place the barometer next to the building in the sun then measure the height of the barometer, the length of the barometer's shadow, the length of the building's shadow, and with a simple proportion, calculate the building's height;
3. Measure the height of the barometer and then as you climb the stairs inside the building, mark off "barometric units" on the wall, then total the units;
4. Determine the mass of the barometer, tie it on the end of a rope, swing it as a pendulum at the street and roof levels, and determine "g" (the acceleration of gravity) for each location; theoretically the difference in "g" values can provide the difference in altitude for the two locations and, hence, the building's height;
5. Take the barometer to the building superintendent and say, "Here is a very expensive barometer. I will give it to you if you tell me the height of this building."

Can you think of another method?

The method of multiple-working hypotheses also promotes innovation and the *invention* of new procedures and models. It helps one to solve investigative problems with maximum efficacy given the talent brought to bear upon the problem. The curious fact-finder who uses the method of multiple working hypotheses is training his mind to ask questions and accept paradigm shifts. The more hypotheses he can create, given the facts at hand, the greater the probability that a successful conclusion can be reached. Invoking the scientific approach is the shortest and most economical route to this success. Good investigators are limited only by their imagination.

The scientific approach is remarkable in that people who think like geniuses use this ability very effectively and to the ultimate. Geniuses are said to be able to make the impossible possible. Andrei Aleinikov has stated:

> If we are trying to find the nature of genius thinking, one feature is immediately obvious: genius is an ability to see

through to the essential. A genius has a special way of seeing things—all at once, all together and all the way to the core. A genius is able to create the essence from split and isolated parts of the whole. A genius is able to understand the essence without always having all the information.[19]

Fact-finders and others, however, should be cautious and not interpret this as being able to cogently explain completely random phenomena. Analyzing patterns in random data will nearly always provide false conclusions. There may be excessive information or misinformation collected in a complex investigation, and thus, the fact-finder must be able to filter, sort, and identify only the significant pieces and facts.

5. Evaluating Probability

What if scenarios can be mentally constructed and variable "truth values" between 1.0 and 0.0 (from completely true to completely false, respectively) can be assigned to various components of any hypothesis. Assignments may not represent true scientific values but, rather, provide *ballpark estimates* or *best guesses*. These probabilities, or statistical weights, are proportional to the amount (preponderance) and reliability of the evidence. If we can show that any one component or variable is false ($p = 0.0$), we can then eliminate the hypothesis. Any value assigned between true and false on a continuous scale has some degree of possibility. Although a detective may conclude, "John may have killed Mary if John's fingerprints are found on the murder weapon," the only absolute probabilities that have been excluded are 0.0 (John did not kill Mary) and 1.0 (John killed Mary), and thus, the statement is relatively meaningless except for its suggestion that additional investigation is in order. Absolute certainty is as rare in investigation as it is in life. That is why we spend so much time making judgmental decisions.

Measurements (and data) are never exact, however carefully taken. There is no such thing as an exact measurement, except for counting numbers.[20] If tests or experiments are conducted and computations made, the result can be accurate only to the same number of significant digits as was the *least* accurate number used in the computation. Instruments used to take measurements have limited precision; that is, their precision is equal to the smallest scale unit that can be clearly read or interpolated. If an investigation includes calculated numerical values, the percentage of error for each operation must be combined in arriving at the final error or uncertainty.

Because only a cursory introduction is provided here, the reader is urged to review the mathematics of probability from other sources.[21]

Basically, the probability of occurrence for any event is the number of ways the event can happen divided by the number of possible outcomes. Here are several simple unconditional theoretical calculations for mutually exclusive, complementary, and independent events.

- *Mutually exclusive:* The probability of rolling a five on one six-sided die roll is 1/6. The probability of each mutually exclusive event can be added, such as the probability of rolling either a three or a four on one die roll is: 1/6 + 1/6, or 1/3 (0.33).
- *Complementary:* The probability of either success or failure, or of rolling either an odd or an even number on one roll of the die, where the events make up all possible outcomes, is: 1/2 + 1/2, or 1.0. The subjective probability that Henry is innocent is 0.9, and thus, the probability that Henry is guilty is 0.1. The sum of the probabilities is always 1.0 for these events.
- *Independent:* The probability of separate unconnected events, say rolling a two on one roll of the die plus tossing a heads with one fair coin-toss is: 1/6 × 1/2, or 1/12 (0.083). The probability outcome of the die roll does not affect the outcome of the coin-toss and vice-versa, and hence, the two probabilities can be multiplied.

Multiplying probabilities of components of hypotheses to arrive at the importance (truth value) of any given hypothesis is a semiquantitative way of comparing all hypotheses. Initially, in evaluating the overall probability of a given hypothesis, all of the evaluated components of any hypothesis must be totally independent of one another. Second, the probabilities must not be multiplied indiscriminately. Unless values are 1.0, the more variables introduced into the analysis, the smaller the calculated probability value. Hence, it is suggested that in order not to arbitrarily create very small probabilities, the total number of independent variables should be no more than five or six, and they should, of course, reflect the most significant components of the case. If all variables are truly independent, the probability is unconditional and the probability product gives the lowest likelihood or worst-case scenario value.

On the other hand, most of the probabilities we encounter in everyday life are conditional ones because they are made with some prior knowledge that influences our thinking; that is, there may be past events within which the probability assessment is grounded. Knowing that event Y has occurred, what is the probability that event X will occur? If the probability is conditional (overlapping probabilities, or the probability of one event affecting the outcome of another event), the mathematical formula called Bayes Theorem is used to calculate the probability of an event. This theorem relates conditional and unconditional probabilities and is a model for updating information as new evidence becomes available, such as something is learned from observing prior events. With conditional probabilities, the probability of some given event is different for different prior conditions. For investigations, however, application of the formal theorem can be very complex and likely does not need to be invoked. In conditional probability, the condition is that at least one reasonable motive or sufficient circumstantial evidence has been established and the fact-finder/assessor can simply justify assigning appropriately higher probabilities to each component of the hypothesis. Motivation and the existence of circumstantial evidence are powerful elements in most cases, and by our very nature we tend to weight them accordingly. We know that people tend to commit intentional acts after making a risk-benefit assessment. Even if the benefit cannot be understood by the rational mind, it may have play in the mind of the irrational. With the exception of the psychopath, we are motivated by fundamental needs. Noted psychologist Abraham Maslow developed a hierarchy of these needs and suggested that people's actions are motivated when these needs go unmet.

- Physiological: the basic needs of air, water, sleep, food, and sexual gratification
- Safety: the need to establish and maintain security and eliminate chaos
- Social: the need to belong to groups and escape the feelings of loneliness and solitude
- Ego: a need for self-esteem, attention, and recognition
- Self-actualization: the need for personal fulfillment and inner peace

Occasionally it is the task of the fact-finder to determine the perpetrator's motive in order to solve the crime. By better understanding fundamental human needs and the circumstances surrounding the event in question, motive can often be determined. Then using our abstract notion of probability, the motive can then be used to better understand the perpetrator and in many instances, identify him.

Language plays a role as well. Language has a degree of ambiguity and is inherently vague. For example, the famous Sorites paradox is, "How much is a heap of sand?" The answer is that it can be anything because regardless of how many times one grain of sand is removed from the heap, it is still a heap.[22] The removal of a single grain should not make any difference. But when only one grain is left, is the heap a heap? An argument can be made that it is a heap or that it is not a heap. It is a matter of relativity. What is considered small by one individual may actually be considered large by another. Experienced interviewers know this all too well. A subject's responses can appear either very deceptive or very truthful, depending on the interviewer's perception of the words used by the subject and his past experiences under similar circumstances. For example, suppose the subject stated: "I took only a small amount of the cash." Each of us has our own idea of what that amount of cash might be. But if the missing cash were over a million dollars, the amount taken by the subject could be anything less than the entire amount.

Similarly, a knowledgeable investigator should be able to precisely articulate the meanings of *beyond a reasonable doubt* or *probable cause*, and the intervening degrees of *preponderance of the evidence* and *clear and convincing?*[23] However, not everyone will agree with his determinations. Because of this imprecision in language and operational definitions, scales of truth values have been arbitrarily constructed and qualities assigned, such as completely true, very true, fairly true, 50 percent chance of being true or false, fairly false, very false, and completely false. Each of these seven values has corresponding numerical values, respectively, of 6/6, 5/6, 4/6, 3/6, 2/6, 1/6, and 0/6.

The American Academy of Forensic Sciences and the American Board of Forensic Document Examiners have gone even further and adopted certainty values, or operational definitions, that are applied to questioned documents. On the 1.0 to 0.0 scale, the examiner has nine degrees of certainty. They are, respectively, identification (definite conclusion of identity), strong probability (highly probable, very probable), probable indications (evidence to suggest), no conclusion (totally inconclusive, indeterminable), indications did not, strong probability did not, and elimination.

Likewise, if components of hypotheses can be rated by *truth values*, then the final hypothesis has a composite truth value. This makes comparisons among many hypotheses less subjective and more valuable. Low-value components are areas of the case that may need more work and very well may be nothing more than pure *coincidences*. In such instances we must then ask ourselves what test can be done to verify, increase, or decrease its value? Is there a cause or justification for our finding or is this value the result of pure chance?

As we shall now see, our inductive logic can extend to events of the past, such as might be encountered in the typical investigation. Consider this conceptually simplified but worthwhile example of a geologic resource assessment that begins with the question: "What is the probability that an undiscovered, economically exploitable, 100-million-barrel oil field will be found at any particular location?"

For this oil field to exist today, five major extraordinary independent events or prerequisites must have occurred in a given order. Each process or event can be evaluated and rated for its own probability. First, a hydrocarbon source rock must have been deposited rich enough to supply the organic material for oil formation; second, a porous reservoir rock with an impermeable seal must have been deposited into which the oil can migrate; third, a structural or stratigraphic trap must have formed, for example, an anticlinal fold structure; fourth, the source rock must have been buried deep enough to convert the organic material into oil and expel it so that it migrates until trapped by the anticline; fifth and finally, the geographic area must not have been subjected to a detrimental tectonic history such as intense faulting that could destroy the trap or extreme temperatures that would overcook the oil and destroy it. If an assessor assigns unconditional probability values of 0.25, 0.75, 0.10, 0.95, and 0.50, respectively, for events one through five, the final probability that this hundred-million-barrel field will exist is the product of all probabilities, or 0.0089. This is a slightly less than 1 percent chance, or one in 112 similar cases. If the geologic province or sedimentary basin has already produced some oil or gas, however small the quantity, the problem now becomes a conditional probability problem and the final *truth value* increases because conceptually the outcome of event B depends on the outcome of event A (the probability that B occurs given that A has occurred); that is, B is conditioned by A, and all events that produced the phenomenon (oil accumulation) have some interdependence. The truth value is dynamic in the sense that it moves between 0.0 and 1.0 depending upon the amount and quality of new information that may be continuously brought to bear upon the problem.

If a geologic prospect is being assessed for a much smaller one-million-barrel oil field, the assessor might elevate each factor one number higher. Thus, each factor in the probability product is dynamic and ultimately depends on the assessor's overall knowledge and experience in his particular area of expertise. If the same problem is given to five or six different knowledgeable assessors (interpose fact-finder) with somewhat differing areas of expertise and experience, their probability answers could be averaged or amalgamated. This is called the *Delphi* method. With Delphi inquiry methodology, the experts must be honest and unbiased for this group decision-making process to work. Also, over time the distribution of these probability estimates can be tracked to gain additional insight into the validity of any one hypothesis. This is particularly important if the composition of the Delphi group changes. For the potential oil field assessment above, if any one of these five factors or events was rated 0.0, regardless of how high the other factors were rated, the oil field could not exist because zero times anything is zero. A zero is the same as completely false and it correlates to exculpatory evidence in criminal cases. For example, DNA from semen of a rape victim that does not match that of a suspect completely rules out the suspect (truth value, or $p = 0.0$) but yet does so without identifying the perpetrator.

In more complex situations where there are independent variables in a case, a similar procedure may be used by a creative investigator to evaluate the possibility of any occurrence. I recently attended a seminar for law enforcement investigators that was held at a resort hotel. One of the sessions included a mock crime scene investigation in one of the guest rooms that served as an apartment for a private party. The scenario involved a witness who had called 911 and reported an explosion in his neighbor's apartment. He had reported that upon arriving at the scene he found a dead dismembered female on the floor. My student-partner and I were dispatched to investigate. Upon arriving we were met at the door of the apartment (guestroom) by the reporting party and our instructor posing as a local police officer. The officer reported that he had just arrived and only quickly looked at the scene and decided to wait. The officer also told us what he had seen inside the apartment. He said he had observed no one except the victim, blood stains on the wall, empty beer cans scattered around the room, a gun on the floor, no shell casings, two different sets of footprints on the rug, a knife on a table, and what appeared to be bomb-making components near the door.

This scenario contains enough evidence and variables making it worthy of analysis. An investigator should be able to construct at least four or five most-plausible hypotheses to fit the information provided and several least-plausible *off the wall* hypotheses. Clearly, the first question to ponder; was this a suicide, an accident, or a homicide? Should we initially photograph the crime scene, look for latent fingerprints, collect fibers, document the orientation of all objects, search for tool marks and other evidence of a breaking-and-entering burglary, measure angles in the blood spatter, examine the weapons, collect air samples for the K9 unit, make impressions of the footprints, or interrogate the reporting party? Could the reporting party be involved or even be a suspect?

Consequently, our initial response was not to enter the crime scene but rather, to interview the reporting party and then have the local officer escort him to the police station for additional questioning. This proved correct as the reporting party had an electronic detonator in his hand; he had placed a bomb at the crime scene and was planning to use it to kill the first responders (unfortunately not an uncommon scenario). Our process approach, conservative strategy, and recognition that the reporting party knew the victim (possible motive) allowed us to sense danger (deductive reasoning) based on the evidence available (inductive reasoning). Our cognitive processes enabled us to distill the facts to the essence of the problem and anticipate a potential hazard. The fact that my partner and I were the only investigators at the conference to survive the mock crime-scene scenario says something about the closed-mindedness and lack of methodology of investigators in general.

My colleagues and I recently investigated a matter where four anonymous and very threatening e-mails over a two-month period (pre- and post-*Columbia* space shuttle disaster, February 1, 2003) were sent to the chief financial officer of a large engineering firm. None of the e-mails was apparently traceable. However, one of the firm's male scientists was terminated a short time before the first e-mail for reasons his employer refused to reveal to us. Thus, the firm's internal security had a possible suspect. Having just the four e-mails, our role was relegated to conducting a threat assessment on the suspect. We did not have access to personnel files or any other evidence or information. Our preliminary research uncovered that the suspect lived about 3,000 miles from the office of the CFO and had no criminal history. However, an Internet investigation produced a wealth of information. The suspect's wife and one family member had Web sites that provided enough information to characterize these individuals and heighten our suspicions. Our dynamic process branched outward to include more possible hypotheses. In so doing, we were able to make broad connections between the content of these sites and the information contained in the e-mails. The information strongly suggested ("very true" value) that the suspect's wife was in fact the most-likely perpetrator. When we presented our findings and interpretation to the client, the response was utter surprise. Because of the detailed content of the e-mails no one had suspected anyone other than an employee or former employee. Of course without the benefit of interviewing the subject and his wife, we are not absolutely positive ($p = 1.0$) of our conclusion, but we had at least a very defendable position for our most viable and strongest hypothesis.

Another real example is taken from Gerald van Belle.[24] For the first time, van Belle used six apparently independent variables to show there was an extremely low probability that someone other than the accused had committed a crime. The empirical facts are as follows.

In 1964 in Los Angeles, a blonde female with a ponytail snatched a purse belonging to another female. The thief fled on foot but was later observed entering a yellow car driven by a black male who had a beard and a mustache. A woman matching the thief's description was later located and charged with the crime. The prosecution assigned probabilities to the empirical facts as follows: blonde hair (0.33), ponytail (0.10), yellow car (0.10), black male with beard (0.10), mustache (0.25), and an interracial couple in a car (0.001). The product of these values calculates to about 1 in 12 million. In other words, at the time in question, in the city of Los Angeles, there was a 1 in 12 million chance (more than the population of city at the time) that a couple, other than the accused had committed the crime. Resultantly, the court convicted the couple.

The case was appealed to the California Supreme Court and overturned. Although the court had tossed out the conviction for its own reasons, the prosecution's problem may have been that they did not really know if each piece of evidence was completely independent of the others. This is not a coin-toss experiment where everything is known to be independent; that is, each toss has to be either a head or a tail and each toss does not affect the outcome of subsequent tosses. Perhaps black males with mustaches have a genetic disposition to drive yellow cars. Perhaps blonde females with ponytails have a tendency to associate with men with beards. Krantz indicates that in 1970 1 in 145 marriages were interracial.[25] Of these marriages, the male was black and the female was white in one couple in six. This means that $p = 0.0011$. But, is it not more probable that a black male and white female combination might exist if the *just friends* and *co-workers* subsets of the sample and the *married* subset were all combined? It is also unlikely the prosecution looked at the demographics of the area of Los Angeles where this crime occurred. Is it not possible that the 0.0011 probability presented by the prosecution does not fit the subdemographics of the location in question? Moreover, what if the witnesses' descriptions of the man, women, or vehicle were incorrect? How would we know? The point is that each *category* of evidence—not each little piece of evidence—needs to be carefully evaluated, particularly for independence, at the highest level.[26] These categories, traditional to the investigative process, include the questions of *who, how, when, where, what,* and *why.*

6. The Concept of Simplicity

Any hypothesis that explains, say, five or six observations or facts has a greater probability of being true than a hypothesis that tries to explain ten or twelve. This is because the ten-fact hypothesis has a greater chance of having one of the facts falsified as the investigative process runs its course and, hence, the conclusion becoming more improbable or false. The principle of simplicity and economy, or the *rule of parsimony*, in designing and choosing hypotheses is known as Ockham's razor (also known as Occam's razor).[27] Ockham's razor is a method by which one cuts out and excludes all of the elements of the hypothesis that cannot be observed. A perfect application of this principle is found in celestial geometry, that is, in an Earth-centered (geocentric) versus Sun-centered (heliocentric) model of our solar system. The currently accepted Copernicus-Kepler heliocentric model fits all of the elliptical-motion observations, including retrograde motions, particularly noticeable for Mercury and Mars, and is much simpler than the extremely complex circular orbits of the sun, planets, and moon required by Ptolemy's model. With its hierarchy of nested circular orbits, the Ptolemy model looks more like the intricate movement of a Swiss watch, and hence a good candidate for the application of Ockham's razor.

Ockham's razor thus provides a guideline for preferring, all else being equal, the least complex explanation. It is an intuitive principle that suggests *simpler is better* and that "plurality should not be assumed without necessity."[28] Another way to state Ockham's razor is that the most brilliant argument is no better than the weakest assumption; one should not invent more hypotheses than are necessary because the simplest explanation that will fit the facts is most likely the best. The interpretation of facts and inferences is made easier and is less convoluted by using fewer models. If one stretches the line of reasoning too far to explain the observations, even when not proven wrong, perhaps the alternative, simpler approach is closer to the truth. The razor thus separates the reasonable from the merely conceivable. Time, personnel, financial support, material resources, and investigative energy must be properly apportioned relative to the value of each hypothesis's probability calculation.

Trap: The merely conceivable (say, the $p = 0.05$ to 0.001 range), however, must not be completely ignored in hypothesis development, for it is in this range we find the domain of coincidental occurrences.

The following is a fascinating yet tragic example of an investigation not completely and systematically adhering to an analytical strategy and scientific approach. Fourteen-year-old Elizabeth Smart was abducted at knifepoint from her bedroom in Salt Lake City, Utah, at about 1:30 to 2:00 A.M. on June 5, 2002, by a Caucasian male subject. The only eyewitness was Elizabeth's younger sister, Mary Katherine, age nine. Nine months later, on March 12, 2003, Elizabeth Smart, now 15, was found in Sandy, Utah, about 15 miles south of her home. She was under the control of her alleged abductor and rapist, 49-year-old religious fanatic Brian "Immanuel" David Mitchell, and his third wife, 57-year-old Wanda Ilene Barzee. The trio had lived a vagabond lifestyle during the nine months of Elizabeth's captivity. During the first three months they actually camped in the hills within a few miles of the upscale Smart family home in Federal Heights.

As the investigation unfolded, police considered Richard Ricci, a drifter and Smart family handyman, to be the prime suspect. Investigators had even told reporters that they were 99 percent certain that Ricci was Elizabeth Smart's kidnapper and that the teenage girl was dead. Richard

Ricci had a lengthy criminal record and was known to have stolen tools from the Smarts. Let us call this hypothesis number one. Unfortunately for investigators, Ricci, having denied any involvement, died of a stroke on August 30, 2002, while incarcerated for parole violation.

On the other hand, Brian David Mitchell's background and probability of being involved was actually downplayed. Call this hypothesis two. Brian Mitchell's history included: (1) he was a self-appointed religious prophet, drifter, and polygamist; (2) he lost custody of a daughter by a previous marriage; (3) he was hired for a day by Lois Smart, Elizabeth's mother, in November 2001, as a handyman to do roof repairs; (4) he was positively identified as the abductor in October 2002 by Mary Katherine; (5) his sketch was released, against the advice of the Salt Lake City police, a month prior to Elizabeth's being found; *America's Most Wanted* television program with narrator John Walsh broadcast the sketch and photographs on February 12, 2003, and again on March 1, 2003; (6) he had been incarcerated from February 12, 2003, to February 17, 2003, by the San Diego County Sheriffs Department for vandalism of a church (note the overlapping date of February 12, 2003); (7) he was controlling and abusive of his children; and (8) he was seen by thousands of people in Salt Lake City's Pioneer Park panhandling with several women who were dressed in loose robes and wearing face veils; hundreds of these people, including store owners of the area, knew Brian "Immanuel" Mitchell. Mitchell's motive may have been related to polygamy or an illusion of Elizabeth Smart as a surrogate daughter. He had made statements years before the kidnapping that as a prophet, he should have seven wives.

After Elizabeth Smart was found alive and well, the general consensus of the experts was that they expected her to be found dead within several hours of her abduction. Several days after her disappearance, most experts concluded that the police should be looking for a body. After her rescue, the police reaction was one of utter surprise. Everyone involved in the case, from the police to the psychologists and even the public, was calling her return a *miracle*. Even the *Larry King Show* (CNN) discussed this case (March 12, 2003). One ex-prosecutor, legal advisor, and expert on the show said, "There is no way police could have ever dreamed up that a religious freak panhandler bum would have kidnapped Elizabeth Smart nine months ago." Prior to Elizabeth's rescue this same expert stated that Ricci was *the* perfect candidate for being the kidnapper. Tragically, everyone had focused on a single hypothesis and blindly invested their resources on the wrong suspect.

Given the totality of the circumstances and facts known by the authorities at the time, hypothesis two should have been given the highest priority. Even a novice would have come to the same conclusion. Consider this:

- Mary Katherine Smart had identified "Immanuel" as the intruder;
- Brian Mitchell was not a complete stranger to the Smart family, and moreover, he was familiar with the layout of the residence;
- An eyewitness had sighted Mitchell lurking around the Smart family home on May 31, 2002, just days before the abduction;
- Mitchell had personally expressed a motive to numerous people;
- Ricci had a credible alibi;
- The chronology of events involving the kidnapping and Mitchell's activities coincides;
- Mitchell had allegedly made comments prior to his arrest that he was going to kidnap Elizabeth Smart's cousin;
- The logic supporting hypothesis number two is not complicated and requires less bending of the mind than hypothesis one.

By invoking perfect 20-20 hindsight, I assert that hypothesis two was a no-brainer. The Mitchell hypothesis should have demanded greater attention, and although overwhelmed by this case at the time, the Salt Lake City Police Department today would also have to agree. The Smart family made a cogent comment when they said, "It's important never to give up no matter what the statistics say, no matter what the worst-case scenario; until you know otherwise, never give up." For additional details, readers are encouraged to see Maggie Haberman and Jeane MacIntosh's account of this investigation.[29]

Tip: Investigators of all experience levels need to maintain an open mind throughout their investigation. The most successful investigators are flexible enough to think and work outside the box and pursue more than just one hypothesis.

---

7. Chaos Theory and the Limits of Predictability

Scientists are always rethinking science, and they do not all agree on the logic and philosophy of investigative techniques.[30] They aim for the epicenter of insight, but sometimes the target moves or the true center is actually on the fringes. Even as this book was being written, legitimate challenges to Albert Einstein's theory of relativity, stating that the speed of light is the same for all observers in the universe regardless of their velocity, are being waged with claims that the speed of light may in fact not be the universal speed limit.[31] And just as quantum mechanics went beyond classical Newtonian physics (predictable cause-and-effect linear systems) to explain the duality of particles and waves (electromagnetic radiation) of the subatomic world and became respectable by the 1920s, the 1960s and 1970s saw an emerging science of chaos that revolutionized the way scientists think about and analyze complex dynamic nonlinear systems.[32]

Categorically, all natural phenomena exhibit chaos; it is characterized by an irregular, irreversible, non-repeating, unpredictable, unstable, and disordered behavior. Although this behavior is seemingly random, there is a magnificent underlying order and structure. According to the laws of thermodynamics, entropy (a measure of disorder in systems) increases with time; henceforth, we know that our universe is unwinding like a mechanical clock. Yet against the grain of increasing disorder, order seeks a *strange attractor* and manifests itself. Every system that acts randomly has a strange attractor or *sink*. Motion, trajectories, and events converge on the attractor. This is a complicated concept, but suffice it to say that attractors are characterized by their dependence on initial conditions and are essentially states to which the chaotic system eventually settles, that is, the stable or ordered part of the chaotic system. Examples of a strange attractor in a cultural sense could be the chief of an organization or tribe, or the dogma of a particular religion.[33]

Systems emerge and evolve from chaos. Systems are ordered entities containing like or related elements attempting to reach equilibrium that changes with time. Because chaos surrounds and resides in all systems, perfect equilibrium can never be achieved indefinitely. Systems can spontaneously self-organize and then just as mysteriously, destruct. Their components are interconnected by feedback loops. The process of learning is an example of feedback loops in the brain, and a hormonal imbalance would be an example of a brain chemistry disorder.

Studies of systems show that there is an interconnection among all the variables in each system, and that all systems affect one another. Examples of organizations that develop from chaotic systems are the knowable universe, a galaxy, a solar system, the Earth's atmosphere, all life forms, oceanic circulation, the history of a civilization, a nation, a war, a political party, the Internet, and of course, an investigation. Chaotic behavior was first studied within the unstable turbulence of streams, fluids, and gases (air and weather), and now has been applied to turbulence associated with airfoils, economics, human behavior, epidemics, and the rise and fall of civilizations.

In chaos theory, very small initial details or perturbations are very important. The effect of rounding or truncating the sixth or seventh digit of a number with six or seven significant figures may not seem important in the grand scheme of things; one part in a million or ten million should be inconsequential. But indeed it is important. This is analogous to a seemingly insignificant event changing the course of history, or the breaking of the 15 grouped balls on a pool table with the cue ball. No opening shots can ever result in identical positions of all of the balls because there is sensitivity, dependence upon and magnification of very small initial differences each time the cue ball breaks the group. This is called *sensitivity to initial conditions* or the *butterfly effect*. Conceptually, it is impossible to predict the effect of a butterfly in Asia flapping its wings one time upon the weather patterns months later in the United States. We do not know the effect of the single butterfly wing flap, and we do not know if this flap has more or less effect than any other butterfly wing flap elsewhere. However, we do know that the butterfly effect of chaos creates diversity in nature. Again, conceptually, replace butterfly flap with any other event or process of your choosing and consider the implications for any system, including an investigation. In the French film *Les Sept Peches Capitaux* (The Seven Capital Sins), a minor domestic argument over a fly in the soup provokes anger and leads to a world catastrophe.[34] Perhaps the best example for sensitivity to initial conditions is an apparently trivial or random decision someone makes while growing up that eventually influences and alters the course of his life, and even history: think Hitler.

The new geometry of chaos, defined as the pattern of irregular shapes, is shown with fractal geometry, or fractal sets, as studied and illustrated by Benoit Mandelbrot.[35] A fractal is a repeating geometric pattern of an irregular shape or surface. Surprisingly, the geometry of fractals is inherent in all natural things. Fractals show self-similarity or symmetry without regard to scale; they are patterns within a pattern. Scale invariance is shown when fractals are subdivided; each part is a small copy of the whole, even with an infinite number of subdivisions, the degree of irregularity always remain the same. The irregularity of objects such as coastlines, mountains, lakes, clouds, trees, and the skyline of a city can all be modeled using fractals. Upon closer view, all surfaces become irregular and a regular irregularity is discernible.

Complex nonlinear components of chaos can lie within linear systems; the converse is also true. There are always subtle relationships between the simple and the complex. Most deterministic linear systems actually have small errors that inevitably lead to huge unpredictable changes and limit our understanding of the future. Even systems with only several degrees of freedom can become chaotic showing irregular behavior. Weather provides the classic example. Air pressure, temperature, wind velocity, humidity, and hundreds of other interrelated variables are sensitive to initial conditions, and hence, weather is a chaotic system that precludes absolute predictability on any scale from global, continental, regional, to local.

With analytical simulation one can compute decent odds of winners in football games but cannot predict the outcome with 100 percent accuracy. The same applies to daily or yearly stock markets, the forecasting of technological developments, and the financial health of a Fortune 500 company 10 to 20 years from now.[36] In 1975 could anyone have accurately forecasted the disparate financial health of K-Mart and Wal-Mart? History is a study of causes and effects. All inventions and technological advances are connected, per James Burke, because every invention or development would have been impossible without the contribution of the inventor's predecessors.[37] Technology as well as the corporate investigation conform to the popular notion that everything is related to everything; therefore, it is up to the fact-finder to trace and define the historical limits of the system being investigated.

In nonlinear systems when the output of an event is folded back into the input of the next event so that the result becomes more complexly altered, intermediate-term predictability suffers and long-term predictability becomes impossible. The consequences of each perturbation and iteration may be unexpected, and the ultimate impact cannot be known. This means that models of systems that we construct today may indeed be ephemeral and tend to limit our understanding of phenomena over the long term. We indeed live in a dynamic and amorphous society teeming with chaos and uncertainty. The mathematician John Paulos has succinctly and cleverly demonstrated the following points about uncertainty:

- Whenever we read an article containing numbers, we should always ask ourselves if the precision is really there.
- Can we know the difference between meaningless and real coincidences?
- What systems are stable and which ones are very sensitive to tiny perturbations?
- Are we being too vulnerable to the anchoring effects of untenable suggestions?[38]

In many ways a corporation is an ecosystem attempting to reach equilibrium of maximum efficiency and profit. In so doing it is absolutely subject to the principle of sensitivity to initial conditions. It is a dynamic system superimposed on the system of natural human behavior influenced by a complex assortment of other systems internal and external to it. Negative perturbations (influences), however, can cause disruptions. Disruptions like the increased cost of money, trade embargos, labor disputes, and the introduction of a new technology by a competitor create chaos and, on the macrolevel, irreversibly alter the history of the organization. More subtle disruptions such as a misfiled invoice, a single employee who occasionally works while impaired, or a missed appointment are more like the flapping of a butterfly's wings. As with the Heisenberg Uncertainty Principle that states: "The position and velocity of a quantum particle cannot be known simultaneously with absolute accuracy," the problem arises as to whether a corporate investigation can be conducted so it does not interfere with or intrude upon and irreversibly alter the entity being investigated. Because chaotic behavior is scale invariant and the given macroscale of the *corporate ecosystem,* the investigation should not impose itself on the outcome. The corporate investigator needs to appreciate that the uncertainty and inherent intricacies of complex nonlinear systems are subject to the minor perturbations created by his actions. Consequently, the corporate investigator needs to think deeply about what is possible, and then invoke an investigative methodology rendering the least amount of disruption to the system and minimize the quantity of chaos he creates.

Every experienced fact-finder has witnessed this phenomenon. Consider for a moment the investigation of an allegation of sexual harassment. Who should be interviewed first? In what order should the witnesses be interviewed? What allegations should and should not be shared with the alleged perpetrator, and what facts about the perpetrator should be withheld from the accuser? The experienced fact-finder ponders these questions and orchestrates his investigation with the precision of a master chess player. He knows each action (move on the board) will influence each subsequent action, and that the sum total of his effort will influence the behavior and very possibly the future of everyone involved. His decisions, actions, and inactions will ultimately determine the outcome of the investigation regardless of the facts. Very much, he alone will determine the fate of the accused and much of what will take place in his life thereafter. Therefore, we can never be too careful.

Whether we analyze a one-time event that occurred in the past by using inductive reasoning, or analyze a scenario that is still under way by using inductive and deductive reasoning, the ramifications of chaos theory, as it relates to systems attempting to achieve stability, affect every investigation we conduct. Because we must accept uncertainty in our work, we must be capable of describing our findings honestly by using our knowledge of subjective probability. We must muster all of our intuition, question everything, find the order among the complexities, and always be truthful.

B. Employee Theft Investigations

Statistics gathered by the U.S. Chamber of Commerce indicate that employee theft is a billion-dollar criminal industry.[39] For years the Chamber has warned us that one-third of all businesses fail because of employee theft. In 1995, the Association of Certified Fraud Examiners reported that fraud and abuse was costing employers an average of $9 a day per employee, or roughly $400 billion a year.[40] In its 2002 Report to the Nation, the ACFE reported that 6 percent of the nation's business revenues were lost as a result of occupational fraud and abuse. When applied to the U.S. gross domestic product, the amount equates to losses of approximately $600 billion, or about $4,500 per employee per year. The report goes on to claim that small businesses are the most vulnerable and that the average scheme in a small business causes $127,500 in losses. The average scheme in the largest companies is only $97,000. The report also reveals that the most common method for detecting workplace theft in 2002 was through tips from employees, customers, vendors, and anonymous sources. The second most common method of discovery was by accident.[41] Experts claim that for every $1 lost to shoplifting, employees steal another $15. In the food service industry, employee theft imposes a 4 percent tax on every customer dollar spent.

Unarguably, employee theft is a problem that cannot be ignored. However, the problem is more than just the dollars lost. The problem impacts morale, increases insurance costs, and decreases competitiveness as well as profits. Less profits mean lower investor returns, less capital in the market, and lower tax receipts at all levels. Moreover, losses due to theft are costly to make up. Depending upon margins, in order to recover a $100 loss, the average for-profit organization must sell nearly $3,000 in additional products or services. In low margin industries such as consumer electronics and groceries, the recovery multiplier is significantly greater. Intuitively, the lower the margin, the more difficult it is to recover the loss.

Employees don't just steal steaks and CD players. More than anything else, employees steal time. The commodity of choice of most workplace thieves is measured in minutes. Efficiency consultants have known this for years. Attempts to improve processes and systems to increase workplace efficiency were undertaken the day after the industrial revolution began. From Henry Ford's first assembly line to the implementation of modern robotics, industrialists have slaved (no pun intended) to improve worker efficiency. But diminishing it, from the dawn of time when man first sold his labor to another, the theft of time has been every employer's nemesis. Ponder this: If each employee of a 200-person organization were to steal 10 minutes a day, the employer would loose 2,000 minutes per day. If the work year had 260 work days, our hypothetical employer would have suffered a loss of 520,000 minutes, or the equivalent of 4.1 man-years. Effectively the workforce of 200 individuals is doing the work of 196. The cost of each employee stealing just 10 minutes a day translates to about $200,000 a year! Reducing wasted time by just one minute a day per employee creates a savings of $20,000 a year. No wonder efficiency consultants are in such popular demand! Just for fun, do the math for your organization; then run the numbers for Wal-Mart (it has roughly 1,200,000 employees). Staggering isn't it?

Some commonalities among these types of offenses:

- They are most often perpetrated by insiders with access.
- Time, finished goods, scrap and waste, and intellectual property (IP) are the most frequent assets stolen.
- Lack of supervision and effective processes are primary contributors.
- Employers should look for secretive relationships, missing documents, indictors of substance abuse, irregular hours of operation, or building entry.

1. Who Steals?

Stealing is the act of taking an asset or the removal or reduction of an interest in the asset where one does not have permission or lawful right to do so. The act of stealing is theft, and under most circumstances theft is a crime. In today's society, values that were once pillars of strength have begun to crumble. A variety of factors have influenced our new moral compass. In recent years the country has been plagued by a poor economy in which few citizens feel they have control of their lives or futures. We have also become a society whose members have no guilt. The victim mentality is so pervasive that even murderers can claim victimhood.

According to a study conducted by the University of Minnesota Sociology Department a number of years ago in which employees and employers were asked about theft in the workplace, the following was discovered:

- Workers who stole were also involved in other counter-productive workplace behaviors.
- The greater the opportunity for theft, the greater the chance that it would occur.
- Employees who are satisfied with their jobs are less likely to steal.
- The greater chance of detection, the less likely employees will steal.
- A strong commitment to deter theft reduces losses.
- Theft on the job is not necessarily correlated to external factors or influences.
- One-third of all employees claim to have stolen from their employers.
- Peer pressure and attitude significantly affect employee attitudes toward theft.

In short, workplace theft is widespread. Without specific policies and management commitment theft cannot be controlled. The employee that does become involved in theft usually falls into one of three categories: the greedy, the needy, or the foolish.

a. The Greedy

The greedy employee usually is first tempted to steal when his income can no longer support his lifestyle. After a series of rationalizations, the individual formulates the justification to initiate the crime. At first stealing in small quantities, the thief becomes increasingly bold and selfish. Rationalizing that what he is doing is justified, he finds it easier and easier to steal. In the final analysis, the greedy often conclude that theft is permissible given their condition and desires.

b. The Needy

The needy employee usually steals because of perceived or real needs. This individual may steal so he can support a drug habit, pay off a debt, or support a family. The need is so urgent that the act of theft outweighs the risk.

c. The Foolish

The foolish employee is one who succumbs to temptation. Given sufficient greed or need they are able to justify their behavior and whisk away their values and principles during a moment of weakness.

2. The Anatomy of a Workplace Theft Investigation

Because workplace theft is most often perpetrated by insiders, it is normally discovered from within. Occasionally, a customer or vendor will report it to a business, but most often it is detected by someone inside the organization. Usually, the discovery is made during routine operations. An item, such as a tool, piece of equipment, or inventory, is discovered missing by someone looking for it. In other instances routine processes or operations (such as a scheduled inventory) cause the loss to be discovered. Only rarely does an audit discover a loss. Regardless, like all successful workplace investigations, the theft investigation requires process. Let's briefly look at each of the components.

a. Preparation and Planning

As I have comprehensively detailed in the previous chapters, the first critical step is to prepare and plan one's effort. A project manager should be assigned. He should constitute the appropriate team, and some preinvestigation fact-finding should be performed. Based on the amount and type of the loss the project manager and the decision makers should decide the objectives, a budget, a timeline, and the standard of proof to be pursued. Often this effort uncovers more information and answers many questions.

b. Information Gathering

Based on the fact pattern and the circumstances surrounding the loss, the project manager and his team will decide which investigative methods will be employed and how they shall be used. Usually randomly interviewing and talking to employees to obtain their opinions regarding what may have taken place is not an investigative method, it is wasteful and counterproductive. Here is a better approach:

1. Based on the information available, formulate one or more working hypotheses.
2. Working one hypothesis at a time, attempt to develop a suspect pool. If the universe of suspects is too large, use this method to reduce it to a more manageable size.
3. Determine, if possible, if the loss was a one-time occurrence or if those responsible will attempt to steal again. Depending on your determination, use the proper information gathering tool(s) either to catch the perpetrators in the act or to identify them.
4. Work all of your appropriate investigative tools and test your hypothesis.
5. Chisel away at your suspect pool until you have identified the perpetrator(s) or the most likely perpetrator(s).

c. Verification and Analysis

Now interview the suspects. Exercise extreme care in selecting the order you interview these people. If you are reasonably sure who is responsible, interview that person first. You likely have the most information on this person(s) and he or she had the most to lose. If you are less sure who the thief is, begin interviewing those on the fringe of your suspect pool and work toward the center. In this fashion, you should be compiling ever-greater information with each subsequent interview—eventually identifying the responsible party.

Tip: Place each interviewee on administrative leave regardless of what he or she says or admits. Discipline no one until you have completed all of your interviews.

In the likely event admissions are obtained, memorialize them. Use a witness if appropriate, and at a minimum, obtain a written admission from each of those willing to provide one. Remember, if an interviewee is unwilling to write his own statement, offer to write one for him. The statement should contain language to that effect and be signed by both the interviewee and the interviewer.

Tip: In the event an interviewee reveals he still possesses some of the stolen property, ask that he return it, even it is only a partial roll of tape. Physical evidence of any type speaks volumes in the event an interviewee later recants an admission.

---

d. Disbursement of Disciplinary or Corrective Action

After all of the interviews have been completed, package your result and present it to the decision makers. Remember, the fact-finders should not be part of the decision-making process.

e. Prevention and Education

Based on what is learned, determine how this type of incident might be prevented in the future. Present your solution to the appropriate parties only after you have received their approval to do so.

3. The Use of Informants

As mentioned earlier, the Association of Certified Fraud Examiners' 2002 Report to the Nation revealed that the most common method for detecting workplace theft was through tips from employees, customers, vendors, and anonymous sources. It is a fascinating conclusion at several levels. First, consider the societal level. Our society holds informants in fairly low esteem. Consider the hurtful words we use to describe them: snitch, narc, Five-O, tattletale, stoolie or stool-pigeon, rat, fink, brown nose, scab, weasel, and teacher's pet. What do we call a person who is concerned, ethical, and honorable enough to come forward and share information with someone whom they often do not know in order to stop or prevent the commission of an improper act against another? The only one I can think of is *hero* and its feminine equivalent, *heroine*. So we have at least a dozen derogatory words for an informant, and only one which is complimentary; a rather interesting yet sad commentary on our culture and its values.

Our criminal justice system appreciates the value of informants and has used them effectively for centuries. These important participants are frequently called confidential informants (CIs). Because of the seedy nature of those that often become CIs, even the word *informant* has unfortunately acquired some negative connotation. Recognizing this sad fact, I prefer to use the term *cooperative individual* for my informants. In using the acronym CI, both my client and law enforcement can understand me. Moreover, cooperative individual so much better describes the 60-year-old grandmother who sheepishly comes to her employer and offers information about an employee theft ring.

CIs are valuable because the information they provide often helps to accelerate our investigative process. In many instances they have done much of the information gathering for us and in doing so, allow us to fast-forward to the verification and analysis phase of our investigation. Often CIs are able to provide information that is unavailable by any other means. Like the undercover investigator, they often are afforded the opportunity to not only see what takes place, but participate as well. They provide a unique insight into the minds of the participants and their behavior.

a. The Qualifications of a CI

Not all CIs are created equal. Some are reluctant, others are too eager, yet others could care less. CIs also come in all shapes, sizes, and colors. But in order to be of value to the fact-finder, they must have certain minimal qualifications. CIs must be

- Truthful and credible (more on this later)
- Willing to affirm and stand by their information or allegations
- Trustworthy

Notice that my small list does not include innocent or willing to testify. Fact-finders frequently make the mistake of thinking that in order for a CI to be of any real value, she must be innocent of any and all offenses. This is patently untrue. Although innocence tends to increase the credibility of the CI, one's involvement in the offense is not necessarily a disqualifier. Moreover, we know from experience most workplace informants gained their knowledge from actual participation. Rarely are they innocent bystanders. It is usually some event after-the-fact that causes the individual to come forward. Knowing this unpleasant fact, fact-finders should ask the CI some tough questions about the source of her knowledge, and her employers should be prepared to face the possibility that they will have to discipline the CI just as they might any other offender.

Regardless of the guilt or innocence of the CI, she must be credible. If the CI has no credibility, that is, she is not trustworthy or cannot be believed, her information is worthless. The determination of credibility is both subjective and objective. Clearly, from an objective viewpoint, the CI who has a history of lying and a reputation of being untruthful should be deemed as having little credibility. On the other hand, if the CI does not have a reputation of lying or ever coming forward and accusing others of misconduct, that person may be considered credible, if only subjectively. Also having a bearing on the credibility of the CI is the strength and quality of her information. Vague innuendo and speculation is far less reliable than a pointed conviction based on firsthand observations. It is somewhat obvious then, the determination of credibility must be made on a case-by-case basis. But, as a very general rule of thumb, absent indications to the contrary, the workplace CI should be considered credible.

However, the CI poses yet another problem for the fact-finder. As mentioned in some detail in Chapter 2, CIs do not always want to testify. The easiest work-around to this common dilemma is not to use the informant's information directly. Instead, use the information provided by the CI to further the investigation from another direction. That is, the CI's information is used only as intelligence. With it, the project manager and his fact-finders can engineer another investigative solution. The results of that effort then become the primary evidence for the purpose of deciding discipline and taking corrective action.

The reader should note that an unwillingness to testify is not the same as an unwillingness to affirm and stand by the information or allegations. Regardless of the cooperativeness of the CI, the fact-finder should ask him to affirm that which he has offered in written form. Asking the CI to provide a written statement is the easiest way. As discussed in detail in Chapter 3, the taking of statements is an integral component of professional interviewing. It is this statement that becomes the foundation on which the fact-finder relies and furthers his investigation. The written affirmation of the CI also gives him credibility. The failure to commit his allegations to a written form may be an indication that the information is inaccurate or, worse yet, false.

Tip: The CI's refusal to provide a written statement does not necessarily disqualify him or his information. However, it should serve as a likely indication that there is much the fact-finder does not yet know about the CI and his motive.

The last attribute the CI must possess is trustworthiness. Because the CI will become a participant in the investigation, he will naturally be exposed to information that must be confidential. For example, it may be essential that an investigation be kept confidential. Once the CI is exposed to the fact-finder(s) and asked to provide a statement, he will know about the investigation and possibly one or more of its objectives. The misuse or improper disclosure of this information can be very disruptive. In some instances it can put the entire process at risk. In the most extreme circumstances, a compromised investigation could put people's lives in danger. Fact-finders should disclose as little as possible to their CIs. As in all aspects of the project, the dissemination of information should be restricted to those with an absolute need to know.

Trap: Resist the temptation to completely trust your CIs. Although their intentions are often good, they usually have underlying motivations that may not always be apparent to the fact-finder. Those motivations may not always be consistent with the objectives of your investigation.

---

b. Developing the CI

I am sometimes asked where one finds a CI. They are not usually found; rather, they are developed. Those that are not developed usually surface on their own volition. Motivated by guilt, shame, or fear, they engage in *approaching behaviors* attempting to find the right person in the organization with whom to share their information. The CIs often want to keep their involvement to a minimum. They frequently share only the information *they* think the fact-finder needs to solve the problem. As such, CIs that come in from the cold often do not share everything they know. They often hedge and offer their information in bits and pieces. The fact-finder should be very much aware of this and continuously probe the CI for more and more information.

Developed CIs are usually more forthright. Because their motivation is more instilled than innate, they tend to be less driven by agenda. CIs can be developed in the following ways:

- A workforce can be surveyed and individuals with information concerning a particular problem can be asked to come forward. The surveys can be constructed to ask for information and volunteers to come forward with useful insight to an issue or problem.

An anonymous incident reporting mechanism such as an employee hotline or tipline can be offered to the workforce. One such system is called MySafeWorkplace.com. It allows users to make confidential or anonymous reports via the telephone or the Internet. This powerful system allows reports, upon their submission, to be instantaneously distributed to designated recipients in the organization. For more information on anonymous incident reporting systems (AIRS) please see Chapter 7.

Management can single-out individuals they know are loyal to management and sympathetic to its agenda. Often these individuals are more than eager to cooperate and provide information. All they are waiting for is management to ask them for their assistance.

Management, or someone representing them, could approach those who have cooperated and come forward in the past. Occasionally these individuals, whether employees or not, are again willing to assist management and provide otherwise unavailable or difficult to obtain information.

Trap: Employers should avoid running their CIs like undercover investigators. Cooperation and the occasionally providing of limited information are much different from working undercover. Moreover, the more formal and lengthy the relationship, the greater the expectations of the parties involved.

---

4. Additional Considerations

Of all of the considerations possible during a theft investigation, one of the most important aspects is recovery and restitution. Employers and the fact-finders who work for them frequently think of prosecution. Calling the police is often the first thing an employer does upon discovering a suspicious loss. Theft is personal. Even when the victim is a business or a large corporation, the people associated with it feel like victims when the business suffers a loss due to theft. It is natural for one to feel personally violated when a theft at work is discovered. In Chapter 2, however, I pointed out that prosecution is but one of three potential outcomes of a workplace investigation. The other two outcomes are termination and restitution. Do not let personal pain and emotion get the best of you. Make restitution a top priority. Whenever possible recover the losses from the perpetrators. Better yet, recover the losses and the cost of your investigation. There is no better deterrent, nor is there any better way to maximize the return on investment of your investigative dollars.

C. Workplace Drug Investigations

Unfortunately, substance abuse is a problem that reaches into every corner of our society. It discriminates against no one. According to the U.S. Drug Enforcement Administration (DEA), the international illicit drug trade is a $300 billion a year industry.[42] Moreover, the DEA estimates that 60 percent of all illicit drugs produced in the world are consumed in the United States.[43] Indeed, this nation has a serious drug problem.

Some commonalities among these types of offenses:

- They can be perpetrated by anyone regardless of age, race, sex, or position in the organization.
- Off-shifts (swing and graveyard) are most at risk.
- A lack of supervision and poor preemployment screening are primary contributors.
- Employers should look for secretive behavior, declining performance, absenteeism, declining production, and unexplained losses.

1. Why Not Call the Police?

As with the discovery of a suspicious loss, upon discovery of a workplace drug problem, employers instinctively call the police. They expect the police to swoop in, round up the usual suspects, and merrily cart them off to jail. You can almost picture it. A group of executives gleefully congratulating themselves, all smiles with chests puffed out, as handcuffed employees are paraded out of the facility into a waiting police van. If the problem were that easy to solve, neither this country nor any other would have a drug problem. The truth of the matter is that law enforcement cannot solve America's workplace substance abuse problem alone. Law enforcement has neither the time, the resources, nor the skill to conduct consistently effective workplace substance abuse investigations. Because the standard of proof for a successful prosecution is so much higher than that needed to discipline an employee, involving the authorities adds both complexity and cost to the investigation. Unfortunately, this troubling and expensive problem is most often left to the employer to solve.

Tip: As a general rule of thumb, by involving law enforcement in any workplace investigation, the employer decreases its chance of success by one-half while doubling the cost of its investigation.

---

2. The Anatomy of a Workplace Drug Investigation

In many regards, workplace drug investigations are very similar to other types of workplace investigations. They should unfold incrementally and follow a defined plan. Here are the basic ingredients.

a. Preparation and Planning

A concerned employee or someone having a relationship with an employee, a spouse, for example, typically brings workplace substance abuse problems to the attention of management. Concurrently, there are usually other indicators, such as decreased productivity, frequent absenteeism, employees engaging in secretive and suspicious behavior, and physical evidence (a good example might be alcohol containers found in the employee parking lot).

If a reliable, CI comes forward, the employer should have this person thoroughly interviewed by a professional. This preinvestigation fact-finding is important because to some degree it will enable the employer to determine the size and scope of the problem. Thus, the employer will be better equipped when deciding which investigative/fact-finding tools it should deploy.

Tip: CIs who come forward alleging a workplace substance abuse problem are often the employer's best
source of information. Employers should resist the
temptation of not involving these people and should
have them thoroughly interviewed before investing
more time and resources in their investigation.

b. Information Gathering

The tools most suitable for investigating workplace substance abuse are
undercover and *interviews*. I have discussed undercover in great detail in
Chapter 3, so here let me briefly address interviewing.

Because substance abuse is frequently a social behavior, those who
are involved in it often know others who are also involved. In the case
of illegal drugs, this is particularly true because the user must know
someone from whom to buy drugs. Conversely, the distributor must know
users in order to peddle his wares. As such, in a workplace where
substance abuse has taken more than a toehold, many members of the
organization know about the problem and those involved. If these people
can be identified, have them interviewed. Be sure each is asked who else
has information and should be interviewed.

c. Verification and Analysis

As in a theft investigation, now interview your suspects. Exercise extreme
care in selecting the order you interview them. If you are reasonably sure
who is most involved, interview them first. You likely have the most
information on them, and they have the most to lose. If you are less sure
who is at the heart of the problem, begin interviewing those on the fringe
of your suspect pool and work toward the center. In this fashion, you
should be compiling ever-greater information with each subsequent interview—eventually identifying primary players.

■ Place each interviewee on administrative leave regardless of what
  he says or admits.
■ Ask each interviewee if he possesses an illegal drug or alcohol on
  his person, in locker, or personal vehicle if parked on the premises.

If so, collect it. Establish a proper chain of evidence and dispose of it properly when appropriate.

■ If the police are involved (as in the case of an undercover investigation), do not have employees arrested on the premises.

■ Discipline no one until you have completed all of your interviews.

d. Disbursement of Discipline or Corrective Action

When the interview process has reached a point of diminishing return, the interview team should stand-down and compile the results.

■ Decide appropriate discipline and disburse it equitably (see Exhibit 2.8 in Chapter 2 for assistance). Refer to the organization's substance abuse policy for guidance.

■ Consider all extenuating and mitigating circumstances.

■ Be aware of past organizational precedents and practices.

■ Seek the advice of a qualified employment attorney.

Trap: Employer's are often tempted to impose more serious discipline on drug dealers than users and purchasers. Although this may be lawful, it is sometimes difficult to defend. From a criminal standpoint, the dealer and his customer have committed the same crime. From that standpoint it is appropriate they both receive the same punishment. Moreover, is it not the impairment that results from drug use that makes this behavior so inappropriate in the workplace—if so, why then would one treat the user any differently from his dealer?

---

e. Prevention and Education

Based on what is learned, determine how it might be prevented in the future. Present your solution to the appropriate parties only after you have received their approval to do so.

Tip: "This is your brain on drugs" training is insufficient. Organizations seeking training for their employees should seek out professionals. They should avoid using the training services offered by law enforcement. Although police officers may understand street-dope, most are unaware of the intricate mechanisms of workplace substance abuse. Hire an expert outside of law enforcement to do your workplace substance abuse awareness training.

3. *Additional Considerations*

An aspect of workplace drug investigations that is often given insufficient attention is evidence management. Unless granted some form of immunity or the DEA has provided you a license, it is unlawful to possess illegal drugs for any reason. The manager or fact-finder who stuffs drug evidence that is confiscated or found in the workplace in his desk drawer or file cabinet is breaking the law. Most likely, he is also violating his organization's substance abuse policy. I have yet to read a corporate substance abuse policy that provides any form of immunity to an employee who is conducting a workplace drug investigation. Simply because management is conducting an investigation or attempting to enforce its policies does not necessarily give it license to break those very same policies. For more information on this important topic, I suggest you return to Chapter 3 and review the section on undercover.

Tip: If drug evidence is obtained during your investigation, seal it in a plastic bag and immediately establish a chain of custody. Secure the evidence in a safe place and notify the authorities. If the police ask that the evidence be remanded to them, do so and request that it be tested. Document your effort and properly maintain the chain of custody.

Rarely does a workplace substance abuse problem involve only one or two individuals. Most often these cases involve a large number of employees. As a result, this type of investigation is painful and disruptive. It is recommended that an employer not undertake a drug investigation unless it has the experience and resources to do so properly. If in doubt, seek the assistance of outside professionals.

D. Fraud and Embezzlement Investigations

Fraud is the crime of theft by means of deceit or deception. There are but three ways to illegally relieve a victim of his money: force, larceny, or trickery.[44] Thus, the thief who uses deceit or deception to cover up or disguise his crime has likely committed fraud. Embezzlement differs from theft in that the property or assets stolen were entrusted to the party who took them. Embezzlements share three common elements:

- A person in control of the asset or in a position of trust who allows access to the asset
- Misappropriation or unlawful use of the asset that has been entrusted to that person
- The owner of the asset not providing permission or consent

The most common embezzlement schemes include one or more of the following or variants of them:

- Personal use of an employer's computers, telephones, office equipment, and mail services
- Personal use of an employer's machinery, vehicles, supplies, vendors, or other assets
- Misuse of reimbursable expense accounts
- Unauthorized loans or loan manipulations for personal gain
- Misapplication or diversion of customer credit for personal gain
- Forging or altering documents for personal gain
- Journal entries and other unnecessary accounting manipulations for personal gain
- Creation of ghost employees, vendors, and customers for personal gain
- Unauthorized discounts or favoritism for personal gain

This is by no means an exhaustive list. Each of these offenses has variations as diverse as the people who employ them. I will make no attempt to even begin to describe them all. Suffice it to say, however, most of these offenses ultimately involve the theft of liquid assets and involve to some degree financial manipulations or distortions. Contrary to the expectations of many who investigate these crimes, they are typically simple schemes that exploit process and system vulnerabilities. Sometimes they are occasionally carried to remarkable ends and can resultantly harm many victims and involve huge sums of money.

The cornerstone of fraud is concealment. As opposed to other types of workplace offenses, the perpetrator of fraud takes definitive steps to conceal his actions from the victim. Acts of concealment include the commission of acts too small to be recognized, destruction of documents or records, alteration of documents and records, and the inaccurate recording of transactions. Concealment can often be proven by demonstrating that the acts (or omissions) had no other purpose than to conceal.

Some commonalities among fraud offenses include:

- They are often perpetrated by those who are most trusted. Perpetrators typically have routine access to the assets they eventually steal.
- Liquid assets are most at risk. These crimes usually involve money.
- Simple but effective policies and practices are deficient or nonexistent (that is, requiring two signatures on checks over a certain amount or inadequate segregation of duties for critical functions).
- Lack of supervision and effective audit and review practices are the primary contributors. Another contributor is the lack of good preemployment screening. Many perpetrators are repeat offenders and research would have likely revealed the potential for problems if the victim-employer had taken the time to look.
- Employers should look for secretive behavior, missing or altered documents, accounting irregularities, unusual transactions, and questionable relationships.

There are two fundamental categories of fraud. They are corruption and asset misappropriation.

1. Corruption

Corruption includes conflicts of interest (purchasing and sales schemes), bribery (invoicing kickbacks and bid rigging), unethical (or illegal) gratuities, and economic extortion. The most common of these are purchasing and sales schemes. These offenses are usually uncomplicated yet relatively easy to identify. They require system and process manipulations, which can usually be demonstrated by routine testing and document examination. Alternately, bribery, unethical gratuities, and economic extortion are usually far more complicated schemes. Because they require the perpetrator to manipulate and take advantage of other people, witnesses and physical evidence rarely exist. Usually in these cases, the CI who comes forward was at one time an unwilling participant in the scheme (or in some way, associated with it).

2. Asset Misappropriation

Schemes involving asset misappropriation are the most common frauds and embezzlements committed. Most frequently misappropriated are cash (no surprise there) and inventory. In offenses involving cash, the perpetrator employs diversion or misappropriation schemes, sometimes just skimming small amounts from large transactions.

Recall the urban myth of the bank teller who stole only a penny from each customer transaction (ostensibly so no one would notice) and then retired a millionaire? Let's see … $1 million would be 100,000,000 pennies, so $5 million would be 500,000,000 pennies. That would require the teller to have handled anywhere from 100 to 500 million transaction during his or her career. For simplicity let's say he handled just 300 million transactions (more than one for each man, woman, and child in America). If each theft of one penny took just 30 seconds to setup, commit, and cover up, the perpetrator would need nine billion seconds, or would roughly have had to work for about 72,115 *years* to make off with his millions! Even if he got away with only $1 million and each transaction took *only one second* he would have had to work roughly 800 years. Yet another reason the fact-finder needs to be skeptical and always do the math.

Inventory schemes involve product diversion, misuse, and misappropriation of equipment or property and larceny. The most successful of these schemes do not require the perpetrators to get their *hands dirty*. In other words, they physically do not have to touch the asset that is abused. Underinvoicing a customer and receiving a gratuity for the trouble is a perfect example. Another classic example is receiving a gratuity for making voluntary adjustments to invoices. These schemes are simple, clean, and very easy to execute. Like other thefts, they also directly hit the victim organization's bottom line.

3. The Anatomy of a Fraud and Embezzlement Investigation

a. Preparation and Planning

It has been my experience that workplace fraud and embezzlement problems are typically brought to the attention of management by a concerned or disgruntled employee. Usually the informer is subordinate to the person(s) reported upon. I have also found that the perpetrators of these offenses usually commit their first offense within the first year of employment. I have been involved in several cases where the offender began embezzling within the first 30 days of employment. Concurrently there are usually other indicators, such as employees engaging in secretive and suspicious behavior, missing documents, frequently altered documents, regularly circumvented processes and practices, and defensive responses when challenged.

As in other types of workplace investigations, if a CI comes forward, the employer should have her thoroughly interviewed by a professional. This preinvestigation fact-finding is important because it will enable the employer to determine the size and scope of the problem. It will also permit the employer to better judge the credibility of the allegations. Additionally, a better understanding of the problem will help determine which investigative/fact-finding tools should be deployed. It will also help identify which documents and records should be safeguarded. Once the investigation becomes common knowledge, offenders may be tempted to remove or destroy documents and other evidence. The CI can be helpful in identifying which items are most at-risk and how they might be best protected. The CI can also assist in the identification of friendly and hostile employees/witnesses. If capable, the CI can help determine who else should be interviewed and for what reason.

b. Information Gathering

The tools most suitable for investigating fraud and embezzlement are *forensic analysis* (think document examination), *interviewing,* and obviously *research and audit.* The initiating circumstances and allegations will determine which tools to use and when.

Fraud and embezzlement are not social behaviors; those who commit these offenses often work alone and do not involve others. Offenders usually begin with the commission of small procedure violations or the intentional omission of simple tasks. In doing so they are able to test the system for weaknesses and evaluate the effectiveness of routine checks and balances that are meant to detect errors and problems. Evidence of this type of system testing is often the mess these people leave behind. Long after these crimes have been uncovered, it is not uncommon to regularly find little things out of place, math errors, improperly filed documents, and falsified reports. When first discovered, these anomalies instinctively suggest more fraud. They should not distract the fact-finder. Often it is determined that these irregularities were the result of carelessness and disorganization. You will likely find some were simply *system tests* performed by the would-be offender.

Another fascinating commonality among fraudsters is their unusual record-keeping habits. Because many fraud schemes require the perpetrator to keep an extra set of *books*, some degree of additional record keeping is necessary. Depending upon a host of factors, these records may be fastidiously kept in an electronic spreadsheet. Others keep a handwritten journal or diary. Cell phones and PDAs can even be used to keep records. Look for, and ask for, records regarding the crime during your fact-finding effort. Look under desktop ink blotters, under keyboards, in unusually labeled file folders, inside desk calendars and diaries, and of course, within computer files.

Tip: Electronic data files can be named nearly anything. They can easily be hidden inside application folders and in root directories. If you are unfamiliar with computer forensics and suspect your subject has hidden data on his workstation or the organization's network get professional assistance. It is very easy to destroy evidence and to render records unusable if you do not know what you are doing.

Another very valuable source of information is co-workers, vendors, and customers. If those with information can be identified, they should be interviewed. These will likely be administrative interviews. The purpose is to obtain a broader understanding of the fraud, the mechanism used to perpetrate it, and those involved in it. Although the sequence of these interviews is important, the questions asked are critical. Here are a few of the typical questions that should be asked:

- What is the source of their information?
- Why have they agreed to cooperate and chosen to tell the truth?
- What documents or other evidence exists that support their allegation(s) or suspicion?
- Do they have any involvement or have they personally ever committed a similar offense?
- Have they shared their knowledge regarding the problem with others, and if so, with whom?
- Who else is involved?
- Who else would be useful to interview and why?
- Would they be willing to testify if necessary?

- Does the subject know others suspect him (or her)?
- How might the fact-finders best go about investigating the matter?

Because every investigation is unique, tailor your questions to suit your particular situation. Use caution. As with all interviews, the subject is also capable of gleaning information from the interview. Never reveal information that you would not want the subject to know until he is interviewed. Document your effort carefully and, if appropriate, obtain a written statement.

Benford's Rule

Of the forensic tools available to the fraud investigator, Benford's Rule, sometimes called Benford's Law, is the most fascinating. It predicts the frequency of numbers (digits), and hence an anomaly, in naturally occurring data sets. When used properly, it allows the fact-finder to identify suspect values in a given data set. For example, it is particularly suitable for identifying vendors that submit fraudulent invoices. Using Benford's Rule, nonconforming invoice amounts are flagged as systemic errors that corrupt the data set. These fraudulent invoices reveal themselves because the amount (dollar value) does not correspond to a predicable Benford-type distribution when compared with the other invoice amounts in the sample.

Newcomb first published the law in 1881 in the *American Journal of Mathematics*. It appears that a simple but powerful mathematical phenomenon exists that quickly predicts the distribution of numbers for "pointing suspicion at frauds, embezzlers, tax-evaders, sloppy accountants, and even computer bugs."[45] Frank Benford, rediscoverer of this phenomenon, was a physicist for General Electric Company who in 1938 recognized that certain nonrandomly behaved numbers in nonnormally distributed data sets (i.e., those that are highly skewed, not uniform in distribution, and not bell-shaped) followed the algorithm defined by Benford's Rule (see Exhibit 6.2).

Exhibit 6.2   Benford's Rule

$$P(n) = \log(n+1) - \log(n)$$

Where $P(n)$ is the probability that n is the first digit; the logarithms are to the base 10, and probability is defined as all numbers between 0 and 1, where 0 is impossibility and 1 is absolute certainty.

Source: Frank Benford, "The Law of Anomalous Numbers," *Proceedings of the American Philosophical Society* 78 (1938): 551–72.

The sample of numbers in the Benford-type data sets should be large enough to give the predicted proportions a chance to assert themselves and they must be free of artificial limits; that is, they should be allowed to take any value they please.[46] A critical feature of the Benford distribution is that it is invariant of scale; that is, it is base-invariant and independent of the choice of units and can be used to evaluate data sets of any value: square miles, dollars, tons, gallons, or invoice numbers in any proportion or amount. Benford's Rule does not offer a mathematical solution to a problem, but rather, it models the data set against the probability distribution of each digit as it appears in any number. This is a predictive tool called digital frequency analysis (DFA). The numbers could be data in a set that measures mass, volume, or all numbers on the front page of the *Wall Street Journal*. Benford manually analyzed over 20 thousand data sets of various categories and found that all of the seemingly disparate numbers followed the same first-digit probability pattern. Subsequent analyses of thousands of more data sets have confirmed Benford's distribution.

Most people intuitively believe that in any string of numbers of a naturally occurring data set each digit, one through nine, has an equal probability of being the first digit. Benford's distribution showed that this intuition is incorrect. It is this belief and practice of the fraudster that all digits should be *regular* that creates data sets that evoke suspicions of fraud. A database with as few as ten numbers can begin to show a trend of honesty or fraud. It should be obvious that the greater the sampling of numbers (the bigger the database), the more closely the distribution of digits follows Benford's Rule. It does not prove fraud, but does indicate the potential for a data set to be partially or entirely unnatural (fraudulent).

Benford's Rule is so powerful in its ability to detect fraud that even the IRS uses it to detect tax cheaters. The idea underlying the method is the analysis of deductions in tax returns to determine if they more or less match the frequencies and ratios predicted by Benford's Rule. The IRS knows that when a database (the taxpayer's return) contains systematic errors, the creator of the database (the taxpayer) has knowingly or unknowingly entered false data into the set. According to Browne, "The income tax agencies of several nations and several states are using detection software based on Benford's Rule, as are a score of large companies and accounting businesses."[47]

Benford's probability distribution (in percentage) of the *first digit* of any number within a database that meets the criteria described above should be like that in Benford's Distribution Table (see Exhibit 6.3).

What fraudster would intuitively know that the first digit of fabricated numbers should appear in this frequency? Whether the numbers in any database are normally distributed or nonrandomly behaved, the probability distribution of the *third digit* of any database is equally divided and hence

Exhibit 6.3   Benford's Distribution Table

1 = 30.10	4 = 9.69	7 = 5.80
2 = 17.61	5 = 7.92	8 = 5.12
3 = 12.49	6 = 6.69	9 = 4.58

should be very close to 10 percent for each of the ten digits. Thus, analysis of the third digit can independently provide a clue as to whether the numbers have been manipulated. Together, the first and third digit analysis provides a very strong indication of whether the numbers are naturally occurring or have been manipulated. For even further analysis, one could examine the second digit frequency distribution as well. In the second digit analysis, the number zero should appear about 12 percent of the time and the number nine should appear about 8.5 percent of the time. The sequence, one-zero (10) should be the most frequent *first two* digits of any number (occurring 3.612 percent of the time), and the sequence, nine-nine (99) should be the least frequent *first two* digits of any number (occurring only 0.389 percent of the time).

Here is an actual example of this powerful tool in use. My client had nearly completed the construction of a $25 million manufacturing plant. The project had been a problem from the very start. Budget overruns, work stoppages, and a host of other problems had plagued it to the point that management was completely frustrated. Shortly before the plant was to go on line, an anonymous informant had called headquarters and provided some troubling information. The female caller alleged that the project manager (soon to be plant manager) was "on the take" and a considerable number of the contractors were paying kickbacks to him. Shortly after receiving this disturbing news our assistance was requested.

After some routine planning and preparation, we asked the client to provide a copy of its accounts payable (AP) database for all of the location's vendors and contractors. This database was segregated into subsets by vendor or contractor and downloaded into an Microsoft Excel® spreadsheet. The frequency distribution of the first digit of each subset was analyzed and several were found not conforming to Benford's Rule. After eliminating subsets containing corrupted or unreliable data (data set too small, vendor had provided only a single item which it delivered and invoiced for on a regular basis, and so forth), we were able to identify systematic errors buried in some of the subsets. One such subset had a normal first digit frequency distribution; however, each number had a fairly large variance:

1 = +16.5 percent
2 = +22.3 percent
3 = −21.2 percent

$$4 = -14.2 \text{ percent}$$
$$5 = +32.1 \text{ percent}$$
$$6 = -21.8 \text{ percent}$$
$$7 = -31.0 \text{ percent}$$
$$8 = -63.8 \text{ percent}$$
$$9 = -19.4 \text{ percent}$$

The high frequency of ones and twos made the curve much too steep and hence suspect. Additionally, the high frequency of fives and low frequency of eights raised red flags. Further analysis was thus warranted to find the source of this distortion. The same data set was reanalyzed without the credits, reducing our set to 297 data points. To our astonishment, the results showed an almost identical distribution with only 0.70 or less percentage difference for each digit. Apparently the credits were not distorting the data and the initial analysis was correct. To further substantiate the conclusion that some invoices were corrupting the data set, a third-digit analysis was performed on the set. The result indicated that the following digits occurred too frequently:

$$5 = +25.4 \text{ percent above prediction}$$
$$6 = +22.0 \text{ percent above prediction}$$
$$0 = +42.9 \text{ percent above prediction}$$

Each of these numbers in the third-digit spot should have been very close to 10 percent in frequency. The result also indicated that the following digits occurred less frequently than predicted:

$$1 = -19.9 \text{ percent}$$
$$4 = -23.3 \text{ percent}$$
$$8 = -26.8 \text{ percent}$$

Both first-digit and third-digit analyses showed that the number five was too frequent and the number eight was too infrequent. We presumed the worst and decided to drill deeper. So next we examined the actual invoices. We found the following fraud indicators:

■ Overlapping invoice dates (sloppy recordkeeping).
■ Every invoice number in the data set was sequential (indicating the vendor had no other customers).
■ No federal taxpayer ID number on the invoice (not required or unlawful, but suggests a degree of inexperience or unprofessionalism on the part of the vendor).

- No vendor phone number (very suspect).
- Vendor's address was a post office box number (very suspect).
- Proof of delivery (required by organizational policy) not attached to invoice (very suspect).
- Multiple invoices in large dollar amounts frequently dated and submitted for payment on the same day (very suspect).
- Some invoices that had been submitted for payment had no approval signature (possibly indicating sloppy handling, however, given the other indicators this was deemed very suspect).[48]

The next vendor's data set also appeared corrupted. First-number and third-number analyses were performed on the 32 invoice amounts (data points). Although the data set was relatively small, the data revealed systemic corruption in several places. The first number distribution was all over the place:

1 = +19.9 percent
2 = +6.8 percent
3 = −75.2 percent
4 = −35.1 percent
5 = −60.8 percent
6 = −60.8 percent
7 = +62.1 percent
8 = −100.0 percent
9 = +37.0 percent

The third-digit analysis of the same 32 data points showed all numbers from zero to nine were far from a predictable distribution frequency. Although each number should have been evenly distributed occurring at about 10 percent, none was. This distribution (not variance) in percentages was as follows:

1 = 3.1 percent
2 = 15.6 percent
3 = 3.1 percent
4 = 3.1 percent
5 = 12.5 percent
6 = 15.6 percent
7 = 6.3 percent
8 = 6.3 percent
9 = 21.9 percent
0 = 12.5 percent

Every number except five and zero in this subset was an *offender*. Look at the frequency of the number nine. The foolish fraudster unwitting believes that prices (for either products or services) must contain the number nine. Examination of the physical invoices revealed more clues. Again we found overlapping invoice dates and sequential invoice numbers. But the biggest red flag was invoice numbers out of date sequence. We immediately advised our client to withhold further payment to the suspected vendors.

My colleagues and I had seen enough evidence for potential fraud; we packed our bags and flew to the new facility. Upon our arrival we performed additional auditing and more document examination. We also interviewed stakeholders of key functions (finance, receiving, and maintenance). After more analysis we identified what we thought were the four most suspicious vendors. Anxious to get their past-due invoices paid, the principals of these vendors agreed to attend a meeting. Upon their arrival, each was separately interviewed. Ultimately, three admitted "some" of their invoices were "incorrect" and two of them admitted outright fraud. Without the threat of prosecution or any intimidation, the three admitted they had improperly invoiced my client nearly $500,000. One of the vendors, a painter, actually admitted he had his 13-year-old son on his payroll and had charged my client $195 per hour for his services (the boy's name was Smiley, honestly). One of the projects on which the young boy had worked was repainted three times, and my client was charged each time! In other instances, upon *doing the math*, we learned that in some instances my client had been charged over $680 per hour per painter. The arrogance of some criminals has no boundaries. For more information about fraud and embezzlement schemes and the methods of detecting them, I suggest Joseph T. Wells's *Occupational Fraud and Abuse* (as cited in note 44).

c. Verification and Analysis

Once the information-gathering process has been completed, you are now ready to interview your suspect(s). In most instances you will know precisely whom to interview and what questions to ask. As in other types of investigatory interviews, after your introduction begin to address the minor issues and offenses first. The object is to find the truth and obtain an admission. If you start with the most serious offense first, you will likely frighten your subject causing him to clam up and resist admitting anything. For a refresher, go back to Chapter 3 and reread the section "Interviews and Interrogation." Here are a few more recommendations:

1. Place your investigative interviewee on administrative leave regardless of what he or she says or admits.
2. Ask the interviewee if he or she has documents or physical evidence regarding the offenses. Establish a proper chain of custody and secure it properly.
3. Ask the interviewee what he or she did with the money that was stolen or diverted. Obtain as much information as possible regarding the disposition of the funds. Ask for bank account numbers, bank statements, and deposit histories. If you are bold enough, ask for a copy of the subject's recent income tax returns and see if any of the stolen money was reported as income. Tax returns are also a good place to look for other assets and the ability to pay restitution in the event a recovery is later desired.
4. Be careful of offers of restitution. If contained in an admission, the document may constitute a contract and bar some forms of discipline or more aggressive recovery actions. Involve counsel if restitution arrangements need to be made.
5. Discipline no one until you have completed all of your interviews and analyzed the results.

Tip: Investigations involving fraud and embezzlement are often complex and they are filled with legal traps. Always get competent counsel involved if you haven't the training or experience in handling these types of investigations.

---

d. Disbursement of Discipline or Corrective Action

When the interview process has reached a point of diminishing return, the interview team should stand down and the results should be compiled. As in all other types of workplace investigations, the results are then presented to the decision makers for disposition.

Tip: If restitution is desired, it is acceptable to offer the offending employee the opportunity to resign in lieu of termination in exchange for his cooperation. Involve counsel to draft the necessary documents and make the proper arrangements.

---

e. Prevention and Education

A recent survey by the Association of Certified Fraud Examiners reveals that organizations with fewer than 100 employees are over *100 times* more likely to be the victims of employee fraud than larger organizations. Although the U.S. Chamber of Commerce reports that internal employee theft is responsible for one-third of all small business failures, employee fraud and dishonesty remain below the radar of most employers. While hiring honest people is critical, sound policies, separation of duties, and routine audits are also a must. My advice:

- *Properly screen applicants.* Exclude those with a criminal past or substance abuse problems.
- *Segregate duties.* Separate the custody of assets from the recording of assets.
- *Audit regularly.* Establish audit and process testing procedures and use them frequently.
- *Let employees know the organization cares.* Provide employees a hotline or an anonymous incident reporting system to report improper or unethical behavior.
- *Discipline offenders.* Forgiveness is nice, but action speaks louder. The best punishment is termination and restitution.

Based on what is learned, determine how the problem might be prevented in the future. Present your solution to the appropriate parties only after you have received their approval to do so.

Trap: Outside auditors are not usually incapable of identifying fraud, nor do they typically look for it. Seek the assistance of a certified fraud examiner or a CPA firm that specializes in fraud detection if you want help auditing for fraud and establishing new fraud prevention measures.

4. Insurance Recoveries

Most organizations of any size carry fidelity insurance (the largest, how-ever, are often self-insured). Fidelity insurance is coverage against employee theft and embezzlement. It is often a *thrown-in* as a component of the property and casualty package. Many organizations do not even know they have it. If purchased, it is usually very inexpensive because of the high deductible (typically not less than $50,000) and low-loss experience. That is the bad news. The good news is that these claims are easy to file and recover. It is often not necessary to even prove the exact amount of the loss, a rough number will usually suffice. The employer should include the cost of the investigation and all of its expenses in its claim. The fees paid to outside professional investigators are often com-pensable and will often be paid with little fuss. What better way to justify one's investigation and drive a high return on investment than having someone else pay for it! There are a few caveats, however.

- Policies typically stipulate that they be notified of the potential claim within 30 days of discovery. This does not mean within 30 days of completion of your investigation, but within 30 days of your determination there might be a problem and a compensable claim. Insurance companies are not flexible on this point. Once a fraud or embezzlement is flagged, have risk management call your carrier. Affirm this notification in writing.
- Carriers will typically reserve subrogation rights. This means, they want assumption of any rights to the claim, including recovery. A sloppy admission, an offer of immunity, or an attempt to facilitate a recovery could void coverage. Once the claim is deemed com-pensable, the insurance company, not your organization, owns all rights to recovery and restitution.
- Recoveries and restitution are credited to the insurers' payout, not your deductible. Only after the insurance company is made whole will any excess be applied to the deductible. As such, there is little incentive for the insurer to pursue a full recovery. *They do not get to keep any more than the amount they paid you.*
- Policies typically require that a timely police report be made if a crime is suspected. This is nothing more than a check-off. However, it has to be done if the policy stipulates it.

Tip: Fidelity claims are easy to pursue and should not be overlooked. When theft or embezzlement is suspected, one of the first action items for the investigative project manager to accomplish is to notify risk management.

5. Additional Considerations

Although most frauds and embezzlement schemes deploy simple ruses and routines, not all crimes are created equal. The manipulations can be extremely complex and involve huge volumes of documents and records (and money—think Enron). The investigative team should be prepared for the worst. In almost every instance, the event that triggered the investigation and the initial evidence is usually only the tip of the iceberg. Fraudsters evolve. Over time they get better and bolder. Look for multiple schemes and attacks by your subject. Do not overlook the simplest and smallest exposures. I have investigated CFOs who have embezzled hundreds of thousands of dollars, yet cheated on their reimbursed mileage while driving their own car and took $5 from petty cash.

Tip: Once the fraudster has crossed the line, he is often capable of doing almost anything. Fact-finders should leave no stone unturned and examine every potential exposure under the control of the subject and the processes to which he had access.

E. Harassment Investigations

Sexual harassment is insidious, painful, and expensive to businesses. Despite heightened awareness, better communication, and training, the problem continues to torment individuals and organizations. It has damaged lives, ruined careers, and left entire organizations publicly tarnished. In order to address the problem and reduce the damage when complaints are made, employers must investigate. In fact, employers have an ethical and lawful duty to investigate. However, their investigation must be thorough and impartial. The investigator must be properly trained, adequately skilled, and fair.

HR experts purport that harassment of all types costs the typical Fortune 500 company an estimated $6.7 million in increased absenteeism, diminished morale, lowered productivity, and employee turnover.[49] A total of 84,442 charges were filed with the U.S. Equal Employment Opportunity Commission in 2002, an increase of 4.5 percent from 2001.[50] Exhibit 6.4 reveals the cases filed with EEOC sorted by category from 1992 through 2002. Note the spike in 1994.

Under federal and state laws, an employer has an absolute affirmative duty to investigate a complaint or suspicion of harassment or discrimination. Employees are protected by the following federal laws:

- Title VII of the Civil Rights Act of 1964 (Title VII), which prohibits employment discrimination based on race, color, religion, sex, or national origin
- The Equal Pay Act of 1963 (EPA), which protects men and women who perform substantially equal work in the same establishment from sex-based wage discrimination
- The Age Discrimination in Employment Act of 1967 (ADEA), which protects individuals who are 40 years of age or older
- Title I and Title V of the Americans with Disabilities Act of 1990 (ADA), which prohibit employment discrimination against qualified individuals with disabilities in the private sector, and in state and local governments
- Sections 501 and 505 of the Rehabilitation Act of 1973, which prohibit discrimination against qualified individuals with disabilities who work in the federal government
- The Civil Rights Act of 1991, which, among other things, provides monetary damages in cases of intentional employment discrimination

The U.S. Equal Employment Opportunity Commission (EEOC) enforces all of these laws. EEOC also provides oversight and coordination of all federal equal employment opportunity regulations, practices, and policies.

In spite of the vast body of laws already protecting employees against discrimination and mistreatment, the U.S. Supreme Court issued landmark decisions in the sexual harassment cases—*Burlington Industries, Inc. v. Ellerth*, 524 U.S. 742 (1998) and *Faragher v. City of Boca Raton*, 524 U.S. 775 (1998). Since decided, both federal and state courts have followed the principles enumerated in these cases and applied them to other types of harassment. Effectively, these sweeping decisions impose liability on employers for the harassment by their supervisors who engage in "tangible employment action(s)," and issues such as demotion, termination, and denial of benefits. In doing so, these decisions have diluted some of the

Exhibit 6.4 EEOC Cases Filed 1992 through 2002

	FY 1992	FY 1993	FY 1994	FY 1995	FY 1996	FY 1997	FY 1998	FY 1999	FY 2000	FY 2001	FY 2002
Total Charges	72,302	87,942	91,189	87,529	77,990	80,680	79,591	77,444	79,896	80,840	84,442
Race	29,548	31,695	31,656	29,986	26,287	29,199	28,820	28,819	28,945	28,912	29,910
	40.9%	36.0%	34.8%	34.3%	33.8%	36.2%	36.2%	37.3%	36.2%	35.8%	35.4%
Sex	21,796	23,919	25,860	26,181	23,813	24,728	24,454	23,907	25,194	25,140	25,536
	30.1%	27.2%	28.4%	29.9%	30.6%	30.7%	30.7%	30.9%	31.5%	31.1%	30.2%
National Origin	7,434	7,454	7,414	7,035	6,687	6,712	6,778	7,108	7,792	8,025	9,046
	10.3%	8.5%	8.1%	8.0%	8.6%	8.3%	8.5%	9.2%	9.8%	9.9%	10.7%
Religion	1,388	1,449	1,546	1,581	1,564	1,709	1,786	1,811	1,939	2,127	2,572
	1.9%	1.6%	1.7%	1.8%	2.0%	2.1%	2.2%	2.3%	2.4%	2.6%	3.0%
Retaliation											
All Statutes	11,096	13,814	15,853	17,070	16,080	18,198	19,114	19,694	21,613	22,257	22,768
	15.3%	15.7%	17.4%	19.5%	20.6%	22.6%	24.0%	25.4%	27.1%	27.5%	27.0%
Title VII	10,499	12,644	14,415	15,342	14,412	16,394	17,246	17,883	19,753	20,407	20,814
	14.5%	14.4%	15.8%	17.5%	18.5%	20.3%	21.7%	23.1%	24.7%	25.2%	24.6%
Age	19,573	19,809	19,618	17,416	15,719	15,785	15,191	14,141	16,008	17,405	19,921
	27.1%	22.5%	21.5%	19.9%	20.2%	19.6%	19.1%	18.3%	20.0%	21.5%	23.6%
Disability	*1,048	15,274	18,859	19,798	18,046	18,108	17,806	17,007	15,864	16,470	15,964
	1.4%	17.4%	20.7%	22.6%	23.1%	22.4%	22.4%	22.0%	19.9%	20.4%	18.9%
Equal Pay Act	1,294	1,328	1,381	1,275	969	1,134	1,071	1,044	1,270	1,251	1,256
	1.8%	1.5%	1.5%	1.5%	1.2%	1.4%	1.3%	1.3%	1.6%	1.5%	1.5%

Sources: The data are compiled by the Office of Research, Information, and Planning from EEOC's Charge Data System—quarterly reconciled Data Summary Reports, and the national data base. Courtesy the EEOC.

employers' traditional affirmative defenses. Those traditional affirmative defenses include:

- The complainant's failure to take advantage of the employer's harassment policy and make a report
- The employer's prompt and effective response
- A prolonged delay by the employee in making a complaint

As a collateral effect, the *Burlington* and *Ellerth* decisions have also imposed a new burden on employers to conduct effective and proper workplace investigations. Although this burden has existed since the enactment of Title VII (see Chapter 5 for more detail), the courts have become less tolerant of sloppy investigations by employers. The courts have more clearly defined what constitutes harassment and what necessitates an employer to investigate. This list is by no means comprehensive:

- Unwanted sexual advances.
- Offering employment benefits in exchange for sexual favors.
- Inappropriate leering, gesturing, and noise-making.
- Inappropriate or obscene calendars, posters, art, graffiti, or drawings.
- Verbal conduct such as derogatory comments, epithets, slurs, or jokes.
- Written communications of any form that are derogatory or stereotypical based upon gender, race, national origin, ethnicity, religion, and so forth.
- Verbal abuse, graphic verbal comments, use of degrading words to describe an individual, group, sex, or physical attribute.
- Unwanted physical touching, brushing, impeding, or blocking movements.
- Retaliation for making harassment reports or threatening to report harassment.[51]

Intuitively, one can surmise there are obvious defenses other than the affirmative ones offered above. Among the most useful is the employer's reasonable care to prevent and correct harassment. For this defense to be viable, the employer has limited time to act once the violation is noticed. The action as well as its promptness will in part determine the employer's liability. Employers should also be aware that the Civil Rights Act of 1991 expanded the remedies available under Title VII to include compensatory damages for pain and suffering, humiliation, and embarrassment in instances of intentional discrimination, and additional punitive damages in cases where the employer acted in a malicious or reckless manner.[52] Never before has there been more incentive to conduct a thorough and prompt workplace investigation.

Listed here are some commonalities among these types of offenses:

- Offenders are often authoritarians who believe they are entitled to abuse and mistreat others.
- Offenders frequently have abusive tendencies and have a history of similar behavior.
- Lack of enforced policies and effective training are primary contributors.
- Unusual behavior, conflicting explanations or claims, authoritative personalities, and questionable relationships may be present.

1.   The Anatomy of a Harassment Investigation

Harassment investigations pose unusual challenges to both the employer and the fact-finder. For one, these cases are capable of producing plaintiffs from both sides of the issue. Both the accused and the accuser are potential plaintiffs and frequently are. Either party can claim mistreatment and suffering. This poses some interesting challenges for the investigative team and the decision makers. Additionally, because of the sensitive nature of the allegations, extra care must be taken to protect the privacy of the individuals involved. This is particularly challenging when the behaviors in question spill outside the workplace or involve spouses and others who may not be employees.

a. Preparation and Planning

In addition to the routine investigative preparation and planning, the critical first step is to determine who the complainant (the accuser) is and whom she or he has accused. As absurd as it may appear, this is not always clear. The organization's harassment policy should also be examined to ensure it is followed properly and that any nuances or subtleties are identified. Poorly written policies include those that detail who should be interviewed and in what order. Be aware of these encumbrances and ensure the policy is properly followed.

Some limited preinvestigation fact-finding should also be performed. The credibility of the complainant and her claim needs to be determined. The fact-finder should also secure personnel files and other organizational records that may be needed later. Counsel should be brought in early to protect the attorney-client privilege and attorney work-product privilege. If this is determined, all documents should be marked accordingly.

b. Information Gathering

The principal information gathering method in workplace harassment investigations is interviewing, and the first challenge that must be addressed is the order in which the parties should be interviewed. Usually, but not always, the complainant should be interviewed first. In order to fully understand the complaint and the assorted issues surrounding it, the complainant is most often the best source of information. In doing so, the complaint and all allegations should be tied down. In order to avoid the expansion of the complainant's claim, the fact-finder should tie it down as tightly as possible. Should the allegations be weak or unactionable, a complainant may be tempted to embellish her claim and expand it in order to keep the matter alive. This can easily be avoided by having the complainant memorialize her allegations in a written statement. The statement should include

- The precise nature of the claim and all supporting allegations
- Identification of all physical or electronic evidence that support the allegations
- Identification of all witnesses and other possible victims (if known).
- The complainant's agreement to testify, if necessary
- The complainant's agreement to continue to cooperate with management and participate in the investigation as requested (that is, to produce records and documents or submit to an additional interview)
- The complainant's agreement to report any future contact by the accused and any retaliation she may experience
- The complainant's agreement to keep the matter confidential and not discuss the complaint or the investigation with others who have no need to know
- Affirmation that the claims and allegations are true and that any intentional misrepresentations or false statements may result in discipline
- The opportunity to add anything that they wish to their statement

The statement should be written (or typed) and signed by the complainant if possible. It should be witnessed as well. When interviewing members of the opposite sex, be sure to have a member of the same sex as the subject present as a witness.

Trap: The complainant will frequently ask for a copy of his or her statement. Unless the organization's policy (or the law) dictates otherwise, resist giving a copy of a statement to any interviewee during the fact-finding phase. Copies can always be provided later. If given, obtain a written acknowledgment of such and admonish the recipient as to the appropriate protocols regarding confidentiality, distribution, and disclosure. Employers should remember that any evidence developed during the investigation is property of the employer. Unless otherwise required, a witness has no right to any evidence, even if he or she created it.

Proceed to interview other material witnesses once you understand the issues. Use the appropriate elements of the checklist above during those interviews. Obtain statements whenever possible. Do not neglect to ask each witness if he or she too may have been a victim. Management may resist this line of questioning; however, it is absolutely necessary. Because of the big dollar value of these claims, once word gets out many witnesses may also *claim to be victims*. Be careful and adhere to your plan.

Tip: Take detailed notes and retain them. Record the start time and finish time of each interview. Document both the questions and the interviewee's answers. Use a witness when appropriate and practicable.

c. Verification and Analysis

Next, interview the accused. Regardless of the sex of the accused, use a witness. Carefully craft the questions so they are not leading or offensive. Obtain a statement regardless of the interviewee's answers. Again, it is important to lock down his or her testimony. Be sure the statement contains the following:

■ The precise nature of the claim and all the allegations against him or her.

- A detailed admission (if an admission is obtained) and any extenuating or mitigating circumstances surrounding it.
- The accuser's acknowledgment that he or she is aware of the organization's harassment policy and that violations of it may result in discipline.
- Identification of all physical or electronic evidence that supports his or her guilt or innocence.
- Identification of all witnesses (for and against him or her) and other possible victims (if known).
- An agreement to continue to cooperate with management and participate in the investigation if requested (that is, produce records and documents or submit to an additional interview).
- Agreement not to contact the complainant and report any contact by the complainant while the investigation is still under way.
- An agreement to keep the matter confidential and not to discuss it or the investigation with others who have no need to know.
- Affirmation that the statement provided is true and that any intentional misrepresentations or false statements may result in discipline.
- The opportunity to add anything he or she wishes to the statement.

Exhibit 6.5 is similar to the checklist my investigative firm uses for these types of interviews. Use this form only as a guide. Circumstances should determine the types of questions that are asked and the format of the interview. Following the interview the subject should be placed on administrative leave until the investigation is complete and an employment status determination made. I recommend that the leave be paid. To do otherwise is punitive and inconsistent with management's claim that discipline has yet to be decided.

d. *Disbursement of Disciplinary or Corrective Action*

Once all interviews have been completed and all reasonable leads followed, the interview team should stand down and compile the results. As in all other types of workplace investigations, the results are then presented to the decision makers for disposition. Once again, it is permissible to allow the subject to resign in lieu of termination. This sometimes allows the subject to leave with his dignity and self-respect intact. It also reduces the chances that he or she will become a plaintiff. Most people incorrectly believe that by resigning, they waive most if not all of their rights. However, in allowing the subject to resign, the employer should obtain something in return, such as an agreement to never return

Exhibit 6.5   Written Declaration Checklist

Subject: _____	Written Start: _____
Interviewer: _____	Break Start/Finish _____
Witness: _____	Break Start/Finish _____
Witness: _____	Written Finish: _____
Witness: _____	Date: _____

Initial each item as covered with interviewee. Substitute N/A for those items that do not apply. If interviewee is unable or unwilling to write a statement, ask if he or she will allow you to write it and he or she can sign it when completed.

_____   Complete opening paragraph according to guidelines.

_____   Detail when, where, and last time and type of incident (verbal/nonverbal/physical).

_____   Document known or observed witnesses to incident.

_____   Document incident (complete detail; use subject's language).

_____   Document response to incident.

_____   Document if consent existed. If so, was it implied or explicit.

_____   Document to whom the subject related the incident and his or her response.

_____   Document why the subject was truthful during the interview.

_____   Provide subject the opportunity to add anything in his or her own words.

_____   Close statement as a declaration according to guidelines.

_____   Ensure all present sign statement.

Note: The guidelines mentioned in this checklist are internal to my organization. Readers should develop their own form based on needs and circumstances.

---

to the worksite, to never contact the complainant again, or to simply go away quietly.

e. Prevention and Education

Based on what is learned, determine how the problem might be prevented in the future. Present your solution to the appropriate parties only after you have received their approval to do so. Because of the employer's liability and the foreseeability of future claims, education and training are often very appropriate following a harassment investigation.

Another tool an employer might consider is an anonymous incident reporting system (AIRS). AIRS have grown in popularity in recent years and are commercially available in a wide assortment of designs and formats. The best systems allow users (complainants) to make anonymous reports via the telephone or the Internet. Reports are taken by trained call-takers at a call center or via a form completed on the host's Web site. Once submitted, the reports are immediately disseminated to designated recipients in the reporting party's organization. The better systems allow the reports to be sent via e-mail or telephone text messaging. The reports are retained in a secure database and available to the designated recipients at anytime via an Internet connection.

Not only do AIRS provide the employee a means to report issues of concern anonymously, they provide enormous legal protections to the employer providing them to their employees. Because damages in harassment and discrimination claims are largely determined by the egregiousness of the allegation and duration the complainant suffered, AIRS provide a bar to retroactive claims when the victim asserts he had no one to whom he could report the mistreatment. With an AIRS in place the victim-plaintiff cannot assert he simply had to endure the mistreatment because he had no place to turn. A failure to use such a system, if available, could significantly diminish damages or invalidate the claim. For the same reasons, AIRS are useful for addressing many other forms of workplace misconduct.

However, having a confidential, anonymous incident reporting system for some employers is no longer a luxury. The recently enacted Sarbanes-Oxley Act of 2002 has made such systems mandatory for publicly traded companies. The act requires covered companies to establish procedures for employees and others to submit confidentially and anonymously their concerns relative to questionable accounting and auditing matters. Specifically Section 301 of the act requires audit committees to provide a mechanism for employees to remain anonymous when reporting concerns about questionable accounting or audit matters. Additionally, the audit committee must provide a process for the "receipt, retention and treatment" of complaints regarding financial irregularities.

The Association of Certified Fraud Examiners 2002 Report to the Nation concluded, "The presence of an anonymous reporting mechanism facilitates the reporting of wrong-doing and seems to have a recognizable effect in limiting fraud losses." The ACFE also concluded that properly implemented employee hotlines can reduce losses "by approximately 50% per scheme." To learn more about some of the AIRS systems available, search *employee hotlines* on Google.com.

F. Proprietary Information and Trade Secret Investigations

Modern workplace thieves have more to steal than their predecessors. Topping the charts today is the theft of intellectual property (IP) and trade secrets. Although the terms *IP* and *trade secrets* are often used interchange-ably, trade secrets are a form of IP and are defined as information that provides its owner a competitive advantage, that is not generally known, and that the owner takes reasonable measures to keep secret.[53] In *Kewanee Oil Co. v Bicron Corporation*, the U.S. Supreme Court offered this definition:

> a trade secret may consist of any formula, pattern, device or compilation of information which is used in one's business and which gives one an opportunity to obtain an advantage over competitors who do not know or use it. It may be a formula for a chemical compound, a process of manufacturing, treating or preserving materials, a pattern for a machine or other device or a list of customers.[54]

On the other hand, IP includes all matters of proprietary information, such as trade secrets (product pricing, unique business processes, formu-las, and methods), copyrights, trademarks, and patents. The value of some IP is priceless. It is estimated that during the cold war the Soviets stole enough American secrets to save them over $500 billion in research and development costs. Yet, ironically, they still went broke trying to beat the United States.

The theft of IP also saves the recipient of the information time, and in many industries time is more valuable than money. Consider for a moment the computer chip industry. What is the value of a manufacturer's ability to leap-frog a competitor's newest design, using stolen R&D in an industry that reports that the cost of engineering a new processor exceeds $1 billion? In such a fast-moving and capital-intensive industry, the loss of such valuable information could spell the difference of life or death for the organization.

Proprietary information and trade secrets are business assets, yet most businesses fail to identify and protect them. When businesses do, they can turn their information assets into dollars. It is essential that businesses become vigilant and systematic in safeguarding their IP. Educating busi-nesses and helping them protect that valuable property has become a thriving industry.

In order to properly define and value proprietary information, the question of ownership must first be answered. Often the answer involves determining the rights of an employer versus the employee and her invention. Laws vary from state to state, but generally three aspects of ownership must be contemplated:

1. If an employee is hired to invent and if the discovery falls within the assigned work area, then the idea belongs to the employer because the invention simply fulfilled part of the job requirement.

2. If the discovery is outside the scope of the employee's duties, but the employer's resources were used to produce the invention, the employer has a *shop right* to the idea. This is sometimes considered the equivalent of a *nonexclusive, royalty-free license to use* idea. The value of such inventions is questionable because shop rights cannot be sold.

3. When an employee discovers an invention without using employer's resources, and when the task is not considered within his *hired duties*, the invention belongs exclusively to the employee.

It is quite common for employers to require employees to assign to their employer all inventions made during their term of employment. The enforceability and interpretation of restrictive agreements within invention contracts vary from state to state. In general, the law takes precedence over any contract and employees are permitted to keep inventions that were created on their own time, with their own resources, and that do not relate to the work performed for their employer. An employee cannot use information *carried in one's head* after leaving a job. However, an employee can keep and freely use any general knowledge of skills acquired on the job.

There are three recognized methods of protecting intellectual property: patent, copyright, and trade secret.

Patents

The federal government grants patents to an inventor or company designated by an inventor to legally monopolize the use of a product. One of the patent requirements is public disclosure. Disclosure is presumably *safe* because for a limited amount of time (usually 17 years) the inventor has the sole right to exclude others from making, using, or selling the invention. Qualifying an idea as a patent is not a simple process. The invention must be truly new and unique. The public patent files must be extensively searched to determine whether the invention differs from previous technology or is similar to any other existing invention. A patent must be applied for within one year of the first public use or offer for sale of the invention. Public use can occur if a model is shown to a potential investor. The importance of a patent is that it gives an invention legal protection. And from that protection, the invention derives certain value, especially if the invention has a desirable use and broad application.

There are some risks involved in the patent method. Patents are expensive and do not guarantee wealth. They can even be ruled invalid by a court. The individual or entity awarded a patent is responsible for discovering and prosecuting any infringements of it. The holder of a patent is less likely to get an immediate injunction against the infringer's use of the invention than if the invention was not patented and considered a trade secret.

Copyrights

Copyright protects the form of the idea, not the idea itself. It is especially appropriate for literary works, music, and computer software. For most types of technology and business information, however, copyright is not the appropriate form of protection. In a long line of cases, the courts have rejected copyright protection for works that were actually *mechanical* in nature. The 1980 amendments to the Copyright Act allow copyrighting of computer programs. Today, most software (developed for public and private use) is copyrighted. Where mass marketing of these programs makes trade secret protection (by contract) impractical, copyright registration is often considered the best alternative.

Copyright is governed by federal law and gives the owner exclusive rights to sell, reproduce, or prepare derivative works, usually for the life of the author plus 50 years. Copyright protects against copying by anyone, regardless of any confidential relationship with the owner. Original works may be registered in order to receive greater protection. To register a copyright, the statute requires the owner to deposit two copies of the work with the Register of Copyrights in Washington, D.C., within three months of publication. However, this provision does not apply to technical drawings or machine-readable data.

Tip: Copyright protection begins at the moment of creation and even unregistered works have copyright protection. Registration provides additional protection and statutorily increases the damages when rights are infringed.

Trade Secrets

Unlike patents and copyrights, trade secrets are protected in concept, and the laws regarding trade secrets vary from state to state. The courts have been largely responsible for creating the current state of trade secret law in their constant effort to establish *fair competition* in industry. Although a trade secret is any information that is uniquely used thereby providing an advantage over competitors, businesses must be able to describe precisely what they are claiming as a trade secret. Fundamentally, a trade secret differs from a patent or copyright in that the idea or invention need not be absolutely unique to the owner but rather derives its value from *the way it is used*. For example, the ingredients of a recipe might not be a trade secret, but the *way* they are combined could be. Therefore, trade secrets could extend over an entire range of know-how and business practices.

Another interesting distinction between a patent and a trade secret is that a patent awards exclusive, monopolistic rights for a period of 17 years. A trade secret offers protection for potentially an unlimited duration. However, it only protects the secret from those who obtain it and use it *unfairly*. Rights are not violated by anyone who can prove acquisition of the trade secret by independent, separate discovery, whether by research or by accident. In this respect, trade secret protection can be like a sieve, with the competitive advantage gradually eroding through independent discovery by others.

The Uniform Trade Secrets Act

Trade secret law has developed over centuries of court decisions. Businesses operating in more than one state have faced a confusing array of standards. As a result, in 1979, Congress passed the Uniform Trade Secrets Act that has since been adopted by many states. Most interestingly, the act protects information that has *potential* value. This means that a piece of information, such as a simple method or idea, can be treated as a trade secret. This prevents the employee, whose design idea was temporarily rejected, from walking off with it, under the assumption it has no value. The method, design, idea, or process is still the property of the employer. However, the act requires that the plaintiff clearly demonstrate that reasonable care was taken to protect the trade secret. If the secret nature of the information is obvious from looking at it, then simple, limited measures may be enough; for example, blueprints of a product under development that carry a notice they are confidential and may not to be disclosed may be sufficient.

Although the Uniform Trade Secrets Act focuses on the value of the information and on efforts to keep it confidential, the courts consider the following factors when deciding whether information qualifies as a trade secret:

- How extensively is the invention disclosed in a patent? If information describing an invention is omitted or unclear, the patent can be invalidated. Conversely, in the case of a trade secret, the more information that is disclosed, the less the trade secret is protected.
- How extensively is the information known outside the organization? Generally, the wider the dissemination of the trade secret, the more

protective measures a court will want to see before conferring trade secret status.

■ How much information is known among employees? The best policy is to disseminate confidential information on a need-to-know basis.

■ How easily can the information be independently acquired? This often becomes the critical factor in cases involving customer lists, where the former employee is charged with unfair solicitation of the former employer's customers. The mere possession of a *list* is not unlawful. The issue is one of how the list was created or obtained.

■ How novel is the secret? The reason for requiring some degree of novelty is to ensure that information does not interfere with an employee's right to use personal skills and general knowledge. However, it is sufficient for a trade secret to combine well-known ingredients or concepts in a new way or to apply known techniques to a new field.

■ How can the secret be distinguished from an employee's skills and general knowledge? This is the greatest challenge facing a judge in a trade secret case. Businesses must be sure their claimed trade secret can be distinguished from an employee's personal skills and knowledge.

Licenses

IP derives its real value from its ability to make or save money. One of the most frequent ways this is done is to sell or license it. For reasons stated above, licensing a patent is easier than licensing a trade secret. Licensing a trade secret will normally require time and money to monitor the security measures the licensee uses to protect the secret against unauthorized use or disclosure. Trade secrets are rarely licensed. In the case of commercial software, like that used to write this manuscript, the developer licensed me the use of its copyrighted code. I do not own the software. I have only a license to use it. Patents are also frequently licensed. Individuals and organizations have derived huge fortunes from licensing their copyrights and patents. The licensing of drug patents by modern pharmaceuticals is fine example.

Contracts and Nondisclosure Agreements

Contracts are also used to help protect proprietary information. For the best protection, contracts should be signed with all those who may have access to the proprietary information. There are two basic types of restrictive agreements. Nondisclosure agreements (NDAs) stipulate that the signer cannot disclose certain information without permission; this mechanism is frequently and effectively used in relations involving employees, consultants, independent contractors, vendors and customers. Noncompetition agreements prevent the signer from competing with a particular business for an agreed length of time. These are very effective tools; however, they have limited value in many states and some states do not recognize them at all.

These tools provide a substantial amount of protection. However, there is no substitute for good policies and sound practices to safeguard proprietary information and trade secrets. A good IP policy should be simple, manageable, and auditable. Suspected violations should be swiftly investigated and any appropriate discipline should be firm.

There are some commonalities among these types of offenses:

- Most often they are perpetrated by insiders with access. Without exception, employees pose the greatest threat.
- Lack of policies and effective processes are primary contributors. Employee carelessness and sloppiness are also significant contributors.
- Employers should look for secretive relationships, sloppy record-keeping, missing documents, indictors suggesting a compromise, irregular hours of operation or building entry, and changes in lifestyles.

1. The Anatomy of a Proprietary Information Investigation

Proprietary information investigations are usually precipitated by the discovery that information has been lost or stolen. In most instances, the first knowledge comes from the field. Sales representatives in the field usually learn first that IP has been compromised and the competition has gained an unlikely advantage by having access to it. The impulse to believe that offices and telephones have been bugged and that the organization's computers have been breached is usually without merit. Unlike theft cases, where everyone suspects the janitors, in these situations the competition usually acquired the information without breaching security or using tools or technology. They got the information from someone on the inside. And in most cases, they did not even pay to get it.

a. Preparation and Planning

Remarkably one of the first things that can be done upon discovering an IP loss is to call the party who is believed to have received it. In some instances, the recipient that received the information had not asked for it and may not even know it was stolen. Alternatively, the recipient may not yet know they have the information. Ethical people and organizations do not want to gain a competitive advantage improperly. Most organizations are law-abiding and have no patience for dishonest business practices. A simple telephone call to the right person, such as the CEO or owner, very often does the trick. Before launching headlong into a complex and expensive investigation, analyze what you know about the recipient (if identifiable) and determine what he might do if he were told that he possessed valuable IP that did not belong to him.

As I have comprehensively detailed in the previous chapters, the first critical investigative step is to prepare and plan one's effort. A project manager should be assigned. He or she should constitute the appropriate team and some preinvestigation fact-finding should be performed. Based on the type and nature of the loss, the project manager and the decision makers should decide the objectives, a budget, a timeline, and the standard of proof to be pursued. Often this effort uncovers more information and answers many questions.

b. Information Gathering

Just as in the typical theft investigation, based on the fact-pattern and the circumstances surrounding the loss, the project manager and his team must decide which investigative methods will be used. Randomly interviewing and talking to employees is not an investigative method. It is wasteful and counterproductive. Hastily making accusations and turning the organization upside down is destructive. Here is a better approach.

1. Based on the information available, formulate multiple working hypotheses.
2. Working one hypothesis at a time, attempt to develop a suspect pool. If the universe of suspects is too large, work your hypothesis to reduce it to a more manageable size. Team-consult with the stakeholders responsible for the information that was lost. Do not overlook the possibility the culprit was a former employee, part-timer, or consultant. Remember tradeshows, press releases, and trade publications can be huge sources of leaks. Examine every possibility before assigning guilt to anyone. Mistakes at this phase waste valuable time and are expensive.
3. Determine, if possible, if the loss was a one-time occurrence or if those responsible will attempt to do it again. Depending on your determination, use the proper information gathering tool(s) either

to catch the perpetrators in the act or to identify them. Your most powerful tool is interviewing. But if the item in question was an original document, see if you can get a copy of it. Originals, and sometime good quality copies, can provide information about where the document came from and who had it last.

4. Work your investigative tools and test your hypotheses. Eliminate hypotheses by proving them wrong. If documents, electronic or otherwise, are involved consider the use of forensics. Document examiners and computer forensic experts can offer a great deal of assistance. Search out the best of these and use them. Good ones will be able to tell you immediately if they will likely be able to help.

5. Chisel away at your suspect pool until you have identified the perpetrator(s) or the most likely perpetrator(s).

6. Interview everyone with access to the information that was stolen. Ask tough questions and do not overlook the obvious. On one occasion, while chasing the leak of some government contracting information, I learned that employees in a classified work area shared floppy disks with those in an unclassified area because there weren't enough to go around.

If the loss was an intentional leak, consider setting a trap. One very effective technique is called the *canary trap* or *beryllium pill*. It is very simple, yet I rarely see it used. The technique requires the minute alteration of targeted documents and the recovery of one if stolen. Each recipient or custodian is provided a uniquely altered copy (a punctuation mark or small typo unique to only that specific copy). In the event of a compromise of one of the uniquely altered documents, examination of it could reveal whose copy was leaked. The compromised document can be recovered by either asking for one or through discovery should litigation proceed. The U.S. government has used this tool since the eighteenth century!

c. Verification and Analysis

Now interview your suspects. Exercise extreme care in selecting the order you interview these people. If you are reasonably sure who is responsible, interview them first. You likely have the most information on them and they have the most to lose. If you are less sure who the offender is, begin interviewing those on the fringe of your suspect pool and work toward the center. In this fashion, you should be compiling ever-greater information with each subsequent interview—eventually identifying the responsible party.

Tip: It is perfectly permissible and lawful to interview former employees or nonemployees. Remember, however, they have no obligation to submit to an interview or to cooperate.

In the likely event admissions are obtained, memorialize them. Use a witness if appropriate and, at a minimum, obtain a written admission from each of those willing to provide one. Remember, if an interviewee is unwilling to write his own statement, offer to write one for him. The statement should contain language to that effect and be signed by both the interviewee and the interviewer. If you need to interview the employees of a customer or vendor, do not ask permission first. It will likely not be granted and your investigation will be intentionally compromised. Interview first, ask permission later.

Tip: In the event an interviewee reveals he possesses evidence, ask that he (or she) surrender it to you. Physical evidence of any type speaks volumes in the event an interviewee later has a change of heart and recants an admission.

---

d. Disbursement of Disciplinary or Corrective Action

After all of the interviews have been completed, package your results and present it to the decision makers. Remember, the fact-finders should not be part of the decision-making process. Monetary recoveries are often possible and litigation is likely. Ensure your case file is in good order and do not destroy any documents or records. In the event of litigation and discovery, much or all of your work product will need to be produced.

e. Prevention and Education

Based on what is learned, determine how the offense might be prevented in the future. Present your solution to the appropriate parties only after you have received their approval to do so. Because employees are the most significant source of confidential information leaks, it is in a business's best interest to monitor and educate all employees, especially those applying for sensitive positions. A business must impress upon prospective and departing employees the importance attached to confidential information. From the first day of employment to the last, employees should be educated and encouraged to respect and protect proprietary information.

In whole or in part, the misappropriation or improper disclosure of IP and trade secrets is a crime. However, in order to seek legal remedies, organizations must take affirmative steps to limit disclosure. The careless and indifferent treatment of IP diminishes the protections provided under the law. Right from the start, at the preemployment interview, employees should be told about the protection program for proprietary information. Before employees are hired, they should be carefully screened and their background and references checked. Requiring new employees to sign nondisclosure agreements is also prudent.

Employers should:

- Identify all information that should be protected.
- Mark reports, lists, and other critical documents as CONFIDENTIAL.
- Restrict access. Password protect computer files, lock file cabinets, and prohibit unauthorized copying.
- Provide policy statements to all employees, stressing the importance of protecting IP and trade secrets.
- Shred all discarded documents.
- Continually educate employees about the importance of confidentiality, specifying the particular obligations of the protection program and the organization's expectations.
- Require those with access to sign confidentiality agreements.
- Train the sales force and limit its access to confidential information.
- Provide incentives to keep employees, vendors, and customers honest.
- Conduct exit interviews to ensure that former employees understand their continued obligation of confidentiality. Have departing employees acknowledge they have returned all confidential documents and stress that the taking of trade secrets is legally actionable.
- Pursue violators and discipline those who break the law and violate policies.

G. Computer Crime Investigations

The technology of today allows anyone with a computer to hopscotch the globe. Personal computers with an Internet connection enable people to connect with one another and organizations of all types. The process is simple and costs very little. Other technologies such as e-mail, instant messaging (IM), wireless connections and networks (LANS, WANS, and VPNs), online banking, computer viruses (yes, this is a technology), and a host of others have made investigation of computer-related crimes one of today's more demanding endeavors. Solving crimes that employ these technologies is complex and time consuming.

1. Computer Crime Is a Growing Industry

Computer crimes can also be very costly. The lack of experience, knowledge, and proper tools make these investigations extremely challenging to solve and expensive to the business. According to the FBI, the average computer-assisted embezzlement nets $450,000, while a similar crime committed without the aid of a computer nets only $19,000.[55] An IBM study of 339 computer-related crimes determined the average loss to be half a million dollars. The study also found manufacturing companies to be as vulnerable as banks.[56] Other studies suggest that the typical perpetrator is a well-educated, skilled professional. Apprehension of these individuals frequently reveals they are well respected by their employers and the community. They rarely have a criminal record. This may be because the crime not only provides monetary rewards, but it is also exciting and challenging.

Categorically, we can divide computer crimes into three groups. The first group includes those in which the computer is the target. These include activities such as theft of the computer or the information in it, erasure or modification of the information, and destruction or improper dissemination of the information. The second group includes crimes in which the computer is used to commit the offense. Some examples include the theft and diversion of money or assets, commission of commercial fraud and deception, identity theft, and forgery. Of this group, identity theft has received the most attention because of its surging magnitude.

a. Identity Theft

Incidents of identity theft in the United States have steadily increased over the past several years, much to the dismay of law makers and law enforcement. The FBI says that the Internet, and all the information it makes available, is the principal reason for the increase. The Internet provides a cloak of anonymity, so businesses and governments have stepped up their efforts to protect the credentials of consumers and identify fraud more quickly.

The Federal Trade Commission (FTC) released a survey in 2003 indicating that 27.3 million Americans have been victims of identity theft in the past five years, including 9.9 million people in the past year alone. According to the 2003 survey, identity theft losses to businesses and financial institutions totaled nearly $48 billion and consumer victims reported $5 billion in out-of-pocket expenses. The agency also released a commission report detailing its ID theft program since its inception.

The FTC is the nation's consumer protection agency. Since 1998, the FTC has had an Identity Theft Program to assist identity theft victims and provide guidance on how to resolve the problems, provide law enforcement training, maintain a nationwide database of ID theft complaints available to law enforcement, refer complaints to criminal law enforcement agencies, and provide business and consumer education. The FTC also maintains the nation's primary identity theft Web site, www.consumer.gov/idtheft, which provides critical resources for consumers, businesses, and law enforcement.

A number of laws limit consumers' liability if they are the victims of identity theft. Not all costs are covered, however. The survey reviewed the different impact on victims who had existing accounts misused and those victims where the thieves had opened new accounts in their names. Where the thieves opened new accounts, the per-victim dollar loss to both businesses and victims was higher and the time spent resolving the problems was greater. The survey found that in the past 12 months 3.23 million consumers discovered new accounts had been opened, and other frauds such as renting an apartment or home and obtaining medical care or employment had been committed in their name. In those cases, the loss to businesses and financial institutions was $10,200 per victim. Individual victims lost an average of $1,180. Where the thieves solely used a victim's established accounts, the average loss to businesses was $2,100 per victim. For all forms of identity theft, the average loss to business was $4,800 and the loss to consumers was $500.

According to the survey results, 52 percent of all ID theft victims, that is approximately five million people in the last year, discovered they had become victims of identity theft by monitoring their accounts. Another 26 percent—approximately 2.5 million people—reported that they had been alerted by companies such as credit card issuers or banks of suspicious account activity. Eight percent reported that they had first learned when they applied for credit and were turned down.

Although most identity thieves use consumer personal information to make purchases, the survey reports that 15 percent of all victims—almost 1.5 million people in the year prior to the survey—reported that their personal information was misused in nonfinancial ways, for example, to obtain government documents or falsify a tax form. The most common nonfinancial misuse took place when the thief used the victim's name and identifying information when stopped by law enforcement or when caught committing a crime.

The survey also reports that 51 percent of the victims—about five million victims—say they know how their personal information was obtained. Nearly one-quarter of all victims—roughly 2.5 million people in the year prior to the survey—said their information was lost or stolen, including lost or stolen credit cards, checkbooks, or social security cards. Stolen mail was the source of information for identity thieves in 4 percent of all victims—400,000 in 2002.

For more information about identity theft, download from the FTC's Web site the consumer guide, "Identity Theft: When Bad Things Happen to Your Good Name." The FTC has distributed 1.2 million copies of the booklet since its release in February 2000.

Identity Theft in the News

Here is a sampling of some of the higher profile cases: In late 2003, Phillip Cummings was arrested for his alleged involvement in the biggest case of ID theft yet. According to authorities, Cummings netted $2.7 million selling information stolen from his employer, Teledata Communications. As of this writing the matter is still under investigation.

Internet job site Monster.com recently acknowledged a growing problem for the online recruiting industry by sending millions of job seekers a terse e-mail warning that fake job listings were being used to gather and steal personal information. The e-mail from Monster cautioned, "Regrettably, from time to time, false job postings are listed online and used to illegally collect personal information from unsuspecting job seekers." The warning focuses attention on a problem some security professionals have warned about for years. And although Monster and competitors such as CareerBuilder.com and HotJobs.com all caution their users about such dangers, most claim identity theft is rare. Experts, however, say sites such as Monster.com, with 24.5 million resumes available, is fertile ground for criminals hoping to steal personal information. Most vulnerable are those new to the job market. First-time job seekers eager to land a job often provide more information than they should. Prospective employers that ask for Social Security numbers and dates of birth should be considered suspect. Some cunning thieves posing as employers charge small "processing fees" in order to obtain an applicant's credit card number. Once provided, the number is used for unauthorized purchases, with the merchandise often shipped overseas.

Tip: Do not give personal information to a perspective employer until after a job offer has been made and you have been provided the proper releases. Honest employers do not charge "processing fees" and never ask for a credit card number to "hold a position."

b. More Examples of Computer Crimes

Best Buy Co., Inc. also recently disclosed that a deceptive spam message sent to thousands of consumers bearing its name was in fact a cunning fraud. The e-mail, which requests personal information such as social security number and credit card information purports to originate from the BestBuy.com fraud department. The company was forced to do everything in its power to alert consumers of the ruse. Best Buy subsequently claimed none of its systems had been compromised and that its online business was secure.

One Web-based scam targeted college-bound students and their parents. For a fee of $895, the scammers pledged to procure 100 percent of the funding students would need to attend college. In fact, they procured no money for the students. Instead, they provided consumers with readily available scholarship information that consumers could have obtained free. Similar schemes have been used to defraud consumers seeking government jobs.

Two different cases against participants in an e-mail chain letter scheme that promised participants significant earnings pledged that the scam was legitimate, and urged recipients to contact the FTC's associate director for marketing practices, who they claimed would vouch for the legality of the illegal schemes. The FTC stopped the illegal schemes, and settlements with the defendants barred them from participating in illegal chain e-mail schemes in the future.

Another Web-based scam claimed that consumers who paid a one-time fee of $49.95 were guaranteed to receive a "100% unsecured" VISA or MasterCard credit card with a credit limit up to $5,000. Consumers who clicked on the "Claim your card NOW" icon on the Web site and entered their checking account information received a confirmation page or e-mail that typically stated, "Approved! Congratulations! Your membership has been approved." In fact, according to the FTC, what consumers received was access to a Web page containing hyperlinks to various companies that purportedly issue credit cards—a list of hyperlinks that would have been available free to consumers who used a search engine.

Tip: If an online offer sounds too good to be true, it probably is. Organizations should educate their employees about cyber crime and e-mail scams. The investment is trivial compared with the potential adverse impact on the organization and its people.

The third category of computer crimes is the most frightening and to date has been the most costly. It is the use of computers to terrorize and disrupt.

c. Viruses, Worms, and Other Villains

Viruses, worms, and other variants have become the new tools of the terrorist and anarchist. The SoBig worm that rocked business and home computers in 2003 will likely be deployed again, but with more potency and viciousness, say some computer security experts. "We've only seen the beginning," Scott Chasin, chief technology officer for MXLogic, told the *Denver Post*. "It's a matter of bracing for the impact." Other experts agree. In 2003 there were at least six new versions of SoBig released, each subsequent iteration of the code fixed bugs and increased the virus's performance and virility. Experts expect the next generation of the menaces will be smarter, more sophisticated, and able to take orders remotely. Unlike other rogue programs—which take the form of viruses, worms, and trojan horses—these new technologies will no longer need e-mail to spread or infect computers. Already we have seen viruses spread using wireless technologies and conveniences as innocent as the cell phone. At this time the best defenses are limited to:

- Antivirus software and frequent updates
- Regular automatic updates for all operating systems and applications
- Firewalls
- Blocking executable attachments to e-mail from entering networks
- Deleting spam
- Careful use of free file-sharing services (they are often used to spread viruses)

There are some commonalities among these offenses:

- They are often perpetrated by those who are most trusted. Perpetrators must have routine access to the systems and networks they misuse. Employee perpetrators are usually motivated by greed or revenge.
- Most perpetrators are well-educated professionals who have no criminal history.
- Simple but effective policies and practices are deficient or nonexistent (that is, lax password discipline, poor use of virus detection software, undisciplined Internet use).
- Lack of supervision and effective audit and review practices are the primary contributors. Another contributor is the lack of good preemployment screening. Many perpetrators are repeat offenders and research would have likely revealed the potential for problems if the victimized employer had taken the time to look.
- Employers should look for secretive behavior, missing or altered documents, accounting irregularities, unusual transactions, and questionable relationships.

2. *The Anatomy of a Computer Crime Investigation*

Computer crime investigations are usually precipitated by (a) the discovery that information has been lost, stolen, or corrupted; (b) employee, customer, and vendor complaints; or (c) accounting, banking, or business process irregularities suggesting a computer crime or the use of a computer(s) to commit a crime. In the worst scenario, law enforcement or government regulators notify the organization. Regardless, the impact is often devastating and will likely be very distracting. The inclination is to panic. As in the other types of investigations we have discussed, panic must be resisted. The organization should have an emergency preparedness plan. If it does, it should use it. At the point it is necessary to launch an investigation, the first step, as usual, is to prepare and plan.

a. *Preparation and Planning*

After analyzing the facts the project manager should decide what assistance she will need. She should constitute the appropriate team using the organizational resources available to her. The typical team might include the director of security, IT and network specialists, general investigators, corporate counsel, and auditors. Following some preinvestigative fact-finding, the project manager and the organization's decision makers should decide on the objectives, a budget, a timeline, and the standard of proof to be pursued. Of particular importance is an evidence management plan. Because much of the evidence is electronic, consideration has to be given to how it is gathered and preserved. For example, how does one capture a Web site and preserve it as evidence, or how might one demonstrate information was maliciously deleted from a server?

b. Information Gathering

Just as in the typical theft investigation, based on the fact pattern and the circumstances surrounding the loss, the project manager and her team must decide which investigative methods will be deployed and how they will be used. Randomly copying files, collecting information, and talking to employees to "get their take" on what may have taken place and who might be responsible is clumsy and, worse yet, it may result in the destruction of evidence. The simple act of rebooting a computer alters files and could destroy useful information. Hastily digging and looking for evidence is counterproductive and disruptive. Here is a better approach.

1. Based on the information available, formulate multiple working hypotheses.
2. Working one hypothesis at a time, attempt to establish an audit trail. Whatever is done may have to be reconstructed for prosecutorial purposes. Inherently, computer criminals do not leave fingerprints or footprints.[57] Document every effort. If appropriate, *mirror* hard drives before examining them. Work with copies and preserve originals in their original state. If at all possible, take the computer off-line and isolate it. Preserve all evidence in a safe and controlled location.
3. Attempt to reduce the size of the suspect pool. If the universe of suspects is too large, work your hypothesis to reduce it to a more manageable size. Team-consult with others in the organization in order to better understand what might have taken place. Mistakes at this phase waste valuable time and are expensive.
4. Determine, if possible, if the problem was a one-time occurrence or if those responsible will attempt to strike again. Depending on your determination, use the proper information-gathering tool(s) to either catch the perpetrators in the act or to identify them. Again, your most powerful tool is interviewing.
5. Work your investigative tools and test your hypothesis. If documents, electronic or otherwise, are involved consider the use of forensics. Computer forensic experts can offer a great deal of

assistance. Search out the best and use them. Good ones will be able to tell you immediately if they will likely be able to help.

6. Plug vulnerabilities as they are identified. Because of the damage computer crimes can inflict on the organization, do not wait until the completion of your investigation to take corrective action.

7. Chisel away at your suspect pool until you have identified the perpetrator(s) or the most likely perpetrator(s).

8. Interview everyone with access to the information and systems in question. Ask tough questions and do not overlook the obvious.

The Internet

The Internet can be a powerful investigative tool. Hackers and other villains of the electronic world often have their own Web sites. Search for them. If you do not have the expertise to do the research yourself, hire someone who does. Experts in this area abound. Check their references and be sure to understand how they charge for their services. Like all consultants, computer experts must be managed. In spite of the urgency, manage them like any other consultant the organization might engage. The Internet can be used to research:

- Possible Web sites owned or operated by the suspect.
- Blogs and wikis owned or operated by the suspect. Blogs (short for Web logs) are the electronic equivalent of a personal diary. These fascinating inventions have captured the interest of millions of people. They allow users, called bloggers, to create an online diary. They frequently are open and viewable to any visitor. Blogs frequently contain photographs of the blogger and a personal profile. Visit Patrick Web's blog at www.PatricWeb.com to get the idea. Web is a retired IBM visionary who muses on technology. His blog is viewed by thousands every day. Wikis (*wiki-wiki* is Hawaiian for "quick") are in many ways the world's simplest Web sites. A member can add or edit pages and content on the fly, survey visitors, and link to other wikis. A fine example is Wikipedia.com. It is an *open encyclopedia* and as of this writing contains over 300,000 articles posted by members. Use the search engine Google to determine if your suspect has a blog or wiki.
- Possible articles or books written by your suspect or about him.
- Public records containing information about your suspect.
- Commercial databases containing information about your suspect.

Google

Google.com is the Internet's number one search engine. Google is fast and surprisingly thorough, in spite of the 32 billion Web sites it currently has indexed. Each day it receives tens of millions of search requests from users around the globe. Here are a few search tricks you might find useful:

- To find or research a person, type in his "full name" (include middle initial if known).
- To find a person's phone number, type in "name" + "city" + state abbreviation.
- To obtain a business address, type in the business's phone number.
- To obtain a business phone number, type in the company name + "contact us."
- To get the lowest price on a product, type in the model + "price comparison."

Google ignores most common words and characters such as "where" and "how," as well as certain single digits and single letters because they slow down a search without improving the results. Google will indicate if a common word has been excluded by displaying details on the results page below the search box. If a common word is essential to getting the results desired, you can include it by putting a "+" sign in front of it (always include a space before the "+" sign).

Another search method is called a *phrase search*. To conduct a phrase search put quotation marks around two or more words. Google also supports the logical "OR" operator. To retrieve pages that include either word A or word B, place an uppercase OR between the words or terms.

Tip: Before discarding or giving away an old computer, you should be sure all confidential files are deleted. Merely dragging and dropping them into the trash bin and selecting "empty" is not enough. Instead use a program such as Norton CleanSweep, which comes with Norton SystemWorks Professional Edition. Alternatively, reformat the hard drive and all discarded diskettes. Better yet, remove and destroy the hard drive.

Spyware

The misuse of workplace computers is a common employer concern. With an Internet connection employees can surf the Web, download music, shop, view pornography, and play games on work time. Resultantly, investigations periodically require the fact-finder to monitor how employees use their computer at work. Although these situations pose privacy issues for the employer, absent an employee's reasonable expectation of privacy, an employer may monitor workplace computer use. In fact, many do. Studies suggest that more than 25 percent of all employers monitor their employees' use of computers at work. The commercial software that assists them is frequently called *spyware*. Spyware allows an administrator to monitor e-mail traffic, chats, and instant messaging, Web sites visited, and applications opened by the target. Features frequently include keystroke loggers and screenshot captures. Applications such as eBlaster (available at www.eBlaster.com) can be remotely installed if the administrator does not have physical access to the target. eBlaster also claims to be the only software that will capture incoming and outgoing e-mail and immediately forward it to someone else. Even Hotmail, Yahoo! mail, and AOL Web-based e-mail services can be monitored. eBlaster's Web site promotes safety:

> In addition, Spector Pro (eBlaster's top-tier product offering) will actually examine what is being done and analyze it to see whether you should be NOTIFIED RIGHT AWAY—if something bad is happening to your loved ones while they are surfing the Internet. Combine visual snapshot recording, e-mail recording, chatrecording and keystroke recording with INTELLIGENT & INSTANT Notification when content you specify is encountered, and you have the most POWERFUL Monitoring and Surveillance spy software you can buy anywhere.

Spyware should be used cautiously. Because of the privacy implications its use creates, employers and fact-finders should think carefully before installing spyware on any system. A policy concerning computer use and misuse should be promulgated first. Employees should acknowledge the policy and proof of such, and it should be obtained in writing. Upon login, employee-users should be notified that the computer they are using is the property of their employer and the employer reserves the right to monitor all use of it. Consult an attorney that specializes in workplace privacy for guidance.

c. Verification and Analysis

It is now time to begin to interview your suspects. Similar to other types of workplace investigations, exercise extreme care in selecting the order in which you interview these people. If you are reasonably sure who is responsible, interview that person first. You likely have the most information on that person, and he or she has the most to lose. If you are less sure who the offender is, begin interviewing those on the fringe of your suspect pool and work toward the center. In this fashion, you should be compiling ever greater information with each subsequent interview—eventually identifying the responsible party.

Tip: It is perfectly permissible and lawful to interview former employees or nonemployees. Remember, however, they have no obligation to submit to an interview or to cooperate. It is illegal to threaten them with prosecution in order to obtain their assistance.

In the event admissions are obtained, memorialize them. Use a witness if appropriate and at a minimum, obtain a written admission from each of those willing to provide one. If an interviewee is unwilling to write his own statement, offer to write one for him. The statement should contain language to that effect and be signed by the interviewee, interviewer, and any witnesses. If you need to interview the employees of a customer or vendor do not ask permission first. It will likely not be granted and your investigation may be compromised. Interview first, ask permission later.

Tip: In the event an interviewee reveals he or she possesses evidence, ask that him or her to surrender it to you. Physical or electronic evidence of any type speaks volumes in the event an interviewee later has a change of heart and recants an admission.

---

d. Disbursement of Disciplinary or Corrective Action

After all of the interviews have been completed, package your results and present them to the decision makers. Remember, if possible, the fact-finders should not be part of the decision-making process. If prosecution is desired, confer with the team's legal counsel and identify the statutes possibly violated and the pertinent elements of proof. If the circumstances do not fit any current statute in the state the crime was committed, federal statue should be examined. Many cases that do not fall under existing state or federal statute fall under larceny or theft-of-services statutes.

If you have not done so already, consider inviting the prosecutor into the case at this juncture. The prosecutor should be able to provide valuable insight regarding the prosecution and what will be needed in order for the prosecution to be successful.

e. Prevention and Education

Because the most sensitive and important information an organization possesses is likely in an electronic form, computer crimes, and the resultant investigations that follow them, are becoming commonplace. It is likely that computer crimes or crimes involving computers will be the most common investigative issue confronting employers in the near future. The ability to conduct these investigations successfully is already a necessary quality of workplace management at all levels. At a minimum every organization should:

- Identify vulnerabilities and that which should be protected. Engage someone from the outside to conduct a vulnerability assessment. Use the results to map your strategy and plan capital expenditures.
- Establish procedures regarding electronic information management and systems administration.
- Clearly establish policies regarding computers, computer technologies, and computer use.
- Establish access protocols and strictly limit who has access and the limits of their access.
- Educate employees about the importance of computer security, specifying their obligations and the organization's expectations.
- Require those in the IT function to sign confidentiality and security agreements.
- Hire a consultant. Because of the ever-changing technologies, the world of computers and the business of protecting them should be left to the experts. Find a consultant that fits your organization's needs and engage that person. The dollars expended will be well spent.
- Pursue violators and discipline those who break the law or violate policies.

Fact-finders should remember that although computer crimes by their very nature are complex undertakings, they are committed by people. The fact-finders should not lose sight that their investigation ultimately involves the investigation of people. Accordingly, the process of investigation should be the same as in any other workplace investigation.

H. Accident and Workers' Compensation Investigations

The cost for workers' compensation insurance has risen much faster than inflation. The $75 billion paid by employers in 2003 is twice the amount of 1997, although the cost of living has risen less than 25 percent. The average cost of a claim has more than tripled over the past ten years and in 2003 exceeded $19,000. The two primary sources of the increases are the spiraling cost of health care and litigation. Medical costs for workers' compensation claims have risen 50 percent faster than U.S. health care costs. In 1990, while claimants (those injured and entitled to receive benefits) collected $7 billion in compensation, the amount spent on litigation was about twice that.[58] Costs have also risen because many employers cannot require their injured employees to see their physician of choice and because there are no deductibles or copayments. Arguably there are no incentives to reduce doctor visits or the treatments they provide.

It is estimated that more than 6.8 million occupational injuries/illnesses occur each year and that some form of drug/alcohol abuse is suspected in at least half of them.[59] Workers' compensation fraud investigations typically are designed to assist organizations in uncovering fraudulent claims and malingering claimants. Most claimants know that a key ingredient in determining their benefits is the extent of disability. In order to maximize benefits, claimants may be tempted to exaggerate their injuries and the extent of their disabilities. Because of a lack of manageable incentives, claimants often malinger and accept treatments and therapy they do not need. Covert investigation often provides the administrator and claims examiner the only opportunity to objectively examine the claimant and determine the extent of his or her limitations and ability to return to work.

1. The Cause of Insurance Fraud

Insurance fraud is any deliberate deception perpetrated against an insurance company or agent for the purpose of unwarranted or improper financial gain. It can occur during the process of buying, using, selling, and underwriting insurance. Underwriting is that portion of the process in which benefits are determined and distributed to the insured. For our purposes I focus on underwriting as it applies to the claimant.

First statutorily imposed in 1911 in California to protect the employee and eliminate the need for litigation while providing speedy benefits, workers' compensation is America's oldest social program. Benefits and compensation are rightfully biased toward the injured worker. The worker is given the benefit of every doubt during the claims process, making fraudulent claims easier and, unfortunately, more lucrative. The claimant with dishonest intentions is easily motivated by the prospect of receiving up to 66 percent of his regular pay while off the job. Greedy claimants frequently take a second job while collecting benefits.

A 1995 Roper study for the Insurance Research Council found that 24 percent of Americans felt it was acceptable to pad a claim in order to make up for premiums paid in previous years. Nearly 40 percent of residents in large cities found the practice acceptable, as did those in New York, New Jersey, and Pennsylvania. An earlier Roper study found that 32 percent of Americans said it was acceptable to underestimate the miles they drove when applying for auto insurance coverage. Another 23 percent said it was permissible to lie about where they garage their vehicles in order to obtain lower auto premiums.[60] Others justify fraud because they feel the insurance premiums they pay are unjust. On the other hand, employers claim insurance companies unwittingly promote fraud by settling and paying questionable claims rather than fighting them. Insurers often reason that it is less expensive to pay the claim than to legally challenge it. Insurers are also concerned that challenging a claim could precipitate a multimillion-dollar *bad faith* lawsuit.

The most common examples of insurance fraud are claims for injuries not suffered on the job and those that are exaggerated or unnecessarily prolonged. Faked and staged injures make up the balance. Fraudulent claims usually involve soft-tissue traumas with subjective symptoms such as headaches, whiplash pain, and muscle strains that limit specific objective diagnosis by clinicians. Claimant fraud also includes multiple claims filed under multiple identities and a claim filed just before or after an individual is terminated from a job or is disciplined.

- A 1992 audit of workers' compensation policies in Florida indicated 46 percent of employers underreported the level of their payroll or misclassified their employees in order to reduce insurance premiums.
- A 1995 study by the Rand Institute for Civil Justice concluded more than 35 percent of people hurt in auto accidents exaggerate their

injuries, adding \$13–18 billion to the nation's annual insurance bill—much of it left on the shoulders of employers.

2. The Anatomy of a Workers' Compensation Investigation

Workplace accidents and injuries do occur. Unfortunately, dishonest employees sometimes make fraudulent claims and report injuries they know are neither the responsibility of their employers nor compensable. There is no single indicator that suggests fraud exists. Even several indicators, while indicative of possible fraud, do not confirm it. The following indicators, sometimes called *red flags*, can help the employer and its fact-finders determine the credibility of a claim and possibly reduce fraud.

- The claimant is never home to answer the phone or is *sleeping and cannot be disturbed*.
- The injury coincides with layoffs or plant closing.
- Information from co-workers or others that the claimant participates in sports, other work, or physical activities.
- Rehabilitation reports reveal the claimant is suntanned and muscular and has calluses on his hands or grease under his fingernails.
- Claimant is in line for early retirement.
- No present organic basis for the disability. All indications are that the claimant has made a full recovery.
- The claimant receives mail at a post office box and will not disclose his or her home address.
- The claimant has relocated out of state or out of the country.
- The claimant has a history of self-employment or is a tradesman (for example, plumber or hairdresser) who is able to work "under the table" while feigning disability.
- Excessive demands for compensation or special treatment.
- Disability appears beyond that normally associated with claimed injury.
- A history of malingering by the claimant.
- Contradicting medical information: One doctor says the claimant is disabled, another says he is not.
- The claimant did not notify the employer in a timely fashion when the injury occurred.
- There is an unusual lack of witnesses to the accident or injury.
- There are inconsistencies and discrepancies in the claimant's story.
- The claimant is a disgruntled employee.
- Co-workers allege the claimant's injury is not legitimate.

- The claimant received a negative review for performance or attendance and is or has been subjected to progressive discipline.
- The claimant requested time off and it was not granted.
- Prior to the injury, the claimant had abnormal or excessive personal problems.
- The claimant failed to seek medical attention promptly.
- There are other known injuries or illnesses not related to work.
- Injured claimant is in seasonal work that is about to end.
- Absence of an objective finding of injury upon medical examination.
- Claimant has financial difficulties.
- Accident occurred late Friday afternoon or shortly after the claimant arrived at work on Monday.
- Accident occurs just before a strike or near the end of a probationary period.
- Diagnosis is inconsistent with treatment.
- The claimant is nomadic and has a history of short-term employment.
- Accident occurred in an area where the claimant should never have been.
- There is a history of drug or alcohol abuse.

If fraud is suspected, it should be investigated. If the employer is self-insured, this is just a matter of organizing and conducting an investigation. If the employer is not self-insured, the matter is best left to the insurer or administrator. Some carriers allow their clients to conduct their own investigations; others do not. If unsure, call either your adjuster or administrator.

a. Preparation and Planning

Upon deciding to conduct an investigation and after determining whose responsibility it is to conduct it, a project manager should be assigned. The project manager and decision makers should decide the objectives and other administrative details pertaining to the effort. These are generally not complicated investigations but timelines and budgets should still be established.

b. Information Gathering

The principal information-gathering tool in workers' compensation investigations is physical surveillance. Most often it is covert and usually done for several days if the subject is *active*. Because evidence of malingering will be used to modify or deny benefits, it is best to document several days of activity. Remarkably, a single day of skiing or roofing may not be enough evidence to prove the claimant is not as injured as he claims.

The following general guidelines apply when conducting covert surveillance. Regulations and laws vary from state to state, so know the law before conducting or directing any form of surveillance.

- Ensure all surveillance is conducted from publicly accessible areas. In situations when viewing must be done from private property, obtain appropriate permission first.
- Commit no act, such as trespassing or breaking and entering, prohibited by criminal statute or public law.
- Make every effort to conceal the investigative effort from the subject of the investigation and from others. Nosy neighbors can easily burn the best-planned surveillance.
- Do not tell anyone of the investigation or the identity of the subject unless legally required. When conducting surveillance in a residential area, it is appropriate to provide the police a courtesy notification. Unless they insist, do not tell them who you intend to watch or why.
- Limit the scope and duration to that which is absolutely necessary. Excessive surveillance can give rise to privacy claims. Remain on public property and respect the subject's right to a reasonable expectation of privacy.
- All efforts should be conducted in good faith. Use common sense and good judgment. Do not trespass or peer into windows or over fences.
- Discontinue surveillance and photographic and written documentation of embarrassing activities that may be unrelated to the investigation or the party you are investigating.
- Exercise reasonableness and care. Do not frighten your subject or others who may be in the vicinity.
- Document your effort with high-quality video evidence. Do not record voices or sound. Craft simple, concise, and complete reports. Timeline reports are best and the easiest to create. Document all efforts and do not exclude evidence that may be favorable to the claimant.
- To be safe, secure prior approval from counsel for any operation, including those efforts where known frauds exists.

In addition to using surveillance, the fact-finder should not overlook the other methods of investigation. Interviewing witnesses, co-workers, and others can help provide insight into the activities of the claimant and the veracity of his claim. If it is suspected that the subject is self-employed, research public records to see if that can be confirmed. Many years ago, during an investigation, I once made an inquiry at the Department of Motor Vehicles to see if my subject owned a vehicle. To my surprise I learned that he owned over 30 buses! Guess what business my claimant was in and what he did during the day? Valued at about $60,000 each, he had quite a racket going. Think outside of the box and use all of the methods of investigation available to you.

c. Verification and Analysis

Unless the subject is represented by counsel, the malingering claimant should be interviewed. My experience is that most employers and the insurance companies that insure them do not do this or approve of it. This is unfortunate. Like all other cases involving workplace misconduct, an admission is the best evidence an employer could have. If resistance is met, ask why. Remind the nay sayers that while on disability, the claimant is still an employee. Unless the attending physician does not authorize it or there are extenuating circumstances (such as being represented by an attorney), press to interview the subject.

d. Disbursement of Disciplinary or Corrective Action

It is unlawful to terminate an employee simply because he files a workers' compensation claim. However, it is not unlawful to fire an employee who has committed fraud. Seek the advice of counsel before interviewing and disciplining a claimant.

Insurance fraud is a crime in most states. If fraud can be proven beyond a reasonable doubt, it should be prosecuted. The victim of fraud should consider prosecuting all of the parties to the fraud including doctors, therapists, and claimants. Seek the advice of competent counsel before deciding anything.

e. Prevention and Education

One of the best ways for an organization to control their workers' compensation costs is to control the frequency of insurance claims—legitimate and fraudulent. A well-orchestrated safety program and a zero-tolerance policy toward fraud should be standard operating procedure. The following tips can help fight fraud and reduce insurance costs.

- Do a better job screening job applicants. Verify everything provided on the employment application and check references.
- Provide all new hires with a written statement about the organization's workers' compensation policies and a separate statement concerning workplace safety.
- Tell employees that fraud is illegal and that those who perpetrate fraud will be terminated and prosecuted.
- Once a reasonably serious injury has occurred, promptly advise the proper representatives. The sooner an injured employee can receive assistance, the greater the chance of avoiding costly litigation and bigger doctor bills.
- Honestly and quickly answer questions the injured employee may have concerning benefits. If applicable, offer the employee modified duty to help the employee feel positive about his recovery and self-esteem. Communicate an honest concern about his condition and his value to the organization.
- In several states, employers have the right to determine which medical providers are to be used by the injured employee for the initial 30 days after the injury. If that is the case in your state, manage the claim to the fullest. Remain involved and look out for your interests.
- Aggressively investigate all suspicious claims and any allegation of fraud. Make it well known that fraud and abuse will not be tolerated.
- Upon separation, have all departing employees certify that they have not been injured or have a pending claim. Those with injuries or existing claims should be processed according to policy and state law.
- Display fraud awareness and prevention posters and promote workplace safety.

I. Employment Screening and Background Investigations

Employers who fail to adequately screen their applicants today will likely hire their competitor's rejects tomorrow. No tool better enables the employer to build a quality and stable workforce than effective preemployment screening. Background investigations of employment applicants or current employees being considered for significant promotion or transfer are appropriate and helpful to (a) verify the accuracy and completeness of statements made by the candidate and (b) develop additional relevant information concerning the candidate necessary to make an informed decision.

The value of an objective, fair, and competent investigation is that it will permit determination of facts not otherwise verifiable or known by the employer. In effect, a properly conducted employment investigation ensures that what the candidate has claimed is truthful and sufficiently accurate and allows a fair evaluation of her employability.

In most cases, this is far easier said than done. Federal, state, and local laws control to some degree what the employer can and cannot do when conducting employee background investigations. Penalties for violating these laws can be stiff; as a result, many employers play it safe and check the background of no one. The price of doing nothing may be even higher, leading to all sorts of problems later in the relationship. With increases in employee substance abuse and crime in the workplace, employers face ever-shrinking bottom lines and also the risk of very costly litigation later.

1. *Specific Statutory Prohibitions and Restrictions*

a. *Antidiscrimination Laws*

Employers are prohibited in most cases from making any oral or written employment inquiry that directly or indirectly identifies characteristics protected by federal law (Title VII, 42 U.S.C., Americans with Disabilities Act) or state law (Fair Employment and Housing Act). Both direct questions about protected status and the use of indirect inquiries that disproportionately screen out job candidates of a protected group are prohibited. The protected groups are: race; color; national origin; ancestry; sex; pregnancy, child birth, or related condition; marital status; religious creed; physical handicap (includes drugs/alcohol); cancer or related condition; and age over 40.

b. *Federal Fair Credit Reporting Act*

The Fair Credit Reporting Act (FCRA), originally enacted in 1970, was extensively amended in 1996. The bulk of the amendments to the law went into effect on September 30, 1997, and affects most employers. The changes primarily deal with the obligation of the CRA (Consumer Reporting Agency) and the user (employer) to furnish notices and disclosures to the consumer (applicant). Although there were many changes to the FCRA that affected the credit industry, the following should shed light on the law and its impact on the applicant screening process.

Definitions

- *Consumer Reporting Agency (CRA)*: Anyone who engages, in whole or in part, in the practice of assembling consumer credit information or other information on consumers for the purpose of furnishing consumer reports to third parties.
- *Consumer report (CR)*: Any report from a CRA reflecting the credit worthiness, credit standing, credit capacity, character, general reputation, personal characteristics, or mode of living which is used solely or partially for the purpose of serving as a factor in establishing the consumer's eligibility for credit, insurance, or employment purposes.
- *Investigative consumer report*: A consumer report (or portion thereof) in which information on a consumer's character, general reputation, personal characteristics, or mode of living is obtained through personal interviews.[61]
- *User*: A recipient of a consumer report or investigative consumer report.
- *Consumer*: The individual who was the subject of the consumer report or investigative consumer report.
- *Adverse action*: Relating to employment: a denial of employment or any other decision for employment purposes that adversely affects any current or prospective employee.

The amended Fair Credit Reporting Act (FCRA) requires a Consumer Reporting Agency (CRA) and users (employers) to provide several types of notices and make specific disclosures to the consumer. The FCRA establishes the following consumer rights and the obligations of a CRA and the user:

- The intent to obtain a consumer report must be disclosed in a stand-alone document.
- The consumer must authorize, in writing, the procurement of a report.
- When used for employment purposes, FCRA requires the user to provide a copy of the report to the consumer in advance of any adverse action, along with a prescribed notice of consumer rights [§607(c)].
- Information is limited that antedates the report by more than seven years (criminal records are exempt).
- The CRA is required to obtain certification of compliance of the law from users.
- Penalties and legal fees for violations of the FCRA are provided [§616, §619].

Obligation of Users (Employers)

- Prior to obtaining a CR for employment purposes, the user must disclose to the consumer his intent in a clear and conspicuous disclosure (stand-alone document) [§604(b)(2)(A)].
- The user must obtain from the consumer written authorization prior to procurement of the report [§604(b)(2)(B)].
- If an investigative consumer report is obtained, the consumer must be notified of its preparation no later than three days after the date on which the report is first requested.[62] The consumer must be advised of his right to request additional disclosures as to the nature and scope of the report and be given a copy of the prescribed summary of consumer rights [§606(a)(1)].
- The user must certify to the CRA that all laws will be adhered to and that all notices and disclosures will be provided to the consumer [§604(b)(1)] [§604(f)].
- Prior to taking any adverse action, based in whole or in part, upon information provided in the consumer report (or investigative consumer report), the consumer (applicant) must be given a copy of the consumer report (or investigative report) and a copy of the consumer summary of rights [§604(b)(3)].
- If adverse action is taken, the user must notify the consumer either in writing, orally, or by electronic means. The user must provide the consumer with the name, address, and phone number of the CRA that provided the report. The consumer must be advised: (1) that the CRA did not make the adverse decision and does not know why the decision was made; (2) that the consumer has a right to obtain a free copy of the report from the CRA if ordered within 60 days; and (3) that the consumer has a right to directly dispute with the CRA the accuracy or completeness of a report [§612] [§615(a)].

Obligation of CRA (Vendor)

- A CRA cannot report negative information that is more than seven years old, ten years for bankruptcies[63] [§605(b)].
- A CRA has a duty to maintain accuracy of public record and other information [§606(d)(3)] [§613] [§623(a)(1)].
- A CRA is required to provide a notice to users of the CRA's responsibilities under the FCRA (user notice) [§607(d)].
- When an adverse decision is made based upon information provided by a CRA, the CRA will respond to consumer inquires within the time frame prescribed [§611-612].

Consumer Rights (Applicant)

- The consumer must be told if information in his file has been used against him. Anyone who uses information from a CRA to take action against a consumer (i.e., denying an application for credit, insurance, or employment) must tell the consumer prior to taking any adverse action and give him the name, address, and phone number of the CRA that provided the consumer report.

- At the request of the consumer, a CRA must give the consumer the information in his file, and a list of everyone who has requested it recently. There is no charge for the report if a user has taken action against a consumer because of information supplied by the CRA, if requested within 60 days of receiving notice of the action. A consumer is entitled to one free report every twelve months, upon request, if the applicant certifies that (1) he is unemployed and plans to seek employment within 60 days, (2) he is on welfare, or (3) the report is inaccurate due to fraud. Otherwise, a CRA may charge up to $8.00.

- If a consumer tells a CRA that his file contains inaccurate information, the CRA must investigate the claim (usually within 30 days).

- Inaccurate information must be corrected or deleted. A CRA must remove or correct inaccurate or unverified information from their files, usually within 30 days after a dispute. In addition, the CRA must give an applicant a written notice stating it has reinserted the item. The notice must include the name, address, and phone number of the information source.

- A consumer can dispute inaccurate items with the source of the information. If an applicant tells anyone, such as a creditor who reports to a CRA, that there is a disputed item, he may not then report the information to a CRA without including a notice of the dispute.

- Access to a consumer's file is limited. A CRA may provide information about a consumer only to those with a legitimate permissible purpose as recognized by the FCRA, usually to consider an application with a creditor, insurer, employer, landlord, or other business.

- A consumer's consent is required for reports that are provided to employers, or reports that contain medical information.

- A consumer may choose to exclude his name from the CRA's lists for unsolicited credit and insurance offers. If a consumer requests, completes, and returns the CRA form provided for this purpose, the consumer must be taken off the lists indefinitely.

- A consumer may seek damages from violators in state or federal court if an FCRA violation has been made.

The FCRA is onerous at first blush. However, if implemented properly, it should cause few problems or disruptions for most employers. In summary, employers should:

- Separately disclose a report request's potential and obtain written consent from the consumer.
- Certify to the CRA that disclosures and consent have been made and obtained; provide preadverse action disclosures and investigative report disclosures.
- Prior to adverse action, provide consumer report and summary of rights.
- Provide postadverse action notice to consumer stating: (1) CRA contact information; (2) that CRA is not the decision maker; (3) his right to obtain a free copy of the report; and (4) his right to dispute.

c. Employee Polygraph Protection Act

The Employee Polygraph Protection Act (EPPA) of 1988 prohibits most employers from using the polygraph for preemployment screening purposes. It also prohibits discharging employees who refuse or fail to submit to an exam. Even in situations in which testing is permissible; an employer cannot use the result as the sole basis of making an employment decision. The following must exist in order to use the polygraph for investigative purposes:

1. There is a legitimate and credible reason to suspect the employee in question.
2. At the time the offense occurred, the employee had access to the missing property.
3. The examination is part of an ongoing investigation regarding a business loss or industrial espionage.
4. The employee is provided 24-hour advanced notice of the examination and is provided the questions that will be asked.
5. The employee is notified of his rights and told that he may refuse to submit to the examination and that he cannot be disciplined for doing so.
6. The employer executes and retains an affidavit describing the circumstances justifying the test.

Some exceptions apply to government employers, security firms, and drug companies, but these apply to all employers engaged in or affecting commerce. Violations of the EPPA may result in fines of up to a $10,000.

Civil remedies are also available to the employee. If the employer is interested in using the polygraph for employment screening purposes, an attorney specializing in employment law should be consulted.

d. Criminal Arrest and Criminal Records

It is unlawful for most employers to ask a job applicant to provide information concerning an arrest or detention that did not result in a conviction. Employers can ask about any arrest with respect to that which the individual is out on bail or on personal recognizance and criminal action is pending. In most states there are exceptions applicable to health facilities regarding arrests for sex offenses and possession of narcotics. As an example see California Labor Code 432.7 and 432.8.

Employers are permitted to use conviction records for employment purposes in most states. Some restrictions apply. Consult with an attorney if you are unsure.

e. Employment Physical and Substance Abuse Screening

Federal and state handicap laws regulate the manner in which an employer can conduct a preemployment drug test or offer a postemployment physical exam. The intricate web of laws and statutes would be impossible to detail here. If interested in either using preemployment drug testing or postemployment physicals consult with an attorney who specializes in these areas. For drug testing information of a general nature and some idea of the current state of the law where you do business, visit www.Laws-InHand.com.

2. What Should Be Done

In many instances, what employers are left with is the search of public records. The information available is voluminous. It is also reasonably accessible and inexpensive. Here are a few of the sources and types of records available.

a. Criminal Courts

Criminal court records can be an invaluable source of information. For the most part, these records are public and available to anyone. Convictions for minor infractions to major felonies are found here. Files include full details of the case and ultimate disposition. Record retention policies vary by jurisdiction. As a rule of thumb, employers should use only conviction records when making employment decisions. Only a few states maintain state-wide databases. In most states the records are maintained at the county level. Thus, thorough searches are time-consuming and expensive. Within reason, employers should check records in all jurisdictions in which the applicant has worked or lived.

b. Civil Courts

Civil court records are segregated by plaintiff and defendant. Uncovered will be all civil actions to which he has been a party, as well as judgments, notices of default, and any unlawful detainer. Divorce records are kept here as well. A litigious applicant may become a litigious employee.

c. Department of Motor Vehicles

The Department of Motor Vehicles is an excellent place to search for a history of substance abuse. Revealed will be all convictions for driving under the influence of alcohol or drugs. Convictions for lesser violations will also be disclosed in full detail. Additionally, vehicle registration information and birth date may be obtained in some states. Note that it is unlawful to make an employment decision based on age. Age, in this instance, is used for identification purposes only.

d. Secretary of State

Corporations and other legally organized entities (LLCs, PLCs, for example) are registered with the secretary of state. Filings typically include the names of all officers and directors, street addresses, and agent for process of service. This is a particularly good place to search if the applicant is a corporate officer or is suspected of being one. Also found on the state level are the licensing boards for the various professions. Nurses, doctors, contractors, teachers, hair stylists, private investigators, and even mattress rebuilders must be licensed in most states. If the position requires a license, it is often worth the effort to check if the applicant is properly licensed.

e. Federal Bankruptcy Court

All bankruptcies are handled in Federal Bankruptcy Court. These records are public and often reveal valuable information about one's ability to handle his or her financial affairs. Note that the Federal Bankruptcy Code prohibits an employer from considering a past bankruptcy when making an employment decision. Some exceptions exist.

3. The Screening Process

a. Start with a Checklist

Search strategies and procedures vary widely. However, your strategy should always fit your specific need and be well thought out. In order to avoid discrimination claims, all applicants should be screened similarly. To facilitate this end, it is suggested that an *applicant screening checklist* or *guide* be developed.

The applicant-screening checklist should detail all that must be accomplished prior to making the employment decision. The following are a few of the actions that are on my firm's checklist:

- Job application completed and signed
- Prescreening interview(s) completed
- I-9 form completed
- References verified
- Previous employment verified
- Education verified
- Credentials or license verified
- Current address verified
- Notification of company substance abuse policy
- Driver history reviewed
- Criminal courts searched
- Civil courts searched
- Management interview completed
- Drug screen results reviewed

The checklist should provide space for the date each item was accomplished and room for the initials of the individual who completed it. The checklist should be made the cover of the employment package. Using such a system precludes disparate treatment and prevents making an offer to someone who did not meet your qualifications.

The items and their order on the checklist should be given much thought. Although the checklist can be revised, it is best to get it right the first time. Thought should be given to the goals of the screening process and the experiences of the organization. It is best to use the same checklist for every applicant. At the very least, employers should establish a consistent *process.*

b. Basic Searches

At a minimum, employers should consider performing the following searches.

Driver's History

As mentioned above, this is the single best place to search for a history of substance abuse. Driver records are also kept at the state level, not the county. They are statewide records of the individual's driving history and generally go back at least seven years. Even if the position applied for by the applicant does not include driving responsibilities, a driver's history search is invaluable. In addition to revealing potential alcohol and substance issues, a driver's history indicates something about the individual's ability to handle responsibility. A history of speeding and reckless driving indicates recklessness and disrespect for rules. Citations for failing to appear in court when required demonstrate disrespect for authority and disregard for the law. It is easy to conclude that an applicant with such a record would likely not make a good employee. If I were permitted to conduct only one background search I would insist on doing a driver's history.

Criminal History

Remarkably, about 10 percent of the American population has a criminal record. If these records are not being searched, statistically one out of ten new hires will have a criminal past. Conducting a criminal search only in the jurisdiction of residence is not foolproof and in many cases individuals who have been convicted of a crime may have moved from the jurisdiction where the conviction occurred. Others may use variations of their name in order to hide their past. Conduct a thorough search and look beyond the county or jurisdiction in which the applicant currently resides.

Public Filings

Filings uncovered will be bankruptcies, tax liens, debtor judgments, notices of default, Uniform Commercial Code filings, and other pertinent civil actions.

c. *Advanced Searches*

For more sensitive positions, more comprehensive in-depth searches are recommended. In addition to the basic searches these investigations may include:

- Verification of current and prior addresses
- Social security number verification
- Verification of education
- Verification of previous employment

- Business ownership
- Fictitious business name filings
- Real estate ownership and financing history
- Vehicle, watercraft, and aircraft ownership
- Civil court involvement and litigation history
- Criminal history
- Corporation ownership or directorship
- Personal credit history
- Professional affiliations
- Professional licenses
- Internet search

Unlike routine employment backgrounds, these investigations are tailored to the position. Exercising care upfront can prevent many problems later when the applicant is already employed.

Consumer Credit Reports

Section 604 of the Fair Credit Reporting Act details the permissible uses (sometimes referred to as *permissible purposes*) of consumer credit reports. It specifically states that a consumer reporting agency (CRA) may furnish a credit report under the following circumstances:

- In response to the order of a court having jurisdiction to issue such an order.
- In accordance with the written instructions of the consumer to whom it relates.
- To a person who the employer has reason to believe intends to use the information in connection with a transaction involving the consumer on whom the information is to be furnished and involving the extension of credit to, or review or collection of, an account of the consumer.
- To a person who the employer has reason to believe intends to use the information for employment purposes.
- To a person who the employer has reason to believe intends to use the information in connection with the underwriting of insurance involving the consumer.
- To a person who the employer has reason to believe intends to use the information in connection of the consumer's eligibility for a license or other benefit granted by a government instrumentality required by law to consider an applicant's financial responsibility or status.

■ To a person who the employer has reason to believe otherwise has a legitimate business need for the information in connection with a business transaction involving the consumer.

If you are unsure that you have a permissible purpose for obtaining a consumer report consult an attorney who specializes in employment law.

Verification of Education

Research by the American Psychological Association indicates that as many as 67 percent of all job candidates provide some untruthful information on their job application.[64] In one study, applicants were asked if they had ever supervised others using a fictitious piece of equipment. Of the 221 applicants questioned, 76 (34.4 percent) stated they had. Other independent studies reveal that as many as 50 percent of all applicants inflate their educational and managerial experience. With such statistics, it is obvious the employer must do everything possible when screening applicants. The least accomplished is the verification of education.

Typically, colleges and universities will verify degrees over the telephone (although this is becoming less common). Some require signed releases or they verify only by mail. When attempting to verify education, ensure you have the correct school and campus. Contact the admissions office or the registrar's office. Some of the larger schools have offices that do nothing but verify information and provide assistance to perspective employers.

Verification of Prior Employment

Verification of prior employment begins with the job application. It is not enough to ask for the name of the applicant's former supervisor. Ask for the names of other people with whom the applicant worked or supervised. Subordinates are more likely to provide information than personnel managers or former supervisors. Former co-workers also can be useful sources of information. Unfortunately, due to the increased number of defamation claims, employers are increasingly careful when providing references. Unfortunately, most employers only provide dates of employment and position held.

Prepare your questions ahead of time. When calling, ask first to speak to former co-workers or subordinates. Ask for them by name. Ask them not only questions about the applicant, but also about the organization in general. Their responses concerning their employer will provide some insight into their attitude and the amount of reliance that can be placed on their answers. Next, speak to supervisors, and finally, to the personnel or human resources office. Also helpful are verification of employment letters. If brief and to the point, these will be answered about 50 percent of the time if postage is prepaid. Exhibit 6.6 is an example of an employment background investigative report prepared by my organization for commercial purposes.

d. Employment Interviews

The employment interview, as a reliable applicant selection tool, has been widely criticized. Many people believe applicants put on a different face for an interview. They correctly suspect that during an interview an applicant will be on his best behavior. They conclude that the interview is a perfunctory part of the process and provides little value. However, when conducted properly, applicant interviews often provide insight and information not otherwise available. Research continues to develop methods to improve its effectiveness. As a selection tool, the interview performs three key functions:

1. Fills in information gaps and provides details not normally provided on an application.
2. Assesses skills and human characteristics that can only be measured with face-to-face interaction.
3. Provides a forum to sell the organization to the applicant. When conducted properly, even rejected applicants can leave with a favorable impression of the organization.

The Structured Interview

Traditional employment interviewing is boring, causing interviews to be highly susceptible to distortion and bias. They are rarely entirely job-related and too often incorporate personal questions that infringe on the privacy of the applicant or violate the law. Interviewers also tend to look for qualities that they prefer, and then to justify the hiring decision based on these qualities. Untrained interviewers tend to prefer people like themselves. They have a natural bias toward those who hold the same values as they do. Unskilled interviewers often overlook applicant weaknesses if they identify with the person and his or her background.

An alternative to the traditional interview is the *structured interview*. These interviews are highly structured and standardized. Every question asked, the sequence in which it is asked, the way responses are interpreted, and the value given to those responses should be managed and

Exhibit 6.6   Sample Background Report

<table>
<tr><td></td><td style="text-align:right">Business Controls, Inc.
Confidential
Background Report</td></tr>
</table>

Recipient		Number
		D04869208
Ms. Jane Doe		Type
Any Company		Inquiry I
Any Street		Prepared by
Any Town, Ohio 00000		WCD
Requested by	Requested Date/Time	Date Completed
Ms. Margie Knight	03/09/04 10:00 a.m. MST	03/12/04

Last Name	First Name	Middle	
Doe	John	N.	
Address	**City**	**State**	**Zip**
5999 Bear Creek, #310	Bedford Heights	XX	00000
	Driver's License		**Social Security**
Date of Birth	**Number**	**State**	**Number**
02/14/77	XXX 747828	XX	000-00-0000

Driver History

The driver history for the State of Ohio, license No. XXX 747828, shows that the subject's license is currently suspended, due to financial irresponsibility (failure to provide proof of insurance). The record indicates the subject has one citation for speeding. The citation occurred September 22, 2003.

Criminal History

A search for misdemeanor convictions was conducted in the county of Cuyahoga, State of Ohio, from 03/09/1994 to 03/09/2004. *No records were found matching the search criteria.*

A search for felony convictions was conducted in the county of Cuyahoga, State of Ohio, from 03/09/1994 to 03/09/2004. *No records were found matching the search criteria.*

Social Security Trace

Social Security Number XXX-XX-XXXX was issued in the state of Ohio. The name identified with the social security number does not match the provided information.

Continued.

Exhibit 6.6   Sample Background Report (Continued)

Credit History

A consumer credit report search was conducted to determine the status of the subject's credit and payment history. The subject was identified having 13 accounts (SSN 000-00-0000), all were active. The subject's credit limit was identified as $30,700.00 with a current balance of $25,322.65. The subject's monthly payments total $670.39. The following accounts are 90 days past due:

Master Card (Cincinnati, Ohio)	**$769.00**
Visa International (Dayton, Ohio)	**$8,904.00**
American Home Mortgage	**$12,000.00**

Employment Verification

City of Houston
Houston, Texas

The city confirmed that the subject was employed with the city from October 14, 1991 to January 11, 2004. The subject was employed as the Director of the Controller's Office. (The source was unsure if the title of City Auditor was the same.) The source was unable to provide any further information, due to organizational policy.

carefully choreographed. The use of a structured interview is recommended because it reduces subjectivity and inconsistency inherent in the traditional, informal interview.

Development of Interview Questions

A structured interview typically contains the following four types of questions. Each category of questions is uniquely tailored to the position. The process can by systematized and the questions retained on a shared server or Intranet for convenience.

- Practical Questions: These questions assess general job knowledge and expertise. As the category name suggests, these questions should be practical and pertain directly to the qualifications and basic skills of the applicant. For example: How well can you type, use a Windows-based operating system, operate a postage machine, drive a truck, deliver a baby (just kidding), and so on?
- Technical Questions: These questions pertain to specific technical aspects of a particular function or task. For example: (1) While using MS Word, how are headers and footers added to a document, and can the first page of a document have a different header or footer than the rest of the document? (2) Are Perl and XML

compatible and with which do you prefer to build tables? (3) What is the V^{max} of the Boeing 777 Bravo and at what airspeed does gear over-speed occur?

■ Situational Questions: These questions are designed to challenge the applicant's thought processes while probing his or her technical abilities. By using a hypothetical example, the interviewer probes the applicant's ability to reason and make good decisions. For example: Suppose you are the EMS first-responder. Upon your arrival you quickly determine that the ninth and tenth floors are fully ablaze and casualties are already beginning to pour into the street. Company 11 and 12 are enroute but both report to be held up in traffic. What are the first two things you should do?

■ Environmental Questions: These questions include the applicant's ability and willingness to work in various environmental conditions. For example: (1) What is your opinion of co-workers who smoke? (2) What temperature range do you like your work area? (3) Do you prefer to work outdoors or indoors? What was the most challenging aspect of the environment in which you worked last? Notice these are not yes-or-no questions. They probe and attempt to provide insight.

Unstructured Questions

To gain a deeper understanding of an applicant's motivations, goals, interests, and performance potential it is appropriate to also ask unstructured interview questions. Notice again, these are not easily answered with a yes or no. They probe below the surface and cause the interviewee to think and make choices.

■ Why do you want to work for this organization?
■ Why should we hire you instead of other applicants who have applied for this position and may also be qualified?
■ How long will it take you to become a contributor?
■ What could cause you to fail?
■ Why haven't you found a new position yet?
■ What did you like least about your last position?
■ What did you like the most about your last position?
■ If we hired you, how long would you stay with our organization?
■ What are your greatest strengths?
■ What are your greatest weaknesses?
■ What is your plan to address those weaknesses and how will you measure your success?

- How do you define success? By that definition, how successful have you been?
- What motivates you?
- What did your last employer do to motivate you?
- Where would you like to be in five years?
- What is your plan for getting there?
- With what type of people do you like to work?
- Do you prefer to work alone or to work in a group?
- What is the most important quality a leader should possess?
- Where do illegal drugs fit into your life today?

Some probing questions about illegal drugs are appropriate. They should be fashioned to determine attitudes toward illegal drugs, not reveal a history of chemical dependency or addiction. The Americans with Disabilities Act puts boundaries on this line of questioning. If you are not familiar with the ADA and limitations it imposes on employment screening, seek the assistance of an expert.

Conducting an Effective Interview

The following guidelines are offered to help improve your process and results. Share them with the rest of your team.

- Use only skilled interviewers. Select well-adjusted, stable individuals with above average intelligence who are interested in the job. Do not leave this important task to just anyone.
- Provide your interviewers proper training. Employment interviewers need to be trained in interviewing techniques and the law. Interviewing is a skill that is learned through training and experience. Audit your trainers and their training.
- Conduct your interviews in a suitable place. Maintain an area that is clean, well lighted, private, and comfortable. Create a positive impression upon the interviewee.
- Plan your interviews. Applicant selection is one of the most critical functions in the organization. Determine in advance the purpose of the interview, as well as what information is desired and what questions will be asked.
- Study the job description before the interview. This will enable you to ask pertinent and clear questions and respond to specific questions from the applicant.
- Admit your prejudices and biases. We are human and instinctively like and dislike certain things about people. Be aware of your

personal likes and dislikes and do not let them adversely influence your opinion of the applicant.

■ Make the applicant feel at ease. Make the interviewee feel comfortable psychologically and physically. Be friendly and personable. Let the interviewee relax.

■ Allow yourself enough time for the interview. Do not rush the process or the applicant. Be patient and invest the time necessary to obtain the information desired.

■ Become a good listener. Interviewers frequently make the mistake of talking too much. Remember your purpose—let the interviewee do most of the talking.

■ Close the interview on a friendly note. Let the applicant know the next step and when he or she can expect to hear from you next. Be polite—this person may some day become your supervisor!

■ Document the interview and retain your notes. Do not write on the applicant's application or résumé. Subjective thoughts should not be recorded. The purpose of the structured interview process is to obtain as much objective insight as possible. Do not dilute your results by peppering it with subjective and off-handed comments in your notes.

Interviewers should remember that the applicant interview is a tool, not a test. Its purpose is to provide better information about the applicant and her skills, knowledge, and abilities. It is not an oral exam or a beauty contest. It should not be used to weed out the weak or test the toughness of the applicant. An employer once told me he used the process to see what kind of *skin* the applicant had. He said he drilled the applicant to see if he could make them cry. What could be the purpose of that? I guess his customers did not want him to hire crybabies or maybe crying was a work rule violation.

Applicants also evaluate the interviewer. They will consciously or unconsciously evaluate the interviewer and everything about the experience. They are likewise shopping. Like the prospective employer, they are looking for the best opportunity and best return on *their* investment. Every contact with you and your organization will be a *moment of truth*. The applicant will continuously evaluate and assess the opportunity. Every impression and moment of truth will be evaluated at some level. Make it a practice to make the best of every opportunity. Even applicants who are rejected could some day become customers, suppliers, or even your boss. Treat every applicant with dignity, respect, and professionalism.

e. Substance Abuse Screening

The U.S. Chamber of Commerce recently reported that about 65 percent of those entering the full-time labor market for the first time have used drugs illegally. However, more alarming is the fact that teenage drug use has increased since the late 1990s. These young people will soon be seeking jobs. Some of them will apply for one with your organization. If their illegal behavior continues and spills into the workplace, they will consume three times the medical benefits of other employees, they will be absent four times as often, and they will be six times as likely to injure themselves while on the job. The U.S. Department of Labor estimates that each of these young abusers will cost his or her employer $9,600 per year more than their nonabusing co-workers.

A drug-free workplace begins with a substance abuse policy. As noted earlier in this chapter, that policy should include provisions for drug testing. Specifically, it should delineate (1) who will be tested, (2) under what circumstances they should be tested, (3) what drugs should be tested for, (4) in what manner positive results will be treated, and (5) how an employee should contest a result with which he does not agree.

The policy should be properly communicated and no one should be left with any doubt that management supports the policy and embraces a drug-free workplace. Employees should know precisely where the organization stands. When violations occur, management should respond swiftly and consistently. Foremost, the policy should be fair and enforced equitably. Do not allow different standards for hourly and salaried employees. Be fair and be consistent.

Testing

Employment drug screening technology is designed to detect the metabolites of a controlled substance in a specimen. The window of detection for each metabolite is different. The aim of testing is not to determine intoxication or impairment. Drawing such a conclusion from a positive result is improper. Only for alcohol is there a threshold that legally establishes a condition. Depending upon the circumstances, the threshold is established by state or federal law. For all other substances, the threshold of intoxication and impairment does not exist.

Once collected, specimens are tested in one of several ways. In the case of urine testing, most laboratories conduct initial screening via thin layer chromatography (TLC). The test is relatively inexpensive and easy to perform. If the metabolite of a controlled substance within the designated panel is detected, a confirmatory test is normally performed. The test method typically used for confirmation and to obtain quantitative results is gas chromatography mass spectrometry (GCMS). Though quite expensive, the accuracy of this procedure is unmatched. As a matter of good policy, all positive results should be confirmed.

Testing Accuracy

The accuracy of drug testing has received abundant attention. Claims have been made that the tests are inaccurate, unreliable, and subject to interference from foods, beverages, therapeutic drugs, and normal human behavior. The majority of these claims are without foundation. Using proper methods and government-recognized protocols, drug testing today produces highly reliable and legally defensible results. Technology is so precise that results are reported in parts per billion, or nanograms. False positives—situations where a laboratory falsely reports the presence of a metabolite—are extremely rare. False negatives are equally rare and the concern about them is largely misplaced. For more information about workplace drug testing, visit www.LawsInHand.com or www.DrugTestingNews.com. A Google search of *drug testing* produces more than 4.9 million results. In 2003, a search of *how to beat a drug test* produced about 500,000 results!

J. Workplace Violence Prevention and Intervention

Workplace violence touches everyone. It affects the way we think, feel, and behave. The threat of workplace violence affects the emotional stability and productivity of our employees and ultimately the organization's profitability. Although the incidence of actual physical violence at work is fortunately relatively low, workplace violence affects the lives of hundreds of thousands of innocent Americans each year. These unfortunate and often-preventable crimes can destroy people, families, and entire organizations. Even when the act of aggression is nonphysical (only psychological), it can still be painful and costly. More locks, fences, and guards are not the answer. Employers need strong policies, effective security protocols, and a well-conceived strategy to confront the potentially violent employee and prevent workplace violence.

Employers have a moral duty to provide a safe workplace for their employees. As public citizens they have the responsibility to the community and the people. They also have statutory obligations to provide and promote a safe and violence-free work environment. Inclusive of these responsibilities are the requirements under the Occupational Safety and Health Administration (OSHA) and state workers' compensation laws. Vicariously or directly, employers may be liable for the harm brought to others by workplace violence. Moreover, public companies have a fiduciary duty to their shareholders to safeguard their investment and protect it from unnecessary risk.

This intricate and ever-expanding web of statutes, court decisions, and regulations creates a legal minefield for employers. Like harassment, the prevention and management of workplace violence is complicated and time-consuming. Wading through that minefield is precarious and expensive. Rarely has the challenge for employers been greater or posed more risk. Fortunately, there are solutions.

1. Avengers and Aggressors

Workplace violence does not occur in a vacuum nor is it spontaneous. The typical workplace aggressor follows a sequence of ever-escalating behavior called a progression. An aggressor typical suffers a traumatic, insoluble (or so he or she believes) experience and projects the blame for it onto others. Egocentric and often narcissistic, they believe that everyone is against them and that their needs trump those of others. Unable to resolve personal, interpersonal, and work-related conflicts, these individuals sometimes resolve conflict with aggression and violence.

Progressions can be detected, although predicting an aggressor's future behavior is a considerable challenge. Experts agree that without careful evaluation and analysis, it is reckless, if not dangerous, to predict the future behavior of anyone. Without the help of an experienced clinician or other qualified professional, it is impossible for the typical organization to psychologically assess an emotionally troubled employee and determine his or her potential dangerousness. However, many workplace aggressors share common behaviors and characteristics. They often relate poorly to people, they strongly believe they are victims, and they are obsessed over their perceived lack of control. Invariably, they also have a history of violence, be it of the domestic form, public or workplace.

Some common behaviors and characteristics include:

- Few friends or interests outside work
- Self-esteem depends heavily on the contribution they make at work
- Strong sense of injustice to oneself, beliefs, or values
- A history of personal failures and disappointments
- Externalizes blame and habitually projects responsibility for undesired outcomes on others
- Poor people skills and difficulty getting along with co-workers and others

- A history of substance or alcohol abuse
- History of violence (domestic, public, and at work)

a. The Motivation toward Violence

We are a culture steeped in violence. We are bombarded by an entertainment industry that thrives on violent content. Economically, many of us face the threat of a corporate down-sizing, restructuring, or layoff. As a result, we are afraid and feel helpless. Many have chosen to accept less personal responsibility while expecting more from others. Much of our society is cynical and angry. In the meantime, the sanctity of the workplace has been challenged as never before.

Those who act on these emotions in inappropriate ways fall into several motivational categories:[65]

- *Economic*—The aggressor believes the target is responsible for undesirable economic conditions affecting him, his family, or his group.
- *Ideological*—Ideologically, the aggressor believes that the target is imperiling principles he or his group considers extremely important.
- *Personal*—The aggressor possesses distorted feelings of rage, hate, revenge, jealousy, or love.
- *Psychological*—The aggressor is mentally deranged or clinically psychotic—a condition often exacerbated by drugs or alcohol.
- *Revolutionary*—The aggressor obsessively desires to further political beliefs at any cost.
- *Mercenary*—The aggressor is motivated by opportunity for financial gain. Often he is hired to commit a crime that the avenger does not have the ability or courage to commit himself.

Tip: Contrary to the myth, those who commit workplace violence don't simply snap without warning. Abundant research has shown that aggressors tend to exhibit inappropriate and disruptive behavior prior to committing an act of violence.[66] To the observant, this behavior serves as a warning sign and allows time for intervention.

The visible and incremental escalation of violent behavior, or *ramping-up,* may occur over weeks or even years. During this progression, the aggressor becomes increasing disruptive and dangerous. For educational purposes, I have segregated the elements of this progression into three phases. Not all aggressors demonstrate every element nor are they always exhibited in this order.

- ■ Phase One
    - ■ Refuses to cooperate or follow instructions.
    - ■ Spreads rumors to harm others or cause disruptions.
    - ■ Is argumentative or resists compromise.
    - ■ Acts belligerently toward customers or clients.
    - ■ Makes inappropriate comments or gestures.
- ■ Phase Two
    - ■ Increasingly argues with others.
    - ■ Refuses to obey policies/procedures.
    - ■ Repeatedly probes established boundaries of expected behavior and protocols.
    - ■ Engages in subversive or manipulative behavior.
    - ■ Sends inappropriate messages to co-workers or management.
    - ■ Expresses repeated claims of victimization or mistreatment.
    - ■ Escalates inappropriate communications.
    - ■ Intimidates others.
- ■ Phase Three
    - ■ Sabotages equipment and steals property for revenge.
    - ■ Vandalizes private property.
    - ■ Threatens suicide and makes references to the after-life.
    - ■ Threatens physical violence.
    - ■ Physically and verbally assaults coworkers and others.
    - ■ Commits a violent crime.

Once set in motion, rarely does this progression reverse itself or abate without intervention. Even if the individual is terminated, he will often continue to harass and disrupt. In some instances we have observed, the individual continues the progression at his next place of employment, effectively picking up where he had left off. One of the few things that does change upon moving to another job is the identity of the target.

b. Intervention Planning

Intervention is the process of interrupting the escalation of inappropriate behavior while helping the employee regain control of his life. To successfully intervene, management must have the will to redefine boundaries and affirm its expectation. Upon recognition of inappropriate or disruptive behavior, management must act immediately and put the employee on notice. If a progression is identified early enough, the first warning is usually verbal. Verbal warnings often suffice to cause behavior changes and halt further misconduct. When such warnings are not enough, written warnings should follow. If the progression continues, the aggressor may be referred to the organization's employee assistance program (EAP) or an outside resource for counseling and to help modify his behavior. Managing performance and behavior is called performance-based management. It provides structure to the work environment while at the same time offering the employee choices.

In extreme circumstances, progressive discipline and professional counseling may not be enough. Under these circumstances, termination, temporary restraining orders, hospitalization, or prosecution may be the only solutions available.

Threat Management Team

Successful intervention is not possible without a well-conceived strategy. That strategy is developed and implemented by what is often called a threat management team (TMT). TMT will develop and drive the intervention. Depending on the circumstances, the TMT will consist of professionals from the following areas or disciplines:[67]

- Project management
- Human resources
- Security/executive protection
- Employment/labor law
- Public law enforcement
- Clinical psychology/psychiatry
- Private investigation/fact-finder
- Incident/crisis management

Each member of the team has a different but important role. Every member should be familiar with others and have a firm understanding of the dynamics of workplace violence. As such, they should be carefully selected and have the skill and experience to make difficult decisions quickly. Once the members are identified, the team should meet and determine basic strategies in the event of an emergency. Later, in situations requiring their attention, the team should decide preliminary objectives and begin the planning phase. Safety of the intended target should always be considered first. Protection of property, inventory, and equipment is secondary. When the lack of information makes decision-making difficult, a comprehensive fact-finding effort should be undertaken. One or more team members should be assigned to collect the necessary information. That process may involve discreetly interviewing the target, witnesses, co-workers, supervisors, former employers, or family members.

c. Information Gathering

A professional background investigation of the aggressor may also be appropriate. The typical background investigation includes the detailed research and examination of criminal records, civil indices, driver's history, registration of vehicles and weapon (if possible), all public filings including bankruptcy records, ownership of real estate, and, of course, the Internet.

Additionally, the aggressor's personnel file (if available) should be reviewed. Treating physicians, law enforcement officials, and other professionals can also be contacted for additional information whenever possible. As in all employment situations, however, the privacy of all parties should be respected and carefully considered. To ensure that the balance between need and privacy is adequately struck, the team attorney must be consulted during the entire information-gathering process.

The assignment of such tasks and the overall coordination of the intervention process is usually the responsibility of the project manager. The project manager must have the experience and leadership skills necessary to steer the TMT and facilitate the decision-making process.

The following summarizes a simple yet effective intervention strategy. However, these suggestions are designed to serve only as a guide. Actual circumstances and identified risk factors can influence the sequencing and effectiveness of actions taken. Due to the paramount risks associated with these situations, organizations should consider their response to them on a case-by-case basis.

For the purpose of this study, let us assume that an incident has occurred in which an employee has exhibited inappropriate behaviors or engaged in such conduct that compromises the safety of all of those concerned. In this event, the individual should be immediately and physically removed from the workplace and placed on administrative leave pending further investigation.

Removal from Premises

Upon learning of the incident, a preliminary safety assessment of the situation should be conducted. If there are injuries, professional aid should be immediately summoned and first aid administered. If appropriate, professional assistance should be summoned. Absent injuries, the parties involved should be separated and questioned. The questioning is for the purpose of preliminary safety determinations, not to determine responsibility or guilt.

If the instigator or responsible party is known, he or she should be placed on administrative leave with pay. Indicate that a thorough investigation of the matter will be undertaken and, until it is completed, the responsible party shall remain on administrative leave with pay. The employee should be told that he is not to return to the facility, call the facility, or contact anyone at work, especially the victim, until given permission or instructed to do so. The employee should also be told that a failure to comply with these instructions will be considered insubordination and, in and of itself, such behavior will be punished. The communication might read like this:

> [Insert subject's name here] as you know [name of organization] has been built on a reputation of treating all employees with respect and dignity. Unfortunately, your behavior has not been consistent with that reputation or our policy regarding workplace behavior. As such, we have no choice but to place you on temporary administrative leave with pay pending a review of your behavior and a decision regarding you and your continued employment with this organization. Allow me to stress this point—you are not fired, but you are now placed on temporary administrative leave with pay.

Also communicate the following:

> We expect to complete our review and investigation of this matter in the next several days. We will notify you immediately once we have completed our effort. How might we best reach you? In the meantime we ask that you remain at home and do not (1) call work, (2) return to work or visit the facility, or (3) contact any employees. However, communications with (counsel, the union) or our EAP is permissible. Thank you. Your cooperation is appreciated.

Note that the tone is nonaccusatory, yet firm. Already, new boundaries are beginning to be established. Do not engage in a discussion of details or in any way defend your decision. Emphasize that the organization is simply following policy for which there are no options. One might communicate, "Under these circumstances, our policy requires institution of temporary administrative leave with pay. There is no choice in the matter." It is helpful to explain that the action is not personal, but simply a matter of policy. Make sure you obtain any organization property the employee may have (such as keys, badges, computer access, and credit cards) before he leaves. Depending on the perceived level of threat and the employee's emotional stability, consider physical security needs. Eliminate the employee's access to the organization's computer system and electronic entry to its buildings.

Upon placement on administrative leave, do not allow the individual to return to his locker, desk, or work area under any circumstance. Any personal property should be obtained for the employee. The employee should not be left alone at any time. Upon providing any necessary personal effects, the individual should be escorted to the front exit and instructed to leave the premises. The individual should be watched until he leaves the property. All building entrances should be secured and the appropriate access control measures should be initiated if not done so already.

Local law enforcement should be notified and a report filed. This is appropriate if the individual has behaved inappropriately and made threats. A protective or restraining order might also be considered. Also if appropriate, secure the services of a contract security vendor and notify the appropriate parties at your headquarters and the union, if required.

Dialogue with the workforce is not recommended at this time. Your investigation is still under way and no final action has been taken. It would therefore be inappropriate to communicate information regarding the individual in question. However, dispelling rumors and inaccuracies and resuming normal business operations are in order. A suggested script for this situation is:

> As many of you know, [insert subject's name here] has been placed on administrative leave. An internal investigation is under way and we are working to bring this matter to a swift conclusion. In the meantime, we are mandating that no one speculates, theorizes, or in anyway impedes our process. Furthermore, it is unfair to [insert subject's name here] to talk about him [her] and what you have heard has taken place. However, [insert subject's name here] has been instructed not to have any contact with you or [name of organization]. Should he [she] contact you or return to the facility, contact [name of contact] immediately. Until this matter is completely resolved, I expect every individual to put this issue aside and focus on his or her work. At an appropriate time, and as soon as practicable, we will provide updated information. Thank you.

Additionally, you should relate that the organization has examined the need for additional security and for the time being no further security is necessary (or other appropriate response). Document every action and communication. Script and rehearse everything.

Now interview the targeted individual and witnesses. Obtain statements from those who are willing to provide them. Similar to the harassment investigation discussed earlier in this chapter, the statement should include the following:

- The facts surrounding what took place or what was witnessed. If interviewing the target, detail all supporting facts and allegations.
- Identification of any physical or electronic evidence that supports the allegations.
- Identification of all witnesses and other possible targets/victims (if known).
- The subject's agreement to testify if necessary.
- The subject's agreement to continue to cooperate with management and participate in the investigation as requested (to produce records and documents or submit to an additional interview).
- The subject's agreement to report any future contact by the aggressor.
- The subject's agreement to keep the matter confidential and not to discuss it or the investigation with others who have no need to know.
- Affirmation that the information provided is true and that any intentional misrepresentations or falsities may result in discipline.
- The opportunity to add anything to their statements they wish.

In some situations a violence risk assessment or other psychological evaluation will need to be performed. The determination of dangerousness of the aggressor is one of the primary goals of the fact-finding effort. A competent professional with expertise in this area should be utilized for this assessment. Most employers are not capable of making an accurate determination of dangerousness and should not be involved in the process. If an assessment is to be performed, the individual should not return to work until the results of that evaluation are completed and reviewed.

d. Verification and Analysis

In most situations, the aggressor should be interviewed before any decision is made regarding her continued employment. A properly conducted interview also allows one to assess the individual and ask questions about her intentions. It is perfectly acceptable to ask if she intend to carry out her threat or if she is capable of it. Employers and their fact-finders are often hesitant to ask tough questions. Resultantly, they often do not obtain the information that would most help them or their process. Aggressors often want to talk and discuss their grievance(s). Sometimes the source of their anger is the belief that no one will listen to them. If given the opportunity, it is appropriate to ask them what outcome they want and how it might be amicably achieved. I have conducted more than 200 such interviews and almost always found the subject to be agreeable to discuss his or her issues and possible solutions. This opportunity should not be overlooked.

If aggressors cooperate, also obtain statements from them. In this statement ask them to explain what took place and why they behaved the way they did. If they make an admission, ask that they acknowledge that the behavior in question was inappropriate and as a result, discipline up to and including discharge may be appropriate.

e. Disbursement of Disciplinary or Corrective Action

If the results of the investigation lead the decision makers to decide the individual in question should be terminated, the decision should be communicated to the individual as soon as possible. Depending upon the circumstances, communication of this decision may be accomplished via mail or telephone. In some instances, it is appropriate to communicate the decision face-to-face. In that case, the following suggestions are recommended:

- Remember, safety is the first order of business. Take the necessary security precautions and do not leave safety to chance.
- An organization communicator and witness/note-taker should be designated. The company communicator should call the individual and arrange for a meeting off the organization's premises at a designated time. The time and the day of the week will be determined by the nature of the circumstances leading up to the action.
- Prepare a termination notice and a resignation notice with releases.
- If a severance package is to be offered, tie receipt of it to the future behavior of the subject. Plan to indicate that any further inappropriate conduct will result in cancellation of any consideration offered.
- Prepare a final paycheck and any severance package materials.
- If appropriate, contract security should be made available and properly briefed.
- If appropriate, law enforcement should be notified. Call the local watch commander and notify him or her that the organization is

planning to disciple a difficult individual but that you do not expect a problem. Do not go into any further detail. Tell him or her you will call if assistance is necessary and ask that a patrol car be in the vicinity at the appointed time.

Upon arrival, the individual should be escorted to a convenient and private area. Once seated, the designated communicator should say in a warm, yet professional tone:

> [Insert subject's name here] as you know, our organization has been built on a reputation of treating all employees with respect and dignity. Unfortunately, your recent behavior has not been consistent with that reputation, nor has it been in accordance with our policy regarding workplace behavior. As such, and consistent with our policy regarding such behavior, we have no choice but to terminate your employment.

Do not engage in a discussion of details or dialogue defending the decision. Stress that the decision is simply a matter of policy. Offer the individual an opportunity to resign in lieu of termination (only if the individual is also willing to sign a release). Offer to pay the individual for the balance of the day or through the next business day. Ask that the individual return any remaining property belonging to the organization he or she may possess. If asked, indicate whether unemployment benefits will be contested. Indicate that organizational policy will be adhered to relative to the request for references or the verification of employment.

Prior to the meeting, collect any remaining personal property and arrange for it to be delivered to individual's home *after the meeting*. Do not allow him to return to his locker, desk, work area, or the premises under any circumstances. Personal property should be gathered by a management representative for the individual and an inventory taken. The process should be witnessed and any valuables afforded appropriate handling.

At the completion of the meeting, the now ex-employee should be watched until he leaves the location. If appropriate, law enforcement should be notified and a report made. Again, determine the need for contract security and make the necessary arrangements. Notify the appropriate parties at headquarters. Allow the supervisor of the individual to communicate to his department that the terminated individual is no longer an employee and that he will be replaced immediately (if appropriate). Change locks, security codes, and passwords to ensure that the former employee is unable to gain access to the facility at a later time.

To aggressively quash all rumors about the employee and his sudden departure, some dialogue with the workforce is recommended at this time.

Final action has been taken and it is appropriate to communicate necessary information to other employees. However, emphasis should be made to quash rumors and encourage the return of normal operations. Here is a suggested script to follow:

> As many of you know, [insert subject's name here] was recently placed on administrative leave. An internal investigation has been completed and [insert subject's name here] is no longer an employee of our organization. It is imperative that no one speculates, theorizes, or in any way speaks disrespectfully of [insert subject's name here]. Furthermore, it is unfair to talk about him and what has taken place. However, [insert subject's name here] has been instructed not to have any contact with you or the organization. Should he contact you or return to the facility, contact [name of appropriate party] immediately. I expect every employee to put this issue aside and focus on his or her own work. Thank you.

If asked about employee safety, indicate that the organization has examined the need for additional security and for the time being no further security is necessary (or other appropriate response). Document every action and every communication. Later, reiterate the organization's policy regarding violence in the workplace and its commitment to maintaining a safe working environment for everyone. Debrief the target and other concerned parties. Ask that they maintain a security mindset and report any unusual or inappropriate behavior or contact by the aggressor immediately.

Debrief the team and determine if any further action is appropriate. Remind team members and employees that they can help protect themselves and their co-workers by exercising the following simple steps:

- Plan head and prepare for the unexpected.
- Treat co-workers with respect and dignity.
- Respect clients and customers.
- Be aware of strangers of their surroundings.
- Report inappropriate behaviors and activities immediately.

f. Prevention and Intervention

Though an employer cannot be expected to provide an impenetrable island of safety for its employees, supervisors and managers are expected to do as much as possible to promote safety and prevent workplace violence. Employees can be trained to deescalate tense situations and avoid conflict. Supervisors and managers can also enforce company policies fairly and consistently and allow employee complaints and grievances to be heard. As noted earlier, aggressive behavior is disruptive and dangerous and often is the by-product of unresolved grievances. Consequently, supervisors and managers must provide employees the opportunity to resolve problems and air grievances. The perfect vehicle is an anonymous incident reporting system (AIRS). AIRS, as described earlier in the section on harassment investigations, is inexpensive and easy to administrate. In almost every case of workplace violence in which I have had involvement or studied, someone knew of the intentions of the aggressors. Unfortunately, and all too frequently, those who knew of the impending danger had neither a safe nor convenient way to communicate their information. If your organization does not currently have an AIRS, use what you have learned in this chapter to make the case for one. Do it without delay.

Training and education are also important in creating a safe and violence-free workplace. Employees must understand what is expected of them to create a violence-free work environment. Every employee must also understand that violence or the threat of violence will not be tolerated and that policy violations may result in immediate termination or prosecution.

In summary, organizations should:

- Make a commitment to workplace safety.
- Create practical and sound policies that address workplace violence and aggression.
- Screen applicants thoroughly and identify individuals with problems before they are hired.
- Allow all grievances to be heard and resolve workplace problems early.
- Quickly address poor performance and inappropriate workplace behavior.
- Hold supervisors and managers accountable.
- Teach kindness.
- Never hesitate to call for help.

K. Ethics Violation Investigations

Ethics and responsible corporate governance have become "the buzz" of almost every industry and in every sector. Wall Street and other investors around the globe have been shaken by recent high-profile corporate scandals. Here is a rundown of a few of the companies and firms under recent investigation for allegations of accounting irregularities, insider trading, or misleading their investors.

In 2002, Xerox said it would restate five years of earnings and reclassify more than $6 billion in revenues. Just prior to the announcement, the company settled charges that it used *accounting tricks* to mislead investors and inflate market values.

WorldCom Inc., the telecommunications company responsible for providing most of the Internet's backbone, reported that it hid $3.85 billion in expenses in 2001. The company fired its chief financial officer and quickly began cutting 17,000 jobs, roughly equal to 20 percent of its workforce.

ImClone Systems Inc., the now product-less biotech firm, has been under congressional investigation and the regulators for more than two years to find out if it properly informed investors that the U.S. Food and Drug Administration had declined to review its experimental cancer drug. Samuel Waksal, its former chief executive, was successfully prosecuted for insider trading. In 2004, friend and investor Martha Stewart was convicted for capitalizing on information she received from Waksal. Federal investigators allege the information saved her from a potential $67,000 loss on ImClone stock. Difficult to fathom such shenanigans when one considers Stewart made about $1 billion when her firm, Martha Stewart Living Ominmedia, Inc., went public several years ago. Let's do some math. If Stewart's $1 billion holdings were liquid and she was to live for another 50 years, she would be able to spend $54,794 a day and not go broke!

Enron Corp., formerly the nation's largest energy trader, collapsed into the largest-ever U.S. bankruptcy debacle in December 2001, amid an investigation surrounding off-the-book transactions that were allegedly used to hide debt and inflate profits. Roughly 5,000 employees lost their jobs and the average employee 401K account lost about $87,000 in value.

Arthur Andersen, the accounting firm founded in 1906 that later became Enron's auditors, was found guilty on June 15, 2002, of obstructing justice in the government's investigation of Enron. Arthur Andersen has since been dissolved.

Adelphia Communications Corp., a cable operator, filed for bankruptcy in 2002. The company is under investigation by the U.S. Securities and Exchange Commission and two federal grand juries for multibillion-dollar, off-balance-sheet loans to its founding family, the Rigases.

Tyco International Ltd., a huge conglomerate and parent of ADT, is under investigation of whether top executives used corporate cash to buy art and a private residence. Tyco's former chairman, Dennis Kozlowski, resigned in June 2002, a day before he was indicted for evading about $1 million in New York sales taxes on art he had purchased.

Merrill Lynch & Co., the largest U.S. brokerage house, in May 2002, agreed to pay $100 million to settle a probe by the New York state attorney general into charges it tailored stock research to win investment banking business.

Global Crossing Ltd., a telecommunications company, also faces probes by the U.S. Securities and Exchange Commission and the FBI regarding its accounting practices. Allegedly the telecommunications giant engaged in network capacity swaps with other rivals to inflate revenue and defraud investors.

Computer Associates International Inc., agreed to pay $638,000 to settle charges brought by the U.S. Justice Department that it violated premerger rules after announcing it would acquire Platinum Technology, Inc.

Although such scandals have shaken investors and destabilized the markets, Congress has not remained idle. With almost $1 trillion in shareholder equity wiped out, law makers had had enough. With much debate, the Sarbanes-Oxley Act of 2002 redefined corporate ethics and governance. Combined with the Federal Sentencing Guidelines (enacted in 1991) and the Racketeer Influenced Criminal Organization Act (RICO) the nation's top cops have the tools they now need to stop greedy corporate elitists and bring them to justice. But Sarbanes-Oxley puts most of the compliance burden on the organization. Ominously, it provides for stiff criminal penalties for CEOs and CFOs of public companies who cheat and steal. Specifically:

- *Section 301*—Requires audit committees to provide a mechanism for employees to remain anonymous when reporting concerns about questionable accounting or audit matters. Additionally, the audit committee must provide a process for the "receipt, retention and treatment" of complaints regarding financial irregularities.
- *Section 404*—Requires that the organization's annual report contain a statement regarding the effectiveness of it internal controls.
- *Section 806*—Prohibits whistleblower retaliation and permits employees to sue their employers if retaliated against.
- *Section 1107*—Allows criminal sanctions against managers found guilty of retaliation with sentences up to ten years in prison.

In addition to stiff criminal penalties, noncompliant organizations may be delisted. With indictments now starting to be handed down, the message has been lost on no one; unethical behavior will not be tolerated.

There is no equivalent of Sarbanes-Oxley for private companies and nonprofit organizations. Legal authorities, however, suggest that they too will be held to a higher standard because of Sarbanes-Oxley. It will be the stick by which organizational ethical behavior will soon be measured. I must agree. Evidence abounds to support this assertion. Ethics and corporate governance have become "the buzz" of the private sector. One can barely discuss the topic of workplace misconduct and not mention ethical misconduct as a component. Yet the literature is largely devoid of any mention of ethics investigations. Of the literature cited in this book, and that contained in my extensive corporate library, I could not find a single reference to ethics other than my own in *Undercover Investigations in the Workplace.*[68] Here are some of the more common unethical workplace behaviors (in no particular order):

- Misuse of a reimbursed expense account
- Gratuities and kickbacks to vendors and others
- Failure to report or correct known hazards to employees, customers and vendors
- Under-reporting taxable income
- Manipulation of financial reports or records for any purpose
- Failure to disclose actual or potential conflicts of interest
- Lying
- Cheating
- Stealing
- Dirty dealing

Peter Drucker said it best: "No professional, be he a doctor, lawyer, or manager, can promise that he will indeed do good for his client. All he can do is try. But he can promise that he will not knowingly do harm. And the client, in turn, must be able to trust the professional not knowingly to do him harm."[69] Like it or not, ethics plays a role in every aspect of business. Correctly, it ought to govern the way we behave and treat others. There are some commonalities among these types of offenses:

- They are most often perpetrated by insiders with access. Frequently, these are people with control and power. By the nature of their jobs, they influence the outcome of many business transactions and how they are accomplished.
- Perpetrators are typically greedy and care little about others.
- Primary contributors include a lack of supervision and effectiveness.
- Secretive relationships, unusual business dealings, and questionable behaviors exist.

1. Anatomy of Ethics Violation Investigations

a. Preparation and Planning

As I have comprehensively and so frequently detailed above, the first critical step is to prepare and plan one's effort. A project manager should be assigned. He or she should constitute the appropriate team and some preinvestigation fact-finding should be performed. Based on the amount and type of information (or allegation), the project manager and the decision makers should decide on the objectives, a budget, a timeline, and the standard of proof to be pursued. Often this effort uncovers more information and answers many questions about the problem. Because ethics violations, or allegations of them, are so often brought to the attention of management by a concerned individual (CI), the preinvestigation effort should clearly identify the source of the allegations and determine their willingness to further cooperate.

b. Information Gathering

Based on the fact-pattern and the circumstances surrounding the loss, the project manager and his team should decide which investigative methods should be deployed and how they shall be used. Once again, randomly interviewing and talking to employees or others to get their take on what may have taken place is not an investigative method. It is wasteful and counterproductive. Here is a better approach:

1. Based on the information available, formulate multiple working hypotheses.
2. Working one hypothesis at a time, attempt to refine your investigative plan.
3. Similar to a theft investigation, determine if the event was a one-time occurrence or if those responsible will attempt do it again. Depending on your determination, use the proper information gathering tool(s) to either catch the perpetrator(s) in the act or to identify him or her. Witnesses and CIs should be used to the fullest extent possible. Do not overlook the potential to interview non-employees. In ethics investigations, it is frequently necessary to interview outsiders.
4. Work your investigative tools and test your hypothesis. Preserve and catalogue your evidence.
5. Keep upper management informed. If the law has been broken and government disclosure is necessary, make the necessary reports. Seek the advice of counsel before communicating with anyone outside of the organization.

c. Verification and Analysis

Now interview your suspect(s). Exercise extreme care in selecting the order you interview these people. If you are reasonably sure who is responsible, interview that person first. You will likely have the most information on that person and he or she has the most to lose. If you are less sure who the perpetrator is, begin interviewing those on the fringe of your suspect pool and work toward the center. In this fashion, you should be compiling ever-greater information with each subsequent interview—eventually identifying the responsible party.

In the likely event admissions are obtained, memorialize them. Use a witness if appropriate, and at a minimum obtain a written admission from each of those willing to provide one. Remember, if an interviewee is unwilling to write his own statement, offer to write one for him. The statement should contain language to that effect and be signed by both the interviewee and the interviewer.

d. Disbursement of Disciplinary or Corrective Action

After all of the interviews have been completed, package your results and present them to the decision makers. Remember, the fact-finders should not be part of the decision-making process. Remind decision makers that organizational policy might dictate the appropriate discipline. Additionally, government disclosures may be necessary. Customer and vendor contracts might also require disclosure or reporting. Do your homework and seek the advice of the entire investigative team before closing your investigation or moving on to the next phase.

e. Prevention and Education

Based on what has been learned, determine how the offense might be prevented in the future. Present your solution to the appropriate parties only after you have received their approval to do so.

Tip: The role of the fact-finder is not to make policy, but to provide information so that it may be enforced. Fact-finders should resist the temptation to judge and, instead, seek the truth.

Notes

1. J. W. Osterburg and R. H. Ward, *Criminal Investigation—A Method for Reconstructing the Past* (Cincinnati, Ohio: Anderson Publishing Company, 1992), 875.

2. William Poundstone, *Labyrinths of Reason: Paradox, Puzzles, and the Frailty of Knowledge* (New York: Anchor Books, 1988), 274; Les Krantz, *What the Odds Are* (New York: HarperCollins, 1992), 296; David Ropeik and George Gray, *Risk* (Boston: Houghton Mifflin, 2002), 485; Gerd Gigerenzer, *Calculated Risks* (New York: Simon and Schuster, 2002), 310.

3. B. N. Waller, *Critical Thinking—Consider the Verdict,* 4th ed. (Upper Saddle River, N.J.: Prentice-Hall, 2001), 460.

4. J. R. Franchi, *Math Refresher for Scientists and Engineers*, 2nd ed. (New York: John Wiley & Sons, 2000), 308.

5. W. F. Bynum, E. J. Browne, and Roy Porter, eds., *Dictionary of the History of Science* (Princeton, N.J.: Princeton University Press, 1981), 494.

6. James Franklin, *The Science of Conjecture: Evidence and Probability Before Pascal* (Baltimore: Johns Hopkins University Press, 2001), 497.

7. A. H. Soukhanov, ed., *Encarta World English Dictionary* (New York: St. Martin's Press, 1999), 2078.

8. Jon Norby and S. H. James, eds., *Forensic Science: An Introduction to Scientific and Investigative Techniques* (Boca Raton, Fla.: CRC Press, 2003), 689.

9. Stuart Kauffman, *Investigations* (New York: Oxford University Press, 2000), 287.

10. William Neblett, *Sherlock's Logic* (New York: Dorset Press, 1985), 290.

11. T. C. Chamberlin, "The Method of Multiple Working Hypotheses," *Science* 15 (1890): 92–96; reprinted vol. 148 (1965): 754–59.

12. F. B. Jueneman, *Limits of Uncertainty* (Chicago: Industrial Research, 1975), 229.

13. J. A. Paulos, *Innumeracy: Mathematical Illiteracy and Its Consequences* (New York: Hill and Wang, 1988), 180.

14. Ibid.

15. James Burke, *Connections* (Boston: Little, Brown and Company, 1995), 304.

16. "Blackout of 2003," *Newsweek* Special Report (August 25, 2003): 68.

17. W. A. McGeveran, Jr., ed. dir., *The World Almanac and Book of Facts 2003* (New York: World Almanac Books, 2004), 1008.

18. Laura Berman, "What Makes Creative People Tick?" *Times Record,* Brunswick, ME (October 20, 1977).

19. A. G. Aleinikov, *Mega-Creativity* (Cincinnati, Ohio: Walking Stick Press, 2002), 228.

20. J. R. Taylor, *An Introduction to Error Analysis, the Study of Uncertainties in Physical Measurements* (Mill Valley, Calif.: University Science Books, Oxford University Press, 1982), 270.

21. S. F. Wagner, *Introduction to Statistics—HarperCollins College Outline* (New York: Harper Perennial, 1992), 369; Carol Ash, *The Probability Tutoring Book* (Piscataway, N.J.: IEEE Press, 1993), 470; Derek Rowntree, *Probability Without Tears: A Primer for Nonmathematicians* (New York: Barnes & Noble Books, 1994), 169; Lloyd Jaisingh, *Statistics for the Utterly Confused* (New York: McGraw-Hill, 2000), 318; David Salsburg, *The Lady Tasting Tea: How Statistics Revolutionized Science in the Twentieth Century* (New York: W. H. Freeman and Company, 2001), 340; Ian Hacking, *An Introduction to Probability and Inductive Logic* (New York: Cambridge University Press, 2001), 302.

22. Dan Cryan, Sharron Shatil, and Bill Mayblin, *Introducing Logic* (Lanham, Md.: Totem Books USA and National Book Network, 2001), 176.

23. Osterburg and Ward, *Criminal Investigation,* 34–35; H.C. Black, *Black's Law Dictionary,* 6th ed. (St. Paul, Minn.: West Publishing Company, 1997), 1657.

24. Gerald van Belle, *Statistical Rules of Thumb* (New York: John Wiley & Sons, 2002), 221.

25. Ibid.

26. Ibid.

27. James Trefil, *The Nature of Science* (Boston: Houghton Mifflin, 2003), 433.

28. Ibid.

29. Maggie Haberman and Jeane MacIntosh, *Held Captivity, the Kidnapping and Rescue of Elizabeth Smart* (New York: HarperCollins, 2003), 342.

30. T. S. Kuhn, *The Structure of Scientific Revolutions,* 2nd ed. (Chicago: University of Chicago Press, 1970), 210; R. D. Tweney, M. E. Doherty, and C. R. Mynatt, *On Scientific Thinking* (New York: Columbia University Press, 1981), 459; Karl Popper, *The Logic of Scientific Discovery* (New York: Routledge Classics, 2003), 513.

31. Joao Magueijo, *Faster Than the Speed of Light: The Story of a Scientific Speculation* (New York: Perseus Publishing, 2003), 279; Tim Folger, "At the Speed of Light," *Discover* 24, no. 4 (April 2003):

34–41; Robert Kunzig, "Taking a Shot at Einstein," *U.S. News & World Report* (May 26, 2003): 48–50.

32. C. G. DePree and Alan Axelrod, eds., *Van Nostrand's Concise Encyclopedia of Science* (Hoboken, N.J.: John Wiley & Sons, 2003), 821; Stephen Hawking, *A Brief History of Time* (New York: Bantam Books), 212; J. P. McEvoy and Oscar Zarate, *Introducing Quantum Theory* (Lanham, Md.: Totem Books and National Book Network, 1996), 176.

33. Ziauddin Sadar and Iwona Abrams, *Introducing Chaos* (Lanham, Md.: Totem Books USA and National Book Network, 1999), 176.

34. Philippe de Broca and Claude Chabrol movie directors, 1962.

35. B. B. Mandelbrot, *The Fractal Geometry of Nature* (New York: W. H. Freeman and Company, 1977), 468.

36. R. D. Hof, "The Quest for the Next Big Thing," *Business Week* (August 18–25, 2003): 91–94.

37. Ibid.

38. J. A. Paulos, *A Mathematician Reads the Newspaper* (New York: Random House, 1995), 212; J. A. Paulos, *Once Upon a Number* (New York: Basic Books and the Perseus Books Group, 1998), 214.

39. In order to avoid a significant amount of redundancy, from this point forward in this chapter I will not discuss each aspect of any particular investigation type in complete detail. If interested in a refresher, the reader is encouraged to return to Chapters 1 and 2. For ease of reading, I will instead hit the highpoints that differentiate one type of workplace investigation from another. I will also offer comments and suggestions to provide additional insight and assistance. However, my brevity should not distract the reader and cause him or her to forgo the now familiar fundamentals of the process. As I have mentioned so frequently throughout this book, the project manager and his or her team should incrementally unfold a strategy that is structured and rational during every investigation they undertake. That carefully orchestrated progression defines the *process of investigation.*

40. Association of Certified Fraud Examiners, *Report to the Nation, Occupational Fraud and Abuse* (1995).

41. Association of Certified Fraud Examiners, *Report to the Nation, Occupational Fraud and Abuse* (2002).

42. E. F. Ferraro, *Undercover Investigations in the Workplace*, 1st ed. (Woburn, Mass.: Butterworth-Heinemann, 2000), 105.

43. Ibid.

44. Joseph T. Wells, *Occupational Fraud and Abuse* (Austin, Tex.: Obsidian Publishing, 1997), 4.

45. M. W. Browne, "Following Benford's Rule, Or Looking Out for No. 1," *New York Times*, August 1998.

46. Robert Matthews, "The Power of One," *New Scientist* (July 10, 1999): 26–30.

47. Browne, "Following Benford's Rule."

48. Unapproved invoices that have been submitted for payment in and of themselves are not indicators of fraud. However, when the practice is intentional, it provides the perpetrator plausible denial if ever questioned.

49. E. F. Ferraro, *The Process of Investigation* (Golden, Colo.: Business Controls, 2000).

50. U.S. Equal Employment Opportunity Commission Web site, http://www.eeoc.gov/stats/charges.html (2003).

51. *The National Employer* (San Francisco: Littler Mendelson, P.C., 2002), 148.

52. Ibid.

53. John J. Fay, *Encyclopedia of Security Management: Techniques and Technology* (Woburn, Mass.: Butterworth-Heinemann, 1993), 736.

54. Ibid.

55. Ibid., p. 153.

56. Ibid.

57. Ibid, p. 156.

58. Ferraro, *The Process of Investigation*.

59. Ibid.

60. Ibid.

61. An interview, in this context, is asking questions that go beyond the scope of verifying factual information (for example, dates, degrees) and call for opinion (for example, performance or character). These include, but are not limited to, contacts made with past employers, educational institutions, neighbors, friends, references, or associates of the consumer.

62. It must be clearly and accurately disclosed that an investigative consumer report includes information as to character, general reputation, personal characteristics, and mode of living, whichever are applicable.

63. Interestingly, according to the law, employers may not use bankruptcy information when making an employment decision.

64. Ibid.

65. Ferraro, *Undercover Investigations in the Workplace*, 18.

66. James Cawood, *A Plan for Threat Management* (Santa Monica, Calif.: Protection of Assets Manual, 1994).

67. Ferraro, *Undercover Investigations in the Workplace*, 19.

68. Ibid.
69. Peter F. Drucker, *Management, Tasks-Responsibilities-Practices* (New York: Harper & Row, 1974), 369.

Chapter 7

Improving Results

A. Investment and Cost Management

A successful workplace investigation requires the investment of time, money, and patience. In addition to all of the other prerequisites, these three elements must be available in ample quantities if the investigation is to be a success. The size, scope, and nature of the problem will determine the amount the employer must invest. There is no magic formula. One thing is certain: the bigger the problem, the bigger the investment. However, employers can manage their investment in many ways. The experienced employer knows that the problem that initially precipitated the investigation is often not the only one. Frequently, the initial problem is only the tip of the iceberg. Beneath the surface may loom other issues and problems that may be significantly more serious. The best example is vandalism.

Over the years I have been asked to conduct hundreds of investigations into apparent vandalism in the workplace. Frequently targeted were the vehicles and property of employees. For years I handled these matters as routine investigations. And while I contemplated motive to help me identify a suspect pool, I rarely thought beyond it. Today, I know better. I know now that the vandalism of personal property does not occur in a vacuum. In fact, vandalism is a critical component of a far greater problem—potential workplace violence. Workplace violence erupts after a progression of ever-increasing inappropriate behaviors is left unmanaged. Research and experience show that the aggressor is typically a self-proclaimed victim who over time, morphs into an avenger. One of the less recognized behaviors during the journey is often vandalism. Vandalism is an expression of anger—anger resulting from frustration. Instead of focusing on the source of that frustration, for example, a supervisor, the aggressor attacks the property of the supervisor. The property is seen as an extension of the individual. Unable to yet muster the courage or determination to inflict bodily harm, the aggressor substitutes the property for the person. Having an acute appreciation for this phenomenon, today I approach every instance of workplace vandalism much as I would if it were workplace violence.

Anyone who has ever conducted a sexual harassment or discrimination investigation also knows that the initial allegations are often also just the tip of the iceberg. Rarely do complainants of any type tell the whole story when they initially come forward. Some do this unintentionally; others do it purposefully. Some victims will tell their employer only that which they think they need to know in order for them to stop the undesired behavior. This is typical in domestic violence cases that spill into the workplace. In other instances, the victim is afraid or untrusting. In yet other instances, the victim may derive some psychological or personal benefit by dribbling out information and evidence. Regardless, my point is simple; more often than not, workplace investigations are ultimately more complex than they first appear. The employer's investment is tied directly to that complexity.

1. Establish Milestones and a Budget

Establishing and using milestones and budgets is a fundamental business practice, yet few fact-finders do it. Experienced managers and executives will sometimes insist on it. A contract investigator may even suggest it. Unfortunately, in practice, few ever actually do it. Establishing milestones and managing a budget take time. They tend to be tedious and often appear unnecessary. Decision makers want to see people on the ground, they want to see action, and they want to see results. As such, this essential aspect of planning is ignored. Instead of taking a little time to chart one's course, almost everybody wants to get started.

Do yourself a favor and stop. Take the time to commit some milestones to paper. Even if they are only preliminary, take the time to do it. Put some numbers to them and determine the amount of time and money it will take to achieve your goals. The exercise will surprise you in several interesting ways. First, you will realize that you have actually crafted a *project plan*. The project plan serves as a blueprint from which you will work your investigation. If done properly, you will have identified the incremental steps that when sequentially executed, will produce a completed investigation. The second thing that will become apparent will be any actions or steps originally overlooked. It will be hard to complete the exercise without exposing gaps in your process. Collectively your project plan, milestones, and budget provide the springboard from which your investigation takes life. The time, money, and resources to be allocated to it are now justifiable. The process enables everyone involved to know what is to be expected and the investment anticipated.

The process is no different if an external resource is used. Similarly, the vendor should propose a project plan with corresponding milestones and a budget. A vendor that does not is either naive or very unsophisticated. The practice leads to misunderstandings and unmet expectations. It frequently leads to wasted time and money. The employer-client generally ends up paying more and receiving less. If you have read the preceding chapters you will easily appreciate this. If you have, you know it will be nearly impossible to achieve one's objectives without stating them in advance. Without planning, no project plan is possible, no budgets can be established, nor is it likely any goals will be attained. It is a recipe for disaster.

Tip: Do not engage vendors who offer investigative services if they do not first offer a project plan, articulate milestones, and propose a budget. To accept anything less is reckless and may be fiscally irresponsible.

---

2. Fees for Professional Investigative Services

Professional investigation firms charge fees for their services. In most instances those fees are charged on an hourly basis. There are some exceptions and on occasion my firm has provided services on a flat-rate basis. The best examples include routine employment background investigations, some forms of consulting, and employee training. By and large, however, most reputable firms that propose to perform an investigation of any complexity charge by the hour. Their rates vary but generally the fee corresponds to the experience level of the individual or class of individual who provides the service. For example, an organization can expect to pay more for an executive-level investigator than for a field investigator. The vendor should have established rates and be willing to provide them in advance of accepting the assignment. The hours necessary to reasonably complete the proposed task(s) multiplied by his or her hourly billing rate becomes the budget for that particular individual. That amount combined with the estimated fees for the other members of the investigative team, plus expenses becomes the project's budget. The vendor's proposal (see Chapter 4, Section B) should clearly articulate these calculations and provide the justification for them. High billing rates alone should not disqualify a vendor. Remember, value is not based on fees; rather, it should be based upon return on investment (ROI). Think of it in terms of efficiencies. In the event of a medical emergency one can either walk to the hospital or ride in an ambulance. The ambulance is clearly more expensive, but it is far more efficient. The ROI may be the difference between life and death. In some circumstances, workplace investigations are no different. If the vendor has not adequately demonstrated how the proposed solution will yield a justifiable ROI, consider another mode of transportation.

Although overcharging is common, undercharging is far more typical. But because it is counterintuitive, this apparent blessing is destructive. Undercharging destabilizes the market. It exerts downward pressures on the fees good vendors are able to charge. It unfairly erodes their profits and inflicts pointless financial pain. It causes weak vendors to take unnecessary risks and cut corners. It diminishes every vendor's ability to pay his or her investigators adequately and provide proper benefits. Over time, the net effect is a loss for the consumer. Businesses, even good businesses, cannot continue to provide products and services for which they cannot make a profit. Undercharging creates a market filled with inexperienced cutthroats chasing eroding margins, while providing the consumer products and services of ever declining quality and value. Unfortunately, the private investigation industry is no exception. Many an aspiring entrepreneur has shared with me his secret marketing plan of low-balling the competition, rapidly capturing market share, and then quickly raising his fees. In no time these hustlers exhaust their seed capital, struggle for a while, and then go under, only to be replaced by another entrepreneur with the same secret plan. It is classic and terribly frustrating. As one who runs a modest consulting and investigation firm, I wish it would stop. The practice pushes experienced firms out of business and spawns new ones, which lack the experience and resources to do the job properly. Become a discriminating buyer. Do not purchase the services of a low-baller. Remember, you usually get what you pay for.

B. Civil Recovery and Restitution

I have addressed the value of civil recovery and restitution extensively in previous chapters. When used properly, these powerful tools can vastly increase the ROI of a project. Not only can losses often be recovered, but frequently so can the cost of the investigation. By carefully engineering one's investigation, losses as a well as the employer's total investment can be recovered. Beyond the fidelity insurance, which covers internal losses due to employee theft and dishonesty, the fact-finding team should look for ways to return value to the organization. Traditionally this can be accomplished by:

- Stopping the losses
- Altering procedures and processes to improve efficiency and reduce losses or waste
- Increasing productivity and reducing headcount
- Obtaining concessions and adjustments from vendors or customers

Rarely do businesses go after their employees or customers. This is unfortunate. Often by simply demanding restitution, an employer can make a substantial recovery. Without using coercion or threatening litigation, employers can frequently convince an offender to come to the table and negotiate. At this stage of the investigation any recovery falls to the bottom line. So even if the amount is small, the real financial impact is significant. If, for example, earnings before interest, taxes, depreciation, and amortization (EBITDA) is 10 percent, the organization would have to generate $10 for every $1 recovered in order to throw the same profits to the bottom line. Accordingly, a $1,000 recovery is the equivalent of $10,000 in new sales, *without producing a single thing.* If EBITDA is a more realistic 3 percent, a $5,000 recovery becomes the equivalent of $150,000 in new sales.

In fraud cases recovery or restitution is particularly easy. In most instances the fraudsters are sophisticated enough not to have spent all of their ill-gotten gains. Frequently, the fraudsters will invest or keep some of their proceeds liquid. It is perfectly acceptable to negotiate a repayment schedule with these individuals. First, ask that the liquid assets be remanded and then make arrangements to liquidate those that remain (for example, the house, condo, or vehicles). Use the initial proceeds to further finance your investigation and recovery efforts. In complicated matters involving multiple wrong-doers, getting someone to pony-up early can quickly make the project self-funding. Professional investigators that specialize in judgment recovery do this all the time. They quickly determine which defendant has the least protected assets, and then they quickly go after the lowest hanging fruit.

Even small, incremental recoveries can actually have a significant impact on the bottom line. For example, accepting the repayment of $100,000 at 7 percent interest over a 12-year period translates to a $200,000 recovery. This item can be reflected on the organization's balance sheet and shown as an asset. Although the losses have already been absorbed on the profit and loss (P&L) statement, the $100,000 note has become a tangible asset that replenishes the asset side of the balance sheet and translates into an increase in equity.

Obtaining concessions and adjustments from vendors and customers is often overlooked as well. Many victims do not want to upset their relationship with those with whom they do business. However, a reluctance to take some risk can be very expensive.

Years ago during the course of a product diversion investigation, we learned that the principal in the scheme was an employee of a vendor, the provider of major overnight shipping and delivery services. My client did sufficient business with this vendor that it justified four full-time vendor employees at his facility. Once the diversion scheme was unraveled we convinced our client to allow us to negotiate some relief from the vendor. Quickly recognizing that without its employee's involvement, my client's losses would not have been possible, the vendor agreed to adjust its last invoice by more than $150,000. Additionally, it agreed to lower its shipping rates several points for the remainder of the existing contract. Totaled, these adjustments and concessions were the equivalent of the loss plus the cost of our investigation. My client and its vendor preserved an important relationship simply through fair and honest negotiations. In most instances when a third party is involved, arrangements of this sort are possible. Be open to them and be creative. As the old saying goes—*you won't get it unless you ask for it.*

One aspect I have not addressed previously is criminal recovery and restitution. The criminal courts provide for victim restitution in a number of instances. Relative to property crimes, restitution is frequently ordered as an attempt to make the victim whole. In theory this is commendable and obviously appropriate. However, in reality it is ineffectual and almost cruel. According to an independent study on the state of the criminal justice system in California in 2004, less than 3 percent of those ordered to pay restitution to their victims ever do.[1] In spite of the threat of being jailed, 97% of those ordered to pay restitution never pay a dime! The system is a joke. Employers that look to the courts as an easy way to recover losses are sure to be severely disappointed. In most instances, it is a waste of time and resources.

Trap: Do not look to the criminal courts to recover from those who steal or commit fraud. Those who do are ensured disappointment. Do not make the criminal court system a part of your recovery strategy.

C. Prosecution

The prosecution of wrong-doers is a fundamental component of our criminal justice system. In cases of criminal misconduct, the accused, when found guilty, is subject to criminal sanctions. Although this system is sound in many regards, from the standpoint of punishing wrong-doers in the wake of a workplace investigation, it is significantly lacking. Typically it is unrealistic to expect the criminal courts to clean up an employer's mess. Although workplace investigations may, in fact, yield prosecutable cases, the decision to pursue them should be made for business reasons only.

The belief that criminal prosecution is an effective deterrent to workplace misconduct is largely false. Employees that intend to commit crimes against their employers already know they face criminal prosecution, yet they still do it. If the crime is premeditated, the perpetrator has already conducted a cost-benefit analysis. Those who go forward and commit the crime already know the possible consequences. The threat of prosecution is always present, yet they make the decision to go forward anyway. Some claim that actual prosecution validates this threat. In truth we really do not know. We do not have statistics on crimes that have not been committed. Intuitively, we suspect some crimes are deterred, but we really do not know. Admittedly, this analysis runs contrary to mainstream thinking, particularly in the criminal justice community, but because of the complexity and cost of criminal prosecution, I think it deserves further consideration.

First-time offenders also tend to get lesser punishments. Particularly in matters involving crimes against an employer, the offending employees are more often than not new to the criminal justice system. As first-time offenders they are frequently able to plead down charges and vacate others. The net is often a slap on the wrist in exchange for the promise to behave in the future. This can be frustrating. An employer who sets out to make an example for the rest of the workforce finds instead that the system achieves the opposite result. A punishment of six months' probation for stealing $50,000 may indicate to some employees that the potential gain is worth the risk. For others it may do nothing more than reinforce their cynicism and diminish their respect for the system.

Employee prosecution is also expensive and time consuming. Crafty defense attorneys will use criminal discovery to find weaknesses in the employer's investigation and decision-making processes. If those weaknesses are perceived as vulnerabilities, defense attorneys might decide to craft civil complaints against the employer. The employer then finds itself prosecuting a criminal case and defending a civil one. Such strategies work. The employer can easily be compelled to withdraw from the criminal case in exchange for settling the civil action. In the worse case scenario, the perpetrator escapes the criminal charges and collects damages from the employer. I know of one such case and the settlement was a cool $5 million. Not bad for breaking the law and selling illegal drugs at work. The only party who was punished and ultimately deterred was the employer.

Alternatively, what if the defendant-employee is found not guilty? The criminal justice system is imperfect. A technicality or defect can result in a not-guilty verdict or a mistrial. The impact on the employer can be devastating. Having cooperated with the police, permitting the employee to be arrested at work and dragged out in handcuffs exposes the employer to claims of false arrest, malicious prosecution, defamation, and intentional infliction of emotional distress. In this scenario the employer has no bargaining chips. Instead, it finds itself on the wrong end of a lawsuit with a criminal court that has found that the employee did not commit the very offense for which the employer had terminated him. These cases are costly and time consuming. They are most often resolved by settling. In the end, the offending employee gets his job back and a big fat check to boot.

The goal of employee prosecution is not a strategy. It may be a component of the overall process and even an investigative objective (though I disagree with this), but it should not be the focus around which an employer wraps its investigation. Employee prosecution is not an effective deterrent and should not be considered one.

D. Process Improvement and Analysis

1. The Importance of Measuring Results

The measuring of our investigative results is difficult and frequently impossible. Few fact-finders like to do it, even fewer attempt it. Typically at the completion of one's investigation, the last thing the fact-finder and his team want to do is spend more time critiquing their effort and measuring the return on that effort. Frequently the return cannot be immediately measured. In some instances, the result is more subjective than objective. In other situations, there is no perceived return by measuring the results or evaluating its value to the organization. However, in practice, all investigative efforts should always be measured. Without some form of measurement, analysis, or critical review of the investigative process, neither process improvement nor best practices development is possible. It seems strange to me that we apply these fundamental business practices to every other aspect of our operation and business, but rarely are they applied to the process of investigation.

Furthermore, if the individual responsible for the investigation doesn't measure the results, someone else almost always will. Be it one's immediate supervisor when conducting personnel performance reviews, the budget review committee when deciding the proper allocation of corporate resources, or the criminal justice system, someone will almost always measure the results of our investigative endeavors. It makes little sense that the professional fact-finder allows others to determine his value. To abrogate this important responsibility to others makes little professional sense. To obtain the most from your investigations, measure your results.

2. Collect Information

Workplace investigations are fluid and dynamic, and the fact-finder must be creative and resourceful. In the final analysis his effort will be judged. At the very least some form of cost-benefit analysis will take place. Whether the fact-finder, his investigative team, or his employer does it, some form of analysis will likely take place. Anticipating this, the experienced fact-finder begins his preparation from the moment the investigation is assigned to him. During the preparation and planning phase, the fact-finder identifies milestones and benchmarks by which he will measure his results. During the preparation of his proposal, he will have articulated a measurable ROI and justified his strategy. Like the other professionals in his organization, he has taken a business approach to solving his problem.

Process improvement begins with measuring. Keeping accurate records and measuring one's results is essential to any process improvement effort. Workplace investigations are no different. Depending upon one's volume of cases here are a few things that might be measured:

- Incident or investigation type
- Number of cases in each category
- Number of cases cleared in each category
- Incident location
- Amount of loss
- Number of employees and nonemployees involved
- Man-hours invested to resolve each case
- Total investment per case
- Number of successful prosecutions
- Recoveries made per case
- ROI per case

3. Analyze the Information

With sufficient data, we are quickly able to conduct a trend analysis. Not only are we able to see trends relative to the type and volume of our cases, we are granted insight into the real damage being done to the organization. In determining an ROI, we can determine which type of matters cost the organization the most and which ones deserve more or less resources. The data will also provide insight to where process improvement is possible. If, for example, the data reveal a prevalence of inventory problems, more attention can be focused on that problem. If property crimes are prevalent, yet recoveries are low, new emphasis can be directed to these matters. Over time, the fact-finder and his organization can drill into the data and determine the root causes of problems and engineer reliable solutions. With confidence, resources can be allocated where they will produce the most benefit. Remarkably, few organizations do this with any consistency.

In order to facilitate process improvement, the fact-finder also needs tools. Using a database to collect and manage the data is essential. Among all the tools available, some of the most cost effective and easiest to use are those commercially available. Convercent, a firm with which I have affiliation, offers such products. Convercent designs and builds HRIM (human resources information management) and asset management tools, which it provides via the Internet. As an ASP (application service provider), Convercent provides a host of risk management tools that allow organizations and their designated administrators to document, track, and investigate workplace incidents of all varieties. Because its products are Web based, a user with Internet access can document and track incidents, assign investigators, conduct statistical analysis, and manage a huge case load from any place, any time. Its CIMS (comprehensive incident management system) product allows a designated report recipient to receive new incident reports instantaneously and manage them electronically. Reports can be routed to investigators or others in the organization for attention and handling. Analytical features allow the generation of statistical reports by type, location, or any number of user-identified variables. For those without Internet access, the system can be accessed via the telephone. Available 24/7 users can interface with their records and manage their information and data. For just pennies a day, organizations can track workplace incidents and issues and have the insight to manage them as never before. For more information about this power resource visit www.Convercent.com.

4. Put the Information to Use

Another way to put the information to use is *flow-charting*. Flow-charting is a process-improvement strategy widely used in business. As the name suggests, it charts a process from a flow standpoint. Similar to an electrical wire diagram, a flow chart outlines a process in the form of a schematic.

The chart guides the user through a process in a step-by-step fashion and illustrates pathways through which certain outcomes are possible. Corcoran and Cawood do this spectacularly in their work, *Violence Assessment and Intervention: The Practitioner's Handbook.*[2] For the purpose of illustrating the proper handling of the incident assessment and resolution process, they provide readers a detailed incident flow chart. Using the tool, threat managers can easily path their way to one of several predetermined outcomes. Because flow charts can be works-in-progress, they are uniquely suited for dynamic problem management, resolution, and ultimately process improvement. Think of them as roadmaps. Using a map one can predetermine a route to almost any destination. If one route proves too difficult or time consuming, the user can select another route. Unlike a map, however, a flow chart can be modified. New pathways can be created to any destination. The user is not limited to those offered by a static map.

As a starting point, flow chart some of your basic investigative and fact-finding processes. Keep each chart to one page. Start with the receipt of the report and work your way toward resolution. Use *yes* or *no* options as switches at junctures where choices can be made. Use a charting software application such as Microsoft Visio® to make the task easier. After use of the chart, modify it where improvement would have been possible. Over time you will have created a collection of flow charts any capable fact-finder in your organization can use. The quality of your investigations and others in your organization will improve. Moreover, you will have memorialized processes, which will enable the production of predictable results time and again. You will have brought the spirit of process improvement to every investigation you and your organization conduct.

E. Alternatives to Investigation

No analysis of process improvement is complete without asking the basic question, is the investigation under consideration indeed necessary? Remarkably, few fact-finders ponder this question. Professional fact-finders by their very nature perceive the value they offer by engineering investigative solutions to most problems they are tasked to solve. This is unfortunate and frequently unnecessary. By failing to ask this basic question, the fact-finder is easily lured into a possibly expensive no-win situation. Undertaking an investigation when one is not necessary is wasteful and risky. It consumes unnecessary resources and exposes the organization to possible liability. It wastes time and delays an otherwise quick solution. It also does very little for the reputation of the fact-finder.

Before undertaking any investigation, the fact-finder must ask—*is the investigation necessary and is there a suitable alternative?* At first blush, alternatives may appear scarce. However, upon closer analysis and some basic preinvestigation, investigation alternatives invariably reveal themselves. These alternatives may not be suitable, some may be reckless, and others may be simply irresponsible. Regardless, the fact-finder owes it to himself and his customer to ponder them. Here are a few of the more common alternatives I have encountered:

- Eliminate the suspects through reassignment or termination.
- Eliminate the temptation by separating duties or physically access.
- Reduce the possibility of reoccurrence by changing processes.
- Reduce the exposure by improving methods of early problem detection.
- Increase physical security.
- Increase electronic security.
- Increase employee awareness.
- Do nothing and rely on the intervention of some higher power.

Depending upon the circumstances each of these may have arguable merit. Combined in some fashion they may, in fact, constitute a viable alternative to undertaking an investigation. The fact pattern of the given circumstances, the employer's objectives, its past practices and policies, and the law will likely influence which action is appropriate. The fact-finder must not avoid these alternatives. She should honestly consider them and offer them (if appropriate) to her decision makers. In some instances a simple cost-benefit analysis will be sufficient. If the estimated cost to investigate a cash shortage of $500 is $5,000, the decision to pursue an alternative to investigation should be easy. Alternatively, if the allegation is widespread sexual harassment, the decision not to investigate may even be unlawful.

The reader will note that the common theme among the aforementioned alternatives is prevention and early detection. This is not only because it is so intuitively obvious, but also because there are no other alternatives. Research shows that the incidence and magnitude of workplace conduct is a function of three fundamental elements:

- The quality of people the organization hires;
- The environment in which those people are placed;
- The quality of supervision managing that environment and those people.

When problems at work are examined closer, it is easy to see what is at their core. Quickly, we see people who should have never been hired. We see those same individuals placed in environments with inadequate controls, overseen by untrained or incompetent supervisors. If it is the desire of management to control its workplace and prevent employee crime and misconduct, it should not procure more locks, gates, and guards. It should look introspectively at the core of the organization, its people, and its values. It has been my experience, and I suspect yours as well, that most of the offenders we have investigated had no business enjoying the jobs they did and should have never been hired in the first place. Stopping the problem at the door makes sense. Continuing to contaminate one's workforce with individuals who intend to hurt the company is the definition of irresponsibility. For just a moment consider the last internal investigation you conducted. If the perpetrator had in fact not been an employee, would the crime have ever been committed? Would your investigation have been necessary? It is the responsibility of every employer to foster a safe and productive workplace. Workplace investigations are essential tools that help make that possible.

Notes

1. *Reforming California's Youth and Adult Correction System*, Corrections Independent Review Panel, The State of California, www.report.cpr.ca.gov/corr/ (June 30, 2004).
2. M. H. Corcoran and J. S. Cawood, *Violence Assessment and Intervention: The Practitioner's Guide*, 1st ed. (Boca Raton, Fla.: CRC Press, 2003), 7.

Appendix A

Glossary of Common Investigative Terms and Terminology

This glossary is not intended to be exhaustive but instead offers the reader exposure to some of the more common investigative words and terms. Please also note that while many of these items have legal definitions, I have provided the more common lay definition as used in the industry.

Accomplice Criminal cohort or conspirator. One who aids and abets others in the commission of a crime or offense.

Action A lawsuit brought in court.

Actionable A matter that may be subject to a legal action or intervention.

Addendum A statement prepared by an interviewer on behalf of himself, not the interviewee. In it, the interviewer should include information not contained in the interviewee's statement (if one has been provided) or elsewhere during the investigative process.

Adjudicate To legally resolve and bring to formal closure.

Administrative interview Interview conducted for the purpose of gathering information, versus *investigatory interview,* which is conducted for the purpose of obtaining *admissions.*

Admissibility The legal authority permitting the entry of evidence into a legal proceeding.

Admissible Evidence that may be formally considered in a legal proceeding.

Admission The simple admission to the commission of an offense, work rule or policy violation, or violation of the law. Differs from a confession in that it may or may not contain all of the elements of the offense or crime in question. Not to be confused with *confession.* A properly obtained admission is a valuable piece of evidence in most workplace and private sector investigations.

Affirm To uphold or establish.

Answer Respond to a formal allegation, normally in writing.

Appeal An application to a higher court to correct or modify a judgment rendered by a lower court.

Arbitration An informal means of alternative dispute resolution without the use of a judge or jury. An arbitrator presides over the proceedings and at its conclusion renders a decision in favor of one party or the other.

Arrest The taking of a person into custody in a manner provided by law for the purpose of detention in order to answer a criminal charge or civil demand.

At-will employment A policy (public or private) that allows an employer to terminate one's employment for any lawful reason or no reason at all. Such policies also permit the employee to quit at will.

Benford's Law A mathematical principle that affords the ability to predict the frequency of digits appearing in numbers of a given data set. Benford's Law (or Benford's Rule) says there are more small things in the universe than there are big things.

Beyond a reasonable doubt The standard of proof necessary to obtain a conviction in a criminal proceeding.

Case file The tool used by fact-finders to organize and maintain their records, documents, and reports during an investigation.

Chain of custody A record detailing those who handled or possessed a piece of evidence. Synonymous with chain of evidence.

Chain of evidence See Chain of custody.

CI See Concerned individual.

Circumstantial evidence Indirect evidence which in and of itself does not prove a material fact. Often gathered and used cumulatively to prove a fact.

Claims made insurance Insurance coverage which is only available during the period in which the coverage is in force.

Coercion To compel by force or deception.

Cold hire A means used to place undercover investigators on the job without any outside influence or assistance.

Commercial fraud Any type of fraud committed against a business or organization.

Compensatory damages Damages awarded to a plaintiff that are intended to compensate for a loss or other hardship.

Concerned individual A person who voluntarily comes forward and provides information not otherwise available to the recipient of that information. Often called an *informant* in the public sector. Referred to as *CI* in the trade.

Confession A comprehensive admission to the commission of an offense or violation of the law that contains all of the elements of the offense or crime in question. Not to be confused with *admission*.

Controlled hire A means used to place undercover investigators on the job using outside influence or assistance.

Corporate investigations Investigations performed at the direction of the organization, for the organization. Usually involve the investigation of crimes and offenses committed against the organization. Differs from workplace investigations in that the subject of the investigation may not be an employee or former employee of the organization.

Covert surveillance Surveillance that is intentionally undetected.

Credibility The reliability or trustworthiness of an individual.

Custodian of record The person or entity responsible for record retention and preservation.

DEA Drug Enforcement Administration.

Defendant The accused. The party whom the plaintiff opposes.

Direct evidence Evidence that proves a material fact.

Discovery The legal process of obtaining information or evidence from a legal opponent.

Disparate treatment Unfair or unequal treatment of an individual.

Diversion The crime of theft that is committed at the source so that the finished goods never reach their intended destination or customer.

Double-hearsay evidence Testimony from a person who has third-hand knowledge.

Due process The collection of rights principally arising from the Bill of Rights, which provides criminal suspects protections against abuses by the government.

Electronic surveillance Any form of surveillance which uses electronic technology and does not require constant human monitoring.

Embezzlement The unlawful appropriation of property or assets of another with which one has been entrusted.

Entrapment Actions that might induce an otherwise honest citizen to commit a crime that without the inducement he would not have committed. Entrapment is a criminal defense and is not crime. In order to use entrapment as a defense, the accused must first admit he committed the offense.

Evidence Any type of proof that when presented, is materially capable of proving or disproving a contention or fact. In order to be used or admissible, the evidence must be material to the matter in question.

Fact pattern The collection of known facts associated with or directly related to the matter in question.

Fact-finder A person engaged in the systematic collection, analysis, and preservation of information or facts related to the matter in question. The fact-finder is often a member of an investigative team working under the direction of a project manager.

False imprisonment The criminal or civil offense of improper arrest or detainment without confinement of a person by force, intimidation, or coercion without proper warrant or authority for that purpose.

FBI Federal Bureau of Investigation.

Fidelity insurance Commercial insurance coverage against employee theft and dishonesty.

Flip The act of turning a suspected or known offender into a witness for the prosecution. May be used in a civil context as well.

Fraud Theft by deceit and deception.

Good faith investigation A fair and impartial investigation conducted by an employer. When used to make a *reasonable conclusion,* it becomes the standard of proof needed to justify employee discipline.

Hearsay evidence Testimony from a person who has second-hand knowledge.

Immunity Protection against prosecution. Typically granted in order to obtain some form of cooperation.

Impeach To render one's testimony useless or diminish one's credibility.

Inadmissible Evidence which cannot be formally considered in a legal proceeding.

Intent A state of mind, which, if proven, demonstrates the intention to commit a criminal act.

Interrogation A highly structured and formal interview intended to yield a confession.

Interrogator One who conducts interrogations.

Interview A conversational exchange for the purpose of collecting information.

Interviewer One who conducts interviews.

Investigative interview A highly structured interview intended to obtain an admission.

Investigative proposal A written document which describes an investigative plan.

IT Information technology. Typically used to describe a functional responsibility or a management position.

Judgment A legal finding of responsibility.

Jurisdiction An area or subject over which a party has authority.

Kick-back Money or something of value improperly provided to obtain something else of value.

Lapping scheme A common fraud scheme in which the perpetrator misapplies receivables to cover previously stolen assets.

Malfeasance Intentional conduct or behavior contrary to the interests of others. Employee theft or substance abuse would be considered employee malfeasance.

Miranda rights and warning Legal rights imparted on those taken into custody when suspected of having committed a crime.

Motive The reason for having committed a crime or offense.

Narc A narcotics detective. Also used as a pejorative to describe those who inform on others.

Occurrence Insurance Insurance coverage which is available regardless of when the claim is made. It is the preferred form of coverage.

Operative An undercover investigator.

Physical surveillance Any form of surveillance that uses people. May be augmented with technology but requires constant human monitoring.

Plaintiff The party which brings a legal action.

Privacy, the right to privacy The expectation of freedom from the unwanted intrusion of others into one's home, papers, or affairs.

Private investigations Investigations performed in the private sector typically for private citizens involving nonworkplace issues.

Private sector The realm under the management, supervision, and authority of nongovernment entities. May include public and privately owned companies, nonprofit organizations, and other private institutions. Those suspected of a workplace offense may be the subject of a *private sector* investigation conducted by their employer or agents, and if determined responsible, punished by their employer.

Privilege A legal protection that permits the lawful withholding of information or evidence from an opponent during the course of litigation. May be used in both criminal and civil cases.

Process of investigation A highly structured and sometimes scientific approach to investigation. Sufficiently structured to provide uniformity and consistency, yet fluid and flexible enough to accommodate most any situation or fact pattern.

Project manager The functional manager leading or directing the investigative process and the investigative team. The project manager is typically the point of contact through whom those outside the investigative team communicate.

Public policy Unwritten expectations relative to one's behavior and conduct.

Public sector The realm under the management, supervision, and authority of the government. Those in public law enforcement are employed in the public sector. Those charged with committing a crime or accused of violating the law may be subject to the rule of law and tried in the *public sector.*

Punitive damages Damages awarded which are intended to punish the defendant and serve as a deterrent to prevent others from engaging in similar behavior.

Restitution The act of making another party whole. Most often, restitution involves the payment of money.

Return on investment The return enjoyed on any particular investment. The return may be monetary or otherwise.

ROI See Return on investment.

Special investigations A generic term used to describe any nonroutine workplace investigation. The investigation of a sexual harassment allegation might be considered a special investigation, whereas a routine employment background investigation would not.

Spoliation Intentional destruction of evidence.

Standard of proof The quality and quantity of proof necessary to make a lawful finding of responsibility.

Subject The individual who is the subject of the investigation or matter in question. Not to be confused with *suspect* as used in the public sector. The subject may or may not be a suspect.

Subrogation The pursuit of another party one deems ultimately responsible.

Surveillance The observing or monitoring of people, places, or things.

Tailgate To follow another person into an area from which one is otherwise precluded from entering.

Trier-of-fact Any person or body charged with the duty of adjudication.

UC See Undercover investigation.

Undercover investigation A method of investigation that entails the surreptitious placement of an investigator into an unsuspecting workforce for the purpose of information gathering. These are typically complicated investigations and should only be attempted after other means of information gathering have been ruled out. Referred to as *UC* in the trade.

Verification and analysis That phase of investigation during which the fact-finder interviews those he thinks are most involved in the matter in question.

Workplace investigations Any investigation taking place in or involving the workplace. May be conducted by those in either the private or public sector. Typically involving the investigation of employee misconduct, workplace policy violations, or work rule violations. The matter under investigation may or may not be a violation of the law. Not to be confused with *private investigations*.

Appendix B

Sample Investigative Report

XYZ COMPANY
777 Straight Arrow Way
Denver, CO 81234
303-555-3333
Re: Anonymous Industries
123 Anywhere Blvd.
Anytown, CA 91234

Executive Summary

On December 15, 2003, Mr. John Smith of XYZ Company ("XYZ"), Denver, Colorado, contacted *Business Controls, Inc.,* and requested investigative and consultative assistance in a matter involving alleged employee and vendor misconduct at the newly opened box plant in Anytown, California. According to Mr. Smith, several employees at the Anytown facility had alleged the plant manager and his plant superintendent had knowingly authorized contractor overcharging and were engaged in other inappropriate activities, much to the determent of the organization. Mr. Smith also stated that independent financial analysis of the box plant's start-up costs and other indicators (see Exhibit A) suggested something was terribly wrong.

The resultant investigation involved on-site information gathering, employee and contractor interviews, and the detailed analysis of hundreds of records, invoices, purchase orders, and requisitions. During the process, the plant manager, Mr. Paul Jones, admitted he had accepted personal services from a painting contractor for which he did not pay and authorized the overpayment of several hundred thousand dollars in invoices. His superintendent, Mr. Robert Miller, admitted to having accepted $2,200 in cash from one contractor (Mr. William Redkin of Handy Services), who himself admitted paying it. Additionally, two other contractors admitted they had overcharged for their services to varying degrees or failed to maintain adequate records to justify their invoices.

The total economic impact and scope of the fiscal misconduct uncovered at the Anytown facility has been impossible to determine. The lack of proper record-keeping, internal process failures, and managerial negligence at the location has frustrated any effort to accurately quantify the damage. However, demonstrably the loss exceeds $500,000.

Investigative Detail

December 18, 2003, Tuesday

Interview of Mr. Roger Gossard

Mr. Gossard stated:

- He has been an employee of XYZ since April 2001 and is currently the plant's maintenance supervisor.
- He had had concerns regarding the ethical relationship of Mr. Robert Miller (plant superintendent) and several contractors nearly from the day he started.
- Chip Miller, the son of Mr. Robert Miller, is an employee of contractor American Electric and has worked in the plant for as long as he can remember.
- Chip Miller appears to do little work at the plant and is most often seen riding a golf cart with his father.

- Chip Miller always immediately leaves the facility anytime corporate visitors are in the plant, so as to not be seen.
- It is alleged by many in the plant that Chip Miller is paid many overtime hours for work he does not perform.
- He had never seen or approved any American Electric invoices.
- He has no idea what "third party" charges are as they appear on the American Electric invoices shown to him.
- Mr. Robert Miller oversees all work performed by American Electric, much of which appears incomplete or not done as needed.
- Mr. Robert Miller possibly has an unethical relationship with American Electric, although he has no proof.
- Alan Rivers of Red Rock Welding ("Red Rock"), a contractor, stated to him that the reason Red Rock's invoices are so large is because that is the way Mr. Paul Jones (plant manager) and Mr. Robert Miller wanted them.[1]
- Both Mr. Jones and Mr. Robert Miller have gone on all-day fishing trips paid for by Red Rock.
- CMB (a contractor that provides equipment and tools) refuses to accept or track purchase orders (PO) for the equipment and tools they sell.
- CMB submitted invoices for band saws, which were never delivered. Upon questioning, CMB canceled the invoice.
- Mr. Robert Miller oversees all work performed by contractor, Handy Services, much of which appears incomplete or not done at all.
- Mr. Robert Miller possibly has an unethical relationship with the owner of Handy Services, William Redkin, although he has no proof.
- William Redkin employs children who are often seen working in the plant.
- Ms. Jane Bond's (office manager) son-in-law (name unknown) was hired by Ms. Bond at a wage that exceeded his skills and experience.
- William Redkin often paints things three or four times.
- He has never seen so many things repainted so many times as William Redkin paints.
- He is currently seeking employment elsewhere.

Interview of Ms. Betty Johnson

Ms. Johnson stated:

- She has been an employee of XYZ since July 2001 and is currently the maintenance clerk.

- She knew Ms. Bond from her previous place of employment, Collins Clothing, and Ms. Bond was known as a liar there, just as she is known to be one at XYZ.
- Ms. Bond hired her son-in-law (name unknown) at a wage that exceeded his skills and experience.
- She was resentful that Ms. Bond rated her performance substandard and intended to appeal it.
- She believes Ms. Bond is out to get her, but that she (Ms. Johnson) will not go down without a fight.
- Former employee Jennifer Roberts should be interviewed because she worked in shipping and receiving and is likely aware of theft by employees.
- She has seen spools of new wire in the bed of Mr. Robert Miller's pickup truck and suspects it was stolen from the plant.
- Temporary stock clerk Jordan Foster can attest to the disappearance of wire and other material from the plant.
- Chip Miller, the son of Mr. Robert Miller, is an employee of contractor American Electric and has worked in the plant for as long as she can remember.
- Chip Miller appears to do little work at the plant and is most often seen riding a golf cart with his father.
- Chip Miller always immediately leaves the facility anytime corporate visitors are in the plant, so as not to be seen.
- Chip Miller often leaves the plant for many hours while apparently charging his time to XYZ.
- It is alleged by many in the plant that Chip Miller is paid many overtime hours for work he does not perform.
- She had never seen or approved any American Electric invoices.
- She has no idea what "third party" charges are as they appear on the American Electric invoices shown to her.
- Mr. Robert Miller oversees all work performed by American Electric, much of which appears incomplete or not done as needed.
- Mr. Robert Miller never followed XYZ purchasing procedures and constantly overruled instructions given to her by her corporate trainers.
- Mr. Robert Miller was constantly working "deals" with the contractors at XYZ.
- Alan Rivers of Red Rock Welding ("Red Rock"), a contractor, stated he is concerned about the amount Red Rock charges XYZ for its services and the materials it uses.
- CMB (a contractor who provides equipment and tools) refuses to accept or track purchase orders (PO) for the equipment and tools they sell.

- CMB has submitted invoices for equipment that was never delivered. Upon questioning, CMB canceled the invoice.
- Mr. Robert Miller oversees all work performed by contractor, Handy Services, much of which appears incomplete or not done at all.
- Mr. Robert Miller possibly has an unethical relationship with the owner of Handy Services, William Redkin, although she has no proof.
- William Redkin employs children who are often seen playing and riding golf carts in the plant.
- William Redkin often paints things three and four times.
- She is currently seeking employment elsewhere.

December 19, 2003, Wednesday

Interview of Ms. Bonnie Lowery

Ms. Lowery stated:

- She has been an employee of Southern Electric Motor for approximately ten years and is currently an outside sales representative.
- She has heard rumors of Mr. Robert Miller's unethical conduct and improprieties while he was an employee at Willamette Industries ("Willamette").
- Employees at Willamette were glad to see him leave and join XYZ.
- It was common for Robert Miller to share cost proposals provided by her and other vendors with contractors Robert Miller favored. She said it typically resulted in the competitor receiving the job.
- Mr. Robert Miller has never asked her for money nor has he ever made any inappropriate overtures.

Interview of Mr. Alan Rivers

Mr. Rivers stated:

- He has been an employee of Red Rock Welding, LLC for approximately nine months and is currently a welder.
- Red Rock has approximately eight employees and he is paid $8.50 per hour and receives overtime for any hours over eight.
- He believes Red Rock invoices are inflated and that XYZ, for whatever reason, consistently overpays its contractors.
- He ordered steel tubing at the request of Chip Miller (son of plant superintendent, Robert Miller), an employee of American Electric,

which Chip Miller subsequently removed from XYZ property for his future personal use.

■ He placed the aforementioned steel on the roof of Chip Miller's personal van so that Chip Miller could remove it.

■ Sometime during the summer (approximately six months prior) at the request of Paul Jones, he delivered a large quantity of plywood to Mr. Jones's home (see his statement, Exhibit B).

Interview of Mr. Robbie Red Rock

Mr. Red Rock stated:

■ He has been the owner of Red Rock Welding, LLC for approximately nine years and currently oversees the work his organization performs for XYZ.

■ Red Rock charges $35 per hour for its services to XYZ and time and a half for anything over eight hours.

■ He knows one of his employees, Alan Rivers, removed material from XYZ using a Red Rock truck at the direction of Chip Miller.

■ He has taken Mr. Jones and Mr. Robert Miller to dinner several times.

■ He has taken Mr. Jones and Mr. Robert Miller on all-expense paid fishing trips several times.

■ He has never offered money or kickbacks to either Mr. Jones or Mr. Robert Miller.

■ He had no explanation why his invoices do not adequately describe the work performed or material consumed (see Exhibit C for a sampling of some of the more anomalous Red Rock invoices).

■ He had no explanation why his invoice numbers where not in date order.

■ He had no explanation why in some cases the man-hours charged exceeded that which the number of people he employed could generate in a single week.

■ He had no explanation why apparently in some cases Red Rock had worked and reworked a task as many as three times (see Exhibit D).[2]

■ He had no explanation why his invoices lacked job numbers or did not clearly describe the work performed.

■ He agreed to cooperate with the investigation and provide whatever documentation was asked of him.[3]

Interview of Mr. William Redkin

Mr. Redkin stated:

- He has been the owner of Handy Services for over ten years and currently oversees the work his organization performs for XYZ.[4]
- He is unsure of his hourly rate, instead he charges by the job (see Exhibit E for samples of his invoices).[5]
- He prepares his own invoices and as such, he sees no need to use invoice numbers.
- He and his organization have not filed a federal income tax return in ten years.[6]
- He pays his employees (his brother and his 13-year-old son) "under the table."
- His 13-year-old son often helped him paint at XYZ on weekends.
- He charged XYZ about $160 per hour for the work performed by his son.[7]
- He has taken Mr. Jones to lunch several times during the business day.
- He has paid Mr. Robert Miller cash on three separate occasions, totaling $2,200. The last time was approximately one month prior to his interview.
- He had no explanation why he had given the money.
- He provided Mr. Robert Miller three bundles of R30 fiberglass insulation as a gift.
- He dry-walled, spackled, trimmed, and painted an unfinished guest room and closet in the home of Mr. Jones as a favor for no charge. The work took him and two other men (one Mr. Redkin's brother) a week to complete.
- He gave Mr. Jones a black powder long rifle (value $100) that had been given to him (Mr. Redkin) as a gift.
- He had no explanation why his invoices did not adequately describe the work performed or material consumed.
- He had no explanation why apparently in some cases he had painted and repainted an area more than once, other than "it needed it."
- He agreed to cooperate with the investigation and provide whatever documentation was asked of him (see his statement, Exhibit H).[8]

December 20, 2003, Thursday

Interview of Mr. Jordan Foster

Mr. Foster stated:

- He has been a temporary employee of XYZ for approximately six weeks and is currently the stockroom clerk.
- Twice he observed Mr. Robert Miller suspiciously put large boxes (contents unknown) into his personal pickup truck and leave.

Telephone Interview of Ms. Jennifer Roberts

Ms. Roberts stated:

- She had been an employee of XYZ for approximately six months as a shipping and receiving clerk.
- She resigned about a week prior to her interview.
- She observed William Redkin put a brand new pallet jack belonging to XYZ into his personal vehicle and leave with it sometime in August 2001.
- She has heard that the owners of Red Rock were paying kickbacks to employees of XYZ, but had no personal knowledge.
- CMB often invoices XYZ for things that have not been received.
- XYZ received two golf carts from CMB. However, now only one is in the plant.
- Chip Miller is the son of Mr. Robert Miller and works for American Electric at XYZ.
- Chip Miller often leaves the facility for hours, but later claims he was at the facility all day.
- She observed Robert Miller put large coils of new wire belonging to XYZ into his pickup truck and leave with them (see Exhibit I).

Interview of Mr. Curt Young

Mr. Young stated:

- He has been the owner of American Electric, Inc. for approximately four years and is currently its chief executive.
- He has approximately 15 employees and charges $42.00 per hour for the services his employees provide.

- He charges time and a half for any work over eight hours and double time for Sundays.
- Chip Miller has been an employee of American Electric for approximately two-and-one-half years and is paid $23.60 per hour.
- He is aware that Chip Miller is the son of Robert Miller and that the conflict is now quite obvious.
- He was unaware Chip Miller often charged 70 hours a week to the XYZ account.
- He has never offered money or kickbacks to either Mr. Jones or Mr. Robert Miller.
- He had no explanation why his invoices did not adequately describe the work performed or material consumed (see Exhibit J).
- He had no explanation why his invoice numbers where not in date order.
- He had no explanation why in some cases the man-hours charged exceeded that which the number of people he employed could generate in a single week.
- He had no explanation why apparently in some cases American Electric had worked and reworked a task as many as four times.
- He had no explanation why his invoices lacked job numbers.
- The "Third Party" charge on some invoices is for work performed by Young Mechanical (a fabricator), of which he is an owner.
- All third party charges are marked up, but he was unsure how much.
- He agreed to cooperate with the investigation and provide whatever documentation was asked of him.[9]

Interview of Mr. Nick Barnes

Mr. Barnes stated:

- He has been an employee of American Electric, Inc. for approximately two years and currently its project manager for XYZ.
- American Electric has approximately 12 to 15 employees and charges $42.00 per hour for the services the employees provide.
- American Electric charges time and a half for any work over eight hours and double time for Sundays.
- Chip Miller has been an employee of American Electric for approximately nine months and was hired for the XYZ project.
- He is aware that Chip Miller is the son of Robert Miller and that the conflict it creates is now quite obvious.
- He was unaware Chip Miller often charged 70 hours a week to the XYZ account.

- He is unsure exactly what services Chip Miller provides to XYZ, but he believes he is a "service representative."
- The only thing he has personally seen Chip Miller do at XYZ was ride around in a golf cart and occasionally operate a forklift.[10]
- He has never offered money or kickbacks to either Mr. Jones or Mr. Robert Miller.
- He had no explanation why his invoices did not adequately describe the work performed or material consumed (see Exhibit J).
- He had no explanation why his invoice numbers where not in date order.
- He had no explanation why in some cases the man-hours charged exceeded that which the number of people American Electric employed could generate in a single week.
- He had no explanation why apparently in some cases American Electric had worked and reworked a task as many as four times.
- He had no explanation why his invoices lacked job numbers or other helpful information regarding the work performed.
- The "Third Party" charge on some invoices is for work performed by Young Mechanical (a fabricator), of which Mr. Young is an owner.
- All third party charges are marked up, but he was unsure how much. He guessed the amount was 15 percent.
- He agreed to cooperate with the investigation and provide whatever documentation was asked of him.[11]

Interview of Mr. Chip Miller

Mr. Miller stated:

- He has been an employee of American Electric, Inc. for approximately a year and a half, and is currently a "service person" for XYZ.
- American Electric has approximately 12 employees of which he is one. He is paid $26.40 per hour and receives overtime for any hours over eight.
- He is the son of Robert Miller and that the conflict it creates is now quite obvious.
- He removed several 20-foot lengths of steel tubing from XYZ without permission. Red Rock had ordered the steel at Chip Miller's request. Alan Rivers loaded the steel onto Chip Miller's personal van. The time was charged to XYZ.[12]
- The steel was for the repair of his home.
- The taking of the steel amounted to theft, for which he was sorry (see Exhibit K).

Reinterview of Mr. Eric Reed

Mr. Reed stated:

- He had spoken to his wife (Marla Reed) and that she was sure all invoices submitted were correct and contained no errors.[13]
- He still had no explanation why in some cases the man-hours charged exceeded that which the number of people he employed could generate in a single week.[14]

Interview of Mr. Robert Miller

Mr. Robert Miller stated:

- He has been an employee of XYZ for approximately nine months and is currently the plant's superintendent.[15]
- Chip Miller, his son, is an employee of contractor American Electric and has worked in the plant for as long as he has.
- He introduced his son and American Electric to Mr. Jones and convinced Mr. Jones the services of American Electric were necessary.
- He is unsure of his son's exact function, but said he was one of the hardest working individuals "out there."
- He approved all of William Redkin's invoices.
- He was unsure of what William Redkin had painted, but was sure XYZ was getting its money's worth from his services.
- He paid William Redkin approximately $9,000 to make repairs on his private residence about one year ago.
- William Redkin gave him cash while in the XYZ employee parking lot on three separate occasions totaling $2,200. The last time was about one month ago when he received $1,000 cash.
- It was a mistake to accept money from a contractor.
- He removed from company premises without permission the following items: tape, copper wire (partial spools), wooden crates, 1,500 pounds of scrap steel, three quarts of liquid soap, and laundry detergent (see his statement, Exhibit L).

Interview of Mr. Paul Jones

Mr. Jones stated:

- He has been an employee of XYZ for approximately 20 years and is currently the plant manager.

- Chip Miller, the son of plant superintendent, Robert Miller, is an employee of contractor American Electric and has worked in the plant for just about as long as Robert Miller has.
- Robert Miller introduced his son and American Electric to him (Mr. Jones) and convinced him the services of American Electric were necessary.
- He is unsure of Chip Miller's exact function, but said his father, Robert Miller, supervised him.
- He last spoke with William Redkin the night before. He said William Redkin was very nervous and wanted him and Mr. Jones to "get their story straight."
- He allowed William Redkin to dry wall, spackle, trim, and paint an unfinished guest room and closet in his home as a favor for no charge. The work took William Redkin and two other men (one Mr. Redkin's brother) a week to complete.
- He received a black powder long rifle (value $100) from Mr. Redkin as a gift.
- He had approved all of the invoices of Red Rock Welding, American Electric, and William Redkin without looking at them or questioning if they were accurate.
- He estimated that his lack of contractor oversight had resulted in the overpayment to those vendors by several hundred thousand dollars (see Exhibit M).

End of Report

Notes

1. Further exploration of this comment revealed that Mr. Rivers was suggesting that Mr. Jones and Mr. Miller were receiving kickbacks from Red Rock. However, upon questioning Mr. Rivers, he had no proof of his suspicion.
2. This is an interesting example where Red Rock fabricated four scrap carts for $3,137 (see Exhibit D invoice #496) and six additional carts for $2,998 (see invoice #4759). Before the work was completed Red Rock reworked four of those same carts and charged $4,602.75 (see invoice #4806). In this same invoice Red Rock charges $400 for fuel. Upon questioning, Red Rock argued it was justifiable. What's interesting is that invoice #4968 (for fabrication) is dated October 9, 2001, and invoice #4806 (for repairs) is dated October 31, 2001. How is it possible the repair invoice has a lower

invoice number than the one for the fabrication? Also note that the charge for repair is greater than the fabrication.

3. Forensic examination of the support documentation subsequently supplied by Red Rock revealed an assortment of accounting and business practices irregularities, including sloppy employee timesheets containing multiple cross-outs and write-overs, rounding up to the nearest quarter hour wherever possible, miscalculations of chargeable overtime, invoice numbers issued out of date order, invoices lacking through-dates or dates service or work rendered, charges for labor but no man-hours stated, and material and equipment charges without descriptions (see Exhibit F for sample Red Rock employee time sheets). However, the greatest exposure to XYZ would have been the practice of charging for hours not worked or tasks not performed. In all likelihood this occurred. The insufficient documentation and the lack of procedural checks and balances relative to routine contractor management make it impossible to prove. The request for documents was expanded on December 27, 2001, and backup documentation was requested for ten selected unpaid invoices (see Exhibit G).

4. Handy Services is not a legal entity and has no federal Employer Identification Number.

5. Forensic examination of his invoices revealed he charged between $110 and $165 per hour. Further investigation revealed that some of his invoices were complete fabrications.

6. He said because he spends all of the profits, there is nothing to tax.

7. Mr. Redkin thought this to be very reasonable. He rationalized his son had given up his weekends to paint at the plant.

8. Although support document for his invoices was requested of Mr. Redkin the day of his interview, he has not been heard from since.

9. Although support document for Mechanical Services' invoices was requested of Mr. Young the day of his interview, he has not been heard from since.

10. Mr. Barnes was rather embarrassed he did not know the true function of Chip Miller and what he did for XYZ.

11. Although support documents for American Electric's invoices were requested of Mr. Barnes the day of his interview, he has not been heard from since.

12. Subsequent review of Red Rock invoices did not reveal that the steel had been charged to XYZ.

13. Mr. Reed was again requested to provide backup to selected invoices provided to him by interviewer, Mr. Eugene Ferraro.

14. In spite of having been shown such discrepancies by the interviewer, Mr. Reed insisted there was no fraud.

15. Mr. Miller was unable to spell "superintendent." His ability to write and spell was so poor the interviewer had to write his statement for him.

Appendix C

Sample Video Surveillance Report

DATE: May 3, 2004
SUBJECT: Jane Doe
LOCATION: 123 Any Street
                  Glendale, CA 91206
START/END TIME: 9:45 A.M.–2:15 P.M.
CASE NUMBER: 298-000-000
CLAIM NUMBER: C-000-0000
DATE OF INJURY: October 12, 2002

CONFIDENTIAL VIDEO SURVEILLANCE REPORT

Executive Summary

Surveillance Results: On May 3, 2004, two surveillance investigators conducted 4.5 hours of surveillance each. The objective was to ascertain if Jane Doe (employee) engaged in physical activity that appeared to exceed her current medical restrictions. During the surveillance, Jane Doe was observed walking, driving, and entering and exiting her vehicle. She was also observed carrying groceries and pushing a shopping cart. Her activities appeared unrestricted and required no assistance.

Physical Description: The subject is a white female, approximately 50 years of age, 5'4", 230 lbs., black hair. During our surveillance, she wore a yellow top and yellow pants. The subject resides in a modest single-story single-family wood frame home situated on a heavily trafficked four-lane thoroughfare.

Weather: The weather during the surveillance was mild and the visibility was unrestricted. Temperatures ranged from 55 to 60 degrees, and the skies were clear, with moderate winds from the southwest.

Video: 15 minutes of video was recorded of the subject while she shopped.

Investigative Detail

At approximately 9:45 A.M., two surveillance investigators departed for the subject's residence located at 123 Any Street, Glendale, California.

At approximately 10:31 A.M., investigator #1 and #2 arrived at 123 Any Street, Jane Doe's residence. Investigator #1 established a position one block east of the residence located on Smith Avenue. Investigator #2 was positioned on Jones Street, two blocks west of the residence. From these two positions, they were able to view the garage, the south side of the property, and the front door of the residence.

At approximately 10:49 A.M., Jane Doe was observed exiting her garage in her white Cadillac (CA license plate 2N3249). Jane Doe drove west on Smith Avenue; moving surveillance was initiated by both investigators and cautiously maintained.

At approximately 11:05 A.M., Jane Doe arrived at the General Store located at 43 Doe Street, Glendale, California. Jane Doe exited her vehicle and entered the store.

At approximately 11:29 A.M., Jane Doe was video taped by investigator #2 as she exited the General Store. Jane Doe then entered her vehicle and directly returned home. [11:29:10 A.M.]

At approximately 1:15 P.M., both investigators arrived at the Business Controls, Inc., office in La Verne, California.

End of Report

Appendix D

Sample After-Action Report

ANY COMPANY
100 Very Marginal Way
Any Town, Any State 92123

POSTINVESTIGATION OBSERVATIONS
AND RECOMMENDATIONS

Executive Summary

A five-month undercover investigation revealed an assortment of problems at the Any Town, Any State, ice cream plant. Those problems included widespread employee substance abuse, unsafe work practices, and reduced productivity. These and the other problems uncovered were the long-term product of:

- Inadequate preemployment screening
- Poor supervision
- Ineffective policies and practices

As in most cases of this type, management's role was significant. However, the following observations and recommendations should not serve as an indictment of that management, but instead augment the continuous improvement process for the good of the organization and the ice cream plant. For the purpose of this report our observations and our corresponding recommendations have been grouped as follows:

- Personnel Screening
- Supervision and Employee Relations
- Workplace Safety
- Security and Asset Protection

It should be noted that *Business Controls, Inc.* did not conduct an internal audit. Our observations, both objective and subjective, were made during our investigation and the employee interviews that followed it. As such, it is recommended a more detailed examination/audit be conducted at some later date.

Personnel Screening

It is often said that the employees make or break an organization. Consequently, a company's success depends on the quality of its people. No other element more greatly impacts our productivity, competitiveness, and profitability than our people. Effective preemployment screening is the only proven technique to ensure quality people are consistently brought into the organization. In this case, a few of the employees involved in substance abuse and other misconduct should not have been hired.

Recommendations:

- Review current preemployment drug testing protocols. During the course of the undercover investigation several employees boasted that they were illegal drug users and had beaten the drug test. A qualified clinician should examine the collection site and the laboratory conducting the test. Audit periodically to ensure process meets needs and expectations.
- Retain the services of a preemployment screening and background investigation firm. Several of the individuals examined during our investigation had criminal histories, including convictions involving violence and substance abuse. Have each candidate thoroughly screened before an offer of employment is made. The background

investigation should include, at minimum: a seven-year criminal conviction history (examine both felonies and misdemeanors), a driving record history, and a public filing history (notices of default, civil judgments, tax liens/bankruptcies). Check other states where the applicant lived over the past seven to ten years. According to most state highway enforcement agencies, driving histories are the single best place to search for, and identify, a history of substance abuse.

- During the preemployment interview, ask penetrating questions that reveal the applicant's ability to solve problems, resolve conflicts, and communicate ideas.
- Have the current employment application reviewed by counsel to ensure it meets current legal standards and asks nothing unlawful.[1] Ensure the application contains an enforceable release of liability and that it provides the necessary protection for conducting background investigations and drug testing.
- Provide training to the supervisors, lead persons, and managers involved in the hiring and training process. The training should be designed to augment their interview skills and ensure they are aware of the legal implications of employment interviewing and screening.

Supervision and Employee Relations

The lack of effective and competent supervision contributed significantly to the size and scope of the problem uncovered at the plant. Two foremen were more involved in illegal drugs than managing their employees. As a result, the absence of supervision allowed a substance abuse problem to permeate the hourly ranks and contaminate much of the workforce. Additionally, we learned that it was common knowledge that employees regularly smoked marijuana in the company parking lot and inside the plant, and that supervision did nothing to stop it. Also, alcohol containers, partially full or empty, were routinely found in the employee parking lot. In two instances partially consumed alcoholic beverages were found inside the plant. Employees returning to work with alcohol on their breath was common.

Furthermore, employees were allowed to work at their own pace and produce only that which they wished.[2] Millwrights and mechanics frequently displayed a complete lack of urgency when called for assistance or assigned a repair. Several of them took pride in allowing production to stop while they casually meandered to an assignment. All the while, foremen failed to inspect the product and monitor productivity. In one instance, a foreman did not inspect his crew's work until 12 pallets of defective product had been produced. Often, senior employees idled, slept on the job, and neglected to assist or train newer employees. Employee hazing and harassment were commonplace. Often, horseplay led to reckless acts endangering employee safety and product quality. Many of the employees openly criticized authority, while those in supervision openly harassed those who questioned them.

During our interviews, several employees indicated they disliked the company and that safety, productivity, and quality were of no concern. Several interviewees expressed explicit disdain for management and organizational values.

Recommendations:

- Reassess the qualifications and skills needed for all positions. Take great care when promoting from within. Provide supervisors and managers better training and communicate expectations.
- Establish performance standards for all levels of the organization including supervision and management. Provide basic training to those employees in need, especially the foremen. Use progressive discipline were necessary. Insist policies and procedures are followed at all times.
- Hold all employees accountable for their actions (or inactions). Ensure that supervisors and managers are accountable for the actions (or inactions) of their subordinates. Be fair, but be firm. Start from the top, train and inform all the way down. Hold more training and safety meetings for all levels.
- Insist that all employees be treated with dignity and respect at all times. Tell employees to report violators and demand an end to hazing and harassing behaviors. Prohibit foul language, horseplay, and rough-housing in the plant.[3]
- Provide alcohol and substance abuse awareness training to all supervisors and managers. Teach the supervisors and managers how to recognize impairment and the at-risk employees. Provide similar training to the hourly employees as well.

Workplace Safety

Workplace safety should constantly be monitored and safety practices reviewed on a regular basis. Safety violations included the failure to lock out while making machine or equipment repairs, failure to wear eye and ear protection, neglecting wet floors, throwing tools, and carelessly operating forklifts and clamp trucks.

Recommendations:

- Conduct a safety audit of the manufacturing operation and office areas.
- Recommunicate safety policies and periodically conduct spot inspections.
- Implement mandatory drug testing for all accidents that occur at work. Communicate to the employees that accidents must be reported immediately. Inform supervisors and managers that discipline will result in cases where the policy is not followed.
- Reward safe behavior, punish unsafe behavior.
- Hold supervisors and managers responsible for safe practices of their subordinates.

Security and Asset Protection

Security in the plant was a concern to a number of employees. The plant's location, design, age, and the nature of the business offer significant security challenges. However, there is much that can be done.

Recommendations:

- Better control employee entrances and exits. Monitor visitor traffic in and about the plant.
- Management may want to implement a program for employees to anonymously report company policy/safety violations. The company may want to consider instituting a toll-free line to use as the anonymous avenue of communication for such issues.
- Employees should be reminded that incorrect documentation of time is theft and a violation of company policy.[4] This includes overstaying breaks or taking breaks when not authorized. Violators should be warned, then punished.

Conclusion

Although no organization is immune to employee misconduct and dishonesty, management can do a great deal to minimize its exposure and significantly reduce its risk. That which is outlined above should serve as a start or at least provide some additional insight beyond our formal investigation.

Notes

1. It is unlawful to ask the dates of military service or high school graduation.
2. Interestingly, this attitude seemed to exist in the front office as well. The tempo of operations in the office was markedly less than the other locations in which we have worked. There didn't seem to be a sense of urgency anywhere.
3. In two separate instances, an open blade knife and a large wooden mallet were thrown directly at our investigator as he worked.
4. Employees routinely left for lunch without clocking out.

Appendix E

Federal Laws Prohibiting Job Discrimination: Questions and Answers

Federal Equal Employment Opportunity (EEO) Laws

I. What Are the Federal Laws Prohibiting Job Discrimination?

- Title VII of the Civil Rights Act of 1964 (Title VII) prohibits employment discrimination based on race, color, religion, sex, or national origin.
- The Equal Pay Act of 1963 (EPA) protects men and women who perform substantially equal work in the same establishment from sex-based wage discrimination.
- The Age Discrimination in Employment Act (ADEA) of 1967 protects individuals who are 40 years of age or older.
- Title I and Title V of the Americans with Disabilities Act (ADA) of 1990 prohibit employment discrimination against qualified individuals with disabilities in the private sector, and in state and local governments.
- Sections 501 and 505 of the Rehabilitation Act of 1973 prohibit discrimination against qualified individuals with disabilities who work in the federal government.

- The Civil Rights Act of 1991, among other things, provides monetary damages in cases of intentional employment discrimination.

The U.S. Equal Employment Opportunity Commission (EEOC) enforces all of these laws. EEOC also provides oversight and coordination of all federal equal employment opportunity regulations, practices, and policies.

Other federal laws, not enforced by EEOC, also prohibit discrimination and reprisal against federal employees and applicants. The Civil Service Reform Act (CSRA) of 1978 contains a number of prohibitions, known as prohibited personnel practices, which are designed to promote overall fairness in federal personnel actions (5 U.S.C. 2302). The CSRA prohibits any employee who has authority to take certain personnel actions from discriminating for or against employees or applicants for employment on the basis of race, color, national origin, religion, sex, age, or disability. It also provides that certain personnel actions cannot be based on attributes or conduct that do not adversely affect employee performance, such as marital status and political affiliation. The Office of Personnel Management (OPM) has interpreted the prohibition of discrimination based on conduct to include discrimination based on sexual orientation. The CSRA also prohibits reprisal against federal employees or applicants for whistle-blowing or for exercising an appeal, complaint, or grievance right. The CSRA is enforced by both the Office of Special Counsel (OSC) and the Merit Systems Protection Board (MSPB).

Additional information about the enforcement of the CSRA may be found on the OPM Web site at http://www.opm.gov/er/address2/guide01.htm; from OSC at (202) 653-7188 or at http://www.osc.gov/; and from MSPB at (202) 653-6772 or at http://www.mspb.gov/.

Discriminatory Practices

II. What Discriminatory Practices Are Prohibited by These Laws?

Under Title VII, the ADA, and the ADEA, it is illegal to discriminate in any aspect of employment, including:

- Hiring and firing
- Compensation, assignment, or classification of employees
- Transfer, promotion, layoff, or recall
- Job advertisements

- Recruitment;
- Testing;
- Use of company facilities;
- Training and apprenticeship programs;
- Fringe benefits;
- Pay, retirement plans, and disability leave;
- Other terms and conditions of employment.

Discriminatory practices under these laws also include:

- Harassment on the basis of race, color, religion, sex, national origin, disability, or age.
- Retaliation against an individual for filing a charge of discrimination, participating in an investigation, or opposing discriminatory practices.
- Employment decisions based on stereotypes or assumptions about the abilities, traits, or performance of individuals of a certain sex, race, age, religion, or ethnic group, or individuals with disabilities.
- Denying employment opportunities to a person because of marriage to, or association with, an individual of a particular race, religion, or national origin, or an individual with a disability. Title VII also prohibits discrimination because of participation in schools or places of worship associated with a particular racial, ethnic, or religious group.

Employers are required to post notices to all employees advising them of their rights under the laws EEOC enforces and their right to be free from retaliation. Such notices must be accessible, as needed, to persons with visual or other disabilities that affect reading.

Note: Many states and municipalities also have enacted protections against discrimination and harassment based on sexual orientation, status as a parent, marital status, and political affiliation. For information, please contact the EEOC District Office nearest you.

III. What Other Practices Are Discriminatory under These Laws?

Title VII

Title VII prohibits not only intentional discrimination, but also practices that have the effect of discriminating against individuals because of their race, color, national origin, religion, or sex.

National Origin Discrimination

- It is illegal to discriminate against an individual because of birthplace, ancestry, culture, or linguistic characteristics common to a specific ethnic group.
- A rule requiring that employees speak only English on the job may violate Title VII unless an employer shows that the requirement is necessary for conducting business. If the employer believes such a rule is necessary, employees must be informed when English is required and the consequences for violating the rule.

The Immigration Reform and Control Act (IRCA) of 1986 requires employers to ensure that employees hired are legally authorized to work in the United States. However, an employer who requests employment verification only for individuals of a particular national origin, or individuals who appear to be or sound foreign, may violate both Title VII and IRCA; verification must be obtained from all applicants and employees. Employers who impose citizenship requirements or give preferences to U.S. citizens in hiring or employment opportunities also may violate IRCA.

Additional information about IRCA may be obtained from the Office of Special Counsel for Immigration-Related Unfair Employment Practices at 1-800-255-7688 (voice), 1-800-237-2515 (TTY for employees/applicants), or 1-800-362-2735 (TTY for employers) or at http://www.usdoj.gov/crt/osc.

Religious Accommodation

An employer is required to reasonably accommodate the religious belief of an employee or prospective employee, unless doing so would impose an undue hardship.

Sex Discrimination

Title VII's broad prohibitions against sex discrimination specifically cover:

- Sexual Harassment—This includes practices ranging from direct requests for sexual favors to workplace conditions that create a hostile environment for persons of either gender, including same sex harassment. (The "hostile environment" standard also applies to harassment on the bases of race, color, national origin, religion, age, and disability.)

- Pregnancy Based Discrimination—Pregnancy, childbirth, and related medical conditions must be treated in the same way as other temporary illnesses or conditions.

Additional rights are available to parents and others under the Family and Medical Leave Act (FMLA), which is enforced by the U.S. Department of Labor. For information on the FMLA, or to file an FMLA complaint, individuals should contact the nearest office of the Wage and Hour Division, Employment Standards Administration, U.S. Department of Labor. The Wage and Hour Division is listed in most telephone directories under U.S. Government, Department of Labor or at http://www.dol.gov/esa/public/whd_org.htm.

Age Discrimination in Employment Act

The ADEA's broad ban against age discrimination also specifically prohibits:

- Statements or specifications in job notices or advertisements of age preference and limitations. An age limit may only be specified in the rare circumstance where age has been proven to be a *bona fide* occupational qualification (BFOQ);
- Discrimination on the basis of age by apprenticeship programs, including joint labor-management apprenticeship programs;
- Denial of benefits to older employees. An employer may reduce benefits based on age only if the cost of providing the reduced benefits to older workers is the same as the cost of providing benefits to younger workers.

Equal Pay Act

The EPA prohibits discrimination on the basis of sex in the payment of wages or benefits, where men and women perform work of similar skill, effort, and responsibility for the same employer under similar working conditions.

Note that:

- Employers may not reduce wages of either sex to equalize pay between men and women.

- A violation of the EPA may occur where a different wage was/is paid to a person who worked in the same job before or after an employee of the opposite sex.
- A violation may also occur where a labor union causes the employer to violate the law.

Titles I and V of the Americans with Disabilities Act

The ADA prohibits discrimination on the basis of disability in all employment practices. It is necessary to understand several important ADA definitions to know who is protected by the law and what constitutes illegal discrimination:

- *Individual with a Disability*—An individual with a disability under the ADA is a person who has a physical or mental impairment that substantially limits one or more major life activities, has a record of such an impairment, or is regarded as having such an impairment. Major life activities are those that an average person can perform with little or no difficulty such as walking, breathing, seeing, hearing, speaking, learning, and working.
- *Qualified Individual with a Disability*—A qualified employee or applicant with a disability is someone who satisfies skill, experience, education, and other job-related requirements of the position held or desired, and who, with or without reasonable accommodation, can perform the essential functions of that position.
- *Reasonable Accommodation*—Reasonable accommodation may include, but is not limited to, making existing facilities used by employees readily accessible to and usable by persons with disabilities; job restructuring; modification of work schedules; providing additional unpaid leave; reassignment to a vacant position; acquiring or modifying equipment or devices; adjusting or modifying examinations, training materials, or policies; and providing qualified readers or interpreters. Reasonable accommodation may be necessary to apply for a job, to perform job functions, or to enjoy the benefits and privileges of employment that are enjoyed by people without disabilities. An employer is not required to lower production standards to make an accommodation. An employer generally is not obligated to provide personal use items such as eyeglasses or hearing aids.
- *Undue Hardship*—An employer is required to make a reasonable accommodation to a qualified individual with a disability unless doing so would impose an undue hardship on the operation of

the employer's business. Undue hardship means an action that requires significant difficulty or expense when considered in relation to factors such as a business's size, financial resources, and the nature and structure of its operation.

■ *Prohibited Inquiries and Examinations*—Before making an offer of employment, an employer may not ask job applicants about the existence, nature, or severity of a disability. Applicants may be asked about their ability to perform job functions. A job offer may be conditioned on the results of a medical examination, but only if the examination is required for all entering employees in the same job category. Medical examinations of employees must be job-related and consistent with business necessity.

■ *Drug and Alcohol Use*—Employees and applicants currently engaging in the illegal use of drugs are not protected by the ADA when an employer acts on the basis of such use. Tests for illegal use of drugs are not considered medical examinations and, therefore, are not subject to the ADA's restrictions on medical examinations. Employers may hold individuals who are illegally using drugs and individuals with alcoholism to the same standards of performance as other employees.

The Civil Rights Act of 1991

The Civil Rights Act of 1991 made major changes in the federal laws against employment discrimination enforced by EEOC. Enacted in part to reverse several Supreme Court decisions that limited the rights of persons protected by these laws, the act also provides additional protections. The act authorizes compensatory and punitive damages in cases of intentional discrimination and provides for obtaining attorneys' fees and the possibility of jury trials. It also directs the EEOC to expand its technical assistance and outreach activities.

Employers and Other Entities Covered by EEO Laws

IV. Which Employers and Other Entities Are Covered by These Laws?

Title VII and the ADA cover all private employers, state and local governments, and education institutions that employ 15 or more individuals. These laws also cover private and public employment agencies, labor organizations, and joint labor management committees controlling apprenticeship and training.

The ADEA covers all private employers with 20 or more employees, state and local governments (including school districts), employment agencies, and labor organizations.

The EPA covers all employers who are covered by the Federal Wage and Hour Law (the Fair Labor Standards Act). Virtually all employers are subject to the provisions of this act.

Title VII, the ADEA, and the EPA also cover the federal government. In addition, the federal government is covered by Sections 501 and 505 of the Rehabilitation Act of 1973, as amended, which incorporate the requirements of the ADA. However, different procedures are used for processing complaints of federal discrimination. For more information on how to file a complaint of federal discrimination, contact the EEO office of the federal agency where the alleged discrimination occurred.

The CSRA (not enforced by EEOC) covers most federal agency employees except employees of a government corporation, the Federal Bureau of Investigation, the Central Intelligence Agency, the Defense Intelligence Agency, the National Security Agency, and as determined by the president, any executive agency or unit thereof, the principal function of which is the conduct of foreign intelligence or counterintelligence activities, or the General Accounting Office.

The EEOC'S Charge Processing Procedures

V. Who Can File a Charge of Discrimination?

- Any individual who believes that his or her employment rights have been violated may file a charge of discrimination with EEOC.
- In addition, an individual, organization, or agency may file a charge on behalf of another person in order to protect the aggrieved person's identity.

VI. How Is a Charge of Discrimination Filed?

- A charge may be filed by mail or in person at the nearest EEOC office. Individuals may consult their local telephone directory (U.S. Government listing) or call 1-800-669-4000 (voice) or 1-800-669-6820 (TTY) to contact the nearest EEOC office for more information on specific procedures for filing a charge.
- Individuals who need an accommodation in order to file a charge (e.g., sign language interpreter, print materials in an accessible

format) should inform the EEOC field office so appropriate arrangements can be made.

VII. What Information Must Be Provided to File a Charge?

- The complaining party's name, address, and telephone number
- The name, address, and telephone number of the respondent employer, employment agency, or union that is alleged to have discriminated, and number of employees (or union members), if known
- A short description of the alleged violation (the event that caused the complaining party to believe that his or her rights were violated)
- The date(s) of the alleged violation(s)

VIII. What Are the Time Limits for Filing a Charge of Discrimination?

All laws enforced by EEOC, except the Equal Pay Act, require filing a charge with EEOC before a private lawsuit may be filed in court. There are strict time limits within which charges must be filed:

- A charge must be filed with EEOC within 180 days from the date of the alleged violation in order to protect the charging party's rights.
- This 180-day filing deadline is extended to 300 days if the charge is also covered by a state or local antidiscrimination law. For ADEA charges, only state laws extend the filing limit to 300 days.
- These time limits do not apply to claims under the Equal Pay Act, because under that act persons do not have to first file a charge with EEOC in order to have the right to go to court. However, because many EPA claims also raise Title VII sex discrimination issues, it may be advisable to file charges under both laws within the time limits indicated.
- To protect legal rights, it is always best to contact EEOC promptly when discrimination is suspected.

IX. What Agency Handles a Charge That Is also Covered by State or Local Law?

Many states and localities have antidiscrimination laws and agencies responsible for enforcing those laws. EEOC refers to these agencies as

"Fair Employment Practices Agencies (FEPAs)." Through the use of "work sharing agreements," EEOC and the FEPAs avoid duplication of effort while at the same time ensuring that a charging party's rights are protected under both federal and state laws.

- If a charge is filed with an FEPA and is also covered by federal law, the FEPA "dual files" the charge with EEOC to protect federal rights. The charge will usually be retained by the FEPA for handling.
- If a charge is filed with EEOC and is also covered by state or local law, EEOC "dual files" the charge with the state or local FEPA, but ordinarily retains the charge for handling.

X. What Happens after a Charge Is Filed with EEOC?

The employer is notified that the charge has been filed. From this point there are a number of ways a charge may be handled:

- A charge may be assigned for priority investigation if the initial facts appear to support a violation of law. When the evidence is weaker, the charge may be assigned for follow-up investigation to determine whether it is likely that a violation has occurred.
- EEOC can seek to settle a charge at any stage of the investigation if the charging party and the employer express an interest in doing so. If settlement efforts are not successful, the investigation continues.
- In investigating a charge, EEOC may make written requests for information, interview people, review documents, and, as needed, visit the facility where the alleged discrimination occurred. When the investigation is complete, EEOC will discuss the evidence with the charging party or employer, as appropriate.
- The charge may be selected for EEOC's mediation program if both the charging party and the employer express an interest in this option. Mediation is offered as an alternative to a lengthy investigation. Participation in the mediation program is confidential and voluntary, and requires consent from both charging party and employer. If mediation is unsuccessful, the charge is returned for investigation.
- A charge may be dismissed at any point if, in the agency's best judgment, further investigation will not establish a violation of the law. A charge may be dismissed at the time it is filed, if an initial in-depth interview does not produce evidence to support the claim. When a charge is dismissed, a notice is issued in accordance with

the law that gives the charging party 90 days in which to file a lawsuit on his or her own behalf.

XI. How Does EEOC Resolve Discrimination Charges?

- If the evidence obtained in an investigation does not establish that discrimination occurred, this will be explained to the charging party. A required notice is then issued, closing the case and giving the charging party 90 days in which to file a lawsuit on his or her own behalf.
- If the evidence establishes that discrimination has occurred, the employer and the charging party will be informed of this in a letter of determination that explains the finding. EEOC will then attempt conciliation with the employer to develop a remedy for the discrimination.
- If the case is successfully conciliated, or if a case has earlier been successfully mediated or settled, neither EEOC nor the charging party may go to court unless the conciliation, mediation, or settlement agreement is not honored.
- If EEOC is unable to successfully conciliate the case, the agency will decide whether to bring suit in federal court. If EEOC decides not to sue, it will issue a notice closing the case and giving the charging party 90 days in which to file a lawsuit on his or her own behalf. In Title VII and ADA cases against state or local governments, the Department of Justice takes these actions.

XII. When Can an Individual File an Employment Discrimination Lawsuit in Court?

A charging party may file a lawsuit within 90 days after receiving a notice of a "right to sue" from EEOC, as stated above. Under Title VII and the ADA, a charging party can also request a notice of "right to sue" from EEOC 180 days after the charge was first filed with the Commission and may then bring suit within 90 days after receiving this notice. Under the ADEA, a suit may be filed at any time 60 days after filing a charge with EEOC, but not later than 90 days after EEOC gives notice that it has completed action on the charge.

Under the EPA, a lawsuit must be filed within two years (three years for willful violations) of the discriminatory act, which in most cases is payment of a discriminatory lower wage.

XIII. What Remedies Are Available When Discrimination Is Found?

The "relief" or remedies available for employment discrimination, whether caused by intentional acts or by practices that have a discriminatory effect, may include back pay, hiring, promotion, reinstatement, front pay, reasonable accommodation, or other actions that will make an individual "whole" (in the condition he or she would have been but for the discrimination). Remedies also may include payment of attorneys' fees, expert witness fees, and court costs.

Under most EEOC-enforced laws, compensatory and punitive damages may also be available where intentional discrimination is found. Damages may be available to compensate for actual monetary losses, for future monetary losses, and for mental anguish and inconvenience. Punitive damages may also be available if an employer acted with malice or reckless indifference. Punitive damages are not available against the federal, state, and local governments.

In cases concerning reasonable accommodation under the ADA, compensatory or punitive damages may not be awarded to the charging party if an employer can demonstrate that "good faith" efforts were made to provide reasonable accommodation.

An employer may be required to post notices to all employees addressing the violations of a specific charge and advising them of their rights under the laws EEOC enforces and their right to be free from retaliation. Such notices must be accessible, as needed, to persons with visual or other disabilities that affect reading.

The employer also may be required to take corrective or preventive actions to cure the source of the identified discrimination and minimize the chance of its recurrence, as well as discontinue the specific discriminatory practices involved in the case.

The Commission

XIV. What Is EEOC and How Does It Operate?

EEOC is an independent federal agency originally created by Congress in 1964 to enforce Title VII of the Civil Rights Act of 1964. The Commission is composed of five commissioners and a general counsel appointed by the president and confirmed by the Senate. Commissioners are appointed for five-year staggered terms; the general counsel's term is four years. The president designates a chairperson and a vice chairperson. The chair is the chief executive officer of the Commission. The Commission has authority to establish equal employment policy and to approve litigation. The general counsel is responsible for conducting litigation.

EEOC carries out its enforcement, education, and technical assistance activities through 50 field offices serving every part of the nation. The nearest EEOC field office may be contacted by calling: 1-800-669-4000 (voice) or 1-800-669-6820 (TTY).

Information and Assistance Available from EEOC

XV. What Information and Other Assistance Is Available from EEOC?

EEOC provides a range of informational materials and assistance to individuals and entities with rights and responsibilities under EEOC-enforced laws. Most materials and assistance are provided to the public at no cost. Additional specialized training and technical assistance are provided on a fee basis under the auspices of the EEOC Education, Technical Assistance, and Training Revolving Fund Act of 1992. For information on educational and other assistance available, contact the nearest EEOC office by calling: 1-800-669-4000 (voice) or 1-800-669-6820 (TTY).

Publications available at no cost include posters advising employees of their EEO rights and pamphlets, manuals, fact sheets, and enforcement guidance on laws enforced by the Commission. For a list of EEOC publications, or to order publications, write, call, or fax:

U.S. Equal Employment Opportunity Commission
Publications Distribution Center
P.O. Box 12549
Cincinnati, OH 45212-0549
1-800-669-3362 (voice)
1-800-800-3302 (TTY)
1-513-489-8692 (fax)

Information about EEOC and the laws it enforces can also be found at: http://www.eeoc.gov.

Appendix F

Sample Search Policy

Illegal Drug, Alcohol, and Search Policy

I. Purpose

The safety and health of employees, protection of the environment, quality of our service, products and financial performance of our Company can be directly and adversely affected by the use or abuse of alcohol, drugs, or controlled substances. Therefore, the following policy is designed to create a safe and drug-free workplace.

II. Policy Statement

A. Preemployment Screening

Business Controls, Inc. will maintain preemployment drug/alcohol screening practices designed to prevent hiring individuals whose use of illegal substances or alcohol indicates a potential for impaired or unsafe job performance.

All job applicants who have received a conditional offer of employment at *Business Controls, Inc.*, will undergo a specimen test for illegal drugs as part of the Company employment process. Any applicant with a verified positive test result will be denied employment.

All individual drug and alcohol test results will be reported to the Company representative authorized to receive such test results or to the Company's "Designated Agent."

All actions taken under the Company Drug Abuse Policy will be maintained in confidence. Information related to investigations, possible violations, medical tests, or test results will be communicated on a strict "need to know" basis. Discussions with individuals tested under this program will be conducted as privately as circumstances permit.

The test sample shall be obtained by a Company-screened laboratory certified for such testing. The laboratory will take all measures necessary to protect both the chain of custody of the sample and the privacy of the individual tested. A signed release from the applicant must be obtained prior to testing. Refusal by an applicant to submit to testing shall result in immediate disqualification.

B. On-the-Job Use, Possession, or Sale of Illegal Substances or Alcohol

1. Illegal Substances[1]

The use, sale, purchase, transfer, or possession, or any offer to use, sell, purchase, transfer, or possess any illegal substance by any employee while in a client facility or while performing Company business, including on a third-party premises, is prohibited. *Business Controls, Inc.* will deem the employee to be in violation of this policy if any illegal drug or like metabolite of an illegal substance is found in the body or body specimen of an employee while performing company business or while in a client facility.

2. Legal Drugs[2]

Except as provided below, the use of and being impaired[3] while under the affect of any legally obtained drug, by an employee, while performing *Business Controls, Inc.* business or while in a client facility is prohibited to the extent such use or impaired state may affect the safety of co-workers or members of the public, the employee's job performance, or the safe or efficient operation of the Company facility. An employee may continue to work, while taking a legal drug, if management has determined that the employee does not pose a threat to his or her own safety or the safety of co-workers and that the employee's job performance is not significantly affected by the legal drug. Otherwise, the employee may be required to take a leave of absence or comply with other appropriate action determined by management.

3. Alcohol

The unauthorized use, sale, purchase, transfer, or possession of alcohol while in a client facility or while performing Company business is prohibited. Impairment while performing Company business or while in a client facility is also prohibited. *Business Controls, Inc.* will deem the employee to be impaired while performing Company business or while in a client facility if alcohol is detected in any measurable amount in the body or body specimen of the employee.

During an investigation an employee may be authorized by a *Business Controls, Inc.* associate/supervisor to consume alcohol for the purposes of furthering an investigation. Under such circumstances the employee is expected to use good judgment. If good judgment is perceived to have not been used, the employee will be deemed in violation of this policy.

C. Disciplinary Action

Violation of this policy may result in disciplinary action up to and including termination, even for a first offense.

D. Illegal Substance and Alcohol Screening

Drug and alcohol screening may be performed in cases where:

1. An employee is involved in an on-the-job accident;
2. An employee's job performance or behavior suggests he or she may be impaired;
3. There is evidence of drug use or reasonable cause to believe employee drug use;
4. Before, during, or after an assignment (investigation) which, in itself, involves drugs or alcohol;
5. At any time so directed by a *Business Controls, Inc.* associate/supervisor, for any reason.

An employee's consent to submit to such a test is required as a condition of employment and the employee's refusal to consent may result in discipline up to and including termination, even for the first refusal.

E. Employees' Reporting Requirements — Legal Drugs

For certain job positions, an employee's use of a legal drug can pose a significant risk to the safety of the employee or others. Employees who feel or have been informed that the use of a legal drug may present a safety risk are to report such risk to their *Business Controls, Inc.* associate/supervisor.

F. Off Company Time and Property Involvement

Off Company time and premises involvement with any illegal drug or controlled substance may result in disciplinary action up to and including termination. Off company time and premises involvement will be reviewed on an individual basis considering such factors as to whether the involvement:

1. Impairs an employees' work performance upon return to work
2. Causes damage to *Business Controls, Inc.* or public property, reputation, or that of a client
3. Jeopardizes an employee's safety or that of co-workers, clients, or the general public
4. Jeopardizes the Company's, our client's, or the public's expectation in confidence of any *Business Controls, Inc.* employee

III. Searches

A. In General

Business Controls, Inc. has the right to inspect Company lockers, desks, and vehicles; packages or other containers brought onto Company property or at a client facility; and other objects brought onto, or existing on Company property that might conceal alcohol or illegal substances.

Searches of employees and their personal property (including employee vehicles) are to be limited to inspecting loose, unsecured personal possessions, asking the employee to turn out pockets and remove shoes and hat, and observing whatever is in plain sight.

Employee cooperation in searches and inspection activities is viewed as a condition of employment and failure to cooperate shall result in discipline up to and including termination.

VI. Involvement of Law Enforcement Agencies

The use, sale, purchase, transfer, or possession of an illegal substance is a violation of the law. *Business Controls, Inc.* management may refer such illegal substance activities to local law enforcement agencies for further actions.

Please sign to acknowledge receiving this copy of *Business Controls, Inc.* **Illegal Drug, Alcohol, and Search Policy**.

I have received a copy of the above and agree to read and abide by this policy. I understand the disciplinary actions that may result if this policy is violated up to and including termination.

_____   _____
Print Name   Signature

_____   _____
Date signed: Witness

Notes

1. "Illegal substance" means any drug (a) which is not legally obtainable or (b) which is legally obtainable, but has not been legally obtained. The term includes prescribed drugs not legally obtained and prescribed drugs not being used for prescribed purposes.
2. "Legal drug" includes prescribed drugs and over-the-counter drugs which have been legally obtained and are being used for the purpose for which they were prescribed or manufactured.
3. "Impaired," for the purpose of this policy, means the employee is affected by a drug or alcohol or the combination of a drug and alcohol in any detectable manner. The symptoms of impairment are not confined to those consistent with misbehavior or of obvious impairment of physical or mental ability, such as slurred speech, difficulty in maintaining balance, or the odor of alcohol. A determination of being impaired will be established by a professional, a scientifically valid test such as urinalysis or blood analysis, and, in some cases, by a layperson.

Appendix G

Sample Nondisclosure Agreement

Confidentiality and Noncircumvention Agreement

Company Name, Company Address, a corporation residing in the Country of _____, State of _____, organized and existing under the laws of the Country of _____ ("we" or the "Recipient"), has received, and/or will receive, certain confidential information from Company Name, Company or its designated employees, agents, representatives, and affiliates (collectively, "you" or the "Disclosing Party") in connection with a potential transaction or venture with the Disclosing Party (a "Transaction"). As a condition to receiving any such information, we hereby agree, for ourselves, and on behalf of any of our partners, employees, affiliates, subsidiaries, agents, representatives, and any corporation which we may form or join in connection with such Transaction, and its shareholders, officers, directors, employees, agents, and representatives (collectively, our "Affiliates") with whom we may share any such information, to keep confidential any information concerning the proposed Transaction or the subject matter of such transaction or participation which is disclosed orally or furnished in writing by the Disclosing Party to the Recipient or its Affiliates in connection with our discussions (the "Agreement"). For purposes of this Agreement, the term Confidential Information shall not include any information which (a) becomes available to the general public other than as a result of a disclosure by the Recipient or any of its Affiliates; (b) was available to the Recipient on a nonconfidential basis prior to the disclosure of such information to it by the Disclosing Party or any agents or representatives thereof; or (c) becomes available to the Recipient from a source which, to the best of our knowledge after due inquiry, is not subject to any prohibition against disclosure of such information to us.

By our execution hereof, we acknowledge that all Confidential Information disclosed or furnished to the Recipient by the Disclosing Party is proprietary to the Disclosing Party, and that neither the Recipient nor any Affiliate shall have any rights to the use thereof unless and until such time as a definitive agreement therefore may be entered into between us, provided, however, that we and our Affiliates may disclose any Confidential Information to our respective partners, officers, directors, employees, and agents who need to know such Confidential Information for the purpose of evaluating the feasibility of the Transaction or any transaction related thereto (it being understood and agreed that such persons shall be informed by us of the confidential nature of such Confidential Information, and shall be directed by us to treat such information in accordance with the terms and conditions of this Agreement).

Neither the Recipient nor any Affiliate to whom Confidential Information is disclosed will use any such Confidential Information in any way detrimental to the Disclosing Party, its partners, employees, agents, or representatives, including, without limitation, by establishing, funding or otherwise assisting any business entity which is or will be directly or indirectly in competition with the business of the proposed Transaction or any proposal therefore.

In the event that the Recipient is requested in any proceeding to disclose any Confidential Information, we will give you prompt notice of such request so that the Disclosing Party may seek an appropriate protective order. If, in the absence of a protective order, the Recipient may nonetheless be compelled to disclose Confidential Information, we may disclose such Information without liability hereunder; provided, however, that we give you written notice of the Confidential Information to be so disclosed as far in advance as is practicable. We shall use our best efforts to obtain assurance that confidential treatment will be accorded to such Confidential Information.

Without your prior written consent, we shall not make any public disclosure concerning any proposed Transaction between us or the subject matter of this Agreement, nor shall we directly or indirectly contact any other party whom you or any of your Affiliates may have approached in connection therewith, or whom you have stated it is your intention to approach. In the event discussions concerning any such transaction between us or other participation shall terminate, the Recipient will promptly redeliver to the Disclosing Party all copies of written Confidential Information furnished to it and/or to any Affiliate hereunder, and shall destroy any memoranda, notes or other writings prepared by it or any of such Affiliates based upon any Confidential Information.

By our execution hereof, we hereby acknowledge and agree that money damages would not be a sufficient remedy for any breach of this Agreement by the Recipient or any Affiliate, and that, in addition to all other remedies to which the Disclosing Party may be entitled, the Disclosing Party shall be entitled to specific performance and injunctive or other equitable relief as remedies for any such breach or threatened breach. The Recipient further agrees to waive, and to use its best efforts to cause its Affiliates to waive, any requirement for the securing or posting of any bond in connection with the exercise of such remedies. The Recipient agrees that it shall not disclose any Confidential Information to any Affiliate unless and until it has fully explained the terms of this Agreement and obtained such Affiliate's consent to be bound thereby prior to his or her receipt of any Confidential Information. The Recipient agrees that it shall not actively solicit the employment or hiring by itself or any Affiliate of any employee of the Company. This Agreement and the Recipient's obligations hereunder shall survive for a period of three (3) years from the date hereof.

By our execution hereof, we hereby represent and warrant that the person signing this Agreement on behalf of the Disclosing Party has full corporate power and authority to enter into, execute, and deliver this Agreement to you for and on our behalf, which Agreement, once so executed and delivered, shall be our legally binding obligation, enforceable against us in accordance with its terms by any court of competent jurisdiction. This Agreement shall be governed by and construed in accordance with the internal laws of the State of _____ applicable to the performance of such agreements solely within the state, without giving effect to any principles of conflicts of law which might otherwise be applied thereby.

The Recipient understands and acknowledges that while you may provide, or have provided, certain Confidential Information which you believed to be relevant to our evaluation of any proposed Transaction, you have not represented and warranted as to the completeness, accuracy, or suitability of such Confidential Information for any purpose, and no such representation or warranty may be deemed or inferred by us unless and until we have entered into a definitive agreement containing such representations and warranties. We agree that neither the Disclosing Party, nor any Affiliate thereof, shall have any liability to the Recipient or any Affiliate thereof resulting from the use of such Confidential Information unless and until such a definitive agreement has been entered into. For purposes of this Agreement, originally signed or facsimile copies of originally signed documents shall be valid and binding between the parties hereto.

We agree with you that, unless and until any definitive agreement is entered into between us in connection with any Transaction, neither the Recipient nor the Disclosing Party shall be under any liability or legal obligation of any kind whatsoever with respect to such a Transaction by virtue of this or any other written or oral expression of intent by either of us or any of our Affiliates except, in the case of this Agreement, for the matters expressly agreed to herein. This Agreement may not be modified or amended except by written agreement signed by both parties hereto.

Signature: By: _____ Date: _____

Printed Name: _____

Address: _____

_____

Telephone: _____ Fax: _____

Approved and Accepted:

By: _____ Date: _____

    Company Officer

Afterword

Thank you for reading this book. I hope you have found it informative and useful. To improve upon it in future editions and any works I might undertake in the future your thoughts and comments would be appreciated. My preferred method of correspondence is e-mail. My e-mail address is eferraro@BusinessControls.com. If you have constructive input or criticism, please share it with me. I will respond personally and will answer all reasonable questions, time permitting.

Also, if you would like to learn more about *investigations in the workplace*, attend one of my seminars on *"The Process of Investigation®,"* or subscribe to my free electronic newsletter, *Security Headlines,* by visiting my Web site, www.InvestigationsInTheWorkplace.com. I hope to see you there!

Index

T

U